Making the International:
Economic Interdependence and Political Order

Project team

Dr Simon Bromley, Course team chair

Dr William Brown, Co-chair

Course team

Dr Suma Athreye
Dr George Callaghan
Dr Ranjit Dwivedi
Ann Garnham
Dr Jef Huysmans
Dr Bob Kelly
Professor Maureen Mackintosh
Dr Giles Mohan
Professor Chandan Mukherjee

Dr Raia Prokhovnik
Dick Skellington
Dr Mark Smith
Hedley Stone
Professor Grahame Thompson
Professor David Wield
Dr Gordon Wilson
Professor Marc Wuyts
Dr Helen Yanacopulos

The OU would like to acknowledge the valuable contribution made to the course team and the development of *A World of Whose Making?* by Dr Robert Garson of the University of Keele.

Dr Hazel Johnson, critical reader
Maria Ana Lugo, St Antony's College, Oxford, critical reader
Kirsten Adkins, BBC
Sally Baker, OU Library
Brenda Barnett, secretary
Pam Berry, composition services
Karen Bridge, project manager
Maurice Brown, software development
Lene Connolly, materials procurement
Mick Deal, software QA
Marilyn Denman, course secretary
Wilf Eynon, audio-visual
Fran Ford, Politics and Government Secretary
Sarah Gamman, rights adviser
Carl Gibbard, designer

Richard Golden, production and presentation administrator
Dr Mark Goodwin, lead editor
Gill Gowans, copublishing advisor
Celia Hart, picture research
Avis Lexton, Economics Secretary
Lisa MacHale, BBC
Vicki McCulloch, designer
Magda Noble, media consultant
Eileen Potterton, course manager
Andrew Rix, audio-visual
David Shulman, BBC
Kelvin Street, OU Library
Colin Thomas, software development
Gill Tibble, BBC
Gail Whitehall, audio-visual
Chris Wooldridge, editor

Contributors to this volume

Dr Suma Athreye, Lecturer in Economics, Faculty of Social Sciences, The Open University.
Aditya Bhattacharjea, Reader in Economics, Delhi School of Economics, University of Delhi.
Dr Simon Bromley, Senior Lecturer in Government and Politics, Faculty of Social Sciences, The Open University.
Dr William Brown, Lecturer in Government and Politics, Faculty of Social Sciences, The Open University.
Dr George Callaghan, Staff Tutor (Economics), Faculty of Social Sciences, The Open University.
Dr Sudipta Kaviraj, Department of Politics, School of Oriental and African Studies, University of London.
Professor Maureen Mackintosh, Professor of Economics, Faculty of Social Sciences, The Open University.
Dr Judith Mehta, Research Associate, School of Economic and Social Studies, University of East Anglia.
Thandika Mkandawire, Director, United Nations Research Institute for Social Development (UNRISD), Geneva.
Dr Amrita Narlikar, Junior Research Fellow, St Johns College, Oxford and Lecturer-Elect in International Relations, University of Essex.
Professor Carlos Salas Paez, Sociology Department, Universidad Autónoma Metropolitana, Iztapalapa, Mexico.
Dr Rathin Roy, Public Resource Management Advisor, United Nations Development Programme (UNDP), New York.
Dr Rafael Sanchez, Associate Researcher, School of International Relations, Universidad Nacional, Costa Rica.
Professor Samuel Wangwe, Principal Research Associate, Economic and Social Research Foundation, Dar es Salaam.
Professor Marc Wuyts, Professor in Quantitative Applied Economics, The Institute of Social Studies, The Hague.

A World of Whose Making?

Making the International:
Economic Interdependence and Political Order

Edited by
Simon Bromley, Maureen Mackintosh,
William Brown and Marc Wuyts

Pluto Press
LONDON • STERLING, VIRGINIA

in association with

The Open
University

This publication forms part of the Open University courses DU301 *A World of Whose Making? Politics, Economics, Technology and Culture in International Studies* and DU321 *Making the International: Viewpoints, Concepts and Models in International Politics and Economics*. Details of these and other Open University courses can be obtained from the Course Information and Advice Centre, PO Box 724, The Open University, Milton Keynes MK7 6ZS, United Kingdom: tel. +44 (0)1908 653231, email general-enquiries@open.ac.uk.

Alternatively, you may visit the Open University website at http://www.open.ac.uk, where you can learn more about the wide range of courses and packs offered at all levels by The Open University.

Library of Congress Cataloguing-in-Publication Data
A catalogue record for this book is available from the Library of Congress.
British Library Cataloguing-in-Publication Data
A catalogue record for this book is available from the British Library.
Edited, designed and typeset by The Open University.
Printed and bound in the United Kingdom by The Bath Press, Bath.
ISBN 0 7453 2136 4 (hbk)
ISBN 0 7453 2135 6 (pbk)
1.1
To purchase a selection of Open University course materials visit the webshop at www.ouw.co.uk, or contact Open University Worldwide, Michael Young Building, Walton Hall, Milton Keynes MK7 6AA, United Kingdom for a brochure: tel. +44 (0)1908 858785; fax +44 (0)1908 858787, email ouwenq@open.ac.uk

Contents

Preface

Making the International: Economic Interdependence and Political Order is part of *A World of Whose Making? Politics, Economics, Technology and Culture in International Studies*, a course from The Open University's Faculty of Social Sciences. As its subtitle implies, *Making the International* is the product of collaboration between economists and political scientists to produce an international text in International Political Economy.

As with other Open University texts, *Making the International* has been produced by a 'course team' of academics and support staff. The Open University has been especially fortunate in that the course team responsible for *Making the International* has included international scholars from outside The Open University and the English-speaking world. This international collaboration was essential to realizing a key aim of the book: namely, to combine the teaching of core theory in economic and political analysis with an exposure to a diversity of voices and standpoints. The editors are extremely grateful to all of our outside colleagues and authors for their time and commitment to the project as a whole, their willingness to work with us, including reworking and editing material, and the ways in which, individually and collectively, they have joined in the course team process and made it possible for us to produce a truly international text. The end result is much richer for their input.

The course team played a vital role in shaping the book as a whole as well as in helping to refine successive drafts into a coherent text. We owe a large debt of thanks to them all. Our external assessors, Professor Anthony Payne and Professor Rhys Jenkins, provided critical and supporting advice on how to improve the text and we are grateful for their careful work on our behalf.

The academic staff of the Open University are also especially lucky to be able to draw on the skills and patience of excellent administrative, production and support staff. Brenda Barnett, Marilyn Denman, Fran Ford and Avis Lexton worked on successive drafts of the text with efficiency and cheerful forbearance. Marilyn Denman also provided great and cheerful support to the course team as course secretary. Mark Goodwin, as lead editor, oversaw the composition of the book with his customary attention to detail, care and good humour, making our lives so much easier despite the perennial difficulties academics have with deadlines. Thanks too to Vicki McCulloch and Carl Gibbard for their work on the design of the book. Gill Gowans oversaw the copublication process with Pluto Press, and our thanks go to her and Pluto for their support in this project. Last, but definitely not least, thanks to Eileen Potterton, our Course Manager on *A World of Whose Making?*

Eileen oversaw the production of *Making the International*, as well as the course as a whole, with such unflappable efficiency, energy and all round goodwill that even the difficult bits were easy.

Making the International is the first of a two book series. Its companion volume (which forms the second half of the course *A World of Whose Making?*) is *Ordering the International: History, Change and Transformation*, also copublished with Pluto Press. Whereas *Making the International* focuses on viewpoints, concepts and models in International Political Economy, *Ordering the International* is oriented towards International Studies as a whole, focusing on states and the states-system; culture, rights and justice; technology, inequality and the network society; and general theories of world order and transformation.

Simon Bromley, Maureen Mackintosh, William Brown and Marc Wuyts

Chapter 1 Economic interdependence and political order: introducing international political economy

Simon Bromley, Maureen Mackintosh, William Brown and Marc Wuyts

1   Introduction

Contemporary debates about the international system centre on two deeply intertwined themes: extensive and increasing economic interdependence and the nature of the international political order. This text sets out to develop an economic and political analysis of the international in the contemporary world. It recognizes that political debate draws extensively on contentious economic arguments and findings, and that economic analysis has to come to terms with key political issues of governance and conflict that profoundly shape economic change. It approaches international political economy, not as a self-contained academic discipline, but as the bringing together of two disciplines, politics and economics, to explore international issues.

This bringing together of the two disciplines is reflected in the organization of the text. It explores some central topics of international political debate, such as the nature and impact of the World Trade Organization, the nature of the bargaining process that has created free trade areas between unequal states, the varied fortunes of different states in the international economy, and the failure of international collective action to address global warming. At the same time it develops, in parallel and through an analysis of these and other topics, the key tools of economic and political analysis needed to understand and evaluate these debates. In our view, the ability to engage with international political economy requires a command of both economic and political analysis. The book has emerged from an unusual collaboration between political scientists and economists, and we aim to convey along the way some of what we have learned about the similarities and differences between the theoretical tools deployed by these disciplines. You need no prior knowledge of economics or political theory to understand this book, but if you come to it with some experience of one discipline we believe that the challenge of interpreting that experience in relation to the other discipline will be illuminating.

1

The content of the book is presented as a genuinely international set of analyses and debates in two senses. First, it is international in the sense that the analyses and arguments that follow are part of a shared, international social science that informs debates among intellectuals and decision makers across the world. Concepts, models and theories drawn from economic and political analysis are used to examine how the international is made, identifying and debating the nature of social agency. Thus the basic tools employed are part of the repertoire of a shared set of international debates in the social sciences. At the same time, however, there are divergent voices to be heard in different parts of the world. Moreover, the international is marked by massive economic inequalities and disparities in political power. We have attempted to recognize and to exemplify these themes in this book. It combines a focus on the dominant tools of economic and political analysis with some recognition of the different ways in which divergent voices employ those tools. And it pays particular attention to issues of inequality and power in the international system.

This approach has shaped the structure and the international authorship of the book. The teaching of economics and politics is integrated across the text as a whole. However, each part is located in particular experiences and vantage points. Parts 2 to 4 address key arguments and shared international concerns from the perspectives of particular regions of the world. Parts 1 and 5 explore core aspects of international political economy from the perspective of particular political debates. Each key question of international concern is thus addressed from a particular vantage point. While the terms and tools of political and economic analysis are shared, there is no single voice in those debates that speaks for us all.

We start, in Part 1, with a view of the international trading regime, and an examination of the World Trade Organization written from the experiences of developing countries both as relatively poor economies with little leverage over the patterns of international trade and as relatively weak states in terms of their bargaining power in international negotiations over trade policy. This gives us a point of entry into, as well as a distinctive perspective on, debates about international trade and the agreements negotiated among states.

Part 2 is located in, and written from, the Indian experience of making state policy since independence. In its political analysis, it addresses general questions about the social shaping of states' interests; in its economic analysis, it examines the roots of industrial growth in capital accumulation and technological innovation. The part gives a strong flavour of these issues as they have been played out in the vibrant context of Indian political and economic debates. In terms of its international politics, India has been a prominent member of the non-aligned countries, and its economic strategy of import-substituting industrialization was similar to that adopted in many other post-colonial states in the first decades after independence. One of the authors in Part 2 draws on an Indian standpoint to set out a view of how state preferences are formed in the international system – a view which contests the dominant approach in political analysis that is set out in Part 1.

This illuminating process of writing general economic and political analysis from a particular standpoint runs through the book. To see the world, as in Parts 1 and 2, from the standpoint of developing countries raises questions about inequality and the exercise of power. These questions are addressed in Part 3, which is rooted in the Mexican experience of economic liberalization and, in particular, the Mexican predicament of proximity to the largest economy and most powerful state in the world: the USA. Mexico is also a developing country; it shares a common border with the USA and has a long history of antagonistic relations with it. The country's membership of the North American Free Trade Agreement (NAFTA) represents a fascinating vantage point from which to consider both the impact of freer trade and investment on inequality within weaker states (a particular issue for middle income economies) and the issue of the exercise of power in the process of international political bargaining.

The fate of weaker states is taken up again in Part 4, which is written from an African perspective. The general theme is Africa's experience of negotiating the shape and direction of macroeconomic policy with international aid donors. The authors draw on African experiences of structural adjustment – and on the particular story of Tanzania – as the basis for economic and political analysis of state autonomy in determining policies for economic development. It also addresses how constraints on autonomy affect the ability of states to give voice to their sovereignty. The African experience since the early 1980s has been one of a struggle with powerful external agencies to define economic policy choices in a situation of acute aid dependency. The authors explore that dilemma within frameworks that also recognize the considerable scope for state agency and political action within the continent.

Finally, in Part 5, we return to the analysis of the international system as a whole – as in Part 1. This time, however, the analysis is situated in the context of collective action (and the failure of collective action) among states. The focus is on the difficulties experienced by the richest and most powerful countries (specifically the USA and the European Union) in formulating a common response to global warming and climate change. Like the earlier parts, Part 5 develops analytical tools of general applicability – in this case, a game theory approach to the collective action problem – and then explores their relevance and limitations in a particular context.

All the contributors to this book take seriously the internationally dominant discourses of economics and politics – and with good reason. These traditions carry significant analytical force and provide real insights into the making of the international system. In our view, they are not to be lightly dismissed. Moreover, dominant actors draw upon these discourses in articulating and defending their conduct, so that the interests of the rich and the powerful are often framed in these terms. This means that, if we are to understand, to criticize and to formulate alternative courses of action, there is no substitute for working through these arguments. If you want to gain a critical understanding of the making of the international economy and political system, and to be in a position to debate it, you have to grasp the tools of political and economic analysis and consider the alternative uses to which those tools may be put.

2   Studying politics and economics in parallel

Each set of issues addressed in Parts 1 to 4 involves economic analysis and debate presented alongside political analysis and discussion. This parallel presentation of politics and economics is our way of bringing the resources of both disciplines to bear on a common set of international issues. In Part 5, the disciplines come together in the game-theoretic analysis of collective action problems.

At the same time, the discussion in each part builds on what has gone before, so that there is a progressive development of the core tools used by both economists and political scientists to analyse the international system.

2.1   Conceptual progression in politics

International political order is rooted in the actions of states in the context of constraints produced by the states system, the different interests and identities of states as they strive to give voice to their own particular concerns, relations of power between and among states, and the ability (or otherwise) of states to act collectively. The politics teaching in this book aims to equip you with the tools to analyse and debate these elements of political order at an international level, and to give you the confidence to make your own judgements about key matters of international politics.

So, in Part 1, we start with the idea of the state as the dominant institution in contemporary politics, and with the basic and stark idea that relations among states are anarchic, that is, ungoverned. International politics is presented as an ungoverned realm in which states pursue power in competition with one another. We explain the concept of international anarchy at work in this realist model, and the ideas of the state and of state sovereignty that lie behind it. We argue that this model provides a powerful insight into the workings of international politics, but that its views of the state and of the character of international politics can be challenged. The processes of governance are not confined to the domestic level; they can and do operate internationally. The idea of international governance opens up a series of questions that run through the book as a whole: how are the interests and identities of states constructed, what is the nature of power and authority in international politics, and how can we understand governance at an international level?

India's national interest and the identity of the Indian state were defined in the context of the country's newly-won independence, when a state-led national strategy of development and anti-colonial non-alignment had the upper hand in an explicitly secular political culture. This is contrasted with the very different context of economic liberalization and the assertion of Hindu nationalism that characterized the Indian political scene from the early 1990s. While altered international circumstances are part of this story, Part 2 looks at the social shaping of the Indian national interest by the particular culture and society of the state. Whereas the realist model explored in Part 1 suggests that the interests of a given state in the international arena are determined by its power position in relation to other states, the experience of post-independence India suggests that the national interest is, to an extent, subject to influences from powerful social groups that are enfranchised by the political system. As societies and political systems change, so will the national interest and even the very identity of the state. This presents an inside-out, bottom-up view of international politics in contrast to the outside-in, top-down view of political realism presented in Part 1. It considers the social shaping of the agency of the state, rather than the constraints that result from the system of states.

Mexico has also experienced a major process of economic (and political) liberalization during recent decades, and it has done so in the shadow of the power of the USA. This provides a fascinating vantage point from which to bring together questions of power and the social shaping of national interests, and it allows us to examine what happens when states interact with one another. It builds on the analysis in Parts 1 and 2 to suggest that interaction is structured not only by the distribution of power between states but also by the nature of the interests they seek to pursue. How the international interests of one state align with those of others is highly variable, ranging from outright conflict, through various forms of mixed co-operation and competition, to a pure harmony of interests. If we assume that both Mexico and the USA have something to gain from mutual economic liberalization, we can expect a process of bargaining to distribute the gains, and Part 3 shows you how to think about the bargaining power of states in these circumstances. The model is then extended to show you how a different kind of power operates: a coercive situation in which the USA is able to impose costs on Mexico, and one in which the latter loses out from liberalization. The general point is that both power and interests are important in shaping international outcomes.

A state's position in the international system can also have profound implications for its ability to realize its sovereign claims and gain sufficient autonomy to manage macroeconomic policy. The contested political and economic experiences of African states, marked by aid dependence and the external influence of other states and institutions such as the World Bank and the International Monetary Fund, illustrate the social shaping of states, their interests and their agency, by other states acting collectively. To what extent is the formal, legal sovereignty of an African state such as Tanzania given voice, and to what extent are Tanzanians able to achieve the autonomy that is required to conduct macroeconomic management? The analyses developed in Part 4 – of sovereignty and, especially, autonomy – show how the international serves to shape, or construct, the nature of the state and the economy.

Finally, in Part 5, we conclude by looking at the prospects for and problems of states acting collectively to achieve mutual benefits at the international level. Given pressing problems such as global warming and climate change, it asks about the circumstances in which states are able to act collectively in the international arena, and whether international interaction can change the nature of states' interests such that co-operation becomes more likely. Part 5 therefore deals with a fundamental question in international politics: how far, and by what means, are states able to act collectively for mutual benefit?

2.2 Conceptual progression in economics

International economic interdependence is rooted in international trading, in the movement of capital, and to a lesser extent labour, around the world, and in the interconnections of policy processes instituted by the exercise of political power across the globe. The economics teaching in this text aims to give you the tools and confidence to dismantle and reconstruct many of the common economic arguments you will come across in the international sphere, and to make effective judgements about the quality of the economic evidence used in these policy debates.

We start therefore, in Part 1, with the theory of comparative advantage: a cornerstone of the economic analysis of international interdependence and the oft-cited basis for many of the claims about the benefits of international trade. We explain the concept and argue for its importance, then use it to explore the distribution of the gains and losses from a policy of freeing trade. Not all countries gain from trade, nor do all groups within countries. In this exploration a theme appears that runs right through the book: the importance of prices and market processes in shaping the international.

International markets are powerful sources of agency that are not easily directed by national policy or collaborative treaty.

Part 2 turns to a consideration of the determinants of growth in the national economy, and focuses on the industrial roots of economic growth. By 'industrial roots' we mean the role of investment by firms in generating growth, the way in which this takes growth in particular directions, and the key role of technological change in economic growth. The part argues that the Indian liberalization of foreign investment – inviting foreign firms into India during the 1980s after 30 years of promoting Indian-owned industrial growth – was driven by a need to import technology, and not by the conventional 'comparative advantage' arguments outlined in Part 1. In the process, it explains the tools of analysis for industrial technical change, and the measurement of growth, and defines the strategy of 'import-substituting industrialization', which came under international attack from free traders in the 1980s.

Free trade can promote growth; it also can, and does, promote inequality. Gainers and losers change as patches of rapid economic growth appear in different parts of the world. A continent that has faced serious problems in trying to benefit from rising economic interdependence is Latin America. Part 3 turns to address free trade in conditions of inequality from the perspective of Mexico. In this middle income country, inequality rose under trade liberalization in the 1980s and 1990s. In asking why, Part 3 develops some general tools of analysis for wages, wage setting and the pattern of inequality. Liberalization of trade and investment is seen from the perspective of labour, and the authors emphasize that workers' agency, in labour bargaining, and the links between Mexican organized labour and both the Mexican state and activists elsewhere, are key variables in understanding how trade influences workers' incomes.

A core role of governments is to manage the national economy, but when economies run out of control through inflation, economic crisis and the failure to pay debts, international agencies move in, under the control of (and largely funded by) rich countries. The resulting substitution of action by aid donors for government control can create a long-term loss of state capability, with severe consequences for development prospects. Part 4 explains what is meant by macroeconomic stabilization, and examines how aid-dependence colours policy formation within the national economy, using the changing character of Tanzanian macroeconomic policy as an example. The part explains the tools of macroeconomic management – national accounting, the balance of payments, and the foreign exchange market. It then uses those tools to argue that the core policy problem for low income countries – and Tanzania is one of the poorest in the world – is to bring together structural change in the economy and effective management of the country's role in trade in such a way as to promote growth. The current international trade and policy regimes exercise sharp constraints on the autonomy and capability of states attempting to undertake such macroeconomic management.

Finally, Part 5 identifies a core aspect of economic policy both within and between countries: the need for collective action to create economic goods and services that cannot be provided efficiently by markets. It argues that economic incentives frequently block effective collective action, and uses game theory to analyse these incentive problems. Game theory is used as a tool of analysis by both economics and politics, which is not surprising as this is the area of economic behaviour that is fundamentally inseparable from political activity (and vice versa). Again, these are methods of general applicability. Part 5 completes a progression of economics teaching that will provide you with many of the core tools used by economists to analyse economic interdependence, and, we hope, will allow you to apply a critical eye to the debates that employ those tools.

3 Looking forward

Several features of the text are designed to support your study. Each part has its own introduction, and this sets out in detail the key features of the chapters. In addition, the chapters contain in-text questions and study activities that will allow you to pause and reflect on the analysis as it unfolds; to develop your understanding and use of the key concepts and models; and to consolidate and check your grasp of the main ideas. Marginal notes provide easy reference to the key concepts and important definitions, and some suggestions for further reading are provided at the end of each chapter.

In the final chapter of the book, we shall return to some of the issues raised by an attempt to understand how the international is made using the tools of economics and politics. We hope that you will gain as much stimulation and enlightenment from studying this book as we have gained from producing it.

Part 1   Trade and states

International trade in goods and services is one of the most important forms of international economic interdependence between countries, exercising an enormous influence on the living standards of people across the globe. International trade is a market process, shaped by opportunities to make profits from buying, selling and investing. It is also strongly governed by international negotiations, international treaties and the trade policy decisions of sovereign governments. As a result, in this arena, economic analysis is highly politically charged, and politics is deeply imbued with assumptions and propositions about economic change.

In Part 1, we begin with international trade, and we start with a view from the developing countries. In Chapter 2, Aditya Bhattacharjea argues that the current governance of international trade through the World Trade Organization (WTO) is systematically weighted against low and middle income countries, and it identifies a tendency for rich countries to prescribe free trade for others but not for themselves. The following three chapters pick up different aspects of this challenge. In Chapter 3, Maureen Mackintosh explores the economic case for free trade, arguing that there are enormous economic gains from trade, but that markets inherently distribute those gains unequally between and within countries. In Chapter 4, Amrita Narlikar turns to the politics of the WTO, picking up the issue of bias in trade rules, examining the politics of rule making within the organization, and asking whether the WTO rules are necessarily a reflection of the dramatically unequal power of states or whether they can be a force for change. Finally, in Chapter 5, Simon Bromley in turn asks about the concepts of international politics that underlie these alternative positions about the WTO. Is international politics fundamentally conflictual, a reflection of the unequal coercive power of states? Or, on the contrary, can we understand international politics as a more co-operative exercise than this, as a system of multi-level international governance?

We hope that you will gain from Part 1, not only knowledge of the debates about the WTO, but also some tools from economics and politics that will allow you to analyse those debates with evidence to hand. The economics in Chapter 3 develops some of the core economic theory and evidence that are deployed in political debates about trade. The politics in Chapter 5 presents some of the core political theory that underpins political differences about the nature of sovereign states and the governance of trade.

The two modes of thought, economic and political, are very different, yet there are a number of common strands in the theories presented here. Perhaps the most striking is the contrast, in both the economics and the politics, between theories that analyse international relationships as entailing the ungoverned interaction of agents (countries, firms or people) and theories that allow for international governance of those relationships. In economics, the basic models of markets are 'anarchic', that is, independent buyers and sellers operate without any specified framework of law or governance. In politics, the realist theory of international politics is also anarchic, seeing only sovereign states exercising power. Both frameworks examine the characteristics of an 'anarchic order', that is, an ordered outcome of ungoverned interactions. In both economics and politics, these anarchic models of reality are challenged by frameworks that emphasize the governing of markets through policy and rule setting, and the possibility of collaborative international governance. The contrasts introduced here will reappear elsewhere in this book, and in particular are contemplated afresh in Part 5, when we turn directly to analyse co-operation and failures of co-operation at the international level.

Chapter 2 Playing by the rules? Developing countries in the world trade regime

Aditya Bhattacharjea

1 Introduction

The Ministerial Declaration adopted by WTO members at Doha on 14 November 2001 fails to address the most pressing needs either of the poorest countries or of the world's most vulnerable communities. This means that the people who most need a share in global prosperity are still those least likely to obtain it.

(A joint statement by Actionaid, CAFOD, Christian Aid, Oxfam, Save the Children and five other charities and non-governmental organizations, January 2002)

Underlying the WTO's trading system is the fact that freer trade boosts economic growth and supports development. In that sense, commerce and development are good for each other.

('Ten common misunderstandings about the WTO', WTO website: www.wto.org, 20 October 2002)

In December 1999, the world's attention was focused on riots and demonstrations taking place in the streets of the American city of Seattle, where trade ministers representing more than a hundred countries were in conclave. The organization under whose auspices this controversial meeting was held, the World Trade Organization (WTO), had come into existence barely five years earlier. It was supposed to have created a system of unanimously accepted rules governing international trade, which would lead to worldwide economic benefits, but it became evident at Seattle that not everyone shared this view.

The demonstrators who received the greatest media attention were American trade unionists protesting against job losses which they blamed on cheaper imports, and environmentalists protesting against ecological damage which they blamed on free trade. Both groups claimed that they were also speaking for poor people in developing countries. Almost drowned out in the media

Seattle police use tear gas to push back WTO protesters on 30 November 1999 (left); President Clinton addresses a lunch in honour of ministers attending the WTO meeting on 1 December 1999 (right)

coverage of what came to be known as 'the Battle in Seattle' were the voices of the official representatives of those developing countries, who felt they were being excluded from the decision-making process. They too had serious concerns about the WTO, some of which were diametrically opposed to those of the demonstrators who were claiming to speak on their behalf. Whether because of the protests outside or inside the conference rooms, the Seattle meeting was a failure in that it ended without agreement.

Ministerial meetings of the WTO are held every two years. Learning the lessons of Seattle, the next one was held in November 2001 in Doha, in the Middle Eastern state of Qatar, where strict control could be exercised on the entry and behaviour of potential demonstrators. Here the developing countries managed to extract several concessions in the final declaration, and indeed the new round of international negotiations launched at that meeting is known as the 'Development Round'. But many developing countries remain unhappy, and as the first quotation above indicates, their unhappiness is shared by influential groups in Britain.

This chapter will, I hope, help you to understand the concerns of developing countries under the WTO regime, and the problems they face in trying to extract a better deal from the Development Round negotiations launched at Doha. The roots of these problems lie in the Uruguay Round (UR) agreements that gave birth to the WTO, and further back in the international trading system as it evolved after the Second World War. Section 2 gives a potted history, and also introduces the major rules and principles regulating international trade. Section 3 spells out what went wrong with the UR agreements: the developing countries' expectations that were unfulfilled, and the onerous costs they had to incur. Section 4 explores aspects of the road ahead from Doha, with particular attention to the two issues that so exercised the demonstrators at Seattle and are likely to come up again at future meetings: environmental damage and labour standards.

In examining the WTO trade regime from the point of view of developing countries, I shall also establish several key themes of this first part of the book. International trade – that is, the buying and selling of goods and services between countries – has a hugely important influence on countries' economic growth and development, and negotiated rules governing trade strongly influence who benefits most, a theme picked up in Chapter 3. High-profile trade negotiations among states that are formally sovereign reflect unequal power and modify the exercise of national sovereignty in practice, a theme developed in Chapters 4 and 5.

1.1   The WTO

What is this organization, the WTO, to raise such passions? Misconceptions abound: in particular, that it is a kind of supranational government that imposes its policies on sovereign nations. Although there is much that is wrong with the WTO, this particular complaint is off the mark. The WTO deals with the rules governing international trade, but neither devises nor enforces them. It provides a forum for international negotiation, in which the rules are usually agreed by consensus. This is not to say that the process of arriving at the consensus is a convivial one, nor that everyone is happy with the outcome. There is hard bargaining involved, and the resulting trade regime reflects the asymmetries of a world in which countries differ widely in respect of their economic and political muscle. But there is no 'WTO view' that is forced on countries: in principle, the rules have been agreed by all members and ratified by their parliaments, and no country is forced to become a member.

Trade regime
A trade regime is a framework of rules and institutions governing international trade.

Most WTO members are states. As the agreements concern trade policy, administrative units that govern trade policy for a particular region can also be members. For example, the European Union has free trade between its member states and a unified policy on trade with non-members, so it is a WTO member in its own right, as are its member states. Hong Kong, a founding member of the WTO in 1995, retained its membership even after reunification with China; China itself joined only in 2001 as a distinct member with a very different trade policy.

The WTO has a mechanism for periodically reviewing each member's compliance with the agreed rules, and another mechanism for impartially settling disputes between them, but it cannot enforce its rulings. In these respects, it is unlike the two international organizations with which it is frequently clubbed: the World Bank and the International Monetary Fund (IMF). Both these organizations have their own very definite views on economic policies, which overlap considerably in what has come to be known as 'the Washington Consensus' (explained in Chapter 8). These financial institutions ensure that sovereign governments in developing countries take their advice seriously by lending them vast amounts of money, often conditional on compliance with elements of the Consensus.

The WTO does not make loans; it is an organization set up to administer a set of international agreements governing international trade. In its ardent advocacy of freer trade between nations (as exemplified by the second quotation with which this chapter began), it does promote one key element of the Washington Consensus – but in principle it does so only to the extent that its members have agreed to reduce barriers to trade and subject themselves to a rule-governed trading system. That, at least, is the formal position, clearly and forcefully stated on the WTO's official website.

However, many critics (including the present author) see a definite attempt to impose policies on developing countries, not by an autonomous WTO bureaucracy, but by the richer countries. It may seem paradoxical that this can be built into a formally democratic and consensual organization which has no teeth to enforce its rules. This chapter illustrates how it has come about, while Chapter 4 explores WTO political decision making in more depth.

1.2 Developing countries

Question

Which countries in the world are classified as 'developing countries'?

There are various definitions of 'developing countries', none entirely satisfactory. The WTO allows members to classify themselves as developing, and lists some 30 of them as 'least developed' (poorest) members for special treatment. For the purpose of this chapter, it would be simplest if you were to think of developing countries as comprising all countries *other than* the USA, Canada, the countries of Western Europe, Singapore, Japan, Australia and New Zealand. So of the 145 WTO members (as of 2002), over a hundred are developing countries. Their gross national incomes (GNI) per head (a crude but common measure of economic development of a type discussed further in Chapter 7) ranged in 2000 from around $500 dollars a year in the least developed countries such as Sierra Leone and Tanzania to around $8000 in typical 'upper middle income' countries such as Malaysia. By way of comparison, the United Kingdom figure was $23 550, Japan $26 460 and the USA $34 260 (World Bank, 2002a, pp.232–3).

I shall argue in this chapter that many of the benefits these developing countries were promised would follow from joining the WTO have so far proved illusory, because of loopholes in the agreements. In particular, they expected that signing on would enable them to get better access for their major exports in the markets of the developed countries, and an impartial mechanism for settling disputes with them. We shall see that things did not quite work out that way. There were also large costs in complying with the rules, some of which could have been foreseen, and others which became apparent only after the ink was dry and the developing countries were faced with implementing agreements that they perhaps did not fully comprehend. And if you are already asking why they do not just quit, the answer is that cutting themselves off from the international economy is likely to be even worse. In an unequal world, being a junior member of the gang is often better than being excluded altogether. After reading this chapter and the next one, I hope you will understand why developing countries find themselves in this predicament.

2   The road to Doha

The WTO was created by the eighth in a series of multilateral trade negotiations that have taken place since the signing in 1947 of the General Agreement on Tariffs and Trade (GATT). The GATT was designed to prevent a repetition of the experience of the 1930s, when individual countries had tried to claw their way out of the widespread unemployment that was characteristic of the Great Depression of those years by restricting imports and subsidizing their exports to other countries. For an individual country, this policy seemed to make sense, because it prevented cheaper imports from displacing workers in vulnerable industries, and promoted employment in export sectors. However, when implemented by many countries simultaneously, it amounted to a 'beggar-thy-neighbour' policy which only made the overall situation worse, as one country's imports are another's exports. (Think of someone standing up to get a better view at a sports event: it makes sense for the individual, but if everyone stands up, no-one gets a better view and everyone gets exhausted.)

Two kinds of import restrictions were especially prominent: tariffs and quantitative restrictions (for more details of how tariffs work, see Chapter 3). Under the GATT, contracting countries agreed to restrict their use of such policies. Tariffs were 'bound' at maximum levels, while quantitative restrictions and export subsidies were abolished. The tariff reductions were negotiated on the principle of reciprocity: country A agreed to reduce tariffs on particular products which it imported from country B, in exchange for B reducing its tariffs on products exported by A.

Seven 'rounds' of multilateral negotiations took place under the GATT between the 1940s and 1970s, resulting in a significant reduction of tariff barriers for most manufactured goods traded between the *developed* countries. However, although developing countries comprised a majority of the original 23 GATT signatories and their number proliferated in subsequent years, they remained suspicious of the motives of the richer countries and of

Multilateral trade negotiations
Multilateral trade negotiations take place between many countries simultaneously. (Bilateral negotiations are negotiations between pairs of countries.)

Tariffs
Tariffs (customs duties) are taxes on imports or exports.
Quantitative restrictions
Quantitative restrictions (quotas) are limits on the amount of imports; for example, 'not more than x tonnes of steel'.

the idea of free trade itself, and most did not participate fully in this process for 40 years (for reasons explored further in Chapters 6 and 7). They neither reduced their own tariffs and quantitative restrictions, nor did they obtain reciprocal concessions from the developed countries for their major exports, notably agricultural products, textiles and clothing.

This changed in the 1980s. The economic performance of the developing countries that had gone furthest in restricting imports was disappointing, and industries shielded from foreign competition were chronically inefficient. Also influential was the 'East Asian Miracle', the spectacular success of countries such as South Korea, Taiwan, Hong Kong, Singapore (and later China) in achieving rapid economic growth by promoting exports. Along with pressure from the World Bank and the IMF, these experiences swung developing countries in the direction of trade liberalization.

Trade liberalization
Trade liberalization refers to the reduction or abolition of barriers to trade (such as tariffs and quotas).

The tide was therefore turning when the eighth round of GATT negotiations got under way in 1986 with a conference in Punta del Este in Uruguay. The Uruguay Round, as it came to be known, was in comparison with earlier rounds the most protracted (it lasted eight years), the largest (it involved many more countries), and much more far-reaching. Some 30 agreements and 'understandings' were signed at the conclusion of the round in 1994, one of them setting up an entirely new organization, the WTO, to supplant the GATT as an institution.

For the first time, the developing countries made significant concessions and opened their markets, in exchange for the developed countries agreeing to bring agriculture and textiles (important developing country exports) back into the framework of rule-bound trade liberalization. In particular:

- Most developing countries agreed to reduce and bind their tariffs, to reduce their subsidies, and to refrain from using quantitative restrictions.

- They agreed to integrate agriculture into the framework of reciprocal concessions, exposing their farmers to intense foreign competition.

- They agreed to extend trade liberalization, which had earlier been confined to trade in goods, to services (for example, banking, insurance and telecommunications).

- They agreed to include protection of intellectual property rights (patents, copyrights, trademarks and so on) in the GATT/WTO framework.

Although similar concessions were also made by the developed countries, we shall see that their very different economic conditions, and their ability to exploit loopholes in the agreements, meant that similar concessions often entailed very different outcomes in developed and developing countries. Some elements of 'Special and Differential Treatment' were retained for developing countries: for example, they were given a few more years to comply with some of the agreements, allowed to make smaller tariff reductions, and the 30 or so 'least developed' (poorest) countries were exempted from having to reduce their subsidies. Many other provisions exhort, but do not force, the developed countries to show special consideration in enforcing the rules on developing countries. Despite all this, the impact of the agreements has been quite severe, as we shall see.

3 What went wrong?

3.1 Market access: expectations unfulfilled

A key objective of developing countries in trade liberalization negotiations is access for their exports to the markets of developed countries. However, the rules have been played out by developed countries in ways that block the hoped-for rise in exports.

Agriculture

According to the UR Agreement on Agriculture, import quotas were to be abolished, but since no country was prepared to expose its farmers abruptly to the rigours of free trade, quotas were to be replaced by 'equivalent' tariffs, which were to be reduced over time. However, the calculation of equivalent tariffs is subject to wide margins of error, and since it was left to each country to determine its own tariffs, most were set at extraordinarily high levels – exceeding 200 or even 300 per cent – for many products. This effectively raised the price of imports by the same percentage, making them unable to compete with home-grown produce. (Chapter 3 explains how tariffs work.) The European Union, Japan (which set a tariff of 550 per cent on rice!) and the USA were the worst offenders in this process, which came to be known as 'dirty tariffication'. Reducing tariffs as agreed was quite meaningless when they were set at such high levels to begin with.

This effective denial of market access in agriculture was compounded by another loophole in the agreement. These same developed countries vastly increased the amount of money they paid their farmers in the form of subsidies, enabling them to compete against farmers in developing countries who could produce the same products more cheaply, but whose governments could not afford these levels of support. Most commentators agree that, as a result of these various circumventions of the UR agreement, there has been no significant liberalization of trade in agriculture.

This issue was hotly debated at the 2002 Earth Summit in Johannesburg, and negotiations were under way at the WTO to reduce these subsidies, but at the time of writing it remains to be seen whether the European Union in particular will be willing to confront its politically influential farm lobby. The next chapter returns to this theme, with some pertinent examples, facts and figures. To be fair, this issue is not one that pits all developed countries against all developing countries: some of the former, such as the USA, Canada, Australia and New Zealand, are leading the charge to open the European market for their agricultural exports, while many developing countries import rather than export food and would actually be losers if developed countries reduced their subsidies.

Textiles and clothing

Here, the conflict is largely between developing country exporters and developed countries that were reluctant to expose their textile producers to cheaper imports. Here too the UR agreement had a proviso to soften its immediate impact, and a loophole that developing countries seem not to have anticipated. In order to enable textile producers in developed countries to adjust gradually to increased import competition, quantitative restrictions were to be phased out over ten years, starting in 1995, with 49 per cent of the restrictions to be removed only at the end of the ten-year period. This much the developing countries knew at the time of signing. What they perhaps did not expect is that developed countries would fulfil their intermediate targets by the clever expedient of including items that were not under quantitative restrictions in the first place, with the result that even by 2002 quantitative restrictions had been removed on relatively few items.

Tariff escalation

Added to this was the fact that, although the developed countries had reduced the average level of tariffs on manufactures to low levels as part of the UR agreements, this average concealed much higher tariffs on products that were imported mainly from developing countries. Moreover, higher tariffs were retained on products involving a higher degree of processing. In the EU, for example, cigars are subjected to a higher tariff than raw tobacco, processed foods to a higher tariff than unprocessed foods, and fabrics to a higher tariff than thread. (Many finished garments remained under quantitative restrictions, which is even worse.) This 'tariff escalation' means that developing countries are discouraged from graduating from their traditional colonial trading pattern of exporting raw materials and simple manufactures. Even if they can produce processed products more cheaply than the developed countries, tariffs tilt the balance against them.

3.2   The costs of liberalization in developing countries

Social disruption

In return for being granted enhanced market access by developed countries, which turned out to be somewhat illusory, developing countries agreed to open up their own markets. Indeed, for supporters of the UR, this was its biggest achievement. As Chapter 3 explains more fully, one of the central propositions of economic theory is that under certain conditions free trade is beneficial to a country – but there are inevitably winners and losers. As a country adjusts to free trade, some sectors of the economy advance, while others decline; colloquially these are referred to as sunrise and sunset sectors. Consequently, some incomes rise, some fall. Nor is this a one-time adjustment: greater openness to trade means that a country's producers will be continually buffeted by changes in technology, consumer tastes and government policies in the rest of the world.

Developed countries have unemployment benefits and retraining pro-grammes that help to cushion the effects of these changes and, as you saw above, they have generously compensated their farmers for exposing them to greater international competition. There are no doubt several deficiencies in these provisions, and retraining is seldom effective: it is hard to retrain a displaced coal miner or steelworker for a job in information technology or financial services. But at least unemployment does not threaten the very survival of the workers and their families, and the next generation is likely to be better equipped to get the new jobs in the sunrise sectors. The point is that no developing country has a system of general unemployment benefits, much less the enhanced benefits and retraining facilities given to workers and farmers whose losses are directly attributable to import competition.

In addition to this kind of social insurance for individuals, the European Union allocates generous 'structural funds' to its poorer regions, especially those that have been badly hit by the closure of industries. Few developing countries can afford this kind of transfer from richer to poorer citizens. Nor do most developing countries provide national health services, old age pensions, food stamps, and financial assistance to families with young children. The absence of these 'safety nets' means that a family can be completely devastated if its earning members lose their jobs. The prospects of the displaced workers, and even of their children, in the new sunrise activities are blighted by their lack of access to health facilities, education and nutrition.

As the Harvard economist Dani Rodrik has pointed out, greater trade liberalization among developed countries after the Second World War went together with a substantial enhancement of social spending by their governments – which was more generous in countries that were more open to trade (Rodrik, 1997). Instead of being able to set up these safety nets, governments in developing countries are under pressure from organizations such as the IMF to *cut* government spending. Although the stated targets of these cuts are inflated bureaucracies and inefficient government corporations, too often the axe falls on what little these countries have been spending on health, education, anti-poverty programmes and social services (more on this topic in Chapters 10 and 11).

Thus, even if trade liberalization had been carried out even-handedly in both developed and developing countries, it would have had very different social consequences. As it happens, the massive increase in subsidies to agriculture in developed countries has not only deprived developing countries of expanding farm exports, but it has also turned the tables and allowed European and American produce to invade developing country markets, displacing millions of small farmers. Wrenching dislocations, growing economic insecurity, and widening inequalities in countries with no safety nets exacerbate social divisions and tensions within those countries. This becomes a source of concern for developed countries when it shows up in the form of political instability and extremism and in waves of desperate migrants fleeing poverty and violence in their native countries.

The protection of intellectual property: the costs of TRIPS

Apart from the internal redistribution of income resulting from greater exposure to the world economy, the effects of one of the UR agreements in particular have achieved a certain notoriety because the agreement clearly imposes huge costs on farmers and consumers in developing countries, to the benefit of corporations in developed countries. This is the agreement on Trade-Related Aspects of Intellectual Property Rights (TRIPS), which strengthens international rules governing patents, trademarks, copyrights, the design of integrated circuits, and certain 'geographical indications' (such as 'Scotch' or 'Champagne'), restricting the use of these names to products produced in those regions. These are all means of establishing intellectual property rights (IPRs), that is, legal ownership of intangibles such as a new invention, a brand name, a work of literature, or the lyrics to a song. Here I explain the costs of TRIPS by concentrating on patents, which protect new products and processes from being copied without the holder's permission.

Patents serve an essential purpose. The kind of research and development that goes into the making of a new drug, for example, costs millions of pounds, takes many years, and runs the risk of not yielding a commercially viable product after all the trouble. A patent gives the pharmaceutical company monopoly rights over its new invention, to produce it itself or license the formula to other firms in exchange for the payment of royalties, thereby enabling it to recoup the costs of developing it.

This of course comes at the expense of consumers and other firms who would gain from free access to the new product or process. But if access were free, most such products would not be developed in the first place: think of computer software or a cure for AIDS or music CDs. (The last category is actually protected by copyrights rather than patents, but the idea is the same.) However, a permanent monopoly would undeservedly enrich the innovator forever and retard the spread of a valuable technology. (Imagine what would have happened if the descendants of Watt and Newcomen had retained the right to their ancestors' idea of the steam engine, or if the Fleming family had the rights to penicillin and all antibiotics derived from it.) Patent laws have always struck a balance, giving the innovator a *temporary* monopoly, after which the idea can be freely used by anyone.

Before the TRIPS agreement, different countries used to protect innovations for anything between five and twenty years, often discriminating between different types of products, or between patents granted to products and to processes. TRIPS commits WTO members to harmonize their laws governing IPRs, tightening them up considerably. In particular, it extends the duration of the patent monopoly to twenty years, and covers products that many countries had earlier not considered patentable: in particular, new plant varieties. Drugs and seeds are in fact the two major bones of contention between the developed and developing countries, with most of the scientific development taking place in the former, and the greatest need for easy access in the latter, where there are great deficiencies in the provision of basic health facilities and nutrition. TRIPS raises prices by preventing copying by local producers, and consequently restricts access to such products to those who can afford them. It will inevitably involve a large transfer of incomes from farmers, patients and consumers in poor countries to patent holders in richer countries, as the World Bank explains:

> IPRs are generally more beneficial to industrial countries than to developing countries. Developing countries are net importers of technology, while, in general, industrial countries are the producers of technology. Industrial countries therefore reap the static benefits of higher prices resulting from the market power provided by IPRs, at the expense of developing countries. It has been estimated that the United States stands to gain $5.7 billion in net transfers from TRIPS, while Germany, Sweden and Switzerland are also expected to receive substantial net inwards transfers. In contrast, developing countries are expected to experience net outward transfers, amounting to $430 million for India, $434 million for Korea, $481 million for Mexico, and $1.7 billion for Brazil.

(World Bank, 2002a, p.147)

Furthermore, strong patent protection limits the ability of developing countries to assimilate and adapt new technology to their own needs, processes that have historically been the basis of technological change across the world (Chapter 7).

Another concern that has been raised in regard to TRIPS is that of 'biopiracy'. This refers to the appropriation, by Western corporations, of biological materials found in plant and animal species native to developing countries, and the patenting of products derived from them. This, it is feared, will convert traditional forms of knowledge (such as herbal remedies) that have been widely used for centuries in developing countries into commercially exploitable IPRs which will bring profits to the patent holder, and not to the countries from where the knowledge was appropriated. Instead, producers and consumers in those countries would henceforth have to pay the patent holder for the privilege of using knowledge that was hitherto freely available.

The alternative is to fight costly legal battles in Western countries, as India has done to prevent the patenting of products based on extracts of *neem* (a tree native to India) and *haldi* (turmeric), whose medicinal properties have been known since ancient times. Fortunately, India could present evidence that these properties had been documented in classical texts, but for many such products there may be no documentation of their traditional use by indigenous peoples, and many developing countries may not be able to afford the legal and technical expertise required to contest the patent claim.

To be sure, the picture is not entirely gloomy. The TRIPS agreement permits countries to grant compulsory licences under certain conditions. These licences compel the patent holder to share its knowledge with other firms, allowing them to produce the patented product on payment of royalties. Brazil and South Africa have used the threat of compulsory licensing to induce pharmaceutical companies to supply drugs at lower prices, and at Doha it was explicitly conceded that governments would have the right to use this provision to protect public health by facilitating the manufacture of essential drugs.

Nor are all developing countries passive consumers of knowledge developed in the West: for example, India can also benefit from stricter IPR protection of the drugs developed by some of its pharmaceutical firms, its computer software, and its 'Bollywood' films. But on the whole, for most developing countries (including India, as the earlier quotation shows), TRIPS entails massive payments to IPR holders in developed countries. And, incidentally, the agreement on geographical indications so far protects only the nomenclature of wines and spirits, principally those of European origin. Place names in developing countries that add value to a product (such as Darjeeling tea) have not yet been granted protection, despite the efforts of countries like India.

Fighting on too many fronts

Although I have dwelt on the agreements relating to agriculture, textiles, and intellectual property, there are some two dozen others, each involving intricate legal and technical details. These include agreements on:

- Sanitary and phytosanitary (SPS) measures: these are standards applied to imported agricultural products so as to protect plants, animals and humans in the importing country. However, these standards are often arbitrarily used to restrict imports in order to favour domestic producers. The relevant agreement regulates how such standards can be applied, although they are still abused.

- Subsidies and countervailing measures: export subsidies are in most cases prohibited, but there are elaborate rules defining what constitutes a subsidy, and when and how the importing country can impose a 'countervailing duty' to offset it.

- Trade-related investment measures: this agreement prevents countries from forcing foreign firms operating in their territories to use domestically produced components (for example, a Toyota plant in India cannot be forced to use spark plugs made in India) or to export a minimum amount of their output.

The apparently diverse agreements in this short list, like most of those discussed in greater detail earlier in this chapter, all try to ensure that there should be minimum government interference with international trade. In particular, they require that domestically produced products should not be given direct or indirect protection from import competition (although of course loopholes exist).

Question

Can you think of an exception to those generalizations among the agreements discussed?

If you are wondering how the TRIPS agreement fits in, you share the puzzlement of many commentators, who believe that it had no business being part of an international trade agreement in the first place, and that the first two letters of the acronym are mere window-dressing. The fact is that the USA threatened to walk out of the negotiations (which would have doomed the Uruguay Round) unless TRIPS was included, a threat widely seen as a response to corporate pressure from large US companies in industries such as pharmaceuticals, software and biotechnology (more on determinants of government behaviour in Chapters 6 and 7).

There is also a deeper purpose to my terse listing of some of the UR agreements (and there are many more!). If your head is spinning with all these issues, imagine the plight of producers in developing countries, having to deal with unfamiliar rules in a foreign language; rules that can affect their profits and perhaps their very existence. Imagine also the plight of governments of many of these countries, with few trained specialists, having to negotiate agreements on issues that they do not fully comprehend. It is difficult to understand the implications of getting into an agreement when it relates to a subject on which one has little experience. This might account for the loopholes that developed countries were able to retain and later exploit.

Even after agreements are concluded, each of the subjects (and the new ones listed for negotiations) is reviewed and discussed by a separate committee or working group at the WTO headquarters in Geneva. According to one calculation (Blackhurst, 1999, p.38), the various WTO committees and working groups between them held an average of 46 meetings *a week* in 1996 – and the workload has only increased and proliferated since then. Each issue requires technical expertise. Several developing countries cannot afford a permanent diplomatic mission in Geneva; many others can maintain only a small embassy staffed by general-purpose diplomats who also deal with the other international organizations that have their headquarters there (for example, the International Labour Organization, the International Committee for the Red Cross, the World Health Organization ...). Ranged on the other side of many of the issues are developed countries with well-staffed missions, backed by legions of economists, lawyers and technical personnel specializing in WTO-related issues in their universities, government agencies and think tanks.

Apart from bearing the economic and social impact of the agreements themselves, developing countries therefore have to incur the costs of setting up administrative institutions to comply with their requirements. They must calculate, for example, the tariff equivalent of quotas, or permissible countervailing duties. They must also retrain their customs inspectors, and set up agencies to evaluate patent applications and to check for violations of technically complex patents or sanitary standards established in other countries. Such agencies were only established in developed countries once they had attained a certain level of economic and institutional development, and these countries therefore already have a stock of the relevant expertise and experience. In many developing countries, such agencies now have to be set up from scratch to comply with the UR agreements, before these countries have reached a comparable stage of economic development. Setting up institutions characteristic of mature economies may not be the best use of their limited resources. According to one calculation, the implementation of just three agreements (on customs valuation, TRIPS and SPS) would cost each country about $150 million – an amount exceeding the entire development budget of many countries (Finger and Schuler, 2002).

Dispute settlement

The lack of expertise in the developing countries shows up at a subsequent stage as well. One of the undoubted plus points of the WTO, compared with its predecessor the GATT, is its streamlined mechanism for settling disputes between members – on the whole quite impartially. But although many of the larger developing countries have won cases against the most powerful members like the EU and USA, the smaller ones are hamstrung by their inability to field lawyers specialized in international trade law, and seldom bring complaints. They are further handicapped by not being able to *enforce* the rulings of the WTO's dispute settlement bodies, which is left to the aggrieved parties themselves: if the 'guilty' member does not modify its behaviour, or compensate the complainant, the latter has the right to restrict its imports from that country in order to penalize it.

This kind of retaliatory punishment can be quite comprehensive, since all but one of the UR agreements constitutes a 'Single Undertaking' (see also Chapter 4). This allows a country that does not fulfil its commitments under one agreement to be punished by suspending commitments made to it under other agreements. For example, a country that does not enforce European patents, whether deliberately or because it does not have the expertise to do so, can have its garment exports to the EU blocked by punitive tariffs. However, a small developing country would find it virtually impossible to impose this kind of punishment on a much larger WTO member: by shutting out imports (the bulk of which typically consist of essential machinery, drugs, or food) from the USA or the EU, it would only hurt itself without inflicting much pain on the offender. (Think of who would be hurt more if you alone were to boycott your local supermarket.) Of course, if the punishment is the other way around – a developed country punishing a developing one – it can be devastating to the victim at little cost to the punisher. (No prizes for guessing who would be hurt more if your supermarket decided to boycott you!)

To sum up, most developing countries are simply overwhelmed by having to implement existing agreements, negotiate new ones, and argue their cases in the dispute settlement process on such a wide range of issues, each of which is technically complex.

Question

So, if the UR agreements are so bad, why did so many developing countries sign on, why do they not quit, and why are so many more applying to join the WTO?

One reason, just argued at some length, has undoubtedly been the developing countries' lack of comprehension of what many of the agreements entailed for them, and the loopholes that limited their benefits. But the more crucial reason is set out in detail in Chapter 3: trade is a key part of developing countries' strategies for growth, and whatever the pains and disappointments of being WTO members, they would certainly have been worse off had they stayed out and had their exports shut out of developed country markets altogether. Without the WTO, the kind of trade sanctions I discussed in the previous paragraph could be used quite arbitrarily by powerful countries. In an unequal world, as I ruefully admitted above, being a junior member of the gang is better than being excluded.

4   The rocky road ahead

Several attempts have been made to form a united front of developing countries to negotiate a better deal at the WTO. They have met with little success because there are substantial conflicts of interest between them, for example between agricultural importers and exporters, and between small countries and those larger developing countries that have been able individually to use the lure of opening their markets to get a better deal from developed countries. Conflicts of interest arise too between those inside and outside regional trade agreements or special arrangements that bring preferential access to the markets of particular developed countries. Mexican membership of the North American Free Trade Agreement – discussed in Chapters 8 and 9 – and duty-free treatment of Caribbean banana exports to the EU are prominent examples. More recently, the EU has allowed free import of 'Everything but Arms' from the least developed countries – but that displaces the competing exports from other developing countries. Chapter 4 examines WTO negotiating procedures and the problems of coalition building.

Nonetheless, developing countries have been vocal in their protests. At the Doha Ministerial meeting, they tabled more than a hundred 'implementation' issues: matters concerning the way rules are interpreted and implemented that they wanted discussed as a matter of priority. The Ministerial meeting itself took few decisions, but referred them to various committees with suitable exhortations. The picture that is emerging at the time of writing (early 2003) is that developed countries will agree to substantive concessions relating to the implementation of Uruguay Round agreements only if developing countries make new concessions of their own in the continuing Doha Round negotiations.

The one concrete decision, already referred to above, was the clarification that TRIPS would not prevent governments from taking measures to protect public health. However, this was a declaration rather than a legally binding agreement, and it is not clear what weight it will carry in formal dispute settlement proceedings. Besides, the facility of compulsory licensing for the manufacture of essential drugs (discussed above) will not be of use to the vast majority of developing countries who do not have the necessary manufacturing facilities – and at the time of writing, the USA has blocked an amendment that would allow them to import their requirements from other developing countries.

The developing countries did succeed, for the time being, in regard to two potentially dangerous issues – environmental and labour standards – that pressure groups in the EU and USA had been trying to insert into the WTO framework. Environmental standards were circumscribed and labour standards were kept out, but as pressure for their inclusion remains it is worth examining them further.

4.1 Environmental and labour standards

Question

Look back at Section 1. Why do trade unions in rich countries take up the cause of poor environmental and working conditions in developing countries as they did at Seattle? And why are developing country governments unwilling to have these issues raised in international trade negotiations?

It may seem puzzling that developing countries' governments were apparently so dead set against protecting the environment or improving the working conditions of their own people. These are complex issues, and there is more discussion later in this book (see Chapter 8). My short answer is that developing countries' governments saw these noble objectives, promoted by well-intentioned individuals and organizations, being hijacked by employers and trades unions in 'sunset' industries in the developed world in order to restrict imports from countries that threaten them with cheaper products. To avoid the restrictions, developing countries would have to incur the additional costs of implementing higher environmental and labour standards, making their products uncompetitive.

What is meant by 'environmental and labour standards'? To begin with the environment, the GATT/WTO framework already allows countries to restrict imports if they pose a danger to human, animal or plant health, based on the characteristics of the product (contaminated seafood, for example). Implicitly, this concerns dangers posed to the *importing country*. The issue is whether this should be extended to imports produced by processes (for example, fishing techniques) that do not embody the standards of the importing country, or damage the environment *in the exporting country*, or that damage the 'global commons' (such as the atmosphere, oceans, or endangered plant or animal species).

Labour standards (often referred to in European debates as the 'social clause'), likewise, mean many things to many people. The GATT/WTO already permits restrictions on the import of goods produced by slave or prison labour; the question is whether this should be extended to other practices that people find exploitative or abhorrent, for example child labour. Some supporters of labour standards go further and call for restrictions on the import of goods produced by workers who do not receive wages or other benefits on a par with those in developed countries.

There are both economic and moral arguments against the imposition of external standards. Consider labour standards. Low wages give developing countries an advantage in international markets in selling goods produced using unskilled labour. Imposing costly labour standards such as higher payments to labour would deny them this advantage and deny developed country consumers cheaper goods. From this perspective, to say that low wages give developing countries an 'unfair' advantage is no more valid than saying that workers in developed countries have an 'unfair' advantage because machinery is more widespread and advanced in those countries. (You will examine this argument in Chapter 3.)

None of this is to condone the deplorable disregard of environmental standards and working conditions in most developing countries. But I am arguing that is a matter to be left to environmental activists and trade unions in those countries, with technical and financial assistance from sympathetic outsiders; they have nothing to do with trade policy, unless the product itself poses a threat to the importing country. Indeed labour or environmental standards, or trade sanctions used to enforce them, can end up harming the very causes they are intended to promote. For example, workers who lose their jobs with firms that cannot implement higher environmental standards may turn to other, more environmentally harmful, activities (such as chopping down trees) in order to survive. Similarly, banning the import of goods produced by child labour, without providing any alternative source of livelihood, can force children into a life of crime or prostitution. Nor will the external imposition of wage and benefit standards help adult workers whose employers cannot afford to implement them: workers may lose low paid jobs, and surely low wages are better than no wages.

Nor do I wish to belittle the genuine concern of citizens in developed countries who feel strongly about these issues. However their support for environmental and labour standards necessarily implies that they are willing to pay more in the form of higher prices for goods whose imports they wish to restrict. They would be better advised to donate the same amount to charities and activist groups working towards providing better alternatives in the developing world. They should also apply pressure on their own governments to reduce barriers to the import of agricultural products, clothing, footwear and simple processed manufactures which the world's poor can sell to them.

It is also often argued that some environmental and labour standards amount to imposing one country's social norms on another. One society might find it repugnant to kill a particular species of animal, which is a staple food or source of livelihood in another country. Landmark disputes that have come to the WTO include American restrictions on imported tuna and shrimp caught with nets that might have killed dolphins and sea turtles, respectively. One society might believe that labour standards should include workers' participation in decision making while another might regard this as anathema. However, one should not push this argument about alien norms too far, lest one end up regarding even basic human rights as culturally relative.

But again, trade restrictions are not the answer. Just as there are international agreements on human rights, there are also agreements such as the Montreal and Kyoto protocols negotiated outside the WTO framework to try to tackle activities that have environmental effects (depletion of the ozone layer and global warming, respectively) beyond a country's borders. (Chapters 13 and 14 examine the Montreal and Kyoto protocols.) Other international agreements regulate trade in endangered species, hazardous wastes, and genetically modified organisms. Conventions of the International Labour Organization prescribe and monitor mutually agreed labour standards, though the ILO cannot enforce them.

Beyond these global norms, it should be left to each country to set its own standards, and the degree to which it is willing to compromise on them in the interests of economic development. The West, it must be recalled, industrialized on the strength of tariff protection of its new industries, highly polluting technologies, and brutal exploitation of labour both at home and in the areas under colonial domination. Yet it now tries to impose free trade, environmental and labour standards on much poorer countries. The experience of developed countries shows that people themselves demand better standards as they become richer. Why is this privilege being denied to the world's poor?

Activity 2.1

I have made a strong argument about a controversial subject on which sharp disagreements abound. Look back at the arguments in the preceding paragraphs. Then think of a particular environmental or labour standard you have heard about through the media and write some brief notes as follows. Do you agree with its objectives? Who gains and who loses from the imposition of such a standard? Are there any better ways in which to meet its objectives? Chapter 8 returns to these issues in a different context.

4.2   Asymmetry between labour and capital

Finally, stepping back to get a broader picture, I would like to point to the asymmetry built into the emerging institutional framework governing international economic relations, of which the WTO is one important pillar. The various WTO agreements encourage free movement of goods and certain kinds of services. Possible agreements on cross-border investment and competition policy may allow for freer international movement of capital, already encouraged by the IMF. Yet there is no move towards opening up the international movement of labour; if anything, barriers are being raised rather than dismantled.

This asymmetry is particularly evident in a Uruguay Round agreement that has not been discussed so far in this chapter: the General Agreement on Trade in Services (GATS). Under the GATS, restrictions are being dismantled on cross-border provision of services such as telecommunications, banking and insurance through the setting up of branches of multinational corporations. This again is encouraging the free movement of capital mainly from developed to developing countries. (Chapter 7 discusses foreign investment and multinational companies). Developed countries have shown far less interest in liberalizing services involving the movement of people. What concessions have been made relate mainly to the *temporary* movement of business visitors and of managers and technicians employed by companies in the services markets dominated by Western corporations. In contrast, note that the movement of capital is not treated as temporary, that the transmission of technology has been severely *restricted* by the TRIPS agreement, and that no one is talking about allowing free migration of the vast army of skilled and unskilled manual workers who constitute the vast majority of the labour force in the developing world.

5   Conclusion

International economic relationships are constituted in large part by international trade and investment. I have argued that the current trade regime, apparently one of voluntary adherence to negotiated rule-making, is actually systematically weighted against the needs of developing countries. This asymmetry is rooted in a context where rich countries are eager to prescribe free trade for others but reluctant to impose it on themselves and able to avoid doing so. Its consequences are exacerbated in many developing countries by the social dislocation that trade liberalization has caused.

The current world trade regime has a mixed record in promoting growth and reducing poverty, a point developed in the next chapter. Developing countries furthermore are being pressured to forego the right to implement policies that the developed countries used to attain their present level of affluence, and are being forced instead to set up institutions and implement standards that have historically emerged at a much later stage of development in the West.

In September 2003, the Ministerial Conference of the WTO at Cancun (Mexico), which was due to have taken the Doha agenda forward, collapsed without any agreement, largely because of determined and united opposition from developing countries. On a positive note, in an agreement that was hammered out on the eve of the conference, the USA finally agreed to allow developing countries that lack the capability to produce patented drugs to acquire cheaper emergency supplies by granting compulsory licences to manufacturers in other developing countries. But two of the issues discussed in this chapter proved to be the rocks on which the conference foundered. First, the developed countries obstinately refused to make meaningful reductions in their escalating agricultural subsidies, even as they tried to get the developing countries to reduce their tariffs on agricultural products. Something that received much publicity was the observation that each cow in the EU is subsidized to the tune of over two US dollars a day, which is more than the daily earnings of over a billion poor people in developing countries. The second deal-breaker was the attempt by the EU to load new issues (notably rules governing international investment and competition policy, as mentioned briefly in Section 4) onto the agenda, against the wishes of most of the developing countries, who argued that they did not fully comprehend the implications. It is not all clear what, if anything, can be salvaged from the Cancun wreckage. Is there any wonder, then, that developing countries are less than enthusiastic about the WTO?

Further reading

A critical view of WTO from the point of view of developing countries is Das, Bhagirath Lal (1998) *WTO Agreements: Deficiencies, Imbalances and Required Changes*, London, Zed Books.

A well documented report that goes over much of the same ground as this chapter is Oxfam (2002) *Rigged Rules and Double Standards: Trade, Globalization, and the Fight Against Poverty*, London, Oxfam [online]. Available from www.maketradefair.com [Accessed 20 March 2003].

For an official WTO viewpoint, see the organization's website: www.wto.org

You may also like to consult Chang, Ha-Joon (2002) *Kicking Away the Ladder: Development Strategy in Historical Perspective*, London, Anthem Press. This fascinating little book delves into history to show that in the process of climbing to their present levels of affluence, developed countries have used all the policies that they are now trying to get the developing countries to abjure – whence the book's title.

Chapter 3 Gaining from trade?

Maureen Mackintosh

1   Introduction

> To many in the developing world, trade policy in the more advanced countries seems to be more a matter of self-interest than of general principle. When good economic analysis works in favour of self-interest, it is invoked. When it does not, so much the worse for economic principles.

(Stiglitz, 2001, p.9)

Joseph Stiglitz, a Nobel prize-winning economist, was for a time Chief Economist at the World Bank and chaired US President Clinton's Council of Economic Advisers. He is raising here, in typically combative style, two themes that are central to this chapter. First, he shares Aditya Bhattacharjea's view, put forward in Chapter 2, that developing countries' governments and citizens generally perceive the current world trade regime as weighted against them and in favour of wealthy countries. And second, he is emphasizing that economic theory is a key source of propositions and recriminations in international debates on trade policy.

This chapter aims to convey a critical understanding of key elements of the economic analysis, and associated evidence, that is so often invoked in the noisy and embittered debates about international trade policy and 'globalization'. By the end of this chapter you should be able to examine critically, using economic analysis, a general proposition that underlies Chapter 2: that international trade generates gains that are large but unfairly distributed, and that that unfairness emerges in part (but only in part) from trade policy and from the negotiations that shape the world trade regime.

In order to examine this proposition, we need to separate out carefully three different questions. The first is the potential and actual gains from international trade for the citizens of trading countries. There are good reasons to think that trade creates economic benefits that are potentially large, in the form of higher incomes and more diverse goods and services to consume, although it also brings economic costs such as environmental damage. The source of these 'gains from trade' is a core question for this chapter, and is the subject of Section 3.

The second question is the *distribution* of those gains from trade: who gains and who loses? Even without the intervention of trade policy, there are good economic reasons for expecting international markets to distribute the gains

33

from trade unequally. Sections 4, 5 and 6 examine some reasons why this is so – and what might be done about it.

Which leads us to the third question: what is the effect of trade *policy*, and specifically of trade liberalization, on the scale and distribution of the gains from trade? Trade policies are interventions by governments to change the extent and pattern of trade. To assess the effects of these policies, we therefore need first to understand trade itself and then to analyse the effects of interventions in trade. Section 2 introduces the problem, and argues that some economic theory is needed to tackle it. Sections 6, 7 and 8 return to it.

As I work through these three questions, I aim to argue the following case. International trade brings large economic benefits: the world would be much, much poorer without trade. But the distribution of those benefits among countries, and among groups of people within countries, depends upon the *terms* on which different countries are inserted into the international trade regime: what resources countries have for production; the goods and services they can export; how expensive those goods and services were to produce, and the prices they command; and the extent to which countries offer markets for the goods of others. Countries can get stuck, producing few exports for a declining market, or experience success in expanding and diversifying exports. A country's experience depends on a mix of economic activity and trade policy, and I shall examine some elements of that mix in this chapter.

2　International trade and tariffs: political economics

'International trade' – often just called 'trade' in this chapter – means the buying and selling of goods and services across national borders. In this section I put forward and present some evidence for four economic propositions about international trade. Each of these propositions plays a role in political debate on trade policy. Taken together, these propositions support and elucidate Aditya Bhattacharjea's argument in Chapter 2 that developing countries face an invidious choice between the high costs of exclusion from important export markets and the doubtful benefits of being 'junior members of the gang' within the WTO. The propositions are as follows.

1　Trade and wealth tend to go together.

2　However, participation in trade can make poverty worse.

3　The current world trade regime favours the rich countries.

4　Yet international market integration forces countries into trade in pursuit of wealth.

2.1   Trade and wealth go together

There are a number of ways in which high incomes and international trading success can be observed to go together. First, international trade is strikingly dominated by the richest countries in the world: mainly the industrialized countries of Europe, North America and Australasia plus Japan (Table 3.1).

Table 3.1   World trading relations: direction of trade (percentages of world merchandise trade), 1998

Origin	Destination		
	High income countries	Low and middle income countries	World
High income countries	58.5	17.3	75.8
Low and middle income countries	17.0	7.1	24.2
World	75.6	24.4	100.0

The numbers may not add to totals because of rounding of figures to one decimal place.
Trade is valued at export value f.o.b. (free on board, not including insurance and freight charges).
The figures are for trade in goods only; trade in services (which is less well recorded) is not included.

Source: World Bank, 2000a

Question

Stop and look carefully at Table 3.1. It compresses quite a lot of information into a small table. State in your own words the extent of the dominance of high income countries in world trade.

Three-quarters of world goods trade originates in high income countries. Over half of world trade is trade between high income countries. Less than one-quarter of world trade originates from low and middle income countries, and only about 7 per cent of world trade is *between* low and middle income countries.

Activity 3.1

Check your understanding of Table 3.1 by describing how important low and middle income countries are to each other as a destination for exports. That is, more precisely, what percentage of low and middle income countries' exports goes to other low and middle income countries?

This dominance of world trade by high income countries is all the more striking as they had only 15.6 per cent of the world's population in 2001. It does not arise because richer countries trade more relative to their total output than poorer countries; on the contrary, they exported about 22 per cent of their total output in 1999, while low and middle income countries exported about 27 per cent. The dominance arises because, in 2001, average income per head in the rich countries was *23 times* the average income of citizens in the rest of the world (World Bank, 2002b, calculations in US dollars). Hence, rich countries' exports and imports dominate world trade.

However, this picture is not static. A number of lower income countries have grown much faster than the world average, and much of their growth has been 'export-led', that is, built on export success and involving a rise in the ratio of exports to total output. This is the second way in which trade and wealth are observed to go together: countries that have been most successful in rapidly raising the incomes of their populations since 1950 have done so, in part, by successful participation in trade. The most striking examples are the rapidly growing Asian countries, led after 1950 by Japan, and followed by the so-called 'Asian Tigers' (South Korea, Singapore, Taiwan, Hong Kong) and then by other Asian exporters including China, India and Bangladesh.

2.2 Trade participation can make poverty worse

However, there are examples of countries that have increased trade – or have continued to export a substantial part of their output – while failing to reap benefits in terms of a reduction in poverty. This, unfortunately, has been the fate of a number of countries in sub-Saharan Africa.

Table 3.1 disguised differences among low and middle income countries. Of the 24.2 per cent of world trade originating in those countries (Table 3.1), almost half (46 per cent) was in fact exported by East Asian and Pacific countries, and only 5 per cent by countries in sub-Saharan Africa. Yet countries in sub-Saharan Africa exported, on average, 28 per cent of their output. It is not that the African countries do not participate in trade, but that they have not managed to grow richer through trade.

Instead, trade seems to have led some very poor African countries into a poverty trap: I shall explore its mechanisms in Section 6 of this chapter, and Part 4 will return to these issues. One aspect of the trap is worth noting here, however: exporters in sub-Saharan Africa and in Asia sell quite different types of goods. The successful Asian exporters have focused on selling manufactures, and their success has formed part of a major shift in the composition of world trade since 1945 away from primary products and towards manufactures and services.

Table 3.2 shows the outcome of that shift. The table distinguishes primary products (agricultural products and unprocessed minerals, including oil); manufactured goods of all kinds; and services. 'Services' is not an easy category to define: it includes insurance, financial services and health services (basically, 'everything you cannot drop on your foot').

Table 3.2   Exports by category, selected regions and the world (percentage of total exports), 1998

Region	Percentage of total exports		
	Primary	Manufactures	Services
Middle-East and North Africa	67	18	15
Sub-Saharan Africa	55	35	11
Latin America and the Caribbean	44	44	12
South Asia	16	63	21
East Asia and the Pacific	14	73	13
High income countries	12	68	20
World	15	66	19

Source: Findlay and O'Rourke, 2001; based on World Bank, 2001a

In the high income countries, as in the world, exports are dominated by manufactures. East and South Asia have both switched strongly to manufactured and service exports, while the Middle East, Latin America and Africa depend heavily on primary exports. Trade and growth are more likely to go together when trade is in manufactures, while primary products seem a less reliable route to higher incomes except for a few Middle East oil-producing countries with relatively small populations.

2.3   The world trade regime favours the rich countries

This is the most controversial of the four propositions.

Question

Look back at Chapter 2. What does Aditya Bhattacharjea suggest is the main reason developing countries have found many of the promised benefits of the current trade regime to be illusory?

Chapter 2 argues that the process of trade liberalization, presided over by the GATT and WTO, has been *asymmetrical*, discriminating in practice against the interests of developing countries. The author gives a number of examples of developing countries' key exports, such as agricultural products and textiles, facing restricted access to wealthy countries' markets because of trade policies designed for that purpose.

To see how this regime can create an African poverty trap, let me start, then, by recounting an exemplary tale of the Aditya Bhattacharjea kind. In the 1970s, I lived for several years in Senegal, a West African country that was at the time developing fruit and vegetable production for export, mainly to Europe. As part of this development, Senegalese farmers rapidly increased the quantities of tomatoes they grew. Some were exported fresh, and many were turned into tomato concentrate – much used in home cooking. By 1990–91, Senegal was producing 73 000 tons of concentrate and exporting it to neighbouring countries.

However, it was not to last. The largest producer of tomato concentrate after the USA is the European Union (EU). EU tomato farmers are paid (at the time of writing in early 2003, and it seems set to continue) a minimum price that is higher than the world price; EU tomato processors are paid a subsidy to cover the difference between that price and the world market price of tomatoes. The processors in turn need markets for their concentrate. In 1994, Senegal removed its tariffs on imported tomato concentrate as part of broader trade liberalization commitments. Senegalese producers, with no subsidies and outdated equipment, then ceased to be able to compete with the European producers. Imports of concentrate jumped from 62 tons in 1994 to 5348 tons in 1996. Senegalese processing firms closed – now only one remains – and local production fell to 20 000 tons. European imported concentrate now dominates the local market (UNCTAD, 2002a, p.160).

Here was a small country benefiting from agricultural trade and moving into trade in processed (manufactured) goods. Both Senegal and the EU countries had been 'protecting' their producers from the full effects of international market competition. One country, the poorest, weakest one, removed the protection. The others, a rich group of countries, did not. In some sense trade had become 'freer' after 1994 since one side had liberalized the entry of goods. But the asymmetry of trade policy that Aditya Bhattacharjea complained about is strikingly evident. The poorest country lost its processing production and its export trade.

How tariff protection works

To see just how that happened, let us look more closely at the workings of tariff protection. Tomato concentrate is a standard product, with many producers of tubes or tins. You can think of the world market, therefore, as having a single 'going price' in dollars per kilo of concentrate. If Senegal puts a tariff on imports of concentrate, it means that it imposes a tax which is levied when the product crosses the Senegalese border.

Question

Just how does that tariff 'protect' local producers? Try to explain it to yourself before reading on.

When the tariff is imposed, the price of imported concentrate in Senegal should rise. Overseas exporters are unlikely to be making so much profit from a standard product on a competitive market that they will pay the tax by reducing profits; rather, they will raise prices in Senegal. The price rise allows local producers both to increase their own prices and to increase sales since they pay no tax and so can compete more successfully with imports. The losers are the local consumers – paying more for their tomato sauces – and the overseas exporters; local workers, taken on by local tomato processing firms, benefit. The local firms are thus protected from the full force of price competition on the world market.

EU farm subsidies similarly protect European farmers and processors within the European Union market from the full force of external competition from producers with lower costs. If both European and Senegalese protection had been lowered simultaneously, trade liberalization would have been fairer as well as more extensive – and the Senegalese producers might have survived.

Activity 3.2

Check your understanding of tariffs before reading on, by running the argument about Senegalese protection in reverse. What happens when the tariff is removed?

Asymmetric trade liberalization

Trade liberalization, defined in Chapter 2 as the reduction of tariffs, quotas and subsidies, therefore implies the reduction of protection of local ('home' or 'domestic') producers. The level of tariff protection for a particular item produced in one country can be measured by the height of the tariff as a percentage of the sales value of the good. Measuring average levels of tariff protection for industrial sectors or countries involves some complicated averaging across the tariffs on many goods, and also taking into account tariffs on inputs used in production, but the measures all tell the same general story – sweeping but uneven liberalization across the world in the latter half of the twentieth century.

Figure 3.1 sets this in a longer historical context. It shows one estimate of tariff levels over nearly a century and a half, for 35 countries (high, middle and low income today) for which a long data series could be constructed. The two breaks in the series are the two world wars. The huge escalation of tariffs in the economic depression of the 1930s (referred to in Chapter 2) stands out sharply, as does the post Second World War liberalization, particularly from the mid-1960s to about 1980 and then again in the 1990s.

Figure 3.1   Unweighted world average tariff, 35 countries (per cent)
'Unweighted' means that the tariff rate for each country is calculated and then averaged across countries; no account is taken of the fact that some economies are larger than others.
Source: Clemens and Williamson, 2001

Not all of this liberalization has been the result of GATT negotiations and WTO agreements; much has been unilateral, instituted with the aim of benefiting the country concerned. As Chapter 2 noted, much of the decline in protection before 1980 occurred in the rich industrialized countries, while in the subsequent two decades, tariff protection was reduced by most middle and lower income countries (Figure 3.2), driven quite strongly by trade negotiations. The fall in protection was particularly sharp in South Asia (liberalization in India is examined in Chapters 6 and 7). However, in the late 1990s, as Figure 3.2 shows, average tariffs were still lower in rich countries than elsewhere. In this sense, rich countries can and do argue that they have more liberal trade policies than developing countries: that, contrary to my proposition, the trade regime *dis*favours the rich countries (see Section 5).

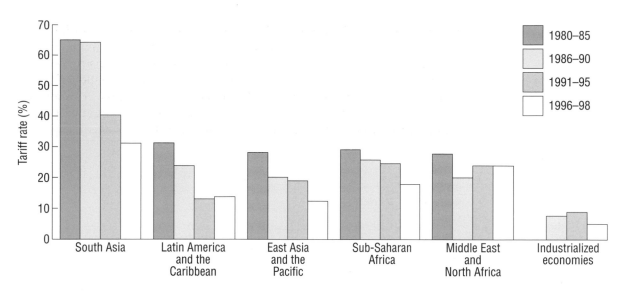

Figure 3.2   Average tariff rates by region
Source: based on World Bank, 2002c, p.9

Activity 3.3

Check your understanding of Figure 3.2 by explaining what the height of each bar indicates.

Average tariff calculations can be misleading, however. Industrialized countries have low tariffs in general, but they have retained some sharp tariff 'peaks' (as Chapter 2 explains). These are high tariffs on particular goods, strikingly those of particular interest to low income exporters, such as agricultural products and clothing and textiles. Agricultural items make up most of the peak tariffs over 50 per cent, and rich countries' tariff rates rise in some cases as agricultural products become more processed, depriving low income countries of opportunities to move into manufactured exports. The result is that, on average, high income countries protect their markets against developing countries more strongly than against other rich countries.

Question

Discuss the extent to which Table 3.3 supports the statement that, on average, high income countries protect their markets against developing countries more strongly than against other rich countries.

Table 3.3   Average tariff rates by country group, 1995 (per cent)

Exporting countries	Importing countries	
	High income	Developing
Manufactures:		
high income countries	0.8	10.9
developing countries	3.4	12.8
world	1.5	11.5
Agriculture:		
high income countries	15.9	21.5
developing countries	15.1	18.3
world	15.6	20.1

Source: Hertel and Martin, 2001

Read down the first column of figures. Average tariffs imposed by high income countries on imports of manufactured goods were 3.4 per cent if the goods were exported by a developing country and only 0.8 per cent if they came from a high income country. The same effect is *not* visible for agricultural exports. However, agricultural exports face much higher tariffs than manufactured exports, and this damages those developing countries – including the poorest – that rely predominantly on agricultural exports.

Chapter 2 argues that a key reason for this pattern of protection is political pressure within rich countries from groups (farmers, clothing workers) who would lose from freer trade. Joseph Stiglitz agrees (2001, pp.8–9):

> What are developing countries to make of the rhetoric in favour of rapid liberalization, when rich countries with full employment and strong safety nets argue that they need to impose protective measures to help those adversely affected by trade? Or when rich countries play down the political pressures within developing countries – insisting that their polities 'face up to the hard choices' – while excusing their own trade barriers and agricultural subsidies by citing 'political pressures'?

2.4   International market integration forces countries into trade

Aditya Bhattacharjea argues in Chapter 2 that developing countries had little choice but to join the WTO regime: that staying out was worse. Let us explore the basis for that statement. As international trade has grown in volume since the 1950s, it has brought with it a process of international market integration that forms part of what is meant by that highly political term 'globalization'.

When economists talk of 'markets', we do not generally mean particular trading locations (as in, going to the local town market), but rather processes of buying and selling and the setting of prices. As incomes have risen,

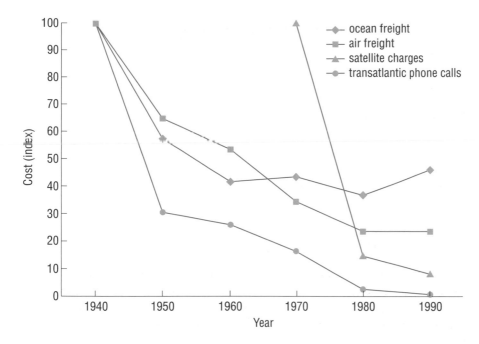

Figure 3.3   Falling transport and communications costs since the 1940s
The vertical axis shows costs as an index: 1940 = 100 for ocean and air freight and transatlantic phone calls and 1970 = 100 for satellite charges.
Source: based on Baldwin and Martin, 1999

markets that were locally bounded – local producers selling to local buyers – have joined up and become national or international. Food markets are a classic example: supermarket chains in high income countries have created national retail markets for food, and their buying has created international markets for food supply. Some suppliers have created international retail markets for particular food or drink items – Coca Cola for example – but this is harder to do, as food tastes are strongly nationally patterned.

The more goods and services can move unimpeded across borders, the more firms come to see their market opportunities in international terms. Falling transport and communication costs have underpinned the integration of markets, allowing Europeans to eat green beans all year round and UK firms to move call centres to New Delhi. Figure 3.3 shows freight and transatlantic phone costs from 1950 to 1990 compared with the costs in 1940, and satellite charges in 1980 and 1990 compared with the charges in 1970.

However, the most dramatic change in the last two decades is not shown in Figure 3.3: the rise of the Internet since the mid-1990s that has allowed US firms, for example, to employ software programmers in South India as a means to cut costs (a move discussed in Chapter 7). In 1993 there were about

26 000 Internet domain names; in 1999 there were around 5 million websites. In 1993 estimates had about 3 million people connected to the Internet; in 1999 about 2000 million people were connected world wide (*Internet Economy Indicators*, 2002).

Mutual knowledge resulting from migration and trade also reduces 'distance' in a social sense, as does the experience of working for the same employer in different countries, or a shared sense of foreign economic and political domination. The trade flows bring with them knowledge and information, from access to new technology to cultural goods and services such as films, music and media gossip about celebrities.

This international market integration is patchy, however. Transport costs still influence trade patterns, and world wide there is still a clear tendency for countries to trade predominantly with neighbours. This has been reinforced by regional free trade agreements such as the North American Free Trade Agreement (NAFTA) (which you will study in Chapters 8 and 9). But for services that depend on costs of communication that have truly been 'murdered' by the Internet – such as bulk software code writing – distance has ceased to protect producers in one country from competition from abroad.

For, in the end, market integration is all about *competition* – a topic about which we shall have a lot to say in this book. The more market integration there is, the less local producers are protected from competition from producers elsewhere. For this reason, a commonly used measure of international market integration is the extent to which prices for particular goods are similar across the world. If there are high transport costs and producers sell predominantly on to local markets, we would expect prices to be very different on different continents. As markets integrate and it becomes cheap to trade, prices are likely to converge. One reason is that very different prices allow people to profit from *arbitrage*: buying in one place and selling in another. This in itself pulls prices closer together. Economic historians calculate that between 1820 and 2000 price gaps between prices for the same traded good across the world fell dramatically, by 92 per cent. This was made up of a huge drop of 81 per cent in the long nineteenth century (to 1914); then a reversal, with price gaps doubling back to 1870 levels, when trade collapsed between the two World Wars; then another big drop after 1950 (Lindert and Williamson, 2001, Table 1).

Finally, as markets integrate, we would expect the ratio of trade to output to rise world wide, as the economic importance of national borders erodes. Migration of people, too, is likely to be encouraged by the 'death of distance' (Cairncross, 1997). Figure 3.4 illustrates these two aspects of 'globalization' since 1870.

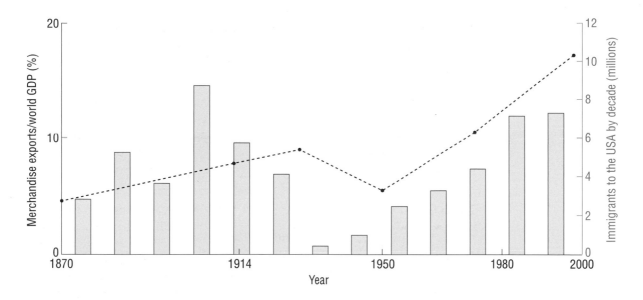

Figure 3.4   Waves of globalization: movement of goods and people

Sources: World Bank, 2002c, p.23 (immigration to the USA); Maddison, 2001, Table F-5 (merchandise exports/world GDP)

Question

Stop and look carefully at Figure 3.4. Describe succinctly to yourself what it shows.

The height of each of the bars shows millions of immigrants to the USA, measured on the right-hand axis: the data are being used as a 'proxy', that is, a reasonable substitute for unavailable data, in this case total migrants in the world. The broken line shows merchandise exports (that is, not including services, which are poorly documented) as a percentage of total world GDP at selected dates. The percentages are shown on the left-hand axis. This line will be higher, the greater the percentage of output traded. It is drawn as a broken line to remind you that it connects up just a few dates: 1870, 1913 (just before the First World War), 1929 (just before the Great Depression of the 1930s), 1950 (just after the Second World War), 1973 and 1998. It does not show what happened to the trade/output ratios between these dates, for example during the 1930s. It does show that trade/output ratios were lower in 1950 than they had been in the 1920s, and that the ratio was higher in 1998 than at any of the previous dates. Migration to the USA peaked before the First World War, fell towards zero between the two World Wars, and then rose to a historically high level in the 1980s and 1990s.

Policy-driven trade liberalization is thus only one force for increasing international market integration. The more markets integrate, the less choice individual governments have about participating in trade, as the protection of distance and market boundaries erodes. The policy issue for governments is then the *terms* on which the country's producers succeed in participating in international markets.

3 The gains from trade

The economic case for an open trading system based upon multilaterally agreed rules is simple enough, and rests largely upon commercial common sense ... According to the principle of comparative advantage, countries A and B still stand to benefit from trading with each other even if A is better than B at making everything.

(World Trade Organization, 2002a)

I shall now return to the first proposition in Section 2, the link between trade and wealth, and explore the economic theory that the WTO puts forward as providing the fundamental justification for its activities.

3.1 Trade, markets and economic reasoning

One of the most powerful ideas in economics and political economy is the idea that there are mutual gains from trade for trading partners. Any understanding of the economic debates underlying trade policy must start with the economic analysis that supports this basic idea. Strictly, the argument is that there are gains to be had from *specialization* and trade. The key assumption in the economic analysis is that people *differ* and so do firms and countries: they differ in their desires, resources and abilities. Therefore, if each 'economic agent' (firm, person, country) does what he, she, it does best, and each trades some of the results for what others do best, then everyone can be better off in terms of the amount of goods and services available to them.

This argument for the gains from trade is thus not only about international trade; it has had a long career in debates on the politics of economic policy. At its most general, it is an argument for freedom to specialize and trade on *markets* in general. It was formulated in general terms by Adam Smith, the eighteenth-century writer who was one of the founders of economics, and who argued for lifting of restrictions on freedom to trade on markets.

The way I explain the theory here, in relation to international trade, looks back to its main originator, David Ricardo. Ricardo was an economist who was also a Member of Parliament in early nineteenth-century Britain, and he was deeply involved in the economic policy questions of his day – including trade policy. He argued strongly for the repeal of the Corn Laws, which imposed tariffs on wheat imported into Britain.

To understand both the robustness of the theory of the gains from trade and its limitations, you need to understand how economic theory works. Economic arguments are generally built up rather formally. Assumptions are made that allow the theorist to isolate and focus on the particular economic problem to be studied, and implications are deduced from those assumptions. The demonstration of the gains from trade is an example of that deductive style of economic argument (sometimes called economic 'modelling') and is called the theory of 'comparative advantage'. Ricardo's core proposition is still repeatedly cited in economic and political debate, as it is by the WTO in the quotation at the start of this section.

Understanding economic 'models' of this type requires a certain amount of patience with simplifying assumptions and the process of deducing implications. The strengths of this kind of formal reasoning are considerable, however, not least in that you can see precisely what you are being asked to agree with or think about. If you disagree, you can locate precisely the step in the reasoning that you reject. To attack economic theories of this deductive type you need to attack the assumptions, or to attack the logic, or to argue that the conclusions drawn are not substantiated empirically. To defend them, you need to defend the simplifications as robust and relevant, the logic as coherent, and the implications as supported by empirical evidence.

3.2   The theory of comparative advantage

So, let us examine how the economic theory of comparative advantage demonstrates the gains from trade between two countries. I shall compare two imagined situations: a complete lack of trade ('autarky') and free trade (no trade barriers such as tariffs). I shall suppose (here come the assumptions) that there are two countries, a low income country and a high income country. Both produce two goods: an agricultural good, unprocessed food ('food'), and a manufactured good, which I shall call 'medicine'.

The low income country produces *both* goods much less efficiently than the other country (the situation the WTO is referring to above). A simple way to specify this clearly is to suppose (more assumptions) that production of each good uses only labour. (I shall forget about machinery for now, otherwise our model would get more complicated because the machinery would have to be produced too.) The low income country uses more labour than the high income country to produce each unit of food *and* each pill.

If there is no trade, each country is truly a self-sufficient economic 'island'. Each will produce a mix of food and medicine for its population. However, if trade opens up between the countries, then both can gain higher levels of consumption of both goods, *despite the fact that one country is absolutely more efficient at producing both goods.*

It is in that last italicized point that the political clout of this model lies, as the WTO clearly implies above. It has seemed natural to many to suppose – in Ricardo's day and in our own – either that countries with highly efficient production have little to gain from exchange with less efficient trading partners, or, alternatively, that less efficient countries will be necessarily damaged by trade with more efficient countries. The model of 'comparative advantage' shows that – on certain assumptions – neither supposition is correct.

A numerical example

To see why this is so, the simplest method is to illustrate the argument with fictional numbers. Even if you do not find numerical examples particularly engaging, it is worth working carefully through this one: it clearly demonstrates the logic of the model. Suppose the low income country has the larger population: it has 1500 workers. The high income country has 200. A worker in the high income country can produce 100 bags of food or 20 boxes of pills a month. In the low income country, a worker can produce only 20 bags of food or 1 box of pills a month.

Figure 3.5 is a graphical illustration of what this implies for output and average incomes. It shows the size of each of the economies by drawing the maximum production possibilities of each country in the absence of trade. Look at Figure 3.5 carefully, starting with Figure 3.5(a), which shows the high income country. On the vertical axis of the figure is plotted food produced, measured in bags per month. The horizontal axis shows medicine, measured as boxes of pills per month. If the country produces no medicine, it can produce 20 000 bags of food (point A); if no food, 4000 boxes of pills (point B). Or it can produce any mix of food and medicine along the solid line AB joining those two points, that is, on the production possibility frontier. All points along the line AB, such as point C, are *maximum* production levels. We assume the country uses all its labour as best it can, so it produces along AB and not at a point such as D.

Activity 3.4

Give a similar description of Figure 3.5(b).

Question

Now look back at both parts of Figure 3.5. Can you show, just using Figure 3.5, that people in the country shown in Figure 3.5(b) consume, on average, less than people in the country shown in Figure 3.5(a), that is, that they are much poorer?

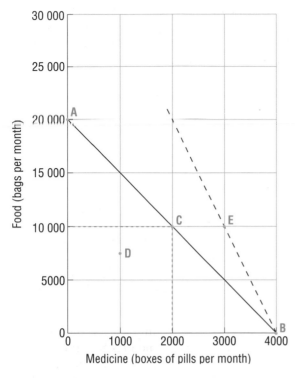

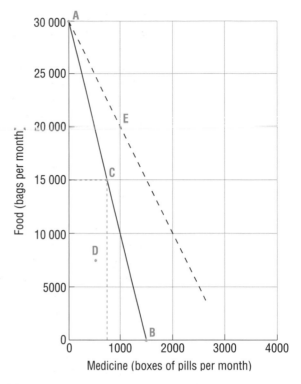

(a)   High income country (200 workers)

(b)   Low income country (1500 workers)

Figure 3.5   Production possibility frontiers for two countries

There are far more people who need to eat and who need to be treated for illnesses in the country shown in Figure 3.5(b). Therefore, for consumption to be equal, the economy in Figure 3.5(b) would have to be much larger than that shown in Figure 3.5(a). You can see at a glance that this is not the case. Indeed, this is one of the uses of figures like this: they summarize numerical information clearly, so you can see what it means. In the absence of trade, each country must produce a mix of food and medicine for its population. Suppose that they each produce half of their total production possibilities of each good (point C). Then in Figure 3.5(b) each worker (and his or her family) has at his or her disposal just 10 bags of food and half a box of pills a month. In Figure 3.5(a) workers have 50 bags of food and 10 boxes of pills each.

Trade can raise output and incomes

So can trade help raise these low incomes? Consider what might happen if these countries can trade. Then each could specialize in one good and trade some of it for the other good. But which to specialize in? To answer the question, look at the rate at which each country can swap food for pills, as workers move from one industry to the other. Suppose that the high income country – Figure 3.5(a) – starts from point C and wants to produce an additional box of pills. How many bags of food have to be given up? Think of one worker moving from food to pills: the country loses 100 bags of food and gets 20 extra boxes of pills: that is, the 'cost' of each box of pills is 5 bags of food. Economists call this the opportunity cost of the box of pills: the country has lost the opportunity to consume 5 bags of food.

The opportunity cost
The opportunity cost of a good is the output that would have been achieved by the best alternative use of the inputs used to produce it.

Now consider a move the other way. A worker moves to food from medicine. The country loses 20 boxes of pills and gets 100 bags of food; the opportunity cost of each bag of food is one-fifth (0.2) of a box of pills.

Question

If the low income country wants to produce an extra box of pills, how much food does it have to give up?

If the low income country reallocates a worker from food to medicine it loses 20 bags of food and gets a box of pills. The 'cost' of a box of pills is 20 bags of food. Going the other way, the opportunity cost in the low income country of a bag of food is 0.05 or one twentieth of a box of pills. Table 3.4 summarizes these calculations.

Table 3.4   Opportunity costs in the two countries

	High income country	Low income country
Opportunity cost of a box of pills in terms of food	5	20
Opportunity cost of a bag of food in terms of medicine	0.2	0.05

Although the high income country produces both food and medicine much more efficiently than the low income country, nevertheless the low income country is *relatively* more efficient at producing food. That is, the opportunity cost of producing food in terms of medicine is lower in the low income country. To say the same thing another way, the low income country has a *comparative advantage* in food production. Conversely, the high income country has a comparative advantage in medicine.

This implies the following strong conclusion: if the low income country specializes in producing food, and the higher income country specializes in producing pills, and they trade, then both countries can be better off. There are gains to be had from trade.

Activity 3.5

Convince yourself that this conclusion is correct. Assume that both countries specialize according to comparative advantage. What is world output (that is, the total output of the two countries together)? How does it compare to world output if both countries produce at point C on Figure 3.5?

I shall turn below to some of the 'buried' issues in this story, notably the prices at which countries trade, which country benefits more and who is actually doing the trading. But before I do that, let me note how strong this argument is. In its most general and robust form, it says that, where countries (it might be people, or firms) have different abilities, then they should specialize in what they do best and trade, *even* where one trading partner is better at producing everything. Then everyone can be better off. The formal nature of this argument (deducing implications from stated assumptions) – together with the reflection that each country will surely enter into trade only if it *does* make it better off – makes it a compelling and influential one.

4   Sharing the gains: the terms of trade

The comparative advantage model tells us that, on stated assumptions, countries *can* benefit from specialization and trade. But do all trading countries actually benefit? So far, we have established only that total 'world' output rises. To understand how the gains from trade are shared between trading countries – a key question raised by Chapter 2 – we need to consider the *prices* at which countries trade.

4.1   The terms of trade

When countries trade, they exchange their goods for goods of another country at market prices. In the real world, there are numerous goods, and prices are set in money terms. Money in the form of tradeable foreign exchange (dollars for example, or euros) allows a country to sell to one country and buy from another. These money prices allow us to compare relative prices of goods: to say that one thing costs, say, twice as much as another.

Economists refer to the price of a country's exports relative to the price of its imports as its terms of trade. These terms of trade are very influential in determining the distribution of gains from trade between countries. To show this, I shall use the numerical example in Section 3 one last time. In that simple two goods/two countries model, we can forget money and just consider relative prices, asking how much food a country can buy for medicine on the international market and (therefore) how much medicine for food.

Terms of trade
A country's terms of trade are given by the ratio of its export prices to its import prices.

Question

Think about the high income country in Figure 3.5(a). It specializes in producing medicine. How much food will it require on the international market (from the low income country) in return for each box of pills?

The answer follows straightforwardly from the discussion of opportunity cost in the last section. If the high income country produces one fewer box of pills, it will get five bags of food from home production (Table 3.4). So to persuade it to trade, it will need to get *more* than five bags of food for each box of pills. Any higher relative price – such as 10 bags – will imply that, by trading some medicine for food, it can increase the total consumption possibilities of people in the economy.

Look at the dotted line in Figure 3.5(a). It represents the high income country's trading opportunities at a relative price of 10 bags of food per box of pills. Suppose the high income country specializes in medicine and trades 1000 boxes of pills for 10 000 bags of food. Then you can think of the country starting from point B on Figure 3.5(a) and trading out along the dotted line to reach point E. Since point E, and the whole dotted line, lie outside the high income country's production possibility frontier, the country is richer at any point on the dotted line than it would be if it did not specialize and trade.

Question

Tell a similar story about specialization and trade for the low income country using Figure 3.5(b).

Exactly the same effect operates for the low income country. It specializes in food. The price of a box of medicine on the international market is, as above, 10 bags of food. The low income country starts at point A and exchanges 10 000 bags of food for 1000 boxes of medicine, trading out along the dotted line to point E. The citizens of the country are still a lot poorer than those in the high income country, but their consumption possibilities (their real incomes) have increased. Both countries gain from trade.

The terms of trade, furthermore, determine *how much* of the benefits go to each country.

Question

Suppose the relative price at which the countries are trading is 10 bags of food per box of pills. The price of medicine falls to 8 bags of food per box of pills. Which country loses and which gains?

I hope you can see that, in this case, the low income country gains. Since the relative price of medicine has fallen, each bag of food the low income country sells buys more medicine. Conversely, the high income country loses: the medicine it trades buy fewer bags of food, although the country continues to benefit from trading as compared with autarky (just not as much as before).

4.2   Real world terms of trade

Let us now take our two-country model of comparative advantage and the terms of trade back into the real world, and ask how prices work in practice to distribute gains from trade. Look back at Table 3.1, which divides trade between countries by income level. The high income countries (top left on the table) tend to have diversified exports and imports. However, the low and middle income countries' trade is often concentrated on a few goods: think of oil producers, of poor countries that rely on a few agricultural exports such as cotton or cocoa (in Chapter 2, Aditya Bhattacharjea refers to this as the 'traditional colonial trading pattern'), and of those whose manufactured exports are concentrated in a few sectors (such as clothing and textiles in Bangladesh).

So it is the trade between low/middle income countries and rich countries (middle of the first column of Table 3.1 and top of column 2) that best fits the comparative advantage model of countries specializing and trading very different goods with each other: food for medicine, minerals for financial services, and so on. And it is the low and middle income countries with a narrow range of exports that are particularly vulnerable to changes in the terms of trade. If the price of a key export drops sharply, while other prices stay the same, so the country's terms of trade decline, then it can buy fewer imports with the same quantity of exports, and incomes in the country fall. Rich countries with more diversified exports can hope to offset falling prices for some goods with rising prices for others.

Figure 3.6 shows some evidence of what has happened since 1960 to the terms of trade of agricultural exporters. The figure shows the ratio of agricultural commodity prices – for agricultural raw materials (such as cotton), food (such as wheat and rice) and tropical beverages (such as coffee and tea) – to prices of manufactured goods on international markets. The ratio for each in 1980 is set equal to 100, and the earlier and subsequent ratios are shown relative to the 1980 ratio.

Question

Describe the trends shown on Figure 3.6.

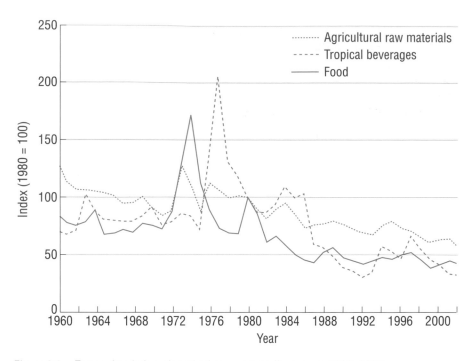

Figure 3.6   Terms of trade for selected primary commodity groups, 1960–2002
Source: UNCTAD, 2002a, p.138

All three price ratios show a peak in the mid-1970s at a time when oil prices were also very high. The variation – or 'volatility' – is greater for food and beverages than it is for agricultural raw materials. All three are lower in the 1990s than in the 1960s, showing that agricultural exporters (which include rich countries such as the USA and the EU as well as lower income countries) were earning fewer manufacturing goods in return for a given volume of agricultural goods.

Table 3.5 gives just one example of the scale of the economic crisis that can be generated in this way in low income countries. In the second half of the 1990s, coffee prices fell steeply. The table shows the scale of the decline, in cash terms, for several of the poorest countries in the world.

Table 3.5 comes from a report by UNCTAD, the United Nations Conference on Trade and Development, on the problems of the least developed (that is, the poorest) countries. This is their comment on the data:

> Prices paid to coffee growers have declined between 1995 and 2000 by over 50 per cent in 10 out of 14 LDCs [Least Developed Countries] for which data are available ... The implications of this for livelihoods in these countries, particularly in those almost completely dependent on coffee exports, cannot be over-emphasized.

(UNCTAD, 2002a, p.141)

Table 3.5   Coffee prices received by selected Least Developed Countries (US cents per pound, current prices), 1995, 1998 and 2000

Country and coffee type	1995	1998	2000
Tanzania:			
Columbian milds	71.32	70.95	64.00[a]
Robustas	48.14	27.13	17.78[a]
Uganda:			
Milds	109.80	117.34	76.29
Robustas	94.41	115.02	26.07
Malawi:			
Milds	108.96	67.36	48.99
Madagascar:			
Milds	88.61	52.14	20.82
Robustas	66.46	43.45	17.35
Ethiopia:			
Brazilian naturals	73.32	88.68	49.86

[a]*Figures for 1999.*
Source: UNCTAD, 2002a, p.143; from International Coffee Organization data

Transporting coffee beans, Quibdo River market, Columbia

Conversely, coffee-consuming countries have to trade fewer of their own exports for coffee. The terms of trade are thus a very powerful influence in distributing the gains from trade between countries. You will come across this general theme about international prices a number of times in this book: big changes in relative prices can restructure economies, redistribute resources and change lives.

5   Gainers and losers within countries

Trade changes the economic structure of countries, sometimes drastically, as Chapter 2 notes. The two-country example in Section 3 illustrated that proposition in a simple sense: in the high income country, complete specialization in medicine requires all the country's farmers to stop farming and retrain for pill production; in the low income country, the converse is true. For countries to gain from trade, this kind of structural change must happen. If it does not, people will be stuck in unemployment as some industries lose the competitive battle, and the industries benefiting from trade will not find the labour to allow them to expand.

This section asks: how can we know who is likely to gain and lose from trade *within* countries? In particular, it is widely predicted that freeing trade will benefit those on low incomes, notably those doing low skill and unskilled jobs. I shall look at the source of that prediction, and at the strong assumptions necessary for it to be true.

5.1   What determines comparative advantage?

So far I have written about comparative advantage as if it was a given feature of countries: some countries just are relatively better at producing some things than other things. But why? To investigate that question, I first need to drop the assumption made in Section 3 that goods are produced only with labour. That was not a key assumption for the basic proposition of comparative advantage, just a useful simplification of the arithmetic.

Factors of production
Factors of production are the inputs, such as labour, capital and raw materials, used in the production of goods and services.

Instead, let us now recognize that goods are made using a mix of factors of production (that is, inputs) including raw materials, machinery ('capital'), and highly skilled and lower skilled labour. An influential extension of the comparative advantage model then argues as follows. A country's comparative advantage depends on its 'endowments', that is, the factors of production it has available at any moment. A country with good mineral resources will have an advantage in extracting and exporting them; a country with lots of sunny days will grow better oranges relative to its other options than a grey northern land.

Those are the easy cases. You can apply a similar argument, however, to capital and labour. A country which already has a large installed manufacturing base should be *relatively* better at automated manufacturing than at, say, handicrafts. Conversely a country with lots of low skilled labour and little highly skilled labour should be *relatively* better at producing goods that require a lot of low skilled labour, and less relatively efficient at high-tech production.

However, the capital equipment and the skills of a country's labour force are not 'endowments' in the sense that countries may be endowed with abundant land, mineral wealth or long hours of sunshine. On the contrary, the stock of installed machinery is the result of a country's history of capital investment in manufacturing by firms and governments. Similarly, the balance between unskilled and skilled labour is a result of a country's educational and industrial history. A higher skilled labour force is created by government, by firms and by people themselves undertaking training and education.

In other words, comparative advantage is *dynamic* not static, it changes over time and is influenced by policy. This is a recurrent theme in this book, and is developed further below and in Chapter 7.

5.2   Does unskilled labour benefit from trade?

> ... in countries where unskilled labour is abundant, such as Bangladesh, China and Vietnam, the gains from integrating into the world economy can be significant for unskilled labour.

(World Bank, 2001a, p.71)

An influential argument for trade liberalization is that opening trade benefits the poorer members of a low income country's workforce, notably unskilled labour. This argument too draws upon the comparative advantage model, and it is one of the implications that give the model its political clout. I shall consider these implications here.

So far I have not discussed payments to labour for working and producing. But once we introduce different kinds of labour, such as highly skilled and low skilled, then wages are likely to differ. When countries specialize and trade, the demand for some kinds of labour will rise, and the demand for other kinds of labour will fall.

I shall use as an example trade in clothing and textiles. Despite the failures to liberalize market access in rich countries, charted in Chapter 2, exports of clothing, textiles and footwear from developing countries grew by over 10 per cent a year from 1980 to 1998, among the fastest growing categories of exports (UNCTAD, 2002b, p.70). China by 2000 sold 23 per cent of world clothing exports (Strange and Newton, 2002).

Items such as clothing use a lot of labour in production relative to machinery: that is, they are *labour intensive*. Furthermore, workers in these industries need and acquire skills, such as the use of sewing machines, but their skills are not ones that require long years of schooling or apprenticeship. So clothing is intensive in its use of low skilled labour.

Now suppose two countries differ in the skill composition of their labour force. One country has a lot of low skilled labour and few highly skilled workers; another has a much higher proportion of workers with high technical skill levels. The low skill country is likely to be relatively more efficient in producing goods such as clothing that use such labour intensively. Conversely, the high skill country will be relatively better at producing, say, computers and telecommunications equipment, which are intensive in the use of highly skilled workers. Comparative advantage follows relative endowments (at a given time) of skilled and unskilled labour, as well as other factors of production.

Suppose both countries produce both goods and consider the structural change within the countries as trade expands. In the country specialising in clothing, demand for low skilled labour rises, pushing up the wages of low skilled workers. In the other country, specialising in, say, computers, the wages of highly skilled labour rise but low skilled workers lose jobs and their wages stagnate or fall.

Now suppose that the low skill country is also low income. What this argument suggests is that trade in line with comparative advantage can reduce poverty by raising the wages of poorer workers. Alternatively, if there is widespread unemployment in the country or large numbers seeking to move out of small scale farming, the expansion of clothing exports (for example) may not raise wages in clothing greatly (as there are lots of people standing in line for the next job). But it may increase employment, tackling poverty by raising average incomes among the poor as poor farmers move into rather better paid (though still low paid) wage jobs.

Conversely in the, let us suppose, richer computer exporting country, lower skilled, lower income workers face unemployment and see their wages drop further behind. Internationally, there is a rise in lower incomes, concentrated in poor countries, the point the World Bank was making above, but there is also a rise in higher incomes concentrated in rich countries, a point less widely emphasized.

This, remember, is a theoretical argument not a statement of fact: it requires testing against the evidence. And the evidence is mixed. In parts of Asia, export success in labour intensive industries such as clothing appears to have reduced poverty by this route, and the World Bank's examples above are therefore Asian. However, trade liberalization elsewhere in the developing world does not appear to have had this effect. For example, if countries with somewhat higher incomes try to compete in the low skill labour intensive export sectors they may experience falling wages. And some developing countries do not have an abundance of available labour for export production.

Question

So what is the answer to the question at the head of Section 5.2?

I would summarize the answer as: yes, if (a) the exporting country is low income and has large numbers of people willing and able to move into producing goods such as clothing for export, and (b) the country does successfully build up industries to export these goods. There is nothing inevitable about such export success; it involves creating and sustaining an industrial exporting sector. Some reasons why it may go wrong are discussed below and there is more on industrial investment in Chapter 7.

As increasing trade requires change in the economic structure of countries, there are gainers and losers within countries. People's interests conflict, and this section therefore has told us something about who may oppose trade liberalization. In the USA, the declining wages of low skilled workers led unions and employers to demand protection from imports from low wage countries, as Aditya Bhattacharjea noted in Chapter 2, despite protests from free trade advocates that imports were far too small relative to production to have driven such a huge change in wages (Krugman, 2000).

David Ricardo, who formulated comparative advantage and advocated repeal of the Corn Laws in nineteenth-century Britain, was aware of these conflicts of interest. Factors of production also include land. Liberalizing wheat imports at that time would have brought in cheaper grain and made some farming in Britain unprofitable. Ricardo deplored the opposition of landlords, on the basis of their own interests, to 'all the benefits which would follow from importing corn at a cheap price' (Ricardo, *Essay on Profits*, 1815; quoted in Henderson, 1997, p.324). He went on to argue that, if imports were 'unfettered by legislative enactment', 'we should gradually withdraw our capital from the cultivation of [poor] lands, and import the produce which is presently raised upon them' (Ricardo, *Essay on Profits*, 1815; quoted in Gootzeit, 1973).

6   Losing from trade

Trade creates gainers and losers across the world. The losers can be groups within countries (Section 5), but whole countries can also lose. As the world economy expanded in the last two decades of the twentieth century, many of the poorest countries in the world saw their economies stagnate, despite high ratios of trade to output and increasingly liberalized trade policies (UNCTAD, 2002a). This section looks at how that came about.

6.1   Trade and growth

Trade restructures economies; it also leads to expansion. Trade and growth can go together, as Section 2 noted. There are two ways in which a country can get richer through trade, and they can be compared by looking back at Figure 3.5 once again. One method, discussed in Section 3, is to specialize, moving labour from food to medicine (or vice versa), and then to 'trade out' beyond the production possibility frontier to gain more of both goods than the country could produce. This produces an increase in each trading country's *national income*, that is, the amount of goods and services available to its citizens after production and trade. It expands total world output, but it does not produce growth in the production possibilities of each country. Specialization changes the mix of goods each country produces, but each country's total production possibilities remain the same.

> *Question*
>
> Suppose, however, that the production possibilities of the high income country in Figure 3.5 increase. How would you show that on Figure 3.5(a)?

Figure 3.7 shows the answer. The whole production possibility frontier of the country has shifted outwards from the line AB to the line EF. The country can now produce more of both goods. This shift is what is meant by economic growth: an expansion of the country's output and production possibilities.

Economic growth
Economic growth means an expansion of a country's total production possibilities.

Activity 3.6

Check your understanding of growth. Suppose that the low income country shown in Figure 3.5(b) expands its ability to produce medicine, with no change in its ability to produce food. Show the country's growth in its production possibilities on a diagram based on Figure 3.5(b).

So how does this growth happen? This is explored in detail in Chapter 7, but let me just note here that two major sources of growth are changes in the amounts of factors of production available to a country, and changes in

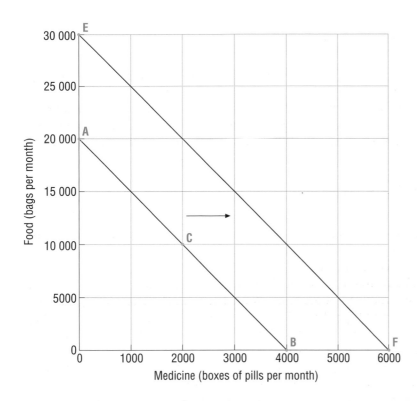

Figure 3.7   Economic growth: an expansion of a country's production possibilities

technology. As the concerns of Ricardo described at the end of Section 5 illustrate, countries' factor 'endowments' change drastically over time. Landlords are no longer a dominant class in British economic policy debates. An increasingly educated labour force, or new mineral discoveries, change a country's production possibilities. Expanding production of goods and services, and creating new industries, requires large amounts of capital investment in machinery, buildings and equipment, which have to be funded in turn by flows of financial investment. The accumulation of capital over time is essential to increasing a country's possibilities of production and trade (Chapter 7).

6.2   Trading into a poverty trap

Section 2 also notes that trade can make poverty worse. Let us now look more closely at the ways in which this can happen. A majority of the poorest or 'least developed' countries in the world depend heavily on non-oil primary commodity exports (Section 4), and these are the countries for which trade seems to be particularly unable to act as an engine of economic growth.

To see why this is so, we need to bring demand for products into the discussion. Demand influences prices; when demand for a product rises it may push up market prices, at least until new supplies arrive. However, the pattern of demand differs in different export markets. Markets for some primary products can be slow growing, dependent on a slowly rising demand for food for example, or on industrial demand for raw materials. They may also be volatile, since a shift in industrial technology – away from copper wire, for example, or away from natural corks in wine bottling – can create a sudden sharp drop in demand for a product. Concentrating exports on current comparative advantage of a 'natural' sort – in tropical fruit, particular minerals, tropical beverages – therefore brings inherent risks.

If market demand is static for an export product on which a country depends heavily, then that country also faces a danger of a terms of trade 'trap' that may impoverish the population. The basic economic model of how this can happen is very simple, although its importance is much debated. Imagine that a country is exporting, say, raw cotton. It expands its output sharply, perhaps by encouraging farmers to invest in equipment that raises output per hectare and per worker in cotton growing. There is economic growth.

What then happens to the price it receives for its increased cotton exports? The answer depends in part on whether the country's exports are large relative to the total size of the market for cotton. If the country is a very small producer in relative terms, then it is likely to be able to add, say, 50 per cent to its output of raw cotton and still sell it at the current world market price.

But if it is a large producer *relative to the market* then that is not so. A 50 per cent rise in its output will greatly increase the quantity of cotton available to buyers. What will happen next? It is likely that the result will be to drive down the price. This is because there may now be more cotton on the international market than buyers want at the current price. The only way to sell the whole crop may be to lower the price, encouraging garment producers to switch from other fibres to cotton and consumers to buy more cotton garments. The country's terms of trade have therefore fallen.

What are the implications for the exporting country? It may be that a large increase in output – such as the 50 per cent I assumed above – will still produce more revenue for farmers and more export earnings for the country even if there is a small fall in price. And, so long as the cost of making the agricultural improvements was not larger than the extra revenue, people may end up better off.

But a large price fall is another matter entirely. If prices fall sharply enough, then the output expansion may leave country and farmers worse off: producing more, but earning less. This effect is called 'immiserizing growth': a process of growing into worsening poverty.

The danger a country faces of trading into this kind of poverty trap therefore depends on a number of aspects of its trade and economy. First, the nature of the demand for the product is important. If demand for a product can be increased only by a large drop in price, immiserizing growth through investing in more exports is a potential danger. Existing producers may be damaged if they expand, or if a new large producer enters the market. The United Nations Conference on Trade and Development (UNCTAD) (2002a) suggested that this problem particularly besets some Least Developed Countries that have been pushed – partly by multilateral lending institutions such as the World Bank – into concentrating on exploiting for export their comparative advantage in primary products. These countries have been losing their capacity to process their own commodities (remember the Senegal example above), retreating to export of unprocessed goods. They have seen their share in world trade decline and their poverty rates rise.

The possibility of immiserizing growth also arises in manufactured exports, though it is much less likely. Fear of market demand constraints in primary products is one reason why developing countries seek to move into manufactured exports: these markets are thought to be more 'buoyant' in the sense that demand is growing more rapidly and market opportunities are more diverse. In general, the evidence supports this proposition. However, there are exceptions that, again, may particularly affect some of the poorest countries.

Consider again the example of clothing and textiles. The high income countries have continued to protect their own clothing and textile industries with tariffs and quotas (Chapter 2). The effect of these policies is to restrict the demand for low income countries' garment and textile exports. Rapidly increasing supply, for example from China and South Asia, may then drive down prices. If this happens, it can create the 'poverty trap' (UNCTAD, 2002a) whereby countries expand exports on the basis of low wage labour intensive exports without generating sustained economic growth, because their terms of trade turn against them as described above.

There is some evidence that suggests that low income exporters of labour intensive manufactures may be facing this problem, with some experiencing a deterioration in their terms of trade in major rich country markets (UNCTAD, 2002b, pp.118–9). For example, a study of South African furniture exports identifies this problem (Kaplinsky *et al.*, 2002). The problem is particularly likely to face very large developing countries, such as India and China, though at present, the rate of expansion of China's exports is outweighing the revenue losses from terms of trade effects. China's accession to the WTO, furthermore, will allow it to benefit along with other producers from the promised relaxation of protection of developed countries' clothing markets by 2005 (if indeed it occurs).

7 Dynamic comparative advantage: escaping the trade poverty trap

Look back at Table 3.2. It showed that the exports of East Asia and the Pacific and South Asia, like those of the high income countries, are dominated by manufactures. And I commented that trade and growth appear more likely to go together when trade is in manufactures. The last section suggested one reason: more rapidly expanding and diverse markets for manufactured goods than for primary commodities. To explore the link between manufactured exports and growth in a bit more depth, we have to look more closely at the implications of increasing international market integration (Section 2.4), and in particular to move the focus away from trade between countries, to consider the firms that actually do the production and trade.

7.1 Big firms, increasing returns and trade policy

Many of the manufacturing firms participating in international trade are very large, in terms of turnover and in relation to their markets. The consequences of the size of these firms for their production and costs give us another reason why trade in manufactures helps generate growth.

In many manufacturing industries, as a firm's output expands, its costs per unit of output decline. That is, the firm benefits from *increasing returns*. This concept is now used to refer to a wide range of different reasons why firms' costs can decline over time with rising output. There may be large unavoidable set-up costs for a manufacturing plant, and these are then spread over larger and larger output, so that the average cost per unit of output falls as the firm expands. Furthermore, as a firm's output becomes very large, it may be able to invest in more cost-efficient production methods, for example greater use of automation.

It may be, in addition, that as a firm grows it *learns* to produce more efficiently by using its basic production set-up more effectively ('learning-by-doing'). It may also happen that available technology changes in ways that allow firms to reduce costs: this effect may be particularly marked in new industries where technology is changing fast (such as the early days of the personal computer industry). Finally, the firm may innovate, finding new production methods to reduce costs as output expands.

In manufacturing, increasing returns is a widespread phenomenon, and the links between falling costs, technical change and growth are explored in detail in Chapter 7. Here I want to identify just one implication for a country's ability to obtain gains from trade. Increasing returns imply that larger firms have a market advantage over smaller rivals: they can undercut rivals' prices while remaining profitable themselves since their costs per unit sold are lower. Since established firms are quite likely to be larger than new entrants to an industry, it is then hard for new firms to get into an established market. The problem is that it can and does take *time* for a firm to establish itself at a level of cost per unit that allows it to be internationally competitive.

The more international markets integrate, through falling transport and communications costs and declining trade barriers, the more scope there is for large firms to exploit increasing returns. This has serious implications for a country's trade policy. Consider a country that wants to encourage the development of an export industry in, say, pharmaceuticals. How are the firms to get started and to grow into successful exporters without going out of business in the early stages?

These considerations generate a strong argument for protection of nascent export industries in low income countries. This is often called the 'infant industry' justification for protection. Tariffs or export subsidies allow firms based in new manufacturing export locations time to grow to an efficient size, and time to learn efficient working practices.

Question

Look back at Section 2, and explain how protection could work in this way.

Consider a large country with low or middle incomes on average, but with a sizeable middle class and a substantial domestic market. The country has industrialists capable of developing firms producing pharmaceuticals. It might be Brazil, say, or India, both of which have such an industry. In its early stages, the firms can grow their production systems, technological capabilities and trained labour based on production for the home market. But they can do this only if they can compete with imports.

So the countries put a tariff on imported pharmaceuticals of, say, 30 per cent. This raises the prices of imports in the home market and helps the local firms to compete. Over time, they become more efficient (the 'infants' grow up) and then they start to export, as the Indian pharmaceutical companies do. So protection has helped new firms to emerge into the international market. At that point, lowering protection of the home market would be unlikely to undermine the firms' viability (which does not mean that the firms will not fiercely oppose such a suggestion – quite the contrary!). This 'infant industry' argument is one of the strongest cases to be made for protection of the home market and the resultant substitution of imports by domestic production.

7.2 Dynamic comparative advantage: the flying geese

The implication of these reflections is that successful export of manufactures can be cumulative: once the firms from a particular country establish competitive success in a particular international market they can hope to build on it. Firms may start by establishing a cost and price advantage, then expand the market by bringing in new products and establishing a reputation for quality. The competitive success of the firms changes a country's comparative advantage over time. The roots of comparative advantage in this more dynamic sense are found in the capabilities of the firms located in a country, the abilities of the country's labour force, and the technical capacity of its universities and research institutions.

All this can be built up, and government policy plays a role. The highly successful developing countries in East Asia, such as South Korea and Taiwan and now China, have been engaged in just this kind of process of changing comparative advantage. They have shifted over time from primary to manufactured goods production, and from goods and services requiring less skilled to those requiring more skilled labour. In Japan, this group of developing countries has been pictured as a formation of flying geese, led historically by Japan, a country which over time has moved to higher skilled, higher technology manufacturing and exports, and has provided (through large Japanese multinational companies) markets, inputs and technology for 'follower' countries – initially South Korea and Taiwan. These in turn moved up the ladder of dynamic comparative advantage, again providing a stimulus to other followers in the flying 'V' formation behind them, including South East Asian countries and China (Rowthorn, 1996; UNCTAD, 1996).

In the 1990s the economic crisis in Japan and continuing expansion of China and South Korea changed the pattern of Asian development, but the underlying point remains compelling: middle income countries' abilities to move 'forward' into higher value export goods requiring higher skills, and to provide new markets for imports as their incomes rise, are key to low income countries' being able to move along behind them.

All of the successful East Asian manufacturing exporters have in the past used protection to support their industrialization. The South Korean government for example, from the 1960s, actively promoted manufactured exports, using selective export subsidies (including lower taxes, cheap credit and privileged access to tax-free importation of inputs) only for exporting firms which proved successful, punishing those which did not. The government selectively nurtured 'infants' and actively promoted Korean exports abroad, deliberately shifting the country's comparative advantage towards skill-intensive exports (Amsden, 1989).

Look back at the conclusion to Chapter 2. What does the author say there about the WTO regime in relation to this kind of active trade policy?

He suggests that the WTO regime now blocks low income countries from following in the trade policy footsteps of the East Asian countries and the current high income countries. I consider this argument further in the final section of this chapter.

8 Do openness, 'outward orientation' and 'globalization' reduce poverty?

The WTO trade regime is built on the premise that trade liberalization promotes a process of international market integration that is also being driven by the other influences such as falling transport costs (Section 2.4), and that liberalized international market trading promotes benefits for all. In support of this proposition, it is widely argued that 'openness' to trade is closely associated with growth. As an influential paper put it, 'open economies tend to converge' (Sachs and Warner, 1995), that is, the poorer 'open' countries catch up with the richer ones. There is evidence in support of this proposition: for example the observed economic convergence between countries within the European Union. However, on an international scale the proposition suffers from a problem which is very important for policy: what exactly do we mean by 'openness'? And if defined carefully, and independently of economic success, can it really be shown to be a reliable source of economic growth?

8.1 'Openness' and 'outward orientation'

There are a number of widely used measures of a country's 'openness' to trade. In essence, they measure either a country's trade/output ratio (*how much* it trades) or the extent of trade liberalization (*policy*-based openness to trade). Neither tells us reliably, case by case, which countries will successfully climb a trade and growth ladder. Consider Figure 3.8 which compares the trade/output ratios of sub-Saharan African and East Asian countries.

The ratio of trade to output is a problematic measure of a country's openness to trade, since big countries have lower trade percentages. (China and the USA are so big they have a lot of internal trade between states and provinces; small countries need to specialize and trade more across borders.) However, Figure 3.8 tells us something useful. It shows that, since 1960, African countries have always had a high degree of openness to trade in this sense. Yet African countries have stagnated, on average, since 1980 and their share

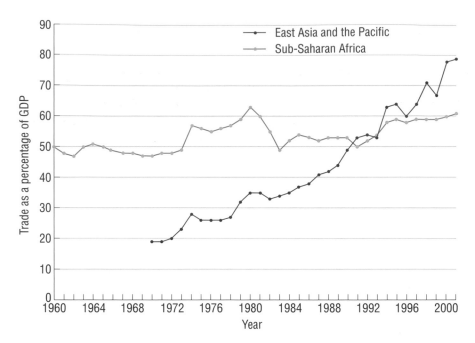

Figure 3.8   Trade (imports plus exports) as a percentage of GDP

Source: data from World Bank, 2002b

of expanding world trade has been falling sharply. The East Asian and Pacific countries in 1970, the first year for which there are data for this series, were quite 'closed' in this sense. They have had very rapidly rising trade/output ratios since then, although they surpassed African levels only in the 1990s (Figure 3.8). Yet in their case these rising trade ratios were associated with an *expanding* share of world trade – indeed, they have been instrumental in growing that trade.

Another measure of openness is the extent of trade liberalization. A number of studies find country by country associations between measures of trade liberalization and growth, and in particular they find high levels of economic benefit from reducing tariffs when trading partners are doing the same (Clemens and Williamson, 2001). However, East Asian countries, the spectacular success story, do not have tariffs that are very low by international standards (look back at Figure 3.2), and in the period of export acceleration this was also true.

To explain therefore why East Asian countries succeeded in trade-led growth without liberalization, another concept was invented to fit their case: 'outward orientation'. This is a label for a package of trade policy measures that *combines* quite high levels of import tariffs with an *absence* of incentives to produce primarily for a protected home market. That is, firms face equal incentives to produce for the home and export market, *yet* nascent exporters are given quite high levels of initial market protection – so long as they perform. 'Outward orientation' means an absence of bias against exports.

One striking feature of these trade policy measures is that they are in practice as much industrial policy as trade policy. They are designed to promote the *trading* success of particular domestically owned or locally based foreign firms. In this they seem to fit the WTO's stated objectives: the WTO, at the top of its website at the time of writing (late 2002), had the following:

What is the WTO?

The World Trade Organization (WTO) is the only global international organization dealing with the rules of trade between nations. At its heart are the WTO agreements, negotiated and signed by the bulk of the world's trading nations and ratified in their parliaments. The goal is to help producers of goods and services, exporters, and importers conduct their business.

(World Trade Organization, 2002b)

Note the emphasis on supporting business. Yet the type of detailed and discretionary trade policy conducted by the East Asian exporters, notably the emphasis on export subsidy, is not in fact in the spirit of the WTO rules.

8.2 Globalization and poverty

Recent globalization has been a force for poverty reduction.

(World Bank, 2002c, p.18)

Divergence, big time.

(Pritchett, 1997)

'Globalization', unlike liberalization, is not just a *policy* concept. It refers in part, as suggested in Section 2.4, to a process of international market integration to which governments can and do contribute but do not manage. The extent of market integration, and the economic benefits accruing to countries that can take advantage of international markets to export on a large scale, mean that the penalties of staying out of international trade are high. This is what Aditya Bhattacharjea was referring to when he suggested that developing countries knew that they were better off in the 'gang' – that is, benefiting from the market access for their exports opened up by the WTO membership – than shut out, despite the asymmetry of the agreements.

The World Bank has been keen to promote the benefits of globalization. The first of the two quotations above is from a report by two high profile World Bank economists, Paul Collier and David Dollar. To support their argument, they identify a category of developing countries that they label 'the new globalizers' (World Bank, 2002c, p.31). These are the countries that have most successfully increased their participation in global trade since 1980. The more 'globalized' countries are thus defined by their increase in trade relative to income. They are then shown to have increased incomes and output faster than other developing countries, and to have on average reduced tariffs faster.

Note that as a way of studying the sources of successful development and its links to 'globalization', this argument dices with circularity. It proceeds by identifying the success stories over a period, and then comparing their average characteristics to those of other developing countries. This is quite a different procedure from developing hypotheses – for example, that liberalization raises growth – and testing them. The World Bank's results depend strongly on the success of a few large countries, including China, India, Brazil and Argentina. The collapse in the Argentinian economy and the fragility of Brazil's success at the time of writing (2003) may alter some of the results in the next decade. Nevertheless, they demonstrate strongly one outstanding pattern that I have already discussed: those developing countries which succeeded in growing rapidly in the last two decades of the twentieth century generally did so through strong and successful integration into the international economy via manufacturing exports.

Hence, as the other author quoted above put it, 'Divergence, big time' in the world economy. That is, the gap between the poorest and the richest countries continued to widen in the later decades of the twentieth century. The worst losers have been low income countries that have liberalized into a poverty trap, seeing their share of world trade decline and their terms of trade turn against them over long periods. Figure 3.9 shows the consequences, testing the World Bank's assertion above that globalization reduces poverty. It shows changes in extreme poverty rates for 43 of the world's poorest countries, grouped by extent of trade liberalization. The evidence does not support the view that liberalization is associated with falling poverty rates in these countries. The authors are rightly cautious about drawing conclusions from small numbers of countries, but Figure 3.9 suggests rather the opposite association: that moderate trade restrictiveness has been best for poverty reduction.

Note that it is possible for both of the quotations at the start of this subsection to be true. Globalization in the sense of integration into international markets may be associated *both* with falling total numbers in poverty in the world *and* with severely worsening poverty in some countries – indeed that appears to

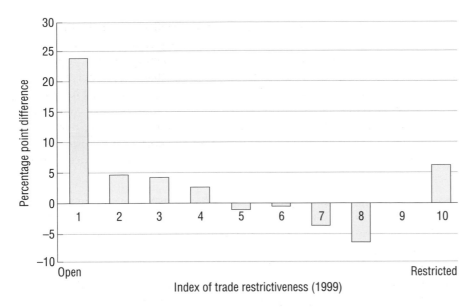

Figure 3.9 Trade liberalization and poverty trends in the Least Developed Countries during the 1990s: changes in $1-a-day poverty, 1987–89 to 1997–99 (averages)

Source: UNCTAD, 2002a, p.117

be the case. And divergence between the poorest and richest countries can and does coexist with the convergence visible between some successfully growing countries which were previously low income, notably China, and the better off.

9 Conclusion

This chapter has explored some economic theory and evidence that play a political role in the trade arena. This economics is the currency of trade policy debate, and of negotiations between governments over the rules of the world trade regime. Since policies and rule making influence the gains from trade and their distribution, to understand trade we need to understand *both* how international markets work *and* how those markets are 'governed' by national trade policies and international trade rules.

The core argument of this chapter has been that a country's gains from trade are determined by the *terms* on which a country trades on international markets. This is not just a matter of prices, though they are very important. Success or failure in international trade is influenced by a country's factors of production; by the capacities of its firms and workers; by the demand for its products on international markets; by the country's ability to generate new sources of comparative advantage over time, particularly in manufacturing and services; and by the success of government trade and industrial policy in supporting such dynamic shifts in comparative advantage.

The theory of comparative advantage analyses international trade as if 'countries' do the trading. This makes sense in that we are interested in the costs and benefits of trade to citizens of particular countries. But, as later sections of the chapter make explicit, it is the decisions of firms and individuals about what to produce and sell, in the light of the prices they can obtain, that create trade flows. Markets are essentially 'anarchic', their outcomes a form of spontaneous order generated by the interaction of masses of independent decision makers: they are not run by governments. Countries' governments can, however, *influence* trade and its outcomes, through decisions about tariffs and through negotiations over market access abroad. They also influence it through international negotiation on trading rules – the international governance of trade – and that is the subject of the next two chapters.

I have argued that free trade – 'free', that is, of tariffs, quotas and other restrictions – can benefit trading countries, but may not do so. Some countries trade into poverty, while some get into an upward spiral of trade-led growth. Furthermore, while some countries grow through trade, groups within them lose out from economic restructuring. The divergence is exacerbated by a world trade regime which, while encouraging liberalization, leans towards the economic interests of firms and lobbies within rich countries. As a result, international trade and market integration are associated across the world with both growth and impoverishment.

Further reading

The journal *The World Economy* publishes informed commentary on economic issues written for non-specialists. The following articles are relevant to this chapter and to Chapter 2.

A very critical point of view on the WTO and Doha can be found in Finger, J.M. and Nogués, J. (2002) 'The unbalanced Uruguay Round outcome: the new areas in future WTO negotiations', *The World Economy*, vol.25, no.3, pp.321–40. A more balanced, but still critical point of view, is Panagariya, A. (2002) 'Developing countries at Doha: a political economy analysis', *The World Economy*, vol.25, no.9, pp.1205–33.

For more on the terms of trade for manufactures and the 'poverty trap', see Mayer, J. (2002) 'The fallacy of composition: a review of the literature', *The World Economy*, vol.25, no.6, pp.875–94. The fallacy in question says that if one country can grow through, for example, the exports of manufactures, then necessarily many other countries can do the same.

For more on trade and poverty, see Winters, L.A. (2002) 'Trade liberalisation and poverty: what are the links?', *The World Economy*, vol.25, no.9, pp.1339–67. For contrasting but by no means wholly opposed official views, two accessible references cited in the text are World Bank (2002) *Globalization, Growth and Poverty: Building an Inclusive World Economy*, Washington, DC, World Bank, and UNCTAD (United Nations Conference on Trade and Development) (2002) *The Least Developed Countries Report 2002: Escaping the Poverty Trap*, Geneva, UNCTAD.

Chapter 4 Who makes the rules? The politics of developing country participation and influence in the WTO

Amrita Narlikar

1   Introduction

The birth of the WTO on 1 January 1995 came almost 50 years after an abortive attempt to establish an International Trade Organization (ITO) shortly after the end of the Second World War. Compared with the GATT, the WTO put the political framework for negotiating and implementing the rules of the international trade regime on a much firmer footing. And the attention and publicity that the WTO has received so far, for instance at the 'Battle of Seattle' in 1999, show that this youthful organization has already become the focus of immense controversy.

Chapter 2 argues that many of the rules of the international trade regime are established and implemented in biased ways, while Chapter 3 makes the point that the question of who gains from trade liberalization – both within and between countries – depends in part on how that liberalization takes place. This chapter picks up from the economic analysis in these chapters and examines the politics of the promise and problems of WTO participation for the majority of its members, namely developing countries. Why and how are decisions taken in the WTO that disadvantage developing countries, given that the latter constitute a majority of the membership? Can developing countries use their position in the WTO to change in their favour what Chapter 3 refers to as the 'terms' of their insertion into the international trade regime?

These, then, are the two central questions in what follows: first, who gets to make trade rules (and how); and second, what, if anything, can developing countries do to shape those rules such that they better serve their interests? In short, what are the prospects that the powerful and expanding organization that is the WTO might help mitigate international power inequalities rather than simply reproduce, or even exacerbate, them?

In Section 2 I begin by tracing the history of developing country participation in the forerunner to the WTO, that is, the General Agreement on Tariffs and Trade (GATT). This first section compares the present day participation of developing countries in the WTO with their involvement in the GATT and explains the continuities and changes in that pattern. Section 3 turns to the substance of WTO rules and negotiations, and takes a closer look at the so-called Development Round of trade talks in Doha (Qatar) in 2001. Section 4 shows how the failure of developing countries to find a voice in the WTO can at least partly be explained by the decision-making processes of the organization, which impede their effective participation. Section 5 proposes possible strategies that may be adopted to facilitate more effective participation by developing countries. Section 6 offers some general conclusions about the problems but also comments on the potential of the WTO for helping developing countries to shift the international trade regime in their favour.

2 From the GATT to the WTO: a historical perspective

The WTO may be a recent invention, but at least some of its rules and workings have a long history in its predecessor the GATT, which was accepted on a provisional basis and entered into force in January 1948. Even though the ITO charter was finally agreed in that same year, ratification proved difficult in many national legislatures. The US government's announcement in 1950 that it would not seek Congressional ratification of the Charter effectively rendered the ITO a non-starter. Thus the 'provisional' GATT continued to provide the rules for the multilateral trading system until the formation of the WTO in 1995.

Despite the fact that some developing countries were original signatories to the GATT, they maintained a low profile and made little individual or collective effort to shape its agenda. At first glance, this is somewhat surprising, especially as the GATT was a one-member-one-vote organization. Given that the developing countries soon came to occupy a significant majority in the GATT, why did they not operate in successful and influential coalitions? Instead, they took their grievances with the trading system outside the GATT into the United Nations Commission on Trade and Development (UNCTAD) and the General Assembly of the United Nations, and referred to the GATT as the 'Rich Man's Club'.

There are several reasons for this course of action. As Aditya Bhattacharjea explains in Chapter 2, developing countries were 'suspicious of the motives of the richer countries and of the idea of free trade itself'. Unlike the stillborn International Trade Organization, the original articles of agreement of the GATT made no mention of development, for example. However, there were also institutional and procedural features of the GATT that prevented developing countries from operating successfully within it. Although the GATT was *formally* a democratic, one-member-one-vote, institution, it was also set up to operate so that consensus rather than majority voting would be the basis for most decisions. 'Consensus' decisions were arrived at in private consultations between industrial countries in the GATT's Green Room (see Section 4), to which few developing countries were invited. Under the consensus principle, there was little opportunity to use the power of large numbers through voting, especially as developing countries feared that a call to vote would simply result in a complete bypassing of the GATT by the developed countries in favour of more exclusionary forums. Such threats were indeed put to use by the developed countries during the 1986–1994 Uruguay Round. So, in practice, the desire to achieve a consensus, and the need to include the high income countries in any consensus, meant that the formal principle of one-member-one-vote counted for little. The problems of consensus decision making in the WTO are discussed further in Section 4.

Another way that the procedural features of decision making worked against developing countries was by means of the application of the 'principal supplier principle'. This meant that negotiations took place between the principal exporting (suppliers) and importing countries and were then extended to other members on the basis of Article 1, which granted most-favoured-nation (MFN) status to all members. The MFN principle says that a trade concession granted to one member must be granted to all. Developing countries were seldom the principal suppliers or consumers, and so could gain the benefits that flowed from MFN status without having to do anything. But it also meant that developing countries were not directly involved in negotiations. The participation of developing countries in reciprocal negotiations was further impeded by the fact that products in which they enjoyed a comparative advantage, such as agricultural products and textiles, were excluded from the purview of the GATT through various exceptions made by industrial countries. These exceptions meant that developing countries were unable to realise whatever little measure of bargaining power that they had.

Even where they wished to take a more active role, developing country delegations often lacked the technical expertise and the diplomatic resources needed to participate in GATT negotiations, and the provisional nature of the GATT agreement meant that there was little institutional support to compensate for these limitations. Taken together, these institutional and procedural features translated power balances between the developed and developing worlds into the internal workings of the GATT. The overall consequence was that developing countries chose instead to insist on Special and Differential (S&D) treatment, that is, trade concessions not matched by reciprocal measures, and refused to engage in reciprocal negotiations. As a result, they became 'second-class members' and reinforced the image of the GATT as a 'Rich-Man's Club'.

Activity 4.1

Check that you understand how the procedures of the GATT undermined its formally democratic character. Re-read the section above and write a short explanation for yourself.

2.1   The role of the WTO

As you have seen in Chapter 2, the Uruguay Round included a new GATT agreement (GATT 1994), TRIPS, an agreement on trade in services (GATS), a new dispute settlement mechanism, a trade policy review mechanism, plurilateral agreements (which only some members signed up to) and the Charter of the WTO itself. With the inclusion of these new issues suddenly much more was at stake than ever before. These new issues are sometimes called 'behind the border' measures – in contrast to the 'at the border' measures such as tariffs and quantitative restrictions on trade – because they impinge on the conduct of government policy as it affects economic activity within the national territory. As its name suggests, the GATT had mainly covered measures applied to trade in goods as they crossed national borders. Within this framework, members were free to determine their own national economic policies.

Thus, the inclusion of the new issues would take the new GATT firmly inside state borders and into areas that were seen to hold the key to the health of national economies. Initially, many developing countries sought to oppose the new measures, but subsequently they participated actively and bargained for the inclusion of issues pertinent to their interests – most importantly, in agriculture and textiles – in return for going along with the new demands of the developed countries. The result was what has been described as the 'Grand Bargain' of the Uruguay Round (Ostry, 2000), in which concessions by developing countries on the new issues (as per the demands of the developed countries) were accompanied by apparent concessions by the developed countries on traditional issues such as textiles and agriculture that had eluded the GATT remit for years (as per the demands of the developing countries).

Not only would the new issues take the purview of the WTO 'behind-the-border' but also the adoption of the WTO Charter had the effect of raising both the costs and the potential opportunities associated with the international trade regime, since the new organization possessed a vastly extended mandate as compared with that of the GATT Secretariat.

There are several ways in which the WTO is a much stronger institution than the GATT. In the first place, members are bound to the WTO agreements through the Single Undertaking, which means that all the provisions apply to all members unless specified otherwise (for example, the plurilateral agreements). Under the GATT, while all members were bound by the procedural rules (Part III), the MFN principle and the tariff concession obligations (Part I), members could claim 'grandfather rights' on many of the substantive obligations relating to customs procedures, quotas, subsidies, anti-dumping duties and national treatment (Part II, Articles III–XXIII). (These 'grandfather rights' were effectively rights not to implement GATT provisions where those provisions were in conflict with national legislation that had been in place at the time of accession to the GATT.) John H. Jackson, a specialist in international trade law, says that 'each GATT contracting party was entitled to "grandfather rights" for any provision of its legislation that existed when it became a party, and that was inconsistent with a GATT Part II obligation' (1997, p.40). The Protocol of Provisional Application, allowing grandfather rights, called for the implementation of Part II 'to the fullest extent not inconsistent with existing [national] legislation'. The Uruguay Round abolished grandfather rights. Thus, not only are all members bound to all the rules, but also the rules themselves go far deeper into what had been national spheres of legislative competence.

Secondly, the Dispute Settlement Mechanism (DSM) of the WTO has much greater bite than that of the GATT due to the requirement of a 'negative consensus', that is, all the members must oppose the findings of the independent dispute panel in order to overrule it. Moreover, the agreements allow for cross-sectoral retaliation in cases of violation of commitments or rules, as explained in Chapter 2. Legally, too, the WTO is quite a different animal from its predecessor, even though it retains some of the procedures of the GATT – aspects of decision making, its member-driven character and small Secretariat (discussed further in Section 3). The GATT, even though it survived for over 40 years, was applied on a 'provisional basis', whereas WTO commitments are permanent and form part of international law, as do the adopted findings of its dispute resolution panels.

As a result of its extended mandate and powers described above, the reach of the WTO intrudes much further behind the border than the GATT ever did, and its members enjoy more power to enforce its rulings than they did under the GATT. The WTO is now an arena in which states make rules on issues such as food safety and animal and plant health regulations. Through the General Agreement on Trade in Services (GATS) and the TRIPS agreement, and more recently through the Singapore issues (government procurement, trade facilitation, competition policy and investment measures) that were

Single Undertaking
A Single Undertaking means that members have to sign up to whole agreement and cannot opt in to some parts while staying out of others.

included in the Doha Development Agenda, the WTO's remit has expanded into areas where states had traditionally exercised their sovereign rights of legislation and managed national development policies with greater autonomy. And finally, states on the receiving end of an unfavourable dispute settlement ruling can no longer veto the outcome.

Developing countries have concluded that the only hope they have in working this elaborate and powerful system of rules to their own advantage is through active participation in the rule-making and rule-enforcement process within the WTO. So it is not surprising that the over half of the 200 proposals that were presented at Seattle (1999) came from developing countries and that they continued to play a proactive role at the Doha Ministerial (2001). The developing countries' assumption is that working inside the rules-based framework of the WTO is better than being outside, where they were more susceptible to the less regulated pressures of the more powerful economies. How far has this assumption been borne out by events?

3   Making the rules for international trade

Of the 145 members of the WTO in 2002, over 100 are developing countries. An additional 32 non-member governments have observer status and all of these are either developing countries or countries in transition. Some are already in the process of negotiating their accession to the WTO while others are scheduled to begin doing so within five years of being granted observer status. These expanding numbers suggest that developing countries believe that membership of the WTO brings some advantages. You have already encountered an economic argument to the effect that even if the rules of the international trade regime are biased against developing countries, the costs of being shut out of the markets of developed countries are even greater.

Question

What political advantages in terms of influencing the trade regime might developing countries reap from being inside the WTO?

The high income (developed) countries are all members of the WTO, so the political choice for developing countries in the international trading system is stark. They can either seek to bargain individually with their trading partners on a bilateral basis and, since those partners are for the most part the high income industrial countries, face a bargaining situation characterized by a marked imbalance of power. Or they can join the WTO and seek to use their collective influence within that organization to shape the international trade regime in their favour. Inside the WTO, developing countries can form coalitions to negotiate and vote together, thereby attempting to use their majority position in a rule-based pattern of diplomacy to mitigate the effects of the disparities in bargaining power that arise from their comparatively weak position in the international economy. For countries that individually have little economic leverage, multilateral bargaining has several distinct political advantages over bilateral trade negotiations, especially when that bargaining is based on principles that treat the parties as formally equal members of a rule-based organization (this central point is analysed more fully in Section 4).

Suppose we accept that there are indeed benefits to a country from trade liberalization. It can nevertheless be a mistake for a developing country to liberalize unilaterally, as the internal costs of adjustment can be high (Chapter 2, Section 3.2). The potential benefits of liberalization are higher, and the political costs are lower, if trading partners liberalize as well, as firms involved in exporting to other countries are then likely to gain. Reciprocal liberalization involving all or most of one's trading partners, as happens in the multilateral WTO because of the MFN principle, in which there is an exchange of 'concessions', helps to ensure that there is at least the potential for various parties to gain market access in preferred areas. This is also preferable to bilateral liberalization, in which the stronger economies are often able to impose their favoured rules on the weak. Hence the underlying logic of the participation of developing countries in the GATT and the WTO: 'by making liberalization conditional on greater access to foreign markets, the total gains of liberalization increase and in the process liberalization becomes feasible politically' (Hoekman and Kostecki, 2001, p.27).

In addition, WTO commitments, especially as backed up by the powerful Dispute Settlement Mechanism, have the benefit for governments of 'tying one's hands'. Governments that want to liberalize can defend unpopular decisions by pointing to the costs of compensation and possible retaliation that would likely arise if they reneged on WTO commitments. Also, multilateral negotiations are less likely to be held up by non-trade related political issues, as when China's MFN status in US trade had to be annually renewed in the US Congress and, thus became embroiled with US concerns about China's treatment of human rights. In these ways they provide developing countries with a degree of stability and predictability.

The 'Grand Bargain' resulting from the Uruguay Round negotiations promised developing countries some important gains, particularly through the inclusion of agriculture and the agreement to phase-out of the multi-fibre agreement (MFA) that had restricted the ability of developing country textile and garment producers to export to the developed countries. (As Chapters 2 and 3 show, the extent to which these promises will be kept remains to be seen.) But the concessions that developing countries made were in the new areas such as services and TRIPS, and the creation of a new institution – the WTO itself.

Many of the new issues were highly technical and not fully understood by developing countries. During the negotiation of the UR, one of the initial reasons given by the G-10 (a group of 'hard-liners' led by Argentina, Brazil, Egypt, India and Yugoslavia, and including Cuba, Nigeria, Nicaragua, Tanzania and Peru) for their opposition to the new issues was that they were not sufficiently understood to allow informed negotiation. Within the Single Undertaking framework, countries had to sign up to all or none of the Uruguay Round; this bargain was put before the developing countries on a take-it-or-leave-it basis. The trade policy specialist Sylvia Ostry writes, 'So they took it but, it's safe to say, without a full comprehension of the profoundly transformative implication of this new trading system' (2000, p.5).

Aditya Bhattacharjea discussed the unequal nature of the economic deal embodied in the Uruguay Round and the asymmetric nature of the costs and benefits involved in its implementation. These became the 'implementation issues' that were discussed at the Geneva Ministerial (1995), provided a key unifying point for the Like-Minded Group of Developing Countries (the original members were Cuba, Dominican Republic, Egypt, Honduras, Indonesia, India, Kenya, Malaysia, Sri Lanka, Tanzania, Uganda, Zimbabwe and Jamaica; the group has expanded since then to include some countries such as Mauritius in an observer status) and proved to be one of the issues that contributed to the failure at Seattle.

3.1   The Doha Ministerial Declaration

Given the difficulties of implementation and problems of managing such a bloated agenda, it is not surprising that most developing countries sought to slow the pace of liberalization. And yet, irrespective of the pressures already facing developing countries, a new round was launched at Doha in 2001. The Doha Ministerial Declaration that resulted has an ambiguous legal status, and it is too early to assess what was achieved and lost at Doha because the declaration allows considerable flexibility on how the new round of negotiations will actually evolve. However, it is already possible to see at least some balance: even though a new round has been launched, developing countries have not come away empty-handed. Simply naming the Doha declarations and decisions and subsequent negotiations as the Doha Development Agenda (DDA) is a telling indication. References to the needs of developing countries and Least Developed Countries (LDCs) abound in the DDA.

The Ministerial Declaration, for example, states that 'The majority of WTO Members are developing countries. We seek to place their needs and interests at the heart of the Work Programme adopted in this Declaration'. Similarly, 'We recognize the particular vulnerability of the least-developed countries and the special structural difficulties they face in the global economy. We are committed to addressing the marginalization of least-developed countries in international trade and to improving their effective participation in the multilateral trading system.' Even those pointing to the limitations of the DDA agree that the outcome at Doha was more favourable to developing country interests than the accomplishments of all previous ministerials.

The achievements of developing countries at Doha lie in the realm of agenda-setting, in shaping the range of issues that are to be negotiated and decided upon. The most widely cited 'victory' lies in the Declaration on the TRIPS agreement and public health. In the Declaration it was agreed that 'the TRIPS agreement does not and should not prevent Members from taking measures to protect public health ... . In this connection, we reaffirm the right of WTO Members to use, to the full, the provisions in the TRIPS Agreement, which provide flexibility for this purpose'. The context for this was the campaign by many developing countries to get cheaper access to expensive, patented drugs used in the treatment of HIV/AIDS and the desire of the US government to mass produce an inoculation against anthrax in the wake of a series of terrorism scares after September 11 2001. It is true that the Declaration is essentially a political one, but its importance goes well beyond the symbolic. The US economist Jeffrey Schott (2002) argues that the Declaration will make it politically very difficult to bring a dispute against a country that uses compulsory licensing or parallel imports of patented medicines in response to public health emergencies. The Declaration reinforces the considerable leeway that member governments have in determining what constitutes a national emergency.

Besides the Declaration on TRIPS and public health, developing countries were promised improved market access in non-agricultural products through the reduction or elimination of tariff peaks, high tariffs, tariff escalation and non-tariff barriers to trade. In fact, the main Declaration referred to these reductions 'in particular on products of export interest to developing countries'. In agriculture, the Declaration agreed to special and differential treatment for them in order to ensure that their development needs, including food security and rural development, are met. Implementation-related issues found mention in the main Declaration, which agreed to a new work programme under the auspices of the General Council to examine the problems of small and vulnerable economies and to facilitate their integration into the multilateral trading system. Two new working groups were set up in areas specifically of interest to developing countries, namely the Working Group on Trade, Debt and Finance and the Working Group on Trade and Transfer of Technology. There was also a focus on enhancing technical assistance and capacity building in developing countries.

Special attention was paid to the needs of the LDCs, with instructions to the Sub-committee for Least-Developed Countries to design a work programme. Seen by many as one of the biggest 'concessions' by the USA, the Declaration

Ministerials
Ministerials are formal meetings of the member states' trade ministers. They meet at least once every two years – Singapore, Seattle, Doha, for example.

sets the agenda for 'clarifying and improving disciplines under the Agreements on Implementation of Article VI of the GATT 1994', that is, anti-dumping duties, subsidies and countervailing measures. And in contrast to the Clinton administration's last minute attempt to put labour standards onto the negotiating table at Seattle (1999), the main Declaration only reaffirmed the decision reached at the Singapore Ministerial (1997). There, ministers had declared their commitment to the observance of internationally recognized core labour standards, but had identified the International Labour Organization as the 'competent body to set and deal with these standards'. The Declaration had also explicitly rejected the use of labour standards for protectionist purposes and had emphasized that the comparative advantage of low wage developing countries 'must in no way be put into question'. Taken together, these are no small achievements. The question is: do these achievements outweigh the costs?

Even if the above commitments are taken at face value, a closer inspection of the DDA reveals some serious losses for the developing world. The most serious perhaps is that 2005 was set as the deadline for the completion of the new round. As noted above, the developing countries were not fully aware of what they had signed up to in the Uruguay Round that took eight years to negotiate. At Doha, they were expected to negotiate agreements that are even more complicated, and to do so much more quickly. Classic examples of the new, complex issues that have been brought within the WTO mandate are the 'Singapore issues' (liberalizing government procurement, trade facilitation, investment and competition policy), which the developing countries have resisted with a fair degree of consistency. It is true that a small grace period is available, as negotiations are scheduled in these areas only 'after the Fifth Session of the Ministerial Conference on the basis of a decision to be taken, by explicit consensus, at that Session on modalities of negotiations'. However, it is still unclear if the qualifying phrase 'by explicit consensus' will in practice introduce any additional safeguards beyond those built into the consensus requirement anyway. The introduction of the complex Singapore issues into the WTO agenda had an air of *déjà vu* about it. It was strongly reminiscent of the way services were brought into the work programme of the GATT in 1982: although the programme initially committed countries to national studies and exchange of relevant information in international organizations 'like the GATT', developed countries had interpreted this work programme as a preparation for the new round with services in it. Developing countries, at the launch of the UR at Punta del Este, were assured of the dual track mechanism, that is that services would be kept separate from traditional GATT issues, but what eventually resulted was the Single Undertaking.

In other words, developing countries have been made promises on procedure in the past only for them to be broken soon after. They may have reason to believe that, in spite of qualifications on procedures, the Singapore issues have already made their backdoor entry into the WTO. On the 'implementation' issues, developing countries had raised the demand that these be addressed before the launch of a new round. But by being mentioned in the DDA, they have been linked to the negotiating process of the new round in exchange for new commitments. In some ways, this means that developing countries will 'pay twice' for the problems caused by the Uruguay Round; that is, in order to get outstanding issues from the UR addressed, developing countries have had to make additional, new commitments. And even in areas that have been explicitly devoted to the interests of developing countries, such as technical assistance and capacity building, debt and finance, LDCs, and the new work programme on small economies, it is still too early to guess how these issues will play out in the actual negotiation process. Even though the impact of developing countries in setting a part of the DDA is clear, it would be premature and dangerous to claim victory on behalf of developing countries.

In order to explain how the DDA came to incorporate issues that developing countries had opposed until the very last minute, it is important to note that one issue that might have surfaced did not do so – that of transparency and internal reform of the WTO. Despite talk in the run-up to the Ministerial that a working group on institutional reform would be set up, no such group actually materialized. The exclusionary processes in operation at Seattle (see Section 4) had brought issues of institutional reform of the WTO to the fore and did bring about certain changes in the run-up to Doha. However, some reports of the Doha Ministerial indicate that, while exclusion of developing countries was not as flagrant as at Seattle, several procedural inadequacies persisted. This raises the question of the extent to which the decision-making processes of the WTO itself are responsible for this marginalization.

4 Decision-making processes and developing countries

Murmurs of discontent with the decision-making processes of the WTO go back to GATT days when closed-door meetings in the Green Room (from which many developing countries were excluded) contributed to the impression that the GATT was a 'Rich Man's Club'. The Seattle debacle however transformed the quiet dissatisfaction of developing countries into a public uproar about exclusionary decision-making processes of the WTO. Examples of the exclusionary processes that took place in Seattle include the failure to invite developing countries to many closed-door deliberations; some reports even say that developing country members were not informed (or were misinformed) about the venue of meetings. The US Trade Representative who chaired the talks, Charlene Barshefsky, did not improve matters when she stated that if the process did not reach a consensus text, 'I fully reserve the right also to use a more exclusive process to achieve a final outcome. There is no question about either my right as the Chair to do it or my intention as the Chair to do it.' Some reform measures were introduced subsequently, but Doha also revealed serious inadequacies regarding the inclusion of developing countries. This section analyses ways in which the very process of everyday working of the WTO has impeded the participation of developing countries.

In terms of providing formal equality of status to developed and developing countries, the WTO is a very egalitarian institution on paper. It is a one-member-one-vote organization (as per Article IX:1) and, as such, differs considerably from the World Bank and the International Monetary Fund (IMF) where countries have votes based on their quotas, which in turn are a function of their respective weights in the international economic system. Further, meetings of most of the formal decision-making structures in the WTO are open to the entire membership of the WTO. And with respect to procedures of counting of votes, Article IX:1 states that decisions will be taken by a majority of votes cast, unless otherwise provided for in the agreement or the relevant Multilateral Trade Agreements. Given that developing countries command an overwhelming majority in the WTO, it would seem reasonable to expect that the WTO's voting system gives them a powerful bargaining advantage.

Unfortunately, the potential advantages of having a one-member-one-vote system with majority voting are seldom realised due to the norm of consensus-based decision making and the importance of informal processes that are crucial for reaching consensus. Indeed, Article IX:1 states that: 'The WTO shall continue the practice of decision making by consensus followed under GATT 1947'. Consensus is arrived at 'if no Member, present at the meeting when the decision is formally taken, formally objects to the proposed decision'. The requirement of consensus contradicts the formal equality of majority voting, since it gives members a veto power. Notice also the key assumption of *presence*. The *WTO Directory* (2000) shows that 24 countries have no permanent representation in Geneva. These countries cannot object to the so-called consensus that various bodies of the WTO arrive at in their everyday workings. Even among the countries that enjoy diplomatic representation in Geneva, the size of their delegations is small (the average size of developed country delegation is 7.38 versus 3.51 for developing countries) and they are unable to attend many of the overlapping meetings that are organized in the everyday workings of the organization. Given that almost 1200 meetings are held every year, developing countries with scarce resources and small delegations that have to cover all the international bodies located in Geneva (for example, the World Health Organization and the International Labour Organization) find that their ability and preparedness to attend these meetings simply does not compare with the presence exercised by developed countries.

Because reaching agreement is not an easy task when many actors are involved, the GATT and WTO have evolved elaborate practices of informal meetings to forge a consensus. Some informal consultations involve the entire membership of the WTO, for example, meetings of the Heads of Delegations. Smaller group meetings are also a commonly used device to reach consensus. Informality certainly offers the advantage of flexibility, which is key to any successful negotiation involving many actors. But the first and most obvious problem with informal consultations is that they can lack transparency. Informal meetings were often by invitation only or through a process of self-selection by a small clique within the WTO. The most infamous in this genre were the Green Room meetings, where the Secretariat often treated the list of the invitees as confidential in order to avoid a flood of requests for participation from the excluded (Rege, 2000).

After the exclusion of many developing countries from informal meetings in Seattle, some attempt was made to reform the system and make these informal meetings more inclusive. Three important steps were made in this direction in the intervening years between Seattle and Doha. First, the schedules of informal meetings and the list of invitees were announced. Members who thought that they had a strong interest in the discussion could also participate. Second, it was emphasized that the meetings were directed purely towards consensus-building and had no decision-making powers. And third, minutes of at least some informal meetings were circulated among the whole membership. It is almost amusing to note that the bad connotations of 'Green Room' diplomacy have led to the replacement of the term with 'small group meetings'. These reform measures certainly presented a step in the right direction, but old habits die hard and many of the problems of small group diplomacy recurred at Doha. Describing the exclusionary diplomacy at work at Doha, Chakravarthi Raghavan (2002) reports on the 'shenanigans and abuse of procedures' as follows.

> That conference started with the adoption of its agenda at the ceremonial opening session, saw the use of named and unnamed facilitators to create an artificial consensus on the Ministerial Declaration and work programme, and ended with consultations among a small number of invited delegations (the so-called Green Room meetings), in which the ministers present were asked to agree to formulations and drafts on new issues that were only brought up there at the last moment.

It is possible that the voice of the developing world would be more difficult to ignore if developing countries were better prepared to identify their interests and then demanded a place in the small group meetings. One way of making the leap, from active participation to an informed and active participation that rivals developed country participation, would be through some extra help from the Secretariat. However, the member-driven character of the WTO means that the Secretariat is small and has neither the resources nor the power of its counterparts in staff-driven organizations like the IMF and the World Bank. In the absence of this extra help, power hierarchies outside of the WTO simply get translated into the institution itself, with the developed countries far better equipped to set the agenda and negotiate than developing countries. Recent years have, if anything, only seen these power differentials exacerbated due to the expanded agenda of the WTO and the even greater strains that this puts onto the scarce diplomatic and research resources of developing countries.

Even the limited role that the Secretariat plays in giving technical assistance (and which receives considerable attention in the Doha declarations and decisions) is controversial. Developing country delegates have told the present author that the promotion of a new round of talks in the run-up to the Doha Ministerial represented an open advocacy of a position which was opposed by a majority of the members and that this considerably undermined the credibility of the WTO as a neutral broker. The figures for developing country representation on the Secretariat staff are also not particularly reassuring: in 2001, of the 552 staff positions available, only 94 were occupied by persons from developing countries.

The problems of informal and formal meetings that overlap, and a pace of liberalization that developing countries find extremely difficult to keep up with, are further compounded by the requirement of the Marrakesh Agreement, which concluded the UR in 1994, that the Ministerial Conference 'shall meet at least once every two years' (Article IV.1). The built-in agenda, notification requirements and so forth mean that developing countries already have their plates quite full, without needing to add the extensive preparatory work that has to be put in before the Ministerial. Some developed countries effectively use these meetings to press developing countries into accepting new obligations that they are ill-prepared and unwilling to accept (Rege, 2000). A recent paper by the Like-Minded Group proposes that it would help if Ministerials were not accompanied by the presumption of starting a new round.

Institutional reform is clearly necessary if WTO decisions are to have legitimacy in developing countries. However, the question of institutional reform has to be approached with great caution, since it might replace the informality and consensus-based decision making of the WTO with a permanent steering committee or executive board. Proposals for such a board have come in many guises from various sources and have received significant attention in the media, among academics, and within the WTO.

The number of such proposals and the attention that they have received is interesting especially as developing countries themselves have baulked at the idea, fearing that it might institutionalize their unequal position (as is the case in the IMF and the World Bank, for example).

5   Strategies for developing countries

As we have seen, the constraints on effective developing country participation in the WTO are both procedural and institutional. But the WTO is both a member-driven organization and a relatively young institution, where the terms of inter-state interaction are still evolving, so developing countries still have considerable scope to improve their position. There are several strategies that developing countries can adopt independently of procedural change.

The first and most important tool available to developing countries to improve their ability to participate in the WTO lies at the national level. Not even the most well-intentioned and adequately funded technical assistance programmes can be completely free from the influence of the great powers and their agenda. Even if funding goes directly to the developing countries, its direction and targets are likely to be selected in keeping with dominant ideological and power-political positions. Among the causes that developing countries identify for their marginalization from the WTO, an important one is the weak interest that domestic governments have in international trade policy matters, even today. One developing country delegate told the present author that trade rules seldom have election making (or breaking) potential in developing countries, and hence governments choose not to invest adequate resources in capacity building at home or at the delegation level. Furthermore, there is little policy co-ordination between the governments and their respective delegations in Geneva, which means that while delegations have considerable negotiating leeway due to their independence from domestic pressures, they are deprived of the research-base and political back-up that is needed to negotiate effectively. Some LDCs point out that they have hardly any national structure for international trade policy making, especially in the context of the technical and complex issues covered by the WTO. Developing countries recognize that they need to somehow increase their Geneva presence, increase co-ordination between Geneva and their governments, and increase interest, resource, and research commitments at the national level in order to allow more informed participation in the WTO. This acknowledgement of limitations at the domestic level presents a remarkable contrast to the developing countries' former dismissal of the GATT as a 'Rich Man's Club' and the accompanying refusal even to try to participate on equal terms.

Besides working on their individual capacity and Geneva presence, the second way of improving the participation of developing countries in the WTO is by bargaining collectively, that is, through forming coalitions. Coalitions allow a pooling of organizational resources, and enable countries with poorly identified interests to avail themselves of the research efforts of allies and a possible country-wide division of research and labour across issue areas. In addition, by bargaining together, developing countries occupy greater weight in terms of trade shares and political clout and can hence exercise more influence than when they bargain alone. Even at Doha, the impact of developing country coalitions was clear. Several coalitions were in operation, which had begun as joint research initiatives and persisted into the ministerial. Examples include the group of LDCs, the group of small and vulnerable economies, the Africa group, the group of ACP countries (countries in Africa, the Caribbean and the Pacific linked to the European Union through preferential trade agreements), and the Like-Minded Group.

Further, coalitions need not operate only at an inter-state level. At Seattle, the links between the USA and the labour lobby had already shown the strength that states could derive from NGOs and vice versa. At Doha, there was a similar de facto synergy, this time between developing countries and developing country NGOs, which may have contributed significantly to the declaration on TRIPS and public health described above.

The third strategy for improving their participation in the WTO is one that developing countries have learnt the hard way. Until the Uruguay Round, developing countries had mainly followed a strategy of *blocking* initiatives. It was only with the failures of the G-10, which had opposed the inclusion of the 'new' issues, particularly services, in the pre-negotiation phase of the Uruguay Round and the successes of the Café au Lait coalition and the Cairns Group in the 1980s to early 1990s that the importance of having a positive agenda dawned on developing countries.

The Café au Lait grouping began as an investigative forum to explore the services issue and its possible inclusion in the new round, in the pre-negotiation phase of the Uruguay Round. It derived its name from the fact that this initiative was led by Colombia and Switzerland. The initiative crystallized into a coalition that offered developing countries an alternative position to the hard line taken by the G-10. The resulting coalition of developing countries was the G-20, which liaised with developed countries, eventually producing the G-48. It was the proposal of the G-48 that provided the basis for the Punta del Este declaration and finally brought about a compromise between the positions of the hard-liners and the 'Quad' (the EU, the USA, Japan and Canada). Its importance was that it heralded a new form of diplomacy in that the coalition straddled both developed and developing countries and acted as a mediating rather than blocking coalition (Narlikar, 2003).

The Cairns Group of agricultural exporters, formed in 1986, was seen as crucial in providing a *modus vivendi* between the EU and the USA on agriculture, thereby finally facilitating an inclusion of agriculture within the purview of GATT, with the launch of the Uruguay Round. The original members of the Cairns Group were Argentina, Australia, Brazil, Canada, Chile, Colombia, Fiji, Hungary, Indonesia, Malaysia, Thailand, New Zealand, Philippines, and Uruguay (by 2002 it comprised 17 members).

Blocking sometimes works, but only when sparingly and carefully used by a group whose consistently positive agenda has already won it legitimacy and credibility. The threat of the six Latin American members of the Cairns Group at the Montreal Mid-Term Review of the Uruguay Round was effective because they had shown themselves to be enthusiastic members of a bridge-building, mediating coalition. The walkout staged to counter EU intransigence, as well as the risk of a deal between the USA and EU at the expense of other agricultural exporters, was taken more seriously because it was unusual – in contrast with the persistent blocking techniques that the G-10 had adopted.

Similarly, the opposition of developing countries to incorporating labour standards in trade agreements has been effective because of their proactive and positive participation in other areas. Another example of successful blocking was by the Association of South-East Asian Nations (ASEAN) and other developing countries in 1999 over the leadership issue and the compromise that resulted. As a result, Mike Moore and Supachai Panitchpakdi (supported by the ASEAN, many developing countries and even developed countries such as Japan) were appointed to the post of Director General of the WTO for three years each with no possibility of a renewed term for either. Overall, there was strong evidence at Doha of the value of a positive agenda and with fairly technical and detailed proposals coming from developing countries and their coalitions (as opposed to blocking and long wish-lists). At least some of the hard work paid off and it is not surprising that Doha, in spite of its many failings and inadequacies, has been judged as the best ministerial decision that developing countries have achieved to date.

6   Conclusion

Viewed from the perspective of developing countries, a multilateral system is preferable to one where the weak are susceptible to bilateral pressures from the strong with no rules to mitigate such pressures (see Section 2). The WTO makes trade liberalization more feasible politically and also promotes greater certainty through its system of established rules. However, multilateral rules may be unresponsive to, even weighted against, the interests of the weak. This is especially so if the internal workings of the organization are shaped by informal political processes that reflect the external disparities in power. There are four reasons why the WTO harbours the risk of swinging in that direction.

First, it is far from clear that the substance of the negotiated agreements (including the Doha Development Agenda) allows an equitable balance between the agenda of the developed and developing countries. This affects the political feasibility of liberalization begun under WTO auspices by developing countries, and thereby also the sustainability of its rules. WTO agreements have been found to generate huge costs that developing countries can ill-afford.

Second, while part of the reason for the lop-sided nature of agreements lies in the weaknesses of developing countries as major trading economies, the decision-making procedures of the WTO tilt this international imbalance further, rendering the formal equality guaranteed to developing countries ineffective through the operation of informal procedures ranging from consensus decision making to small group diplomacy.

Third, the member-driven nature of the WTO is a double-edged sword. While it ensures that the WTO's Secretariat lacks the influence of the staff of the IMF and the World Bank and places the onus of participation on the countries themselves, it also means that countries with limited capacities find themselves unable to participate effectively. This is especially so with the LDCs, some of which even lack diplomatic representation in Geneva; the problem, however, extends to the larger developing countries whose representatives are severely over-taxed with the complicated new issues, and receive only minimal support from their governments.

Finally, the scope of WTO regulation represents a significant expansion from its predecessors, with a tendency to penetrate further and deeper into the domestic regulatory domains of its members. If current trends continue, the WTO will risk generating a serious institutional over-stretch. It will be regulating in areas that traditionally fell within domestic jurisdictions of states. Its developing country members will be even more marginalized due to their inability to participate in the making and implementation of these new rules.

All the dangers cited above notwithstanding, it may still not be injudicious to end on an optimistic note. The WTO is a young and still evolving organization. In its formal rules (one-member-one-vote, no executive council) at least, the WTO is considerably more democratic than the IMF and the World Bank. And its member-driven character allows the possibility of some initiative to developing countries in contrast to staff-dominated organizations. If the WTO is able to guard against rampant institutional over-stretch, and if developing countries are able to sustain and further develop their joint efforts at proactive involvement, especially if they can continue to form creative coalitions, including making common cause with some developed countries, there is a possibility that they may be able to set up a virtuous cycle in shaping the evolution of the WTO and its agenda to their great advantage.

Further reading

A thorough review of the economics and politics of the world trading system, particularly focused on the role of the WTO and multilateral trade rounds, is to be found in Hoekman, B. and Kostecki, M.M. (2001) *The Political Economy of the World Trading System: The WTO and Beyond*, second edition, Oxford, Oxford University Press.

For a study of the legal and political structure of the WTO and its implications for the policies of member states by one of the world's leading international trade lawyers, see Jackson, J.H. (1997) *The World Trading System: Law and Policy of International Economic Relations*, second edition, Cambridge, Mass., The MIT Press.

A study that expands on many of the cases and examples discussed in this chapter, and gives a fuller account of the position and experience of developing countries in the WTO, is Narlikar, A. (forthcoming in 2003) *International Trade and Developing Countries: Coalitions in the GATT and WTO*, London, Routledge.

WTO official documents can be accessed at www.wto.org

Chapter 5 International politics: states, anarchy and governance

Simon Bromley

1 Introduction

In Chapter 4 you were introduced to an important debate about how we might understand the politics of the World Trade Organization (WTO). Can the WTO as a system of trade rules mitigate the inequalities between states? Or does the operation of the WTO reveal an exercise of power by the richer states to the disadvantage of the weak? Amrita Narlikar argues that, while the developing countries have felt that the WTO has too often been an arena in which the rich have got what they want, there is nevertheless some hope that a more co-operative system of trade rules might be created through the WTO.

In this chapter I want to take this debate and investigate some of the arguments which underlie it. For, in many ways, the contrasting positions which Narlikar identifies reflect very different understandings of the nature of international politics. In part this difference lies in different views of what politics itself is, and in part in contending ideas about the difference, and relationship, between *domestic* and *international* politics.

On one reading, the World Trade Organization (WTO) is a multilateral forum in which the rules of the international trade regime are negotiated. As both Aditya Bhattacharjea's and Amrita Narlikar's discussions make clear, the members of the WTO are sovereign states and, in principle, WTO rules 'have been agreed to by all members ... and no country is forced to become a member'. Politically speaking, the international system is indeed a world of sovereign states, in which states attempt to monopolize political life within a given territory and claim to speak for the people of that country in international institutions. Each sovereign state is constitutionally independent and states are equal to one another in matters of international law. That is to say, each state has the same right to determine its internal (or domestic) affairs and cannot be bound by international laws that it has not consented to. The creation of international trade rules which, as Narlikar says, have 'expanded into areas where states had traditionally exercised sovereign rights of legislation' is in this view not problematic if the member states have consented to those rules.

Indeed, consent is often taken to be the basis of domestic politics, at least in liberal democratic states. People obey the laws of their state, it is said, because they are *their* laws in the sense that the laws serve general, common interests and have been made by their elected representatives. The defenders of the WTO argue that a parallel argument applies in relation to states and the rules of the international trade regime.

I am going to examine these kinds of argument rather closely because they rest, I think, on some very questionable assumptions about the nature of politics, both domestic and international. You have already seen that the idea that developing countries have consented to what is done in their name in the WTO is questionable. In fact, for many, the realm of international politics is based more on coercion by the powerful than consent among equals.

I shall begin by considering the difference between domestic and international politics and in order to do that I need to establish the nature of 'politics' itself. Accordingly, in Section 2, I outline the origins of the view that political decision making is fundamentally about the co-operative exercise of *consent*, before offering a rather different account of the fundamental basis of politics that sees it primarily as a form of *co-ordination* in Section 3. In these sections, my discussion will focus on politics within the state, that is, domestic politics, though I shall note some implications for thinking about international politics.

With these understandings of politics to hand, in Section 4, I turn directly to the character of the international system of sovereign states and outline what is arguably the dominant view, in both academic and popular discussions, of the nature of international politics: namely, that the international is a field of interaction defined by relations of power, in which powerful states are able to set the rules and get others to do what they want.

Thus, Section 4 develops the argument that there is a fundamental *difference* between domestic and international politics. While domestic politics is based on either consent or co-ordination and is therefore a fundamentally co-operative enterprise, international politics is basically conflictual and involves states striving for coercive power. (We shall consider the nature of power more carefully in Chapter 9.)

Section 5 begins to develop some criticisms of this 'realist' model of international politics and takes a closer look at the nature of the modern state and the precise character of its sovereignty. This closer look suggests that there are real elements of co-ordination, perhaps even consent, involved in international politics as well as domestic politics, and that the hard and fast distinction that realism wishes to draw between the character of domestic and international politics may be increasingly unsustainable.

Section 6 attempts to put some concrete substance on this rather abstract argument by outlining a model of international politics that views it as one part of a world of multi-level governance, in which the distinction between the domestic and the international is somewhat fuzzy. If this model is at all accurate, the idea that the rules of the international trade regime could modify the power relations between states, such that international politics becomes more co-operative and less conflictual, is at least plausible.

As I go through this discussion, I shall also note two dimensions that the *political* analysis of the WTO introduces, compared with the analysis of international trade from an *economics* stance (Chapter 3). The first of these is the different ways in which the question 'who gains from trade?' is analysed in political and economic analyses. Economics tackles the question in terms of models of trading on markets, while politics focuses on how trade rules are made and whose interests are served. This is central to the debate I noted at the start. The second comparison is between different conceptions of 'anarchy' and anarchic order in the two frameworks and their relation to governance. These concepts in economic analysis were introduced in Chapter 3, Section 9, as a contrast between pure market models and an examination of the impact of policy and negotiation. In this chapter, the key debate that concerns us reflects a comparison of political concepts of anarchic and governed order: between the idea that the politics of the WTO reflects the anarchic, ungoverned, interplay of states using power in their own interests (discussed in Section 4), and the idea that the WTO demonstrates the existence and possibility of some kind of conscious 'governance' of international trade (discussed in Section 6). (The terms 'anarchy' and 'governance' are explained more fully below.)

1.1 The nature of political enquiry

Before I start, I want to raise a couple of issues to do with the nature of political enquiry. First, the academic attempt to understand politics is inseparable from the object of study – political activity itself. This is a result of the fact that political activity is shaped by human agency and is therefore coloured by the beliefs and ideas that people have about politics. The terms, concepts and arguments at play in political activity are taken into political analysis, where they are then subject to academic scrutiny, elaboration and refinement, and thence may flow back out into the political world. The language of politics, which is common both to ideologies oriented towards action in the political world and to theories oriented towards understanding and explaining the context for political action, is forged in the political world as much as, if not more than, by academic analysis.

Consider the arguments of the developing countries about the WTO, which Narlikar discussed in the previous chapter, and what I have already said about how we are going to try to understand international politics in this chapter. You have already seen that the debates about international trade in and around the WTO itself use concepts such as power and arguments about the ways that the powerful states 'get what they want' in the WTO. Yet, as I shall discuss, these arguments and concepts are also used to analyse and understand international politics more generally. In a similar way, concepts like sovereignty, which I discuss in Section 5.3, are both part of the theories oriented towards understanding, and of the arguments being used in and around the WTO. Academic debates about 'what sovereignty means' both reflect and help to shape the substance of 'what sovereignty means' in the political world.

This does not mean that there is no distinction to be drawn between political analysis, on the one hand, and political ideology, on the other. Unlike political analysis, political ideologies involve concerted action and hence organization, decision making and therefore control. Political analysis can certainly aspire to be independent of concerted action and decision making, though it need not. What it cannot do is be independent of political language, that is, the concepts and forms of reasoning used in 'real life' political arguments. And it is important to see that this is not a weakness but a strength, since it is precisely what makes it *possible* (it is not always achieved!) for political analysis to have a purchase on the world, and what enables it to operate as a form of practical reasoning, that is, a form of thinking about what we have reason to *do* and *become*.

Arising more or less directly from reflection on the nature of political activity, the tasks of political theory are, first, to make clear the nature of the values, beliefs and interests at work in actual political action as it now stands, as well as to clarify the context in which these operate and the consequences of their interaction, and second, to reflect on the coherence and justifiability of different values, beliefs and interests as a way of trying to think about how we might want the world to be or become. We must also judge how and by what means we can reasonably move from the first to the second. The techniques of political theory are as diverse as its subject matter: sometimes it turns to history to elucidate the nature, context and consequences of political action; sometimes it employs conceptual analysis to interrogate the meaning and implications of the values and beliefs found in the political world; and sometimes it develops models (similar in kind to those economic models discussed by Maureen Mackintosh in Chapter 3) to clarify the context and consequences of political action.

I hope this chapter will help you to think about international politics in new ways. I aim to show you some examples of political analysis and to provide you with some tools and theories so that you can begin to make your own evaluations and judgements.

The second issue I want to raise about the nature of political enquiry is the use of 'Western' terms and concepts. It is, I think, a fact of life in the contemporary world that all of the key terms and concepts that are used to discuss political activity, and to analyse political causality, are to a greater or lesser extent shaped by a tradition of thinking that can be called 'Western'.

Since we are examining politics in the context of an international system that comprises *all* of the world's cultures, I want to reflect on the significance of this fact. The Western tradition of political theory self-consciously traces its roots back to the ancient civilizations of Greece and Rome and no account of that tradition can afford to ignore these antecedent roots. I will argue, for example, that our very conception of what political activity consists of is due in part to the Greeks, and specifically to the account of Greek politics given to us by Aristotle. Thereafter, this tradition continued to develop and change in Europe and in areas of European settlement in the non-European world.

But, as the contemporary political theorist John Dunn has claimed, it would be both 'culturally offensive' and 'impossible to defend' the idea that the history of political theory is confined to this tradition. 'Wherever there have been literate civilizations of any political scale and longevity (in China, in the Islamic world, in Japan, in India, in Indonesia, in nineteenth century West Africa)' says Dunn, 'there have developed traditions of understanding of prominent and undeniably important aspects of politics' (1996a, p.14).

If this is so, how can I justify the exclusive focus on the Western tradition of political thought in what follows, save by an honest admission that it is the only one with which I am at all closely acquainted? While the latter is, indeed, regrettably true, I share Dunn's belief that this does *not* render what I have to say merely parochial, let alone culturally offensive and impossible to defend. Dunn's answer as to why this particular tradition has a serious claim on our attention is that, while there may be many other rich and diverse experiences, they have all, at some point, been forced to come to terms with modern politics and the intellectual categories forged in the West to understand it.

> As matters now stand, no one thinking seriously and on any scale about political agency in the world in which we live can ignore for any length of time the legal, administrative and coercive apparatus of the modern state ... or the recalcitrant dynamics of the world trading system. These are all historical realities that were first analysed with any rigour and profundity in the west; and it seems clear that ... they are still more intensively and deeply understood by thinkers who have chosen to adopt the categories of western political and economic analysis (with whatever amendment) for their own than they are by any traditions which have sought to insulate themselves as best they could from the imaginative pollution of western conceptions of value, purpose and causality.

(Dunn, 1996a, pp.15, 16)

I would add to this the point that Dunn's judgement, which I fully share, is itself contested in some parts of some cultures in the world, including parts of the 'West'. That is to accept that the place and relevance of Western political theory in the contemporary world, and the view I am taking of it here, is itself subject to political argument and dispute.

2   The nature of politics

Even within the Western tradition of thinking about politics, there is no single account of the nature of political activity that commands universal assent. However, there are some themes that recur in most contemporary discussions which, as I noted above, can be traced back to ancient Greek thinkers such as Aristotle (384–321 BCE). Aristotle's *Politics* opens with what is at first sight a highly dubious claim that:

> Every state is a community of some kind, and every community is established with a view to some good; for everyone always acts in order to obtain that which they think good. But, if all communities aim at some good, the state or political community, which is the highest of all, and which embraces all the rest, aims at good in a greater degree than any other, and at the highest good.

(Aristotle, 1996, p.11)

Aristotle was in fact remarkably clear sighted about the realities of political life in the Greek city-states of his time (he was tutor to Alexander the Great), so, before we dismiss his comments as wishful thinking, it might be useful to see if we can make some sober sense of what he is saying. There are, I think, at least three enduring insights that we can derive from Aristotle and which continue to shape a great deal of contemporary thinking about politics.

In the first place, Aristotle is insisting that politics is fundamentally a co-operative activity. Aristotle says that forms of association among individuals must serve some common or shared interests among their members, otherwise people would not join them. But he goes on to say that the 'state or political community' embraces other communities and 'aims at good in a greater degree than any other'. This is a complex argument but Aristotle seems to mean *both* that the things that people require if they are to live together well are fragile and require protection, *and* that some of these things – especially those relating to the security of people and possessions and the pursuit of the good life – can only be provided for collectively, by co-operating with one another.

Thus, the most basic form of political activity is that concerned with the collective regulation of social life, the making and enforcing of rules and policies. Political activity involves collective choices, forms of co-operation where the outcome is binding on all. The need for this kind of political activity arises because people are social beings – they must live together if they are to live at all; and if they are to live together, there must be some minimal level of social order. At a minimum, social order presupposes the physical and material security of persons. But social order may be threatened both by individuals and groups within a political community, or from outside by other political communities. Politics understood as the activity of collective choice is thus directed towards making and upholding (or enforcing) the rules and policies needed to sustain and protect social order.

Second, however, the subject matter of politics is potentially limitless. Aristotle believed that the purpose of the state was to provide the conditions in which people could pursue the 'good life', not merely guarantee security of persons and property. The state, says Aristotle, aims 'at the highest good' and 'comes into existence, originating in the bare needs of life, and continuing in existence for the sake of a good life' (1996, p.13). Actors often seek collectively binding rules in order to pursue interests and to affirm or express their identities and values, especially those interests and values that can only be provided for collectively. Thus, political activity can be oriented towards the construction and pursuit of collective interests, identities and allegiances, which in turn often serve to define the boundaries of a political community. What about the relations *between* political communities? I shall return to that below.

Third, even within a stable political community, people's interests, values and identities differ, so that these aspects of political life are inherently conflictual to some extent. Conflict is certainly an ever-present fact-of-life between and within political communities today as it was between the city-states of ancient Greece. Moreover, people, groups and whole political communities vary in their ability to secure favourable political outcomes: that is, some have more power than others. Indeed, perhaps the simplest and most commonsense understanding of politics is that it involves the struggle for power, where power is understood as the ability to secure one's interests and values in conflict with others.

Political activity, then, invariably involves a mixture of co-operation and conflict. Without some conflict, there is no need for politics; and without co-operation, there is no collective choice, only strife and potentially war. Nevertheless, co-operation is the primary element in political life.

Question

Can you think of ways in which we might challenge the conception of politics described above?

While the understanding of political activity I have sought to extract from Aristotle might seem intuitively compelling, even obvious, it can be and has been challenged. First, we might challenge Aristotle's claim that politics is essentially co-operative with the idea that in fact politics is a form of domination, a conflict-ridden process whereby some are able to coerce and control others. This rival view sees co-operation among some as being structured by, as arising from, their conflicts with others. This more pessimistic view of politics has been a recurring, if minority, feature of the Western tradition and is well represented in the writings of Aristotle's teacher, Plato, and a host of recent conservative thinkers such as Carl Schmitt as well as in the socialist tradition, for example, in the political writings of Marx and Lenin. Importantly for our purposes, it also forms the basis of the 'realist' view of international politics (see Section 4).

Of course, Aristotle did recognize the conflictual elements of political life but he distinguished politics from domination. Domination involves one person or group of people subordinating another or others, so that the subordinate are controlled or coerced into following the rules of the dominant. In Aristotle's time an obvious instance of domination was slavery. Aristotle remarks that 'the rule of a master is not constitutional rule, and ... all the different kinds of rule are not, as some affirm, the same as each other. For there is one rule exercised over subjects who are by nature free, another over subjects who are by nature slaves' (1996, p.19). Politics for Aristotle is therefore, the realm of a co-operative endeavour (among non-slaves) in the pursuit of common or shared interests and values. Those humans who are not slaves 'by nature' are 'by nature' fitted for politics, according to Aristotle; and 'he who is unable to live in society, or who has no need because he is sufficient for himself, must be either a beast or a god .... A social instinct is implanted in all men by nature' (1996, p.14). For Aristotle, these people will, for the most part, agree about what constitutes the good life. As noted above, Aristotle believed that some people are 'naturally' slaves. However, if we ignore that aspect of his thinking, it is possible to appreciate that we could see politics in a much less sympathetic light than this, as the realm of domination first and foremost, with co-operation as a secondary activity.

Second, Aristotle encourages us to see politics as a realm of choice, as a field of agency, rather than of fate, in which the political community is able to choose the collective features of the good life. This is surely an even more precarious assumption than the first. While we may grant that politics involves choices and that it can, therefore, be viewed in terms of agency, we cannot assume from this that political *consequences* are in some sense completely under our control. Political activity may be less a conscious collective pursuit of the good life, and more action and reaction to circumstances and constraints that are beyond collective control. If the latter is the case, then political analysis becomes less a reflection on the conditions of the good life, and more an attempt to calculate constraints and opportunities. Politics here becomes a realm of fate, not choice. As you will see, the realist view of *international* politics is very much that it is a realm of fate (see Section 4).

2.1   Politics and consent

In Aristotle's time and place, the political community was organized as a city-state comprising a self-governing citizenry, in which all citizens had the right to participate directly in the making of legislation and the administration of justice. (Women, slaves and foreigners were not citizens.) Citizens were free to leave the city-state with all their property. Thus, citizens could be expected to obey the laws of the state because the laws were *their* laws. At this point, I want to define the notion of political authority. The authority of a political body, in this case a city-state, is that 'which authorizes (i.e. makes legitimate) the acts and commands exercised in its name' (Scruton, 1982, p.32).

In Aristotle's account, the ground of political authority, the source of the obligation to follow the commands of the state, was *consent* as to the nature of the collective interests and values involved in the good life. When rule is anchored in consent, citizens take responsibility for conforming their actions to the rules of the state because those rules are, in some sense, their own. In short, political authority derives from the active consent of the citizenry. Arguably, consent remains an important component of political obligation in those contemporary states that respect the civil and political rights of citizens, uphold the rule of law and select their governments by some form of representative democracy. But even in the best of these, let alone in those states where the opportunities for genuine consent are more limited, consent is not the only source of political obligation.

> **Political authority**
> The authority of a political body authorizes (legitimates) the acts and commands exercised in its name.

Activity 5.1

Supposing that we can move from the level of the state to international politics, would Aristotle's view of politics be a potential model for understanding the 'political community' of the WTO? Look back at the outline of the debate about the WTO in Section 1. Which side of the debate would this tend to support and why might you question it?

In fact there are good reasons to doubt that we can easily transplant a view of politics *within* a political community to politics *between* political communities as Activity 5.1 supposes. This is because the nature of political communities has implications for the kinds of relations which can occur between them. Why is this so? To answer this I need to consider a rather different proposition about the basis of political communities.

3 The state and the political community

I noted above that contemporary states are (for the most part) constitutionally independent of one another, that they attempt to monopolize political life within their territories, and that they claim to speak for their people in the international arena. In other words, states claim political authority over, and on behalf of, the people in their territory and recognize no external or higher authority than their own. This is what is meant, roughly speaking, by saying that states are 'sovereign' or possess 'sovereignty' (I shall be more precise about this in Section 5). However, this implies that, in claiming authority over and on behalf of the people, states are making a stronger claim to obligation from their populations than is implied by the notion of participation in rule making, and consent about the good life, which Aristotle advances. Furthermore, the claim by the state to an exclusive and supreme form of authority domestically leaves the realm of politics between states without any overarching authority. These implications are important for how we understand the WTO and international politics in general. To explain this I need to turn to the argument for political obligation that was made clearly and forcefully by Thomas Hobbes in the seventeenth century and elaborated upon by David Hume in the eighteenth century.

3.1 Thomas Hobbes and political obligation

Writing in the context of violent upheavals in Europe just after the conclusions of the Thirty Years War and the English Civil War, Thomas Hobbes was searching for a basis for stable and durable political authority in circumstances where there was widespread and often violent disagreement about the proper ends and means of politics. Rival ideas about what constituted the good life had led many people to merciless and brutal religious warfare, including especially civil war. In this context, Aristotle's view seemed to have lost all purchase on reality. If people's interests and values differed so violently, then what could provide a *common* basis for political authority? What could create an obligation to conform to the commands of authority?

Hobbes's answer was but one contribution to a complex set of ideas and practices that, in effect, invented the idea of the modern sovereign state in the late sixteenth and early seventeenth century. However, his answer is still studied because, as John Dunn has noted: 'The problem of political obligation was best stated – and perhaps most nearly resolved – by Thomas Hobbes in the middle of the seventeenth century' (1996b, p.68). In my view, Hobbes's theory of political obligation – that is, an account of why people should and would accept the commands of what he called the *sovereign*, the highest or final source of political authority in a given territory – remains one of the sharpest statements of the fundamental basis of modern political order.

At the centre of Hobbes's account was the absolute priority of material and physical security of individuals over all other human values and interests. For Hobbes this was not a question of biological or cultural fact, he did not believe that individuals and peoples valued self-preservation above all other goals. Clearly, those involved in religious warfare valued the conversion of other souls – or the safeguarding of their own – more highly than their own earthly existence. However, Hobbes thought that 'it was a matter of right – that no human being could rationally deny to other human beings the natural right to do their very best to preserve their own lives and to judge what actions such preservation required' (Dunn, 1996b, p.69). The problem, as Hobbes saw it, was that when individual judgements over what is necessary for self-preservation are in conflict, there are no correct answers, no facts of the matter – there is just a plurality of individual wills. Accordingly, Hobbes argued that in the 'state of nature' – that is, in the absence of overarching political authority – life is 'solitary, poor, nasty, brutish and short', since there exists a 'war of every man against every man', in which each person must enforce their rights and protect their material and physical security as best they can.

Faced with these circumstances, Hobbes argued that the only way of escaping from the state of nature was if all individuals agreed to subordinate their individual judgements as to what was necessary for self-preservation, as well as their individual capacities to enforce their natural rights, to a common power that is, by definition, *sovereign*. The establishment of a sovereign power would bring peace and security to social life by creating a political authority that could both impose a uniform judgement as to what is required for self-preservation and establish an effective monopoly over coercive power. Citizens would thence be obligated to the sovereign power by virtue of the guarantee provided for their individual and collective self-preservation. Stable and durable political authority, for Hobbes, results from the creation of a common source of security by a given people in a particular territory: an impersonal public power whose first and overriding duty is to ensure the individual and collective security of its citizens, thereby creating a reciprocal obligation on the part of the latter to obey the commands of the sovereign power.

Activity 5.2

Check that you understand Hobbes' argument so far. If in doubt, re-read the previous two paragraphs and note down the various steps in the argument.

3.2 A theory of political rule as co-ordination

Hobbes envisages the political problem in terms of the lack of an objective basis on which individuals can judge and enforce their rights to self-preservation. There is no basis for collective agreement about the good life, no consensus of values to support the authority of the state. Thus Hobbes presupposes a state of moral or ethical uncertainty and conflict. This is not Aristotle's world and the authority of the state cannot be founded in consent as to the nature of the good life.

Question

Whose depiction of the nature of politics do you find more compelling – Aristotle's or Hobbes's – and why?

Hobbes's central claim is that, if an artificial power can be established, a sovereign body capable of exercising coercion over and on behalf of those who find themselves in this position, people will prefer this to a continuation of the state of nature. In short, any system of centralized rule is preferable to no rule, so long as the sovereign does, in fact, secure the context for their self-preservation. The authority of the sovereign power stems from this fact, creates the obligation on the part of the population to obey its commands, and enables it to uphold its coercive monopoly without challenge. Even if the people might have preferred a different kind of rule (say, a democracy rather than an authoritarian state) this preference will be set aside in order to achieve security.

Hobbes terms the agreement to establish the sovereign a 'contract', or a 'covenant', in which individuals (implicitly) renounce their right to individual judgement in matters of self-preservation, and erect a sovereign to undertake this task, as long as others do likewise:

> It is fair to say that the contract in *Leviathan* [the book in which Hobbes set out his argument in its fullest form] has little independent moral force: we stick with our agreement to align our judgements because (as long as everyone else does so) there is no reason for us to defect from that arrangement. ... it does not matter (on Hobbes's theory) *who* makes the judgements about our preservation, as long as we all make the same judgements ...

(Tuck, 1996, pp.xxxii–iv)

People will abide by the contract (that is, they will not 'defect' from it), according to Hobbes, because peace and security are so obviously preferable to the state of nature. As there is no objective basis for choosing one kind of rule over another, the only thing that matters is that the people abide by the same form of rule. It is thus co-ordination rather than consent that establishes the basis of political order, where co-ordination is defined as independent choices by everyone on a single, mutually beneficial solution. Individuals align their intentions and expectations with others who are trying to achieve the same end. What is needed for co-ordination to work is that the people concerned have convergent interests (peace and security) and that they are able to align their mutual expectations and intentions on something that allows them to satisfy those interests. Once that thing, the sovereign state, has been established, future compliance is more or less self-enforcing because it is in no one's interest to defect from the covenant and, when individuals do defect, there is always the fear of the sovereign's sword to instil obedience: 'covenants without the sword are but bits of parchment', as Hobbes put it. But, and this is the crucial point, the ability of the sovereign, metaphorically speaking, to wield the sword against the few presupposes a prior and ongoing act of co-ordination on the part of the many.

While many have wondered whether Hobbes's argument succeeds in giving a satisfactory explanation of political obligation, I think that its overall logic is sound enough and that he was fundamentally right to see the creation of political authority as a form of co-ordination (though he would not have described it quite in those terms). We may no longer be able to subscribe to the specific ideas in which Hobbes's arguments were framed but, in my view, he was not wrong in identifying the massive mutual advantage involved in aligning decisions about self-preservation on a common, impersonal power.

This basic argument was shared by the Scottish philosopher and near contemporary of Adam Smith, David Hume, in the eighteenth century. Hume argued that it was 'on opinion only that government is founded' in particular the 'opinion of interest', that is, the public interest in 'the general advantage which is reaped from government' (David Hume, 'Of the first principles of government', 1741). However, what Hume adds to Hobbes's account is the important insight that once a sovereign power is established by means of co-ordination, the state can seek to promote further forms of co-ordination to even greater mutual advantage. What Hobbes portrays, somewhat unrealistically, as a one-off, static process of covenanting, Hume more realistically sees as an ongoing, dynamic process of co-ordination to mutual advantage.

In fact, Hume ridiculed the idea that any actual state had arisen from a covenant. But whatever the actual historical origins of the state, the reason why political authority survives and prospers is that it serves the function of mutually beneficial co-ordination. Russell Hardin has called this the 'co-ordination theory' of political rule: 'The central value of government that makes it easy to assent to is that it enables us to co-ordinate in the production

Co-ordination
Co-ordination is defined as independent choices by everyone on a single, mutually beneficial solution.

of enormous gains' (1999, p.98). We return to this idea – of further forms of co-ordination for 'enormous gains' – in Section 6. We also return to some of these ideas more formally in Chapter 13.

3.3 Sovereign states displace anarchy to the inter-state level

I noted above that this way of understanding the nature of politics within states has important implications for understanding politics between states. The important and immediate consequence of this process of establishing a sovereign power is that while the formation of a sovereign state remedies the depredations of the state of nature between *individuals*, it creates an *international* state of nature (assuming there is more than one such state). Although *states*, by virtue of their monopoly of physical coercion, pacify the *domestic* realm, they now confront one another *internationally* thus reproducing an inherently violent state of nature between one sovereign and another. The authority of the sovereign and the obligations of the citizens are bounded by the territory of the state yet between sovereigns politics is characterized by anarchy. By anarchy I do not mean 'chaos' but the dispersal of political authority, a relative absence of political specialization and institutionalization, and a corresponding dispersal of the coercive means necessary to enforce collective decisions. Violence between political actors in such a situation is always possible, however. Hobbes's solution to the anarchy of the state of nature between individuals necessarily creates anarchy between states.

Anarchy
Anarchy is the dispersal of political authority, a relative absence of political specialization and institutionalization, and a corresponding dispersal of the coercive means necessary to enforce collective decisions.

Thus even in times of peace many analysts argue that international relations are anarchic in the sense that there is no overarching authority internationally. Here, each state must look to itself to guarantee its security against (potential) threats from other states, and, at least in relation to questions of security, states are locked into conflict, and the security of one or some is often bought at the expense of the insecurity of others. This is because of what is known as the security dilemma: because it is often difficult, if not impossible, to distinguish between offensive and defensive military capabilities, the forces that make one state feel secure are seen by other states as threatening and vice versa. 'The nature of war', Hobbes says in Leviathan, 'consisteth not in actual fighting, but in the known disposition thereto during all the time there is no assurance to the contrary'. These anarchic, potentially hostile, relations among states are the defining feature of international politics according to many analyses of the international system. On this account, the key contrast between the anarchy of international politics and the sovereign authority found in the domestic realm turns on the different ways in which the means of physical coercion (force) are organized.

Security dilemma
A security dilemma exists when military capabilities that make one state feel secure are seen by other states as threatening.

The leading exponent of contemporary realist theory, Kenneth Waltz states in his *Theory of International Politics* that:

The difference between national and international politics lies not in the use of force but in the different modes of organization for doing something about it. A government, ruling by some standard of legitimacy, arrogates to itself the right to use force. ... A government has no monopoly on the use of force, as is all too evident. An effective government, however, has a monopoly on the *legitimate* use of force, and legitimate means here that the public agents are organized to prevent and counter the private use of force.

(Waltz, 1979, pp.103–4)

Waltz is here following in the footsteps of the great German sociologist, Max Weber, who defined the state as follows.

A 'ruling organization' will be called 'political' insofar as its existence and order is continuously safeguarded within a given *territorial* area by the threat and application of physical force on the part of the administrative staff. A compulsory political organization with continuous operation will be called a 'state' insofar as its administrative staff successfully upholds the claim to the *monopoly* of the *legitimate* use of physical force in the enforcement of its order.

(Weber, 1978, p.54)

State
A state is a compulsory political organization, operating in a given territory, that successfully upholds a claim to a monopoly of the legitimate use of physical force in the enforcement of its order.

As Helen Milner remarks: 'Legitimacy then appears to be the linchpin upon which conceptions of government rest. It ... is what distinguishes domestic and international politics' (1993, p.152). And, as we have seen, for Hobbes and Hume that legitimacy derives from 'the sheer practical expediency of settled political authority' (Dunn, 1996b, p.86). For Aristotle, by contrast, legitimacy was a result of an active consensus as to the nature of the good life shared by a people.

What the government of a state possesses internally – that is, a monopoly over the legitimate use of force – is precisely what is absent as between and among states at the international level, and it is this difference that defines the nature of domestic and international politics, respectively (see Table 5.1). This Hobbesian and Weberian view argues that political power is, in the last instance, the combination of authority and physical coercion (or force) exercised over a given territory and population. In the case of domestic politics force is centralized and legitimate; internationally the use of force is both decentralized, since each state possesses its own means of coercion, and lacking a common source of legitimacy, since each state judges its own cause in terms of its own particular interests and identity – states owe no obligations to one another.

Table 5.1 The organization of force within and between states according to Hobbes and Weber

	Domestically, inside the state	Internationally, as between states
Is force centralized?	Yes	No
Is the use of force legitimated?	Yes	No

We saw above that if politics is grounded in consent, then international politics as represented by the WTO, for instance, can also be viewed in a similar way. What would be the parallel in the case of Hobbes's theory of political order? Logically, the answer is co-ordination among many sovereign states on a single source of coercive power, that is, a world state. In the absence of the latter, political co-operation is limited by the fact that each state is judge, jury and executioner in its own cause. This fundamental difference between the domestic and international realms provides the starting point for the *realist* theory of international politics.

4   Waltz's realist theory of international politics

Kenneth Waltz is perhaps the best-known international relations theorist and his statement of contemporary realist theory is the starting place for much analysis and debate about international politics. Waltz in fact started off studying economics but moved on to study international relations and began, in the wake of the Second World War and the Korean War (he served in the US army for both) to formulate a 'theory of international politics'. His first book *Man the State and War* was published in 1959, but it is his *Theory of International Politics*, first published in 1979, which is one of the most influential works in the field. While the overall arguments of these two books are remarkably similar, what sets the latter apart is its explicit attempt to build a model of the political structure of the international system in order to elucidate the context and consequences of international interaction between and among states. The model-building aspects of realism have developed, mainly in the post-Second World War period, in an intellectual climate in which political analysis sought to borrow forms of reasoning from economics and in an intimate relationship with foreign policy discussions in the USA.

Explicitly drawing on his understanding of economic models, Waltz develops a theory of the workings of international politics from a series of deductions derived from a simple model of political structure based on a few abstract assumptions. The point of this exercise, Waltz maintains, is that if the conclusions he derives from his model fit what we know from historical and comparative inquiry, and if the simplifying assumptions on which the model is built are still appropriate, then the theory can be used as a guide to current and future developments in international politics. So, in thinking about Waltz's theory of international politics, you need to consider whether the simplifying assumptions of the model make sense, how far his deductions follow from that model, and how well those deductions are supported by the evidence.

4.1   The structure of international politics

Waltz's principle aim is to develop a theory of the *structure* of international politics. Theories of structure are common in the social sciences. Something – in the present case, the system of states – has a structure when it is composed of a number of parts that are arranged together by means of a set of interrelations. A model of structure abstracts the essential features of an arrangement and the interrelationships among its parts. And structural theories seek to use such models, that is, models of the arrangements among the parts, not models of the parts (states) themselves, in order to account for the workings of the system. Waltz's key claim is that only a structural explanation can properly account for the character of international politics.

Waltz argues that the structure of any political system can be defined in terms of three criteria: the *organizing principle* among the actors or institutions (what Waltz calls the 'units') that comprise the system; the degree of *functional differentiation* among the units; and the *distribution of capabilities or resources* across the units. It is easiest to see what Waltz means by following his contrast between domestic and international political systems. Among the actors and institutions that comprise domestic political systems making up a sovereign state, the principle of organization is hierarchical. This means that there is a ranked order of political authority with the sovereign power at the top; all other authorities and powers are subordinate to the sovereign. As between and among states there is no such hierarchy: each state judges and acts in its own interests, and the organizing principle is thus anarchy (as defined earlier). Thus far, Waltz is simply following Hobbes's account of sovereignty.

Hierarchy
A hierarchy is a ranked order of political authority, with the sovereign power of the state at the top.

Organizing principle

Waltz's first simplifying assumption, then, is that the units of the international political system are sovereign states and, therefore, that its principle of organization is anarchy. It is important to be clear that, for Waltz, the relations between states are anarchic *because* they are sovereign internally in relation to their territories and people. In addition, Waltz assumes that just as self-preservation is the overriding goal of individuals in a state of nature, so it is for states in an anarchical system – an international 'state of nature'.

Remember these are simplifying assumptions, conceptual abstractions from the messy reality of actual political practice, not simple statements of fact.

Functional differentiation

The clearest contrast between domestic and international political systems therefore, is that in the former the organizing principle is hierarchy whereas internationally it is anarchy. However, according to Waltz, this principle, together with the overriding priority given to security, has profound consequences for the second element of political structure, the degree of functional differentiation among the units. By functional differentiation, Waltz is referring to variations in what states do, or seek to do. In an anarchical system, each unit must attend first and foremost to its own security and, Waltz argues, this will radically limit its ability to specialize because to do so would mean becoming dependent on others for the necessary requisites of self-preservation. As states have to rely on themselves for those matters that bear directly on their material and physical security – because there is no 'sovereign' to guarantee it – they will tend to be functionally similar to one another.

In hierarchical political systems (that is, within states), by contrast, where the basic problems of self-preservation have been resolved by establishing a common authority with the power to guarantee security, actors and institutions can afford to specialize and become interdependent with one another, taking advantage of the efficiency gains brought about by an advancing division of labour.

Activity 5.3

In Chapter 3, Maureen Mackintosh outlined the economic theory of comparative advantage, the argument that specialization and trade among agents (individuals, firms or countries) can lead to gains for all (see Chapter 3, Section 3.2). To what extent does Waltz's argument identify different considerations as to whether to trade or not?

Waltz draws attention to the fact that while specialization and trade may make all agents better off, by becoming interdependent with one another – and interdependence is just another way of saying 'mutual dependence' – a potential vulnerability is created in that agents come to rely on others for the fulfilment of their needs. In a hierarchical system this does not matter since the common authority and power of the state guarantees these needs. Under anarchic conditions, however, dependence on other agents may directly threaten the security of an agent, since the agent may come to rely on others for the fulfilment of basic needs relating to self-preservation. Adam Smith recognized this in his *An Inquiry into the Nature and Causes of the Wealth of Nations* when he observed that 'defence is more than opulence'. For example, Waltz argues that it is unlikely that states will rely *solely* on the workings of comparative advantage and free trade to ensure that they have access to the food necessary to feed their populations or the weapons required to equip their armed forces. In short, Waltz is suggesting that market relations and the specialization and vulnerability they entail operate best under a kind of Hobbesian protection and that this is absent from the international sphere.

Distribution of capacity and resources

The conclusion of this argument is that states in an anarchic international political system will tend *not* to specialize in matters relating to security. In fact, Waltz makes the simplifying assumption that, for the purposes of international politics, all states are functionally alike. In an anarchic system, what differentiates states is not function, that is, what they (seek to) do, but rather capabilities – what they have the resources to accomplish. It is the power of states, not their common purposes (survival), that differentiates one international political system from another. The structure of an anarchic political system is thus given by the third of Waltz's criteria, the distribution of power across the states. International systems may be unipolar, bipolar or multipolar depending on whether one, two or several states hold the preponderance of power.

Moreover, the distribution of power across the states system is the central *dynamic* feature of international life. States strive to increase their own power as best they can, and they form shifting alliances with one another to balance against the power of potential enemies, but they cannot, either individually or in alliances, fully control the processes by which the relative capabilities of states change over time. Rather, states must respond to the ever-shifting distribution of power by means of internal and external efforts at self-preservation, that is they must act on calculations of the balance of power. Writing in the eighteenth century, not long after European states had entered into a lengthy epoch of more or less violent rivalry with one another, focused on commercial competition, David Hume described the balance of power, that is, action based on prudent considerations of interest and power, as founded on 'common sense and obvious reasoning' (1994 [1752], p.157). Martin Wight describes this understanding of the balance of power as 'an application of the law of self-preservation' (1986, p.169).

Balance of power
The balance of power is the attempt by states to maintain or improve their power position by internal or external efforts aimed at preservation in an anarchic system.

Once again, Waltz argues that there is an important difference between hierarchical and anarchical systems in respect of considerations of power. Just as states will seek to avoid forms of interdependence that create vulnerability in relation to issues of security, so they will seek to avoid becoming subordinate to others in terms of power, since the superior power of some may also threaten the security of the weak. In hierarchical systems, actors can afford to concentrate on what they themselves can and cannot do, they may even be indifferent to how their capabilities compare with those of others; but under anarchy, since each is potentially a threat to the survival of another, all must be concerned primarily with how their capabilities compare with those of others – their concerns about power must be *relative* not absolute. We shall return to these issues in more detail in Chapter 9.

In short, international political systems comprise an anarchy of similar, competing political authorities in which each strives to maintain or improve its relative power. Politics in the international arena revolves around the relative power of states; outcomes – that is, the results of diplomatic negations and military conflicts, but also the rules and institutions that regulate interactions among states (including trade) – are determined by the structure of power.

Activity 5.4

Check that you can identify the key differences between anarchical and hierarchical systems as seen by Waltz. If you have difficulty, re-read this section and note the features of each.

4.2   A summary of Waltz's model

I have now finished my exposition of Waltz's realist model of the political structure of the international system. I have covered quite a lot of ground and so I'm going to summarize it briefly. The starting point is two assumptions: first, that the basic units of the international political system are sovereign states and, therefore, that the principle of organization is anarchy; and second, that in a structure of anarchy, the overriding goal of all states is self-preservation, or security. From these premises, Waltz draws the conclusion that states will be functionally alike in relation to matters that bear on their security. The structure of anarchy imposes a uniform logic of survival on agents subject to it. Given that anarchy is a constant of international politics, and because the logic of survival under anarchy produces functionally equivalent states, what differentiates one international system from another is the distribution of capabilities within it. International political systems are defined not by the mix of purposes of their component states (since all states have the same overriding purposes – to avoid vulnerability and maintain or expand their relative power), but by the distribution of power. Relative powers, not purposes, and means, not ends, determine outcomes at the level of international politics.

4.3   Explaining international co-operation

This model generates some powerful conclusions about the extent to which states can co-operate with one another in circumstances that would deliver absolute gains for all parties.

Question

Assuming that states would gain by pursuing freer trade with one another and that to realise the gains they need to co-operate in the making and implementation of rules to liberalize trade, how can Waltz's model account for the frequent failure of co-operation?

There are two implications of Waltz's model that are relevant. I have already drawn attention to the first of these: namely, that the gains from co-operation arising from specialization and trade can create a form of dependence that threatens the security of the state (for example, by becoming dependent on another, potentially hostile, state for a technology that is crucial to military power). The second is implicit in what I have said about the importance of relative power. Suppose that the *distribution* of the gains from co-operation worsens the relative position of some of the parties, even as their absolute welfare is improved, then just as states will forego specialization and interdependence that improves their economic fortunes if it creates vulnerabilities that bear on security, so they will also forego interaction with other states that threatens to subordinate them in terms of power. As Waltz says, 'even the prospect of large absolute gains among parties does not elicit their co-operation so long as each fears how the others will use its increased capability' (1979, p.105). Actors that have to guarantee their own self-preservation – that is, individuals in a state of nature or states in an anarchic international system – will not willingly co-operate if the result is an increase in vulnerability and/or a decrease in relative power. These are rather strong conclusions about the limits to international co-operation, and they will be criticized in Chapter 9.

Still, if Waltz's conclusions are robust, they pose some searching questions about the kinds of co-operation currently on the agenda of the WTO. As you have seen, some analysts argue that, for the poorest economies and the weakest states in the least developed countries, the kinds of trade liberalization pursued under the auspices of the WTO have precisely been associated with both a worsening of their relative position vis-à-vis the more successful countries and growing concerns about their ability to ensure their material and physical security on an independent basis. Towards the end of Chapter 3, Mackintosh raised the possibility that the kinds of policies that the middle and high income countries used in the past to avoid vulnerability and improve their relative position are now being denied to the low income countries by the WTO. Aditya Bhattacharjea raises the same issue in

Chapter 2. Why, then, have these countries participated in the WTO negotiating process?

Perhaps they did not foresee the consequences of their actions. This is the explanation offered by Chakravarthi Raghavan:

> The Uruguay Round and the WTO entered the developing world like a thief in the night, without much awareness or discussions – either in parliaments or among the public or among domestic enterprises and sectors. Now, with the obligations kicking in and biting, the WTO as an 'animal' has been identified and has become well known.

(Raghavan, 2000, p.503)

Another view, often articulated in developing countries, is that the WTO represents an exercise of power through which the rich countries and strong states have imposed their interests on the low income economies and weaker states. Especially now that the 'thief' has been identified, many argue that low income countries have been effectively coerced into going along with the direction of change, that they are unwilling participants in a process they cannot control. This means that the appearance of co-operation is spurious and that it is only the exercise of coercive power by countries with rich economies and strong states that ensures the continuing (and selective) drive towards freer trade. Realists like Waltz and many in the developing countries would no doubt agree that this serves as an accurate characterization of the WTO.

This kind of argument can be stated much more generally. The view that the rules and institutions of the international political arena reflect the interests of the powerful rather than of all states is one of the strong conclusions of Waltz's model. It is also a central claim of a long tradition of thinking about international politics going back at least to Hobbes. The historian and theorist of the modern international system, Martin Wight, was drawn to the general conclusion that 'while in domestic politics the struggle for power is governed and circumscribed by the framework of law and institutions, in international politics law and institutions are governed and circumscribed by the struggle for power. This is indeed the justification for calling international politics "power politics" *par excellence*' (1986, p.102).

Activity 5.5

In Section 1 I introduced two comparisons between economic and political analyses: one to do with how the outcomes from international trade are explained; the other with the different uses of the contrast between anarchic and governed orders.

1 In your own words outline how a Waltzian approach would explain outcomes from international trade and the rules formed by the WTO.

2 What role does the concept of anarchy play in Waltz's argument?

Recall that Aristotle saw politics as co-operation based on consent and that Hobbes and Hume regarded co-ordination on the rule of the sovereign state as a form of mutual advantage. According to realists such as Waltz and Wight, international politics is a realm of domination where the strong impose their interests on the weak. The international is not really a realm of politics at all, in the sense that Aristotle, Hobbes and Hume understood politics.

5 Questioning Waltz's realist model

Probably the most common criticism made of Waltz's theory and of realism in general is that it is 'state-centric', that it privileges the role of the state in political life. Realists like Waltz argue that a focus on states as the basic units of the international political system is less 'a privileging of states than an open recognition and proclamation that states have seized and are seized of privileges' (Buzan *et al.*, 1993, p.218). As you may have guessed, I regard this starting point as reasonable. In my view, a more interesting question to ask is what does Waltz's concept of the 'state' refer to?

5.1 Hierarchy and anarchy

One way of questioning Waltz's model is to question the idea that political systems are either hierarchical or anarchic. Waltz's concept of the state is a Hobbesian one, in which there is a strong two-way link between the obligation to obey authority and the (territorial) monopoly over coercion needed for security. Hume makes explicit what is implicit in Hobbes – that co-ordination on an impersonal public power brings great gains for everyone. For Waltz, this is simply a fact of contemporary political life – hence his simplifying assumption that a hierarchical structure exists within states but not between them.

The idea of classifying phenomena as a dichotomy – as either hierarchy *or* anarchy, for example – is often a useful abstraction, and can serve as a powerful analytical device. However, it can blind us to the fact that phenomena may also be conceptualized in more relational ways that seek to highlight connections and similarities instead of differences. Instead of 'either/or' we may focus on 'both/and': that is, rather than seeing domestic political systems as hierarchical and international systems as anarchic, it may be useful to explore the possibility that all political systems contain different mixes of both hierarchy and anarchy.

The distinction between the domestic and the international may then seem more one of degree than of kind, and historical shifts in the balance of hierarchy and anarchy within each may be easier to detect. As Helen Milner has asked: 'May not some domestic systems lack centralized authority and legitimacy, while certain international systems ... enjoy high levels of legitimacy? Can and should we draw a rigid dichotomy between the two on the basis of anarchy defined in [Waltz's] way?' (1993, p.153). (I shall return to this in Section 6.)

5.2   States and self-preservation

A second way in which I want to question Waltz is over the assumption that self-preservation is the overriding goal of states and that as a consequence, in the form of the balance of power, this concern dominates international politics. This assumption of the priority of self-preservation seemed to follow from Hobbes's argument that I reviewed in Section 3. But let us take a closer look. Hobbes gave priority to self-preservation because he thought that nobody could reasonably deny that right to others and because all other human values and interests presuppose survival. Let us grant that claim for individuals. Why should it apply to states? In effect, Waltz is asking us to accept an analogy between individuals in the state of nature and states in an anarchic international system.

Question

Can you think of any reasons why the analogy between individuals and states that Waltz employs may break down?

Analogies between individuals, on the one side, and corporate bodies such as states or firms, on the other, have a long history in the social sciences but they must always be inspected carefully. In Hobbes's case, the analogy was rather complex. On the one hand, Hobbes did personify the artificially created sovereign, calling it a Leviathan (after the sea monster from the Book of Job in the Bible). And his contention is that what makes the sovereign 'authority an effective custodian of its desperately vulnerable subjects is its combination of independence (impartiality), unity of will and judgement, and effective capacity for coercion' (Dunn, 1996b, p.77). This is the state in the image of an absolute ruler, albeit a form of absolutism that is limited or governed by the natural right to self-preservation that individuals possess in the state of nature (Tuck, 1989).

On the other hand, since it is in fact an artificial entity, Hobbes thought that the potential for sudden death does not exist in the case of states (he was writing some time before the advent of nuclear weapons!). More importantly, Hobbes reasoned that the effects of anarchy on individuals and states would, therefore, be different; and, indeed, that whereas the anarchy of states was tolerable, that between individuals was not. That is to say, Hobbes did not believe that there was a single logic of survival under anarchy; a structure of anarchy establishes constraints but what those constraints mean depends in part on the nature of the actors subject to them.

Whereas individuals cannot pursue any purposes unless they are alive, the individuals that collectively comprise a state can continue to pursue their goals even if their state 'dies', as long as they can find security elsewhere. Unlike the death of an individual, the death of a state is not necessarily, or even usually, the death of the people who comprise it. In short, while security must remain an overriding concern of individuals in the way that Hobbes supposes, the logic of this argument does not carry over into a generalization about the ultimate purposes of all states. Waltz may therefore be wrong to assume this similarity between individuals in the state of nature and states in the international system – too literal an analogy between personal security and the security of states may be misleading.

5.3   Sovereignty

To pursue these two areas – the dichotomy of hierarchy or anarchy and the analogy between the survival of states and individuals – we need to have a closer look at the concept of sovereignty which underlies both. There is a case for saying that Hobbes presents things in a rather one-sided manner – that states establish sovereignty domestically and then confront one another in a new international state of nature. This image is central to Waltz's theory too. But the particular circumstances in which Hobbes was writing might prompt us to look at things the other way round.

In Hobbes's time, establishing the authority of the sovereign was centrally bound up with the religious politics of the day. Religious institutions wielded considerable power – not just spiritual – over people's lives and many took up arms against their rulers and against other rulers on behalf of their religion and their co-religionists in other states. One way of reading Hobbes's solution to the problem of political obligation is to see it as an answer to these conflicts.

The religious institutions that competed for the allegiance of many of the subjects of the state were no respecters of territorial borders. Peace agreements signed by some of the leading European powers in the seventeenth century attempted to put an end to these conflicts and are seen by many as crucial in the historical development of state sovereignty. In this context, Paul Hirst has argued:

The agreement of most of Europe's most affected states [that is, affected by violent religious conflicts] to avoid interference in the religious peace of other states changed the terms of conflict between territorial authority and confessional groups in the former's favour. To a significant degree the capacity of state elites to assert 'sovereign' control over territory came from *without*, from agreements between states in the developing society of states. To a considerable degree, therefore, the capacities of the state grow inward from the *international* recognition of its rights to certain key powers by other states. ... the territorial sovereign state was able to develop its distinctive attributes at least in part because of international agreement between states to limit intervention in each other's affairs in matters of religion. Modern nation states have been built on these seventeenth century foundations. Sovereign power did not originate at the national level alone.

(Hirst, 1997, pp.222, 229)

Question

What does the phrase 'the capacities of the state grow inward from the *international* recognition of its rights' mean?

Hirst is arguing against the view that sovereign control of territory is forged purely internally and that states then interact in the anarchic realm of international politics with other states. He considers that the achievement of sovereign authority – the capacities of the state – is at least partly the product of agreements between states in the form of recognition of each others' sovereign rights.

The domestic sovereignty of states is therefore, in part, a product of an international agreement between states – this agreement is not *hierarchical* authority to be sure but, if Hirst is right, it suggests that the authority claims of sovereigns were addressed not only to their population but also to other states and, crucially, that the effectiveness of the former may have been dependent on the recognition of the latter. Waltz's clear division between hierarchy in the domestic sphere and anarchy in the international starts to look a little shaky from this perspective.

What, then, are the main features of these sovereign states? Contemporary states are said to have sovereignty, a term I have already used many times without ever defining it precisely. 'Sovereignty' is one of the most difficult and contested words in the political lexicon. This complexity is, in part, a result of the fact that sovereignty is a practical concept. It is a term of art used in the political and legal discourses through which states interact with one another. One consequence of this is that there is an internal, two-way interaction between the changing practices of states, on the one hand, and the

Sovereignty
Sovereignty is a form of authority, the power of command associated with a socially recognized right to rule.

meanings attributed to the term sovereignty, on the other. Sovereignty is, in large part, shaped by what states that call themselves 'sovereign' do. (This is a specific example of the point I made in Section 1.1 that the language, concepts and arguments used in political analysis are shared with the language of political activity.)

Sovereignty is also a difficult term because although it is conventional to attribute it to states, the picture of sovereignty as a property that states may or may not have captures only part of what the term has historically referred to. It is more accurate to say that sovereignty is a relationship between an authoritative claim to rule, on the one side, and the recognition of an obligation to obey, on the other. Sovereignty is a form of authority, the power of command associated with a socially recognized *right* to rule. But rights involve relationships: they are claims one party makes in respect to others, and their effective realization depends on a degree of acceptance or recognition, on how far obligations are in fact accepted.

A further complication comes from the fact that the claims to rule made on behalf of a putatively sovereign state are addressed not just to the people within its territory, as Hobbes emphasized, but also to other similarly constituted sovereigns in the international system. As Hirst points out, ever since the early modern era in Europe when Hobbes was writing, state sovereignty has related *both* to the rights claimed by states in relation to their territories and populations *and* to the reciprocal claims they make of one another.

And finally, sovereignty does not entail a singular right to rule: rather it has always involved a complex bundle of different rights and the precise bundle of rights, relationships and recognition involved in state sovereignty can vary from one state to another, from time to time and from issue to issue. That is to say, sovereignty does not come in fixed chunks, it is not simply present or absent, it is rather a basket of 'attributes and corresponding rights and duties. While every state has a basket, the contents are by no means the same' (Fowler and Bunck, 1995, p.70).

Activity 5.6

Think of any arguments or claims about sovereignty that you may have come across in your previous studies or more generally. How do they illustrate this understanding of sovereignty?

So, sovereignty is something that has an ongoing history, and is not fixed once and for all. It is best understood relationally rather than as a property of states and the relations of authority and obligation involved in sovereignty pertain both to the territory and people of a state as well as to other states.

Furthermore, these relations are complex rather than simple and best understood as a basket of attributes, which may differ from one state to another, and from time to time. For all these reasons, as John Dunn has argued, the notion of sovereignty 'was never intended to be a description of how things were, a simple statement of fact. Rather, it was a deeply motivated political aspiration' (Dunn, 2000, p.68).

5.4   Varieties of sovereignty

State sovereignty faces two ways: inwards, towards national territories and populations; and outwards, towards other states. Hedley Bull (1995) defines the *external* or *international* sovereignty of the state as the ability to maintain constitutional independence in relation to external sources of authority (such as other states or religious organizations), and its *internal* or *domestic* sovereignty in terms of the ability to exercise supreme authority over rival domestic sources of authority. I am going to use this framework to discuss some different understanding of state sovereignty, starting with Hobbes.

As I have argued above, Hobbes's understanding of sovereignty founds the realist tradition of international political thought. Sovereignty is primarily a matter of domestic sovereignty, it refers to the coincidence of a sovereign power and a given territory and people. External sovereignty, then, is merely the recognition of this fact by other states. As Wight says, it is the 'existence of what is recognized that determines the act of recognition, and not the other way around' (1986, p.46). States recognize one another's sovereignty because of purely prudent considerations of power and interest. What sustains international order is the workings of the balance of power, that is, the striving by all states, whether by internal means or external alliances, to maintain their position and independence in the system.

As Martin Wight put it: 'The alternatives to the balance of power are either universal anarchy or universal domination. A little reflection will show that the balance of power is preferable to the first; and we have not yet been persuaded that the second is so preferable to the balance of power that we shall submit to it' (1986, p.185). This is why realists are adamant that although the necessity of the balance of power may appear to be a pessimistic conclusion, the alternatives are worse. Unlike domestic politics, international politics is not susceptible to collective choice: it is a realm of fate.

A rather different view of the basis of international order argues that some aspects of international sovereignty are conferred upon states, mutually and reciprocally, in what Hedley Bull called the *anarchical society* of states. From this perspective, the nature of international anarchy derives not simply from a plurality of sovereign states but is also socially *constructed*, or negotiated, by states interacting with one another. While the minimum features of international sovereignty, that is, constitutional independence from external authority, may be accomplished domestically and simply recognized by others, Bull argued that international recognition was capable of conferring rights, and the correlative duties, on states that they could not, even in principle, achieve simply by virtue of their domestic accomplishments. In fact, if Hirst is right, even the consolidation of domestic sovereignty presupposes a degree of international recognition at least as far as non-intervention is concerned.

According to Bull the core elements of the society of states are the notions of legal equality among sovereign states under international law, the principal of *pacta sunt servanda* (treaties must be obeyed) and the laws of war and neutrality. None of these follows from the mere fact of a plurality of states successfully establishing their internal or domestic sovereignty. Rather, they are evidence of the existence of a *'society of states* (or international society)', in which 'a group of states, conscious of certain common interests and common values, form a society in the sense that they conceive themselves to be bound by a common set of rules in their relations with one another, and share in the workings of common institutions' (Bull, 1995, p.13).

It is important to be clear that for Bull this remains an *anarchical* society in so far as its most important rules and institutions are essentially ones of *coexistence* and do not presuppose that states share common purposes, save what he calls the 'elementary, primary, universal' goals of states that define order at the international level. These include: the 'preservation of the system and society of states itself'; 'maintaining the independence or external sovereignty of individual states'; 'the absence of war ... as the normal condition'; and 'the common goals of all social life: limitation of violence resulting in death or bodily harm, the keeping of promises and the stabilization of possession by rules of property' (1995, pp.16–18).

I would therefore pose the following questions. If individuals in a state of nature can co-ordinate on a common structure of authority and thereby gain 'the general advantage which is reaped from government', then why can states not do likewise? Even without creating a world state, why can states not co-ordinate on non-security issues? And if states come to share a conception of the good life, then why can Aristotle's view of politics as based on consent not apply to international politics? Might not the view of the WTO as rules based on consent, or if not consent, then co-ordination, come back into the picture?

Activity 5.7

How would a realist reply to the questions I have just posed?

5.5   Renegotiating sovereign authority

At this point, it might be better to think of a spectrum of possibilities, with the kind of sovereignty Waltz describes (and consequently the organizing principle of anarchy between the sovereigns) at one end. Further along the spectrum authority over some activities can also be shared between states as in the case of the genuinely supranational elements of systems such as the European Union. At the far end of the spectrum, in empires, authority is formally organized into a hierarchy in which one political system uses its power to dominate another or others. Somewhere in between, in informal empires, authority is in reality hierarchically organized between what are formally independent states. Sometimes informal empire is called 'hegemony', and in this sense hegemony is therefore consistent with formal, supranational arrangements to share sovereignty.

To what extent does the character of international sovereignty in the society of states reflect the interests and values of all of its members, as is approximated in the EU, and to what extent is it determined by the interests and values of the most powerful, as in an informal empire? And how far do the practices and discourses of international sovereignty influence the shaping of domestic sovereignty? Are there processes at work that, first, enable the most powerful states to shape the accepted norms of behaviour at the international level and, second, lead to a reshaping of domestic authority claims in line with international norms? Might not the evolution of the WTO be one such process?

Whatever the answers to these questions, the idea that the claims to political authority inherent in the notion of state sovereignty are, to a greater or lesser degree, negotiated among states is a challenge to the realist claim that a sharp distinction can be drawn between domestic and international political systems. However, it also means that the answer to Waltz's (and our) question – as to what the organizing principle of international politics *in general* is – is rather more open, depending on the nature of sovereignty shared between states.

We can also use this idea to look at particular aspects of international politics, like the WTO. This brings me back to the debate with which I started: does the WTO simply reflect the distribution of power among states in an anarchic international system? Or does it represent some kind of governance by which states create an international authority specifying the rules by which trade will be conducted between them? Or is there some combination of both whereby authority maybe shared between states to govern trade but that the character of those rules, and their implementation, is nevertheless informally skewed to the interests of the powerful?

6   Anarchy or governance?

If the WTO is understood as an instance of international governance then how might we explain it? The term governance has been defined by Stokke as 'the establishment and operation of a set of rules of conduct that define practices, assign roles, and guide interaction so as to grapple with collective problems' (1997, p.28).

This can be contrasted with government, which is 'the collection of offices in a political system' which 'successfully upholds a claim to the regulation of the legitimate use of physical force in enforcing its rules within a given territorial area' (Dahl, 1970, pp.11–12). Aspects of international politics like the WTO can thus be understood as systems of *governance* without *government* – a means of establishing and operating collective rules without a single, unified government.

I want to ask about the relation between the authority of (international) systems of governance and that of states. Let me begin with the explanation closest to the ideas I have been discussing thus far, which builds on Hobbes's analysis of the state. Remember that, for Hobbes, the sovereign could command allegiance *because* it was able to discharge the purposes for which it had been established. However, as I noted above (see Section 3.2), Hume added to Hobbes's insight by arguing that 'the general advantage which is reaped from government' might not be limited simply to the provision of security but that government might be a more general instrument for co-ordination. What does he mean by this? Hume was arguing that once a state is established it could then provide a means by which co-ordination on rules for other areas of life could be achieved. Hume had in mind particularly the institutions that make market exchanges possible: legal systems and contracts, currency, unified systems of weights and measures and so on. The purposes of the state can thus extend beyond simply ensuring security.

Now, if as we have already seen, states can establish common norms, rules and institutions in order to achieve their 'elementary, primary, universal' goals that Bull spoke of (see Section 5.4), might they not also do this in order to realize other purposes which they share? Proponents of multi-level governance argue that states do indeed do this, by sharing their sovereignty. Sharing sovereignty can take one of three forms: pooling, delegation and federation.

The pooling of sovereignty involves creating decision-making procedures in which member states take decisions collectively but do not have an individual right of veto, so that a given state can be bound by the decisions of others. Sovereignty is delegated 'when supranational actors are permitted to take certain autonomous decisions, without an intervening interstate vote or

Governance
Governance has been defined by Stokke as 'the establishment and operation of a set of rules of conduct that define practices, assign roles, and guide interaction so as to grapple with collective problems' (1997, p.28).

Government
Government is 'the collection of offices in a political system' which 'successfully upholds a claim to the regulation of the legitimate use of physical force in enforcing its rules within a given territorial area' (Dahl, 1970, pp.11–12).

unilateral veto' (Moravcsik, 1998, p.67). If the pooling and delegation of sovereignty includes the right to make laws (legislative competence) and if the resulting laws are directly applicable in the legal systems of the member states, then a form of supranational authority is thereby created. This is precisely what has happened in some elements of governance in the European Union and it is one possible way in which the WTO might yet evolve. Federation involves an extensive transfer of sovereign rights to a higher body, such that the higher body becomes sovereign in its own right in certain specified areas. In this case, the hierarchy of authority is transferred from the level of the state to the federation.

There are two things that follow from this. First, you can see that even if we start from independent sovereign states, there are ways in which new patterns of authority can be created by states. That is to say, even in the absence of a covenant among states to create a world federation, states may be able to reach a consensus or co-ordinate with one another on issues apart from security, such as the rules governing international trade. Thus, patterns of regulation governing different areas of social life will not necessarily match up with the territorial boundaries of state coercive power.

There is still the question, second, of the precise relation between these new sources of regulation created by states and the Hobbesian sovereignty of the state. While there are many signs of emerging supranational authority in world politics, of which the WTO is a prominent example, there are very few signs of the supranational organization of the means of coercion (although few, if any, states acting independently can guarantee the security of their citizens). Realists rightly contend that this means that the new sites of authority such as the WTO lack their own means of enforcement. But if the WTO is really the result of consensus or co-ordination this need not matter, since states will see the rules as their own or have no reason to defect from them. In fact, the rules of the international trading system appear to have a considerable degree of authority for the members of the WTO. The degree of compliance by states with international economic law is, in fact, very high as compared with the compliance of individuals with domestic law.

In other words, the patterns of multi-level governance may derive their authority from more than one source. It may derive indirectly from the member states that created them (by pooling or delegating sovereignty), since these states are themselves directly legitimated by their role as guarantors of security. They may also derive directly from the fact that they represent either a consensus or a form of co-ordination among states. In short, the WTO may be legitimated, first, by the fact that *governments* created it, and second, by the contribution it makes to the *governance* of international trade. The idea here is that while governments are essential to setting up new forms of governance, these forms of governance may come to develop their own independent authority. At least, that is what some theorists of multi-level governance contend. Regulatory governance, for example, is often argued to derive its authority from the need for co-ordination in pursuit of economic efficiency. An example might be the internal (or 'common') market of the European Union. Something similar might yet apply to the WTO.

Importantly, what some advocates of multi-level governance maintain is that we may be moving towards a situation in which there is no necessary hierarchy in the sites and sources of authority, with the security concerns of states at the top. Where this idea of governance without (or at least beyond) government diverges sharply from that of Hobbes, Weber, Waltz and a long tradition of Western political theory is in its argument that *different* sites and sources of authority can coexist without the need for any formally organized hierarchy anchored in a monopoly of the means of coercion. Here we are close to returning to Aristotle's view of politics based on consent, or Hume's view of the co-ordinating role of government, at the international level. The idea that state sovereignty, in the Hobbesian sense, is the fundamental building block of international governance is being questioned here in a rather strong way.

In short, we have three possibilities: first, all governance is conducted by governments domestically and at the international level there is a pure anarchy; second, while governments remain central, they are capable of sharing their authority in order to create forms of international governance that go beyond that which governments are able to provide on an independent basis; and third, these forms of international governance can develop sources of authority that are, in some measure, independent of the authorities which created them, such that governments become simply one source of authority among others.

Whatever the precise relation between the authority deriving from governments and that which results from international governance, if governance can exist beyond governments, if there are relations of authority and obligation between states, then the meaning of international anarchy must be somewhat different from the traditional realist understanding. If this is right, then the prospects for international co-operation are not as limited as our discussion of Waltz (see Section 4.3) suggested.

7　Conclusion

I want to conclude by drawing some of the threads of this discussion, and that of Part 1 as a whole, together.

Aditya Bhattacharjea and Amrita Narlikar have both shown how international trade within the rules of the WTO disadvantages many developing countries. You have seen how the economic analysis deployed by Aditya Bhattacharjea and Maureen Mackintosh can explain both why countries might seek to gain from trading with each other, and why the benefits from that trade are distributed unequally. The analysis of the politics of the WTO has focused on the issue of whether the rules within which trade takes place are or can be the product of voluntary co-operation between member states, or whether they are a field dominated by relations of power.

On this latter point, in this chapter you have seen that Hobbes's most fundamental point was that when conflicts of judgement arise, especially over matters as vital as those of self-preservation, there is no objective basis for deciding between the contending parties and such issues can only be resolved by a sovereign. Realists contend that this means that an international politics based on consent or co-ordination is inherently limited by the security dilemmas facing states under anarchy. International politics cannot really be a realm of co-operation and, as such, constitutes a realm of fate where the kinds of concerns that inform domestic politics cannot apply. The idea of shared sovereignty and distributed multi-level governance is a direct challenge to this view. It argues that co-ordination and consent can operate internationally, that states can learn to share their sovereignty in new ways, and that anarchy does not dictate a single logic of conflictual interaction and domination among states. The contours of the debate defined by Amrita Narlikar reflect this divergence.

Finally, you have also learnt some important tools of analysis for understanding international trade drawn from the disciplines of economics and politics. You have also seen some comparisons between these two disciplines. The economic analysis of trade presented in Part 1 focuses on trade as a process of international market integration. Firms buy and sell across frontiers, in response to opportunities for profit, and the comparative advantage model considers the outcome for trading countries' citizens. So the basic model is of trading by independent economic actors in markets: a model of an anarchic process and its outcomes. However, Chapter 3 also examined the effect of trade policy and agreed trade rules: the shaping of trade by processes of governance. It is this realm that is at the centre of political analysis. Political analysis, by contrast, is more concerned with how the rules that affect the outcomes from trade are formed and operate and how far the power of states determines these (we return to the question of power in detail in Chapter 9). Thus, here too, there is a contrast between understanding international processes (this time political processes) as a realm of fate – an anarchic interplay among unequal powers – or as governed activities in which some element of choice and consensus may be possible. At root, these are debates about our understanding of how the international is 'made'. And on these the future of the international trade regime rests.

Further reading

For a short and accessible introduction to the thought of Thomas Hobbes, situating his arguments in their historical context and including some observations on their continuing relevance, see Tuck, R. (1989) *Hobbes*, Oxford, Oxford University Press.

For an important discussion of the concept of governance and, in particular, a review of how the concept of governance helps us to think about international politics, see Stokke, O.S. (1997) 'Regimes as governance systems' in Young, O.R. (ed.) *Global Governance: Drawing Insights From the Environmental Experience*, Cambridge, Mass., MIT Press.

The classic, contemporary statement of the realist theory of international politics, and a central reference point for the subsequent debates, is Waltz, K. (1979) *Theory of International Politics*, New York, Random House.

Part 2 Making state policy

The economic and political analysis developed in Part 1 focused on relations between and among countries. The theory of comparative advantage is a general explanation of the gains from trade between different countries, and realist theory suggests that in an anarchic states-system all states are constrained to seek security by maximizing their power in relation to one another. But Part 1 also recognized some of the limits of these ways of thinking, powerful though they undoubtedly are, by noting that states are rarely simply the bearers of these international forces of trade and anarchy. On the contrary, many states make strenuous efforts to change their terms of trade and to create forms of governance at the international level.

In other words, states and their economies, cultures and societies are sites of agency and change as well as actors constrained by a wider international system. A key aspect of this agency – and the focus of Part 2 – is the making of state policy in relation to national political and economic priorities, especially the objective of economic growth, and the corresponding international alignments of the state that go with these priorities. States make and implement policies in order to achieve specific national objectives, for development, say, as well as to change their position in the international system.

This part contains two chapters that address the politics and economics of economic liberalization and industrialization. Both are written from and located within the experience of India. On the politics side, the theme of Chapter 6 is the making of state policy, drawing on liberalization as the source of evidence and analysis. Chapter 7 then explores the economic logic behind the key arguments outlined in Chapter 6, unpicking the trail from an economic policy rooting industrialization in planning to one locating a core source of industrial growth in liberalized trade.

We start, therefore, with a fascinating discussion of some central aspects of Indian politics. In Chapter 6, Sudipta Kaviraj argues that the formation of the interests of the Indian state can be understood only by paying close attention to the national context, to the specific historical and cultural circumstances within India, and to the internal evolution of Indian society. Through an analytically structured narrative, Chapter 6 looks at the ways in which social interests are translated into political programmes, at the languages or discourses of politics within which people perceive and express their political choices, at the role of legitimacy and identity in shaping the character of the political system, and at the bargaining processes and the coalitions of interests that make up the lived experience of politics in a vibrant and complex society.

Chapter 6 also traces the implications of these processes and pressures for the changing international alignments of India. It thus presents a very different way of thinking about the international interests of states from that provided by the realist model outlined in Chapter 5, which assumed both that such interests derived from the position of the state within the inter-state system and that political leaders are able to pursue these interests independently of the interests, values and identities of the social and economic groups that make up the society.

In Chapter 7 Suma Athreye examines the economic policy issues at the heart of the narrative in Chapter 6, especially the attempt to craft a strategy for industrialization in India. In lower income countries, industrialization is a key route to the objective of economic growth. Chapter 7 explains why, tracing the roots of growth in capital accumulation for industrial expansion and in technological change. Suma Athreye shows how and why an initial success in Indian industrialization – built on tariff protection, a significant role for the public sector in allocating resources, and direct industrial production – subsequently ran into the sand. She argues that, while capital accumulation could drive industrial growth, technological change was also essential but was blocked by the relatively 'closed' nature of the economy. The result was a pattern of partial trade liberalization in the 1980s driven by the purpose of acquiring new technology. Indian economic liberalization in the 1990s was built upon this foundation. Chapter 7 contrasts the Indian economic purpose of liberalization – aiming to build new export capabilities on the earlier foundation of industrialization and sustained access to new technology – with the analysis lying behind pressure for liberalization from external agencies such as the International Monetary Fund, which focused on promoting exports on the basis of existing comparative advantage.

We hope that you will gain from Part 2 not only a new political analysis of states, interests and identities, and an economic analysis of the sources of growth and the importance of industrialization, but also a sense, informed by the richness of the Indian experience, of the importance of national processes in making state policy, and the ways in which these processes can shape the nature of development and the alignment of states in the wider international system.

Chapter 6 The politics of liberalization in India

Sudipta Kaviraj

1   Introduction

This chapter will trace how a particular definition of the Indian national interest was formulated after independence was achieved in 1947. It will examine how the definition evolved over time and was subsequently radically redefined in the context of a process of liberalization and a basic shift in the nature of Indian politics and political culture. The argument of this chapter is that the particular national interest that a state pursues in the international arena is strongly shaped by internal, domestic processes. The particular social purposes that the state may be seeking to realize, the things that make it a historically and culturally specific political order, and the relation of the state and the political system to the society it aims and claims to rule, are of prime importance in understanding its international purposes. I aim to show that the way in which a state's interests are constructed, through the expression of interests arising from a given national society in its dominant political discourses, as well as the ways in which those interests and discourses are enfranchised in the political system, plays an important role in international politics. This involves some consideration of the particular history of the state, of the nature of its political system and the dominant discourses in which a consensus over major issues of public policy are fashioned and expressed, and of the coalitions of interests that support those policies. Each of these aspects – the nature of the state and political system, the discourses in which interests are articulated, and the particular coalition of interests expressed in public policy – differs from one state to another and from time to time in any given state.

> **National interest**
> The national interest of a given state is set of interests, values and identities that it seeks to pursue and express in the international arena.

You will see that in India domestic and international changes were important in this process, and that the political process was embedded in a wider series of social and economic transformations. Over time, it was primarily domestic changes that redefined the content of India's national interest. Thus I examine the social and economic forces and context that shaped Indian politics after independence (Section 3), and show how these gave rise to a particular definition of the Indian national interest in international affairs (Section 4). I then consider how the forces and context shaping Indian politics changed over time, leading to a reshaping of Indian politics and an impetus towards liberalization (Section 5). In Section 6 I examine both the process of liberalization itself and the new character of Indian politics, demonstrating in turn how these contributed to a new definition of the national interest. I conclude with some observations on the character and understanding of Indian politics. While I largely follow a narrative format, my aim is to develop a series of related analytical arguments – about different forms of states, interests and political discourses, about the importance of legitimacy and definitions of political identity, about the role of social groups and their interests, and about the character of the political process and the bargaining and coalitions that are essential to political life, especially in democracies. I hope that these arguments will speak to the general condition of many societies and states.

I am going to focus my narrative and my analysis around the shift from a model of political and economic development that involved a highly protected national economy with strong elements of public enterprise and planning to a more liberalized order in the 1990s and beyond. Accordingly, in Section 2 I start by considering the meanings of economic liberalization and the different social and political contexts within which it can occur. India is a particularly interesting place from which to address these issues, and to view their implications for thinking about international politics. It is a large, democratic country with a vibrant political life and a lively and contested political and intellectual culture, in which these questions have been debated in relation to India's international alignments ever since it gained its independence from the ruling colonial power, Britain. India played a major role in the non-aligned group of post-colonial states, a grouping that sought in various ways to pursue anti-colonial policies and to avoid being dragged in to either side of the Cold War division of world politics after the Second World War. Of course, international events and processes affected the subsequent redefinition of India's international alignments, but this was also driven by the evolution of domestic circumstances. This fact also makes India a valuable place from which to address the social and cultural construction of state interests, the particular identity of the state, and the impact of this identity on the national interest.

2 States and the politics of economic governance

You have already studied one element of economic liberalization, namely, moves towards freer trade. More generally, economic liberalization in the Indian case, as elsewhere, included measures to free up the movement of capital into and out of the country, and to remove many of the regulations that constrained industrial development. Market forces and competition took the place of administrative measures and state monopoly (the economic reasoning behind these initiatives is discussed in Chapter 7). Liberalization is an excellent topic for the study of political economy, that is, the necessary entanglement of economic policies with political conflict, because although it refers to a set of internally interconnected *economic* policies, the introduction of these policies is, in most cases, an intensely contentious *political* process. Liberalization also affects the nature of a country's integration into the wider international system (something pursued further in Parts 3 and 4). The changes collectively called 'liberalization' happen in the context of previous conventional, settled habits of policy formulation by governments as well as the general economic conduct of ordinary people. Thus, what liberalization actually means for citizens of a particular state depends to a large extent on the kinds of relations that already exist between the state and the economic sphere.

2.1 States and models of economic governance

States vary substantially in terms of how they conduct their politics. There is an immense variety of distinctive forms of representation, policy making and modes of social and economic governance, but we can bring some order to this diversity by distinguishing a few simple models. No actual state corresponds to any of these models. Rather the models are abstractions from, and idealizations of, the messy reality of political life; they seek to capture some aspects and not others as a way of highlighting potentially important similarities and differences. Like much political theory, these models represent a systematic abridgment of political practice and, as such, they are a starting point for further analysis, not a substitute for the concrete study of real cases.

Since I am concerned with the politics of economic liberalization, I shall focus mainly on some simple models of economic governance. In the first model, society functions on the basis of a very limited conception of the state's economic role. The state aims to provide internal law and order and external defence, the enforcement of property rights and contracts, and the minimal conditions for the efficient operation of the capitalist economy such as a stable currency, a variety of public services and limited social welfare. State intervention in economic life is deeply disapproved of as inefficient, bureaucratic, and also as inducing an economic culture opposed to self-reliance. This is the laissez-faire – that is, non-intervention – model of a liberal capitalist society.

Diametrically opposed to this model, ideologically speaking, is the communist model that provides a simplified account of the economies of the former states in the Soviet Union and Eastern Europe, in which administrative planning displaces a great deal of market activity and most property is owned by the state rather than by private individuals. In this second model, the state does not merely assume overall direction of the economy as a whole, but is also engaged in the management of production through direct allocation of resources and the administrative setting of targets for publicly owned firms. Thus, a vast majority of the people are direct employees of the state, and the state is the primary producer of goods and services. It is also the provider of a comprehensive system of welfare.

A third model, that of the mixed economy, admits elements from both of the previous two, and operates without surrendering the entire functioning of the economy to either the unrestrained logic of the market or the total control of the state. Even allowing for considerable divergence in the exact mix of the two elements and the precise fashioning of the institutional structures, this represents a recognizable third model.

Many commentators contrast the mixed forms of economic and social governance found in the member states of the European Union with the more laissez-faire society of the United States, although in reality the latter has important elements of a mixed economy as well. Likewise, the degree to which planning was able to displace and suppress markets in the former communist economies and the effective reach of public property was highly variable. This simply reinforces the point made above that these models are abstractions from, and idealizations of, the messy reality of political life. Nevertheless, as you will see below, they are helpful in picking out some important distinctions.

These models not only influenced the experience of states in the Western world, but are our means of understanding that experience. Yet, despite the disproportionate influence of these states, the majority of states in the world system are non-Western. In terms of economic governance, many non-Western states, especially under colonial rule and in the early period after independence, would seem to be closer to a fourth model. In this model, the state simply does not have the capacities to regulate economic life in any comprehensive sense. The economic activities of ordinary people's livelihoods and market exchanges all proceeded without much reference to the state. The state exacts a certain revenue from the society's economic activities, where it can, but its taxing and regulatory capacities are extremely limited. In the analysis that follows, one particular distinction is important to bear in mind. Both in the first and the fourth model, the state leaves much of economic activity alone; but these cases should not be confused. In the former case, the state has the capacity to interfere if it wants, and it does, for instance, in cases of war or emergency, and more generally to set the legal framework for market exchange. In the latter, the state simply lacks the capacity for widespread intervention: it is unable to provide a legal and political infrastructure for a market economy in the way that the laissez-faire state does. Again, remember that this is a model and not a statement of empirical fact. The degree to which actual states conform to the model is highly variable.

2.2 'Meanings' of liberalization

Given the diversity among states, these divergent models of economic governance and economic liberalization will mean quite different politics in different cases. First, liberalization can occur in economies that are already following liberal free enterprise policies as a settled habit of economic practice. Such societies are already organized on 'liberalizing' principles. These feel minimal disturbance in their experience of economic life when further liberalization is introduced. Yet in all other types of states, the experiential impact of liberalization can be radical.

Second, liberalizing policies can be introduced in socialist/communist economies in which ordinary people's economic life is largely controlled by the state, and centred on its institutions. The effects of liberalization in such contexts mean nothing less than a total reorganization of economic life. Historically, however, the conversions of communist societies to markets have led to very different trajectories of social change. It affected the heavily planned economies such as the former Soviet Union most severely, taking away secure jobs, destroying social security, creating highly unstable quasi-markets which often collapsed into open lawlessness. Nevertheless, there were other examples of more successful and orderly transitions in cases such as Hungary or Poland. The most intriguing and paradoxical example is in China where a secure and, as yet, unchallenged communist regime has supervised a phased introduction of a booming market economy.

Third, liberalization has occurred in economies where the habits of policy were relatively non-liberal, mixed economies where the people expected large economic benefits from the state's activity. Consequently, the state habitually intervened substantially in economic life either by regulatory structures or by direct management of economic enterprises. In much of Western Europe, where mixed economies flourished, this meant cutbacks in welfare spending by the state, reduction of the political power of trade unions, and large-scale privatization of state-managed companies providing public utilities. While they remained mixed economies, their governance took on a more laissez-faire character in many respects.

Finally, liberalization can happen in societies that have a large, informal economic sector, relatively unacquainted with modern controls of economic life, where economic and productive activities take place in unregulated spontaneity, with the state being indifferent and irrelevant to much of ordinary economic life.

Question

What are the different implications of liberalization in these four cases?

The crucial point is not to confuse liberalization in an already liberal society, where the state provides an infrastructure for market activity and can, in principle, regulate more extensively (though it chooses not to), with liberalization in either the planned second model or the fourth model of limited state capacity. In these latter contexts, liberalization of the economy means nothing less than a major transformation of the settled forms of economic practice. (As its name suggests, the experience of liberalization in a mixed economy is mixed!)

Often economic liberalizers seek to insulate such changes from political conflict by claiming that these changes are 'technical' economic questions, a matter of simple determination of the most effective means for achieving narrowly economic objectives. However, it is in fact never so simple, or so clearly apolitical. These changes affect the life chances and life structures of major social groups who are bound to respond powerfully to such reforms; and this means that liberalization is always serious politics. Liberalization might appear to be 'freeing the spirit of enterprise' of economic individuals and groups, but contrary to ideological images of the process there is nothing spontaneous or natural about it. Treating people as 'economic individuals' with atomistic self-interested inclinations is not to respond to a natural human trait, but to build a policy on a cultural construct. Models of liberalization often assume (albeit implicitly) an already liberal environment.

In the second and the fourth models of economic governance, liberalization means serious reorganization of economic life, which only the state has the legal authority and the sheer social power to carry through. This leads to a major paradox of liberalization: though the eventual and ideal objective of liberalization is to reduce the state's role in economic life, ironically, it is only the state that can reduce the functions of the state. Or, to put it less paradoxically, economic liberalization in most cases requires significant use of political power. In the fourth model, in particular, the state may need *both* to liberalize *and* to intervene, the latter in order to provide the infrastructure for a more market-based economy.

3 The political economy of Nehru's India

Since we are concerned with liberalization in India, let us see where it fits in the typology just discussed. The Indian economy is very large, on a subcontinental scale, extremely diverse and internally complex, but until the reforms of the 1990s its segments were a mix of the second, third and fourth models. In a case such as India, liberalization could not be anything but a deeply contested political affair. I shall not go into the details of the economic policies through which liberalization of the Indian economy was carried on starting from 1991 (many of which are dealt with in Chapter 7). Rather, I shall discuss the politics that went before liberalization and prevented its happening earlier, that went on around it, and made it feasible, and the politics of its likely future. In what follows, I shall view liberalization not as an economic, but a political process.

The Indian nationalist movement, led by Mohandas Karamchand Gandhi until his assassination in January 1948, had achieved independence in 1947. The Congress party (led by Jawaharlal Nehru), which formed the centre of this mobilization in its final stages, ruled India uninterruptedly for nearly 40 years. This long period of Congress rule can be divided into two phases. In the first phase, Congress followed a reformist (some would call it socialist) programme of industrial development devised by a relatively radical elite around Nehru. Yet in the period after Nehru's death in 1964, when leadership of the party passed to Indira Gandhi and then her son, Rajeev Gandhi, Congress policies changed in significant ways. During Nehru's leadership, from 1946 to 1964, a fairly coherent and well reasoned structure of policies was put in place through a discourse of political economy that achieved almost complete intellectual hegemony and turned into a kind of social 'common sense'. Political debate took place within these parameters.

Over the next two decades, however, these policies subtly changed their character, leading to serious unintended and undetected consequences, which eventually undermined those policies. By the early 1980s, that old, reformist, redistributive, state-centred intellectual consensus had lost its persuasiveness. A vague, but distinctly discernible new kind of 'common sense' emerged in economic circles and began to circulate in the political public sphere through academic discussion, journalism, media debates, and even the unceasing flow of political gossip that often plays an important role in opinion making. Initially, through the decade of the 1980s, this remained a subtle change in the climate of elite opinion, without achieving much tangible policy consequence. But in 1991, due to some dramatic turns in political life, a new government took office that decided to introduce policies of economic reform.

The process of liberalization of the Indian economy has to be understood in terms of two contexts. First, it is essential to recognize the internal dynamics that set up pressures for liberalization. In this respect, we need to ask what kind of economic structure did India have before liberalization and why were these earlier policies adopted? What was the intellectual justification for these policies? And how did the development of these earlier settled habits of policy and economic life lead to a liberalizing impetus? India is an interesting case, in part, because liberalization was primarily internally driven. Second, however, there were outside pressures from international agencies and a strand of highly influential contemporary economic thinking informed by laissez-faire models. Interestingly, Indian economists such as Jagdish Bhagwati and T.N. Srinivasan made a significant contribution to that strand of liberal economic thinking. So, before we turn to the internal evolution of policy within India, let us take a brief look at the external context.

3.1 The global context

It is commonplace today to link changes of any large magnitude in national economies with the process of globalization. Yet how revealing or analytically useful this statement is depends on the exact meaning placed on the term. At times, the contemporary trends of globalization are presented as historically unprecedented; but clearly, with a longer view, the present phase of globalization is an accelerated process of a historical tendency continuing for two centuries, at least since the rise of modern industrial capitalism in the West. Globalization as a concept can be construed narrowly or broadly. In the broad sense, it refers to the process of intensifying interdependence and emergence of networks of regular transaction between and across the borders of economies and states throughout the world that began with European colonization and the rise of the modern world economy.

This process was clearly discerned by the more historically perceptive theorists of the nineteenth century, such as Karl Marx. Marx's *Capital*, especially Volume III (1981; first published 1894), contains a sketchy but powerful analysis of the emergence of a world system through the expansion of capitalist development in the West, as does, more famously, *The Communist Manifesto* (Marx and Engels, 2002; first published 1848). This general process, however, went through several distinct stages, keeping pace with the development of productive technology and the evolution of new techniques of political organization, or governance.

Both technology and these new forms of political control vastly expanded the capacities of economies and states to affect the lives of social groups, sometimes at great distances. Undoubtedly, this long-term historical process has recently gone through a qualitatively new phase of acceleration, where such interdependence and capacity to produce reciprocal effects has gone further than ever before. Narrowly, this has been called 'globalization' since the 1980s. This has been caused by the growth of a new technology based on digital communication and corresponding development of political and economic institutions, which can at least encourage and monitor, if not regulate, the networks created by these technological leaps. For a historical understanding of what is happening to our world, it is essential to guard against two common errors – the first is to believe that nothing like this ever happened before, the second to think there is nothing new in the present stage.

In the 1970s, there was already a wide realization that the structure of the world economy was changing. Intensive trade practices had fundamentally altered the structure of the world economy that emerged from the world wars. Governments veered round to the view that greater, more intensive economic exchange between societies was inevitable, and each state had to find a way of turning it to their benefit. Another unexpected development accentuated this trend. It became increasingly clear that the Soviet systems in Russia and Eastern Europe were in serious economic difficulty. The utter collapse of these states at the end of the 1980s removed the imaginative attraction of an alternative economic model. It became possible to simplify this historical trend as 'the end of history', Francis Fukuyama's claim that liberal democracy and market capitalism had triumphed over all other political and economic systems, when only the laissez-faire and mixed economy models were left standing. Widespread reforms towards liberalization of economies occurred in this international setting.

3.2   The Indian context: interests and discourses in Indian politics

The changing international context sketched above may have made liberalization a more attractive and feasible option but we still have to explain why and how India embarked upon this course. This story is as much, if not more, one of internal developments than one of external pressures.

In order to understand policy changes it is helpful to deal with two levels of analysis. The first is the level of intellectual discourses of political economy, that is, the arguments put forward by economists and public intellectuals; the second is the level of governmental policy making, in terms of the attitudes and decisions of major political actors – the bureaucracy, political parties and pressure groups.

In the first case, we should analyse how economists formulate policy directions based on more technical considerations about economic objectives (see also Chapter 7), and how these technical ideas are taken up by political groups who derive their support from particular social constituencies. Many intellectually respectable ideas never have an influence on public policy. To have serious political effect, those 'technical' economic ideas must go through a popular translation. Political parties give those ideas a more accessible, less technical form, so that these then become part of political discourse and are reflected in public meetings, parliamentary debates and journalistic arguments.

At the second level, we must study opinions and interests inside the bureaucracy, the formation of party policies, pressures brought on the government by organized interests, and constraints on government action deriving from the resources and agencies of other actors. These constitute the non-electoral side of democratic politics, which is sometimes neglected by an exclusive focus on elections and government responses to their verdicts.

Political discourse
Political discourses are the languages through which people and groups express their interests. They embody the collective values and identities of a society about the legitimate scope of public action.

Question

What might be gained by studying both discourses and interests?

Both discourses and interests determine actual political events. It is wrong to believe that individuals or social groups have some kind of immediate, pre-theoretical understanding of their own interests, that they can understand their interests the way people feel pain. Rather, people and groups 'perceive' what is in their interests through the languages of political discourse that are necessarily public. These discourses shape the horizons of popular imagination about what is regarded as desirable and possible. The more mundane politics of interest-pursuing actors occurs in the context of such possibilities already shaped by discourse. At some level, then, interests are socially constructed. In other words, they are formulated and given expression in a publicly shared set of terms, concepts and arguments. At any given time, these discourses embody the collective values and identities of a society about the legitimate scope of public action. Section 3.3 explores the interests and discourse embodied in the nationalist movement.

3.3   The legacy of economic nationalism

The nationalist movement that brought independence to India was a wide, broad-based coalition of social groups, economic interests and ideologies. The Congress party represented this large, coalitional, ambiguous nature of Indian nationalism. Although we speak of Indian nationalism in the singular, in fact, several strands inside this broad movement entertained strikingly dissimilar views on what to do with state power once it was won from the British. Since the late nineteenth century, groups of political economists had advocated a 'drain theory' about Indian poverty. This claimed that British dominion led to an economic impoverishment of Indian society – imports of British manufactures undermined artisanal craft production, and the extraction of Indian revenues paid British bills. There existed highly significant differences between various nationalist strands on economic policy; but until independence became a serious prospect, these remained primarily theoretical disputes.

From the late 1930s, however, economic policies were discussed with a new seriousness. It is of interest that Congress always had strong relations with political leaders of the Indian business community. A few years before independence, a group of politically minded industrialists published an outline of the kind of economic policy they thought the state should follow after independence, popularly known as the 'Bombay Plan'. Although primarily a platform supported by industrialists, it advocated policies derived from the tradition of economic nationalism, and championed two key ideas – protectionism and the nationalization of some industries – surprising for those who see capitalism and a liberal model of economic governance as more or less synonymous. Not surprisingly perhaps, the Bombay Plan proposed a strong protectionist policy for the development of indigenous industries, shielding them from the competition of more powerful Western business.

Possibly more remarkably, Indian business, as a social class, saw clearly that while the nationalization of industries could go against their interests, protection against foreign competition required a large role for the state; and a weak state could not pursue economic nationalist policies. Indian business also supported the idea that the state should play a significant role in running industries that the private sector was unable to develop, and provide the necessary infrastructure for the development of an industrial economy. Leftist nationalists, influenced by Marxist and social democratic ideas, had already pressed for such policies.

Question

How does a focus on both discourses and interests help us to understand the convergence of leftist nationalists and the business groups associated with the Bombay Plan?

There was an interesting convergence between discursive advocacy of leftist opinion and that of the capitalist class, which promoted an incipient political consensus in favour of an interventionist state and a mixed economy. True, the leftist forces and the capitalist groups supported the state on the basis of radically different principles and interests, and expected rather different things from its intervention; but they did support the idea of an active state. Such discursive facts often play a very significant role in political life. In India, this consensus was written into the founding political institutions of the state, and shaped the political imagination of elites and ordinary people, structuring political life in particular ways. Section 4.1 explains how this domestic consensus supported the particular international stance taken by Nehru's India in the 1950s and early 1960s.

In countries with a democratic political set-up, the movement of ideas and the formation of public opinion are crucial in the determination of long-term policy, though in the Indian case, due to widespread illiteracy, this effective 'public' was highly restricted. The Gandhian national movement had mobilized huge masses of the people on large general issues such as the right of self-determination; but illiteracy reduced ordinary voters' ability to influence specific questions of policy. In the first two decades of democratic politics, ordinary voters were mainly politically quiescent, leaving an unusually large room for the initiatives of political elites and intellectuals. Sections 5.3 and 5.4 explain how this was subsequently to change dramatically.

3.4 Indian sovereignty and the search for legitimacy

In 1947, gaining freedom from the British Empire seemed a magnificent political achievement. It was hardly surprising that immediately after decolonization, the overriding concern for the new nationalist elite was the protection of this newly won political sovereignty.

There is a great variety of states in the modern world, each of which claims internal and external sovereignty. The idea of sovereignty asserted by these states involves what the historian of political theory, Quentin Skinner, has referred to as a 'doubly abstract notion of public power'. On the one hand, the idea of the state is of a corporate body, a legal entity that is separate from the particular holders of political office at any one time – that is, the government of the day. It includes the entire constitutional order and the means of coercive control that serve to guarantee domestic peace and external defence, i.e. the law, the police, the army and the bureaucratic machinery of the state. On the other hand, the sovereign state is also separate from the political community over which it rules: 'it is the state itself, rather than the community over which it holds sway, that constitutes the seat of sovereignty' (Skinner, 2002, p.386). This is the idea of the state as developed by Hobbes that you will be familiar with from Chapter 5. The complement of this historically specific form of state is often seen to be an equally historically specific form of society, sometimes called civil society, populated by atomistic individuals (and families) whose relations with one another are largely impersonal and anonymous, mediated by institutions such as the rule of law, money and bureaucratic institutions.

Civil society
Civil society is the realm of independent, rights-bearing individuals (and families) and their freely formed associations that coexists with the abstract, impersonal, legally constituted public power of the modern state.

In the case of India, it was British colonial rule that brought this idea of the state as an impersonal form of public power as well as the idea of an individual subject (which was necessary particularly to introduce the new regime of private property and the entire regime of taxes and other obligations) and the notion of equality, whether of rights or the denial of rights. Here, the important thing was the constitution of the political-individual subject, rather than whether the subject enjoyed democracy or suffered subjection. This was also a state which (illegitimately under colonialism) pretended to represent the collective interest of society, and from whose legitimate interference nothing in society was morally immune.

Question

What would you expect the major difference to be between the establishing of sovereign rule in Europe and in colonial India?

The major difference between the introduction of this structure of rule in Europe and in India was that, while in Europe this was seen by the major part of society as a result of experimentation in controlling and reducing irresponsible power, and therefore as liberating, in India it seemed the reverse. The society had to be subject to an abstract power, as a result of the irresistible power of the colonial rulers. This array of ideas, when seen in their totality, constituted the invention of a new political world, or a re-cognizing of the world, and of the position of the society and the state in their modern versions – society as a large complex of impersonal associations and organizations among individuals, and the state as an impersonal apparatus of public power. This colonial structure, which the independence movement was to inherit, represented not only a set of new institutions, but also a set of discourses.

However, the doubly abstract form of power embodied in the sovereign state has never gone unchallenged. The austere reasoning of Hobbes has never been enough to legitimate any actual state. First, the separation of the state from the political community has always been problematic. Even within the Western tradition itself, republican theory – which had its origins in the political thought of ancient Greece and Rome, was rediscovered in the Renaissance, and has formed an important continuing influence ever since – argued that the authority of the state was at best a delegated one, in which the inalienable rights of the political community and the individuals that comprised it remained intact. This latter perspective is sometimes called the theory of popular sovereignty to distinguish it from the theory of state sovereignty associated with Hobbes. One can readily see why colonial rulers would be opposed to ideas of popular sovereignty. Yet for nationalist movements contesting colonial rule, the notion of popular sovereignty was an attractive one.

Second, many critics have questioned the independence of the state from those who are its agents – the actual government of the day – and the interests that the latter seek to represent. The socialist tradition, especially in its Marxist variant, developed a variety of arguments to show that the separation of the state from particular governments and the class interests that they served was illusory. In different ways, conservative and elite theorists throughout the nineteenth and twentieth centuries made similar arguments.

As this form of state was reproduced, whether by imposition or imitation, in the non-European world, aspiring sovereign states faced, and continue to face, these and other challenges to their authority. Most obviously, in colonial contexts, nationalist movements sought to wrest sovereignty from foreign rulers and place it the hands of nationals, or at least in a state of their own. So what did sovereignty mean for the newly independent state in India in 1947 and how would the new rulers seek to legitimate their rule?

Popular sovereignty
The theory of popular sovereignty asserts that political authority ultimately lies in the inalienable rights of the people.

Question

How might the legitimation of a post-colonial state differ from that of a rich and powerful Western state of long-standing political independence?

Both forms of legitimacy are likely to make Hobbesian claims about guaranteeing internal peace and external security. However, unlike an established and powerful state, the post-colonial state might also be centrally concerned with reclaiming sovereignty from an imperial power and giving a commitment to develop the country's people and resources. In the Indian case, nationalists since the early twentieth century had contributed to a strong sense of economic nationalism. They were convinced that Indian poverty and British affluence were both based incontrovertibly on the colonial 'drain of wealth'. From the mid 1930s, this tradition of economic thinking, originally developed by giving an ingenious nationalist twist to Scottish and English political–economic doctrines, which were widely read by Indian intellectuals from the early nineteenth century, was increasingly linked to analytical frames drawn from Marxist critiques of imperialism.

Jawaharlal Nehru's own economic understanding played a significant part in producing a form of 'common sense of the state' – an underlying strand of thought which helped to shape state policies at a fundamental level. Nehru was critical of the political practices of the Soviet Union, but he applied a primarily Marxist framework to the understanding of international politics.

4 Formulating India's national interest

You will recall that the realist view is that relations between states can be explained in terms of the distribution of power among them, but that realism says nothing about how and why power is distributed across the system in the way that it is, nor how and why that distribution changes over time. Marxist theories of imperialism, which were in fact the product of the first international debate about the character of the world order conducted in the international socialist movement between the 1890s and the outbreak of the First World War in 1914, tried to account for the underlying distribution and dynamics of global power. According to these theories, it was the worldwide spread and deepening of market relations, and the distribution of capital across the globe which provided the dynamics of world politics. These theories argued that state power arose from a basis in the institutional organization of economic capacities in general and the global development of industrial capitalism in particular. The development and spread of capitalism on a world scale was not bounded by the territorial borders of states – no matter how hard some states tried to control it – and the uneven and conflict-ridden character of capitalist expansion, as capitalists competed against one another on an increasingly global basis, provided the underlying rhythms of world politics.

In an international system in which power and the competition between states was shaped by the uneven growth and the competitive processes of industrial capitalism, it followed that the protection of political sovereignty was not just a narrowly political or military–strategic question. It depended heavily on India's economic place in the complex structure of the world capitalist system. This was a highly plausible theory, which saw the industrialization of the West as the real source of its colonial power and argued that if ex-colonial societies were to move out of the crippling dependence on the West, they had to industrialize themselves, rather than agree to the disingenuous ideas of static comparative advantage. Continued specialization in agricultural production, which had been India's conventional strength, would lead to a perpetuation of economic backwardness because of the adverse international terms of trade between industrial and agricultural goods.

Significantly, even simple industrialization in consumer goods was not likely to dispel Western economic domination, as this would continue in the form of dependence on Western technology and machinery. Nehru and nationalists feared, like elites in other post-colonial societies, that the West might use its economic leverage to limit their exercise of political sovereignty, and turn them, despite formal independence, into effective satellites. Sovereignty depended on economic independence. True economic independence could emerge only if India could develop her own heavy industries.

Several major policy directions followed from this theoretical perspective. Since indigenous Indian capitalists simply did not have the kind of capital required to establish these large industries, this could be done only by the state. Following this line of reasoning, the state in independent India assumed a large role in direct economic production in certain sectors, particularly in steel, heavy engineering, petrochemicals, power generation and distribution – all lines of economic production regarded as essential for the development of other, consumer-oriented industries. Although this model of economic growth gave the state in India a large and in some ways determining economic role, it was also fundamentally different from Soviet style planning. India was seen as a mixed economy with much economic activity left to private enterprise, but the state was also given large regulatory powers, including licensing to ensure that private industries developed in line with the priorities of the plan.

Question

Why is the Indian economy just described best approximated by the mixed economy rather than by the communist model?

The economic ideal of the Nehru regime could be called 'socialist' in a broad sense because it used an eclectic mix of various leftist ideas; it certainly included a Marxist understanding of the working of the capitalist world system and a social democratic concern about redistribution of income within a democratic political framework. Its economic ideal was the creation of an economy that was self-reliant, not autarkic. This was a major difference between Nehruvian thinking and the communist model exemplified in either the Soviet or the Chinese variety. Nehru saw the Indian model functioning primarily within the structure of the capitalist world economy, not as an alternative or oppositional model. It was a way of improving India's economic position within that system.

However, Nehru believed that the new state's resources and tax base were just too small to attempt serious redistribution, or provision of welfare. In fact, welfare in the strict sense was limited, in Nehru's times, to programmes intended to help the urban poor by providing low fixed-price food through state distribution channels called 'ration-shops'. By the time the Nehru regime had worked out its economic growth model in some detail, by the mid 1950s, the state had established a large role in the economy in two ways – its ability to impose regulatory controls through bureaucratic institutions, and its role in directly running crucial productive industries, which provided infrastructure or essential inputs into other industries. (The railways had been a wholly state-run industry since colonial times.)

This was the overarching intellectual frame for economic policies, but the actual pursuit of these objectives in the real world contained surprising, unintended developments. Interestingly, there was little serious intellectual opposition to this basic policy from any organized social group. Organized labour, under the influence of communists or left-wing Congressmen, welcomed them in any case. The middle classes were largely intellectually persuaded by the cogency of these arguments and a realistic expectation that this policy of industrial growth would materially benefit them by creation of management and technical jobs: engineering education became a great favourite of ambitious middle-class families. The public bureaucracy was enticed by its nationalism and prospects of immense increases in its own size and powers of control. Even business, as we saw earlier, supported this brave protectionist vision of industrial development – resulting in something like a rare economic consensus. Yet pursuing these aims led to surprising events.

4.1   India's international alignments under Nehru

Nehru was always a socialist, but never, after the 1930s, an admirer of its Stalinist model. He admired the Soviet Union's astonishing industrial growth, but was repulsed by the methods of terror used to achieve it. Under Stalin, the Soviets heartily returned his dislike, calling him, at times openly, 'an agent of western imperialism'. Despite Nehru's very early, but short-lived, admiration of Soviet society (which was incidentally shared by many Western socialists in the 1920s), a convergence of policies between independent India and post-war USSR was highly unlikely. In spite of sharp criticisms of Western societies for their colonial past, and the persistence of European colonialism and US support for this, in Nehru's thinking it was states such as the UK and the USA that were the most likely allies of independent India.

The realities of the post-war political world soon altered this perception. Serious friction began between India and the Western powers on both political and economic issues. Immediately after the war, the US-led Western alliance began a frenetic search for allies across the Third World to contain communism by establishing a ring of interconnected military alliances around the perimeter of the communist bloc. Nehru thought these treaties contributed to increased tension, and decided to follow a policy of non-alignment, a strategy condemned initially by both the superpowers as a devious way of siding with the other camp. In fact, the founding principle of the non-aligned movement was its opposition to colonial rule, based on the ambitions of many of the newly independent post-colonial states to turn their formal independence into a meaningful degree of autonomy in international affairs (the struggle over autonomy is examined further in relation to Africa in Part 4). The Western powers also used their economic advantage to put pressure on Nehru on this question, which simply increased his suspicion that they wished to compromise India's political freedom of decision making.

On the economic side, Western governments, especially US ruling circles, looked upon his statist policies with deep suspicion, and feared that they could be a prelude to comprehensive nationalization of foreign and private industries. When Nehru's government sought technology and capital to develop his primarily state-led industrialization plan, the US response, from government and business circles, was hostile and negative. But this led to a mutual misunderstanding of motives. The West thought it had enough reasons to treat Nehru as little better than a communist; Nehru thought the West was little better than imperialist.

Nehru's regime had two options – either to abandon its ambitious plans for industrialization or to look elsewhere. The change of regime and fundamental shifts in Soviet policy after Stalin made this possible. The end of the Stalin era led to not merely some internal changes in the Soviet system, but also to a comprehensive review of Soviet policies towards the world. The Khrushchev regime slowly began to change their attitude towards newly decolonized states, and made cautious overtures towards them, especially as a series of radical nationalist and revolutionary movements came to power in a wave of Third World revolutions and coups.

In part, this shift in Soviet policy was also driven by a crucial and more realistic assessment of the structure of world power. The inflated ideological discourse of bipolarity often confused the real condition of the world. It stated, correctly, that there were only two superpowers – that is, powers with global military capabilities – but often went on to imply, incorrectly, that their powers were broadly equal. In fact, the bipolarity of the post-war world was marked by an asymmetry between the West and the communist world in terms of economic strength and political influence. Only in military power, and even then only after the early 1970s, was there something like an equality of conventional arms and nuclear deterrence. However, the asymmetry meant that the objectives of the two sides were determined very differently. The West generally expected its allies to give full support to its military and political objectives. The communist system, as the weaker player, would have been content if countries such as India did not follow the lead of the West, and the post-Stalin regimes recognized this in their policies. In other words, the Soviet objectives were lower than those of the United States. Therefore, this created a possibility of a convergence between Soviet and Indian objectives, even in the absence of ideological agreement.

A combination of this kind of economic thinking and short-term political moves eventually shaped the outline of the political economic structure that India was to follow for nearly four decades after independence. It was undoubtedly a mixed economy, with a sprawling private sector, loosely or inefficiently regulated, but dominated by a highly visible public sector in crucial industries such as steel, mining, heavy engineering, petrochemicals and oil exploration. Much of the technology and some of the capital needed for this drive towards heavy industrialization came from the USSR. The coincidence of Soviet and Indian policy towards Kashmir and other international disputes sometimes made this convergence of interest look far worse to Western eyes, and to some panicky bourgeois groups inside India. Equally, Western hostility to legitimate ambitions of industrial growth, and the mysterious ways of US foreign policy – that declared itself in favour of freedom yet supported many dictatorships – made Indians increasingly mistrustful of Western declarations. What Indians found particularly strange was how the United States preferred army regimes in Pakistan over elected ones in India.

5   Questioning the Nehruvian legacy

The creation of the new public sector industries led to the elaboration of a system of public administration which classified industries, somewhat like British thinking at the time, into four kinds. There were private enterprises wholly owned by capitalists, and besides these there were, legally, three types of government involvement in industries. 'Joint enterprises' had shared private and state control, usually with a majority share with the state. 'Public enterprises' were funded by the state, but their managements were supposed to enjoy managerial autonomy of decision making. These were, in administrative theory at least, sharply distinguished from 'ministerial departments' such as the railways or the post office, which were entirely controlled by state ministries, and were regulated by ordinary rules of bureaucratic management.

In the Nehru period at least, the public enterprises enjoyed some genuine autonomy of managerial decisions from the bureaucracy. And the initial performance of the public enterprises was encouraging: first, they successfully established these industries in the Indian economy and reduced dependence on external sources of heavy industrial goods; and second, even their economic performance in terms of productivity and costs was fairly respectable. As a whole, the policy generated industrial growth, though at a relatively modest rate, and it created an economy with a large and versatile production base. Most significantly, from the Nehruvian point of view, it helped India, in the thick of the Cold War, to remain impervious to pressures from outside to alter its political policies. India remained more independent of international, particularly of Western, pressure compared to countries such as South Vietnam or South Korea, which were seen derisively as satellites. For three crucial foundational decades, Indian political economy followed this fundamental design.

5.1   Some assessments of Nehru's policies

Historical assessments of Nehru's policies diverge widely. There are two main lines of evaluation. Some economists have argued forcefully, since the 1970s, that the state-led heavy industrialization policies were flawed from the inception, in their very design, and not surprisingly, they delivered sluggish long-term growth. One of the best, and certainly most influential, critiques is that of Jagdish Bhagwati (1993), an Indian economist who has played a prominent role in the international debate about liberalization and has been described by some as one of the main intellectual architects of the Uruguay Round. Raj Krishna (1984), another leading economist, famously derided India's growth rate as the 'Hindu rate of growth', though what it has got to do intimately or causally with Hinduism is unclear. This line of thought begins from the premise that the criteria for assessment of policy should be exclusively economic, in fact narrowly income-oriented and based on stringently narrow calculations of 'economic growth'. Other economists who support broader conceptions of economic development, and advocate wider and more complex criteria such as 'quality of life', judge Nehru's policies rather more positively (see, for example, Bardhan, 1984; Dreze and Sen, 1995).

The other line of thought still asserts the correctness of Nehruvian policies, and blames its two main disappointments – widespread poverty and slow growth – on failures of implementation. Of interest, from a theoretical point of view, is that both these judgements depend crucially on comparison between actual states of affairs and counterfactuals. This is a common feature of much policy evaluation: the analyst is attempting to compare what we know happened given certain policy variables and certain other factors that are taken as external constraints, with what would have happened under different policy variables with the same external constraints. Since one cannot in fact run history twice, what usually happens is a comparison of one country with another that had different policies, or one country in two different periods characterized by different policies; or one develops a theory that allows a prediction (or guess) of what would have happened. Consequently, these judgements always leave a certain margin of uncertainty.

It is possible to suggest a third, more mixed judgement. If the criteria used are mixed – combined economic and political ones – then the historical judgement on the first stage of policies is bound to be more complicated, at least less pessimistic. The evaluation of goods such as political freedom of decision making and political independence would show the performance of Nehru's policies in a far better light than narrowly economic measures. Yet even those who advocate this historical line of judgement must admit that in its two main functions in the economic sphere the state's involvement began to yield diminishing and eventually counter-optimal returns over the longer term. Even after decades of Nehruvian planning, the Indian economy remained plagued by the two problems of slow growth and large-scale poverty.

The problems with the Nehruvian economic design will be discussed in Chapter 7, but for now we can note the political implausibility of expecting politicians and bureaucrats to change policies that were, in the short run at least, successful. By the mid 1970s, there was a widespread perception in the political public sphere, in journalistic debates and in the popular mind that state-run industries were running uneconomically and inefficiently, running up huge losses, which eventually fell on the state. However, the degeneration of the public sector and its growing disrepute was not entirely an economic phenomenon. Political processes were equally to blame.

After Nehru, the administrative distinctions in management styles and structures between ministerially controlled industries such as the railways and post office and relatively autonomous public corporations producing, say, steel were slowly eroded by political interference. Indira Gandhi's attempts to centralize government resulted in increasingly direct bureaucratic and ministerial interference in industry's affairs. By the mid 1970s, there was hardly any discernible difference between the two types of enterprises: public sector industries were run as bureaucratically as ministerial departments. Everyday political commentary and popular gossip was full of speculation about politicians surreptitiously using the resources of the state enterprises for their own political purposes or for straightforward financial malpractice. Thus, the degeneration of the 'public sector' was a somewhat complicated affair. There was no doubt that the public sector had degenerated; but it was, equally truly, not the same kind of a 'public sector'. This had two highly significant results: first, the economic performance of the public industries became uniformly poor, and began to be universally derided, not merely by economists preferring the market, but also by ordinary commentators. Second, it became increasingly clear that the Nehruvian discursive justifications for the sector, for its contribution to the economic strength of the country and preventing concentration of economic power, had ceased to apply.

5.2   The break-up of the Nehruvian consensus

By the early 1990s, then, economic arguments for liberalization were not new or unconventional. Large social groups who had great electoral leverage, and influential and strategically placed elites who commanded wealth and connections, increasingly saw the bureaucratic controls over the economy as serious obstacles to their growth. Nevertheless, the old policies retained solid support from other social groups: first, the bureaucracy, which enjoyed immense powers from these regulations; then the political class who indirectly or corruptly benefited from its assets; and finally organized labour, which profited from vastly improved working conditions. The interest convergence, which had led to the Nehruvian policies without much serious opposition, started fragmenting. Still, it would take a major macroeconomic crisis – a crisis of the management of the national economy – to start serious policy change.

The politics of discourse also began to change, but significantly more slowly and more subtly. Intellectually, a major part of the political intelligentsia still defended a state sector that functioned very differently from Nehru's times by wholly anachronistic reference to high-minded Nehruvian economic ideals. But both politicians and common people recognized that the state sector represented a large vested interest, rather than a welcome counterweight to the power of private capitalists. The genuine policy consensus of the 1950s and 1960s was thus already in jeopardy. Early suggestions towards liberalization mainly stressed two policy recommendations – reducing state controls over licensing of new industries, and bringing in market forces in sluggish sectors of the economy, ending state monopoly. The climate of opinion changed slowly: although a larger section of economists began to argue forcefully for reduction of state control and greater freedom of the market, they met with a stodgy dismissal.

Yet there were discernible changes in practical orientations of economic policy. In any case, Indira Gandhi showed, from the start of her prime ministerial career in 1964, a more flexible, pragmatic approach to macroeconomic policies than her father, certainly less constrained by ideological convictions about development or redistribution. The first major change in economic policy she initiated was the shift to green revolution strategies in agriculture – that is, the attempt to improve output by means of new seeds and the application of chemical fertilizers. This demonstrated how easily she could abandon the egalitarian conviction behind the earlier policies of land reform and institutional change. For the benefit of sharp rises in productivity, she was prepared to accept large-scale inequalities, since access to the new technologies presupposed access to credit, which poor farmers lacked.

More subtly but fundamentally, Indira Gandhi's attitude towards planning was very different from Nehru's. Under her leadership, economic planning changed character. Though the Nehruvian rhetoric of planned development was retained, from the fourth five-year plan onwards, the government in imperceptible degrees gave up the intention of directing economic growth purposively. Planning slowly became a process of setting down targets and large-scale objectives, and the vast apparatus of planning kept itself busy in statistical exercises.

During the short period of the emergency, in an interesting interlude, a section of the Congress leadership, encouraged by Indira Gandhi's second son, Sanjay Gandhi, began to suggest heretically that India should abandon planned development and adopt 'the Brazilian path'. The latter was a transparent code for more liberalized economic policies. (The 'emergency' was the period of 1975–77, when Mrs Gandhi used those powers of the colonial state that had survived in the Constitution of 1950 to respond to political opposition by authoritarian means.) With the gradual decline of the Nehruvian economic thinking behind real control regimes, these policies lost their ideological resilience, and crumbled morally from inside. As a result, the system of bureaucratic controls did not collapse, but it became a gigantic, arbitrary, Byzantine mass of rules capriciously implemented – more to extract bribes or to inconvenience adversaries than to realize defensible policy objectives. This system became more repressive and less justifiable at the same time. Already a certain change in economic thinking was discernible in government circles in the last years of Indira Gandhi's rule. Economists with pronounced liberalizing views were appointed to highly influential and visible advisory positions in the economic ministries. Their presence indicated incipient rethinking in political circles and the high bureaucracy. These economists also made strong attacks on the inefficiency of the conventional state sector and licensing controls, slowly altering the intellectual climate in which government economic policy was formulated.

Arguments for liberalization and market-friendly reforms did not re-emerge in serious public political debates until Rajeev Gandhi came to power. Rajeev Gandhi had a shorter term in power, but his economic tendencies were even more eclectic than his mother's. He clearly pushed for an incorporation of high technology in particular sectors of the Indian economy, especially telecommunications and computers. While general policies were not radically revised, government attitudes were seen to be friendlier towards risk-taking entrepreneurial initiative. Since high technology could not easily come into the Indian economy without market-friendly reforms, this was seen as a natural entailment of his policies. However, Rajeev Gandhi was assassinated before his initiatives could form into seriously worked out general policies.

5.3 The changing face of Indian politics

The latter half of the 1980s was highly significant for Indian politics. Though analysts and commentators generally remember a period of messy, fractious government, in fact, the political universe of Indian democracy was moving from one historical stage to another. Since independence, a majority party, the Congress, had always controlled the central government securely. In 1991, for the first time, Indian society faced the startling fact that no party could secure a majority at the national level. In the elections of 1989, after Rajeev Gandhi's death, Congress was riven by internal factional fights and failed to get a majority. Yet, there was no party that could replace it on a stable basis. Congress had declined, but not enough to disappear electorally; the Bharatiya Janata Party (BJP) had emerged strongly but not enough to form a government (see Section 6.3). Historically, this was an interregnum between strong central governments of powerful, all-Indian political parties and much weaker ones based on coalitions between regionally powerful forces, obliged by the logic of electoral arithmetic to seek support from others.

After the Nehru era, slowly Indian politics underwent a fundamental change towards a newer and deeper form of activation of the common people. By the 1970s, elections had become much more important for both the electors and the representatives. Voters appreciated that while they were consulted only once in five years about who should rule over them, this was a useful opportunity to extract serious concessions. Moreover, due to ministerial instability, such occasions came at shorter intervals than five years, a fact which the voter did not regret. Also, the economic powers of the state and its asset-controlling reach had grown so formidably that elected politicians, at every level, controlled considerable resources for disbursement and use.

However, the collective actors that emerged powerfully into the arena of democratic politics, dominating its conflicts and transactions, were not interests, but identities. In distinguishing between interests and identities, I am drawing attention to the difference between things that individuals and groups want (interests) and the socially defined community with which they identify (identity). In Indian society, despite the inroads modernity has made into traditional forms of communitarian bonding of people, the process of individuation has not remade the entire logic of the social world. Disadvantage is seen more as unjust treatment of whole communities, like lower castes, minority religious groups and tribal communities, which are thus seen as potential political actors for social equality. Certainly, people who are part of democratic mobilizations are predominantly poor, but the principle of their self-identifying action is not poverty but *discrimination*. And the relevant unit of social analysis is not the individual, but the *community* (Chatterjee, 1994). Thus, the individualist picture of society, which is an assumption of political sociology behind much of modern Western democratic theory, is unavailable in India, except perhaps in a few big cities. Even in these, it may be found only in the social behaviour of a small, highly Westernized middle class. Otherwise, the democratic game and its outcomes have become fundamentally different because the game is played by a different species of player.

Interests and identities
As used here, 'interest' refers to an individual's or a group's assessment of what they want, while an 'identity' is a form of identification with a given community.

Activity 6.1

In terms of the distinction between interests and discourses introduced in Section 3.2, how would you describe the transformation of Indian politics noted above?

Democratic theory in the West has tended to assume that the participants in politics are individuals pursuing interests, in effect, that the *demos* (the people) constitute a single identity, or *ethnos*, in which majorities are only temporary and no group of the population is a permanent minority. In India, the activation of the common people in the form of identity politics, as communities rather than as individuals, has resulted in political forces that see themselves as permanent minorities and wish to transform themselves into part of a permanent and invincible majority. These developments have brought into question the cognitive, the political and the moral legitimacy of the whole institutional regime constructed after independence. This critique asks of the regime – the impersonal nature of public power, the rule of law, the democratic order, the idea of a complex and composite nation, a secular polity – whether it is legitimate for a relatively small elite to impose their ideals on others who do not necessarily share them. It also asks if this political form, because of its unintelligibility, can be worked by this people. It must also be clear that these questions are addressed not only to the Indian political or modernist ruling elite, but also to social theory in equal measure because the questions can be logically so directed, and also because it is these theories, which the elite believed, that gave them the intellectual justification to do what they had undertaken.

Activity 6.2

Think of some recent political issues in a Western country. How convincing do you find this contrast between the individualistic and interest-based character of politics in the West and the community and identity nature of politics in India? Does your answer give you any reasons to question the critique mentioned above?

5.4   The politics of liberalization

Full-scale liberalization, when it arrived, was full of paradoxes. The government that P.V. Narasimha Rao formed in 1991 was the weakest central government in modern Indian history. In parliament, the government did not command a majority. Its survival depended on voting support from some opposition groups – mainly leftist and lower-caste parties. Rao was not secure inside his own party, with a major section of political leaders openly declaring their loyalty to Rajeev Gandhi's widow, Sonia Gandhi, and obstructing his policies. Rao was the weakest Prime Minister both in parliament and inside his own party. Yet his government undertook what was undoubtedly the most radical reform of the Indian economy since Nehru's times. (The nature of these reforms is discussed in Chapter 7.). How was this possible? How could the most radical reforms be carried out by the weakest regime since independence? Four reasons could be advanced to explain this paradox.

The first explanation examines the changing international context within which Indian policy makers had to operate. By the 1970s, the structure of the global economy and the nature of economic relations had changed radically. These changes seemed to make fears of neocolonial control by ex-colonial powers unrealistic, and therefore policies meant to guard political sovereignty unnecessary. In addition, countries that had been derided as satellites (such as South Korea) showed, through their prosperity, the great economic advantages of intensified trade and a policy that opened economies out to the world rather than closed them in the name of self-reliance. The spectacular economic growth of the East Asian economies was analysed by Indian observers, and this fuelled speculation that given proper government policies, Indian business could emulate their prosperity. Ideologically, the global collapse of communist systems in the late 1980s seemed to undermine the philosophical legitimacy of socialist economic thinking in general, and thus nationalistic arguments that relied on those concepts carried a fading power of persuasion. The relevance, but also the limits, of this kind of account were noted in Section 3.

A second explanation considers the changing interests of the various social groups in the Indian political economy. Economic changes from the 1950s had led to a slow, imperceptible recomposition of social classes, altering the balance of economic power in the society. The most significant change was the rise of the new capitalist farmers in the green revolution areas who were the main beneficiaries of the absence of agricultural income tax, and of some of the regime of subsidies. The professional middle classes, initially the prime beneficiaries of industrial growth because they monopolized the new job opportunities in both the private and the public sector industries, and the bureaucracies that supervised them, increasingly felt their economic life had reached a point of stagnation. Until the 1960s, these upper-class groups were entirely dominant in the political world; but from the 1970s, politicians coming from rich farmer and lower-caste backgrounds successfully challenged their exclusive control of the political field. As the professional middle classes became less dominant in the political process due to growing democratic participation, they became more receptive to liberalizing ideas, expecting new opportunities of income growth from global economic changes. A highly skilled section of the Indian professional classes gradually gained access to the international economy, and developed much greater aspirations for wealth than the earlier structure of policies allowed.

Even without a concerted intellectual campaign to open up the Indian economy, the slow dispersal of the Nehruvian consensus in favour of protectionist policies and state intervention to promote industrial development, and redistributive policies, led to the emergence of a new, weaker consensus in favour of liberalization. Curiously, no-one argued strenuously for the market, excepting a small group, but the mistrust of the state grew so immense that it amounted to the growth of a new economic 'common sense' which even the leftist parties could not resist with conviction.

However, this kind of consensus by default, which exists as a background common sense among economic and political elites, cannot translate into economic policy without some political agents to carry them through. Although it is sometimes casually asserted that political democracy and economic liberalism have an elective affinity as both are based on principles of unrestricted choice, in actual historical contexts this relation does not hold so simply. The mere existence of democracy is no guarantee that voters will choose liberalizing policies. It is more likely that voters reflect on the possible effects of liberalization on their own economic interests, and large social groups who rely on benefits from state action will vote against liberalization initiatives. In India, despite this widespread feeling of the inefficiency and unpopularity of state-centred policies, pushing through liberalizing reforms was generally seen as a hazardous, unpopular business. Liberalization, if fully implemented, would help some groups and injure others, and consequently large political parties shrank from taking the first step. Organized political groups would have agreed to allow liberalization policies to go through only if others enacted them, and they could avoid the responsibility.

At this point, a third explanation draws attention to the specific conjuncture of political forces at a particular moment in the evolution of Indian politics. The Rao government came to power without an absolute majority, and it used its position of relative weakness with masterful political skill. In 1991, the macroeconomic crisis was such that radical decisions could not be avoided. Rao's finance minister, Manmohan Singh, was a distinguished economist who became a bureaucrat and eventually a minister, but not a career politician who had to cultivate an electoral constituency. He fashioned a powerful, cogent and eloquent intellectual justification for a package of reforms, bringing the vague drift of opinion among elites to a clear focus (the nature of the economic crisis and the reforms introduced to deal with it are discussed in Chapter 7). Liberalizing reforms were unpopular to a large section of the Congress party itself. But they could not produce a counter-strategy to deal with the immediate crisis. Rao, as the prime minister, resolutely protected his finance minister from pressures inside his party and from the opposition in parliament. Ironically, other parties had, in their own way, come round to similar conclusions about long-term economic strategy, though they were unwilling to admit that publicly. For them, it was in fact advantageous that Congress was forced to take the initiative, and would take the blame. It is remarkable that while in the intense debates in the political public sphere both the Hindu nationalist BJP and the leftist parties criticized the Congress and warned about the effects of liberalization, no political group opposed it hard enough.

Another, fourth, explanation, also focuses on the concrete character of Indian politics at the time. It starts from noting that although the debate about liberalization was a mainly economic one, it did not happen in a vacuum. Academic analysis separates out single problems – like liberalization in our case – and seeks explanatory accounts. People do not live in the comparative luxury of such single issues in real political life; they live within tangled webs of interconnected exasperations. What political actors decide to do about one issue is sometimes determined not by what they think about that problem but what they think about others. In this case, decisions about liberalization were subsumed under the question of how to respond to the rise of the BJP, the Hindu nationalist party, which began to emerge into prominence from the 1980s as part of the shift in Indian politics noted in Section 5.3 above. The actual decisions of Indian political parties in 1991 were determined, not by their thinking on the economic consequences of liberalization, but by the possible effects of a takeover by the BJP and the challenge to the secular conception of Indian politics that this might imply (see Section 6.3).

Narasimha Rao was not a strong politician, but a sly one. With long political experience, he knew how to calculate on the weakness of his enemies. He played the interconnection of the two issues with masterful political adroitness. All political combatants realized that if the BJP was able to form the government at the centre, it would threaten to restructure Indian politics in a fundamental way, changing both the constitutional structure and the common sense of everyday politics. For opposition parties, therefore, the choice was invidious. They could seriously threaten Rao's reforms only by letting the BJP into power. Left parties disliked liberalization, but they disliked the prospect of a communal takeover at the centre even more. Rao gambled, as it turned out quite rightly, that if he pursued liberalization policies forcefully, they would merely criticize him, but not topple his government. By enacting legislation for liberalization, he dared them to dismiss his ministry. Understandably, the leftists and other opposition parties thought liberalization was a lesser disaster than BJP's accession to power. Predictably, they stopped short of voting his government out of office.

6 Liberalization, the BJP and the reshaping of Indian politics

In politics, vagueness is often an unanswerable strength. Liberalization went through successfully partly because of the ambiguity of its meaning, and the great variety of expectations. As Section 2 explained, liberalization means different things to different groups in different contexts. At least, some interested social groups or political parties believed that they would allow some aspects of liberalization to take place and delay or stop others.

Intellectually, those who advocated liberalization – the Congress government and its general supporters – understood its internal logic clearly. Liberalization meant the adoption of a structured set of interconnected policies, the success of each part of which depended on the other parts. Segments of this policy structure could succeed up to a point, but not entirely. Just as Nehruvian planners slowly realized that the structure had an indispensable internal coherence, liberalizers understood the coherence of this alternative set of policies. Liberalization meant several radical changes in the received structure of the economy and, consequently, in the settled forms of economic practices in everyday life. All observers saw some constituents of liberalization as crucial: reducing the labyrinthine regime of industrial licensing, reducing tariffs particularly on import goods, reducing subsidies, creating a flexible labour market giving greater powers to managements to hire and fire workers and determine pay and conditions of employment, and finally, in cases where state sector industries were running at a loss, privatizing them.

Obviously, each one of these measures went directly against the settled policies of the Nehruvian design of political economy; therefore, their adoption would have meant, irrespective of the tact or skill with which they were handled politically, a radical change in the overall character of economic life for all social groups.

As the content of liberalization policies and their theoretical rationale is analysed in Chapter 7, we shall discuss only the political implications – in two stages. First, we will analyse how each component policy of liberalization reforms was likely to affect large, social interest groups. However, social groups have complex and not always predictable relations with political parties, for the translation of group interests into political sentiments is a complex affair, as is the further transfer of these into party policies. Thus, second, we will look at how the actual party politics of liberalization unfolded.

6.1   Social groups and liberalization

Indian liberalization, it is generally acknowledged, proceeded slowly, compared to China or some cases in Africa. Accordingly, its economic and political results were also quite different. This slow progress was not merely because of obstacles, but for deliberate political reasons. The Congress party was itself divided about liberalizing reforms, and a large segment opposed it – out of habit, if not conviction. The part of the leadership that had to push the reforms through, therefore, had to conciliate not merely the opposition, but sections of opinion in their own party. In addition, the reforms progressed slowly out of deliberate political calculation. Let us consider first some of the key organized interests likely to be affected.

Liberalizing economists tend to assume casually that business interests would unequivocally favour opening the market; but that evidently is not true under all circumstances. It depends on whether business expects to do well because of the market opening. While for international business corporations the opening up of the immense Indian market was a tempting prospect, for Indian business it meant, crucially, an end to protection. Competition by international business could drive some indigenous industries to the ground. Thus, the business response was mixed.

On the whole, entrepreneurs welcomed the opportunities for cheaper imports, fewer licensing controls, lower or more rationalized taxes, and openings for easier collaboration with the large international corporations for capital investment and the latest technology. But they had reason to fear unrestricted competition and the great volatility of the international capital markets. Some specific industries, such as software manufacture, which were knowledge intensive and unhampered by the constraints of bad infrastructure, quickly turned these openings to the best use. Yet the success of these industries was partly because of their peculiar nature, their ability to exploit India's social and economic strengths, and the specific conditions of the world market. Other industries could not emulate them so easily. Old-style industries, used to protectionist laws, comfortable with outdated technology and selling to undemanding captive markets, had less reason to rejoice at this impending triumph of the market.

The Indian business world is highly fragmented and stratified. Small business formed a different social group and a distinctive political constituency, with a history of support for right-leaning opposition to the Congress. In north India, small business had conventionally supported the Jana Sangh and the BJP. These groups, who had complained most bitterly against small-time bureaucratic control, leading to extortionate practice and corruption, stood to gain moderately, or to lose nothing. At least in the near future, big international corporations were not going to swamp their businesses.

Professional managerial groups, who play such a significant role in both directing decisions and directing opinion in Indian society, were also likely to approve of liberalization, owing to a peculiarity in opinion formation in social groups. Of course, because of the nature of the Indian economy, this group was divided. Private managers were always in favour of market-friendly policies; bureaucrats and public sector management in favour of controls. But it is important to recognize that sociologically they constitute a single social group. Although divided by their specific interests, they are tied together intimately by familial and social relations, and the common climate of opinion in classes earning similar incomes. As a result of liberalization, bureaucrats as a special group could face a relative loss of their regulatory or discretionary power. But general group opinion often transcends calculation of narrow, individual self-interest. Often bureaucrats would have family or kin in private management or other professional occupations likely to benefit disproportionately from these reforms. Professional-managerial classes could realistically expect long-term expansion of their economic prospects as a social class, if not as individuals or families. Nevertheless, what bureaucrats would lose was often an illegitimate penumbra of power, not legitimate authority, and certainly not their jobs. The bureaucracy generally thus did not have either strong motivations of group interest or ideological conviction to resist liberalizing policies.

However, the initial impact of liberalization affected this group in a specific fashion, by opening up utterly unprecedented income differentials *within* the upper middle classes. Salaries in private management always tended to be higher than government salaries. Now, the more fortunate section that gained access to international companies received a vertiginous rise in their incomes without any chance of bureaucratic salaries catching up – leading to some envy. Yet social opinion of the group could come to the entirely rational conclusion that what one section lost could be more than compensated by what others gained, and by the expectations of long-term gains for the class as a whole.

The likely impact of liberalization on the livelihood of farmers was equally complex, again partly because of the internal differentiation of the Indian peasantry. Farmers who benefited from the green revolution often invested their surplus income into small local or regional businesses. This fraction of their interests was to coincide with those of other small or medium-scale business interests. But there were two central elements of liberalization that went directly against them. All liberalization packages envisaged a reduction and eventual removal of subsidies. This would mean a serious reduction of state support for the entire rural sector, particularly its wealthier sections.

Apart from conventional arguments against subsidies and their effects on government finances, there was an added problem in India. Since agriculture constituted a much larger sector of the economy than the industrial and service sectors, this meant that a smaller sector of the economy was subsidizing a vastly larger one. This was very different from the European case, where a larger and powerful industrial sector subsidized the agricultural. In the latter, subsidies could continue; but in the reverse case of India, such policies simply could not go on indefinitely. Elimination of subsidies would threaten a major source of farmers' prosperity – the large government subsidies in agro-inputs and energy. Any proposal for the rationalization of the tax structure was likely to raise the spectre of an agricultural income tax. If wages of labour in agricultural jobs went up, as liberalizers expected, as employers of hired labour for their farming, especially during the harvest, the farmers were going to lose very heavily.

Liberalization was, therefore, bound to get a mixed reception from the farming interests. Furthermore, the scene had become muddied by competitive bargaining by political parties for the rural vote – with some parties in an election in Punjab promising to provide farmers use of electricity entirely free of charge. There is an enormous tension here. Economically, reducing subsidies is a fundamental part of liberalization. Because the farm lobbies influence votes in the countryside, it is the hardest measure to implement politically. In this case, liberalizing policies were difficult to implement precisely because the political process was democratic, and the state had to find a way of expropriating people with their consent.

Organized labour, a social group that is powerful because of its numbers, organization and strategic location in the industrial economy, looked at liberalization with the greatest anxiety. They expected to be the most serious losers in a comprehensive liberalization of the economy. Due to labour legislation influenced by socialist thinking, employment in the organized sector is permanently secure, irrespective of productivity. Reform of the labour market in line with liberalization policies would certainly entail retrenchment and prospective unemployment on a fairly large scale. Liberalization would affect the working conditions of workers in the state sector in particular, where labourers enjoyed large social benefits, apart from permanent employment. Disinvestment in the public sector industries was bound to end in widespread redundancies, and new labour rules in which workers would face much greater uncertainty. An additional factor was the great reduction of trade union power that was bound to follow.

In India, as elsewhere, the opinion of the working class is sometimes confused with the opinion of trade union leaders, to the benefit of the latter. Not surprisingly, liberalization policies were most strenuously opposed by the representatives of the organized working class, and the political parties which ran the biggest trade unions. But the conventional left parties, communists and socialists, have steadily declined as a force of effective opposition since the 1960s. They simply lacked the political strength to stall liberalizing reforms, and in addition, the overriding anxiety about the Hindu nationalists capturing power through an electoral opening constrained them to give their grudging consent to Manmohan Singh's initiatives. Even in the states where leftist parties control power, and do not face an immediate threat from the BJP, the parlous state of government finances has forced them to ask for assistance from international agencies, contrary to their deepest ideological beliefs.

Activity 6.3

What kind of explanation of politics is used in Section 6.1? You may find it helpful to re-read Section 5.3.

6.2   Liberalization and the political parties

However, this is a very incomplete political sociology, because a majority of citizens in India are not business people, managers, bureaucrats, rich farmers or organized labourers. They are mostly poor unorganized labourers in the cities and the countryside, or poor peasantry, small craftspeople or artisans. Women in very large numbers are housewives and affected by policies through the changing economic fortunes of their families. This vast mass of people, who are not organized through professional interest-articulating institutions, have no regular, uninterrupted contact with policy makers. Their only opportunity of letting the governments know what they think of their reforms is through elections. Both political parties and organized groups, therefore, try to couch their own demands in such a form that they can appeal to a large number of these unorganized people. But exactly how these people have reacted to liberalization is hard to analyse, since the only data collected is through secondary questions at election surveys. We can now consider how politicians responded to this predicament.

Policy makers who introduced the reforms based their moves on political calculations derived from such perceptions of group interest. How the parties moved depended on their sociological support base and institutional structure. Both Congress and the BJP, which had by the 1990s emerged as the major opposition party, were socially universalist. That is to say, they wanted to attract support from all social groups, not just some powerful sectional interests as the communist or peasant parties did. Thus, they had to make sure that introduction of liberalization did not inadvertently produce a grand coalition of social interests against them and destroy their chances of winning elections. They chose their priorities and the sequencing of policies with the greatest care.

Observers have pointed out how the liberalizers selected some policies for early implementation and pushed others down in priority. Some more acute observers of the Indian liberalization programme have noticed that in effect the decision makers made deliberate distinctions along two separate axes. First, actual implementation seemed to separate out policies that were likely to yield short-term results from those that required a long period to succeed; second, and politically more significant, there was a distinction between policies that brought immediate benefits for some groups without affecting others adversely, and those which would mean serious costs to large organized social constituencies. This explains why economic reforms in India have not merely been slow, but selective; or rather, why their slow progress has been due to their selectivity and deliberate sequencing.

As the economic crisis that brought on liberalization was mainly due to a foreign exchange shortage in July 1991, the first moves were to stabilize the economy. Stringent restrictions on foreign exchange were lifted and tariff regimes were relaxed in the early phase. The easing of foreign exchange regulations immediately benefited business and the upper classes. Import of capital goods and technology became easier and made export-oriented industries and upper-class consumers happy. Relaxing licensing rules dealt with a long-term complaint of entrepreneurs. It also helped small entrepreneurs whose main capital was technological skills; its best example was the burgeoning software industry in South India (see Chapter 7). These changes, though quite radical against the context of past policies, mainly allowed new developments without negatively affecting others.

Other policies were politically different because they would cause serious pain to economic groups. Labour market reforms and reducing the size of the public sector would harm workers. Reducing subsidies and tax reform would damage agricultural interests. And if the agricultural sector acted as a single political interest, instead of breaking up into class factions, they had the immense power of numbers on their side. The only way to avoid a grand overwhelming coalition of political forces against liberalization was to select and sequence its constituent policies – make sure that these groups were not antagonized by adverse policies at the same time.

However, economists advocating liberalization pointed out that its success depended on the implementation of the whole package. Many argued that breaking up and sequencing the various parts would make the changes less effective. This was another paradox for politicians: to succeed economically, the policies had to work together; to succeed politically, they had to be pursued separately and in parts.

The actual progress of liberalization in India has been very interesting. While economists have often deplored the fact that the whole package of policies has not been implemented, and therefore, its full beneficial effects could not be realized, others point to its remarkable success given the unpromising initial conditions. In fact, the political history of the period immediately following liberalization was highly volatile. The Congress government, which began the reforms, was followed by a coalition of assorted 'leftist' groups. The latter drew its main support from parties that had been sharply critical of liberalization; but when they came to office they did little to obstruct or reverse it. After a brief and ineffectual period, the coalition went out of office, to be replaced by a coalition government based around the BJP in 1998.

6.3   The BJP and the redefinition of the national interest

Briefly, as a party the BJP is both old and new. After independence, Jana Sangh was the major party of Hindu nationalism, which wanted India to become a Hindu, rather than a secular, state. Its political campaigns have always been strongly anti-Muslim. Interestingly, the JS never had a clearly defined economic programme, though its major political support came from lower government employees and small business people in Northern India. Yet the JS was never able to go beyond modest gains in electoral terms. In 1977, it decided to join the coalition of opposition forces against Indira Gandhi and merged into the Janata Party. Ideological rifts soon began in the Janata Party, and when it broke away it assumed the new name, Bharatiya Janata Party, presumably to emphasize its 'Indianness'/indigenousness,

'Bharat' being the Hindi word for India. In the elections of 1984, the party's fortunes fell to a record low of two seats in the central parliament. It began a highly visible and divisive campaign about the destruction of a mosque at Ayodhya, in the northern state of Uttar Pradesh. In December 1991, activists from Hindu nationalist groups demolished the structure of the Babri mosque at Ayodhya, leading to widespread rioting in the whole subcontinent. Allegedly, the Mughals built the mosque after destroying a temple, and the BJP launched a campaign for 'rebuilding' a long list of such temples after destroying mosques. The campaign was surprisingly successful, and rebuilt the BJP's electoral base. By the time of the liberalization initiatives of the Congress, it had started to threaten to launch a bid for power at the centre.

From the mid 1980s, the Hindu chauvinist party, the BJP enjoyed a startling electoral revival. From a low point of two seats, in 1984, in successive general elections, it stormed to an ever-larger share of seats. In 1989, only an indirect coalition of Congress and left parties kept the BJP out of office. The accession of the BJP to government in the late 1990s led to the most serious ideological change in Indian politics since independence. The BJP finally found a way to power at the centre, although as the major constituent of a coalition. The BJP had always challenged the hegemonic vision of secular nationalism advocated by the Congress, and its electoral success was built directly on the campaign around the demolition of the mosque at Ayodhya. Oddly, however, it had continued the economic indistinctness of its precursor, the Jana Sangh. Nevertheless, as its role changed from a regional North Indian party to a serious contender for national government, the BJP was forced to define its economic policy more clearly. In the event, it developed two somewhat contradictory lines of argument.

In line with its general ideological indigenousness, it began to appropriate the traditional Gandhian economic ideals of 'swadeshi' – a policy that supported cottage industries, voluntary restriction of consumption, a simple rural lifestyle and above all rejection of foreign-made goods. This was incongruous for a party that was directly linked to the RSS (Rashtriya Swayamsevak Sangh) organization, one of whose members had assassinated Gandhi. Yet the strand of indigenousness was quite strong in some sections of the Hindu nationalists, and increasingly they made more assertive claims for swadeshi policies.

However, the BJP, crucially, wanted to entice the upper and middle classes from their traditional habits of supporting the Congress because of its policy of economic modernism; it has strenuously sought to dispel the idea that it was a backward-looking fundamentalist force, opposed to modernity. A large section of its social supporters and leadership advocated strongly modernist economic policies and claimed that, under their leadership, the economy would come out of mismanagement and stagnation. Ideologically, therefore, the BJP did not have a clear line towards liberalization.

Activity 6.4

How would you describe the political strategy of the BJP in terms of the distinction between discourses embodying collective values and identities and interests introduced in Section 3.2?

Both the left parties and the BJP fiercely criticized the Congress for initiating liberalizing reforms, but when they came to power, they did nothing to stop or to reverse them. Since the 1998 elections, the BJP has ruled at the centre with fluctuating and, at times, unruly coalition partners in a strange mixture of broad stability because the BJP was in power and small instability because it was never certain about its allies. In order to keep the coalition together, the BJP had to tone down its own ideological stance and its deeply anti-Muslim agenda. On economic issues, however, it had a free hand as none of the coalition parties were strongly opposed to liberalization. In fact, some of its coalition partners, such as the dynamic Chief Minister of Andhra Pradesh, Chandrababu Naidu, used the opportunities created by liberalizing policies to produce an economic interpretation of federalism and press for faster regional development. The BJP's own formal attitude towards liberalization has been surprisingly conciliatory. Although it criticized the Congress at the time, it kept its own position vague. Rather, after the economic situation started to show remarkable improvement on several counts, others have sought to steal some of the credit.

In character with its general expertise in chauvinism, the BJP, or some sections of it, have kept up a fierce rhetoric of economic nationalism against 'foreign interests', generally unspecified. But rhetoric has not threatened to invade actual policy making. Internally, Hindu nationalists have always been friendly to business, especially small business groups, which were their loyal constituency in the first three decades of independence. Big business did not traditionally support the BJP, preferring the more comprehensive modernism of the Congress. However, instead of alienating big business or the professional classes when it was making electoral strides towards power, the BJP sought to woo them by promising greater efficiency, less corruption and making it clear that it was not advocating a comprehensive re-traditionalizing of Indian society.

This had two reciprocal effects. As its electoral strength grew, and the prospects of its power improved, upper middle-class and big business interests became more drawn to it; and reciprocally, the party put its more modernizing leaders into more prominent roles. Now the party often fronts individual leaders who try to cultivate a highly modernist image that is knowledgeable about international trends, friendly to business and markets, interested in high technology. This is only a partial makeover of its indigenous image, but a very real strand of its quotidian politics.

As it continues in government and gathers experience, the BJP government also realizes that international economic pressures demand a continuation of liberalization. Recently, the BJP government appointed a Committee for Disinvestment, followed by a special ministry to look after the necessarily contentious process of dismantling government enterprises. And even leftist governments such as the Communists in West Bengal have admitted that loss-making state industries will have to be closed. As finances of the state governments are near collapse, the central authorities can use that to force through liberalization.

In these ways, the emergence of the BJP and its stable control of the central government, represents a further stage in the slow redefinition of India's national interest. In the era of Nehru and with Congress under his influence, the post-independence political elite thought of foreign policy as primarily an instrument of protecting sovereignty and securing economic development. India's influence in the world was expected to come from the persuasiveness of its suggestions and the moral validity of its position on issues such as arms control, apartheid, imperialism and so forth. Already, in Indira Gandhi's times, given the increasingly populist character of Indian politics based on the slow activation of the common people, this had changed significantly towards a clearer orientation towards power; and Indian policies plainly sought regional hegemony.

The BJP's orientation towards the international society has continued and intensified those tendencies: the reinvention of identities and values within Indian politics has parallels in the way that the BJP envisages India's role in international politics, especially in relation to its immediate neighbours. For example, the BJP dramatized its acquisition of new nuclear weapons. Given its ideology, it naturally emphasizes the idea of sovereignty, but interprets it utterly differently. The BJP's understanding of sovereignty implies a more assertive stance based on increased military power and, more dangerously, an internal connection of sovereignty with an exclusivist Hindu definition of Indian nationalism. Thus, the power of this redefined 'Hindu' nation is used to threaten internal minorities, such as Muslims. Some of the BJP government's foreign policy initiatives are likely to strengthen the drive towards economic liberalization. Its attempts to improve political relations with the United States, for instance, are likely to accelerate liberalization subtly. If foreign investment into India's economy is to be radically increased, its first condition is greater liberalization of economic controls. Yet the strand of swadeshi should not be dismissed entirely. Although the supporters of economic swadeshi are not in dominant positions, they are likely to remain a major part of the Hindu nationalist politics. Advancing liberalization is bound to exacerbate internal conflict within the BJP on this question.

7　Conclusion

It appears then that the logic of liberalization has taken on a life of its own. Irrespective of which political party comes to office and what they say rhetorically, their economic administrations are constrained to enact legislation, which carries forward the next step of the 'logic' of liberalizing reforms. That, after all, is the central objective of the liberalizing policies – to emancipate the economy from the direct control of the state and the uncertainties of electoral politics, and to render this entire process irreversible. It appears that in India, despite large and unpredictable complexities in this process, the state has gone some way in freeing the economy from itself. At the same time, there has been a marked reshaping of Indian politics, away from the elite-dominated secular, non-aligned nationalism of Nehru, towards a communally based activation of the common people into political life and the emergence of religious and communal definitions of the nation and its interests.

Neither process – economic liberalization or the reshaping of Indian politics – has been the cause of the other, though I have argued that they are related in complex ways. Rather, both represent a profound change in the pattern of Indian political economy established under Nehru, both are in many respects the product of the internal dynamics of the political economy of post-independence'India, and both have significant implications for how India defines its interests and constructs its self-identity in the wider world. It is not necessary to contest the view that the international context within which Indian policy has been formulated has played a role in the developments traced. Yet we have seen that there are important ways in which the definition of the national interest has been shaped by 'particular interpretations and combinations of security, welfare and sovereignty preferred by powerful domestic groups enfranchised by representative institutions and practices', and that these interpretations can and do sometimes change primarily as a result of the internal dynamics within a society (Moravcsik, 1997, pp.519–20).

There are perhaps three main analytical points to emphasize in the preceding study of Indian politics. First, I have argued that in order to analyse the formation of India's national interest we need to look at the collective values and identities found in Indian society, formulated and expressed in its political discourses, and see how these served to shape the articulation of interests. Second, I have argued that the interests of different groups, especially well organized and powerful groups, need to be identified and we need to consider how these change over time in relation to an evolving national and international context. Third, I have suggested that different forms of the representation of interests within the Indian political system can have significant effects, as with the change from the elite dominated politics of Nehru's era to the more popular, communal appeals of subsequent political leaders faced with the wider activation of the common people in India's political life. Each of these – collective values embodied in political discourses, organized interest groups, and the forms of representation – served to shape India's national interest in a given international context.

Further reading

Khilnani (1997) explores the history of independent India as 'the history of a state' and as 'the adventure of a political idea: democracy', asking whether 'a culture and its members can sustain their distinctive character once they entrust their destiny (as they must) to a modern state'. The full reference is Khilnani, S. (1997) *The Idea of India*, London, Penguin.

For a political economy of independent India that explores the changing social and economic context of Indian politics, the transformations of state policy, the rise of Hindu nationalism and the challenges that this poses to India's secularism and democracy, see Corbridge, S. and Harriss, J. (2000) *Reinventing India: Liberalization, Hindu Nationalism and Popular Democracy*, Cambridge, Polity Press.

A series of essays chronicling, analysing and criticising the assertion of Hindu nationalism in contemporary Indian politics can be found in Desai, R. (2002) *Slouching Towards Ayodhya*, New Delhi, Three Essays Press.

Chapter 7 Trade policy, industrialization and growth in India

Suma Athreye

1   Introduction

In Chapter 6 Sudipta Kaviraj examines the politics of economic liberalization in India, drawing out from a complex narrative a general political analysis of the ways in which states define and redefine the national interest. This chapter picks up a theme from that narrative – the relationship between industrialization, economic growth and liberalization – and examines it more closely. In the process I too draw some general lessons, this time about the roots of economic growth in industrialization and technological change.

Ask a politician in any developing country what they wish for in their economic policies and without doubt each would ask for policies for economic growth and development. A nation's political clout in the international economy often depends upon how it is doing economically. We can see a nation's economic strength by how fast its economy is growing, and you saw in Part 1 how developed economies have more power than developing countries in multilateral institutions and negotiations.

I argue in this chapter that economic growth depends upon the twin forces of increased investment and technological change, both of which contribute in different ways to enhancing the productive capacity of the economy. In turn, these forces depend upon the 'openness' of the economy to international trade and investment (remember that 'openness' was defined in Chapter 3). Unfairly perhaps, one needs the international economy to grow, and growth makes a nation much more powerful internationally, as you saw in the discussion of the World Trade Organization (WTO) and the General Agreement on Tariffs and Trade (GATT).

Consequently, it may seem something of a paradox that many developing countries chose in the mid twentieth century to shut themselves away from international trade and markets in order to create a broad based growth in their economy. The first country successfully to do this was the former Soviet Union, whose rapid growth to superpower status in a relatively short time span showed that international markets were not essential for rapid growth. Yet in three decades after it became a superpower, the Soviet Union too appeared to realize the advantages of open markets and the pains of isolation. Its *perestroika* led the way for Soviet integration in the world economy.

The core of this chapter is a narrative of the economic rationale for changing industrial policy in India. It begins from the special appeal of Soviet style development for nations like India who emerged battered from their colonial history but with a fierce desire to catch up with old colonial rulers and to join the ranks of the other industrial powers. In striving for economic growth in the 1950s and 1960s, Indian policy makers relied less on the market and foreign trade and more on planning and public sector investment to meet a large domestic demand. For this strategy, Indian policy makers drew upon the minds and ideas of some of the great economic thinkers of that period. By 1980, many of these dreams had turned to dust. The five-year plans, which had laid the basis of economic growth through planning, consistently failed to meet their targets for growth. Public and private investment became mired in corruption. Industrial growth had stagnated in the mid 1970s and Indian manufacturing was relatively high cost.

Through the late 1970s and early 1980s there was extensive and critical debate about what ailed Indian planning and industrialization, and why it had failed to deliver, particularly on industrial development. The finger of blame began to be pointed at India's policies of planned industrialization. There was a gradual reversal of some of these policies, which culminated in the major policy reversal represented by the New Industrial Policy of 1991.

These days the images that India evokes are no longer stagnation and decline. India has come to occupy the world stage as both a mature and large democracy and a resilient and growing economy. Since the mid 1980s, both the national income, as measured by the real gross domestic product or GDP (explained in Section 2), and the GDP per capita have grown much faster than before (see Table 7.1). Moreover, the attention of the world has been grabbed by the phenomenal success of the Indian software industry and the transformation of the sleepy town of Bangalore in South India into the most popular destination for multinational firms.

Table 7.1 Annual growth rates of the Indian economy (per cent)

	1950–80	1980–90	1990–2000
Real gross domestic product	3.7	5.9	6.2
Real per capita product	1.5	3.8	4.4

Source: DeLong, 2001, p.4

What accounts for the acceleration in growth shown in Table 7.1? Many economists would say it is the liberalization policies adopted by successive Indian governments from 1991. Indeed, the popular perception is that the software industry is the success story of India's liberalization. But is this really true? Some researchers have disagreed, saying that software's success was a vindication of the earlier strategy of import substituting industrialization. After all, could India have changed its comparative advantage and created a world-class software industry had it specialized in tea and jute, its main export commodities in the 1950s?

To analyse these questions about Indian industrialization, I shall employ some tools for the economic analysis of industrial growth. These allow us to sort out the main economic influences upon industrial growth in any economy. Of necessity, this will involve a consideration of some related analytical questions. Why the emphasis on industrialization? What exactly is import substituting industrialization?

A second theme in this chapter was signalled above: how does economic growth affect global integration, and how is it affected by it? Relations with the rest of the world impinge on the growth process in several ways: through the influence of export markets for various commodities; through the import of raw material and other goods that could potentially create a bottleneck for domestic production; by making better technology available in the form of imported capital goods and technology; and, lastly, by making foreign resources available for investment in the domestic economy.

Once again, the Indian experience of growth illustrates this second theme well. India attempted to grow in a self-sufficient way with a minimum involvement in international trade, guided by a notion of self-reliance. Recurrent balance of payment crises and technological obsolescence forced a rethink of this policy. Present-day policies of liberalization are in many ways a complete reversal of earlier policies, an affirmation (however grudging) of India's dependence and desire to integrate with the international world.

The remainder of this chapter is organized as follows. Section 2 begins with a consideration of the analytical toolkit needed to study influences on economic growth. Section 3 outlines the central role of investment, the perceived need for public investment, and the roles accorded to private investment (domestic and foreign) in the policy of planned industrial growth. The section also considers some of the original critiques of India's planned industrialization strategy (often by prominent Indian academics) and the rebuttal of these critiques with arguments surrounding import substitution and dynamic comparative advantage that were important considerations in the adoption of the Second Five-Year Plan.

Section 4 reviews the growth performance of India since independence and contrasts it briefly with the performance of other countries in the same period. Section 5 describes the changes to industrial policy in the 1980s, the rationale for the changes that were introduced, and in particular the greater openness to trade and foreign investment. Section 6 turns to a discussion of the economic rationale for the liberalization of the mid 1980s, which centred upon the rate of growth of productivity. This is contrasted in Section 7 with the International Monetary Fund (IMF) rationale advanced for the full liberalization of the 1990s.

Finally, Section 8 discusses the growth of the Indian software industry, addressing the question raised at the beginning of the chapter: could the software industry have grown without the import substituting policies of an earlier generation? I argue it probably could not have done so. At the same time, the limited impact of the software industry's growth on the overall economic growth of the country is also an illustration of some of the failures of the earlier industrial policy regime in achieving broad based growth. Poverty and inequality continue to pervade the Indian economy even though there are islands of success.

2   The industrial roots of economic growth

2.1   Measuring economic growth

What is economic growth? While development is a broad term that includes improvements in well-being and societal welfare, economic growth is defined more narrowly. It is the rise in the *material* well-being of people in an economy, frequently measured by the change in the economy's production or national income. The gross domestic product (GDP), which is the aggregate value of all goods and services that are produced in an economy, is the most commonly used measure of an economy's production, and changes in GDP are a measure of economic growth.

Another frequently used measure of economic growth is the change in per capita income (income per head) or per capita GDP. The latter is simply the GDP divided by the total population of the economy. It indicates the amount of an economy's production that would be available for each individual if it were distributed equally. We know this does not happen in practice, so per capita GDP does not measure what each individual actually receives. Still, the level of per capita GDP is often used to rank countries as more or less developed, especially by multilateral organizations such as the World Bank, IMF or the United Nations (UN).

All measures of growth and development are problematic because they try to reduce to one number what is essentially a process of qualitative change. Instead of enumerating the many problems of these two measures, however, let me first try to give you some reasons why they might be appropriate, although crude, measures of material well-being and economic growth.

2.2 Understanding growth rates

Conceive of an economy that produces only one good, call it X, using two factors of production: capital (K) and labour (L). All income in the economy is derived from people who either produce X or work for people who produce X. People in this economy can use their incomes, derived from the purchase of X, for importing other commodities such as Y and Z through trade. In this economy a prudent Ministry of Economic Affairs believes in measuring annually the changes in the production of X, and providing its government and the world with evidence of how well the economy is faring. National income is measured by the production of X, and economic growth would be measured by the rate of increase in the production of X.

How can we measure the rate of growth of the production of X? Suppose that in 1999 the economy produced 100 units of X; in 2000 it produced 150 units of X; and in 2001 it produced 120 units of X. In year 2000, the economy added (grew) 50 units of production in addition to the 100 they produced the previous year. To calculate the percentage change, divide the change by the original level and multiply by 100. (Note: I shall use a full stop to represent 'multiplied by'.) Thus, as a percentage of production in 1999 the economy grew in 2000 by:

$$\left(\frac{50}{100}\right) . 100 = 50\%$$

Question

What would the growth rate be in 2001?

In 2001, however, the economy contracted by 30 units relative to year 2000. So, relative to 2000 it grew by:

$$\left(\frac{-30}{150}\right) . 100 = -20\%$$

However, notice that relative to production in 1999, the economy grew over two years by:

$$\left(\frac{20}{100}\right) . 100 = 20\%$$

We can generalize from those calculations to write a formula for the rate of growth (g). If X_t is the production of X in period t and X_{t+1} is the production of X in the next period, $t + 1$, then the rate of growth is:

$$g = \left(\frac{X_{t+1} - X_t}{X_t} \right) . 100$$

Activity 7.1

The following table gives data for 1995 to 1999 for the same hypothetical economy. Calculate the rate of growth of production for each year relative to the previous year and fill in the third column of the table.

Year	Production (in units)	Year on year rate of growth (%)
1995	120	
1996	90	
1997	110	
1998	160	
1999	100	

The Ministry of Economic Affairs may be concerned not only with the increases in production, but also with whether production is sufficient to meet the consumption needs of the entire population. It would then look at the production of X divided by the total population of the economy (N): the ratio $\frac{X}{N}$. This is the per capita income. If this ratio were high, they would be confident that there was enough income around for everyone provided they could achieve a reasonably equal distribution of the income.

2.3 Allowing for inflation

Would the two measures outlined so far be less useful if we considered a real economy where many types of goods are produced? A little reflection should tell you that they can still be used. However, with many goods, there is an additional problem. To add many goods together, we would need to use their prices. We would sum the quantity of each of the different kinds of goods produced multiplied by its price. Such a measure is the total of the nominal or money value of the many goods produced and is called nominal GDP or GDP at current prices. The information this measure gives is not very different from the simpler measure constructed earlier. Increases in the value of this measure would indicate rising levels of production and income in the whole economy.

Nominal GDP
Nominal GDP is the money value of the final goods and services produced in an economy.

Question

When would that last statement be incorrect?

Increases in the value of GDP at current prices will not indicate rising levels of income if they result only from rising prices of the different goods. Nominal or money values can rise because of changes in prices or changes in quantities. What the Ministry of Economic Affairs would like is to have an increase due to a rise in quantities alone. Put differently, the measure we are interested in is a measure of real GDP and also real per capita GDP. That is, we want to adjust the measure of GDP for changes in prices, so that what remains is a measure of increases or decreases in the quantities of the different goods produced.

Real GDP
Real GDP is the nominal GDP adjusted for changes in the prices of goods. GDP at constant prices is one measure of real GDP.

One way to produce such a measure of real changes in production is to use prices from an earlier period when calculating our money value of goods produced in a later period. Let us denote the earlier prices by P_0 where 0 indicates the price of a commodity in, say, 1990. We would measure GDP in 2000 by multiplying the quantities produced of X, Y and Z by their prices in 1990 (P_0). In this way, we have a measure of GDP that we can compare between 1990 and 2000, where the total increase in GDP is on account of changes in quantities produced. This measure is called GDP at *constant prices*.

2.4 The value-added approach to GDP measurement

Finally, there is another problem in measuring GDP. Since in modern economies most commodities are produced using other commodities, a simple addition of the quantities produced of X, Y and Z may be misleading. In so far as the production of X involves the use of Z, simply adding the quantities produced of X and Z counts twice at least some of the Z produced in the economy.

Question

How does adding the values of X and Z 'double count' the value of Z?

This is because in adding the value of X and Z produced in the economy we are including the value of Z twice. First in the output of Z and then because the value of X also contains the value of Z, which is an input in X.

To overcome this problem, GDP is measured by adding together the *value-added* in each sector. The value-added in the production of X is the money value of X produced (price times quantity), less the money value of the inputs used. The value added in the production of X is thus a measure of the contribution of capital and labour to the production of X, but excludes the contribution of Z to the production of X.

2.5   Questioning GDP

There is much controversy about the GDP measure itself and we can think of this as arising from the following main sources of disagreement.

1   Which goods and services should be included?

2   How many goods and services can be measured accurately in terms of value?

3   Which prices should be used to value these various goods and services: in particular, should we use world prices?

The second point is particularly controversial. For example, household chores that are often carried out by women are rarely included in standard GDP measures. Having someone who does these chores certainly allows others in the household to do more paid work, and prevents women who undertake these chores from doing more work elsewhere. Therefore, all our measures of growth are affected by this non-inclusion.

Does this list mean the measure is flawed? We can never have a perfect measure of something as broad or multidimensional as economic growth. The reason for wanting to measure production in an economy is to gain a sense of the material well-being of the people in the economy. For this limited purpose, per capita GDP at constant prices is a reasonably good measure, and was used in this way in Table 7.1.

2.6   Determinants of industrial growth

The Ministry of Economic Affairs will not only want to measure economic growth, but also to devise means of expanding economic growth. What strategies might it adopt to achieve this? Inevitably, it must turn its mind to industrial change, that is, to expanding the output of particular goods and services. The rest of this section sets out a simplified economic model of how goods are produced, using capital and labour. I shall build upon this model a number of times throughout the chapter to explain the sources of industrial change and the way the Indian planners thought about encouraging growth. The key ideas that the model helps us to get straight are outlined below. Look back at these points at the end of the section and check that they are all clear.

First, goods can be produced using many different *techniques*, and we can think of those techniques as requiring different mixes of capital and labour. Second, industrial growth can occur by doing 'more of the same' or by switching techniques; both require investment, that is, the accumulation of capital. And third, a key determinant of industrial growth is labour productivity: the output per head achieved in production. You will not learn about productivity in this section, but I shall return to the determinants of productivity in Section 6.

We shall continue for the moment to think about production in terms of a single good, and denote it by X. This good can be produced using two main inputs, capital (denoted by K) and labour (denoted by L). By capital I mean things such as the machinery that can be used and the tools that are used by workers to produce any good. The firm may be able to choose between one or more techniques of producing X.

Let us consider a hypothetical example: an Indian economy that produces only one good: textiles. Indian producers can produce their textiles using a variety of techniques. Textiles can be produced using many weavers weaving with their hands and with spinners spinning thread. Here, the only capital equipment they need is looms for the weavers and spinning wheels for the spinners of yarn. Think about the spinning machines and power looms as the capital input (K) and the weavers, spinners and supervisors of the machinery as the labour input (L). Using this technique (let us label it technique A), producers know that they can obtain 60, 120 or 180 bales of fabric with the combinations of capital and labour shown in Table 7.2(a).

Table 7.2(a)   Technique A of textile production in India

Technique	Capital input (K) in units	Labour input (L) in numbers of people	Output level (X) in bales
A	4	9	60
A	8	18	120
A	12	27	180

Alternatively, producers of textiles in India could choose from two other techniques, B and C. Spinning machines and power looms can be used with a few supervisors rather than weaver artisans (technique C). Or producers may decide that they will use spinning machines to keep the even quality of their yarn but use weavers on hand-operated looms because this gives them a wider range of textile textures and designs. This is technique B. Again they know the capital and labour inputs required for producing 60, 120 and 180 bales of textiles for each technique. Table 7.2(b) summarizes the three production techniques available to the producers of textiles in India.

Table 7.2(b)   All known techniques of textile production

Technique	Description	Capital input (K) in units	Labour input (L) in numbers of people	Output level (X) in bales
A	Spinning by hand and weaving by hand	4	9	60
		8	18	120
		12	27	180
B	Spinning by machines, but weaving by hand	6	6	60
		12	12	120
		18	18	180
C	Spinning and weaving by machines	18	2	60
		36	4	120
		54	6	180

The information given in Table 7.2(b) relates inputs to outputs and can be depicted graphically. However, if we wanted to plot the information in this table graphically we would need three axes, corresponding to each of the variables X, K and L. You would need to imagine a surface. This is of course very difficult and so we try to reduce the complexity by creating an image of only two axes at a time. We can do this if we assume one variable is fixed at some level and indicate the value of that level. Those of you who climb or sail will be familiar with this simplification. This is how contour maps are prepared. A contour map links up all the points at a particular height, and the height is indicated by a little number on the map. Or, in the case of sea charts, regions of equal depth are linked together on a two-dimensional map.

We can use the same trick. Thus we could plot L against K (for different levels of X) as shown in Figure 7.1. In words, this is equivalent to stating what level of capital and labour inputs are required to produce a given level of output, using each of the three techniques. So Figure 7.1 shows the quantities of capital and labour needed to produce 60 bales of textiles. From Table 7.2(b), we know that to produce 60 bales of cotton we would need 4 units of capital and 9 units of labour (if we used technique A), or 6 units each of capital and

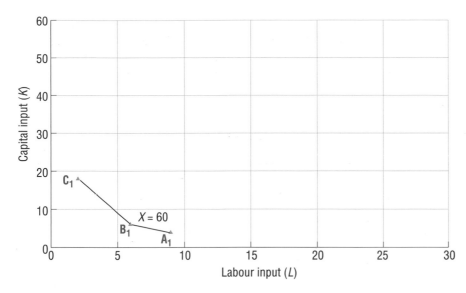

Figure 7.1 Isoquant showing techniques for producing 60 units of textiles

labour (using technique B), or 18 units of capital and 2 units of labour (using technique C). These correspond to the points A_1, B_1 and C_1 on Figure 7.1. We label the line joining these points as $X = 60$ and call it an isoquant, which means 'same quantities'.

Activity 7.2

To ensure that you understand the idea of an isoquant, draw in two more.

Use the information in Table 7.2(b) to draw the following isoquants onto a diagram like Figure 7.1.

1   $X = 120$

2   $X = 180$

Isoquant
Isoquants show the different minimum combinations of inputs that can be used to produce the same level of output.

Once you have attempted Activity 7.2, and drawn the isoquants for $X = 120$ and $X = 180$, turn over the page. Figure 7.2 shows how adding your 'mapping' of the isoquants from Figure 7.6 to Figure 7.1 should look. For each level of production ($X = 60$, 120 or 180) there are three points which correspond to the three different techniques of production, A, B and C. Economists refer to such a representation as the *production function* as it shows the different ways in which each level of output can be produced using different combinations and amounts of capital and labour. Each

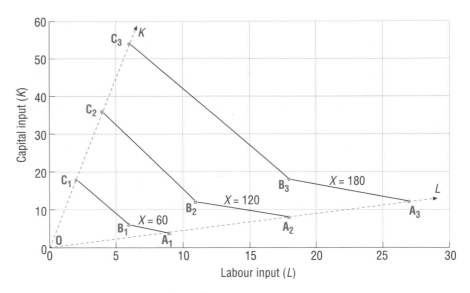

Figure 7.2 Production function for textiles

Technique
A technique is defined as a method of production that uses a specified ratio of capital to labour.

technique is unique because it requires a different combination of capital and labour input to produce the same level of output.

Figure 7.2 is useful because it allows us to see the impact on output growth of varying both capital and labour using the techniques available. The first thing you should note from Figure 7.2 is that no matter which technique one uses, greater production is possible only with a larger capital and labour input. This is the case whether we chose technique A, B or C. From Table 7.2(b) you can see that to produce 120 bales of textiles instead of 60 using technique C would require an additional 18 units of capital. Technique B would require an additional 6 units of capital, while technique A requires the least additional capital, needing only 4 units more to increase production from 60 to 120 bales of textiles.

In other words, the amount of additional capital needed for the growth of textile production depends on the technique of production employed.

Activity 7.3

Stop here and check your understanding by making a similar argument for labour. Using Table 7.2(b) and Figure 7.2, show that the number of extra workers needed to increase production from 120 to 180 bales of textiles depends on the technique of production chosen.

Look again at Figure 7.2. I have also drawn on it dotted lines, or rays, from the origin, joining up each level of output using technique A. This is ray OL. Another ray, OK, joins up all the levels of output using technique C. Moving outwards along OL is in fact what we would do if we were increasing production using only technique A. Similarly, when we move along ray OK, we move from point C_1 to C_2 to C_3, expanding output using technique C alone.

Which techniques would producers actually choose? This depends upon the cost to firms of capital and labour, that is, upon the relative rates of interest and wages. To invest in machinery, firms must borrow funds. If interest rates were low and wage rates relatively high, producers would find it easy to borrow money for capital investment and expensive to employ more people. Producers may then prefer a technique like C that uses more machines relative to workers. In contrast, in many developing countries it is wage rates that are quite low while borrowing can be expensive, and so producers may prefer to choose a technique like A, which uses more labour relative to machines. Economists call a technique like A, using relatively more labour, a labour intensive technique. Conversely, C is a capital intensive technique.

Irrespective of which technique the producers choose, the key strategy implied by this model for increasing output (and hence economic growth) is increasing the capital stock through increased investment. The production of any good depends on labour and the machinery in use. Therefore, if there are more machines available, more labour can be employed in production, and more output can be produced. In other words, the key to increasing production is to install more spinning and weaving machines, through investment by firms, and hence employ more labour. The stock of machines (capital) in an economy increases as more machines are added and as the worn-out machines are replaced. These two processes of replacement and new investment are the main components of what we call 'real investment'.

Early theories of economic growth were built on this economic model. Economic theorists believed that capital accumulation, through increasing investment, was the most important way of increasing the growth of incomes and of output per head. This meant adding more capital and employing more labour to achieve higher levels of output, indicated on Figure 7.2 by moving along one of the rays from the origin, such as OL or OK. The key policy imperative in this view of what determines industrial and hence economic growth was to mobilize enough resources to undertake large private sector and public sector investments. Indian policy between 1950 and 1975 broadly subscribed to this view of what determined growth.

Labour intensive technique
Technique A is more labour intensive than technique B if technique A has a *lower* capital to labour ratio than technique B.

Capital intensive technique
Technique C is more capital intensive than technique B if technique C has a *higher* capital to labour ratio than technique B.

3   Planned industrialization and growth: Indian industrial policy between 1950 and 1980

Accepting the view of growth that focused on mobilizing resources for capital investment meant that an increase in the rate of investment in the economy had to be achieved in order to put more capital in the hands of employable workers. The important questions that remained were:

1   Who would undertake the investments?

2   In which sectors would this investment be concentrated?

3   How should the economy use the external sector, that is, how should it trade?

The answers to these questions would dictate the course of industrial policy in India. Let us examine each in turn.

3.1   Investment and the role of the state

Private Indian firms, the public sector, or foreign (multinational) firms could each have undertaken investment in the economy. India had a fledgling private sector at independence. As was mentioned in Chapter 6, leading Indian industrialists of the time met at Bombay in 1944, just after independence, where they drew up the Bombay Plan. This presented the government of India with a list of industries in which public sector investment was deemed desirable. Many of these industrial sectors later appeared in Schedule B of the Second Five-Year Plan, which listed sectors in which investment was reserved for the public sector. These included industrial sectors requiring heavy investment, where the capital outlays were prohibitively high for the private sector (such as iron and steel, petrochemicals and heavy machinery production), as well as infrastructure sectors where the gestation period before the investment produced profits was considered far too long for the private sector. It was recognized, however, that both these types of investment were crucial for the growth of the industrial economy and of the private sector itself.

Foreign firms were distrusted because of colonial experiences. Many leading Indian business houses saw established British firms as their closest rivals and were hostile to them. Policy makers recognized that the economy could gain from multinational firms' presence, as they were important sources of technological know-how. Nevertheless, the policy makers wished to keep out the foreign investment that simply sought to extract profits from technology currently in use, and to encourage only the efficiency-seeking new investment which would come with new technology. This position gradually

Table 7.3   Countries of origin of the total stock of foreign investment in India, selected years (percentage of total)

Country	1960	1971	1980	1987
UK	76.6	64.5	53.9	51.7
USA	14.5	18.4	21.1	12.9
Germany	1.1	3.1	7.0	16.7
Japan	0.2	0.4	0.4	3.7
Switzerland	2.4	5.0	5.9	3.7
Others	5.2	8.6	11.7	11.3

Source: Athreye and Kapur, 2001, Table 4, p.406

hardened as the new technology-imbued investment from the USA failed to arrive in the quantities hoped for. Indeed, as Table 7.3 shows, a very large part of foreign investment in India in the 1960s and 1970s remained in British hands.

This left the public sector as the other main agent for undertaking investment. In order to execute this investment the public sector needed control over the resources required: foreign exchange and the availability of crucial inputs. Foreign exchange, in the form of dollars or other hard currency, was earned by exports and was needed to import equipment not produced in India. The public sector gained control over resources through a battery of instruments of direct regulation: through the industrial licensing of production capacity, issuing of import licences and the nationalization of financial institutions to gain control over investment finance.

Of these, the use of licensing to regulate the quantity and composition of private investment and imports was peculiar to India and to this period of its industrialization. Indeed, many policy commentators refer to the whole period of the 1960s and 1970s as the 'licence raj'. Under licensing, every private producer had to ask for permission from the state to set up a new plant of stated capacity or to expand an old plant. Import licences did the same with imports. Once these applications were made, the bureaucracy would consider each application for production licence on the basis of plan priorities in investment and the production needs of the public sector. Similarly, import licences were subject to an overall quota based on domestic availability, foreign exchange reserves and the production needs of the importer. In truth, the resource needs of public sector investment would never have been met without such a system of control.

Industrial investment was thus to be done in a mixed economy, public/ private way. This approach met relatively little resistance. Most academic economists of that time accepted a role for the state and did not believe that the structural problems of development could be overcome by the free play of market forces. This belief continued even in the 1970s, when there had been considerable disenchantment with planning and regulation. The following quotation from a book examining what India's development policy meant for America, makes this point:

> For the American who is trying to decide what is the appropriate posture of his government toward the cause of Indian economic development, however, the really relevant point is simply that the Indians, in any event, are already deeply committed – one may safely say, irrevocably committed – to a central economic role for their government during their period of initial accelerated expansion. There would be no chance whatsoever of talking them or bargaining them out of this general position, even if one thought it were appropriate to try ... Outside supporters of the Indian development process who refuse to accept this proposition well-nigh disqualify themselves from the outset.

(Lewis, 1962, p.28)

This is surprising to us today, when market-friendly policies are prescribed in the same breath for very poor sub-Saharan countries and for large diverse Asian countries like India and China. Yet, in the mid 1950s when these issues were being debated, there was a near consensus on the need for a major role for the state in development. The area of the big debates and critiques was different. It focused on the Indian planners' decisions about where to invest and how to use the external trade sector for growth.

3.2 Industrialization strategies

The first important decision for the Indian planners was whether to invest in agriculture or in industry. Why industrialization? Perhaps this was to emulate the colonial powers that had ruled India. It was also part of a quest for self-reliance in production. Yet, even among economists in developed economies, industrialization was widely regarded as urgent and important if economies were to grow rapidly. The reasoning behind this view depended principally on the expectation of diminishing returns to agricultural growth.

What this means, briefly, is that it was thought that the inability to increase the total land available meant that ultimately the additional output to be gained from additional investment in agriculture would decline to low levels. Before the emergence of modern industries, which use means of production, such as machinery, that are themselves industrial products, economies were largely agricultural. The productivity of labour – that is the output per person working the land – was largely determined by the quality of land and irrigation. Furthermore, other uncontrollable factors, for instance, rainfall, determined agricultural output. Low and variable productivity translated into low and variable incomes.

In contrast, the industrial sector had a level of productivity, measured as output per worker, that was both higher than in agriculture and also more controllable. As the industrial sector began to create a larger and larger share of the national output, average productivity in the entire economy grew. And unlike land, the total amount of machinery in the economy could be increased through more investment. This analysis formed, at the time, the main economic argument in favour of industrialization as a strategy for economic growth. Indeed, as the economist Kuznets (1966) showed in his Nobel Prize winning work, all countries that had rising rates of economic growth after 1945 also saw a fall in the share of agriculture in their national incomes.

As awareness of environmental degradation due to industrialization grows in the West, some have argued that industrialization constitutes a wrong notion of development. Interestingly, in India even at independence there was a small group of Gandhians who resisted modern industrialization as the basis of modern growth. Followers of Gandhi argued for small, self-sufficient village communities as the basis for generating economic growth. They were overruled both then and now, but they have been part of recurrent critiques of India's strategy of industrialization.

A focus on industrialization should not of course mean a neglect of agricultural production, for it is also important to feed the growing cities and workers in the new industries. The principal policies adopted for the agricultural sector were no taxation of farming incomes, land redistribution and land reforms. Despite a pre-independence history of famines on account of failed monsoon rains, the amounts earmarked for expanding irrigation were small.

Even in the industrial sector, there were two different sorts of investment strategies that the government could have chosen. The first was a Soviet style strategy of increasing investment in industrial sectors that produced capital goods (machinery). These capital goods would, in the longer term, enhance the economy's capacity for generating self-sustaining growth. The key to self-sufficiency and self-reliance according to this view lay in being able to manufacture all the capital goods required for an emerging, broad based industrialization process.

This Soviet-style industrialization strategy constituted an unbalanced investment strategy since in the initial years at least, high and sustained investment in capital goods sectors would have had to take place at the expense of investment elsewhere. However, over time the potential for growth through this strategy was thought to be very high, as the example of the Soviet Union and Germany before it had shown the world. This was because sustained investment in capital goods producing sectors would eventually produce the necessary inputs to production in the consumer goods producing sectors, creating linkages that would make for a broad and self-sufficient industrial economy.

In any economy, the rate of investment, that is, the proportion of the country's output that is invested rather than consumed, is constrained by the rate of saving. The more a country wants to invest at any time, the less can be consumed and so the more must be saved. (Part 4 examines these macroeconomic relationships more closely.) In a country as poor as India, there were limits on savings possibilities. Thus, if the public sector was to invest in the core sectors in this way, the private sector's investment had to be constrained. In India this was achieved through the complicated system of industrial licensing described above, to control investments in new areas and the expansion of private investment.

Moreover, to pursue this strategy of promoting deep linkages within the economy between the new capital goods industries and the consumer goods producing sectors, the nascent capital goods industry in India would have to be protected from foreign competition. India imposed tariffs and restricted imports of capital goods. Many producers preferred to make do with what was domestically available and this stimulated domestic production of these goods. Consequently, the policy makers thought that this would nurture domestic industry, which would in time 'grow up' and become competitive enough to face foreign competition (Chapter 3, Section 7.1 describes this as the 'infant industry' justification for tariffs). In other words, India pursued an import substitution strategy of development, using tariffs to encourage and protect domestic industrial development.

Import substitution strategy
An import substitution strategy for development uses tariffs to protect the growth of domestic industry.

Initially, India sought to protect its consumer goods industries while importing the machinery it hoped later to produce in India. At independence, India had large foreign exchange reserves. It was thought that these could finance the initial heavy imports of capital goods that the import substitution strategy required. Further demands for imports would, planners thought, die out as domestic industry grew more broadly, replacing imports with domestic production. During later stages, capital goods sectors received greater protection.

There is, however, a second strategy towards industrialization that could have been chosen by the Indian planners. This would have put less emphasis on early investment in capital goods industries, some of which are capital intensive such as textile machinery, and hence generate little additional employment. Instead, it would have been possible to grow in a more balanced way, through both labour and capital accumulation, using a variety of industries already established. For instance, textiles had grown even before independence. The textiles and clothing industries would have generated more employment and the investment required would have been lower. (Go back to Activity 7.3 if you do not understand this.) Such a strategy would have encouraged the growth of more labour intensive industries. The technology required for the growth of these sectors could be imported, and paid for through reliance on the export earnings of the agricultural sector. A strategy of this type was in fact proposed by two Bombay economists Vakil and Brahmanand. What the strategy did have in its favour, and we can see this more clearly with the benefit of hindsight, was that it would have addressed the problem of employment and agricultural poverty more effectively. Further, the alternative approach involved a fundamentally different treatment of the external sector than was implied in the first strategy, as I shall go on to explain.

3.3 Protection and import substitution

That India did not go in for an export-oriented, open economy strategy for growth might come as a surprise to you, having read about the gains from trade in Part 1. This policy issue was the subject of fierce dissent and debate amongst Indian economists, and was discussed extensively in the pages of the widely read Indian journal, *The Economic Weekly* (now *The Economic and Political Weekly*), before the formulation of the Second Five-Year Plan.

An important reason for the choice of an import substituting strategy, as described above, was that there was considerable 'export pessimism'. India's main comparative advantage, at independence, lay in the export of primary products, notably tea and jute. These markets were perceived to have *inelastic* demand. This means that demand in the market does not rise greatly as price falls. You have already seen this problem facing low income exporters in Chapter 3, Section 6.2. As the supply of goods rises in a market with inelastic demand, price falls but demand does not rise enough to compensate. Thus, exporters find themselves producing more but seeing export earnings stagnate. Fearing this trap, Indian planners aimed to change Indian comparative advantage from primary products to manufactures – and thus to change what many regarded as a colonial pattern of exports. Colonial history too had played its part in this choice; remember that India was renowned as the land of the finest woven muslin, and it was only under colonialism that it became an exporter of raw cotton, jute and tea. It had taken decades of discriminatory British tariffs against Indian manufactures for the Lancashire cotton industry to take root and grow. Furthermore, trade in India was a small proportion of national income. This meant that the domestic market was always likely to be more important for domestic producers than the foreign market. For all these reasons, it made sense after independence to protect the domestic market for domestic producers by imposing high tariffs on foreign manufactures in order for domestic manufacturers to grow their own industries.

Notice that the choice of the tariff policy route to industrialization was also a sort of 'second best' policy for industrial growth. Any country wanting to industrialize based on a private sector needs to have many complementary institutions that will weed out the better entrepreneurs from the worse ones, for example, venture capital and lenders who evaluate risky proposals. These institutions give private finance to worthy projects while rejecting the poorer ones (this is the function of stock markets) and offer a well-developed system of commercial and property laws. To provide these institutions would have been the best policy for industrialization. At independence, India had very few of these institutional supports for private sector investment and it was recognized that it would be some time before they could be put in place. In the meantime, tariff protection acted as a second best policy to nurture private enterprise development through domestic competition alone.

Critics of this strategy pointed out that this choice had tremendous costs. The strongest criticism was by Jagdish Bhagwati, a prominent Indian economist with an international reputation in the field of international trade. Bhagwati and Desai (1970) argued that India was not paying enough attention to export growth and to utilizing the export sector for generating the imports required for investment. More importantly, they argued that import substitution constituted an implicit tax on sectors that could generate exports but that did not have the benefit of tariff protection. What was happening was that the protected industries could raise prices (as is explained in Chapter 3) because of the tariff shelter from external competition. Firms that tried to export, however, had no subsidies, so had to compete with world market prices. Worse, they might have to buy inputs from protected firms at prices above world prices, making them uncompetitive on world markets. These price distortions in the economy, Bhagwati and other critics argued, would ultimately hurt competitiveness and growth. The price distortions due to the tariffs meant that industries producing for the home market would appear more profitable for investment than exporting industries when, in fact, on a global scale they were the sectors where the economy was less efficient. Perhaps most of all, the industrial regulations also kept much needed technologically advanced foreign investment out. In the long term, the economy was tying its growth to the rate of growth of demand in the domestic economy, rather than the world economy.

In debates at that time in India, this logic based on free market economics was dismissed as being too *laissez faire* to be practical. It is perhaps ironic that nearly 40 years later, the International Monetary Fund and the World Bank would use the same logic and language to make their case for India's liberalization.

4   Reviewing the growth performance of the Indian economy between 1950 and 1980

The rich excitement of the debates in India on early industrialization and its course was matched only by the trenchant criticism that followed a bitter post-mortem of what went wrong. In reviewing the performance of the Indian economy in the first three decades of development, it is important to realize both what did happen and what did not happen sufficiently. The former perspective is sometimes lost in these debates because of the loftiness of the Indian ambitions for growth at the start of independence.

Look back at Table 7.1. Compared with pre-independence performance when per capita output was growing at a rate of 1 per cent, even the relatively poor rate of growth of GDP at 3.7 per cent per annum was quite good. It outstripped the rate of population growth of just over 2 per cent and left something in the economy that could be reinvested. Though drought and floods still happened regularly, famines of the type that wreaked havoc in Bengal in 1943 never reoccurred. Food imports were high in the early years, but India did later acquire self-sufficiency in food grain production.

As the Indian Nobel Prize winning economist Amartya Sen (1986) has pointed out, impressive strides were made in education, especially scientific education. By some estimates India in the 1980s had the largest stock of scientific labour power next only to the USA, the Soviet Union and the UK. In 1982, it also boasted an impressive percentage of young people in higher education in the 20–24 age group. At 8 per cent, this ratio for India was not only ahead of other countries in the same per capita bracket (China in the same period had 1 per cent), but even countries that had twice India's per capita income did not approach such a high percentage.

Still these achievements paled when confronted with the basic inequity of the development process, which screamed silently through the figures on growing poverty and the swelling army of unemployed youth, particularly in cities. Films made during the 1970s show the stereotype of the unemployed (angry) young man let down by the system around him, which was rife with corruption. More importantly, investment and growth routinely fell short of planned targets, and by the country's own standards of what it sought to achieve, India had failed.

Even sharper was the contrast in performance with the East Asian economies that had pursued the 'path not taken' by India, namely export-led industrialization. Table 7.4 reports both on economic indicators of growth, such as the growth of per capita gross national product (GNP) and exports, and on social indicators of growth that measure the quality of living. Gross national product (GNP) used here includes both domestic output (GDP) and also net income from Indian overseas assets. Table 7.4 reports on the spread of literacy and two indicators of public health: life expectancy and infant mortality. It is notable that India has one of the lowest rates of growth in per capita income and some of the poorest indicators of public health. Also striking is the poor achievement in terms of literacy, in stark contrast to India's achievements in tertiary education noted earlier.

Table 7.4   Indicators of growth for India and selected East Asian economies

	Per capita GNP, average annual growth (%)	Life expectancy at birth (in years)		Infant mortality per 1000 births		Adult literacy rate (%)	
	1980–93	1960	1992	1960	1992	1960	1992
Indonesia	4.2	41	62	139	66	54	84
South Korea	8.2	54	71	85	11	88	97
Malaysia	3.5	54	70	73	14	60	80
Thailand	6.4	52	69	103	26	79	94
India	3.0	44	60	165	89	34	50

Source: Bajpai and Sachs, 1997, Table 3, p.143

The achievements of this early period of growth are well summed up by the following quotation.

> The extraordinary thing about India's post-WW2 growth experience is how ordinary and average it seemed to be – up until the end of the 1980s. It is not nearly as bad as the growth performance in Africa ... It is not nearly as good as growth performance in East Asia ... It is average – suggesting either that India's growth management policies were not that damaging, or rather that *they were par for the course in the post-WW2 world*.

(DeLong, 2001, p.17, emphasis added)

This last point is rather important. Many developing countries had followed the Indian style policy of state-led import substituting industrialization. In an influential paper on the subject, two US economists, Sachs and Warner (1995), found that only 17 countries had followed open economy policies in the 1970s, while 73 developing countries had followed state-led import substituting industrialization. Of these latter countries, 59 also suffered some kind of severe macroeconomic crisis in the 1980s. The crises took the form of either hyper-inflation, a mounting foreign debt on which the interest could not be paid and that needed rescheduling or a default on foreign debt. India was not among these 59 countries. Its impending crisis came much later in the early 1990s and was nipped in the bud rather quickly.

5 Retreating from import substitution: 1981 to 1990

5.1 Criticisms of planned industrialization

Contrary to popular perception, the domestic disenchantment in India with planned industrialization had set in quite early. That excessive regulation was stifling initiative at the firm level and slowing down growth had been recognized in a number of industrial sectors. It also added a new dimension to the competitiveness of firms, since dealing with 'Delhi', as firms in Bombay called this administrative dealing with the government, became an important fixed cost in terms of time and money, and a drag on the economic growth process. Prakash Tandon, the first Indian Managing Director of the multinational subsidiary Hindustan Lever, describes this well in his memoirs.

> Dealing with New Delhi posed me with a delicate task. Large companies had developed their relationships in various ways. Some had a Delhi director, usually chosen for his capacity to foster contacts; others went a stage further and appointed a retired I.C.S [Indian Civil Servant], whose junior colleagues and subordinates would provide convenient contacts for some years to come. He would also know well the anatomy of decision-making and be able to forecast the course of the File. Some companies showed a predilection for employing politically well connected sons and nephews with easy access to power. The easy if not cynical part of this whole process was that mostly everybody got what they wanted, but it had to go through a long-drawn drill that satisfied a series of impeccable desirables in planning and procedures ... but little was ever denied; only everything went slower, and like a sluggish stream less water went through. In fairness, the large international and Indian companies of the professionally managed kind did not ask more than what was their due, but matters that had been theirs to decide at their management's initiative and discretion were now the subject of prolonged negotiations. The time that should have gone into policies went into procedures. Growth was thus painfully slow.

(Tandon, 1980, p.21)

Industrial growth was not the only casualty. A number of key reports starting from 1969 also questioned whose interests industrial regulation was actually serving. The first of these came with the Dutt Committee Report in 1969. The committee was set up to examine the allegation that big business houses were using the industrial licensing system to foreclose competition from new entrants. Its findings confirmed that India's big business houses were purchasing future licensing capacity in particular sectors to prevent entry of other domestic firms. The Monopolistic and Restrictive Trade Practices Act was passed in 1969, which laid a number of controls on the big business houses: both Indian and foreign. To promote the growth of small businesses, a number of industrial sectors and lines of activity were also reserved for village and small-scale industries. There was considerable corruption in the allocation of import licences and quotas. The Narasimhan Committee report of 1978 had suggested the entire economy deal with this by moving to a system of market based financial instruments of control.

All these pressures and constraints soon began to show up in the figures for industrial growth. Rates as high as 9 per cent in the 1960s slowed dramatically to less than 5 per cent in the mid 1970s. There was a very lively debate among academic economists about the causes of the slow down in industrial growth. The limited growth of agriculture, the slow down of public investment and the considerable inequality of incomes in the economy were all blamed as contributing factors. Public sector investments also came in for heavy criticism and it was alleged that their poor performance in core sectors was to blame for the high cost nature of Indian industry. Table 7.5 looks at employment, output and investment in state-owned enterprises in India and other East Asian countries. What is remarkable in the table is that while the state-owned enterprises in India commanded a much higher share of employment and investment than elsewhere in East Asia, they accounted for a similar share of output. That is, other East Asian economies achieved similar levels of output as India with much smaller amounts of investment and employment. This suggests that they were more efficient than their Indian counterparts.

Table 7.5   Percentage of total employment, output and investmentprovided by state-owned enterprises, 1990

	Employment	Output	Investment
Indonesia	1.2	13.0	5.0
South Korea	1.9	10.2	3.3
Thailand	0.9	5.4	4.9
India	8.3	14.1	8.5

Source: Bajpai and Sachs, 1997, Table 6, p.323

Even as the debates about industrial growth were underway, a new line of criticism came from studies on technology absorption and growth in Indian industry. In two celebrated works, Desai (1981) and Ahluwalia (1985) showed that there was considerable technological obsolescence in industry and that this was directly linked to trade policy (high tariffs) and to the lack of competition in particular industries. These factors were symptomatic of a lack of 'openness' in the economy. An open economy tends to trade a large proportion of its output (though large countries tend to trade less, relative to output, than small countries). It is open to international trade and has few of the tariffs and quotas that hinder the flow of trade. An open economy also allows the free flow of international financial capital. Table 7.6 shows that on these indicators India in the mid 1990s was much less open than other East Asian economies, despite liberalization in 1991.

Table 7.6 Measures of openness to trade

	Imports + exports as % of GDP	Percentage of industries under quota restrictions	Average tariff rates	Foreign direct investment (% of GDP)	Openness to financial flows: 5 = high, 0 = low
	1994	1992–94	1994	1993	
Indonesia	55	3	6	1.4	5
South Korea	55	2	4	0.2	3.5
Malaysia	171	2	9	8.0	4.5
Thailand	80	4	9.3	1.4	4.5
India	25	58	33	0.3	2.5

Source: Bajpai and Sachs, 1997, Table 4, p.320

5.2   Opening to the world markets

The response of policy makers to this string of damaging criticisms was a series of ad hoc measures to cope. First, imports were liberalized. As a result, imports ran ahead of exports, so that the Indian economy soon ran out of foreign currency to pay for its imports. You will learn more about such foreign currency crises in Chapter 11. Second, measures were taken to promote the export sectors of the economy with special concessions: they were rewarded with quality imports in return for a good export performance, received tax reductions and subsidies, and were allowed to locate in special export promotion zones where overall infrastructure quality was good.

However, the greatest attention was paid to technology policies. Between 1980 and 1990, there were three separate policy declarations on technology. As Sridharan (1995) points out, there was also a subtle shift in the definition of self-reliance. Through the 1960s and 1970s, self-reliance had become associated with self-sufficiency in production and technology generation. This association had equated import substitution with policies of autarky (see Chapter 3). In the 1980s, for the first time the *costs* of self-reliance were emphasized. The following quotes from the government's Sixth Five-Year Plan (1980–85) make this very clear.

> Self-reliance, as should be obvious, but often is not, does not necessarily mean self-sufficiency in all sections of the economy. So long as a country is able to pay its way, it cannot be said to be dependent on others.

(Government of India, 1980, p.xxi; quoted in Sridharan, 1995)

> However, self-reliance can no longer take the form of indiscriminate import-substitution ... In the eighties, export promotion is as much a part of the drive for self-reliance as efficient import substitution.

(Government of India, 1980, p.10; quoted in Sridharan, 1995)

In particular, imports of technology and capital goods were more freely permitted. In its quest for technological self-reliance, government policy had in the past attempted to separate the benefits of technology transfer, that is, how to bring new technology into the country and build up Indian technological capacity, from the problem of (foreign) ownership. The government had introduced stringent regulations (on royalty payments, capital goods imports and profit repatriation by foreign firms) that would give Indian firms the incentives and protection to develop their own technological capacity. The result of these policies had been to discourage foreign investment considerably, especially in key sectors like pharmaceuticals, machine tools and later electronics, where technological advance was moving far more rapidly than domestic firms could hope to keep up with.

Some of these policies were reversed with liberalization. The early 1980s saw a more inviting government attitude towards technology intensive foreign investments. The position towards foreign investment in general became more conciliatory. A prominent example of this was a joint venture in car production by the public sector firm Maruti with Suzuki of Japan in 1981 set up by an act of Parliament. During the 1980s, the process of approval for foreign investment too became easier, particularly in the technology intensive sectors.

Thus, the retreat from import substitution in favour of integration with the world economy had already started from the early 1980s. Even though there was no move to dismantle the entire regulatory system, small bits and pieces were added to curb the excesses, make procedures simpler and more transparent, and where possible, as in the newly developing electronics and software sectors, the regulatory hand was applied less heavily. Many articles of essential import for these sectors were de-licensed. In some sectors there was also a de-licensing of industrial capacity so that no regulatory permissions were needed to set up firms in these sectors. Software, which is discussed further in Section 8, was a beneficiary of these new measures.

Perhaps the best term to describe this retreat from old policies in the 1980s is 'limited import liberalization'. Tariffs were still high but capital goods and technology imports were liberalized. There was no large-scale dismantling of the regulatory structure yet key sectors were allowed to feel the benefits of deregulation. Certain curious phrases like 'automatic approval' crept into the language of bureaucracy. Whether as cause or consequence, the biggest boom took place in the consumer durables sector as urban Indians discovered the variety in consumption that the international market had to offer, and domestic producers rushed to imitate these offerings.

5.3   Technology and industrial growth

Import liberalization was not without its consequences. Huge capital goods imports during this period undoubtedly caused the major balance of payments crisis that pushed India to seek help from the International Monetary Fund in 1991. Nevertheless, something remarkable happened to growth in this period. Figure 7.3 plots an index of real GDP per capita in India over time. The data in Figure 7.3 are expressed in index form. The real GDP for year 1990/91 is set equal to 100 and called the base year. The real GDP for other years is then expressed as a percentage of the base year. Notice the steep increase in its level after 1980. This rise in the rate of growth happened long before liberalization, and is a much sharper change in trend than the break that occurred with liberalization in 1991. How could we explain that?

DeLong (2001), from whose work this graph is taken, argues that the limited reforms of the 1980s had a huge impact on the economy because even though they were small, they were strategic in terms of their effect on growth and productivity. Import liberalization in the 1980s had achieved a huge expenditure on technologically sophisticated capital goods. Some key sectors such as software electronics and telecom were allowed to grow in a relatively unhampered way. The influence of this on overall growth was immense. Even though the increased imports of technology precipitated a foreign currency shortage, it was one that the economy soon had the ability to overcome.

Though the ad hoc polices adopted in the 1980s fell short of a full liberalization, they had a substantial influence on the policies that could be adopted in 1990s. They had shown what even limited liberalization could achieve economically and, more importantly, scoped ways of implementing such a process. When liberalization finally arrived in the 1990s as part of the IMF conditionality, many Indian administrators and industrialists knew what to expect and were prepared for it. Furthermore, there was a groundswell of support from middle-class Indians for what full liberalization could bring in terms of consumption opportunities.

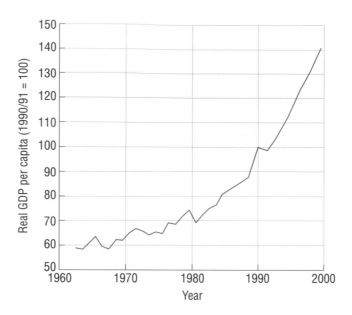

Figure 7.3   Indian real GDP per capita, 1962–2000

Source: adapted from DeLong, 2001, p.23

Activity 7.4

Based on your reading so far:

1   Summarize the main elements of India's industrial policy in the 1960s.

2   List the changes introduced to this in the 1970s and 1980s.

---

6   Technological change and productivity as determinants of growth

You may have noticed the shift in the terminology in this narrative of changes in India's industrial policies. There is less talk about capital accumulation, but technological progress and industrial productivity have become important in discussing the future of economic growth. Is this switch related to what you learned about growth in Section 2? This subsection revisits the basic model of economic growth introduced in Section 2 and explains the relation between productivity and growth. Then the influences on productivity are examined. I hope this will clarify the economic rationale behind the changes in Indian industrial policy in the 1980s.

6.1 Productivity and industrial growth

Consider once more the hypothetical textile producing economy of India. Imagine they have seen for some years that their neighbour and rival, let us say South Korea, has been able to produce more textiles although they are smaller in terms of their working population. South Korea has, let us assume, a higher rate of growth and a consistently higher level of workforce productivity in textile production. We can measure this productivity by looking at the ratio $\frac{X}{L}$ where L is the population employed in the production of X. A higher ratio means that any one person, on average, produces more in Korea than in India.

How is such a difference in productivity of workers possible, if all countries are assumed to have knowledge of the available techniques of textile production, that is, techniques A, B and C? To understand this we need to distinguish between *technique* and technological change. In common parlance, these terms are often used interchangeably. In Section 2, A, B and C were defined as different techniques of production. However, producers of textiles in India, and indeed anywhere in the world, can choose between techniques and can also benefit from technological change.

Technological change
Technological change may allow a firm to use an existing technique more efficiently or it may introduce a new technique of production entirely.

Question

Can you think of examples of sources for what we might mean by technological change?

Here are some examples of possible technological changes in textile production, though this list is by no means exhaustive:

1   Producers could benefit from a generic change to a new source of power from, say, electricity generated from fossil fuels to more reliable solar power, due to advances in solar cell technology. Previously in the history of textiles something similar happened when spinning machines moved from being steam powered to powered by electricity. The result of this move is that they will now be able to have a greater amount of output from the same machines, thus requiring less capital and labour for producing a given output.

2   The development of more specialized weaving and spinning machines, as the result of developments in computerized and numerically controlled machines, may enable firms to have better quality control and also economize on the stocks of different fabrics they hold. On the other hand, these numerically controlled machines also allow producers to hire fewer machine supervisors.

3   Improved means of managing the production of textiles using A, B or C due to learning by the firms allows them to use the existing capital and labour inputs more efficiently.

Question

Are improvements of types 1, 2 and 3 likely to affect the existing technologies A, B and C equally? Are any likely to create new technologies?

These sources of technological change may or may not affect all three techniques equally. Technological improvements such as 1 and 2, above, may not favour any technique in particular. Improvements of type 2 may create a whole new technique. However, improvements of the type in 3 do generally favour one technique more than another, since learning is likely to be about the technique producers have been using.

The effect of technological change on production is to reduce the resources required for production of a given output. It may also add to the variety of output (fabrics) available. Bringing down the labour and capital resources required for production makes the average productivity of both capital and labour higher. To make this clear, let us return to the hypothetical textile producers in India (from Section 2) and see what happens when technological change occurs that affects all the three techniques equally.

The impact of technological change in 2000 on the input requirements for technique A is illustrated in Table 7.7(a) below. The first set of figures (for 1980) is the same as in Table 7.2(a), but technological change in 2000 has made it possible to produce 60 bales of cloth with fewer capital and labour inputs. You now need only 2 machines and 8 units of labour to produce 60 bales of cotton. Similarly, technique B now requires 2 fewer machines and 2 fewer units of labour than in 1980 to produce the same 60 bales of cotton. The largest saving of machines is for technique C, which requires 10 fewer machines than before.

Table 7.7(a)   Effect of technological change on textile producers

Technique	1980			2000		
	Capital input (K) in units	Labour input (L) in numbers of people	Output level (X) in bales	Capital input (K) in units	Labour input (L) in numbers of people	Output level (X) in bales
A	4	9	60	2	8	60
B	6	6	60	4	4	60
C	18	2	60	8	1	60

If we now plot the isoquants for 60 bales of textiles in 1980 and 2000, as in Figure 7.4, we see that the 1980 isoquant has moved inwards towards the origin in 2000. A consequence of the higher productivity due to technological change is that *less* labour and capital are needed to produce the *same* level of

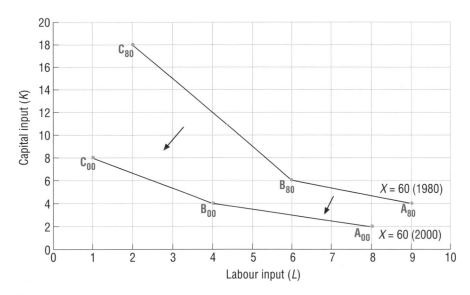

Figure 7.4   Growth in productivity due to technological change

output. Even though all the techniques are more productive due to technological change, this increase has not been even. Technique C has gained the highest increase in productivity due to technological change.

Activity 7.5

Check your understanding of this before moving on. Table 7.7(b) shows the impact of technological change on the production of textiles, giving data for 120 and 180 bales of cotton.

1   Use this information to draw a diagram plotting the isoquants $X = 120$ and $X = 180$ for the year 2000.

2   Compare the isoquants you have plotted with those in Activity 7.2 and Figure 7.2. How have the isoquants changed?

Why is the increase in productivity of labour and capital due to technological change important? The level of productivity is closely connected to economic growth itself because it influences the possible level of investment. When productivity is high, fewer resources are needed to produce the same levels of output. As a consequence, more resources are available to the economy as a whole, over and above its consumption needs, for investment. Greater investment in turn means greater productive capacity in the future, more employment, and more output and income in the next period. Moreover, increasing productivity means more is available to firms as profits. The financial resources required for additional investment come partly from these

Table 7.7(b)   Effect of technological change on textile producers

Technique	1980			2000		
	Capital input (K) in units	Labour input (L) in numbers of people	Output level (X) in bales	Capital input (K) in units	Labour input (L) in numbers of people	Output level (X) in bales
A	8	18	120	4	16	120
A	12	27	180	8	24	180
B	12	12	120	8	8	120
B	18	18	180	12	12	180
C	36	4	120	16	2	120
C	54	6	180	24	4	180

profits and are invested in anticipation of even greater profits. At the same time, old levels of consumption can be maintained. Economic growth thus becomes a self-sustaining and cumulative process.

What factors affect technological change? Technological change may occur inside a firm as it learns, from its experience of production, about new and better opportunities for profit. Alternatively, technological improvement could be imported into the country. The two most common forms of import of technology are through the direct import of machinery, tools and technology licences, or through the encouragement of foreign investment which comes imbued with newer and better technology. Openness of the economy is very important in order to allow the import of technologies. However, so is the economy's own experience of production. Import substituting industrialization, which did not have an export component, constrained India's ability to pay for such technological imports, and insulated the economy against any competition from better technology.

The discovery of the importance of technological change to productivity and overall industrial growth occurred in the Indian economy in the late 1970s and 1980s. Studies on technological change cited earlier had found that productivity growth in the economy had stagnated and several industrial sectors were saddled with obsolete technology. The first impulse to liberalization therefore responded to the needs of an industry starved of access to new technologies, and took the form of a massive import liberalization. Liberalization of capital goods imports then pushed the rate of national income growth to a much higher level than before, as seen in Table 7.1 and Figure 7.3. On the other hand, such large-scale imports with no corresponding increase in export performance pushed the Indian economy to the brink of a foreign exchange shortfall crisis in the early 1990s, and forced it to turn to the IMF for a dollar loan that would pay for the excessive imports.

7 Liberalization in the 1990s

The IMF was able to exercise some leverage over Indian industrial policy because it demanded policy reforms in return for a much-needed loan. The IMF, therefore, demanded the liberalization of the Indian economy as a long-term corrective for avoiding future foreign exchange crises. This demand, however, came at a time when, to some extent, policy had already been softened for such a move. A number of different measures were suggested by the IMF as part of the reform, all of which accorded a larger role to market processes in economic decisions. These included:

- liberalizing imports by reducing tariffs and quotas to promote exports

- a progressive removal of administrative controls including a move to a free market for food grains

- a whittling down of food subsidies

- a reduction of the role of public investment in the economy

- the privatization of publicly-owned assets

- an invitation to multinational companies to invest in priority sectors including infrastructure

- financial liberalization that would remove all bank lending by priority to chosen sectors and all subsidized credit.

Of course, not all of these measures had been examined before and implementing some of them was more problematic than others. The measures that were particularly difficult to effect were the free market in food grains and whittling down of food subsidies, privatization of the public sector, and the abolition of tariffs on a range of manufacturing industries. The progress of reforms has thus been slow and some argue that the smaller improvement in growth after 1991 is directly linked to this delay.

The next sub-section explains the IMF rationale for liberalization, which you will be surprised to know is quite different from the logic that underpinned the self-propelled changes of Indian industrial policy in the 1980s. At the end of this section you should be less surprised that the pace of liberalization is slow in India and yet be able to explain the spurt in India's economic growth.

7.1 The IMF rationale for liberalization

The balance of payments crisis prompted by the import liberalization of the 1980s forced the Indian government to approach the IMF for a foreign currency loan. What is a balance of payments crisis? You will learn more about it in Chapter 11. Here I want you to note that when a country's imports run ahead of its export earnings, there is a shortage of foreign currency to pay for the imports. This is a balance of payments crisis and it can be resolved by incurring foreign debt. As part of the conditions of the loan, the IMF prescribed the full liberalization of the economy to market forces. What was the rationale advanced by the IMF for these liberalization policies?

In order to understand this rationale, you will need to recall the production possibility frontier that you met in Chapter 3. Look back at it now, in Section 3.2, to refresh your understanding, then look at Figure 7.5.

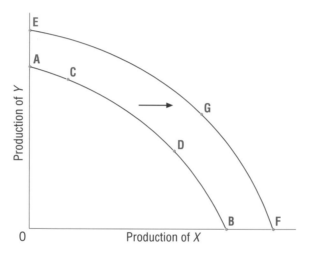

Figure 7.5   Production possibility frontiers: gains from reallocation and reorganization with liberalization

Figure 7.5 shows a production possibility frontier (PPF) like those in Chapter 3, Figure 3.5, except that it is curved. The shape is derived from the idea that, as an economy becomes more specialized, it becomes harder to move to further specialization. So suppose, for example, that in Figure 7.5 good X is farming and good Y is manufacturing. AB is the production possibility frontier for the two goods. Then to shift from a mix of X and Y to rather more Y may be quite easy. But to drop farming altogether may be hard. So as you move towards complete specialization in manufacturing, the extra output of manufactures that you gain by closing one more farm declines. Hence the 'bowed outwards' shape of the PPF in Figure 7.5.

Behind the production possibility frontier (AB in Figure 7.5) lie decisions about how to allocate capital and labour to produce output, as we analysed above using isoquants. Producers in the economy decide how much of a good to produce by looking at the relative prices of X and Y, and deciding which type of production will be most profitable. This depends upon the relative prices in X and Y. If this ratio is high, more of X would be produced and if this ratio was low, more of Y would be produced.

In making those decisions, producers of both X and Y know that they can choose between different techniques of production (such as A, B, C for textiles in India). Each technique in turn employs a different mixture of capital and labour. Producers then look at the prices of capital (the costs of borrowing) and of labour (wage rates). Rates of interest and wage rates will be the same whether X or Y is being produced. Therefore, producers across the economy will choose the technique that is most profitable given these costs and the amounts of capital and labour needed.

You might have started wondering what all this has to do with liberalization. Well, under liberalization the ratio of the price of X and the price of Y facing Indian producers would change. Instead of facing the prices of X and Y generated by the protected home market, the producers will face the world price ratio, which is likely to be different, and producers will want to make different production decisions.

Suppose that before liberalization producers are producing at point C on Figure 7.5. Then suppose that the effect of liberalization is to reduce the price of Y relative to the price of X. The likely result is that some producers move over to producing X, so the output mix of the economy changes to, say, point D.

This change can be seen as a move towards specializing in production in which India has a current comparative advantage, as signalled by world price ratios, and producing less of Y in which India has a comparative disadvantage. Instead of farming and manufacturing, let us think of Y as manufacturing and X as services. Under import substitution and regulation the price of manufactured goods was high relative to the price of services, because of tariffs to protect manufacturing. But in fact, the economy could have obtained those manufactured goods more cheaply through imports. With liberalization, the prices of manufactured goods fall, and the relative prices of services begin to look attractive to producers. This is in truth what happened. India started to produce somewhat more services, where the country's cheap and educated labour has a comparative advantage.

Moving from point C to point D in Figure 7.5 thus changes the allocation of resources to X and Y. It will bring consumption gains, as India exploits its comparative advantage more effectively and trades more output. For this reason, these gains are also called allocative efficiency gains: capital and labour have been reallocated between X and Y and have thus increased the consumption possibilities for the open economy. Consumers in the economy can import more goods from the world markets or producers may use them to buy newer forms of machinery. These are the gains from trade that you studied in Part 1.

However, there is another benefit. New investment is occurring, particularly in X, the newly attractive sector of investment in the economy. Consequently, the PPF shifts over time as well. This is shown by the outward shift of the PPF on Figure 7.5 to EF. The shift is due to more investment in production of X and improved productivity in Y as established manufacturers fight back foreign competition by using improved techniques. The economy may move to a point such as G. In other words, the outward shift on PPF measures the 'reorganization gain' to the economy as a whole.

In this rationale for liberalization, if the progress of reform has been slow, the strength of the reallocation and reorganization effects is weak and their overall impact on growth is also smaller. Notice that this rationale for liberalization is in fact quite different from the rationale for the limited import liberalization of the 1980s that we discussed earlier. The 1980s' liberalization measures were not about comparative advantage. They were about allowing imports of technology for efficient import substitution. The similarity of the IMF position to that of the 1980s' changes is only that it attacks the same faulty instruments of policy, that is, over-regulation of the industrial sector through licensing and the closure of the economy to all competing imports, especially in technology.

Furthermore, current Indian debate on industrial policy centres on three sorts of issues.

1   The advantages and disadvantages of public sector divestment and privatization especially in utilities and infrastructure sectors.

2   How to make manufacturing more competitive. There is debate over why India suffers a comparative disadvantage in manufacture: is it poor infrastructure, high tariffs or less flexible labour laws than in competing countries for firing underperforming employees?

3   The need for competition policies to regulate industry for the benefit of consumers.

These debates should give us some clues about why the progress of some IMF type reforms has been slow. Briefly, policy makers and industrialists are less convinced about the desirability of some elements of the reform package than others. The more difficult question of what to do with the large numbers of the population below the poverty line also remains unanswered. While nobody wants to go back to the policies of the planned era, the current debates reveal a deep scepticism about the free market economy. The free markets logic, which the IMF has championed, still faces considerable dissent in India.

8   Industrial policy and economic growth: the Indian software story

This last section briefly looks at the story of India's success in the software industry. In many ways, this success captures many of the issues this chapter has tried to raise: the static versus dynamic comparative advantage argument; what liberalization did and did not do; and the changing story of how economic growth takes place. Software growth in India was an unintended consequence of the Indian government's efforts at import substitution in computer hardware and a wage advantage in skilled (English-speaking) scientific labour. Its success was triggered by two main events.

The first event was the exit of IBM in protest against the Foreign Exchange Regulation Act (FERA) rules in 1977, which created a huge vacuum in the computer hardware market in India. Other foreign hardware vendors, especially of microcomputers (Boroughs, Honeywell, DEC, Zenith), rushed to fill this vacuum, usually through tie-ups with local firms who would then re-port the mainframe programs from IBM computers to their computers. For private firms like Tata Consultancy Services and Patni Computer Services, this was a great import substituting opportunity – each tied up with a particular hardware producer to migrate data from the IBM operating systems to another proprietary operating system, thus building up a variety of skills in computer software programming (not necessarily taught in universities). This was far in excess of what could be expected given the installed base of computers in India itself. In a bid to avoid the costs of proprietary software, the public sector had also invested in developing UNIX software systems long before UNIX became popular as a common platform.

The second important event was that when import liberalization occurred in 1985, it coincided with a collapse of world hardware prices and a sudden spurt of demand as firms the world over started computerizing operations based on the client-server model. This was followed in 1995 by the Y2K demand, which arose as firms in the West grew alarmed at the consequences of the 'millennium bug', and wrote new software to fix it. In all, the demand boom for software programming lasted for nearly 15 years and allowed Indian firms with data migration capabilities to operate as international subcontractors because of the large numbers of talented, but relatively cheap, programmers in India. As other domestic firms recognized the possibility, there was a resource reallocation along comparative advantage lines. Many domestic firms had moved out from declining profit margins in manufacturing into the software services business.

Foreign firms too identified the cost advantage in locating their computerization facilities in India and this started an influx of foreign investment that pioneered both new ways of organizing the business of outsourced software and novel arrangements to overcome the infrastructure problems created by an inadequate telecom infrastructure in India. Domestic software manufacturers quickly improved their strategies and pressed for permissions to have their own generators for electricity and invest in private satellite links for telecommunication facilities. State governments, limited in what they could do by their own fiscal crisis, nevertheless tried to outdo each other to make themselves attractive for software investment by domestic and foreign firms.

As more and more multinational firms set up subsidiaries in India, wage rates in the sector were bid up. Multinational firms that entered software were in fact quite unlike foreign firms that had come to the Indian economy before. They were not interested in the Indian market for software, which was almost non-existent. Almost all of them came to make software more cheaply for their parent companies. In doing so they competed with Indian firms only in the labour market for that scarce resource, English-speaking, scientifically trained programmers.

This competition then transformed the market for programmers beyond recognition. Professional norms of employment began to be adopted by all firms, salaries for men and women were not different, and all salaries began to rise. To get a sense of the extent of this wage increase consider that software salaries rose from between $3000–5000 per annum in 1991 to between $8000–11 000 in 1995: a rough doubling plus of salaries in four years. By 1997, a software developer could hope to earn between $15 700–19 200 per annum. (Sources: 1991 – *Business India* (1992); 1995 – Institute for Development Policy and Management (2003); 1997 – Arora (2000).) Dollar salaries take into account the depreciation of the Rupee during this period. The rate of increase of Rupee salaries was even higher. The level of salaries was still a fraction of what an entry level programmer in the US would earn, at $4000 a month. Not surprisingly, labour attrition in the industry was also very high (estimated at 20 per cent by NASSCOM, the industry organization). Many software programmers left Indian companies to join foreign firms, especially in the USA.

The rising wage rates and high rates of employee attrition forced Indian firms to adopt more efficient processes and procedures. International norms of employment were imitated: software employees in India enjoy flexi-time work practices and demand work satisfaction and professional freedom. These are norms quite unheard of in other areas of Indian industry. Software firms also adopted several organizational innovations and practices designed to decrease the effects of losing employees on the quality of software. As a consequence of these innovations and investments, productivity in this sector has risen. Some procedures are now slowly being copied in other remote service sectors with similar business models such as call centres, data transcription services, medical transcription and other IT enabled services.

Note that the software story tells us something very different about how growth might happen. The capabilities of firms, that is, how well they can produce particular outputs or use particular inputs, have become the key driver of growth. These capabilities were built by the managerial efforts of domestic firms, by the example set by foreign firms and, last but not the least, the large educational investments undertaken by a government that had wanted to build a hardware industry. As real wages increase, they induce the build-up of firm capabilities and productivity also increases. Firms replace expensive employees with machines and software tools wherever they can, thus moving to a more capital intensive technique of production – as a complementary effect of rising wages. Technological change occurs, in fact, with a change in the techniques of production!

It is likely that this story could never have been told if the first stage of import substituting industrialization had not taken place and all that cheap engineering talent had not been created. Furthermore, the process of change and the move to a more capital intensive technique was slow – it took nearly 15 years of learning under conditions of a sustained boom in demand for a moderate increase in capital intensity to take place in Indian software. These conditions were more favourable than any other industrial sector in India has ever faced.

Yet for all its spectacular growth, the impact of software on India's overall investment, employment and growth has been small. The demand for computerization in India is low. The increasing productivity of Indian software largely benefits US firms that are the main customers. Constraints to growth of manufacturing, namely poor infrastructure and uneven education, also constrain software growth. Thus, software growth utilized the window of opportunity offered by the investments in education and skills made in the period of import substitution. Liberalization allowed firms to tap into the demand boom of the 1990s. However, the growth of Indian software is also limited by the same factors that limited import substitution in India in the earlier period: poor infrastructure, limited domestic demand and willingness to pay for the software services.

Most of India still looks to the growth of manufacturing industry for an overall improvement in its well-being. Nevertheless, this is still the sector where Indian firms have failed to demonstrate any significant comparative advantage, despite all these years of protection. Many believe the real challenge for India's industrial policy still remains in changing this comparative disadvantage to an advantage. Others opine that India's future lies in the growth of its service industry and closer integration with the rest of the world. This will allow the import of manufactures from where they are produced most cheaply. The Indian software industry supports both points of view.

9 Conclusion

In this chapter I have explored the most important influences on the industrial growth of an economy by studying the evolution of industrial policy in India. We have argued that capital accumulation through investment, and improvements in productivity due to technological change are the two key influences on industrial growth. International trade and investment are, in turn, important vehicles for investment and technological change. Foreign investment contributes directly to total investment and to technological change in an economy, while international trade opens up the possibility that new technology embodied in patents, and new machines can be bought by technologically backward countries. The positive impact of the twin forces of globalization (trade and foreign investment) with their impact upon economic growth is the main reason why the last two decades have seen a large-scale adoption of open economy policies by a range of countries.

I started this chapter, however, with the discussion of a policy aiming to reduce openness; that is, import substituting industrialization using Indian industrial policy as an example. The aim of such policies was to change comparative advantage and India was one of many countries that followed this policy in the 1960s and 1970s. Yet since then successive changes in industrial policy have made India's economy more open. An important impetus was the desire to advance technologically and reap the benefits of industrial growth. Closing its door to the world meant the country could not gain from the efforts of others, and productivity increases were restricted to the fruits of domestic initiatives alone.

I also showed, again using India's liberalization as an example, that there were two sorts of cases to be made for openness and its influence upon growth. One case argued for import liberalization, but with continued import substitution aimed at changing comparative advantage in the long run. This propelled the liberalization of the Indian economy in the 1980s. A second case, most forcefully argued by the IMF, sees integration into the world economy based on existing comparative advantages as crucial to growth and sustained development. Both sorts of policies advocate openness, but for different reasons. Perhaps this is why openness continues to be a matter for debate, and Parts 3 and 4 will demonstrate that it is a policy which has resulted in different outcomes for a variety of adopting countries.

Further reading

For an early review of India's planned industrialization, using a political economy perspective, see Bardhan, P. (1984) *The Political Economy of Development in India*, Delhi, Oxford University Press.

Those who have a background in economics may find the following review of Indian development policies of interest (non-economists may find it hard going): Chakravarty, S. (1998) *Development Planning: The Indian Experience* (ninth edition), Delhi, Oxford University Press.

For a review of India's economic performance in the period since liberalization, see Das, G. (2000) *India Unbound*, New York, Viking Press.

A recent article comparing India's post-liberalization performance with the more celebrated performance of its neighbour China, is Huang, Y. and Khanna, T. (2003) 'Can India overtake China?', *Foreign Policy*, July/August, pp.74–81.

Part 3 Inequality and power

Growth and industrialization are sources of economic inequality and also of vast differences in political power among states. In Part 3, we turn from the sources of wealth and power (Part 2) to their implications for people and for political relations between states. The USA is the dominant world power in the early twenty-first century. The economic and political leverage it exercises plays a major role in shaping events across the world, but the impact of its power to influence other states has been felt particularly strongly in its 'backyard': in Central and indeed in South America.

It is from the standpoint of Mexico therefore that Part 3 sets out to examine economic inequality and the operation of power between states. In 1994, the North American Free Trade Agreement (NAFTA) came into force, creating a free trade area for Canada, the USA and Mexico. NAFTA, as Chapter 8 explains, goes beyond opening borders to trade, to include agreements on investment, labour and the environment. The debates about the consequences of some of these 'behind the border' agreements echo the debates in Part 1 about the evolution of the WTO. NAFTA creates a far-reaching integration of two profoundly unequal economies.

In Chapter 8 Carlos Salas Paez and George Callaghan examine the economic implications of trade liberalization and NAFTA for the Mexican economy. The authors explore this issue largely from the standpoint of working people. The economic analysis in Chapter 3 might lead us to expect that free trade between a high income and a lower income economy would benefit low paid workers in the poorer country. Chapter 8 shows that this has not been the case in Mexico. The chapter examines the sources of the impoverishment that has been associated with liberalization for many Mexican workers and documents the persistence of wide inequality within the country.

Chapter 8 thus develops an argument first made in Chapter 2: that free trade has very differentiated effects in both the short and the long run, damaging some as it benefits others. Labour markets, as Chapter 8 explains, are social as well as economic institutions, and the organization of a country's labour markets, including the extent and nature of labour organizing and the leverage exercised by labour over the political system, influences and redistributes the impact of trade liberalization within the country. Chapter 8 introduces and employs an economic analysis of labour markets, labour bargaining and economic inequality to explore the experience of Mexican labour under free trade.

Given the damaging experiences of many Mexicans, as traced in Chapter 8, why did Mexico do it? Why go into NAFTA? In Chapter 9 Rafael Sanchez takes this question as his starting point for an exploration of power and bargaining between states. He picks up from Sudipta Kaviraj's discussion in Chapter 6 of the preferences of states, and asks how a state like Mexico forms a preference for free trade in conditions of economic inequality. He introduces and employs a model of inter-state political bargaining as a game, using this model to identify reasons why a state might prefer an apparently invidious policy choice.

Sanchez explores two possibilities: first, that Mexico gained from the bargain with the USA that resulted in NAFTA, even if the larger share of the gains went to the USA; and second, that Mexico's enthusiasm for NAFTA was an attempt to regain lost ground in an already liberalizing world economy. To discuss these alternatives, Sanchez introduces and employs two different ways of thinking about power relations between states as well as adding an analysis of interdependence among states to the picture of an anarchical states-system developed in Part 1.

We hope that you will gain from Part 3 some tools for analysing power, interdependence and inequality that can be used in a wide variety of contexts: to measure inequality between and within states; to examine the differential impact of trade and investment liberalization; to see the importance of interdependence among states (alongside the role of anarchy); and to explore systematically the processes of political bargaining and the exercise of coercive power between states and their outcomes. The authors of this part also seek to convey a sense of how these relationships of inequality and power look 'from below', drawing on the perspectives of the poorer state in the negotiations and of the working people within that state.

Chapter 8 Labour and free trade: Mexico within NAFTA

Carlos Salas Paez and George Callaghan

1 Introduction

In Chapter 7, Suma Athreye argued that economic growth has its roots in industrial change: in investment, technological change and the movement of capital across borders in search of new opportunities for profitable production. She told a story of changing industrial policies in India, drawing on Sudipta Kaviraj's analysis in Chapter 6 of the political roots of economic liberalization on the subcontinent.

This chapter continues the themes of economic liberalization and industrial change, but we turn from the process of investment to the consequences for labour: for those who work in the factories and are displaced from the fields. We do this through an exploration of a situation that one could almost think of as a laboratory for the effects of economic liberalization on middle income countries: the experience of Mexico within the North American Free Trade Agreement (NAFTA). NAFTA was implemented in January 1994 after an earlier period of liberalization had opened Mexico's borders to increasing international trade and investment. NAFTA is not the first free trade agreement of its kind – Canada and the USA signed an earlier one in 1988, for example – but it was the first such agreement between a very rich industrialized economy and a middle income industrializing one. (NAFTA includes Canada, but the experiences of that country will not be considered here.) The US and Mexican economies are characterized by widely differing levels of output and standards of living (Section 2) and the chapter examines liberalization in the context of such inequality.

NAFTA is also significant in the scale of free trade and openness to investment it instituted, and in the speed with which its measures were to be implemented (Section 3). On both sides of the border, many people had severe doubts about the wisdom of Mexico's accession to the agreement. Mexico and the US have a mixed history of interdependence and conflict through the nineteenth and twentieth centuries that has left a legacy of deep mistrust of US attitudes towards Mexico among people of all social classes in Mexico. Or as the Mexican proverb puts it *Pobre México, tan lejos de dios y tan cerca de los Estados Unidos* ('Poor Mexico, so far from God, and so close to the United States'). Others on both sides were more optimistic, however, arguing that NAFTA would help Mexico shift to more rapid and sustained economic growth.

This chapter examines the changes in wages, incomes and working conditions in Mexico experienced under the combined impact of economic liberalization and the accession to NAFTA. We shall argue that, despite economic growth, the effect of NAFTA has been to impoverish many working people in Mexico. We examine first the changing patterns of employment under liberalization and since accession to NAFTA, and draw out some links between NAFTA's provisions and employment change, notably the impoverishing effect in rural areas of competition in agricultural markets and the consequences of this for wages and labour incomes (Section 4).

We then turn to working conditions and labour organizing in the same period, emphasizing the enduring importance of worker *agency* – that is, the active defence of labour rights and wage incomes – for labour market outcomes (Section 5). We spend some time examining a very particular Mexican experience: the rise of the maquiladora manufacturing plants. These plants were established by US foreign investment in northern Mexico before NAFTA to produce goods for export.

Section 6 then reports evidence for declining real wages in the 1990s. We contrast these findings with the expected effects of freeing trade on labour incomes, as predicted by the economic theory outlined in Chapter 3, and ask why these expectations were unfulfilled. Section 6 then examines the extent to which economic analysis can explain the observed wage decline. Finally, Section 7 investigates the extent to which inequality has changed over the years of increasingly free trade. In this section we introduce some concepts, techniques and theories that are of general use for examining labour market change and inequality of incomes: the distinction between nominal and real wages; the difference between competitive models of the labour market and the concept of segmented labour markets; and how to create and interpret measures of inequality.

In summary, this chapter explores what happened when Mexico's historical institutional and political patterns of organization in its labour markets – including wage levels, patterns of wage bargaining and extensive labour rights – met trade and investment liberalization in the 1980s and then the provisions of NAFTA.

Marchers protesting against the Free Trade Area of the Americas (ALCA) at the World Social Forum, Porto Allegre, Brazil, 4 February 2002

2 Mexico in the US shadow: economic policies and labour relations

Mexico, unlike India, undertook liberalization within the huge economic shadow cast by the richest and most economically powerful country in the world: the USA. Chapter 9 considers the implications of this fact for the degree of free choice that Mexico exercised in negotiating NAFTA: did Mexico choose NAFTA because it believed it would gain from the process, or was the decision a response to the power of its northern neighbour? In this chapter, however, we shall concentrate on the economic consequences for Mexico of liberalization and accession to NAFTA.

2.1 Unequal neighbours

Mexico is a big country, and its income per head places it as a middle income rather than a low income country. Table 8.1, however, shows the scale of the disparity between Mexico and its huge and powerful neighbour. The USA has nearly three times the population of Mexico. Economic output in Mexico measured by GDP per head of the population is only around one-quarter of the US figure. This disparity is also reflected in the incomes available to be spent by households ('disposable' income), meaning that Mexican households have a lot less to save or spend after taxes and social security contributions than do households in the USA.

Table 8.1   Comparative economic statistics, 2000

	Mexico	USA
Population (thousands)	97 379	275 372
GDP per capita at current PPPs (US$)	9152	35 619
Disposable income per capita at current PPPs (US$)	6430	26 448

Source: OECD, Main Economic Indicators, June 2002

Two of the rows in Table 8.1 contain data calculated using current purchasing power parity exchange rates (or PPPs). What do we mean by this term? When economists use one currency, in this case the US dollar, to compare growth and income statistics between two countries, such as the USA and Mexico, that use different currencies (the dollar and the peso) within their economies, then they must decide on a rate of exchange. They could use the prevailing market exchange rate, that is, the rate you would get if you sold US dollars and bought Mexican pesos, but this measure is affected by the continual influence of current interest rates and short-term currency speculation. (Exchange rates are explained in detail in Chapter 11.)

It is to overcome this problem that economists have developed the concept of a purchasing power parity (PPP) exchange rate. This is the exchange rate that would equalize the purchasing power of a unit of one currency in different countries by offsetting the differences between domestic price levels in the two countries. To explore this further, let us consider an example. In reality, the PPP exchange rate is calculated using a basket of goods, but we shall simplify the situation and take just one item, the beloved American doughnut. If, for example, a doughnut costs 10 pesos in Mexico and $1.00 in the USA, then the PPP exchange rate would be 10 pesos to 1 US dollar.

Question

Look back at Table 8.1. Mexican disposable income per capita is $6430. What does this tell us about Mexican purchasing power compared with the USA?

If the Mexican (peso) income were converted into dollars using the PPP exchange rate, the $6430 of disposable income of each Mexican (were national income to be divided equally per person) *really would* buy only about 24 per cent of the goods which could be bought on average by US citizens with their $26 448. In other words, a Mexican could buy 6430 doughnuts while an American could afford the rather daunting number of 26 448.

A serious problem with purchasing power parity exchange rate measures relates to the variety and quality of goods used in the calculations. The goods and services people consume are rarely the same in different countries. However, despite the practical problems, the strengths of this measurement technique are that it gives us a better measurement of comparative purchasing power than market exchange rates, and it can help to tell an interesting story. In this case, it confirms that Mexico has a much lower output and income per head than the USA.

2.2 Economic policies

To understand a bit more about Mexico's economy, and to appreciate what work is like for those citizens in employment, it helps to set its current economic policies in their historical context and to link them to its labour relations history. (Political developments will be covered in the next chapter.) For most of the twentieth century, the *Partido Revolucionario Institucional* (PRI) – the Institutional Revolutionary Party – governed Mexico. The PRI was created after the Mexican revolution of 1910–20 with strong support, not only from the politically active but also from those involved in the labour movement. This close relationship between government and unions – often referred to as 'corporatism' – has been crucial to the direction and implementation of later economic policies and labour relations. (Corporatism is discussed further in Chapter 9.)

One important element of the economic policy that was pursued from the 1940s until the early 1980s was industrialization through import substitution. Chapter 3 and, especially, Chapter 7 describe how this policy works by employing a tariff (tax) on imported goods to protect local manufacturing firms from competition. The aim is to stimulate manufacturing growth by replacing imported goods with home-made products. Unlike India, Mexico did not initially set out to produce machinery for factories. Instead, like other Latin American countries, it began by levying tariffs on imports of consumer durables but imported more freely the large-scale machinery used to make these products. So firms could import capital equipment to make televisions but were discouraged from importing televisions. Other protectionist policies accompanied these tariffs, including direct import controls, government restrictions on foreign direct investment and tax relief for domestic manufacturing firms.

These import substitution policies saw initial success, with the manufacturing share of GDP growing from 18 per cent to 25 per cent between 1940 and 1965. Public sector investment in physical infrastructure, such as roads, power stations and irrigation projects, also helped other sectors of the economy to grow, and this period saw an annual average of 6.3 per cent economic growth in real terms.

Question

What do we mean by growth 'in real terms'? If you are not sure, look back at Chapter 7, Section 2.

If GDP rises in real terms, this means that production of goods and services has increased; the effect of a general rise in prices has been removed from the data. In general, when we speak of variables rising in real terms, we mean that the effects of inflation have been excluded. Later in this chapter, we calculate changes in real as compared to nominal (money) wages, to explore how the purchasing power of Mexican workers has changed over time.

Inflation
A general rise in prices resulting in a decrease in the amount of goods and services a nominal sum of money can purchase.

The next stage of import substitution industrialization involves the domestic production of capital equipment. In this case, Mexico would have moved from making TVs and fridges to producing the assembly line machinery required to manufacture those items. Mexico struggled to move towards this second stage, and continued to rely upon imports of such goods throughout the late 1960s and 1970s. Domestic manufacturing, meanwhile, was becoming increasingly expensive and uncompetitive, so export performance was poor. This deteriorating economic position was masked in the short term by high and expanding public spending, partially financed from oil revenues. Further finance came from borrowing on the international capital markets;

markets that were eager to lend the large savings generated by the oil producing countries after the rise in oil prices during the 1970s.

The crunch came in 1981–82. Oil prices fell and interest rates rose worldwide. Mexico's international borrowing had run up a large debt on which the interest had to be paid in dollars (known as 'servicing' the debt). The fall in oil prices caused Mexico's dollar revenues to drop and the country could no longer service the debt, nor raise the dollars needed for essential imports. Banks were no longer willing to lend, fearing default. The threatened default on debt also threatened the viability of international banks (starting a cycle of Latin American debt crises in the 1980s). The Mexican economy headed into decline. (Chapter 11 has more on international borrowing, aid and debt.)

The ensuing economic crisis in Mexico led to a fundamental policy change. The Mexican government decided that economic growth would have to come, not from state-led industrialization and import substitution, but from deregulation, flexible markets and trade liberalization. Like their counterparts in the USA and Britain, Mexican politicians and policy makers replaced state action with market activity. This move towards liberalization set the context for later trade negotiations such as NAFTA, and was welcomed by US officials, the World Bank and the International Monetary Fund.

These international lending institutions complimented the governments of Miguel de la Madrid Hurtado (1982–88) and Carlos Salinas de Gortari (1988–94) on following the liberalizing recommendations of the Washington Consensus (World Bank, 2000b). This Consensus served as a paradigm of economic policy that helped to shape policies for reform both in Latin America and in other developing countries during the late 1980s and 1990s. It advised countries to open up to trade, liberalize industrial policy, deregulate foreign investment flows, follow exchange rate policies that increased industrial competitiveness, and privatize state-owned enterprises. (Part 4 describes this policy package in more detail.)

Mexico followed many of these polices. In 1984 it removed restrictions on foreign direct investment that had been in force from the mid 1940s through to the early 1970s. It also privatized many large state firms and removed the state monopoly in infrastructure sectors such as road construction and telecommunications. The number of state-owned firms fell from 1155 in 1982 to 232 in 1992. The sell-off included the denationalization of two airline companies, the two largest copper-mining companies, the country's largest telecommunications company and the commercial banks. Mexico also joined the General Agreement on Trade and Tariffs (GATT) in 1986. After 1986, Mexico's maximum tariff rate fell rapidly from 100 per cent to 20 per cent by 1987, and most of the import licences were rapidly eliminated.

2.3   Labour relations

The introduction and implementation of any large-scale changes to economic policy have a major impact on a country's workforce. The full effects of liberalization on workers depend in part on the institutional arrangements in the labour market. In Mexico, these arrangements were dominated by the corporatist relationship between the PRI and the official trade unions. For our present purposes, 'corporatism' refers to co-ordination and agreement on labour issues between a central government and powerful trade unions (see also Chapter 9).

The long history of the corporatist association between government and unions in Mexico gave the labour movement a substantial voice in deciding labour market policies and in determining labour law. Strong labour standards were adopted both in the 1917 Constitution and in the 1931 labour law (Ley Federal del Trabajo – LFT – 1931). The labour-related articles of the Constitution and their regulating law (LFT) comprise a complete set of rights and were used to develop a labour relations model. This model limited employers' discretion on the length of a standard working day and the length of an employment contract. It also allowed for an eight-hour working day, permanent employment after a 28-day contract and a minimum wage. A tripartite commission, the *Comisión Nacional de Salarios Mínimos* (National Commission on Minimum Wages), set the minimum wages. Other aspects of the model included an annual payment equivalent to 15 days' salary; a fund for workers' housing; profit sharing (10 per cent of companies' taxable income); access to health care and social security; pensions; health and safety regulations; the right to collective bargaining; and the right to strike. Overseeing such rights, a tripartite labour justice system (*Juntas Federales y Estatales de Conciliación y Arbitraje*) was created to intervene in the resolution of individual and collective conflicts. Unions were also encouraged to participate in the National Commission on Minimum Wages and in Federal and State Conciliation and Arbitration Boards.

Of course, this kind of protection of labour and domestic wages went against the grain of liberalization policies. Under liberalization, wage rates would depend upon both the productivity of different parts of the workforce and the relative scarcity of different kinds of labour. The policies producing these changes were likely to arouse opposition from the unions. However, the close political relationship between the ruling PRI and the trade union movement, and the extent to which it had resulted in the above raft of labour protection and social security rights, had been used before by Mexican governments to pacify elements of the trade union movement opposed to change and to pursue its own economic agenda.

This occurred again after 1982. For example, the government persuaded the leadership of the large and powerful Confederation of Mexican Workers (CTM) – the largest trade union confederation and an integral part of the PRI – to dampen wage demands and block mobilization. The CTM's agreement to limit wage increases allowed the politicians to bring down inflation, an important element of the economic policy package. Furthermore, as part of its efforts to control wage increases, the Salinas administration after 1988 forcefully used its executive powers to restrict increases in minimum wages, with the aim of increasing the competitiveness of the economy under liberalization.

The labour rights enshrined in the Constitution, the model of labour relations, the minimum wages and the bargaining rights, appeared to provide decent protection for labour in the face of trade liberalization. In marked contrast to the agenda of state withdrawal from regulatory activity that the Mexican economic reformers pursued in other arenas, such as import licensing, government officials during the 1980s and 1990s showed little interest in dismantling the complex array of legal and administrative controls regulating the right to strike, union formation, or wage and contract negotiations. Limiting wage increases in order to reduce inflation was the key element in the strategy towards labour during this period, 'bought' by a retention of other labour rights.

However, there was an important caveat. The interpretation and implementation of labour law are devolved to local government agencies and localized bargaining. Any reluctance to apply regulations at this level reduces the effectiveness of national labour law and seriously weakens the workers' bargaining power. One important example of this, which we shall explore in more detail below, is the maquiladora industrial plants. These factories were established in the 1960s in low wage areas of the country, where employers (mainly US) could use Mexican labour in assembly line production for export using imported inputs. In these zones, the flexible application of labour law led to poor wages and tough working conditions.

In summary, then, the context in which we shall consider the impact of liberalization and NAFTA on wages and labour was one of corporatism, where the official union movement supported the government's low-wage, liberalizing agenda in return for employment protection (however inconsistently applied) remaining in place. It would seem that the price paid by the government for trade union co-operation on wage setting was to exclude the legal protection and administrative structure of labour relations from the liberalizing agenda. Conversely, we can see that the official unions prioritized employment protection over pay.

3 The North American Free Trade Agreement

Under NAFTA, Mexico sought a free trade agreement with the USA, and the eventual deal was built on the existing Canada–USA Free Trade Agreement that had been implemented in 1989. In effect, this agreement expanded to include Mexico, and created an area covering the whole of North America within which goods, services and investment were traded freely. The creation of NAFTA thus involved much more than trade liberalization. It aimed to create a regional block in which capital could move freely – not unlike the Single European Market policies of the European Union.

NAFTA came into operation on 1 January 1994. The scope of the Agreement is very wide, covering rules and procedures for ensuring free cross-border trade (including rules regulating the official origin of goods, and customs procedures); rules seeking to establish equal treatment for local and foreign companies investing in member states; specific sections regulating the agriculture, energy and telecommunications sectors and financial services; provisions on competition policy and on the protection of intellectual property; and a range of procedures for dispute settlement. The objective is market integration and market competitiveness, to allow the free flow of capital and goods and services. The interventions in competition policy and intellectual property (such as patent law) illustrate the extent to which NAFTA goes beyond trade liberalization. In addition, two supplementary agreements, or side-deals, were negotiated on the environment and labour standards.

The broad thrust of NAFTA is pro free trade. Tariffs in many areas were reduced to zero immediately or over a timescale of up to 15 years. Alongside the liberalization of cross-border investment measures, this trade liberalization meant more power moving towards corporations and away from governments. This is particularly noticeable in Chapter 11 of NAFTA, which comprises a set of particularly strong rights and protections for investors: prohibitions on investment-related performance requirements for firms are strengthened and broadened to include subnational governments; foreign investors are protected against discriminatory treatment; and investors can bring complaints about governments to international arbitration.

Some of these provisions particularly favoured foreign investors. For example, Article 11.10 guarantees foreign investors compensation from NAFTA governments for any direct government expropriation or any other action that is 'tantamount to' an 'indirect expropriation', while Article 11.02 provides for 'national treatment' for foreign firms in NAFTA countries. This means that governments must grant all firms treatment similar to that given to locally owned firms. Any firm that believes that a NAFTA government has violated these investor rights and protections can ask for monetary damages before a trade tribunal. These tribunals consist of a three-person panel of professional arbitrators, who listen to the arguments and have the power to award an unbounded amount of government dollars to firms whose NAFTA investor privileges and rights they judge to have been affected negatively. Crucially, these deliberations are closed to public participation, observation or input.

Not surprisingly, a number of companies have used these protections to challenge the prevailing national and local legislation of all three NAFTA countries. By the beginning of 2001, companies had filed more than a dozen complaints, asking for damage payments of more than $13 billion (Tuirán, 2000). One example comes from Metalclad Corporation, a USA-based waste-disposal company, which had invested in industrial waste treatment in the Mexican state of San Luis Potosi. The mayor of the municipality of Guadalcazar denied permission for the company to open its facility, and a NAFTA tribunal dealt with the resulting conflict. Metalclad claimed that Mexico had breached Chapter 11 of NAFTA in refusing permission for a waste-disposal facility. The Federal government, as well as the San Luis Potosi authority, had granted permits to construct and operate a landfill site at the municipality of Guadalcazar. But the local authorities had denied the municipal construction permit. At that point, the state governor called for an environmental impact analysis. The study found evidence that the facility would contaminate the local water supply. As a result, state authorities declared the site part of a 600 000-acre ecological zone.

Metalclad sought compensation of some $90 million for expropriation and for violations of national treatment, most-favoured nation treatment (which states that investors must be treated on the terms offered to the most favoured country) and prohibitions on performance requirements. In August 2000, a three-person panel found that Mexico had breached the provisions of Chapter 11 and awarded Metalclad $16.7 million, the amount it had spent on the facility. Mexico then filed a petition to the Supreme Court of British Columbia (where the case had been heard) appealing the award and arguing that, in accordance with the Mexican constitution, municipalities had the right to regulate land use. However, the Court ruled that it did not have the jurisdiction to overturn the verdict reached by the NAFTA-appointed tribunal. In June 2001, the parties reached an agreement to settle the case for $16.7 million – the amount originally recommended by the panel.

NAFTA thus intensified Mexico's process of economic liberalization, which had begun in the 1980s. It also contained key economic provisions that strongly influenced labour and communities. These included powerful foreign investor rights, the opening up of trade, and sharp reductions in the role of the state. In addition, NAFTA also encouraged the creation of a more flexible labour market. The next section explores the consequences of this for Mexican workers.

4 Mexican labour under liberalization

4.1 Unemployment

A quick glance at Table 8.2 makes it look as if the Mexican economy was doing rather well in the 1990s. In 1992 only 2.8 per cent of those living in urban areas were officially classified as unemployed and, apart from 1995–96 when the peso crisis (which we shall discuss later) pushed unemployment to over 6 per cent, it has stayed between 2 per cent and 4 per cent. These rates compare well with UK unemployment, which was over 6 per cent from 1993 to 1998 (Office for National Statistics, 2002). Mexican unemployment is listed for urban areas only, because of the highly seasonal nature of agricultural labour, which makes it difficult to speak of (open) unemployment in areas where lots of the workers are peasants.

However, such relatively low unemployment figures do not reveal the whole picture of Mexico's labour market and the associated issues of poverty and inequality. To obtain a clearer understanding we must first know more about official definitions of employment and unemployment and about systems of welfare support.

Table 8.2 Urban unemployment rates by gender (per cent)

Year	Women	Men	Total
1992	3.2	2.7	2.8
1993	3.9	3.2	3.4
1994	3.9	3.6	3.7
1995	6.4	6.1	6.2
1996	5.9	5.3	5.5
1997	4.2	3.5	3.7
1998	3.6	2.9	3.2
1999	2.7	2.4	2.5
2000	2.4	2.1	2.2
2001	2.6	2.4	2.4

Source: INEGI, 1992–2001

Mexico's Institute of National Statistics uses International Labour Organization (ILO) definitions to categorize citizens as employed or unemployed. Under the ILO guidelines, anyone over a specified age (in Mexico it is 12) who has been employed in a paid or unpaid capacity in a certain economic unit for more than one hour during the week in which the survey is carried out officially has a job. Those who do not fall into this category, but are immediately available and actively seeking work, are classified as involuntary unemployed. This means that a person working unpaid in a family business for six hours and one paid for working full time in a modern manufacturing plant are both classified as employed. When we realize that this distinctly weak definition is applied in Mexico within a society with no unemployment insurance, and one where there is little capacity for saving, it becomes clear that low headline unemployment figures do not necessarily imply a buoyant and prosperous labour market.

It is also interesting to examine the profile of those described as unemployed. They are mainly young females or males with an above average education. Household heads represent only 20 per cent of the unemployed. The implication is that only those with savings, or those on whom others are unlikely to be dependent, can afford to be unemployed.

Question

What does Figure 8.1 show about the length of time people are registered as unemployed?

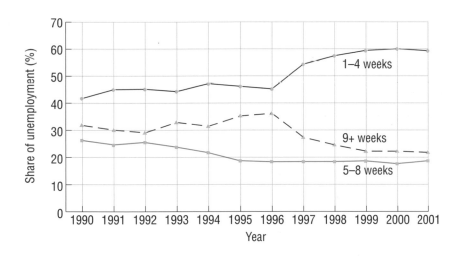

Figure 8.1   Length of time unemployed: share of total urban unemployment by duration unemployed, Mexico, 1990–2001 (per cent)

Source: INEGI, Banco de Información Económica, http://www.inegi.gob.mx

Note: Data do not quite add to 100% because of rounding.

Figure 8.1 indicates that the largest of the three categories of the urban unemployed is those who have been without work for less than four weeks. Furthermore, their share of this category in urban unemployment rose over the 1990s while the share of those without work for longer periods of time correspondingly fell.

This figure supports the image of unemployment as a relative luxury for Mexican workers and implies that the unemployment recorded by the National Institute of Statistics is mostly frictional, that is, it represents the time it takes for citizens to move from one job to another.

4.2 Employment

So most Mexicans have jobs, but what kind of work is done and how have liberalization and NAFTA affected the structure of the labour market? Table 8.3 gives us a way to begin to answer these questions by providing a snapshot of the labour force by industry and gender for the year 2000. The first point to note is the gender profile of the overall labour force – of the 39 million in work or seeking work, 66 per cent are men and 34 per cent are women. This may reflect the greater pressure on women to remain in the domestic sphere, and compares with a situation in Britain where women make up 46 per cent of the labour force (Office for National Statistics, 2002).

Table 8.3   Mexican labour force by sex and industry, second quarter 2000 (millions)

Industry	Labour force		
	Men	Women	Total
Agriculture	6.1	1.0	7.1
Extractive industries	0.1	0.0	0.1
Manufacturing	4.7	2.8	7.5
Construction	2.5	0.1	2.6
Electricity	0.2	0.0	0.2
Commerce	3.6	3.2	6.8
Restaurants and hotels	0.6	0.7	1.3
Food peddling	0.2	0.3	0.5
Communications and transportation	1.6	0.2	1.8
Services	5.7	3.4	9.1
Domestic services	0.2	1.6	1.8
Total	25.7	13.3	39.0

Source: adapted from INEGI, 2000

Question

Think of an industrialized economy like that of the UK. What is strikingly different about the sectoral distribution of employment in Mexico?

One big difference is the relative size of the Mexican agricultural work force. In 2000, over 7 million, mainly male, workers were employed in agriculture. This represented 18 per cent of the total labour force, in comparison with 1.6 per cent in the UK (where the share of agricultural labour is particularly low).

The importance of agriculture to Mexican employment was particularly relevant to the impact of NAFTA, as any changes to the rate of employment in this sector were going to affect a lot of people. Liberalization affected the agricultural and livestock sector in two ways. Increased competition from imports reduced prices for local farmers, and a drop in government investment, production subsidies and price supports reduced farmers' incomes. Corn production in particular was badly affected. Following the implementation of NAFTA, the highly capitalized (and subsidized) grain producers in the USA exported corn to Mexico, forcing agricultural workers out of this sector and, in many cases, making people leave the land completely.

The NAFTA treaty did include an exceptional 15-year transition period for highly sensitive products such as corn and beans, which are food staples. This policy was designed to cushion the impact of NAFTA on Mexican farmers by providing a long adaptation period. However, the option was not fully exploited by the government. In a move that illustrates the important interaction between politics and economics, the Mexican government chose to reduce tariff and non-tariff barriers to corn imports faster than required, resulting in a severe decline in income and employment among small and medium sized agricultural producers. This aspect of trade liberalization resulted in a growing dualism in Mexican agriculture, providing a boost for the comparatively small number of export-orientated producers (firms exporting fruits, vegetables and some livestock) while forcing many less efficient producers out of business, and contributing to further stagnation and decline in the rural economy.

The result was a fall in rural employment from 8.2 million in 1990 to 7.1 million in 2000, and a consequent increase in the urban population. Over the 1991–2000 period the share of the population living in cities of 100 000 plus inhabitants grew from 44.6 per cent to 47.2 per cent. Citizens displaced from the country tended to move into the informal employment sector in cities. This led to an increase in the number of those doing low skill work in small workplaces. Table 8.4 gives a little more detail, and shows that in 2000 over 40 per cent of the workers in the economy as a whole were employed in economic units with five or fewer people. In construction and commerce the percentage was over 50 per cent. The majority of these small-scale firms (including some non-wage work in family enterprises) were in commerce and services, large employment sectors (Table 8.3) where working conditions are generally poor.

Table 8.4   Industry distribution of employment by size of unit (percentage of total by industry), 2000

			Employees			
	1	2–5	6–10	11–15	16–50	51 or more
Manufacturing	5.8	13.6	6.0	2.9	10.2	61.3
Construction	17.6	37.3	9.2	3.8	13.6	18.4
Commerce	21.2	36.5	6.4	3.3	8.6	23.8
Services	18.4	22.9	5.1	2.3	7.2	44.0
Total	15.9	24.4	5.9	2.8	8.7	42.2

Note: Figures are for urban areas of 100 000 plus inhabitants.
Source: based on INEGI, 1991–2001

This prevalence of small scale employers was associated with a trend towards more part-time jobs. Throughout the 1990s around 10 per cent of the urban labour force worked less than 15 hours per week. Most of these were female workers, and their inclusion in the total employment figures can give an exaggerated impression of the economy's ability to provide jobs.

Another emerging trend was the falling number of those receiving a daily wage (known in Mexico as 'salaried' employees). Between 1991 and 1998 the share of salaried employees in total employment decreased from 73.9 per cent to 61.2 per cent. The pattern was for older salaried workers to move from employment in modern manufacturing, construction, trade and communications into self-employment in retail, food and transportation. Younger workers moved into unemployment or low pay/no pay jobs as street peddlers or trade apprentices. Overall, the share of self-employed workers increased by 50 per cent and the numbers of workers having unpaid positions as their first occupation doubled. Also, the percentage of workers aged 12 to 14 who had unpaid jobs jumped from 40 per cent to 60 per cent between 1991 and 1998. Lastly, employment insecurity was evident from the 23.3 per cent (up from 20.5 per cent in 1990) of urban waged and salaried employees without the mandatory social benefits (health care, retirement funds, paid holidays) specified by Mexican labour law.

Thus despite corporatism and its tradition of protection for labour, the plight of many kinds of workers in Mexico actually worsened after liberalization and NAFTA. Some of those most affected were displaced from the agricultural sector and moved to urban areas, where they worked in small establishments on temporary contracts or were self-employed. Another group of disadvantaged workers was women with part-time jobs. None of these groups was unionized or protected by labour laws. In short, they were labour with very poor bargaining power.

Liberalization not only put pressure on people to move from the countryside to the city, but also led to migration across borders. Northbound international migration increased throughout the 1990s, and the number of permanent migrants, in particular, has risen (Tuirán, 2000). The geographical origins of these migrants are very diverse, as many of the new migrants come from Mexican regions with no previous history of migration to the USA. At the same time, more migrants have been leaving from urban areas and they are better educated, providing a stark contrast to the traditional image of rural, illiterate migrants. This shift in migration patterns is a significant indicator of a decline in the supply of good jobs in Mexico, even for well educated and well skilled workers. Migration to the USA not only helps to absorb a number of Mexican workers, but remittances also help those relatives that stay in Mexico to survive, and sometimes to thrive, in their villages and cities. Current estimates of the amount of migrants' transfers from the USA to Mexico hover around 7 billion dollars a year (CONAPO, 2000).

In trying to understand the Mexican labour market we must remember that labour markets are continually changing, adapting to new demands from the market, conforming to (and occasionally confronting) new developments in technology, responding to government policies and reacting to trade agreements and other global events. Mexico's labour market shares this dynamism and complexity. But while we acknowledge the complicated nature of the labour market, it is still possible to identify the impact of increased liberalization and NAFTA. Specifically, the effects have been a movement away from government intervention (including the sustaining of labour rights), an increase in insecurity of employment and a shift to low-end service sector work. And importantly, there has also been a commitment to using low wages to reduce industrial costs and to encourage exports, and thus to act as an incentive to attract foreign investment. This commitment has been especially successful in the maquiladora plants that have developed near the border of northern Mexico. The next section investigates these plants and uses them to discuss the broader issue of working conditions and labour organizing.

5 Working conditions and labour organizing

The maquiladora programme grew out of the border industrialization programme that started in 1965. The aim was to create assembly plants that imported duty free parts into Mexico and then exported finished products made by Mexican labour. Most exports were intended for the US market, and tariffs were levied only on the value added abroad. Thus if US parts worth $1 million were exported to Mexico and, after assembly, were re-exported back to the USA with a value of $1.2 million, a tariff would be levied only on the additional $200 000 (Gereffi, 1996).

Early maquiladora plants were based on the USA–Mexico border and drew on local labour with little industrial experience. As Morales (1999) has pointed out, one possible explanation for the location of these plants was to discourage the migration of low skilled labour to the USA. Initially, the plants were low technology operations assembling clothing, footwear and furniture. The numbers employed grew modestly to 60 000 workers by 1985 and, throughout the 1990s, the labour force increased steadily so that, by 2000, over one million workers were directly employed in maquiladoras (Table 8.5).

Table 8.5   Maquiladora employment (thousands)

Year	Men	Women	Total direct workers
1980	23.1	78.8	101.9
1985	53.8	120.0	173.8
1990	140.0	219.4	359.4
1995	217.6	314.2	531.8
2000	468.7	576.7	1045.4
2001	433.0	526.5	959.5

Source: INEGI, 1991–2001

Employment in clothing has seen a particularly strong rise in numbers, due mainly to the relaxation of Multifibre Agreement quotas under NAFTA (O'Day, 1997). Clothing and apparel production have always been an important part of the maquiladoras, but more recently there has been a shift into electronics and auto part exports (Carrillo and González, 1999). As employment in the maquiladoras grew they moved away from the border. Between 1994 and 2000 the proportion of maquiladora workers in non-border locations increased from 16 per cent to 23 per cent as the population shifted southward to areas such as Jalisco, Mexico City, Puebla and Yucatan.

In many ways the maquiladora programme serves as a microcosm of the labour conditions that were created under liberalization and intensified under NAFTA. Principal among these conditions was the 'flexibilization' of the labour market, as noted by the Chilean author Francisco Zapata (1997). 'Flexibilization' refers to the loss in practice of the forms of labour protection outlined in Section 2, increasing the power of employers over workers. It includes changes in labour market structure of the sort discussed in Section 4, where workers move from salaried to precarious employment, and implies deteriorating employment conditions, falling salary levels, worsening labour contracts and declining union membership. For example, manufacturing saw union membership fall from 1.4 million in 1992 to 1.2 million in 2000. Across the economy, only around 4 million Mexican workers, representing some 10 per cent of the workforce, were unionized by 2000. This compares with an average union density in Britain of 36 per cent (Cully *et al.*, 1999). Some 60 per cent of Mexican union members are male and union density is highest in the services sector, notably in education, health and social security where there are large numbers of government employees.

It is worth noting that NAFTA contains a Labour Side Accord specifically to protect the rights of labour. Unions from all three member countries pressed during negotiations for the recognition of labour rights and succeeded in establishing the North American Agreement on Labour Co-operation (NAALC), which was signed in 1993. This agreement was based on a commitment to a number of guiding principles, including rights to collective bargaining, to organization without interference, to strike freely, to equal pay and to protection for migrant and child workers. These principles supplemented each country's domestic labour laws, which in Mexico's case would seem to offer formidable protection.

However, in contrast to the rules protecting investors (think back to the Metalclad example in Section 3), the sanctions and the administrative structure supporting the appeals process for NAALC are weak. There is a trinational Commission for Labour Co-operation and a National Administrative Office (NAO) in each member state, but there are problems in identifying issues, in the limited sanctions available and in the apparent reluctance to apply those sanctions strictly (Carr, 1999). For example, before any action can be taken there has to be a consistent pattern of non-compliance, then a panel of outside experts is established, and finally, following their recommendations, sanctions can be applied by the relevant NAO. Even then, such sanctions are rather modest and range from consultation between labour ministries to fines in extreme cases.

Sanctions are also infrequently applied. To demonstrate the ineffectiveness of the appeal process, Carr (1999) cites the examples of the Honeywell plant in the city of Chihuahua. Here the Mexican Authentic Labour Front was working with the United Electrical, Radio and Machine Workers of America and the International Brotherhood of Teamsters to organize a local union. This led to 20 workers being dismissed. Since a Strategic Organizing Alliance operated between the three unions, a petition was filed with the American NAO. The NAO accepted that the 'timing of the dismissals appears to coincide with an organizing drive', but no action was taken. So while the NAALC provides an avenue for the expression of discontentment, and offers space for international co-operation between unions, its effectiveness is limited by the strength and consistency with which its rules are enforced.

Working through official unions is one route for workers to express and exercise agency, that is, to demonstrate their engagement individually and collectively with their working environment. Another method of exercising agency is for workers to create their own independent unions. An interesting example of this approach comes from a major maquiladora producer of Nike clothing called Kukdong International. An activist's website describes the developments.

On January 9 of 2001, the workers of Kukdong International (now called 'Mexmode'), an apparel contractor in the town of Atlixco, Mexico, seized control of their factory. Fed up with the factory's rancid cafeteria food, corrupt company-allied union, and the firing of five workers for demanding better treatment, approximately 800 workers, mostly young women in their teens and early 20s, left their stations at midday and went on wildcat strike. For the next three days, they camped in protest in [the] factory's front patio, enduring nights of drizzling rain with little or no cover. Late on the third night, a battalion of riot police, led by the existing union's secretary general, marched into the area wielding clubs and guns. By sunrise, 17 workers needed medical attention. Several were struck unconscious. ...

News of the uprising and violent dispersal, and the fact that Kukdong was a major producer for Nike and dozens of universities, zipped quickly through the internet to student anti-sweatshop activists in the US. Spying another bout with the mammoth apparel firm, students organized support rallies at Nike stores across the country. Meanwhile, a wave of new factory monitoring organizations descended on Atlixco to conduct investigations. Within weeks the story had made it to the pages of the *New York Times*. By late February the factory had reinstated the majority of the fired workers, including several of the leaders originally terminated for organizing – a virtually unprecedented scenario in Mexican maquiladoras. And by mid September, the workers of Kukdong had successfully launched the only independent union for garment workers in all of Mexico with a collective bargaining agreement. They have since won improvements in almost every aspect of factory life. ...

In this case, the workers themselves spearheaded the campaign and established a remarkably strong base of support. The conditions for organizing are daunting. The factory's workforce lives scattered across 64 small rural towns surrounding the factory, some located as far as two hours away. Most workers cannot be reached by phone, so to keep workers informed one has to drive deep into rural areas and simply hope the workers will be around when you arrive.

Source: Blasi, 2003

In this case, determined workers dissatisfied with the official union – which had used violence to keep workers in line – had managed to overcome the barriers to independent labour organizing, drawing on the collective strength within the plant and the broader community. The problem of unions that work closely with employers, rather than prioritizing the representation of employees, is common in the maquiladoras. These unions are known as *sindicatos de protección* ('sweetheart' protection unions), which help employers to control the workers.

Also particularly striking in this case was the role of international support for local labour organization. There were two aspects to this. One was the Internet-based student activism and the publicity it generated – taking the story into the *New York Times*. The anti-sweatshop campaigning on US campuses has included successful pressure to reveal the names and locations of contractors, making this kind of campaigning link-up easier. The other aspect was the 'factory monitoring organizations' referred to in the extract. These included the Worker Rights Consortium, Verité, and the International Labor Rights Fund. They aim to inspect garment and shoe factories and document abuse; to publicise their findings; and to call for basic labour rights. In this case, the Kukdong workforce was able to capitalize on this international publicity and pressure to improve its own bargaining position sharply.

The experience of the maquiladoras is one element of the greater 'flexibility' of labour markets emerging in Mexico in the period of liberalization. Greater flexibility for employers means the abrogation in practice of labour rights, a decline in working conditions and the suppression of labour organizing. NAFTA's failure to create effective labour rights protection – in contrast to its protection for investors – has reinforced this 'flexibilization'. But we have seen that workers do continue to organize and negotiate for improved rights, and that both official and independent Mexican unionism has been able on occasions to draw strength from international collaboration and solidarity.

Activity 8.1

Look back at Chapter 2, Section 4.1. There, Aditya Bhattacharjea argues that trade unions in wealthy countries should not campaign to include labour standards in trade agreements. Do you think that his argument also applies to the Kukdong International story? Are US activists in this case also engaging in protectionism?

6   Explaining wage decline

We know from Sections 4 and 5 that the plight of workers in Mexico is pretty tough. We know that there are laws protecting their rights but that those laws are applied inconsistently. What about the wages the workers receive? Did they change after liberalization and NAFTA? What we find is a pattern of falling wages across the country during liberalization and into the period after accession to NAFTA. This is a surprising result. We might have expected the opposite – rising wages with liberalization and under NAFTA. In this section we shall discuss some possible explanations for the falling wage rates.

6.1   Real and nominal wages

First, how do we measure the rise or fall in wages? Looking at money wages gives us only part of the answer. To measure the extent of a drop in the living standards of those working in wage jobs, we need to measure the decline in the purchasing power of the money wage, that is, in the amount of goods those wages will buy. This will not be the same as the change in the money value of the pay packet because of the effects of inflation. If there is inflation, a given money (or 'nominal') wage will buy less and less over time.

So to measure the fall in wages we need to take nominal wages and *deflate* them, to take out the effect of inflation. Trade unions make this calculation when considering a pay claim. The claim they put in will seek to cover inflation and also give the workers a real rise in pay.

Question

If nominal wages rise by 4 per cent over a year, but the inflation rate is 8 per cent in the same period, what has happened to real wages?

They have fallen. If you thought that they fell by 4 per cent you were not far off. Here is how you calculate the drop. If wages rise by 4 per cent we can think of that as a wage of 100 per cent at the beginning of the year, and a wage of 104 per cent at the end of the year. Price change can be measured as an index in the same way, as does, for example, the consumer price index in the UK. The base year's price for a basket of goods is defined as 100 and inflation is measured from that level. In our example, the base was the start of the year, and prices rose to 108 by the end of the year. The real wage at the end of the year is then measured as:

$$\frac{104}{108} \times 100 = 96.3 \text{ (to one decimal place)}$$

Real wages thus fell by a little less than 4 per cent.

Mexican real wages went into a sharp decline in the 1990s. The benchmark national minimum wage, set at a level agreed between the official unions, employers and federal government, lost 50 per cent of its purchasing power between 1990 and 1999. In industries where wage bargaining is under the supervision of the federal state (described as *salarios contractuales*, that is, 'contractual wages' or bargained wages), pay fell by 21 per cent in real terms between 1993 and 1999. Real wages also declined in manufacturing, dropping by 11 per cent between 1994 and 2000.

Table 8.6 shows some detailed calculations of the evolution of real wages in Mexico after 1994. A drop in real wages in manufacturing, and for those wage and salary earners eligible for social security (as reported by the IMSS, the Mexican Social Security Institute), stands out for 1995 and 1996.

Table 8.6   The evolution of Mexican wages, selected indicators (index 1994 = 100), 1994–2001

Year	Minimum wage	IMSS reported wages	Wages in manufacturing
1994	100.0	100.0	100.0
1995	87.1	84.4	85.3
1996	80.5	75.2	76.9
1997	79.5	73.9	77.8
1998	79.9	75.2	80.0
1999	77.2	75.6	81.7
2000	77.6	79.2	87.0
2001	78.4	83.3	89.0

Source: calculations from data provided by Banco de Información Económica, INEGI and Secretaría del Trabajo y Previsión Social

Why did this happen? One reason was that inflation rose sharply after 1994 without corresponding adjustments in nominal wages. The year of accession to NAFTA (1994) also saw a Mexican currency crisis and a devaluation of the peso. (Foreign exchange markets and devaluation are explained further in Chapter 11.)

If the value of the peso falls relative to the US dollar (the main trading currency for Mexico's external trade), each dollar will buy more pesos. This makes Mexican products cheaper in dollar terms and firms exporting from Mexico will get more orders from the USA. This effect helped to sustain an expansion of maquiladora exports in the following couple of years. However, think about imported goods. The prices of these will be set in dollars, the

Devaluation
A currency has been devalued if a unit of that currency will buy less of other currencies than before.

dominant trading currency. Mexicans now need more pesos to buy a dollar, so the peso price of imported goods will rise. If a substantial proportion of the goods bought by workers are imported, or produced from imported inputs, consumer prices will rise.

In Mexico in the mid 1990s, devaluation of the peso was indeed accompanied by a sharp upward jump in inflation. Figure 8.2 shows the rise in the consumer price index (CPI). Nominal wages did not keep pace; rather, they stayed much the same in nominal terms. In a period of economic crisis, this led to a sharp decline in real wages.

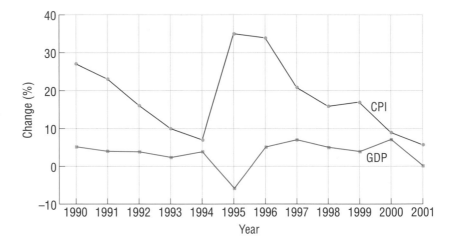

Figure 8.2 Annual change in consumer price index (CPI) and annual growth in GDP at constant prices, Mexico, 1990–2001 (per cent)

Source: World Bank, *World Development Indicators*, online

Question

Why did competition in the labour market not push up wages as prices rose? Look at Table 8.2 and Figure 8.2 for clues.

Figure 8.2 shows that 1995 was a recession year, in which real GDP fell by 6 per cent. Table 8.2 shows that in 1995–96 recorded unemployment was sharply higher than in earlier or later years. This suggests that workers, especially those with 'salaried' jobs, were being laid off. So employers in this period were not facing a need to compete for workers; on the contrary, workers were competing as jobs became scarcer. Thus competitive market pressures were pushing wages down rather than up in the immediate aftermath of the NAFTA accession.

This combination of inflation and economic recession was the immediate cause of a sharp decline in real wages. But what of the longer-term effects of liberalization and devaluation on wages? The next section considers what economic theory can tell us about the reasons liberalization has not brought rising wages to Mexico's workers.

6.2   Liberalization and changes in real wages: economic theory

The decline in real wages is particularly striking because it was the opposite of what many economists expected to occur as a result of liberalization and free trade within NAFTA. To see why this is so, let us pick up some theory that you studied in Chapter 3. One of the big differences between Mexico and the USA is the skill levels of the labour forces. The USA has a higher ratio of more highly skilled to lower skilled labour than Mexico. And Mexican wages are lower on average than wages in the USA.

Question

Look back at Chapter 3. What would you expect to happen to wages in Mexico after liberalization of trade and foreign investment?

Let us start with trade. We would expect Mexico to have a comparative advantage (Chapter 3, Section 3) in producing goods requiring low skill, routine assembly work, such as manufacturing jeans or slotting together computer components. Similarly, we would expect the USA to have an advantage in producing, say, computer software using highly skilled labour.

So when trade is liberalized, we would expect Mexico to specialize and export along the lines of comparative advantage. The expansion of those activities, in turn, should raise the wages of low skilled Mexican workers, or at least expand employment at existing wages (Chapter 3, Section 5.2). Now add the liberalization of foreign direct investment to the model. Again, we would expect, say, US firms to move activities requiring lots of low skilled labour to Mexico, while keeping those elements of production that require high levels of skill in the USA. That expectation is in line with the development of the maquiladora industries, as described above, from the 1980s. And again, the effect should be to increase the demand for lower skilled labour (that is, the majority of Mexican workers) and consequently to raise – not reduce – their wages (although high skilled Mexican workers may lose out). In the USA, lower skilled workers would be expected to lose out – and that is indeed what happened.

So why did real wages in Mexican manufacturing fall? The decline included lower wage earners, so it is not explained by an increase in the relative numbers of the low paid. The first question to ask then is, is the model just outlined the appropriate one, or are some of the assumptions incorrect? The explicit modelling of assumptions and expected outcomes is one of the greatest strengths of economic theory. In simplifying and concentrating on important variables, economic models allow us to analyse carefully an otherwise bewilderingly complex reality. In this case, the failure of the prediction of the standard theory shows that we have to question the model.

Let us do so in stages. First, suppose that we are wrong to analyse this situation using a model with just two countries trading. Remember that Mexico liberalized its external trade relations in the 1980s, before NAFTA. Suppose we add a third country to our comparative advantage model: one with even lower wages than Mexico (Bangladesh, for example). Then, in this three country model, Mexico is the middle income country; let us suppose it has medium skill levels, between the skill patterns of the USA and Bangladesh. Then Mexico's exports of low-skill intensive goods – such as training shoes – are competing with those of Bangladesh in a free trade model. In this situation, Mexican labour producing training shoes is effectively competing with Bangladeshi labour producing training shoes for sale on the international (particularly the US) market. The effect is likely to be rising wages for low skilled workers in Bangladesh but falling wages for low skilled workers in Mexico. Mexico, as a middle income country, will need to find a niche that exploits higher productivity, medium-skill intensive activities, if it is to sustain its levels of wages and compete successfully.

Next, note that underlying the comparative advantage model is a competitive model of the labour market. As trading patterns change, competition for particular types of labour on the labour market drives up wages, while other types of labour lose out. This competitive model can take us quite a long way: we have just shown that we can, with quite a small amendment to the model you are already familiar with, produce one explanation of Mexican wage decline in export manufacturing.

But there is more to the study of labour markets than models of competition, as the previous sections have shown. Labour markets are social and political – as well as economic – institutions, heavily influenced by government and unions. And government pressure in Mexico is a major factor in explaining wage decline. For a number of years, a central element of economic policy has been to keep wages low in order to help control inflation and stimulate exports. To see how this has worked, we have to bring wage bargaining into our understanding of the labour market.

In models of wage bargaining, competition for labour in relation to the supply of different types of labour is not the only determinant of wages. Instead, nominal wages are agreed during negotiations between representatives of management and workers. Then both workers and employers take the agreed wages into account in their labour supply and hiring decisions. The corporatist relationship which has emerged from the long association between the Mexican government and the official unions (Section 2) has meant that such wage bargaining has long been important in Mexico, and its influence can be seen in the central and local negotiations establishing the minimum wage and *salarios contractuales*. As discussed briefly above, the official union movement in Mexico appears to have traded off falling wages, including a deterioration in the minimum wage that formed a benchmark for low wage earners, for an influence on government that allowed the maintenance of labour laws and some continuing employment security. This government policy and bargaining partly explains the widespread wage decline.

6.3 Segmented labour market theory

It is not only in terms of the role of bargaining that labour markets need to be understood as social and political institutions. Labour markets are also deeply influenced by social divisions, as segmented labour market theory explores. Segmented labour market theorists argue that the competitive labour market model, in which wages are set by the interaction of supply and demand for labour, and a rise in demand for labour pushes up wages, is at best a severely incomplete model of the labour market. They argue that social, historical and institutional forces exert a strong influence on labour market inequality, decisions and outcomes. Central to their work is a concern with explaining inequality, in terms of wages, working conditions and employment opportunities, among different occupational, industrial and demographic groups.

This interest in the importance of social forces in shaping labour market outcomes can be dated back to John Stuart Mill (1976; first published 1848) and John Cairnes (1974 first published 1874), who criticized Adam Smith (1982; first published 1776) for paying inadequate attention to the importance of 'social rank' as a barrier to mobility. The argument developed that non-economic phenomena played a role in shaping labour market inequality. Later writers reasoned that non-competing groups of workers were formed in a number of different ways, through the development of an official labour market institution such as a trade union, for example, or via the interaction of social forces such as social class. Such institutions and social groups help to create an occupationally and industrially stratified labour market (Kerr, 1954; Dunlop, 1957; Cain, 1976).

This was built on by influential US labour market economists such as Doeringer and Piore (1971) and Gordon *et al.* (1982), who argued that one model that helps to explain the persistence of poverty and unemployment among certain groups (particularly related to race) is the model of the dual labour market. In this model, social, historical, institutional and political forces combine to create two, essentially non-competing, sectors: a core, primary workforce occupying relatively secure jobs with relatively good pay and conditions; and a peripheral, secondary workforce with insecure jobs and relatively poor pay and conditions. While some argue that the search for evidence of a strict dualistic formulation has led to oversimplifications (Rubery and Wilkinson, 1994), there is broad agreement on the importance of historical, institutional, political and social forces in creating segmented labour markets.

Empirical evidence from Mexico shows that the labour market is segmented in a number of important ways – and one of these ways is gender. Women make up most of the part-time work force and are strongly represented in the informal sectors of the labour market, domestic services and food peddling (Table 8.3). And, although the situation in the maquiladoras has been changing, the historical position has been that women have outnumbered men in this important sector (Table 8.5). There is some evidence that maquiladora industries' employers have sought to employ female workers because they are less unionized and will accept lower pay and poorer working conditions than men (Nauman and Hutchinson, 1997). As the case of the young female workers in the Kukdong factory in Section 5 demonstrates, women do not passively accept such a working environment, but nevertheless when the work is highly routine the management often turns to women.

The structural changes to the economy also point toward stratification. The move to low-end service sector work, often carried out by the self employed or in economic units made up of only two or three people (Table 8.4), increases the type of work that is part of the secondary labour market. Tables 8.3 and 8.4 illustrate the extent of this employment in Mexico – some 41 per cent of those who work in services (around 3.76 million workers) work in units of five or fewer people. Such small-scale workplaces are usually characterized by poor terms and conditions and typify the shift to more 'flexible' labour markets associated with liberalization and intensified under NAFTA.

As discussed in Section 4, one of the reasons people move into self employment and carry out low skill, low pay jobs such as street vending is the absence of adequate unemployment insurance. A final (and more radical) explanation for low wages argues that this lack of welfare support weakens workers' bargaining positions over wages and working conditions, which means that most people are likely to take any job they can get. Such a labour market environment makes the training and education associated with high skill, high productivity work tough to achieve.

So in understanding the falling wages in Mexico associated with trade liberalization we can bring together a number of aspects of the labour market. As people moved from the countryside to the town, as a result of the decline of agriculture, the numbers of people seeking low skilled jobs rose. However, those job seekers were crowding into one segment of the labour market and the competitive model tells us that this will tend to drive down wages in that sector. Furthermore, this segment of the labour market displayed a number of characteristics that tend to produce low wages: high numbers of women and young people, low levels of unionization, and a lack of welfare support. In addition, the government wanted to attract foreign direct investment on the basis of low wage rates, and used its corporatist controls to put downward pressure on wages. This prevented nominal wages rising sufficiently to offset inflation and so real wages fell. The next section investigates the bigger picture of income inequality.

7   Income inequality

We have told so far a complex story of falling real wages in manufacturing; falling incomes and declining employment in agriculture; and a segmented market for labour with many working in 'flexibilized' conditions with few or no effective labour rights. In this section we ask about the implication of these changes for inequality of incomes in Mexico as a whole. To answer this question, we need to measure inequality of incomes in Mexico, and then see if and how it has changed. In this section we shall introduce some different measures of inequality and apply them to answer this question.

We shall use per capita household income to analyse income inequality. It makes sense to choose a measure of income based on household, rather than individual, income because incomes are shared to some extent within households. So someone earning a very low income is much better off if they live with someone who has a good salary than if they live with another low earner. However, if we use household income, we must take into consideration the number of people who share the total income. The easiest way to do this is by dividing the total household income of each household by the number of people in the household. This gives us the *per capita* household income. So in this section household income data have been adjusted in this way to take account of household composition. (Other methods of adjustment treat children in households as fractions of adults.)

Wage labour income is the most important source of household income. According to 2000 data from the National Household Income and Expenditure Survey, about 60 per cent of the total monetary income of households came from labour income. In the same year, income from 'entrepreneurial' activities, that is, income from ownership of a business or self-employment, accounted for 27 per cent of total household income. Income from bank accounts, real estate, stocks and other assets accounted for the remainder.

To see how to measure income inequality, suppose we line up people by the per capita income of their households, with the poorest at the left and the richest at the right, each of them with their corresponding income. This gives you an income distribution ranked from poor to rich. Suppose we then put a marker one-tenth of the way along; that is, we mark off the ten per cent of the poorest people (that is, the people with the poorest per capita household income) and look at the income at this point. Suppose this income is $200. The marker is at the first *decile*; everyone below the marker has a lower per capita household income than $200. Then we put another marker at the 20 per cent poorest, and we look at the income at this level: $350 for instance. That is the income at the second decile. And so on, until the ninth marker leaves just the 10 per cent of the richest people above it. Each of these markers, at an income expressed in terms of the local currency, is at a decile: that is, one tenth of a ranked income distribution. A widely used measure of income inequality is the ratio of the income at the ninth decile (P_{90}) to the income at the first decile (P_{10}). This is often referred to as the decile ratio.

Decile ratio
The ratio of the income at the ninth decile to the income at the first decile of the income distribution: P_{90}/P_{10}.

The decile ratio is a good indicator of inequality because it measures the 'distance', across the income distribution, between someone in a high income and a low income per capita household.

The decile ratio compares two incomes at different places in the ranked income distribution. An alternative way of measuring income distribution is to look at the shares of different groups of poor and rich people. So, once we have everyone lined up (in the computer) by per capita household income, we can calculate the proportion of total income that goes to each one-tenth of the population. This gives us another commonly used method of picturing inequality: the proportion of income that goes to, say, the top 10 or 20 per cent, and the proportion that goes to the bottom 10 or 20 per cent.

Table 8.7 shows some data similar to this for Mexico, for selected years since 1977. In this case, however, the data are for households (not people) ordered by per capita household income. So the 'top 20 per cent' refers to the richest one-fifth of households. Table 8.7 shows that over half the income goes to the richest one-fifth of households, and less than 4 per cent to the poorest one-fifth. The picture is one of a persistently unequal distribution of income between households.

Finally, we can use data of the kind shown in Table 8.7 to find a measure of income distribution that includes both ends of the distribution, the very rich and the very poor, and also reflects what is happening in the middle. If the gap between the ends stayed much the same, but in the middle the lower earners lost ground while the higher earners moved up, we would want to note that inequality had increased. The last measure described here gives us a way to pick up a change of this sort.

Table 8.7   Monetary income distribution between Mexican households, 1977–2000

	1977	1984	1989	1992	1994	1996	1998	2000
Lowest 20%	3.0	3.9	3.4	3.1	3.1	3.4	2.9	3.2
Second 20%	6.9	8.2	7.7	7.1	6.9	7.3	7.0	7.2
Middle 20%	11.8	13.1	12.2	11.4	11.1	11.7	11.7	11.8
Fourth 20%	20.1	21.2	19.5	18.9	18.5	19.1	19.1	19.1
Top 20%	58.3	53.4	57.2	59.5	60.3	58.4	59.3	58.6

Source: INEGI, 1997–2001

The first step is to understand how to draw a Lorenz curve, which is a way of picturing graphically the nature of the income inequality. We can illustrate how this is done using the data in the last column of Table 8.7. The second column of Table 8.8 shows the data in Table 8.7 for the year 2000 only. The third column shows the cumulative percentages of households, and the fourth column shows the cumulative percentages of the total monetary income received by each one-fifth of Mexican households. To construct these cumulative income percentages, start with the percentage of income received by the poorest 20 per cent of households, that is, 3.2 per cent, then add the percentage received by the next poorest 20 per cent (7.2 per cent in column 2) to give the share of the poorest 40 per cent (10.4 per cent in column 4). And so on.

Activity 8.2

Make sure you understand the rest of the figures in column 4 of Table 8.8 before reading on.

Table 8.8   Cumulative monetary income distribution for Mexican households, 2000

(1)	(2) Share of total of monetary income	(3) Cumulative share of households	(4) Cumulative share of total monetary income
Lowest 20%	3.2	20	3.2
Second 20%	7.2	40	10.4
Middle 20%	11.8	60	22.2
Fourth 20%	19.1	80	41.3
Top 20%	58.6	100	99.9

Note: The cumulative share of total monetary income does not quite add up to 100 per cent because of rounding of the data to one decimal place.
Source: INEGI, 2000

From Table 8.8 we can draw a Lorenz curve (Figure 8.3). We measure the cumulative percentages of total monetary income along the vertical axis, and the cumulative percentages of households along the horizontal axis. The Lorenz curve plots the relationship between these two variables.

Activity 8.3

Look carefully at Figure 8.3. The line is curved to the right, as the first 20 per cent of households receive very much less than 20 per cent of the total income. Check that you understand this before moving on.

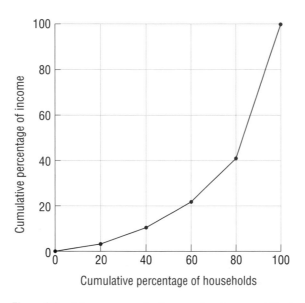

Figure 8.3   A Lorenz curve for the monetary income of Mexican households, 2000

Question

Now suppose that incomes were equally distributed, so that each one-fifth (20 per cent) of households received one-fifth of the income. What would be the shape of the Lorenz curve?

It would be a diagonal straight line. If that is not clear to you, write 20 in each row in column 2 of Table 8.8: each one-fifth of households now has 20 per cent of the income. Now calculate a new column 4 from your new column 2 and plot the curve on a figure like Figure 8.3. Figure 8.4 adds this line of perfectly equal incomes to Figure 8.3.

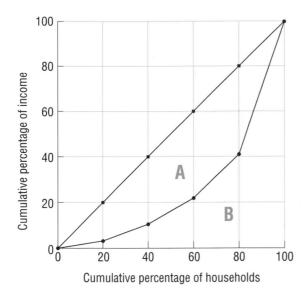

Figure 8.4   The Lorenz curve from Figure 8.3 plus a line showing an equal distribution of monetary income

The further away the Lorenz curve is from the diagonal line showing equal distribution, the more unequal the incomes are. (A perfectly unequal distribution would be one in which one household had all the income and everyone else had none. In that case, the Lorenz curve would run along the horizontal axis to the one rich household and then vertically upwards to 100 per cent of income.)

In addition to income, Lorenz curves can be used to depict inequality of assets, such as land for example. The Lorenz curve is also the basis for a widely used summary measure of inequality that allows us to compare inequality at different times in one country or across countries. This is the Gini coefficient.

Look at Figure 8.4 again. The Gini coefficient is the ratio of the area between the diagonal and the Lorenz curve (the area marked A) to the area of the triangle beneath the diagonal (the area A + B). It varies between 0 in the case of perfect equality and 1 in the case of perfect inequality. The more the Lorenz curve is bowed rightwards, away from the diagonal, the more unequal the distribution of income (or assets) and the larger the value of the Gini coefficient.

So what has happened to inequality in Mexico in recent decades? If you look back at Table 8.7, you will see that it is quite difficult to summarize what has been happening, as there is quite a lot of information to take in. The Gini coefficient provides us with a systematic summary, shown in Table 8.9.

Gini coefficient
The Gini coefficient is a summary measure of income or asset inequality. The larger the Gini coefficient, the greater the inequality.

Table 8.9   Inequality of monetary income, Mexico, 1977–2000: Gini coefficients

	1977	1984	1989	1992	1994	1996	1998	2000
Gini coefficient	0.526	0.477	0.518	0.532	0.538	0.521	0.534	0.523

Source: Cortés, 2001

Question

Summarize the trends in income inequality shown in Table 8.9.

Inequality fell by 9 per cent between 1977 and 1984, during the last part of the import substitution era. It then rose again in the second half of the 1980s, but surprisingly, given the decline in labour incomes, there is no clear trend over the 1990s. One reason may be that the fall in real wages discussed in Section 6 caused households to respond by sending more members out to work. In 1977, 1.53 members of each household were income earners; by 2000, the figure had risen to 1.92. So real wages may have been falling, but total household income may have been sustained because more family members were out earning. This reflects a growing impoverishment among the individual earners, with more people having to earn just to maintain a household's level of purchasing power.

Finally, the data in Table 8.10 shows that levels of income inequality in Mexico are extremely high by world standards. The table gives the Gini coefficients and decile ratios for Mexico, for some transitional countries

Table 8.10   Decile ratios and Gini coefficients, selected countries

	Decile ratio	Gini coefficient
Mexico, 1998	11.55	0.494
Russia, 1995	9.39	0.447
Czech Republic, 1996	3.01	0.259
Hungary, 1994	4.19	0.323
Taiwan, 1995	3.38	0.277
France, 1994	3.54	0.288
Germany, 1994	3.18	0.261
Sweden, 1995	2.61	0.221
UK, 1999	4.58	0.345
USA, 2000	5.45	0.368

Source: Luxembourg Income Study, (accessed 2003)

(Russia, Czech Republic, Hungary), for a rapidly developing Asian country (Taiwan) and for several high income countries. On both measures, Mexico stands out as a highly unequal country. The inequality at the ends of the distribution is particularly striking: the decile ratio is more than twice that of the USA, which in turn is more unequal (on both measures) than other high income countries.

In summary, these economic techniques are useful in measuring inequality within one country and in making international comparisons. Mexico's data shows an economy with a large gap between the rich and poor. Over the 1990s the country's high level of inequality remained relatively constant despite the shift to liberalization, and it is still relatively large by world standards.

Activity 8.4

Check your understanding of Lorenz curves and their interpretation by completing this activity. Using the data from Table 8.7 for 1984, construct a table on the model of Table 8.8 for 1984, showing the cumulative shares of total monetary income for that year. Then plot Lorenz curves for 1984 and 2000 on the same figure, using your calculations and Table 8.8. Show from your results that monetary incomes were more unequal in 2000.

---

8   Conclusion

This chapter opened by suggesting that we could use Mexico's experience of NAFTA as a laboratory within which to explore the impact of economic liberalization on a middle income country's labour market. What have we learned? Our central theme has been that the impact of trade and investment liberalization from the perspective of working people depends on a number of key variables. It depends on the position of the country within a complex trading world: Mexico faced lower income competitors in its strategy for building up export markets. The impact also depends on the existing structure of the economy and the government's economic and political strategy. In addition, the organization and operation of the labour market are important: the wage levels, bargaining practices and labour laws, and the extent to which employers implement or evade them. Lastly, the organization of workers has a role: we have called this 'worker agency', the extent to which organized workers can exercise an influence over their own working conditions. So in coming to a view on liberalization we have to consider how each of these variables helps to shape the labour market.

Mexico came to NAFTA with a high level of pre-existing inequality, which had increased during the pre-NAFTA liberalization process of the 1980s. NAFTA did nothing, it seems, to reduce this inequality of incomes. In fact, as NAFTA was implemented during the 1990s we saw declining real wages in manufacturing and agriculture. Employment in some areas of the economy, such as the maquiladoras, did rise, but the types of employment available became in many ways more precarious: there are now more people in part time and insecure work. There was also a continuing loss of labour rights and a shift of the balance of power in labour relations in the direction of employers, a process we labelled the 'flexibilization' of the labour market. But we pointed out that no matter what the conditions of employment, workers keep trying to influence the organization and rewards of work. The corporatist relationship between government and official unions has added another layer of complexity: negotiations at the national level have prioritized legal protections for labour over pay, but workers continue to press for improved working conditions at the local level.

So although there have been some aspects of economic success in the 1990s, notably in exports and revived economic growth, this analysis does not present NAFTA as of unequivocal benefit to Mexicans. Instead, it has brought impoverishment and insecurity to many. So why did the government do it? Why join NAFTA at all? The next chapter turns to that question.

Further reading

For an exploration of the way organized labour can combine to combat some of the negative effects of globalization, see Carr, B. (1999) 'Globalisation from below: labour internationalisation under NAFTA', *International Social Science Journal*, vol.159, pp.49–60.

A useful collection of essays and case studies on Mexico's economy and labour market is Otero, G. (ed.) (1996) *Neoliberalism Revisited: Economic Restructuring and Mexico's Future*, Boulder, Col., Westview.

For an examination of how the Mexican workforce was affected by economic and policy changes throughout the 1990s, see Zapata, F. (1997) 'The paradox of flexibility and rigidity: the Mexican labour market in the 1990s' in Amadeo, E. and Horton, S. (eds) *Labour Productivity and Flexibility*, London, Macmillan.

Chapter 9 Power among states: Mexico's membership of NAFTA

Rafael Sanchez

1 Introduction

As you saw in the last chapter, the North American Free Trade Agreement (NAFTA) between the USA, Canada and Mexico, which came into force in January 1994, represented the first such agreement between countries of such radically different standards of living and levels of economic development. The USA and Canada, which have a long history of economic integration as well as the longest undefended border in the world, concluded a Free Trade Agreement (FTA) in 1988, but the decision of the Mexican President, Carlos Salinas de Gortari, to seek a similar arrangement with the USA in 1990 represented a fundamental shift in Mexico's international alignments as well as a far-reaching transformation of its domestic policies. The disparities between the economies of the USA and Mexico inevitably raised questions about why Mexico had proposed such a radical initiative and about who gained most from the resulting agreement.

This chapter addresses two main questions. In the first place, why did Mexico propose a free trade agreement with the USA? Did the Mexicans jump or were they pushed? In other words, was the decision on Mexico's part something willingly entered into in pursuit of the country's preferences and, if so, what were those preferences and how was NAFTA expected to contribute to their satisfaction? And second, in the negotiations over the content of the NAFTA agreement, what shaped the nature of the eventual bargain that was struck and who gained from it? In order to answer these questions, I shall develop some simple, formal models of international politics that can be used to clarify questions of power, co-operation and bargaining among states. While my focus will be NAFTA, and especially Mexico's relations with the USA, these models are quite general and can be used to analyse other situations.

In order to simplify matters, the discussion that follows will concentrate solely on US–Mexican interactions and ignore the role of Canada. This is a reasonable simplification, because Canada's main concerns in the NAFTA negotiations were simply to protect the gains it had made in the Canada–USA FTA. More importantly, Mexico had made its original overture solely to the USA, and nearly all the contentious bargaining involved these two countries. By ignoring the role of Canada, we shall not miss much that bears at all directly on our two central questions – why did Mexico join, and who gained what? This chapter aims to equip you with the tools to evaluate these debates about the role of domestic choices and international constraints in world politics.

In order to analyse the changing nature of Mexican politics, I am going to begin by outlining the characteristics of the country's political system and consider the collective social interests and values that have played a major role in its historical development (Section 2). After a brief historical sketch of Mexico's political history, I outline the role of the Partido Revolucionario Institucional (PRI) – the Institutional Revolutionary Party – and the corporatist nature of the political system. Next, I trace some of the political tensions associated with Mexico's corporatist arrangements and examine how the political system evolved in the context of changing domestic and international circumstances in the 1980s and beyond. By examining the development of Mexican politics through to the 1990s, I confront the question of the reasons behind the decision to negotiate a free trade agreement with the USA.

In Section 3, I shall explore some simple models of co-operative bargaining among states, consider some different kinds of interaction and examine the competition between states to secure the gains arising from co-operation. In these models, I assume that states evaluate their gains independently of one another, that is, the USA and Mexico are not concerned about each other's gains. In Section 4, I move on to consider what happens if states evaluate their gains in relation to others, that is, if they are concerned with their position in relation to others.

In Section 5, I consider the governance mechanisms that were established to oversee the NAFTA agreement. As with multilateral arrangements such as the WTO, regional agreements to regulate international trade and investment encompass institutions and rules designed to ensure the ongoing implementation of the agreement and to resolve disputes about the interpretation and application of rules. These governance structures oversee agreements that are necessarily incomplete, in so far as it is impossible to specify all contingencies in advance, especially in the context of fast-changing technical, economic and political circumstances. They also embody varying degrees of supranational decision making based on collective ways of sharing sovereignty. Finally, in Section 6, I conclude by drawing out some general implications of the analysis provided. We shall see that analysing interdependence and bargaining provides an important additional way of understanding international politics to that provided by the realist focus on anarchy.

2 Analysing Mexican politics

After the Mexican Revolution of 1910, which destroyed the dominance of large landowners, foreign firms and the church over the Mexican economy, governments began to assert control over the national territory and its resources. The 1910 Revolution and the creation of the PRI in 1929 fostered a strong nationalist ideology oriented toward maintaining the independence of the country from foreign economic and political influences. Mexican governments were suspicious of foreign entanglement, and sought to exercise their national sovereignty on an independent and largely unilateral basis. A symbol of these changes was the experience of the oil industry. Before the Revolution, the dictatorship of Porfirio Dias (1876–1910) enacted a series of liberal economic measures, especially on land tenure and leasing arrangements, designed to attract foreign investment. This investment was particularly attracted to the oil industry and, by the 1920s, the sector was largely foreign owned, becoming one of the world's largest producers. In 1917, a new constitution was adopted that nationalized land and included restrictions on foreign investment.

The state began to demand greater contributions from foreign investors in terms of taxes, wages and social protection for workers, but the companies involved in oil, railway and mining activities resisted. Following a period of conflict and non-cooperation, in May 1938 president Lázaro Cárdenas took the bold step of expropriating the assets of the foreign oil companies and nationalized the Mexican oil industry. More generally, the Mexican state, particularly during Cárdenas' government (1934–1939), started to play a central role in organizing workers (industrial and agricultural) and small businesses, channelling and mediating their interests.

In this way, Cárdenas introduced corporatism into Mexican politics (I shall define corporatism more carefully in Section 2.1). This corporatism was based on a populist alliance between the government and organized social forces, including labour unions, small and middle sized businesses and the military. The alliance was originally directed against the foreign companies that had refused to co-operate with the social and fiscal policies of the government and against the conservative interests dispossessed by the Revolution. Both of these constituencies were identified with the subordination of Mexican interests to those of its dominant neighbour, the USA. Positively, corporatism was related to a process of nation building, in which the revolutionary elite sought to consolidate its power over the state and society, and to developing a notion of Mexican nationalism as involving the independent exercise of sovereignty.

In contrast to Brazil and Argentina, where corporatism took on a quasi-fascist character centred on a charismatic leader – Vargas in Brazil and Peron in Argentina – who demanded loyalty in exchange for protection, Mexican corporatism was more institutionalized. It did not rely solely on the ephemeral presence of a charismatic leader. Instead, it was based on a lasting and organized political structure, the Partido Revolucionario Institucional (PRI), through which most social interests were represented (Villegas, 1986). These social interests (leaders of different parties, the armed forces, unions, cliques, factions and organizations) gave their allegiance and support to 'the PRI-dominated system in exchange for material benefits and privileges, including the promotion of their own interests and those of their constituencies' (Dresser, 1996, p.178).

Again, in contrast to the position in South America, where workers were to some extent prevented from participating in formal politics and from taking industrial action, organized labour played a militant role within the PRI. Through the participation of workers' representatives in the PRI governments, the labour movement was incorporated into the Mexican political system. In this respect, Mexican corporatism resembled the social democratic systems of Western Europe more than the quasi-fascist models observed in Brazil and Argentina. Its advanced labour legislation, according to Pastor (1993), had more in common with Europe than with South America or even the USA. On the other hand, while small business groups submitted to state regulation and were required to join state sponsored business organizations, those representing large businesses generally remained autonomous from the state (Shadlen, 2000). Large businesses have been reluctant to follow the 'rhetoric of the post-revolutionary leadership, even if in reality their interests have been shared' (Ai Camp, 1999, p.138).

2.1 The PRI and Mexican corporatism

In the period immediately after the Revolution, the new elite was embroiled in a period of infighting in which different factions competed for power, and opposition often took the form of political assassinations and coups. The creation of the PRI in 1929 was a response by President Plutarco Elías Calles to this power struggle, a successful attempt to provide an institutional way of resolving conflict that transformed the country, in his words, 'from a country of a man into a country of laws' (quoted in Villegas, 1986, p.108). The formation of the PRI was not an attempt to establish a liberal democratic system. It represented the integration of the revolutionary forces into a single party that could dominate the political system and impede access to power by the conservative opposition. (It was not until 2000 that the PRI was defeated in an election and forced to hand over power to a president elected by the opposition.) Thus, the PRI operated as a broad political bloc, which largely explains its political success and longevity in Mexican politics. It was, as Dresser puts it, 'a way of life; a system of formal and informal rules, elite circulation, patronage distribution, and clientelist practices' (1996, p.159). (Clientelism is a form of politics in which a patron directly provides benefits to his or her constituents in return for their political support.)

The PRI created a sort of semi-authoritarian political system that gave Mexico long-term political stability (notwithstanding the occasional recourse to violence as when, for example, a large number of students demanding democratic change were killed by the army in 1968). It was sustained through a process of bargaining and co-option between the political elite and its social allies (labour unions, intellectuals, small businesses and a loyal armed forces). In other words, the Mexican political system was a form of corporatism. Philippe Schmitter defines corporatism as follows.

> Corporatism can be defined as a system of interest representation in which the constituent units are organized into a limited number of singular, compulsory, non-competitive, hierarchically ordered and functionally differentiated categories, recognized or licensed (if not created) by the state and granted a deliberate representational monopoly within their respective categories in exchange for observing certain controls on their selection of leaders and articulation of demands and supports.

(Schmitter, 1979, p.13)

Corporatism
Corporatism is a form of interest representation in which functional categories are granted a monopoly of representation by the state.

Schmitter also distinguishes two types of corporatism that are encompassed by this general definition: 'societal' and 'state' corporatism. Societal corporatism is based on a situation where the constituent units (labour unions, business organizations and so on) have a significant degree of autonomy from the state and it tends to emerge in an evolutionary manner. State corporatism, by contrast, involves the subordination of interest associations to the state and has often been imposed in response to a serious political crisis. This understanding has been criticized by some for defining corporatism solely as a mode of *representation*, and for ignoring other aspects of the political system such as the mode of policy making and forms of economic intervention. However, it does help to characterize the Mexican experience, which included elements of both societal and state corporatism in Schmitter's sense of those terms.

Corporatist systems can be compared with dictatorships that dispense with formal systems of representation more or less completely, and with parliamentary or presidential democracies that secure representation through party-based competition for votes in order to form an elected government. In parliamentary and presidential democracies, it is individual citizens who participate in policy making through the exercise of the right to vote for a party (or parties) that will form an elected government. Party-based competition is, in principle, a winner-takes-all process, in which control of the government alternates between different (coalitions of) parties depending on the outcome of individual voting in regular elections. Under corporatism, representation is functional, different groups (workers, peasants, business interests and so on) are incorporated, and all such groups – sometimes called *corporations* – participate in the political process. A single ruling party typically dominates corporatist systems. Corporatist systems are also typically associated with an ideology of national unity, in which a dominant leader or party integrates functionally different parts into an organic whole. Politics is presented as an exercise in conciliation in which all interests share in the determination of policy.

However, corporatist systems rarely occur in a pure form. In practice, elements of corporatism can be combined with dictatorships or party-based democratic systems. This was the case in Mexico. Overall, the Mexican political system was a semi-authoritarian combination of corporatist and presidential forms of representation linked to strong and interventionist bureaucratic apparatuses in the state. Governments were headed by a strong presidency, with elections for a new president every six years, and there was a division of labour between the PRI and the government, 'in which the PRI was centrally engaged in political mobilization, control, and conflict resolution, while the government bureaucracy and its political executives focused primarily on policy development and implementation' (Grindle, 1996, p.49).

Understood in these terms, the Mexican polity was not only a combination of presidential and corporatist elements but also a mixture of societal and statist forms of corporatism. Unlike the more dictatorial, state-centred corporatism found in Argentina and Brazil, in which the military often played a central role, the Mexican system was civilian-dominated and comprised important elements of consensus as well as top-down control. As the political scientist and analyst of Mexican politics, Merilee Grindle, has noted:

> If it was a country of extensive and increasing inequalities between those who had access to power and those who did not, between organized groups of industrialists and workers and captured groups of peasants and lumpenproletariat, it was also a country that escaped the instability and overt brutality and repressiveness of many political regimes in Latin America.
>
> (Grindle, 1996, pp.49–50)

Under the umbrella of this hybrid political system, the interventionist role of the Mexican state was strengthened by the introduction of economic planning, initiated in the 1930s and 1940s and supported by the boom in the oil industry in the 1960s and 1970s. The entrepreneurial hand of the state expanded to cover most economic sectors and, by 1982, there were about 1155 state enterprises involved in activities such as petroleum, steel, mining, railroads, airlines and communications (Moody, 1995). According to Harris, 'the public sector contributed about a quarter of the value added in the gross domestic product and the state employed a fifth of the workforce and paid two fifths of the national wage bill' (1986, p.84). Until the late 1970s, Mexico was viewed as a politically stable country as well as a successful economy that was industrially diversified and growing rapidly.

The oil boom also had the effect of raising Mexico's confidence and room for manoeuvre in international affairs, particularly during the presidency of José López Portillo (1976–1982). Traditionally, Mexico displayed an active and independent foreign policy in support of Third World solidarity in international bodies such as the United Nations and, on a regional basis, it supported the communist government in Cuba. This desire for independence can also be seen in the fact that Mexico neither joined the Non-Aligned Movement, despite its radical sympathies, nor became a member of the Organization of Petroleum Exporting Countries (OPEC). Mexico's relations with the USA – already strained by the policies mentioned above – were further stretched by their opposing positions toward the civil wars that raged in Central America in the 1980s (Castañeda, 1988). While this active foreign policy represented the aims of what Castañeda describes as 'the more progressive sectors of the political establishment', especially the labour unions and intellectuals, it began to sour the relationship between the state and private business. The latter were especially unhappy with the foreign policy stance of José López Portillo because they feared that it would damage their economic interests in the US market.

2.2 Liberalizing the corporatist model

As is noted in Chapter 8, Mexico's economic development during the 1970s was financed in part by a rapidly growing foreign debt. By 1982, rising interest payments on its foreign debt and falling oil prices resulted in Mexico stating that it was unable to service its existing commitments (debt and international payments are discussed in Part 4). The measures taken by President López Portillo to deal with the economic crisis were unsuccessful and created new hardships for the Mexican population, deepening the social differences inherent in the corporatist structure. López Portillo led a coalition made up of public employees, the state bureaucracy and small business groups. This coalition of interests was unwilling to dismantle the corporatist structure of power that had prevailed since the 1930s. The winners from state corporatism were the middle classes and public sector workers, while most workers outside the public sector faced marginalization and a decline in their standard of living, mostly as a result of unemployment and the increasing informalization of the economy.

The deepening of the adjustment policies under Presidents Miguel de la Madrid (1982–1988) and Carlos Salinas (1988–1994) further exacerbated social conflict and eroded the credibility of the PRI and the corporatist model of governance in Mexico. Under the government of President de la Madrid, a new elite, highly educated and with a distinctive technocratic profile, positioned itself at the top levels of policy making. This new elite was willing to make the economic changes that were needed to stabilize the economy and re-launch the internationalization of Mexico with an open economy and a liberalized private sector. However, corporatism remained an essential feature of this process of economic reform, although its aim was no longer to support import-substituting policies and strong state economic intervention, but rather to assist a shift towards export-led growth. The latter depended on keeping the economy open to foreign capital, and this required re-engaging the country with the international financial community and tackling the macroeconomic troubles facing the Mexican economy.

Thus, as a result of the economic crisis and the collapse of the old elite in the PRI, the balance between the statist and societal elements of Mexican corporatism shifted towards the latter, while the ability of the state to direct economic activity declined as firms were privatized and markets liberalized. Big business and foreign multinationals were the key beneficiaries of these changes and their strongest supporters. Through a process of bargaining, the state was able to gain the support, or at least reduce the opposition, of small businesses to the process of economic reform and internationalization. Small businesses followed a strategy of accommodation to the process of liberalization and maintained their support for the government, recognizing that the policy of trade and economic liberalization pursued by the government would, in the words of the director of the largest chamber of small and medium sized businesses (CANACINTRA), 'bring them clear rules and the consideration of their commercial partners' (Ortiz Muñiz, 1992, p.30). Opposition from organized labour was weakened by the continuing privatization of the economy and the subsequent de-unionization of the labour force.

The strategy of economic liberalization increased the importance of relations with the USA and multilateral economic institutions. This led President de la Madrid gradually to abandon the traditional nationalist rhetoric that had characterized the country's foreign policy, especially in relation to US policy in Central America, and this changed the Mexican approach from one of unilateralism to multilateralism. Mexican policy towards the conflicts in Central America was conducted through the Contadora Group created by Mexico, Venezuela, Colombia and Panama in 1983 and involved supporting the efforts of the governments in the affected states. The effect of this was to improve Mexico's relations with the USA.

2.3   The road to NAFTA

In 1986, Mexico joined the GATT, the forerunner to the WTO, and this was followed by the negotiation of a Framework Understanding on Trade and Investment with the USA in 1987, which, in addition to committing both to negotiate freer trade, included new means of settling trade disputes. This further improved the trade relations between Mexico and the USA (Nester, 1995). By these means, Mexico opened its economy, lifting tariffs and non-tariff restrictions to trade in both the manufacturing and agricultural sectors. This was done for two reasons. In the first place, it was a defence mechanism to protect Mexico's trading interests in the face of an increase in protectionist practices in the developed world, especially in the USA – the main market for the country's exports. And secondly, membership of a multilateral organization and a bilateral agreement with the USA served to lock the domestic economic reforms undertaken by the government into international agreements.

President Salinas continued the policy of economic reform and trade expansion, seeking free trade agreements with other states and regions, and he took Mexico into the Organization for Economic Co-operation and Development (OECD) and the Asia-Pacific Economic Co-operation forum (APEC). The Salinas administration realized that Mexico would need abundant foreign investment in order to finance its programme of reform and the policy of export promotion, and that this depended on the confidence of foreign investors. Likewise, the government faced strong domestic demands for further economic liberalization from business groups, parliamentarians, especially senators, and consumer groups. Opposition from labour and some small business interests was averted by co-opting them through a domestic bargaining process, involving political patronage and the promise that the internationalization of the economy would improve welfare for all.

Nevertheless, the implementation of the reforms had a huge political cost for the government. The privatization of public corporations and the opening of the economy were associated with high levels of unemployment and increased poverty. The PRI was losing political support. Salinas's electoral victory in 1988 was considered fraudulent by many, and the opposition was on the rise. In the 1988 presidential election, the opposition obtained 48 per cent of the votes. Facing accusations of fraud, both in the USA and at home, the government carried out some electoral reforms designed to appease the opposition and to gain external credibility.

It was against this background that the government opened negotiations on a free trade agreement with the USA. While the idea provoked opposition, particularly from the left, it also caught the imagination of most Mexicans, heightening the popularity of President Salinas. By the 1991 congressional elections, President Salinas was reaping the benefits. The PRI recovered its majority status, whereas the Democratic Revolutionary Party (PDR), made up of the PRI dissidents who claimed to have won the 1988 presidential elections, was rolled back to a minority status. This gave Salinas sufficient bargaining power in the parliament to ensure the implementation of his government's programme, including approval for NAFTA. The central goal of the Mexican government in negotiating NAFTA was essentially political; it was aimed at 'the search for credibility for the free market reforms undertaken since 1982. Thus, the mere conclusion of those lengthy negotiations was as important, if not more so, than their actual content' (Rubio, 1996, p.76).

Even though the central goals of the government were driven by domestic political considerations, President Salinas' request for an agreement with the USA constituted a major turning point in Mexico's foreign policy, a shift guided by the president's perception that a new geo-economic order was emerging with the end of the Cold War divisions in international politics. The end of the Cold War (1989–1991) triggered a strategic re-evaluation of Mexico's national interests. Salinas realized that the increasing centrality of economic issues, the competition for world market share and foreign investment, meant that the traditional Mexican conception of sovereignty – exercised unilaterally and, especially, independently of ties to the USA – needed to be revised.

During a visit to Europe in 1990, Salinas discovered that East Europeans were hastily moving to embrace market economies and, at a meeting with world business and political leaders at Davos, was told that Mexico had become less attractive to foreign investors as the world economy was being reshaped in terms of regional economic blocs (Cameron and Tomlin, 2000). The Salinas government came to see that, in these changed circumstances, Mexico had to compete not only to attract European and East Asian investment, but also to prevent American investment from relocating to the new emerging economies of Europe. The only way that Mexico could remain attractive to investors was, as Salinas put it, by becoming 'part of an economic trading bloc with the USA and Canada' (quoted in Pastor, 1993, p.20).

Sovereignty, according to Salinas, 'was now not something rigid or codified, but contingent and adaptable in a rapidly changing world' (quoted in O'Toole, 2002, p.9). In an interdependent world, a pragmatic association with the USA would reinforce rather than weaken sovereignty. From such a perspective, NAFTA was not a surrender of sovereignty but a way of exercising it collectively, in the pursuit of mutual gains with others. From

Mexico's point of view, NAFTA was to be a limited form of political integration, the functions of which were to ease the internationalization of the Mexican economy, improve the competitiveness and diversification of Mexican exports, and attract foreign investment, thus enhancing Mexico's bargaining capability in world politics. The real utility of NAFTA for Mexico was that it gave a legal formality to an already existing *de facto* integration that had been going on since 1965 and had accelerated in the 1980s. The real gain would be to commit 'Washington irrevocably to the relationship' (Grugel, 1996, p.141). Moreover, as with its earlier membership of the GATT, NAFTA would also allow Mexico to ward off future pressures in the USA for discrimination against its exports.

Indeed, Mexico was a leading force behind the making of NAFTA. It was President Carlos Salinas who proposed the idea of a free trade agreement between Mexico and the USA to Carla Hills (the US trade representative) in January 1990, during a meeting at the World Economic Forum in Davos Switzerland, thereafter taking the proposal directly to President Bush in February (Cameron and Tomlin, 2000). However, the fact that it was Mexico that initiated the process that resulted in NAFTA does not tell us why it did so – as you have just seen, both domestic changes and a changing international context were important. Certainly, there were several points at which the interests of the USA and Mexico converged.

The key NAFTA preferences for each country could be identified as follows (Smith, 1996). For the USA:

- To preserve stability in Mexico.

- To gain access to the Mexican oil industry.

- To obtain an important bargaining chip in trade negotiations with Europe, Japan and the GATT.

- To consolidate diplomatic support from Mexico on foreign policy in general.

And for Mexico:

- To preserve its social peace through the attraction of investment and the creation of new jobs.

- To institutionalize economic reform in order to ensure its permanence in the long term.

- To bring about international recognition and legitimacy to the political system.

- To increase Mexico's bargaining power vis-à-vis other states.

To a large extent, these elements constituted points of convergence, which, together with the *de facto* process of integration already underway, reinforced the benefits of co-operation between the two states.

3   Interdependence in international politics

The story recounted in Section 2 highlights the fact that *both* the domestic basis of Mexico's political economy *and* the international context had altered dramatically by the late 1980s. As you saw in Chapter 8, the economic asymmetry between Mexico and its northern partners – measured in terms of total GDP and in living standards – is stark. So, given these huge differences, did Mexico's participation represent a capitulation to the power of the giant to the north, or was it an independent initiative in pursuit of Mexican preferences? Did Mexico jump or was it pushed into joining NAFTA? In order to answer this question it is necessary to consider some theories of the conditions under which states interact together in the international system.

Question

Why might a realist analysis predict that Mexico and the USA would fail to co-operate on a free trade agreement?

In Chapter 5, you studied the basic realist model of the political structure of the international system. This modelled the international condition of states as one of anarchy, and argued that this placed strong limits on the extent of co-operation because states would be concerned both to maintain their relative power in relation to one another and to avoid forms of interdependence that might be a source of vulnerability. It was precisely this kind of reasoning that led Stephen Krasner, a US political scientist, to conclude that 'there have been some commercial accords between [the USA and Mexico], but the extreme differences in terms of vulnerability make it very improbable that an agreement as broad as the Canada–USA Free Trade Agreement could be reached' (quoted in Cameron and Tomlin, 2000, p.18). Note that this was view was published in the very year that President Salinas began the process that led to NAFTA.

As an alternative to the realist hypothesis, you also studied – in Sudipta Kaviraj's discussion of India in Chapter 6 – the idea that the preferences that states seek to satisfy in the international arena might be shaped as much by their domestic societies and their economic opportunities and constraints as by their relative position within the system of states. In this section, I shall explore this line of analysis further by focusing on *interdependence* as a feature of the relations between states that is as important as anarchy. That is to say, while I shall assume that states exist in an anarchical world, I shall also consider the implications of the fact that economic interactions – trade and investment flows – mean that the world is also interdependent.

I begin with the assumption that, in the words of Andrew Moravcsik, the international policies of states reflect 'interpretations and combinations of security, welfare and sovereignty preferred by powerful domestic groups enfranchised by representative institutions and practices' (1997, pp.519–20). (You may recall that this was one of the concluding observations of Chapter 6.) In Mexico's case, Section 2 showed how President Salinas sought to redefine Mexico's international policies as the domestic agenda moved towards liberalization and as new interests were enfranchised in the political system. As states pursue their international policies, they encounter other states doing likewise. Sometimes these interdependent policies conflict with one another, sometimes they reinforce one another, and sometimes the result is a mixture of both.

According to liberal theories of international politics (of which Moravcsik is a leading advocate), it is this pattern of interdependent preferences that is the key to explaining how states will interact: 'the expected behaviour of any single state – the strategies it selects and the systemic constraints to which it adjusts – reflect not simply its own preferences, but the configuration of preferences of *all* states linked by patterns of significant policy interdependence' (Moravcsik, 1997, p.523).

We shall see that recognizing interdependence adds an important element to our model of world politics. 'While anarchy is an important condition of world politics, it is not the only one,' writes Helen Milner, 'strategic interdependence among the actors is at least as fundamental' (Milner, 1993, p.167).

In reality, what the governments that represent states internationally want – that is, their preferences – are many different things: more opportunities for their exporters in foreign markets, greater amounts of foreign investment, better equipped and more efficient armed forces, policies to deal with cross-border migration, international co-operation against drugs cartels, and so on. Some of these things are measurable and some can be weighed against other preferences. Others may be important but nonetheless intangible. Complex deals involving bargaining and trade-offs are the stuff of international economic policy. NAFTA, for example, consists of more than 1000 pages of text, covering 22 chapters of agreements and numerous annexes.

Yet, when states act internationally they are often compelled by the very nature of an interdependent world to rank their preferences and to trade one thing against another. International politics is a realm in which states have to make choices. And despite the inherent complexity of such a process, many states do, in fact, exhibit relatively stable, well-ordered preferences. They are able to determine their priorities and evaluate gains in one area against losses in another. Of course, this is a messy and difficult process in which miscalculation and luck play a role as well. (You may recall that Chapters 2 and 4 in Part 1 suggest that many developing countries were not fully aware of what they had signed up to in the Uruguay Round and the founding of the WTO.)

Given this, it is, I think, reasonable to use some simplified models of co-operation and bargaining to try to understand some of the factors that shape international negotiations. These models abstract from the complexity and uncertainty of the real world and so miss out important aspects of the real politics. On the other hand, by simplifying the picture and concentrating on a small number of important factors, they often help to clarify things. In the models that follow, I shall assume that the states concerned have a single preference – for economic gains that can be measured in US dollars ($). States seek to maximize their gains (or minimize their losses) and are in principle able to calculate their best course of action: states are able to work out which policies best contribute to the satisfaction of their preferences.

3.1 Interdependence

Interdependence
Interdependence is a situation in which the gains (and losses) of each depend not only on their own actions but also on the actions of others.

Positive-sum game
A positive-sum game is one in which the total gains are positive.

Zero-sum game
A zero-sum game is one in which the gains of one player are matched by equal losses for the other.

Negative-sum game
A negative-sum game is one in which the total gains are negative, that is, they are losses.

Absolute gains
Absolute gains are gains measured independently of the gains (or losses) of others.

Interdependence among actors implies that the gains (and losses) of each depend, not only on its own actions, but also on the actions and reactions of others. (In what follows, I shall simplify things by considering an interaction between just two actors.) In such situations, rational actors behave strategically, that is, they attempt to calculate the impact of their actions on others and how the actions of others can, in turn, affect them.

Interdependence takes a number of different forms and these can be modelled in terms of different 'games'. In a positive-sum game, the total gains are positive and both players can gain relative to their initial position. In a zero-sum game, the gains of one player are matched by equal losses for the other. In a negative-sum game, the total gains are negative, that is, they are losses.

A key assumption in the models that follow is that a state evaluates its gains (or losses) independently of the gains or losses of the other, and in terms of what it already has, not in terms of how its gains compare with those of the other. In the analysis of international politics, this is often described by saying that states are concerned with absolute gains. (I shall drop this assumption and explain the notion of relative gains in Section 4.)

To see how a focus on interdependence changes our understanding of international politics, let us consider, first, a specific model of one kind of strategic interaction. I assume that there are gains to be reaped from co-operation, and that thus there is a positive-sum game to be played. This model of bargaining assumes that the players can come to a binding agreement about sharing the total gains. This distinguishes it from the game theory you will study in Chapter 13, where players act independently and cannot make binding agreements. Bargaining games – sometimes called co-operative game theory – assume that players can bargain with each other or walk away. One useful aspect of these models for international relations, therefore, is that they can help us to predict what countries will do, given their different capacities to 'go it alone'.

As an example of what I have in mind, imagine that Mexico and the USA are considering whether to negotiate an FTA and that their economic advisers have told them that the total potential gains from liberalization are $100 billion if they co-operate in reciprocal measures. For example, the USA agrees to remove the quotas that had previously limited Mexican textile and agricultural exports to the US market in return for Mexico agreeing to open its banking system to foreigners, including US banks. Their advisers have also told them that if they liberalize their economies unilaterally, the USA will gain $50 billion and Mexico $10 billion. Figure 9.1 illustrates how the total gains from co-operation, that is, the gains from reciprocal liberalization, can be divided between the two parties.

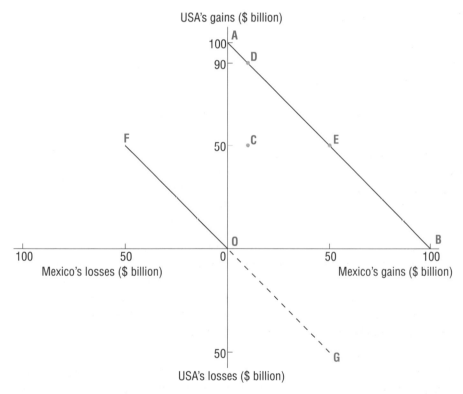

Figure 9.1   Mexico/USA bargaining games

Start by looking at the top right-hand quadrant of Figure 9.1. The vertical and horizontal axes measure the gains going to the USA and Mexico, respectively, as a result of negotiations. At point O (the origin), the game has not started, no negotiations have taken place, so the gains are zero. Once the game starts, the USA and Mexico move away from the origin, both seeking the best deal they can achieve. The points along the line AB represent all the possible divisions of the total gains ($100 billion) between the USA and Mexico. The line AB can be thought of as a possibility frontier like the production possibility frontier you studied in Chapter 3 in looking at the gains from trade. Each country seeks to achieve the best deal that it can along the frontier AB, by instituting reciprocal liberalization and then seeking a division of the gains that benefits their citizens.

Question

What do you think will be the outcome? Will the USA gain all the benefits? If not, why not?

To narrow the range of the expected outcome, consider what might be each country's alternative to making a deal. As Chapter 3 noted, unilateral trade liberalization – without reciprocal market opening from another country – can sometimes bring gains. Suppose that this is so. Suppose that if Mexico undertakes some unilateral liberalization its gains are $10 billion; if the USA does so, its gains are $50 billion. Then point C on Figure 9.1 represents the outcome of the game if there is no co-operation, if the players walk away. This is sometimes called the fall-back position of the parties – what each can get in the absence of co-operation. It is also called a 'threat point', a position with which one can threaten the other in a bargaining situation.

Fall-back position
The fall-back position or threat point in a bargaining model is determined by how each party would fare if co-operation broke down.

We can give a partial answer to the questions posed above. As the USA can get $50 billion without co-operating, it will presumably not accept a division of the joint gains that gives it less than that figure, and similarly Mexico will not accept anything less than $10 billion. Neither party will accept a co-operative outcome that gives it less than its fall-back position.

So, all points between D (where the USA gets $90 billion and Mexico gets $10 billion) and E (where the USA gets $50 billion and Mexico gets $50 billion) are possible outcomes. This does not tell us exactly where the division will occur, but it does illustrate the general point that we can expect the outcome of a bargaining process to be more favourable to the side with the better fall-back position, because that is what it can threaten the other side with. The party with the most to gain from co-operation is in the weaker position; the party with the least to gain from co-operation is in the stronger position. Of course, such threats have to be credible. In this case, it is not unreasonable to suppose that the message that US negotiators regularly conveyed to their Mexican interlocutors – that the USA did not need an FTA with Mexico as much as Mexico needed one with the USA – was indeed a credible argument.

The bargaining game just described is a positive-sum game: there are benefits from co-operating for both parties. Unfortunately, not all the games relevant to international economic and political bargaining take this form. Suppose that, instead of the line AB on Figure 9.1, the relevant available outcomes of liberalization were along the line FG.

This can be thought of as a situation in which, once the barriers to trade are reduced, subsidized US agricultural exporters push Mexican producers out of their domestic markets. Suppose, further, that this implies that, as a result of liberalization, every dollar gained in the USA is a dollar lost in Mexico. Then starting from point O, the countries would move out towards point F as liberalization occurred. This is a zero-sum game: no mutual benefits from co-operation are available to share.

Question

What would Mexico do?

The rational response for Mexico in this zero-sum game is not to liberalize, but to stick at the origin. Mexico's only fall-back position in this game is not to play: it has no other threat point. Only the USA has an incentive to play.

Question

What does the dotted line OG represent?

This line represents a zero-sum game in favour of Mexico. It shows an – admittedly unlikely – situation in which Mexico is in a position to impose losses on the USA in a zero-sum game.

Now, let us return to the game represented by the frontier AB on Figure 9.1. Suppose that, instead of engaging in this game, the USA uses its economic weight in the world trading economy to change the outcomes available. It might, for example, increase its subsidies to agricultural producers before liberalization, in such a way as to impose greater costs on Mexico when the border opens; this, in turn, reduces the total net gains (benefits minus losses) available to the two countries from reciprocal liberalization.

Question

Now look at Figure 9.2. The line HJ represents the frontier of the new bargaining game. Points along HJ again represent different distributions of the gains from liberalization. Is this a positive-sum or a zero-sum game?

This is a positive-sum game. There are positive net gains to the parties from liberalization, relative to the starting point at the origin (O). To see this, start at point O and move to J. Total gains are $50 billion, all going to the USA,

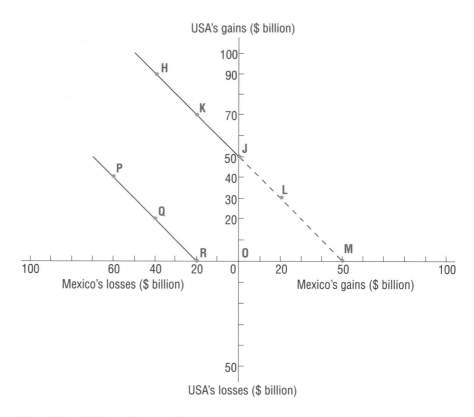

Figure 9.2   A different Mexico/USA bargaining game

while Mexico gains or loses nothing. Then look at point K. There the USA gains $70 billion and Mexico loses $20 billion. Total net gains are $50 billion again. So the sum is positive.

Question

So will Mexico play?

Why should it? It gains nothing. So it will stick to its threat point, which is point O. However, in this game, Mexico does have a possible bargaining tool of a different kind. By sticking to its threat point, it is depriving the USA of a large sum in dollars. Conversely, if the USA can persuade Mexico to liberalize reciprocally, it can afford to make Mexico a side payment and still be much better off than it was at O.

Question

Suppose the USA offers Mexico $20 billion to 'play'. Locate the outcome on Figure 9.2.

The outcome would be at L on the line JM. The game has been effectively extended by side payment; the parties have bargained out along the dotted line into the top right-hand quadrant, where there are positive benefits to both countries. So in a game such as this last one, where there are positive total gains but one net loser, there is potential for a co-operative bargained outcome if one party can afford to compensate the loser. These kinds of payments often play an important role in international bargaining.

Activity 9.1

Consider the bargaining game that has a frontier represented by the line PR on Figure 9.2.

1   What kind of game is this? Is it a positive-sum, zero-sum or negative-sum game?

2   Can the USA make a side payment to Mexico in order to extract the potential gains it can make from playing this game?

Finally, consider the bottom left-hand quadrant. This represents all the outcomes from games in which both countries lose. No country will voluntarily make an agreement that takes them here. But consider a trade war: a situation where Mexico retaliates against a US attempt to benefit its agricultural exporters by raising tariffs and the end result is a cessation of a large amount of trade between the two countries, such that the pre-existing gains from trade across many sectors are lost. Not only is this a negative-sum game; it is one where there are no gains to be had for either party. You may recall from Part 1 that one of the reasons for multilateral trade negotiations in the GATT/WTO is to avoid just such outcomes in which everyone loses.

Activity 9.2

Sketch such a trade war game on a diagram like Figure 9.2.

3.2   Asymmetrical interdependence and power

In the examples discussed in relation to Figures 9.1 and 9.2, neither country was able to change the threat point of the other. Consider again the line HJ on Figure 9.2. We established that although point K represented an outcome in a positive-sum game, Mexico would not play as it could stick at O (no gains are better than loses of $20 billion). Because Mexico could stick at O, the USA would have to offer a side payment to move the game along the line JM, to a point such as L. I now want to consider what happens when one country, say, the USA, is in a position to change another's threat point. How might this be possible?

In what follows, I assume that the use of force is not an option. I also continue to assume that the system is anarchic, that is, that there is no authority shared between states. Finally, I assume that actors know what they want and cannot be persuaded or deceived into changing their beliefs about what is in their interests. Remember that these are the assumptions of my model, not statements of fact. In the absence of force, authority, persuasion or deception, the only way that one state can get another to do something that it would not otherwise have done is to change the costs and benefits associated with the range of options from which it selects. I will call the ability of one party to impose costs on another its coercive power (Barzel, 2002).

Coercive power

Coercive power is the ability of one party to impose costs on another.

Consider again the example of trade. In an influential discussion, the economist Albert Hirschman argued that:

> The influence which country A acquires in country B by foreign trade depends in the first place upon the total gain which B derives from that trade; the total gain from trade for any country is indeed nothing but another expression for the total impoverishment which would be inflicted upon it by a stoppage of trade. In this sense the classical concept, gain from trade, and the power concept, dependence on trade ... are seen to be merely two aspects of the same phenomenon.

(Hirschman, 1945, p.73; quoted by Baldwin, 1989, p.178)

Question

What might affect the ability of country A to exercise the influence that Hirschman is talking about in the quotation above?

Presumably, A gains from its trade with B and would therefore also suffer a degree of impoverishment from a stoppage. Suppose the USA was threatening protectionist measures against Mexico. (In Section 2 above, I pointed out that one reason why Mexico wanted an FTA with the USA was to avert the protectionist measures that began to surface in the latter half of the 1980s.) To assess the likely consequences of this threat on Mexico, we would want to know the expected costs to *both* the USA and Mexico as well as the expected benefits to the USA of Mexico changing its policies as a result of the threat. The USA's threat makes sense only if its expected benefits exceed the costs. If benefits do exceed costs, however, the USA may impose costs on Mexico by unilaterally changing the terms of their interdependence in ways that Mexico cannot prevent.

For example, the USA may impose costs on Mexico by acting with a third party. By negotiating freer trade and investment with Canada, the USA may impose costs on Mexico, as trade and investment links with Mexico would be diverted to Canada. (Wasn't this exactly the kind of fear articulated by President Salinas when he worried that Mexico might find itself outside a world of regional trading blocs?)

We are now in a position to clarify how interdependence may operate as a source of coercive power. The USA may be in a position to alter the terms of its interdependence with Mexico, either unilaterally (by changing its national trade policy) or by acting in coalition with a third party (say, Canada), in such a way that the USA's benefits exceed its costs, while Mexico has no option but to bear its costs. This is sometimes called 'asymmetrical interdependence'. In terms of Figure 9.2, suppose the USA undertakes unilateral actions (or actions with Canada) that move it and Mexico from the origin O to point K. This is not a bargaining game; it is an exercise of coercive power. That is, the coercive power of the USA enables it to take away Mexico's threat point. Once the USA has taken away its threat point, Mexico finds itself in a new situation with new options.

In principle, then, asymmetrical interdependence may form the basis for an exercise of coercive power.

3.3   Go-it-alone power and its uses

Lloyd Gruber (2000) has called the power to impose costs of this kind on another, either by unilateral action or by acting in coalition with a third-party, go-it-alone power. Once one state, say the USA, has exercised (or credibly threatened to exercise) go-it-alone power, thereby changing the position of another state, say Mexico, the latter may 'co-operate' in a subsequent bargaining game. But unlike games that lie along the line JM on Figure 9.2 and the line AB in Figure 9.1, this bargaining takes place *after* the state with go-it-alone power has taken a position that *worsens* the position of the weaker state. Thereafter, even co-operative bargaining may not be enough to get the weaker party back to where it was before that exercise of power.

Often, go-it-alone power is exercised in a coalition with others, as when the USA and Canada signed a free trade agreement in 1988, and the possibility of forming such a coalition is the basis of a credible threat to exclude others. Those threatened with exclusion would prefer that the coalition not form; but once the latter has exercised its go-it-alone power, the outsiders have little alternative but to join as inclusion represents a better outcome than exclusion, even though inclusion represents a loss over the *status quo ante*. Gruber expresses the point as follows:

Go-it-alone power
Go-it-alone power is the ability of one country to deprive another of its threat point and thus change the options it faces.

... institutionalized co-operation by one group of actors (the winners) can have the effect of restricting the options available to another group (the losers), altering the rules of the game such that members of the latter group are better off playing by the new rules despite their strong preference for the original, pre-cooperation status quo.

(Gruber, 2000, p.7)

In our example, Mexico might have preferred it if the USA and Canada had not formed an FTA, but once they had, it was better off joining than remaining outside. The exercise of go-it-alone power can give rise to a 'bandwagoning' dynamic: losers join the winners because 'accession is simply the lesser of two evils' (Gruber, 2000, p.50). The enlargement of the coalition changes the situation for other outsiders, who then experience a similar pressure to follow suit. This kind of logic might help explain why several other South American countries sought free trade agreements with the USA after Mexico joined with Canada and the USA to form NAFTA. (This is an example of what Aditya Bhattacharjea calls being a 'junior member of the gang' in Chapter 2.)

The central point to understand here is that, unlike the co-operative bargaining represented by the line JM in Figure 9.2 and the line AB in Figure 9.1, which must involve positive gains for all parties, 'co-operation' that is enforced by the use (or threat) of go-it-alone power need not be positive sum; indeed, it can even be a negative sum game overall. It is only a co-operative, positive-sum outcome with respect to the new status quo that arises *after* the exercise of coercive, go-it-alone power. Suppose that what Mexico gains by co-operating after the USA has exercised its go-it-alone power is less than its original loss. That is, suppose Mexico loses overall. When 'co-operation' is enforced in this way, that is, after one party has moved the starting point to the disadvantage of the other, the USA's gains may be more or less than Mexico's losses because, as Mancur Olson explains:

The party with power gains from threatening to use or using that power if the cost of doing this is less than the value, *to that party*, of what is obtained: the losses to the victim, and even the size of the losses in relation to the gains to the party with power, do not necessarily bear on the outcome.

(Olson, 2000, p.61, emphasis added)

There is no doubt that the USA was in a favourable position of asymmetrical interdependence with Mexico immediately prior to the negotiation of NAFTA and that it had a stronger fall-back position on most of the issues at stake in the negotiations. Whether in fact the slightly earlier Canada–USA

FTA of 1988 represented an exercise of go-it-alone power that imposed costs on Mexico, as some commentators allege (for example, Gruber, 2000), is more debatable. Indeed, some analysts contend that it was the prospect of a USA–Mexico free trade agreement that alarmed the Canadian government, which feared that a new agreement might erode the gains it had made in the 1988 agreement. In the most fully researched account of the negotiations to date, Cameron and Tomlin claim that Canada sought to join the go-it-alone coalition of the USA and Mexico in order to offset the 'danger of investment diversion' and to 'prevent Mexico from getting preferential access to the US market through a better free trade agreement than the Canada–US one' (Cameron and Tomlin, 2000, p.65).

However, perhaps the most interesting question is whether what Mexico gained from the negotiation of NAFTA was enough to offset any loses it suffered from the prior negotiation of the Canada–USA FTA. That is, was US power able to produce a situation in which it gained overall while Mexico lost, or was US power (to negotiate an FTA with Canada) used to kick-start a process that, unequal as it was, involved net gains for Mexico? Thus far, we have no reason to believe that the USA wanted to impose losses on Mexico. I have been assuming that each country is motivated solely by its own gains. It is more likely that the USA sought to use its go-it-alone power simply as a bargaining tactic to ensure a maximum share of any subsequent gains from bargaining with Mexico. US power was used to bargain for the largest possible share of the gains, but since Mexico achieved gains over the *status quo ante*, what it gained from NAFTA was greater than what it lost from the Canada–USA FTA, its participation was genuinely voluntary. Mexico would have preferred a bigger share of the gains, but it did not have the power to make that wish effective. This was because Mexico's new fall-back position after the conclusion of the Canada–USA FTA was, in many cases, to liberalize its economy whatever the USA did.

In Part 1, it was suggested that a multilateral forum such as the GATT/WTO is likely to be favoured by the weaker party. Mexico's experience casts an interesting light on this suggestion. In this context, it is worth noting that the USA had a long involvement with the GATT prior to the negotiation of NAFTA and was, in fact, negotiating the final stages of the Uruguay Round at the same time as some of the NAFTA negotiations. One aspect of the US fall-back position was that it always had the multilateral negotiations as well. Nevertheless, by negotiating bilaterally with Mexico, the USA was able to extract concessions from a 'developing' country that it could not have got against a coalition of developing countries inside the GATT. Most notably, NAFTA embodied a radical liberalization of agricultural trade. (The USA refused to recognize Mexico as a developing country for the purposes of the NAFTA negotiations.)

For Mexico, however, membership of the GATT proved disappointing. In 1988, Salinas had said that 'I believe that through the GATT we have a multilateral way to deal with our neighbours. There is such a different economic level between the USA and Mexico that I don't believe such a common market [as the Canada–USA FTA] would provide an advantage to either country' (*New York Times*, 24 November 1988; quoted in Cameron and Tomlin, 2000, p.59). Yet, just over one year later he was proposing a free-trade pact to President Bush, who immediately accepted. Mexico had come to value even unilateral liberalization more highly than the outcomes of the multilateral round, so the latter could not serve as a threat point in its negotiations with the USA.

Activity 9.3

Given the rise of regionalism in the world economy, when President Salinas proposed an FTA with the USA he saw that Mexico had four choices: maintain tariffs to support import-substitution; open the economy unilaterally; develop a strategy of negotiated liberalization in the GATT; or negotiate bilaterally with the USA. How did Salinas rank these choices? What were the implications of this ranking for the fall-back position of Mexico during the NAFTA negotiations?

3.4 Evaluating NAFTA

The political impact of NAFTA on Mexico has been ambiguous. The consolidation of the liberalization strategy has deepened social and economic differentiation in the country. The industrial labour force absorbed by the buoyant maquiladora sector and those economic sectors that gained from liberalization has not reaped the benefits in terms of income distribution. The inclusion of agriculture in NAFTA heightened the social conflict affecting the agricultural states of the south, and these have been net losers from integration. They have been affected not only by the liberalization of agriculture, but also by the concentration of the maquiladora industry in the north and centre as industries have relocated from the south to the north. As a result, the southern states of Mexico have seen a process of land concentration following the privatization of communal land known as 'ejidos' as well as deindustrialization.

This helps to explain the Zapatistas' revolt in Chiapas, which began in January 1994. The Zapatistas Army of National Liberation (made up of indigenous peasants from the south of the country) came to life, taking the government and public opinion by storm, on 1 January 1994, the day that NAFTA went into effect. It seized villages in the state of Chiapas in protest against NAFTA and against the neo-liberal policies of the Salinas administration.

By the end of the Salinas administration, the dominance of the PRI within the Mexican political system was crumbling, and the chosen successor of Salinas, Luis Donaldo Colosio, was assassinated in March 1994, forcing Salinas to select Hernesto Zedillo as presidential candidate. However, the political victory of Zedillo did not stop the institutional crisis. Following the election, in September 1994, the Secretary General of the PRI, José Francisco Ruiz Massieu, was also assassinated. Hernesto Zedillo, therefore, was faced with a political crisis on top of the economic turmoil of 1995. The long-term consequence of the lack of political accountability and a decade of liberalization was the loss of power by the PRI in the presidential elections of 2000. This was an unintended consequence as Salinas had seen economic reform as a means of *restoring* the authority of the PRI. Vicente Fox won the presidency. Although not all the political problems faced by Mexico since 1994 have been a direct consequence of NAFTA, it has undoubtedly been a contributing factor in a unleashing social and political crisis and ending the PRI's virtual monopoly of power.

On the positive side, NAFTA has been an important factor in bolstering Mexico's internationalization. Membership of NAFTA increased Mexico's bargaining power in international politics, especially in international economic relations. For Mexico, NAFTA is now what oil was in the 1970s – a currency that has allowed it to reinvent its prestige and influence, particularly in Latin America. Getting closer to the USA has not restrained Mexico's capacity for pursuing an independent foreign policy. This was demonstrated during the US-led war against Iraq (March–April 2003), as President Vicente Fox refused to support the Bush administration without the cover of an explicit UN Security Council resolution authorizing the use of force. As Foweraker pointed out, because of its membership of NAFTA, Mexico 'is asserting itself as the hub of a new hub-and-spoke arrangement (with Chile, Colombia, Venezuela, and Central America) that can maximize both its economic and political interests' (Foweraker, 1996, p.165). The influence of Mexico in Central America, for instance, is impressive.

Until 1990, the Central American governments had refused to get involved in close economic relations with Mexico and trade relations were negligible. Since 1991, however, the governments of the region have been queuing up to negotiate trade agreements with Mexico, partly because they believe that it will give them access to NAFTA. Costa Rica signed a free trade agreement with Mexico in 1994, Nicaragua in 1995 and the other states (Guatemala, Honduras and El Salvador) did so *en bloc* in 2001. Trade between Mexico and Central America has been on the rise, although it is still limited. Another Mexican initiative, 'Plan Puebla-Panama', aims to integrate Central America and Mexico's southern states in a common developmental programme.

For the USA, NAFTA represented a pioneering free trade agreement with a large, middle income developing country, but its primary purpose was probably political. It was aimed at furthering, locking-in and stabilizing the liberalizing measures already taken in Mexico, and at achieving a degree of joint control over the US–Mexican border and, in particular, over illegal immigration across that border.

4   Do relative gains matter?

Question

Why do realists believe that states might forego absolute gains in their international interactions? You might want to look at Chapter 5 again.

There are two closely related reasons. First, as you saw in Chapter 5, realists argue that self-help is the predominant principle of action in an anarchic order. According to realists, self-help means that states must accord priority to security and hence be concerned, not just with their absolute capabilities, but also with the distribution of capabilities across the system of states. If others do relatively well, they must emulate the successful or face the possibility of threats to their survival. Kenneth Waltz calls this the 'balance-of-power theory' and says that it is the 'distinctive' theory of international politics. Similarly, the realist theorist of international co-operation, Joseph Grieco, writes that: 'Driven by an interest in survival, states are acutely sensitive to any erosion of their relative capabilities, which are the ultimate basis for their security and independence in an anarchical, self-help international context' (Grieco, 1993, p.127).

The consequence of this, says Waltz, is that:

> ... even the prospect of large absolute gains for both parties does not elicit their co-operation *so long as each fears how the other will use its increased capabilities.* ... a state worries about a division of possible gains that may favour others more than itself. That is the first way in which the structure of international politics limits the co-operation of states.
>
> (Waltz, 1979, pp.105–6)

Second, there is the idea that some forms of interdependence generate vulnerability, a form of mutual dependence that is sufficiently asymmetrical to give rise to relations of domination and subordination. This is often called 'vulnerability dependence', or just vulnerability, and refers to 'a relationship of subordination in which one thing is supported by something else or must rely upon something else for fulfilment of a need' (Baldwin, 1989, p.174).

Waltz draws attention to this when he notes that 'a state ... worries lest it become dependent on others through co-operative endeavours and exchanges of goods and services' (1979, p.106).

For these reasons, realists maintain that states are concerned with their relative positions vis-à-vis one another. Waltz says, for example, that 'states spend a lot of time estimating one another's capabilities, especially their abilities to do harm' (1979, p.131). Typically, realists have military capabilities in mind. But as economic resources can be turned into military ones – ploughshares into swords, butter into guns – and as the effectiveness of military capabilities often depends on intangible features such as leadership and national will, the estimation of capabilities is not an exact science. Nevertheless, at any given time, a ranking of the major powers is usually a relatively straightforward affair. A rough and ready approximation of a state's relative position might be the country's share of world military expenditure or world national income, or some aggregate of both.

4.1   The zero-sum character of relative gains

Notice that if states evaluate their capabilities in these terms, that is, if they focus on their share of, say, the world's income (or military resources), they are locked into a zero-sum world, in which a gain for one is always a loss for another. To see this, consider a world with just two countries in it, the USA and Mexico, both of which are concerned to maintain their current position. Suppose that, before any co-operation, the USA has 90 per cent of the world's income and Mexico has 10 per cent. What division of the gains from co-operation is consistent with both maintaining their relative position (measured by their share of world income)? There is only one outcome that will satisfy both parties: the USA gets 90 per cent of the gains and Mexico gets 10 per cent. Only a division of the gains that is proportional to the original starting positions of the parties keeps their relative positions the same, if we measure relative positions as a ratio.

Activity 9.4

What happens to the absolute gap in income if a constant relative position (in ratio terms) is maintained? Suppose the world income is $10 trillion and that gains of $1 trillion are shared as above. (A trillion is a thousand billion.)

The example above is very probably overstated. The USA probably wouldn't be that bothered if its share of world income fell to, say, 70 per cent and Mexico's rose to 30 per cent, as long as its absolute standard of living had increased. Nevertheless, consider the following example. In 1990, Robert

Reich, later to become Secretary of State for Labour in the Clinton Administration, conducted an informal poll and asked a series of business and financial leaders, civil servants and politicians which of the following scenarios they favoured. Scenario 1: by 2000, US national income increases by 25 per cent and Japan's by 75 per cent. Scenario 2: by 2000, US income increases by 10 per cent and Japan's by 10.3 per cent. Reich reported that nearly everyone he spoke to (except the economists) preferred the second alternative (Reich, 1990).

The general point is that as soon as states start evaluating their positions relative to one another, the range of co-operative outcomes that is sustainable is dramatically limited by the fact that absolute gains tend to be converted into zero-sum conflicts. And in a zero-sum situation, there is only one point at which nobody loses (and nobody gains), that is, the point at which the relative positions are unchanged.

Notice, however, that Waltz and Grieco are not arguing that states care about their relative positions directly. Rather, states care about their position in the system because of its potential impact on their welfare, security and sovereignty: they fear that a position of weakness or vulnerability may be used against them. Faced with the prospect of absolute gains from co-operation, the reason states also focus on the gains of others, writes Lloyd Gruber, 'is because they fear that by falling too far behind they run the risk of incurring more than offsetting *absolute* losses at some point in the future' (2000, p.24).

In terms of the analysis developed thus far, the realist contention is simply that states pursue absolute gains, subject to the constraint that, in an anarchic system, a position of weakness or vulnerability may be used by another as the basis for an exercise of coercive power that imposes costs. Typically, realists have in mind the use (or threat) of force as the means of exercising coercive power. But you have seen (in Section 3.2) that asymmetrical interdependence can also provide a basis for the exercise of coercive power. And in both cases, similar considerations apply. Whether force or a pattern of interdependence can be used depends on the threat point that a state can (credibly) establish, and that depends on the costs and benefits of using force or changing the terms of interdependence. Even in the case of the use of force, if the costs of war exceed the gains of victory, then a state cannot use a threat of force to establish a credible threat point.

So, it would be surprising if states were concerned with only relative evaluations of capabilities. After all, relative capabilities are a means, a way of safeguarding security, not ends in themselves. In fact, realists do not maintain that states are motivated *solely* by gains in relative capabilities. Grieco, for example, argues that when considering the impact of gains from an interaction on its capabilities a state will seek to maximize its *net* gains, which he defines as a function of its absolute gains *and* its relative gains. How states evaluate this function, that is, how they balance absolute gains and relative considerations depends on what he calls their 'coefficient of sensitivity' to considerations of relative advantage.

In my examples in Section 3, I assumed that states showed no consideration at all for their relative position. But consider, for example, two powerful states that start out with the same national income and identical military forces. Let us suppose that these states are also ideological and political rivals. One might expect them to be very sensitive to any division of gains from co-operation that upsets this balance, and they might also be expected to forego potential absolute gains from co-operation if the result was that the other got a larger share and thereby improved its relative position. In this instance, the states might be concerned only with their relative positions; their coefficients of sensitivity are so large as to drive out all considerations of absolute gains. This is one highly plausible explanation for the marked lack of economic co-operation between the USA and the Soviet Union during the Cold War.

In general, however, Grieco recognizes that the coefficient of sensitivity to considerations of relative advantage will vary.

> It will be greater if a state's partner is a long-term adversary rather than a long-term ally; if the issue involves security rather than economic well-being; if the state's relative power has been on the decline rather than on the rise; if payoffs in the particular issue area are more rather than less easily converted into capabilities within that issue area; or if these capabilities and the influence associated with them are more rather than less readily transferred to other issue areas.

(Grieco, 1993, p.129)

5   Governing interdependence

Agreements such as NAFTA take time to implement, often a decade or more, and they are inherently open-ended in so far as NAFTA's rules cover anything not explicitly excluded by the agreement and, therefore, are intended to govern trade and investment decisions in an inherently uncertain future. This means that some means has to be found of interpreting and implementing the agreement after the formal deal has been done. Negotiations are extremely time-consuming and costly, and they involve the commitment of scarce political resources. Therefore, parties are reluctant to renegotiate agreements. Moreover, the parties want some certainty that others will hold to the commitments made and some may seek to 'lock in'

Relative gains
Relative gains are gains evaluated in relation to those of others. This can be done in various ways. Here we assume that states are concerned with their share of the total income or total military capability, or both.

domestic reforms by means of a binding international agreement. For all these reasons, it is a noticeable feature of regional arrangements such as NAFTA – as well as global freer trade negotiating rounds such as those organized within the WTO – that they are not only wide-ranging and reach deeply into national patterns of policy making but that they also involve the creation of collective governance mechanisms through which the parties agree to conduct their future interactions under the agreement.

These mechanisms of governance can be intergovernmental or they can involve a pooling and/or delegation of sovereignty. Under inter-governmental arrangements, states make decisions collectively rather than individually, but on the basis of unanimity, that is, each has a veto, or at least is not bound by the decisions of others. The pooling of sovereignty involves creating decision-making procedures that do not have a built-in veto for the member states, and so a member may be bound by the decisions of others. And sovereignty is delegated 'when supranational actors are permitted to take certain autonomous decisions, without an intervening interstate vote or unilateral veto' (Moravcsik, 1998, p.67).

In these terms, the governance of NAFTA is primarily of an intergovernmental kind, combined with some elements of delegated sovereignty. The central decision-making institutions of NAFTA are the Free Trade Commission and the Secretariat. The Free Trade Commission, based in Mexico City, is comprised of cabinet ministers or their designates, and operates on the basis of consensus, unless otherwise agreed. It oversees the overall functioning of the agreement and the government representatives are 'charged with the formulation of policies affecting trade in manufactured goods, agricultural products, textiles and financial services' as well as being 'responsible for developing common rules of origin, customs procedures, transportation regulations, sanitary measures, and labelling standards' (Gruber, 2000, p.96). The Free Trade Commission does not operate as a permanent body but convenes at least once a year in regular sessions that are chaired successively by each party. The only permanent bureaucracy is the Secretariat, which has offices in Mexico City, Ottawa and Washington. Each member state appoints an individual to serve as the Secretary for its section. The Secretariat is responsible for the administration of the dispute settlement provisions of the agreement, assists the Free Trade Commission, and provides support for various non-dispute related settlement committees and working groups.

In addition, there are separate commissions for co-operation on the environment, based in Montreal, and on labour issues, based in Dallas, Texas. These commissions were included at the beginning of the Clinton Administration in order to counter opposition from environmentalists and labour unions and to secure the ratification of the agreement in the US Congress. These interest groups, by-passed by the administration of George

Bush Senior, regained centrality during the 1992 presidential campaign. The Clinton campaign was 'aimed at shifting attention from the overall benefits of free trade with Mexico (which was what [President] Bush emphasized in his efforts to use NAFTA as a foreign policy success story for his administration) to the domestic distributive costs and environmental externalities of such an agreement' (Cameron and Tomlin, 2000, p.205). The independent presidential candidate, Ross Perot, who argued that NAFTA would create a huge 'sucking sound' as US firms moved their production to Mexico to take advantage of its cheap labour and lax environmental standards, echoed these concerns.

The main obligations that NAFTA imposes on the member states arising from these two supplementary accords are to enforce their own labour and environmental legislation; not to erode further existing standards in order to attract or maintain investment; to consult with each other in the event of a complaint; and to develop transborder co-operation, particularly between Mexico and the USA. This latter is particularly directed towards the regulation of legal and illegal migration.

Finally, NAFTA includes a system of arbitration to settle trade and investment disputes in which panels of experts exercise powers of judicial review, a form of delegated sovereignty. The decisions reached by these panels of experts are binding for the member states. Moreover, it is a distinctive feature of NAFTA's dispute system that 'private' parties (that is, firms) can sue the member states if they believe that their contracts have been violated in breach of the rules of the free trade agreement. Such cases can be taken either to one of the international arbitration mechanisms provided by the agreement or to the courts of the member states. In the first such case – that of Metalclad, described in Chapter 8 – the supranational authority of the NAFTA-appointed tribunal was affirmed.

5.1 Accounting for supranational governance

Question

Can you think of reasons why states create forms of supranational governance? You might want to look back to Chapter 5.

There are two, possibly complementary, reasons why states adopt forms of supranational governance in order to regulate complex interactions such as NAFTA. The first reason is that a form of governance that facilitates the sharing of information and is able to draw upon sources of technical expertise in an independent manner may enhance the efficiency of decision making. States may realize that if they implement their agreements in a relatively uncoordinated manner, they may fail to achieve all the potential gains. In this context, establishing a form of supranational governance represents an attempt to ensure that states find themselves on the line AB in Figure 9.1, rather than at a point somewhere below it. A second reason for creating a degree of supranational authority is to enable states to bind one another to the decisions they have made, and to prevent subsequent governments from reversing those decisions. As Moravcsik notes: 'Governments are likely to accept pooling or delegation as a means to ensure that other governments will accept agreed legislation and enforcement, to signal their own credibility, or to lock in future decisions against domestic opposition' (1998, p.73). It is this latter point that Gruber also emphasizes: the real purpose of supranational institutions, he suggests, is 'to deter the enacting coalition's successors from mounting a serious challenge to the new regime if they should ever get the opportunity' (2000, p.90). We have seen that President Salinas saw NAFTA as a means of cementing his liberalizing policies in place in the face of domestic opposition in Mexico.

6 Conclusion

The framework I used above to analyse US–Mexican relations is quite general. It can be applied to other forms of interaction in international politics and it can be extended to take account of more than two states, although the model inevitably becomes a little harder to apply. I want to conclude by drawing out some general implications of our analysis for how we think about the prospects for international co-operation under conditions of *both* anarchy *and* interdependence.

We can draw three general conclusions. If, first, the game is positive-sum, and if states are concerned solely with their absolute gains, there is space for co-operative bargaining to mutual advantage. In some cases, side payments may be necessary to persuade one party to play. Anarchy poses no obstacles to co-operation in this world. Second, if states evaluate their positions purely in relation to others (measured by their share of, say, world income or the ratio of their military capabilities to those of an adversary), then all games – even positive-sum ones – are transformed into zero-sum games and there is only one division of the gains: that which divides the gains in proportion to the original disparity between the parties and leaves their relative positions intact. Neither will be prepared to move away from the origin. A concern with relative position, deriving from anarchy, blocks co-operation – as in the example of the superpowers during the Cold War. And third, when states care about both their absolute gains and their relative positions, the outcome is indeterminate and depends on how they weigh the one against the other. If relative considerations do not weigh too heavily in their calculations, states may still find themselves in a positive-sum game.

In other words, the concern with relative positions that is generated by anarchy is not necessarily an obstacle to co-operation when Grieco's 'coefficient of sensitivity' is sufficiently small. Even in Grieco's model, the realist claim that worries about the distribution of gains inhibits mutual co-operation emerges as but one possible outcome. It is a special case, operating where considerations of relative power dominate a concern with absolute gains. Such concerns are likely to dominate, as suggested above, when a position of relative superiority can be used to achieve greater absolute gains than those available from co-operation, or inflict greater absolute losses on another. The general point may be stated more positively. The pattern of interdependent preferences is also part of the structure of international politics and serves to shape outcomes. Realist considerations apply when this pattern is such that the game is zero-sum. I have argued that zero-sum games are a special case, and not the general picture. Both anarchy and interdependence matter.

As Thomas Schelling wrote in *The Strategy of Conflict*, still one of the most perceptive analyses of strategy in international politics:

> Pure conflict, in which the interests of two antagonists are completely opposed, is a special case; it would arise in war of complete extermination, otherwise not even in war. For this reason, 'winning' in a conflict does not have a strictly competitive meaning; it is not winning relative to one's adversary. It means gaining relative to one's own value system ... In the terminology of game theory, most interesting international conflicts are not [zero-sum] games ... the sum of the gains of the participants is not fixed so that more for one inexorably means less for the other. There is a common interest in reaching outcomes that are mutually advantageous.

(Schelling, 1960, pp.4–5)

In general, what explains the difficulty in achieving co-operation is not a fixed feature of anarchy – that relative evaluations (measured in ratio terms) are inherently zero-sum – but rather the likelihood that relative disparities of capability can be translated into outcomes in which one party is able to better its own position and damage the absolute capabilities of another. To reach the realist conclusions of Waltz, that international co-operation is strongly constrained by anarchy, it is necessary to assume that relative considerations weigh heavily in the calculation of states, that states fear that relative positions can be translated into absolute outcomes, specifically that one state's relative position can impose absolute losses on another while achieving gains for itself. These considerations did not apply to Mexico and the USA, and that is why Krasner's prediction that Mexico would not sign a free trade agreement akin to the Canada–USA FTA proved to be mistaken. Not only is the general realist contention that anarchy is a barrier to co-operation unfounded, but we have also seen that states are able to create (albeit limited) forms of collective governance, ways of sharing their sovereignty, to manage their interdependence.

More generally, our analysis has the merit of making explicit what is often taken for granted in realist accounts. You will recall that Waltz says that the structure of the international system is defined by the distribution of capabilities between states and that structure determines outcomes in international politics. Yet, two international systems may have exactly the same structure (as defined by Waltz) and have different levels of co-operation because *their net costs of translating relative positions into absolute gains* differ from one to the other. This is another general point that is often overlooked: the exercise of power involves costs. In some circumstances, a state's share of some resource may be an accurate measure of its power, that is, its ability to impose costs on others. In terms of the analysis developed above, a favourable relative position may be the basis of a stronger threat point in a bargaining game. But this cannot be assumed, as the gains reaped from using a superior relative position against a bargaining partner may be less than the costs.

To see this, consider one final example. Imagine that the USA and the European Union are negotiating an FTA. These have broadly similar levels of national income and, for the purposes of this example, I assume that they are equal. However, in 2002 the USA military expenditure was $364 billion, while that of Europe (excluding Russia) was around $190 billion. But how far could this massive disparity in US military power (almost certainly understated by these figures, given the technological superiority and integrated command of US forces compared with those of the EU) be used to make a credible threat against the EU? Could the USA threaten to bomb French farmers to secure a reform of the Common Agricultural Policy? More seriously, could the USA threaten to withdraw from NATO and leave Europe to face its security challenges alone? And how much might the Europeans be prepared to pay to avoid this outcome? There are imponderable questions, but I hope they are enough to make you question the assumption that a superior relative position can always be translated into a credible threat. Once we recognize that states subsist in conditions of interdependence, just as much as those of anarchy, our considerations of power have to be considerably subtler than asking who has what share of total military capability or world income.

Further reading

A detailed account of the NAFTA negotiations, based on extensive interviews with key participants in all three countries, is Cameron, M.A. and Tomlin, B.W. (2000) *The Making of NAFTA: How the Deal Was Done*, Ithaca and London, Cornell University Press.

For a thorough study of power, bargaining and the development of international governance, including case studies of European monetary union as well as NAFTA, see Gruber, L. (2000) *Ruling the World: Power Politics and the Rise of Supranational Institutions*, Princeton, Princeton University Press.

An important set of essays on how to think about power and interdependence in international politics is Baldwin, D.A. (1989) *Paradoxes of Power*, Oxford, Blackwell.

Part 4 Autonomy, sovereignty and macroeconomic policy

The state is the political institution at the heart of international relationships, and sovereignty is its defining characteristic. But what states do with their sovereignty, the aims they pursue and how far they are able to realize those aims: these capabilities are forged both domestically and internationally. States' preferences – such as the decision to block or liberalize trade – are formed by social, political and economic processes at the national and international level (Chapter 6). And unequal power between states helps to determine the scope states have to pursue those aims interdependently with other states (Chapter 9). The core theme of Part 4 is the question of how the interplay of domestic and international processes determines the autonomy of states, especially their capacity to act effectively in managing and developing the national economy.

The three chapters that follow are all written from an African perspective. Africa is a good vantage point for the purpose of analysing state autonomy and sovereignty because, as Thandika Mkandawire outlines in Chapter 10, the capability of African states has been explicitly contested for many years. Multilateral institutions and powerful states have tried to redefine African states from the outside, notably employing the leverage provided by the donation of international aid. Chapter 10 sets these activities and their consequences in a historical context, including severe economic crisis and continuing poverty. Thandika Mkandawire focuses on the close inter-relationship over time between contending political and economic theories of the role of the state in African development and the changing international and national contexts in which they have arisen.

This theme of the creating and undermining of the autonomy of national states through the interplay of domestic and international agency is continued in Chapters 11 and 12, which both focus on Tanzania. A core role of states is to manage the economy through the instruments of macroeconomic policy. In Africa, as Chapter 10 sets out, this means above all creating the economic conditions for development. In Chapter 11 Marc Wuyts argues that macroeconomic policy is centrally concerned with managing the international economic relationships of a country – trade and investment flows – for domestic benefit. Marc Wuyts explains the basic tools of macroeconomic analysis and the implications of different macroeconomic policies – some externally imposed – in the harsh context of extreme poverty and high external aid dependency. He argues that effective macroeconomic policy has to manage the complex interplay between trade integration and structural change in the domestic economy in a manner that can drive economic development, and identifies the sharp constraints imposed by the current international trade regime and by international economic policy prescription.

In Chapter 12 Samuel Wangwe then takes up the question of how international and domestic forces produce a struggle over the autonomy of the state in terms of a national state's ability to determine and pursue its own development objectives. The story of Tanzania's relationship with international aid donors shows how constrained this autonomy can become in a situation of acute aid dependency. Based on his own professional experience, Samuel Wangwe asks if and how autonomy can be reclaimed and ends the chapter on a note of cautious optimism.

We hope that you will gain from studying this part a deeper conceptual understanding of the different aspects of state sovereignty and the determinants of the autonomy of states, plus an ability to deploy some tools of macroeconomic analysis to analyse policy choices, impositions and constraints. That this conceptual exploration – in itself of general applicability – is written from the perspective of the most economically and political marginalized continent in the world gives it, we believe, a particular edge and urgency, sharpening your understanding of key choices and dilemmas. Above all, it identifies the importance of the two-way interaction of domestic and international agency in shaping the position of particular countries in the world economy and the state system.

Chapter 10 Can Africa have developmental states?

Thandika Mkandawire

1 Introduction

Africa provides an excellent vantage point for understanding how history, theories and ideologies shape the role of the state. I aim in this chapter to explore these influences through the lens of the extremely sharp international and national debates around state activism in Africa – or through the question, 'can Africa have developmental states?'.

Developmentalism, in the sense of the successful promotion of rapid economic transformation, is a core concern of leaders and citizens in African countries. The depth and ubiquity of poverty is central to the African political agenda, highlighting the need for a state response. At the same time, the argument that the state cannot play a positive role in promoting economic development has been taken up in international arenas with great insistence in precisely the African case. The sharpness of these arguments between international agencies and African leaders, and among engaged academics and advisers illuminates competing theories about the proper and possible role of the state. In this chapter, I trace the interlinking of these shifting analytical claims and assertions about African states with changing economic contexts.

The concept of the developmental state can be defined in terms of ideological commitment to economic growth and development, and state capacity to promote it. In Section 2, I examine the concept and follow the role of developmentalism in post-independence nation building in Africa. I then go on, in Section 3, to analyse the international political contestation of African developmentalism in the context of severe economic crisis.

> **Developmental state**
> A developmental state combines a developmentalist ideology with effective capacity to manage resources in order to promote development.

Africa's economic decline in the 1980s and 1990s – the so-called 'lost development decades' – has been the worst of all the major regions of the developing world and, as a direct consequence, Africa has been subjected to much greater external policy interventions than elsewhere. Indeed, the multiplicity of external and internal social actors in African governance points more sharply than anywhere else in the developing world to the complexities of reconciling national efforts with international co-operation. International institutions such as the International Monetary Fund (IMF) and the World Bank, and powerful Western states have argued in this period that African developmental states are an impossibility and foreign advisers have assumed political and managerial roles that would be unacceptable in much of the rest of the world.

The political field on which this external intervention has been played out is that of foreign aid. Overseas development aid has played a much greater role in Africa than in any other part of the world. It is the leverage that aid provides which has allowed external agencies and governments to seek directly to effect far-reaching internal change in African states. The tool has been 'conditionality' – the placing of policy conditions on recipient governments in return for aid in the form of loans and grants. In Sections 3 and 4, I examine the theoretical justifications offered for the forced reduction and restructuring of African states which has been a central element of this conditionality, and track some of the consequences. The theme is taken up again in Chapters 11 and 12. The former examines the economic consequences of aid dependence and forced policy change, and the latter explores the politics of aid dependency.

The extreme nature of the international intervention in Africa provides insights into the construction and destruction of state capability which have wider application across the world. The political conditions just described have encouraged irresponsible experimentation with different policies and strategies in Africa, an experimentation that has amounted, at times, to a confiscation from outside of the ability of national states to define their own role and to give expression to the political community they represent. African experience has also been widely drawn upon in international academic and political debate to develop and illustrate different theories about the possible and desirable role of the state.

The restructuring of African states by external agency has been in large part effected through a broader package of economic policies characterized as 'structural adjustment'. Chapter 11 examines this package in detail. Here, however, I track some of the economic outcomes expected and experienced during the 'adjustment years' of the early 1980s to the mid 1990s (see Section 4). The failure to generate through these policies a sustained increase in African economic growth has been associated with the emergence of a 'second generation' of international reform proposals which gives the state a central role. These proposals introduced discussion of the importance of good governance and an 'effective' state; in Chapter 12, Samuel Wangwe examines the extent to which this international debate can provide a political context for an African state to reassert local political autonomy and initiative.

This chapter thus sketches an empirical *history* of African experience of economic growth and development alongside an *analytical* story of an evolving contest about the role that African states might, and should, perform in the development process. It is not argued that one caused the other; rather I trace the use of evidence in the analytical debate and the feedback into policies that influenced events. To do this, it is useful to periodize these stories of economic and policy change. I will divide the post-independence period into four periods defined in terms of the growth performance of African economies: the 'developmental years' 1963–73; the 'crisis years' from 1973 to the early 1980s; the 'adjustment years' 1982–95; and the 'recovery years' 1996–2001. These form the next four sections of this chapter. Corresponding to each period there have been changes in the perceptions and debates about the role and capacity of the state.

The two stories – a historical one and an analytical one – are briefly summarized in Table 10.1 which you may find useful to guide you through the subsequent discussion. When identifying these periods, I pictured in outline the long destructive cycle of interaction of economics and politics that many African countries have gone through (see Figure 10.1), starting from early post-independence developmentalism, first in the context of economic growth and then economic crisis, and emerging with a shrunken 'adjusted state' in the 1980s. The period of stabilization and slow growth has since reopened policy debates that may – hence the question mark in Figure 10.1 – be taking us back to a renewed acceptance of the possibility of a developmental state. However, as I discuss at the end of the chapter, African states face these new challenges in a weakened condition precisely because of the denial and destruction of their capabilities in earlier years.

Table 10.1 Economic performance and the debate on African state capability

Period	Economic growth record	Role of the state
1963–73: the 'developmental years'	High growth	State-led developmentalism
1974 to the early 1980s: the 'crisis years'	Economic crisis and decline	Attacks on the state as the source of economic crisis
1982–95: the 'adjustment years'	Economic stagnation, macroeconomic stabilization	The thesis of African state incapability
1996–2001: the 'recovery years'	Fragile resumption of growth	The return of the state? Governance, institutional reform and 'partnership'

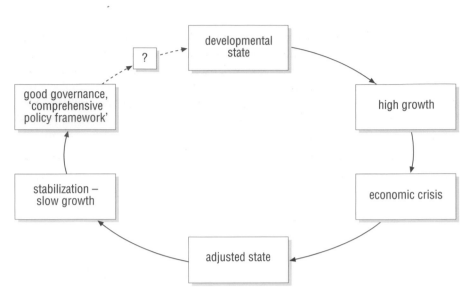

Figure 10.1   The African state: from developmentalism to adjustment – and back again?

2   The developmental years and the African developmental state

2.1   Historical sources of developmentalism

Until 1960, the year when many African countries won their independence, economic development was defined by the imperial or colonial authorities that controlled much of the continent. Although the colonial powers had described their mission as that of bringing civilization to the 'Dark Continent', it was only in the post-Second World War era that the colonial authorities made explicit statements on economic development and 'Colonial Welfare and Development' schemes were introduced.

These schemes were driven by two contradictory forces. The first was the need of the colonial powers, especially in the aftermath of the war, for contributions from the colonies for the reconstruction of the devastated metropolitan economies. These were to be achieved by increasing primary commodity exports from the colonies to provide raw materials for industry in the metropolitan countries. Furthermore, the foreign exchange earned by the colonies' exports was to be held as reserves in the metropolitan countries, and these amounts were quite substantial. The colonies' financial reserves thus helped the European powers' post-war reconstruction by alleviating the 'dollar shortage' from which they suffered and which restricted imports of needed supplies. Finally, the colonies were also to serve as markets for imperial industries.

By its nature, economic development of this kind excluded certain policies that could benefit the colonized countries but would have run against the colonizers' objectives as set out above. The colony could not, for instance, introduce import substitution measures to protect and help develop domestic industry. Moreover, given the reluctance of colonial authorities to train Africans for high positions, little was done to provide secondary and university education in the colonies.

However, the second and contradictory force driving the 'Colonial Welfare and Development' schemes was the clamour by the Africans for social progress and national independence. The colonial governments were under great pressure to address the demands of the many social groups that had emerged and had been inspired by the claims of the imperial powers that their fight against Germany was for freedom and the independence of nation states. The creation of the United Nations and its Universal Declaration of Human Rights also undercut the ideological underpinnings of the 'civilizing missions' of the imperial project. The colonial powers had to demonstrate that not only were they looking after the welfare of the subjects, they were also preparing their colonies for eventual sovereign independence.

With independence, the new states could take advantage of the economic policy instruments available to states in the pursuit of development which had been denied them under colonialism. These included trade policies such as the protection of national industries (discussed in Part 1), the creation of national currencies and regulatory financial institutions, and the opportunity to become members of institutions such as the World Bank and IMF (these multilateral institutions are discussed in Section 3). Serious efforts were also made to expand secondary and tertiary education.

Nevertheless, some feared that what had been achieved was mere 'flag independence' – international recognition of national sovereignty for states whose capability and autonomy in exercising that sovereignty was severely limited. The attainment of independence did not always mean that the state was autonomous and able to act as it pleased; rather states were created whose room for manoeuvre was severely restricted.

One source of constraint lay in the process of decolonization. The outgoing colonial powers made sure that they maintained some leverage over the new states through aid and trade arrangements, diplomatic pressure and military intervention, constructing a set of relationships commonly known as 'neocolonialism'. The more articulate African leaders like Kwame Nkrumah of Ghana, Julius Nyerere of Tanzania and Patrice Lumumba of the Congo raised their voices against this 'neocolonial' domination that sought to undermine their newly-achieved independence. Their fears that the new states might be captured by external forces were often dramatically confirmed by the machinations of the former colonial masters who actively sought to 'divide and rule' the new nations, supporting pliant leaders and removing leaders (through military coups, economic sabotage and assassinations) considered hostile to the neocolonial project.

Furthermore, 'nation building' was a central preoccupation of the new leaders and it provided one of the central ideological supports for state activism. While seeking to exercise national sovereignty in respect of external forces, the new states had also to assert their authority internally. The new states often faced domestic challenges from a variety of social forces, whether regionally or ethnically defined; they had to claim loyalty from and authority over a population with a range of social identities; and they had to cope with wide social and class divisions. Hence, the national project of achieving authority over a divided nation and pursuing the aims of social, economic and political improvement which had driven the anti-colonial struggles was a defining feature of post-independence African politics.

2.2 Sovereignty, autonomy and the 'developmental state' in Africa

The new African states, therefore, found in the post-colonial world a general and widespread international acceptance of the *de jure* sovereignty (that is, formal or legal sovereignty) of the new nation states. This was partly because of the attitude of the USA which had no colonies in Africa; partly because of Cold War rivalries; and partly because of the militancy of the nationalists and their considerable success in winning broad support for national independence. However, *de facto* (in other words, in reality rather than in form), this sovereignty had to contend with many external pressures and internal centrifugal forces.

The concerns about the content of sovereignty were not African alone. As Sudipta Kaviraj said in Chapter 6, across the developing world many states were 'centrally concerned with reclaiming sovereignty from an imperial power and giving a commitment to develop the country's people and resources'. Consequently, when most African countries attained independence in the 1960s with the understanding that the state would play an important role in the development process, they were part of a broad international consensus about the link between developmentalism and the construction of effective sovereignty, and about the need for an active role for the state in economic development.

This consensus on state economic activism found some of its ideological and theoretical roots in the economics of the 1950s and 1960s. After the experience of the 1930s' Depression and of post-1945 reconstruction, economic policy in the developed capitalist economies was interventionist. Both the war effort and the development of the welfare state in much of Western Europe had underscored the view that the state could be used strategically to mobilize and deploy resources for the national purpose. Economic theories, referred to as Keynesian after the influential British economist John Maynard Keynes, provided a rationale for state intervention in the economy that was compatible with the social security and social services provision that had been partly a response to the Depression. In developing countries, the impact of these theories was reinforced by the spectacular industrialization of the Soviet Union, achieved through central state planning of the economy.

At the same time, specific theories of economic policy for development emerged in the new 'development economics'. This drew on historical and theoretical arguments to provide the intellectual basis for interventionist state policies in developing countries. Economic historians suggested that to the extent that development patterns or 'stages' (Rostow, 1960) could be identified from history, there was the possibility of learning how to accelerate or even 'leapfrog' development stages by deliberate state policies. One influential interpretation of the historical record came from the historian Alexander Gerschenkron (Gerschenkron, 1962) who argued that among 'late industrializers' such as post-1945 developing countries, the state assumed a more extensive role than had been the case among the pioneers of industrialization.

Economic theory concerning the role of the state in this era was characterized by an emphasis on macroeconomics, as a key domain of analysis and policy initiatives; this is the topic of the next chapter (the economics you have studied so far has been largely microeconomics).

The macroeconomics of the time identified an important role for the state in steering the economy as a whole, for example, by influencing key macroeconomic variables such as savings and investment which were considered important determinants of growth and development, as Chapter 7 explained. In developing countries in particular, distinct macro-level institutions such as ministries of planning to co-ordinate economic and industrial development were seen as necessary to address macroeconomic problems.

The economic rationale for this state economic activity lay in microeconomics: in identifying failings of markets to promote growth and development. In the context of underdevelopment, some important markets may not exist, for instance, effective stock markets and banks able to provide long-term industrial investment. One solution was to set up state-owned Development Banks, and to turn to international lending institutions significantly including the World Bank.

Furthermore, as Suma Athreye explained in Chapter 7, there was a widely held view that what she called the 'structural problems of development' – the need for different sectors of the economy to develop in mutually compatible ways – required state co-ordination. The state could do this through information and by encouraging compatible decisions by disparate actors

Macroeconomics
Macroeconomics analyses the operation of the national economy as a whole.
Microeconomics
Microeconomics analyses the decisions of individual economic actors such as people, households and firms.

297

(this process was called, at the time, 'indicative planning'), and through its own investments where private investment was lacking. Such gaps were particularly likely in infrastructure and some heavy industry which required massive mobilization of resources that the private sector might not undertake, either because it lacked both financial and managerial capacities or because of the uncertainty of returns. Moreover, the private market would under-provide investments in services such as education that were essential for development, and thus the state had to step in.

These historical and theoretical considerations, which give the state a strategic role in promoting development, were drawn upon by the resurgent nationalism in the post-Second World War era. There was a clamour for economic progress to allow the new states to address issues of poverty, nation building and 'catching up' with the developed countries. Therefore, nationalism gave development the status of an ideology – 'developmentalism' – driven by nationalist aims of 'catching up' and securing the resource base for national defence and security. Formal sovereignty and the unprecedented state autonomy created by independence finally placed economic development squarely on the African policy agenda.

Sovereignty and autonomy

The concepts of sovereignty and autonomy are explored further in Chapter 12 in the context of a study on the politics of aid-dependence in Tanzania. Sovereignty was defined in Chapter 5, Section 5 as a state's claim to authority: its claim to a right to rule rooted in recognition of that right by the state's own citizens and by other states. 'Autonomy', on the other hand, is about the state's *ability* to rule: its ability to make independent decisions such as policy choices around economic development strategy of the type just discussed. While the autonomy of a state may require sovereignty – it must have the recognized right to exercise its authority – sovereignty is not a sufficient condition for autonomous action. And to realize the purpose of sovereignty – to allow a political community to make effective choices – requires autonomy.

To use these concepts to understand the developmental state, we need to distinguish two meanings of state 'autonomy' which are both widely used in the political analysis of African state capability. The first is autonomy of the national state from external pressure. The neocolonial pressures on African states referred to in Section 1 are an example of international constraint on a national state's autonomy of action, as are the pressures from aid donors described in Chapter 12. Economic constraints also limit state autonomy, as examined in Chapter 11. For example, limitations on capacity to import goods constrain industrialization efforts, as do declining terms of trade for a country's exports (see Chapter 3). Poverty and the level of aid donations limit a state's capacity to provide universal access to primary health care and good schooling. A state can only mobilize a certain level of resources and give expression to certain choices of its own political community, according to its particular location in the international economy and relation to other states.

The second meaning of autonomy looks inwards, to the state's relation to its citizens. I wrote above about the difficulty faced by African states in establishing authority over divided societies. The other side of this problem is the need to establish the autonomy of the new states from particularistic social forces in order to allow the state to devise long term economic and social policies, unencumbered by short-term claims of myopic private interests.

The formulation of the importance of state autonomy in this sense goes back to the writings on bureaucracy of the great nineteenth-century German sociologist, Max Weber. He argued that an effective state bureaucracy was a hierarchical structure of authority operating according to clear general rules applied impersonally within the organization and between the organization and its clients. The posts were separate from the private possessions of their office holders and held on the basis of merit. Hence, the state bureaucracy was autonomous from particularistic social interests. This concept of bureaucracy was a model, an 'ideal type', not a description of actual state functioning. Yet it was also an aspiration to create a state capable of serving national rather than particular private interests. The concept of state autonomy in this sense underpins the concept of the developmental state.

Developmental states

The labelling of the newly independent African states as 'developmental states' is retrospective. The states were spawned by the ideological perspective of developmentalism and nation building, and aimed to manage resources strategically for developmental purposes. The concept of the 'developmental state' has been applied particularly in attempts to explain the role of the state in rapid economic growth in East Asia. It has two components: ideological and structural (see the definition in Section 1).

A developmentalist ideology implies that the state conceives its 'mission' as ensuring economic development, usually interpreted to mean high rates of investment and industrialization. Indeed, such states derive their legitimacy from high rates of growth and economic progress. Other sources of legitimacy, such as democratic elections or the ability of the state to protect human rights, may be subordinated to this overriding developmentalism and in fact many developmental states have been authoritarian. In much of Africa, developmentalism provided the ideological scaffolding not only for the state's development plans but all too often for authoritarian governance. It was argued, in the name of both nation building and development, that development needed not only 'strong' states in the sense of autonomous from particular social forces, but also authoritarian ones that could carry out long-term plans unburdened by the short-term and short-sighted concerns of an electorate. Developmentalism thus subordinated all other human rights to the cause of national development.

The structural side of the definition of the developmental state emphasizes the state's capacity to implement economic policies sagaciously and effectively. There is, however, a problem of finding evidence of effectiveness. There is a risk of tautology (that is to say, assuming the answer you seek to establish) because evidence that the state is developmental is often drawn deductively from the performance of the economy. This produces a definition of a state as developmental if the economy is developing, and equates economic success to state strength, while measuring the latter by the presumed outcomes of its policies. Not only is this logically unsatisfactory, it ignores the extent to which policy effectiveness can be a trial and error process of seizing favourable circumstances.

A more satisfactory definition of a developmental state recognizes that unforeseen circumstances, external forces (such as declining terms of trade or wars on your border), and mistakes and plain bad luck can torpedo genuine developmental commitments and efforts by the state. At times, a government's political will and technical capacity may simply prove inadequate to fend off external forces. Recognition of episodes and possibilities of failure leads us to a definition of a developmental state as one whose ideological supports are developmental and one that seriously *attempts* to deploy its administrative and political resources to the task of economic development. We can look for evidence of serious intent (or developmental 'effort') in the state's behaviour, for example, the rate of collection of taxes and the effectiveness and accountability with which it manages public funds.

The 'dependency school'

Finally, the developmentalist ideology of the time had its critics, both in Africa and internationally. One set of criticisms came from radical nationalist circles that identified the state's neocolonial underpinnings and doubted whether its external dependence could allow it to be an instrument of development.

The argument was that in the industrialized countries, capitalist development had been driven by a national bourgeoisie – the owners and managers of large private firms – which had created a state that could be the lynchpin of industrialization efforts. However, African countries peripheral to international capitalism could not produce an African bourgeoisie. The spread of international firms based in the developed countries and investing across the world implied that the African dominant classes were historically condemned to be no more than a 'comprador' or 'lumpen bourgeoisie', subservient to the interests of foreign capital (Amin, 1972; Nabudere, 1985). The African state, it followed, was not up to its 'historical mission' of ensuring capitalist accumulation; there could be no possibility of developmental states in Africa that were either led by a national bourgeoisie or capable of nurturing one.

In the Cold War years, the most radical of these critics sought rupture with the global capitalist system. However, other social movements in the 1970s argued for internal reform and the possibility of 'dependent' capitalist development based on Asian and some African and Latin American experience (Cardoso and Faletto, 1979). The latter argued for a progressive national alliance between the national bourgeoisie and organized labour to create a 'developmental bloc' of forces able and willing to pursue a strategy of national industrial development over the long term. In effect, this presupposed a developmental state, and a literature spelling out the necessary 'developmental alliances' emerged across the developing countries. In Africa, the high performance of economies such as Kenya and Côte d'Ivoire were cited as examples of the possibility of capitalist development (Lubeck, 1987).

2.3 Economic performance in the developmental era

Independence for most African countries came in the middle of the 'golden age' of capitalism with high growth rates through the 1950s and 1960s, increasing trade and high levels of employment in the developed countries. During this period, African countries also experienced what must seem, in retrospect, a golden age of high growth, as Figure 10.2 demonstrates. Figure 10.2 shows average annual growth rates of GDP per head for sub-Saharan African countries from 1961–2001.

Question

How do the developmental years compare with the subsequent African growth experience shown in Figure 10.2?

The average growth rate of real per capita GDP of African countries was higher in nine of the years between 1961 and 1973 than for any subsequent year on Figure 10.2 except 1980. In fact, the average African growth rate for the whole of 1961–73 was 2.4 per cent, a higher rate than that attained in all but one subsequent year on Figure 10.2.

We return below to the data shown on this figure. First, let me note that the main driving force behind these early growth rates was industrialization: the outcome of import substitution (explained in Chapter 7) and some rather

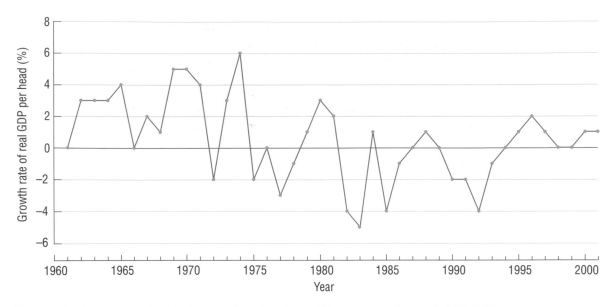

Figure 10.2   Growth rates of real GDP per head in sub-Saharan African countries (per cent), 1961–2001

Source: World Bank, *World Development Indicators*, online

basic processing of countries' main primary export commodities. You can see the effect in Table 10.2. From 1961–73, the 'developmental' years, manufacturing and industry as a whole (which includes manufacturing and also construction, mining and utilities such as electricity generation) grew faster than GDP. Exports also grew, on average, at a respectable 2.3 per cent per year. Agriculture, as Table 10.2 suggests, was the Achilles heel of this developmental exercise, its slow growth threatening to undermine development in countries with large rural populations and reliant to a considerable extent on agricultural exports.

Table 10.2   Annual average growth rates by sector for sub-Saharan Africa (per cent)

Period	Agriculture	Exports	Manufacturing value added	Industry	GDP
Development years	−0.1	2.3	5.7	4.6	2.4
Crisis years	−1.9	−2.6	0.5	−0.8	−0.3
Adjustment years	−0.3	0.8	−1.7	−1.7	−1.1
Recovery years	1.1	2.7	0.1	0.0	0.7

Source: World Bank, World Development Indicators 2002 CD-ROM

Industrialization requires high rates of investment (see Chapter 7) and, in the post-independence period, African countries achieved a rate of investment as a percentage of GDP that compared well with the East Asian countries, though the investment yielded lower rates of growth. Figure 10.3 shows the investment effort: gross capital formation (GCF) is total investment as a percentage of GDP, and this was driven upwards to a high of 24 per cent in 1974 and 1975 and then remained strong until the early 1980s before falling off. Investment was largely sustained by domestic savings, as Figure 10.3 shows. Gross domestic savings (GDS) increased from around 16 per cent of GDP in 1960 to over 23 per cent in 1980. Close to one-third of African countries had savings rates that were higher than 25 per cent by 1980, an indicator of major developmentalist 'effort'.

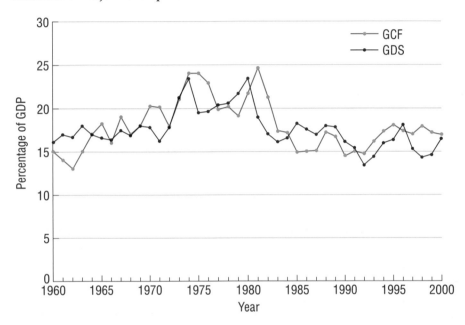

Figure 10.3   Savings and investment as percentages of GDP for sub-Saharan African countries, 1960–2000

Source: World Bank, *World Development Indicators 2002* CD-ROM

As in post-independence India (see Chapter 7), state intervention during this period was extensive. The state intervened in credit markets to direct credit towards preferred investments, mainly through specialized financial institutions such as development banks. Trade interventions included protective tariffs, export promotion and the allocation of import licences (granting permission to import goods) for priority goods. The state subsidized commodities such as food and undertook monopoly purchasing and export of agricultural commodities through state marketing boards. It became directly involved in production through investment in state-owned industries, nationalization of firms and joint public/private ownership. Furthermore, labour markets were influenced through labour legislation, minimum wages and direct provision of jobs.

Question

Do African states in the period 1961–73 meet the definition of 'developmental states' offered in Section 1 and elaborated in Section 2.2?

In addition to the widespread ideology of developmentalism, the impressive array of state efforts to promote development supplies indicators of developmental effort. Growth rates in the period were at a level never since matched. Thus, there are good reasons for accepting the label 'developmental state'.

However, this model of state-led development had a number of weaknesses, making many African economies vulnerable to the crises in the world economy in the 1970s and eventually undermining much of the success.

The first weakness was the great inequality in the distribution of the benefits of growth among and within the African countries. Internally, the growth process was not meeting what the International Labour Office (ILO) termed the 'basic needs' of much of the population, such as food, education and health care. The ILO located the problem partly in capital-intensive industrialization (see Chapter 7) generating too little employment. High rates of urbanization also outpaced wage employment. Where growth seemed to have been mastered, the call now was for 'growth with equity'.

Between countries there was also wide variation in access to the benefits of growth and gaps between countries widened. Table 10.3 divides the economies of sub-Saharan Africa into three categories in each period:

- countries with high per capita growth rates (3.0 per cent and above)

- countries with medium per capita growth rates (above 1.5 per cent but less than 3.0 per cent)

- countries with low per capita growth rates (less than 1.5 per cent).

The division between high and low growth countries in the 'development years' stands out. The highest performing country was Botswana in all four periods.

Table 10.3   Distribution of growth rates of GDP per capita of sub-Saharan African countries, over four periods (number of countries)

Period	High growth countries	Medium growth countries	Low growth countries	Lowest growth rate	Highest growth rate	Standard deviation
Development years	10	7	18	−1.7	9.0	2.5
Crisis years	9	4	28	−6.4	7.1	2.9
Adjustment years	5	2	40	−5.6	4.7	2.3
Recovery years	9	10	25	−6.7	8.4	2.7

Source: World Bank, World Development Indicators 2002 CD-ROM

Activity 10.1

Describe the distribution of growth rates between countries in each period using the information in Table 10.3.

The second weakness of the strategy was the failure to promote exports of manufactured goods. African policy makers were persuaded they could exploit their comparative advantage in primary exports to pay for the capital equipment and intermediate products needed for industrialization. This was in sharp contrast to the East Asian industrialization strategy that used the industrial sector itself to earn some, if not all, of the foreign exchange required for industrialization. The result was extreme vulnerability of African economies to decline in the primary commodity terms of trade (see Chapter 3). The multilateral institutions such as the World Bank encouraged African optimism about these terms of trade, despite a strong contrary view publicized by the Latin American economist Raul Prebisch and others in UNCTAD (Prebisch, 1959).

The third weakness of the African developmental model made this vulnerability worse: the failure to transform agriculture. As a result, urban–rural income gaps widened; foreign exchange earned by exports had to be used for food imports; and key agricultural exports stagnated. There was no African 'green revolution' of the type that transformed farming techniques in Asia, to enhance productivity and the responsiveness of agriculture.

Fourth, there was a failure to encourage a domestic entrepreneurial class. In some countries there was an ideological aversion to domestic capitalists, despite joint ventures by the state with foreign capital. In others, even with pro-capitalist political principles, state enterprises intended for eventual transfer to domestic private ownership remained stuck in state hands partly because of resistance by their managing bureaucracies to privatization.

These economic strategy failings were compounded by a narrow nationalism. African economies were understood to be too small for industrialization on the basis of the domestic market. Nevertheless, a widely discussed report on the need for regional integration (Organisation for African Unity, 1980) was completely side-stepped as each African state sought individual arrangements with external funding institutions.

Moreover, as I have already suggested, African state–society relations were troubled, and this undermined states' capacities to mobilize society for development. Most African states opted for an authoritarian mode of governance, often on the grounds that both development and nation building required 'strong states' unencumbered by the clamour of different interest groups in democratic politics. However, though authoritarianism did produce rapid development elsewhere, Africa was full of cases where authoritarian regimes had become predatory or had mismanaged the economy. In many cases, the state failed to win adhesion of key elements of society for its developmental project. In the more tragic cases, this failure to mobilize society led to an alienation that produced armed conflict.

Partly as a result of economic weaknesses and vulnerability and the resultant aid dependence (examined in the next two chapters), and partly through Cold War era geopolitical and ideological positions, in the 1970s African countries already allowed much greater foreign presence in their policy-making process than anywhere else in the developing world. Though Africans themselves decried this dependence as neocolonialism, its legacy was a lack of African 'ownership' and co-ordination in policy making that has bedevilled African policy to this day (see Chapter 12).

3   The crisis years

The years from 1974 through to the early 1980s were years of severe economic crisis across sub-Saharan Africa. The economic distress was associated with deepening political crisis in many countries and paved the way for international aid donors – specifically the IMF and the World Bank – to get a grip on African policy making to an unprecedented degree. I describe briefly these turning point years, and the multilateral lending institutions that came to exert such power. Section 4 examines the policy content and consequences.

3.1 Economic and political crisis

Question

Look back at Figure 10.2. What happened to African growth rates after 1973?

The average growth rate of GDP per head shot up to the highest level on Figure 10.2 in 1974, then collapsed. From 1975–83, only three years saw any growth; the rest were years of economic decline. The worst year of all was 1983 when African countries' GDP per head *fell on average* by 5 per cent.

Question

Now look back at Table 10.3. How was this economic disaster distributed among countries?

A number of countries did well through the crisis years, while many others did very badly. These were the years of the 'oil crises': in 1973 and again in 1979, the Organization of Petroleum Exporting Countries (OPEC) took advantage of world market conditions to force up oil prices. Several African countries are oil exporters – notably Nigeria and Angola – and the large rise in their export earnings kept up average African growth rates of GDP per head in the crisis years (Table 10.3). The oil price increases were accompanied in the mid 1970s by a brief boom in the prices of other primary export commodities.

Internationally, the 1970s were years of rapid inflation and economic recession. These external economic 'shocks' exposed the vulnerability of the African development model. Exports volumes fell sharply because of recession in developed country markets, and the terms of trade improvements were short lived as demand for commodities fell. The result was a severe balance of payments crisis in many African countries generating economic stagnation and decline (the consequences of the balance of payments crisis are examined in Chapter 11).

There is considerable debate about what African governments should have done in this period. They had, in effect, two choices. To accept the balance of payments crisis as structural and long term, and change their economic development model in order to tackle the trade deficit, or to borrow finance from abroad to cover the continuing deficit. That most chose the latter was in part the result of advice and pressure from external lenders, notably the 'Bretton Woods' Institutions (BWI): the IMF and World Bank.

The Bretton Woods Institutions (BWIs) include the World Bank and the International Monetary Fund (IMF). Set up at a meeting of 43 countries in Bretton Woods, New Hampshire, USA in July 1944, the aims of the BWI were to ensure the stability of the financial and monetary system, to help rebuild the post-war economy and to encourage trade. The first task was assigned to the IMF, which would create a stable climate for international trade by harmonizing its members' monetary policies and maintaining exchange stability. It would also be able to provide temporary financial assistance to countries encountering difficulties with their balance of payments. The task of 'reconstruction and development' was assigned to the World Bank, lending money for post-war reconstruction and to the developing countries. The third task was to have been carried about by an International Trade Organisation (ITO), but until the World Trade Organisation (WTO) was created in the early 1990s trade relations were guided by the General Agreement on Tariffs and Trade (GATT) (see Chapter 4).

Since the end of reconstruction in Europe, World Bank activities have been confined to developing countries. Up to the mid 1970s, the IMF played a minor role in African economies – much less than it had in Latin America. The World Bank was heavily involved in drawing up national plans and financing projects. It was only after the 1973 crisis that the IMF became active in stabilization programmes using models it had developed in dealing with the high inflation rates of Latin America. Ideally, the IMF was to ensure stabilization, while the World Bank continued lending for long-term growth and development issues. In practice, the stabilization programmes of the IMF took precedence, its preoccupations assuming the role of 'fundamentals'. Countries could access World Bank funds only after meeting the conditionalities of the IMF. One consequence of this was that issues of poverty and development that were the mandate of the World Bank simply disappeared from the agenda – a fact that has been acknowledged by the World Bank through its later calls for 'comprehensive development frameworks' or 'second generation reforms' that placed poverty reduction at the core of its preoccupations (Section 5).

In the late 1970s, the BWI were advising African governments, on the basis of their economic projections, that the decline in the terms of trade for primary commodities was temporary, so that temporary external borrowing was advisable. The IMF and the World Bank also pressed countries to borrow at a time when real interest rates (allowing for inflation) were low or negative, and chaperoned many African countries to the private financial markets. Then, in 1981, private external capital flows into African countries were cut off in the wake of the Mexican debt crisis. Mexico's inability to pay the interest on its foreign debt led to private banks across the world cutting off new loans to developing countries, including African ones, leaving African states with no source of financing except the BWI.

Tanzania's experience (discussed at length in Chapters 11 and 12) illustrates these pressures. When in 1977 Tanzania had a foreign exchange bonanza due to sharp increases in coffee prices, the government thought it a passing windfall and preferred to use it to build up its foreign exchange reserves. Donors threatened, however, to withdraw their aid unless Tanzania spent these reserves, leaving the country vulnerable when export earnings turned down again.

The widespread economic crisis in Africa was compounded by a political crisis as the fundamental weaknesses of the state and its vulnerability to external pressure were exposed. There was a loss of legitimacy of the state as a result both of economic distress and the authoritarian style of governance that had denied the state the necessary flexibility in the face of economic crisis.

To understand the nature of the political crisis, we need to revisit the political model associated with the developmentalist strategies. The widespread understanding at the time was that both development and nation building required strong states. Such strong states would have the capacity to mobilize resources (including through forced savings), would impose the discipline required for the difficult task of playing 'catch up' and would bring coherence to the disparate contributions of both the public and the private actors. This was often construed as meaning authoritarian regimes. Developmentalist ideology also tended to accept the view that there was a trade-off between democracy and economic growth, and that democracy was therefore a 'luxury' that poor countries could not afford. One should also recognize the imperatives of nation building. The nationalists in power were apprehensive of the dangers of secessionism and ethnic conflict. One consequence was a politics that often sought to balance different regional and ethnic claims. This was not done through decentralization, as is currently proposed, but through an increased concentration of power at the centre. One consequence of such a concentration was the overloading of the agenda of the central government, further reducing its flexibility.

Authoritarian rule did not, of course, always produce developmentalist states. Authoritarian states in Africa included both developmental and predatory ones. And in all too many cases, authoritarian regimes that started off as developmental ones degenerated into personalized, predatory institutions. The significant point is that, while democracies drew their legitimacy from the fact of being elected, authoritarian regimes tended to derive their legitimacy from the ability of the state to maintain national unity and achieve good economic performance. The consequence of the latter point was that, when the economic crisis struck, the tendency of the authoritarian state was to sustain public expenditure, especially spending on current consumption. And when the state lost all legitimacy because of its failure to manage the economic crisis, it increasingly rested its authority on force and corruption, producing a vicious circle of reduced economic performance and reduced legitimacy.

3.2 Laying the basis for an attack on the African state

Following the economic crisis of the 1970s, there was a sharp shift in the views about the role of the state in both developed and developing countries. In the developed countries, the new conservative governments in the USA and UK blamed inflation on state profligacy and fiscal irresponsibility. And for developing countries, the internationally dominant view blamed the crisis on domestic economic policies and the extensive role of the state in African economies. The titles of some of books and articles published on the matter testified to the unhealthy condition of the African state: 'lame leviathan', 'the bloated state', the 'vampire state'.

One school of thought blamed the economic crisis on the state itself, specifically state interventionism and distortion of markets. It was claimed that national development planning and the strategies of import substitution had undermined Africa's competitiveness, reduced its share in world trade and ultimately led to unsustainable levels of indebtedness. The most influential statement of this position for the African context came in a World Bank report called *Accelerated Development in Sub-Saharan Africa: An Agenda for Action* (World Bank, 1981), known as the 'Berg Report' after its team leader Elliot Berg.

The request for this report actually came to the Bank from African governments dissatisfied with economic performance and the slow pace of economic recovery after 1979, and seeking a strategy of economic growth that would enable African economies to grow as fast as the East Asian economies. The Berg Report was to have enormous impact on policy making and analysis for the next two decades. It argued that accelerated growth could be achieved by freeing markets and reducing the economic role of the state. Given the ability of the IMF and the World Bank to dictate policy terms to African states, these arguments strongly influenced economic policy in the 1980s. They also laid the basis for a thoroughgoing attack on the role of African states. Section 2 argued that this role, legitimated by developmentalism, was in many ways an expression of the political projects of post-colonial states as well as of the received wisdom about development. Thus, the critique of the state-led model was both a challenge to theory and to these 'national projects'. The strongest argument was not that state interventionism could not be justified in principle by economic theory, since the justifications for intervention set out in Section 2 are widely accepted by economists. Rather, the argument was that African states could not intervene effectively for reasons rooted in the nature of the state and the politics of policy making.

Consequently, the critics' most important case against the possibility of developmental states in Africa was not rooted in faith in flawless markets but rather in the view that whatever the degree and extent of market failures, states cannot correct them in ways that do not make things worse. Such views are coloured by the particular ideological predispositions of those making these arguments and their interpretations of cases of state failure. To these arguments we now turn.

4 The adjustment years

The years from the early 1980s to the mid 1990s were a period of wholesale external assault on the capabilities of the African state, and an externally driven redefinition of the purpose of state activity towards economic stabilization rather than development. Led by the BWI, this assault was framed in the concept of 'structural adjustment', a framework that includes economic stabilization (explained in Chapter 11), a major reduction in the scale of state economic activity through privatization and reduction of public expenditure, and the reorientation of policy towards supporting market-led economic activity. In political terms, and especially in the African context where the international institutions exerted most leverage, the earlier criticisms of state policy grew into a full-blown thesis for reining in the role of the state. The analysis and consequences for state capacity are the subject of this section.

4.1 The 'impossibility' thesis and the analysis of the state

Lessons from East Asia?

The thesis that developmental states were impossible in Africa was rooted in tendentious contrasts repeatedly drawn between the African experience and that of the highly successful East Asian industrializers: notably South Korea, Hong Kong, Singapore and Taiwan. These Asian economies performed spectacularly well during the 'lost decades' of development and global recession. Figure 10.4 illustrates this contrast. It shows that, up to the crisis years, the growth performance of sub-Saharan Africa and East Asia (including Pacific countries) was not dissimilar. Beyond those years, the divergence in growth performance was huge.

Early interpretations of this experience, such as the Berg Report, argued that this success showed that 'external forces were not the chief factor' in Africa's poor trade performance (World Bank, 1981, p.17). East Asian experience showed, it was argued, that reliance on markets and export orientation were a better strategy than the state interventionist and import substitution strategies that had been pursued by African states.

This portrayal of the East Asian experience was rapidly challenged by a vast literature demonstrating that the state had played a central and strategic role in the development process. It had, in Robert Wade's words, 'governed' or

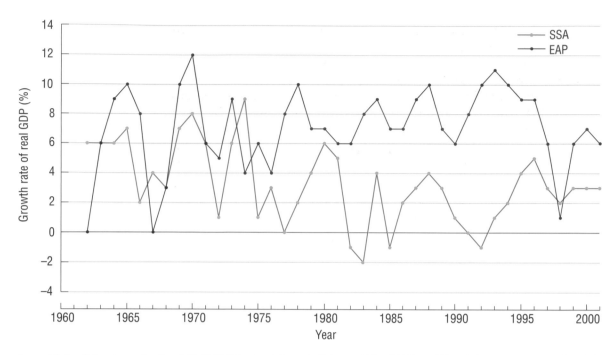

Figure 10.4   Rate of growth of real GDP (1995 prices) for sub-Saharan Africa (SSA) and East Asia and the Pacific (EAP) (per cent), 1962–2001

Source: World Bank, *World Development Indicators*, online

steered the market in developmental directions it thought appropriate (Wade, 1992). Eventually, in a widely debated report called *The East Asian Miracle* (World Bank, 1993), the World Bank admitted (albeit grudgingly) the central role played by the state in the 'miracle'. Indeed, it was in the light of this debate that the term 'developmental states' gained widespread usage, applied both in East Asia and elsewhere in the developing world.

Yet this was not so in the case of Africa. Here the shifting interpretation of Asian experience was used to buttress the denial of the possibility of developmental states in Africa. The replication of the Asian experience was somehow impossible in Africa. For example, Peter Lewis argued that:

> While some aspects of this [Asian] model (for instance, greater political insulation of economic policy makers) could reasonably be achieved in African countries, the extensive coordinated economic interventions of the East Asian States are well beyond the administrative faculties of most African governments.

> (Lewis, 1996)

From Section 2 it follows that I believe this 'impossibility thesis' to be based on a misreading of Africa's development experience. The Berg Report's brief history of Africa's post-colonial development and the role of the state portrayed policy and performance in the first two post-colonial decades as unmitigated and largely undifferentiated disasters. The veracity of this account of the African economic crisis was taken for granted by most analysts of African economies, who generalized from it and set out to provide political explanations for that poor policy performance. And yet the Berg Report had in many ways falsified economic performance during the preceding two decades.

First and foremost, it underestimated the enormous importance to African economies of external conjuncture and the role of foreign expertise. African economies generally do well when the global conjuncture is good and poorly when it is bad: evidence of their extraordinary openness and vulnerability to terms of trade changes. As for foreign expertise, this is one variable that is often conveniently forgotten in looking at the malaise of the African state. Nevertheless, international institutions do, on occasion, admit that their role in African policy making has been a major contributory factor to the policies African countries have pursued. Most policies that are today attributed to weaknesses specific to the African state, such as neo-patrimonialism and rent seeking (see below), were the orthodoxy of the day brought to Africa in well-funded and well-staffed packages by external actors.

Furthermore, I argued above that despite the many distortions of import substitution, up until the second oil crisis many African economies had performed relatively well. Africa had examples of states whose ideological inclination was clearly 'developmentalist' and which pursued policies that produced fairly high rates of growth in the post-colonial era and significant social gains and accumulation of human capital. African bureaucracies were able to extend infrastructure and social services to degrees that were unimaginable under colonial rule. Moreover, in a significant number of countries, the political elite was able to reach arrangements that provided peace and stability.

These arguments run against the international consensus at the time of writing. I explore here the key analytical arguments in the large literature expressing doubts about the inherent developmental capability of African states.

Lack of autonomy

Among Africans themselves, the extent of a developmentalist ideology linked to a nationalist project is a matter of debate. Contrasts are sometimes drawn between the first generation of African leaders, who were aware of the need for a nationalist-cum-developmentalist ideology, and later leaders. Claude Ake (1996) argues that for some African leaders a lack of ideology is inherent in personal rule, and the loyalty of the population is not to some overriding societal goals but to individuals. They often hold highly idiosyncratic ideologies that are not developmentalist in nature, which they themselves flout with impunity and with no moral qualms.

The idea of 'personal rule' forms part of a substantial critique of African states which argues that they are not autonomous from societal pressures. This is the second concept of 'autonomy' defined in Section 2 and, as explained, it is a core idea in the concept of the developmental state: such states must not act on behalf or at the behest of narrow private interests. To deny autonomy to the African state is to attack its developmental capability.

This critique argues that African states are not really or only partially 'modern' in the Weberian sense of rational-legal institutions acting according to general rules and procedures rather than in response to particular social interests. This is the 'modern' ideal of authority residing in the impersonal offices of the state. Weber drew a contrast with patrimonialism, a form of rule that is an extension of the rulers' extended household, in which administration and force are under the direct control of the ruler. The neo-Weberian critique of the African state argues that African states are all imbued with patrimonialism, in which state power is concentrated in the personal authority of an individual ruler regardless of their ideological claims and the moral rectitude of individual leaders.

The consequence for state action is argued to be a lack of autonomy in the sense of an inability of the state to distance itself adequately from society in order to perform efficiently. Instead the state is used to distribute resources to support personal rule. African states, rather than representing the modern side of the modern/traditional dichotomy, were now seen to be hopelessly and incurably steeped in Africa's debilitating culture, in which clientelism and the 'politics of the belly' (Bayart, 1993) guided all social action. The state became mired in activities designed to redistribute resources to personal networks of kin and personal clients. Termite-like, Africa's primordial and patrimonial relationships had eaten into the very core of the edifice of modern administration rendering it both weak and incoherent.

The virulence of this attack is reflected in the language of 'societal failure'. The African state is argued to be inherently unable to provide the bureaucratic order and predictability that capitalists need if they are to engage in long-term investment. The Asian autonomous developmental state is juxtaposed with the African 'lame Leviathan' (Callaghy, 1987), which is so porous and 'penetrated' by society, so beholden to particularistic interest groups, so mired in patron-clientelist relationships, and so lacking in 'stateness' that it cannot pursue the collective task of development which demands insulation from such redistributive demands.

This patrimonialist argument develops the critical contrasts between African and East Asian policy and performance. It runs up against the problem that neo-patrimonial states, in Africa and elsewhere, have pursued a wide range of policies including some that are squarely developmental. In other words, other than indicating the style of governance, neo-patrimonialism does not tell us much about what policies a state will pursue and with what success.

Even more damning is the fact that some of the features of the African state highlighted by this literature as non-developmental have been present in successful developmental states. In particular, accounts of spectacular corruption – an indicator of 'patrimonialism' – in the high performing East Asian economies are widely known, yet in Africa corruption is seen as a uniquely damaging barrier to development. Arguments that African states are afflicted by a uniquely damaging 'pathological paternalism' (Ergas, 1986) do not resolve this conundrum. Rather, we should recognize that though certain 'patrimonialist' practices may be morally reprehensible or culturally unacceptable, we do not have a clear theoretical understanding of how they affect the performance of capitalist economies. Capitalist economies operate with much more moral latitude than is often preached, and a very wide range of morally reprehensible behaviour can be integrated into strategies of capitalist development.

The 'rent-seeking' critique of the state

Alongside these political arguments about lack of autonomy, there was a second set of arguments rooted in economics that used the concept of 'rent-seeking' behaviour to characterize the problems of state interventionism and to argue for rolling back the state. This framework of ideas was particularly fundamental to the World Bank's critique of the state, and it was put forward cogently and influentially in the case made by Robert Bates (1981) against the developmental capacity or inclination of African states.

The analytical point of departure of this critique is that markets generally work well if allowed to function freely. State intervention causes market 'distortions'. For example, state intervention changes prices away from the prices that would be set by freely operating markets. In turn, the effect of such distortions is to create an opportunity for individuals to profit in ways unavailable before the intervention. These profits are described as 'rents', and expenditure by potential beneficiaries in order to gain access to the rents ('rent-seeking' expenditure) is waste in economic terms, since it is unproductive of development. Consider, for instance, the industrial licensing described by Suma Athreye in Chapter 7. An exclusive industrial licence provides a private firm with the opportunity to make monopoly profits, free of competitive pressures from other producers and importers. These licence-based windfall profits are the 'rents', and firms have an incentive to spend (for example, on lobbying and bribes) to achieve access to these rents.

This analytical framework is then used to *explain* state policies. Given that markets work well, why does the state introduce distortions? In Bates' work, the answer lay in the rational pursuit of self-interest groups by organized individuals who pushed the state to adopt policies that generated rent-seeking opportunities for them.

Question

Can you link this explanation of state behaviour to the concept of patrimonialism?

The explanations are compatible. Patrimonialism identifies personalized redistributive activities by the state. The rent-seeking framework adds an economic explanation for particular state policies directed (in patrimonialist fashion) at benefiting particular groups. The state is understood as essentially a rent-generating institution that inhibits efficient allocation of resources. All state activities involving the safeguarding and transfer of rights and resources generate rents; the explanatory force of the model is in its emphasis on expenditure of resources to capture artificially created rents as the origin of state policy decisions.

Drawing on this framework, Bates (1981) argued that African institutions were infested by rent seekers who had captured state policies to serve their narrow interests. This had rendered the state incapable of pursuing long-term development goals. In this view, state bureaucrats were part of the coalition that had produced disaster. The only solution was the removal of the source of such rents by drastically reducing state interventionist policies.

The rent-seeking framework is focused on microeconomic efficiency and was particularly used to attack policies of import substitution: tariffs, subsidies and direct state investment in industrial development. Its denial that active policy making could be beneficial undermined the arguments for active industrialization policies set out in Chapters 3, 6 and 7, pitting high rent-seeking costs against potential benefits.

Yet the comparison with East Asia – so widely drawn in these years – undermines the policy implications once we look closely at the industrial policies in question. Many of the policies attributed to rent seeking and identified as the cause of Africa's failure have been and are still in use by the high performance Asian economies. Once we take into account the benefits of industrial investment and growth it becomes clear that rents can be either 'productive' or 'unproductive' in their developmental effects. Imagine a situation where the pursuit of rents leads a firm to expand efficient productive activity, for example, to capture as large a quantity of low cost export finance as possible. In this case, rent seeking has become a spur to growth, not a block on growth. The difference between this case and the standard rent-seeking model is that rent seeking here generates new resources; in Bates' static model it can only suck existing resources away from productive use.

Much of the writing on Asia, at least up until the financial crisis in the late 1990s, took for granted that the creation and allocation of rents by the state in this way had played a central role in both creating a nationalist capitalist class and promoting accumulation. Writers on Asia point to 'contingent rents' used to encourage contests among private firms for government incentive and co-ordination schemes, thus rewarding growth-enhancing activity by private firms (Yanagihara and Sambommatsu, 1997; Sundaram, 1996). Akyüz (1996) argues that the creation of rents in this more dynamic sense, creating profits for some firms over and above those that would be attained under free market policies, was central to the process of accelerated capital accumulation and growth in Asia, generating new industries and sustaining profits in order to underpin high corporate savings and investment rates in a number of Asian countries.

Rent seeking and neo-patrimonialism have both been used to argue for more autonomous states in the sense of autonomous from particularistic social forces. However, the implied image of state technocracies pursuing development in complete isolation from societal pressures is a myth – an ideal type (see Section 2), not an empirical description of Asian or other developmental states. In seminal work on Asian developmental states, the political scientist Chalmers Johnson (1981) underlined the intimacy of their relationship with the private sector and the intensity of their involvement in the market as a crucial feature, not their distance from these pressures. Subsequent writing on other developmental states has underscored this point, leading to the useful, albeit problematic, notion of 'embedded autonomy' to describe the nature of state autonomy in these societies. This is an autonomy circumscribed by the dependence of the state for its development project on the activities of the private sector and the way the state becomes 'embedded in a progressively dense web of ties with both non-State and other State actors (internal and external) through which the State has been able to coordinate the economy and implement developmental objectives' (Evans, 1992).

In many countries, independently organized business associations have had considerable influence on state polices. In the Republic of Korea, concentration of business and the highly diversified interests of the industrial conglomerates (the *chaebols*) allowed business–government relations managed through direct firm level and even personalistic consultations between the *chaebols* and state institutions (Cheng *et al.*, 1996). The World Bank observes that 'formal institutions that facilitate communication and cooperation between the private and public sectors ... [are] in effect an institutionalized form of wealth sharing aimed primarily at winning the support and cooperation of business elites' (World Bank, 1993, p.181).

With few exceptions, such 'embeddedness' never really developed in Africa and import substitution policies were not the result of lobbying by rent seekers. If there was one thing the state in Africa failed to do, it was to allow the local business class effective presence in policy making. Or, conversely, if there is anything that relatively weak African business classes failed to do, it was to 'capture' state policies for their own ends. The fact that a group benefits from a particular set of policies does not prove that they lobbied for those policies, let alone that they have 'captured' rents that will be sustained through hard times. Synthesizing the results of a number of studies on the interaction between the economics and politics in several developing countries, the two leading theorists of rent seeking, Robert Bates and Anne Krueger, state: 'One of the most surprising findings in our case studies is the degree to which the intervention of interest groups fails to account for the initiation or lack of initiation of policy reforms' (Bates and Krueger, 1993, p.455).

This analysis of Asian and African experience suggests that the use of rent seeking as a general argument against an active developmental state in Africa is simply not credible. The relevant questions are 'rents' for whom, and with what reciprocal obligations for recipients? The answers will depend on the desired income distribution and strategy of development. The denial of an active developmental state for fear that the state will be 'captured' by rent-seeking coalitions is tantamount to the denial of the possibilities in Africa of accelerated development achieved by a deliberate government policy. In the African debates, the fear of the damaging effects of rent seeking has not only sustained the argument for a minimalist state, but has also given the foreign experts, who for inexplicable reasons do not engage in rent seeking like all other mortal beings, a moral upper hand.

The imperial approach

The elevation of foreign experts fed another line of analytical attack on African states which simply questioned from a technocratic point of view their capacity and bureaucratic acumen to be developmental. From this perspective, African states were seen to be in desperate need of technical assistance and external guidance. Such a belief induced a *tabula rasa* view of African institutions, with the cultivation among international institutions and aid donors of a culture of unbridled experimentation in creating new institutional arrangements and projects.

This 'imperial' approach was fundamental to the behaviour of the World Bank and the IMF in the adjustment years. Their construction of the 'problem' asked: how can the aid donors (who wanted 'good policies') get recipient states (deemed to be self-seeking and corrupt) to act in the desired manner? The answer was the regime of conditionalities: conditions on aid receipt which aimed to create incentives for African states to act as required, associated with the creation of institutions to monitor and sanction laxity. This model shaped donor–recipient relationships in Africa through the 1980s and 1990s.

4.2   The political consequences of adjustment

The consequences for the state in Africa were far-reaching. The standard view of the state which emerged from these analytical positions was that it was somehow over-extended. Informed by an unbridled faith in the market, an idealization and even distortion of the history and character of the Asian 'development state', and the conviction that the African state could not replicate the Asian experience, the advice to Africa was not only that greater reliance should be placed on the market, but that the state should be 'reined in'. In addition, specific conditions on aid forced a reduction of the state's role in the economy.

Much of this thinking became such a part of conventional wisdom that radical proposals on state reform have been made without the slightest concern for the implications of such reforms on existing capacities, and without a detailed analysis of the institutional make-up of the state. The reasoning has been largely deductive – a state that performed activities which it should not have performed in the first place must be bloated. There has been no consideration of the fact that a state overstepping its bounds in certain areas could be woefully inadequate in others.

As a result, we witness in Africa the external reinforcement of policies that continually erode the economic and political capacities of the state. In a self-fulfilling diagnosis, the state was first identified as overextended, and the fiscal crisis of the 1980s (the excess of expenditure over taxation) blamed on spending to maintain patronage systems. To cut down on clientelism and rent seeking, the BWI-led reforms of the state aimed to cut public expenditure and promote withdrawal of the state from many of its activities. The effects were predictable: the weakened state would then exhibit an incapacity to carry out its basic functions; as spending shrank, state personnel became demoralized and civil servants sought to make up lost salaries by moonlighting and through corruption. This incapacity could then be used to argue that the state in Africa was not capable of handling development and needed to be stripped down further. This downward spiral of erosion of state capacity ruled out prospects for the self-regeneration of the state, or for its own internal reform into a more effective actor in the development process, and nourished the idea that 'ownership' of policy should be taken away from the state.

And yet, on some measures, comparative research clearly suggests that there has been little difference between states in Africa and in other developing countries, including those that have performed exceedingly well. One way to compare the size of states is by size of the bureaucracy, for example, by comparing the number of civil servants per 100 people in the country. On this count, one study shows that the average ratio for sub-Saharan Africa (1.5) is less than that of Asia (2.6) or of Latin America (3.0) (Schiavo-Campo, 1996). Interestingly, Mauritius and Botswana – the best-performing African countries in terms of growth and with bureaucracies touted as efficient – have more than three times the African average size of bureaucracy: 5.5 and 5.8 respectively.

An earlier study, conducted in the early 1980s by the IMF before the wave of redundancies, estimated the predicted level of public sector employment given levels and pattern of development. Actual public employment in the 17 African countries included was on average 8 per cent *less* than would have been predicted. A more recent study for the 1970s, 1980s and 1990s similarly concluded that, adjusting for the level of development, urbanization and exposure to external risk, public sector employment in Africa was about average for developing countries (Goldsmith, 2001).

Another measure of the size of the state is the ratio of government wages and salaries to other goods. Again, Africa's ratio is below average. For the 11 African countries for which data are available, downsizing reduced the total number of central government workers by 9 per cent during the 1980s and early 1990s. As a consequence, spending on government wages and salaries dropped from 7 per cent of GDP in 1986 to 5.8 per cent in 1996. Only in Botswana and Mauritius, the economic success stories, did total public employment and the share of the central wage bill in total public expenditure increase. The evidence of the African state as bloated simply does not exist. As a World Bank study put it (Schiavo-Campo, 1996), most African countries 'do not need to shrink the workforce but to overhaul the entire civil service system'.

These years thus led not so much to a rolling back of the African state as a drastic erosion of capacity. The loss of spending on social and physical infrastructure undermined state legitimacy. Had the result been accelerated growth, this loss of ownership and of autonomy from international interference might have been worthwhile. The next section considers the economic record.

4.3   Economic performance under adjustment

The ultimate justification for this thoroughgoing redefinition of the role of the state was that it would put African countries back on the path of 'accelerated growth', as the Berg Report had phrased it. Adjustment aimed to combine immediate stabilization of the economy with increasing and diversifying exports, mobilizing domestic investment resources and generating increased inward investment. By the mid 1990s, major changes in African economies had occurred through stabilization and market liberalization: lower inflation, reduced gaps between public expenditure and taxation, liberalization of trade and exchange rates (see Chapter 11), though privatization of state-owned industries had proceeded more slowly. Nonetheless, economic growth rates did not improve.

Question

Look back at Figure 10.2 and Table 10.3 and compare the growth rates in the adjustment years with earlier periods.

Between 1982 and 1995, Figure 10.2 shows *only three years* when the sub-Saharan African countries had, on average, any growth at all in GDP per head. Only 5 out of 47 African countries had growth rates of GDP per head that were over 3 per cent in these years, and 40 had growth rates of less than 1.5 per cent, including some with a decline (Table 10.3). The cumulative effect of this on standards of living in countries whose experience was around or below average is quite hard to imagine for those who have not lived through economic collapse. It looks worse still if compared to recent estimates that growth rates of 7 per cent or more are required to address poverty in Africa.

Adjustment, at best, placed state finances on a sounder footing and it did increase exports. Yet the hoped-for diversification of exports away from primary products did not emerge. In a World Bank study Francis Ng and Alexander Yeats showed that:

> ... no major expansion occurred in the diversity of products exported by most of the Sub-Saharan African countries, although there are one or two exceptions like Madagascar and Kenya. Indeed, the product composition of some of the African countries' exports may have become more concentrated. Africa's recent trade performance was strongly influenced by exports of traditional products which appear to have experienced remarkably buoyant global demand in the mid-1990s.

(Ng and Yeats, 2000, p.21)

However, the biggest disappointment has been the low level of private foreign direct investment (FDI) – the basis on which growth could be achieved in the longer term without remaining overly reliant on external aid. One of the constraints on development is low absolute levels of savings, even where savings ratios are respectable, because of low levels of income. A persuasive promise made by BWI was that adhesion to its policies would attract foreign private investors, thus increasing total investment and growth. Most African governments' acceptance of IMF policies has been based on precisely this claim; that agreements with IMF would catalyze new inflows of foreign capital. Governments were willing to enter a 'Faustian bargain' of reduced national autonomy in return for increased financial flows. Even when governments were sceptical of the developmental validity of BWI policies, the expectation of foreign investment tended to dilute the scepticism.

To the surprise of the advocates of these policies and to the chagrin of African policy makers, the response of private capital to Africa's diligent adoption of structural adjustment policies has, in the words of the World Bank, 'been disappointing'. Private investors appear unconvinced of the attractiveness of Africa for investment. Rather than IMF agreements catalyzing FDI, for many investors the presence of the IMF and World Bank may simply signal economic trouble, a problem of which the BWI seem unaware. The fact that no African country has 'graduated' from BWI support to standing alone maintains this negative impression of Africa among investors. Consequently, despite the fact that rates of return on direct investments have generally been much higher in Africa than anywhere in other developing regions (Bhattacharya *et al.*, 1997; UNCTAD, 1995), an intangible 'risk factor' continues to deter investors. Africa is systematically rated as more risky than is warranted by the underlying economic characteristics, ratings nurtured by a large dose of ignorance about individual African economies (Collier *et al.*, 1999). The outcome has been a trickle of foreign investment into Africa, but not enough to increase Africa's share of global FDI flows.

Question

State carefully, using Figure 10.5, the changing pattern of FDI flows into sub-Saharan Africa relative to world FDI.

FDI flows into sub-Saharan Africa fluctuated between 2 and 4 per cent of world FDI for much of the 1970s; there were high points in the early 1970s and again in the mid 1980s, and then a decline. The early 1990s, when adjustment should have been bearing fruit in increased investment inflow, have been very disappointing. FDI into sub-Saharan Africa other than Nigeria (the largest oil producer) and South Africa (the other large economy) was particularly low, at well under 2 per cent of global FDI during most of the 1990s, and fell below 1 per cent at the turn of the century.

Although the average real inflow increased five-fold, by 1998 sub-Saharan Africa's share of global FDI at 1.3 per cent was less than half that of the mid 1980s (UNCTAD, 2000). A rise in FDI in the latter part of the 1990s has been cited as evidence that globalization and structural adjustment programmes are working (Pigato, 2000); however, this celebration is premature.

Furthermore, the FDI entering Africa is of dubious benefit to longer term, sustained growth. From the mid 1990s, the country concentration of investment worsened, with much of the investment going to South Africa. In

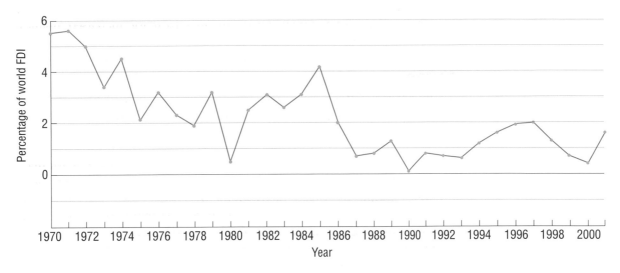

Figure 10.5   Foreign direct investment (FDI) in sub-Saharan Africa as a percentage of world FDI, 1971–2001
Source: UNCTAD, *World Investment Report 2002* and CD-ROM

addition, there is a longer term sectoral concentration on minerals including oil, with little FDI going into manufacturing. Investment in mining is drawn to African countries not by macroeconomic policy changes (as is often suggested) but by the prospects of better world prices, changes in ownership away from state control, and specific sector-level incentives.

Moreover, the limited direct investment has been largely driven by acquisitions of already existing enterprises (often those being privatized under adjustment programmes), rather than being 'green field' investment in new productive enterprises. Privatized plants have been sold by the state under 'fire sale' conditions, and privatization acquisitions made up 14 per cent of FDI flows into Africa in 1998 (UNCTAD, 2000). Some of the new investment has expanded existing capacity, especially in industries enjoying local market monopolies (for example, beverages, cement and furniture), and may taper off when these opportunities have been taken up. For instance, in Ghana, a country hailed as a 'success story' by the BWI, FDI peaked in the mid 1990s at over US$200 million annually. This inflow was mainly due to privatization and rapidly reversed to produce an outflow (Aryeetey *et al.*, 2000; Hutchful, 2002).

Worse still, on top of poor inward investment, capital has been flowing out of Africa, to the extent that it is likely to be a net capital exporter. Data on capital flight are hard to assemble but it has been estimated that in 1990, 40 per cent of privately held African wealth was invested outside of the continent, and that capital flight from Africa per head of its workforce has been higher than from other developing country groups (Collier and Gunning, 1997; Collier *et al.*, 1999). For the whole period of 1970–96, capital flight from sub-Saharan

323

Africa has been estimated at US$193 billion, or US$285 billion including accumulated interest. These figures can be compared to the combined debt of these countries which stood at US$178 billion in 1996. Far from being heavily indebted, many sub-Saharan African countries are net creditors vis-à-vis the rest of the world, since their private external assets, as measured by cumulative capital flight, are greater than their public external debts (Boyce and Ndikumana, 2000, p.32).

So far, financial liberalization has not done much to turn this tide, as the World Bank has acknowledged (Devarajan *et al.*, 1999). Private investment abroad benefits individual African capital owners, but the social benefits of investing those funds in Africa in terms of employment and incomes are lost. As a result, the end of the adjustment years was a pessimistic time. As the World Bank noted, 'In the 1960s governments actively strove for accelerated development. By the mid-1990s simply restoring growth to allow rising per capita income was seen as an achievement for many countries' (2000c, p.38).

5   The years of recovery?

I have argued that in the adjustment years the ability of African states to determine their own development strategies was eroded to the point where an African voice in both policy and analytical debate was drowned out by external intervention and particularly by the BWI. The second half of the 1990s saw a series of changes that held out some prospect of a reversal of this downward spiral of state capability and autonomy from international pressure, including some optimism about economic growth, and a reassessment by aid donors of the state's role in development.

5.1   An economic upturn in the 1990s?

The tone at the end of the 1990s concerning economic prospects was markedly different from much of the preceding two decades. Previously, poor growth in the adjustment era was blamed on the failure of African governments to implement adjustment policies. By the second half of the 1990s, the BWI changed their stance, claiming that growth was rising as a result of the policies they had been promoting in Africa. They suggested that enough time had transpired and enough African countries had persevered in their adjustment to begin now to reap the fruits of the adjustment process.

There were certainly some signs of economic recovery in Africa. Figure 10.2 shows a return to positive per capita growth from 1995, at least for three years, before a dip at the end of the decade. The IMF talked about a 'turning point' in the mid 1990s (Fischer *et al.*, 1998), and claimed that this 'reflected better policies in many African countries rather than favourable exogenous developments' (that is, favourable developments independent of African states' policies) (Hernández-Catá, 2000). This is part of the IMF summary of the policy changes they approved:

> Important structural reforms have been implemented in many African economies in this decade: domestic price controls have been abolished or at least liberalized in several countries; some inefficient public monopolies have been dismantled; and a large number of state enterprises have been privatized. In the external sector, non-tariff barriers have been eliminated in most SSA [sub-Saharan African] countries and import duties have been lowered in some, exchange rates have been freed and unified in most countries ... Most countries also have eliminated direct controls on bank credit and have established market-determined interest rates.

(Fischer *et al.*, 1998)

The president of the World Bank, James Wolfensohn, reported in his 1997 address to the board of governors that there was progress in sub-Saharan Africa, 'with new leadership and better economic policies.' (Wolfensohn, 1997a). Michel Camdessus, managing director of the IMF, at the 1996 annual meeting of the World Bank and the IMF, said: 'Africa, for which so many seem to have lost hope, appears to be stirring and on the move'. The two vice-presidents for Africa at the World Bank wrote an article entitled 'Africa on the move: attracting private capital to a changing continent' (Madavo and Sarbib, 1997), which gave reasons for this new 'cautious optimism'. The major World Bank report on Africa in 2000 stated 'many countries have made major gains in macroeconomic stabilization, particularly since 1994' and there had been a turn around because of 'ongoing structural adjustment throughout the region which has opened markets and has a major impact on productivity, exports, and investment.' (World Bank, 2000c, p.21). Thus, by the end of the millennium it seemed that African countries had been successfully adjusted.

And yet, from 1997, the growth rates began to falter. By 1999, in its report on global prospects and the developing countries, the World Bank revised downwards its prediction of the African growth rate 'despite continued improvements in political and economic fundamentals'. The report blamed the poor performance on worsening terms of trade and the knock-on effects of the Asian financial crisis of 1997, not on policy failings.

In a sense we have been here before. A series of 'success stories' have been told about 'strong adjusters', 'early intensive adjusters' and 'globalizers' (the labels varied) who strutted and fretted on the 'success' stage, only to be heard of no more. Twenty six sub-Saharan countries have been, at one time or another, on the lists compiled by the international institutions of countries experiencing growth attributed to adjustment, and of 15 'core adjusters' listed by the World Bank in 1993, only three (Lesotho, Uganda and Nigeria) appeared in the 1998 list of strong performers (UNCTAD, 1998). As in the past, the African economies remain vulnerable to external terms of trade shifts and external influences such as the economic downturn that followed the Asian financial crisis of the late 1990s.

The World Bank's projection of African economic performance in the decade from 2000 makes depressing reading:

> The forecast is for a halt to the region's lengthy decline and marginalization and even for moderate reversal: The longer term (2003–2010) outlook is for sustained GDP growth – 3.7 per cent – with per capita income rising 1.3 per cent per year. The primary driving force behind the outlook remains better governance and ongoing reforms to the policy environment.

(World Bank, 2001b, p.152)

Such prospects were simply not compatible with any serious notion of development. If this was what Africa had come to after two decades of policy reform, it was obvious that the reforms had managed to place Africa on a low growth path.

5.2   A changing analysis: bringing the state back in?

The changing forecasts of the 1990s were reflected in a new agenda for aid. The World Bank study *Can Africa Claim the 21st Century?* (World Bank, 2000c) not only took a less optimistic tone, but contained a grudging admission that the policies of the past had not worked. The rethinking of the late 1990s was eclectic and of a political and institutional character, rather than focusing on economic reform. The mix encompasses a demand for 'good governance', which includes reforms to the institutions of government, the rule of law, anti-corruption policies and systems of administration.

There was, however, a substantial policy shift underway by the early 2000s, reflecting an admission that too much emphasis had been placed on stabilization, and a recognition that a major task of development – poverty eradication – had been sidestepped in the policies of the adjustment years. The new agenda has been called the 'second generation' reforms. The central theme is a call for poverty reduction to be the goal of development co-operation, expressed in the 'Millennium Development Goals' which were formulated by the OECD, the UN and the BWI, and included the aim of a reduction of the numbers of people in absolute poverty by 2015. Countries receiving aid were asked to draw up Poverty Reduction Strategy Papers (PRSPs) to indicate how they would work towards these goals, all within the limits of macroeconomic stability.

These shifting goals for development aid necessarily prompted a rethink about the role of the state. Significantly, it now became clear that while the narrow agenda of stabilization could be implemented by a small technocracy, the long-promised 'accelerated development' and the goals of poverty reduction required a much more effective state apparatus:

> Far from supporting a minimalist approach to the state, these examples have shown that development requires an effective state, one that plays a catalytic, facilitating role, encouraging and complementing the activities of private businesses and individuals ... History has repeatedly shown that good government is not a luxury but a vital necessity. Without an effective state, sustainable development, both economic and social, is impossible ... development is not just about getting the right economic and technical inputs. It is also about the underlying institutional environment: the rules and customs that determine how these inputs are to be used.
>
> (Wolfensohn, 1997b, p.iv)

In addition, the pursuit of the new objective of poverty reduction was to take place in a new framework of 'partnership' between all the 'stakeholders in development', including international donors, national states and civil society groups. The World Bank sought to maintain an overall 'co-ordinating' role through its 'Comprehensive Development Framework' (CDF) – a matrix within which stakeholders would play their parts in a manner reminiscent of the discarded development plans of an earlier era. And, so the rhetoric went, in a process of intensive consultation between national states and their domestic populations in the formulation of PRSPs, development plans and strategies would (once again) be 'owned' nationally.

Nevertheless, as we have seen, the capacity of the state had been severely eroded in the adjustment years. The paradox at the end of the 1990s was that African states were now being asked to play a strategic role in guiding development; yet this was precisely what they were accused of failing to do in the era when they had greater capacity.

6   Conclusion

So has this story of the denial of the developmental role of the state in Africa and its reworking by actors external to the continent come full circle in the way I suggested in Figure 10.1? In terms of economic growth, the recovery years look doubtful at the time of writing. The fact of the matter is that after 20 years during which the BWI held sway over policy making in Africa, the promised 'accelerated development' did not appear. No single country 'graduated' from these programmes to more rapid development and effective policy making autonomous from international conditionalities.

In terms of the trajectory of analytical debate about the developmental state, there does seem to have been something of a return to a central role for the state, albeit with very different economic policy instruments at its disposal. In its new incarnation, the developmental state faces enormous challenges. These include tackling the enormous 'maladjustment' that African economies have undergone during the 1980s and 1990s, notably in terms of deindustrialization (see Chapter 11). Previously, developmental states thrived when global trade agreements and financial flows allowed a certain latitude for states to pursue their own policies with respect to economic development, welfare and employment. It is not clear that this latitude still exists, despite the rhetoric about the need for national 'ownership' of development. As Chapter 2 suggested, retrieving more local policy scope may need a global governance of trade 'as if development really mattered' (Rodrik, 2001).

Furthermore, the state must also rebuild its own capacities. I noted above that an important aspect of the developmental state was ideological: that is, that developmentalism was an expression of a national project and a legitimating device through which the domestic resources and population could be mobilized behind development. Perhaps the most damaging legacy to Africa of the years of crisis and adjustment was the lowering of the visions and expectations of Africans themselves.

The revised 'technocratic' view of the state's role in the 'second generation' reforms does not spell out clearly what should be the ideological underpinnings of the new developmental state, other than a series of externally agreed upon development goals. While governments may eventually have acceded to a number of internationally spelt-out developmental goals, it should be borne in mind that even in this globalized world development is a local and contextual experience. The motivation to drive both public and private actors towards undertaking developmental initiatives will ultimately have to have local resonance.

Moreover, African efforts to democratize in the 1990s have yet to show that new developmental states can be more democratic than the older version. It is important to imagine developmental states that are democratic rather than authoritarian, and indeed two of the most cited – Mauritius and Botswana – are African. Yet the long legacy of external denial and destruction of African states' developmental role bore on issues which were and are fundamental to the legitimacy of African states: national development, freedom from external control and the development of internal capacities of statehood and the exercise of state authority. This political weakening has made it harder to re-imagine developmentalism, not least by cutting off learning from the early developmental years.

Further reading

For a World Bank view, see World Bank (2000) *Can Africa Claim the 21st Century?*, Washington, DC, World Bank.

The classic attack on African states that generated the rent-seeking literature is the readable Bates, R. (1981) *Markets and States in Tropical Africa*, Berkeley and Los Angeles, University of California.

For a country's experience that is rather different from the one you have just read, see Hutchful, E. (2002) *Ghana's Adjustment Experience: The Paradox of Reform*, Geneva and London, UNRISD/James Currey.

Chapter 11 Macroeconomic policy and trade integration: Tanzania in the world economy

Marc Wuyts

1   Introduction

Macroeconomic policy is a key tool for changing the economic position of countries in the world economy. Macroeconomics, as Chapter 10 explained, is concerned with the management of the national economy, including management of the country's economic relations with other countries through trade, investment and foreign currency exchanges. The smaller and poorer a country, the more important it is for the government to manage these international economic relationships to promote growth and development.

My objectives in this chapter are to explain some of the core concepts used in international debates on macroeconomic management; to illustrate the extent to which macroeconomic policy decisions shape a country's international economic position; and to do this through an exploration of the macroeconomic dilemmas faced by a low income African country that is open to trade. As Chapter 10 showed, macroeconomic management is a battleground of international politics, and ideas about economic management are tools of international intervention in the domestic politics of fragile and aid-dependent states. Here we pay critical attention to these economic tools and debates in the 'adjustment years' (see Chapter 10), drawing on the experience of Tanzania.

1.1   Market prices and static comparative advantage: the prescription for economic liberalization in Africa

As Thandika Mkandawire argued in Chapter 10, Section 3, it was the influential World Bank report on African development published in 1981, the 'Berg Report', that set the stage for the subsequent cascade of donor-inspired economic policy reversals which swept across most of sub-Saharan Africa during the 1980s. The report ushered in the era of structural adjustment programmes in Africa. In addition to the reduction of the size and activity of the state (see Chapter 10, Section 4), the report put forward two core policy prescriptions that will concern us here: the market-based determination of key price ratios, and a retreat to trade policy driven by static comparative advantage.

The report put its key critique of African economic policy as follows: 'Trade and exchange rate policy is at the heart of the failure to provide adequate incentives for agricultural production and for exports in much of Africa' (World Bank, 1981, p.24).

The Berg Report accepted that African economies were 'uncommonly "open"' (World Bank, 1981, p.5) in the sense of a high ratio of trade to Gross Domestic Product (GDP) (see Chapter 3, Figure 3.8). However, it argued that export performance was poor because of mistaken economic policies that had affected two key price ratios: the prices for agricultural relative to industrial goods, and the exchange rate, that is, the price in local currency of the foreign exchange (for example, dollars) needed to buy imports on the international market. It recommended that these price ratios be determined by the market, and so this policy approach came to be summarized as 'getting the prices right'.

The Berg Report, as Chapter 10 noted, also argued against the view that the terms of trade for existing African exports were a key constraint on trade policy. Sub-Saharan African countries, it therefore proposed, should concentrate on creating market incentives for increased exports in line with their prevailing comparative advantage: tropical agriculture and mining. Having read Chapter 10, you should be aware how provocative this argument was at the time of writing. Most African countries had fairly recently emerged from colonial rule with an economic legacy of primary export production and little industrial development. The developmentalism of the early years had focused on import substituting industrialization supported by foreign aid. The strategy was rooted in precisely the argument Berg denied: that African primary exports were problematic because they were subjected to the vagaries of declining terms of trade combined with volatile commodity prices.

Should development follow or change comparative advantage? This is the key question underlying this debate. The Berg Report asserted that existing comparative advantage should lead economic development. In contrast, the early developmentalism asserted that for African economies to develop and to integrate on (more) equal terms within the world economy, a prior state-led or state-guided transition through import substituting industrialization was needed to break away from the sole dependence on primary exports.

My argument in this chapter will be that these two views, while pitched as polar opposites in this debate, each contain aspects which are essentially complementary. The latter view asserts that the economic structure of a country matters in terms of the possibilities it provides and the constraints it imposes on that country's trade and development. The former view asserts that economic efficiency and financial viability, rooted in existing comparative advantage, are important drivers of development through trade, and are also an essential basis for rallying additional resources including foreign aid behind the development effort. Understood as polar opposites, each of these views tends to downplay the importance of the insights provided by the other, yet both aspects matter for the process of development. I track these two aspects of macroeconomic and trade policy through the structural adjustment years, and I argue in the later part of the chapter that effective macroeconomic policy, responsive to local needs, must seek to attend to both of these aspects of trade and macroeconomic development.

1.2 Tanzania: macroeconomic policy in conditions of aid dependency

The United Republic of Tanzania is a small, low income, aid-dependent East African country – and a country with a very lively tradition of intellectual and policy debate. This chapter and the next explore the economics and the politics of aid-dependency through the Tanzanian case, examining the tensions inherent in a policy context where outside actors – in this case, the aid donors – exert great influence over the domestic policy agenda and debates.

Tanzania came into being on 24 April 1964 when the mainland, Tanganyika (which had become independent in 1961), merged with the island of Zanzibar (which gained independence in December 1963). The analysis in this chapter is confined to economic developments on the mainland. As the country emerged from colonial rule, the mainland was predominantly rural in nature. Its agricultural economy had two main components: a plantation economy with sisal, sugar and tea, drawing seasonal and migratory labour from the more remote and less developed regions of the country; and a cash cropping peasantry producing coffee, cotton and cashew for exports. Sisal was the leading cash crop at the time of independence but quickly lost ground, particularly after the dramatic fall in its price in 1964, a trend that was to continue thereafter. The urban population was very small and industrial development relatively insignificant – less than 4 per cent of GDP in 1961 (Rweyemamu, 1973).

I trace Tanzanian macroeconomic and trade policy through the phases established by Thandika Mkandawire in Chapter 10: the early developmental years of import substitution and a focus on basic needs; the crisis years in Tanzania in the late 1970s and early 1980s; the era of structural adjustment when the driving seat of economic policy design was occupied by the World Bank and the International Monetary Fund (IMF); and finally the dilemmas of economic policy at the turn of the century. At the core of the chapter is a critical investigation of the analytical and empirical foundations of the Berg Report's recommendations – the need to correct for the failure of trade and exchange rate policies to stimulate agricultural production and exports – in the context of the Tanzanian experience with structural adjustment from the mid 1980s onwards.

Throughout the post-independence period, Tanzania has relied heavily on aid, that is, external financing in the form of grants and loans. I begin in Section 2 by setting out a macroeconomic framework that we can use to situate the roles of foreign trade and aid in the Tanzanian economy. Macroeconomic analysis is akin to painting with large brush strokes – it gives a sense of structure and of the overall movements of an economy's constituent components. It allows us to understand how the different (aggregate) parts of an economy interact and fit together (or perhaps fail to fit together) to sustain the livelihoods of the people living within it.

Section 2 allows you to engage with macroeconomic reasoning by providing a basic familiarity with national accounting. It also gives you a first look at how the Tanzanian economy interacts with the international economy through trade and aid. Section 3 then takes a more historical approach, surveying Tanzania's economic development since the early 1960s. It draws on the macroeconomic framework in Section 2 to create a more precise definition of the concept of structural adjustment than was possible in earlier chapters.

Section 4 turns to the economic analysis underlying the Berg Report's recommendations of market liberalization. From earlier chapters, you are already familiar with the concept and practice of trade liberalization. In this chapter, I shall focus in more detail on another dimension of openness – the role of the exchange rate. Macroeconomic analysis of prices concentrates on the overall price level in an economy and on major price ratios which influence the whole economy. One of these, central to structural adjustment, is the price of foreign exchange. Understanding the exchange rate allows you to answer policy-relevant questions such as 'How do exchange rate policies affect the level of a country's trade integration in world markets?' and 'How does the exchange rate affect farmers' incentives to produce and export?'

Finally, in Section 5, I investigate the outcome of the period of economic reforms in light of the question posed above concerning the relation between trade integration and economic development. I pick up the claim in the Berg Report that the terms of trade for primary products was not a major constraint on development and ask whether that is so. Is the structural composition of output and of exports indeed of little relevance?

The tools of macroeconomic analysis that you will learn in this chapter are of quite general application. Furthermore, the Tanzanian economy, though a specific case, has many features in common with the experience of other aid-dependent sub-Saharan African countries. I argue that the early Tanzanian macroeconomic policies paid insufficient attention to financial viability in terms of foreign exchange earnings. Yet the 'structural adjustment' years privileged liberalization and 'openness' over the need for structural change in the economy, and could not escape the pitfalls inherent in the continued reliance on volatile and adverse terms of trade. Good macroeconomic policy in low income contexts has to confront the mammoth task of bringing together trade policy and structural transformation while finding the necessary external financial support. The political complexity of this balancing act will be considered in Chapter 12.

2 Foreign exchange, aid and the trade gap: macroeconomic constraints on growth

In Chapter 7, Suma Athreye made the point that investment is the key to economic growth. In Chapter 10, Thandika Mkandawire argued that structural adjustment – a macroeconomic policy framework – had hampered growth in Africa. To see how macroeconomic constraints can limit growth, we need to take a closer look at a key link between trade and investment in open economies: access to foreign exchange. I do this in three stages. First, I set out an accounting framework for understanding a country's national income. Second, I use that to explore the role of foreign exchange, generated by trade or aid, in national income. Third, this in turn is linked to the problem of sustaining investment at low levels of income per head.

2.1 GDP growth in an agrarian economy

In this section I review the growth performance of the Tanzanian economy and subsequently unpack that growth (and decline) into the productive sectors that lie behind it.

Figure 11.1 shows the year-to-year growth rates in Tanzania's real GDP over four decades. Along with annual growth rates in *real* GDP, that is, GDP at constant prices (see Chapter 7, Section 2), the graph features the estimated annual growth rates of the Tanzanian population, indicated by the dashed line.

Question

In which years did GDP exceed population growth? What does it mean if it does not?

Only in slightly more than half of the years under review – 25 out of 48 years – did the growth rate of GDP exceed that of the population. Only when GDP grows faster than population will GDP per capita rise. Thus, the margin of

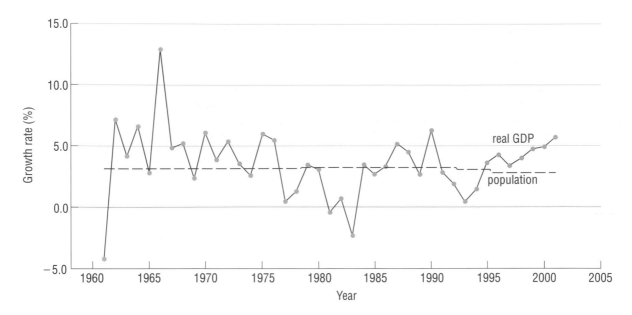

Figure 11.1   Tanzania's growth performance, 1961–2001

Source: National Bureau of Statistics, Tanzania, 1995a, Table 7.1; 1995b, Table 1; 1999, Tables 3 and 4; 2002, Tables 1 and 3 (author's own calculations)

GDP growth over and above population growth has often been precarious and seldom very large.

This is all the more serious since Tanzania is one of the world's poorest countries. The measured GDP per capita was about $261 in the year 2000, much less than $1 per head per day. GDP per head is an important piece of data for understanding poverty. This measure is limited since it tells us nothing about the distribution of income (see Chapter 7). Yet it tells us that the level of output (and, hence, of the incomes derived from it) is so low that even if each person were to receive an equal share, this common standard of living would still be unacceptable. Given this level of output per capita, Tanzania suffers from 'generalized poverty' (UNCTAD, 2002a, pp.69–100). The 2000/01 household budget survey estimates put the percentage of the population living below an (already very low) basic needs poverty line at about 36 per cent (National Bureau of Statistics, Tanzania, 2002, p.80).

The sectors of the economy: adding up GDP

To look behind the growth rates and understand the structure of the economy, it is useful first to review the measurement of GDP. The GDP of a country measures the totality of its output for 'final use' during a given period in time, usually in a given year. By goods for final use we mean, for example, the bread bought in the bakery and consumed at home. The bread is the gross output; into making it went other goods as inputs, including wheat grown by farmers, flour made from the wheat, and salt. These inputs are intermediate goods, not for final use.

Chapter 7, Section 2 explained one method of adding up GDP while avoiding 'double counting' intermediate goods: by adding up the 'value added' produced in the different sectors of the economy. The value added is the difference between the value of the gross output and the value of inputs used in each sector.

This value added consists of *incomes*: it is made up of the wages and salaries paid to those who work in these sectors, the incomes of those who are self-employed (including farmers), the profits of the owners of enterprises, and interest paid to lenders of funds. A look at the sectoral value added in the economy tells us the incomes derived from the activities within each sector.

At the turn of the century, in the year 2000, agriculture accounted for 45 per cent of the total GDP of Tanzania – indicative of the still largely agrarian nature of the economy. Moreover, this agricultural GDP includes both the value of agricultural commodity production, that is, the production of agricultural goods *for sale*, and non-monetary production for home consumption. The production of cash crops for exports, for instance, is clearly monetary in nature and purpose. Similarly, food surpluses are sold in domestic markets to earn cash income. However, part of farm output is produced for own use: grain, vegetables and milk or meat for consumption within the household. Statisticians estimate how much agricultural output is produced for own consumption and then impute a monetary value to it in order to measure its contribution to GDP. In Tanzania in 2000, only 56 per cent of the agricultural GDP was monetary in nature; the remaining 44 per cent was the estimated value of direct production for own consumption. Taken all sectors together, non-monetary GDP accounted for around 29 per cent, most of it in agriculture (National Bureau of Statistics, Tanzania, 2002).

Note, though, that non-monetary production does not include unpaid domestic work – cooking, cleaning and caring for children, the sick and the old – work almost exclusively done by women. As Chapter 7 noted, the output of domestic work is typically not counted or estimated and, hence, is rendered invisible by national accounting practice in most countries.

Agriculture and economic growth in Tanzania

Question

Look back at Figure 11.1. Is there any period where GDP growth rates were exceptionally low or even negative (a fall in GDP)?

First, recollect that when looking at the evolution of GDP over time, economists measure GDP at *constant* prices or 'in real terms' (see Chapter 7, Section 2.3). Value added in each year is calculated at the prices of a chosen base year and not at current prices. Given the length of the period, the data in Figure 11.1 have been constructed by combining several series, each with its own base year. Therefore, Figure 11.1 shows growth in *volume* terms: the increase in the quantity of goods and services available each year, once the effect of rising prices is removed. Consequently, a growth rate below zero is a real fall in volume of output.

Historically, Tanzania's growth performance has fluctuated greatly from year to year. One plausible explanation is that rain-fed agriculture constitutes the backbone of the Tanzanian economy and, thus, is likely to be variable over time. Nevertheless, as we shall see, there are other reasons to consider: fluctuating terms of trade, variations in the availability of foreign aid, and macroeconomic crisis conditions.

However, in the late 1970s and early 1980s Tanzania clearly witnessed a severe crisis when GDP growth rates were consistently low and, in some years, GDP declined. These years, as we shall see, witnessed a veritable 'goods famine' in Tanzania when rising oil prices, declining export production, falling aid and import restrictions all combined to create economic hardship and crisis (Wuyts, 1994). Note that it was in this period that the Berg Report appeared on the policy stage. Something was clearly amiss, a problem the report sought to redress. The early 1980s were the breeding ground for a transition between macroeconomic policy regimes, from import substituting industrialization to market-led development, the effects of which we shall trace.

Question

Mentally divide the horizontal time axis in Figure 11.1 into two parts: the 1960s, 1970s and early 1980s on the one hand, and the mid to late 1980s, 1990s and into the turn of the century on the other. The latter are the reform years under structural adjustment. How does the growth performance compare between these periods?

As in the broader African story told in Chapter 10, it was the period of the 1960s through to the late 1970s which, by and large, witnessed the highest growth rates in Tanzania, ending in the crisis years of the early 1980s. The period of economic reforms, from the second half of the 1980s onwards, led to an economic revival which fell into its own (less dramatic) downturn in the early 1990s followed by the renewal of growth thereafter. Yet growth rates during this later period never matched the growth performance in the heyday of the pre-reform period.

In the recent period, from 1987 to 2001, GDP in real terms grew by about 63 per cent in total. Of this growth momentum, agricultural growth contributed about 30 per cent and non-agricultural growth 33 per cent. Agriculture remains a major player in the economy, not only in terms of its share of GDP, but also in terms of its importance as a contributor to economic growth.

2.2 Trade as a macroeconomic constraint: aid and the trade gap

Over the period 1987–2001, Tanzania has managed to use, for consumption or investment, more goods and services than it has produced; it did so by importing more than it exported. But the economic difficulty of sustaining this, and the international and domestic political consequences, have driven economic policy changes. This section develops a national income accounting framework that allows us to trace the role of the trade gap and the problem of its financing in Tanzania.

GDP, domestic absorption and the trade gap

In addition to adding up value added by sector, there is a second distinctive route to measuring GDP: counting the output produced within the economy for final use only (the *gross* value of the bread and other goods consumed, ignoring all inputs). The final use may be at home or abroad (exports). Imports (produced elsewhere) are also ignored. This method is useful for identifying the relationship between the goods available to people in an economy and a country's trade performance.

Table 11.1 illustrates this approach. It compares the total availability of output in Tanzania with its use for a few selected years during the period of economic reforms. For each year, all totals are quantities of output for final use, expressed as percentages of GDP.

Table 11.1   The availability of output and its use in the Tanzanian economy, selected years

Resource availability	Percentage of GDP			Resource use	Percentage of GDP		
	1987	1995	2001		1987	1995	2001
GDP	100.0	100.0	100.0	Domestic absorption, of which:	117.3	117.5	108.5
				1 private consumption	81.7	83.9	84.5
				2 public consumption	16.9	15.3	6.3
				3 investment	22.1	19.8	17.0
				4 [unrecorded trade and statistical discrepancies]	–3.4	–1.5	0.7
Imports	26.3	41.5	24.5	Exports	9.0	24.0	16.0
Total	126.3	141.5	124.5	Total	126.3	141.5	124.5

Source: National Bureau of Statistics, Tanzania, 1999, Table 5a; 2002, Table 2b (author's own calculations)

Macroeconomists work in totals or *aggregates*. This accounting framework is an example: it is constructed such that total aggregate availability of goods and services equals total aggregate use of them, and it allows us to look at relationships between domestic consumption and trade.

Start by looking at the left-hand panel of the table. Reading down each column, it states that resource availability, in terms of goods and services for final use, originated either from domestic production (GDP) or from imports. Then look at the right-hand panel. This shows how these resources were used: either within the country (domestic absorption) or abroad (exports). Finally, since national accounts data are drawn from a variety of data sources, errors and omissions are inevitable. This is captured in the item of 'unrecorded trade and statistical discrepancies' on the right-hand side of the table.

Question

I said above that Tanzania was using more goods and services than it produced. Can you find this fact – and a measure of its extent – on Table 11.1?

The answer is in the 'Domestic absorption' row in the right-hand panel. Domestic absorption is, as it sounds, the total output for final use that is 'absorbed' (or used) within the economy. In 1987 this was 117.3 per cent of GDP; in 2001 it had dropped to 108.5 per cent. In each year shown it was greater than GDP: more output was used in the economy than was produced.

Domestic absorption is measured as expenditure on goods and services within the economy. It includes private consumption, government (public) consumption and private and public investment.

- Private consumption is expenditure of households on goods and services such as food, clothing, consumer durables, transport, education and health care and so on. Table 11.1 shows that, in Tanzania, this component takes the lion's share of total expenditures and its share in GDP rose slightly over the period concerned – from about 82 per cent to nearly 85 per cent.

- Government (public) consumption is recurrent expenditure by government on final goods and services used in government departments and public institutions: to keep public administration running, to keep the army functioning, to provide social services and so on. The share of this component changed dramatically, from around 17 per cent in 1987 and 15 per cent in 1995 to only slightly more than 6 per cent in 2001.

■ Investment consists mainly of expenditure on fixed capital formation: physical infrastructure, and buildings and equipment to increase the productive capacity of the economy. However, it does not include the expenditure on, for example, education and health which undoubtedly contribute to increasing the economy's productive potential. The latter expenditures are recorded under public consumption (when financed by government) or under private consumption (when financed privately). Investment also includes the expenditure on increases in stocks of goods (inventories) within an economy. For instance, the increase in grain reserves within a given year will be recorded as investment, as are increases in inventories of raw materials, intermediary inputs and finished products. Table 11.1 shows that investment as a share of GDP fell over the period but less dramatically than government consumption, from about 22 per cent in 1987 to 17 per cent in 2001.

This accounting scheme is thus an economical way of examining the changing pattern of use of resources in relation to total output. It works with broad aggregates within an overall framework where both sides of the ledger are made to balance *by construction* (that is, by definition) based on the simple premise that what is available within an economy is used in one way or another, intended or unintended. The fact that accounts balance, nevertheless, does not mean that no mismatches occur between planned production and imports, on the one hand, and the demand for domestic consumption and investment or demand for exports, on the other. This point can be best illustrated with a simple example.

Question

Suppose that, in a given year, a trader imports 1000 radios for immediate sale in domestic markets, but only succeeds in selling half of them. How does this enter our accounting framework?

In terms of Table 11.1, the value of the radios will be included in imports on the left-hand side, but only half of these radios will be recorded under private (or public) consumption on the right-hand side. What happens to the other half? These can be found as increased stocks of merchandise on the shelves in the trader's shop, which will be found under investment as 'increase in inventories'. This way, availability and use are brought in balance by construction.

Yet, clearly, our unfortunate trader will be none the happier for it, and is likely to import fewer radios (or none at all) in the following year. In other words, our trader is likely to adjust his import orders in line with his revised expectations about domestic demand.

This example illustrates an important distinction in economic analysis. At the empirical level, the data we work with are the recorded footprints of the past, moulded within an accounting framework where, by definition, total resources and their uses are made to balance. Commodities left unsold will be recorded as investment, and unsatisfied demand will not be recorded. Accounts, therefore, balance the uses with availability of resources *ex post* – that is, after the event.

At the theoretical level, however, in macroeconomic theory we make no assumption that *ex ante* – that is, before the event – the intended uses of (demand for) resources will of necessity balance with their planned availabilities (supply) across the multitude of independent, yet interdependent, actors operating within an economy. Where such a balance is achieved, economists define the situation as an equilibrium. An equilibrium is a theoretical construction that depicts an economy (or a part of an economy) as at rest. In an equilibrium there is no need for people, firms or governments to revise their plans or to adjust their expectations: no demand remains unsatisfied and no supply unsold. Much of macroeconomic reasoning examines how the national economy adjusts when 'disequilibrium' prevails, and asks whether such adjustments will bring the economy back towards equilibrium. I shall return to this concept of equilibrium in Section 4, when dealing with the foreign exchange market.

Let us return to Table 11.1 and use it to pinpoint the role of the trade gap: the excess of imports over exports. Equating the right-hand side with the left-hand side yields the following expression:

Domestic absorption + Exports ≡ GDP + Imports

Equilibrium
An equilibrium exists when an economy or part of an economy is at rest, and so economic actors see no need to revise their plans or change their expectations.

Activity 11.1

Demonstrate that the above formula applies in Table 11.1, using the figures for 2001.

In economic analysis, the above expression is called an 'identity' – an equation which is true by definition. To indicate that an equation is an identity we make use of the identity sign ($\equiv$). Consequently, whenever you encounter this sign, keep in mind that you are dealing with an accounting identity, true by definition.

Now I am going to rearrange this equation to bring out the link between domestic absorption and the trade gap. Subtract exports from both sides and define the trade gap as imports minus exports; this gives you the following:

Domestic absorption ≡ GDP + Trade gap

Trade gap
The trade gap is defined as imports minus exports.

This latter identity implies that the trade gap is equal to the gap between domestic absorption and GDP. The identity states that if an economy spends more on final goods and services than it produces, its imports will exceed its exports to the tune of the excess domestic expenditures. The higher is domestic absorption relative to GDP, the bigger the trade gap.

Table 11.1 shows that Tanzanian domestic absorption was slightly more than 17 per cent in excess of GDP in 1987 and 1995, but subsequently declined to about 9 per cent in excess of GDP by 2001.

Question

Look back at Table 11.1. What elements of Tanzanian domestic absorption were 'adjusted' downwards to achieve this narrowing of the trade gap?

The answer is that mainly government consumption and, to a lesser extent, investment were adjusted to bring down the level of absorption relative to GDP.

Financing the trade deficit   How could it import more?

How, then, could Tanzania import more than it exports and, hence, maintain a level of domestic absorption in excess of its GDP? How, in other words, does a country pay for its imports over and above what it earns in terms of exports?

What needs to be financed is the trade deficit – the difference between the foreign exchange flowing into the country from its exports of goods and services and the foreign exchange needed to pay for its imports of goods and services. The trade deficit, therefore, equals exports minus imports and is the opposite of the trade gap – equal in size, but with the opposite sign.

> **Trade deficit**
> The trade deficit is defined as exports minus imports.

There are different ways in which a trade deficit can be financed. First of all, a country could rely on other *current* payment flows between countries, the net balance of which might help to offset a trade deficit. These include 'factor payments' and 'transfer payments'.

- *Factor payments* are payments for labour, capital or land across national frontiers. For example, residents of a country work as temporary migrants in foreign countries and remit part of their wages; or a company invests in a venture abroad and repatriates part of the profits earned there; or an investor receives interest payments on financial capital held abroad; or, finally, residents of a country own land in other countries and receive rent payments from abroad. If more factor payments are received than sent abroad, the resulting balance on factor payments can contribute towards offsetting the trade deficit.

■ *Transfer payments* are unilateral payments which are not made in return for factors of production. For instance, money sent to elderly parents by their children permanently resident abroad. Another example is an official grant given by one government or international institution to the government of another country. A grant from one non-governmental organization (NGO) to another across national boundaries is similar in nature. The first is an example of a private transfer payment; the last two are examples of international aid payments. The balance on transfer payments, if positive, can help to offset a trade deficit.

Current account balance
The current account of a country's balance of payments is equal to its trade balance plus the balances of factor and transfer payments.

The current account balance of a country is defined as the sum of its trade balance and the balances on factor and transfer payments.

Table 11.2 looks at the current account balance of Tanzania. I shall take 1995, a year well into the adjustment period, as an example.

Table 11.2   Current account of Tanzania's balance of payments, 1995 (US$ millions)

1	Trade balance	−874.5
	goods balance	−657.6
	services balance	−216.9
2	Balance on factor payments	−110.3
3	Balance on transfers	338.4
	Current account balance	−646.4

Source: Bank of Tanzania, 2001, Table 4.1

Question

Did the transfers and factor payments across the borders of Tanzania help to fund the trade deficit?

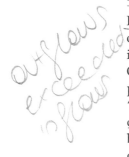

Factor payments did not help; the balance was *negative*, meaning that outflows exceed inflows. This is generally the case in Tanzania. The country is not a major exporter of labour, nor is it a major investor abroad. Consequently, inflows are quite low. The outflows mainly consist of interest payments on previous debts (including loans by foreign aid agencies on 'soft', low interest, terms). Net transfers, however, did fund part of the trade deficit: they were *positive*. Again, this is a general feature of Tanzania. The bulk of transfers are inflows to government: mainly grants from foreign aid donors. Private inflows are also considerable and include transfers paid to NGOs as well as payments to private individuals.

So, what about the remaining deficit – the deficit on current account? How was it financed? Broadly speaking, a country can finance such a deficit either by drawing on its official foreign exchange reserves or through the balance on capital account transactions. Drawing on foreign exchange reserves is a limited option, especially in a country like Tanzania which generally holds few of them. Capital account transactions involve dealings in financial assets, public or private, or direct investment from abroad. It is a distinctive feature of a small, low income country like Tanzania that it has very limited access to private capital markets in the world economy. Few foreign residents or private banks and other financial institutions are interested in acquiring financial assets in a country with an economy as vulnerable and precarious as that of Tanzania. Historically, Tanzania also found it difficult to attract foreign direct investment but, towards the turn of the century, in the wake of extensive financial liberalization and a liberal investment regime aimed at inducing foreign direct investment, the Tanzanian economy witnessed a significant rise in foreign investment, mainly in mining and tourism.

Foreign aid loans at concessionary terms, though, were and continue to be the major item accounting for a positive balance on Tanzania's capital account, though the inflow of new loans is partly offset by the need to repay (amortize) accumulated debts resulting from loans made in the past. This offsetting explains the increased importance of rescheduling of the debts and of debt forgiveness from the mid 1990s onwards.

If we look at the overall picture, we find that two items in particular allow Tanzania to import more than it exports: grants and loans obtained through foreign aid. The former are transfer payments, while the latter are capital transactions. Both, nevertheless, derive from foreign aid. The trade deficit, therefore, has been and continues to be largely financed by foreign aid.

2.3 Aid, investment and the trade balance

How does the trade deficit – and the foreign aid that finances it – affect investment and growth? This is the final step in the trade–growth link.

To make this link, we need to return once more to our accounting framework as illustrated in Table 11.1, and introduce aggregate *domestic savings* into the picture. Domestic savings are defined as the difference between a country's GDP and its private and public consumption of resources. Domestic savings, thus, equal that part of income not spent on consumption, which is available to finance investment.

Activity 11.2

Look back at Table 11.1. What were domestic savings as a percentage of GDP in 2001?

Leaving statistical discrepancies aside (that is, assuming no errors were made), if you subtract the value of consumption from the column totals of both sides of Table 11.1, you are left with domestic savings and imports in the left-hand panel and with investment and exports in the right-hand panel. This is because domestic savings equal GDP minus consumption. It follows that investment is equal by definition to the sum of domestic savings and the trade gap (imports minus exports):

Investment ≡ Domestic savings + Trade gap

The policy implications of this macroeconomic identity are immense. It says that necessarily, as a matter of definition, the excess of investment over domestic savings equals the trade gap (the excess of imports over exports) of any country. However, in Tanzania where aid – whether in grants or in loans – was the main source of foreign finance during most of the period under review, the trade gap and thus investment in excess of savings was largely financed by the net inflow of foreign aid. It follows that, for macroeconomic policy makers, the size of the trade gap is a key variable. Figure 11.2 takes a closer look at the evolution of export and import coefficients for Tanzania, that is, exports and imports as a percentage of GDP. These coefficients are often taken as measures of the level of a country's trade integration within the world economy. The data are for 1975 to 2001 (the period for which a consistent set of national accounts data is available).

Take a careful look at this graph. We note that both the export and import coefficients fell sharply from the mid 1970s to the mid 1980s. They then rose to a peak in the mid 1990s, after which they declined again. The export and import coefficients and their sum are often taken as indicators of the trade openness of an economy: the larger the coefficients, the more open the economy. Therefore, the period of economic reforms witnessed a rapid rise in trade openness, particularly during its first decade, an effect we return to below.

Figure 11.3 gives an overview of the evolution of the different elements of our last accounting result, which stated that domestic investment equals the sum of the trade gap and domestic savings.

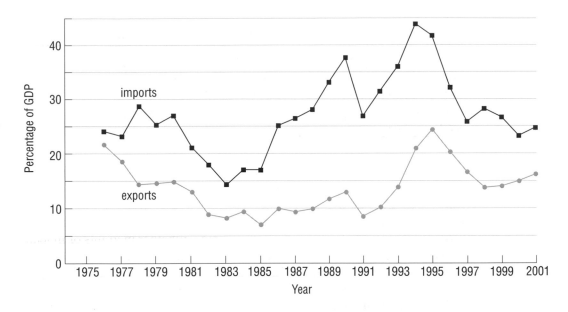

Figure 11.2   Exports and imports as shares of GDP in Tanzania, 1976–2001

Source: National Bureau of Statistics, Tanzania, 1995b, Table 6; 1999, Table 5a; 2002, Table 2b (author's own calculations)

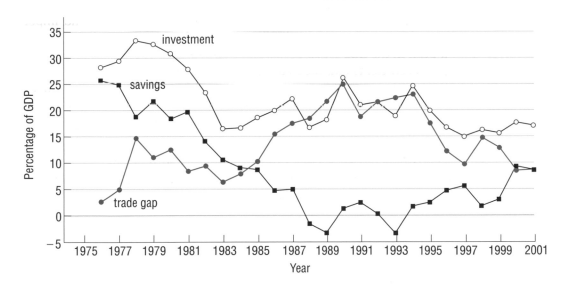

Figure 11.3   Investment, savings and the trade gap in Tanzania, 1976–2001

Source: National Bureau of Statistics, Tanzania, 1995b, Table 6; 1999, Table 5a; 2002, Table 2b (author's own calculations)

Activity 11.3

This activity asks you to make a descriptive summary of the patterns shown in Figure 11.3. Carefully study the evolution of each variable in turn. When was it high, when low? Are there any noticeable differences in the behaviour of each variable over the following periods.

1   The heyday of import substituting industrialization (late 1970s).

2   The crisis years of 1980–85.

3   The subsequent period of economic reforms.

I shall return to the patterns shown in Figure 11.3 when discussing Tanzania's economic development in different periods below. Let me conclude here by pointing out one of the most stunning features of the data shown in Figure 11.3: namely that in the adjustment years the rate of investment – and hence growth – was wholly dependent on aid, a dependency with highly problematic economic and, as Chapter 12 will argue, political consequences.

3   Tanzania's macroeconomic strategy, from structural change to market-led development

In the early days of independence, the main focus of Tanzanian government policies was political consolidation and nation-building. Economic policy was initially non-interventionist and outward-oriented. Justinian Rweyemamu, Tanzania's first major economics scholar, characterized this earlier policy stance on economic affairs as follows.

> There was in fact a belief that the major impulse of the economy was to come from the foreign sector, regardless of the form of that sector. That is to say, there was no expressed intention to alter the ratio of foreign trade to the national product, nor was there a change in the composition of that trade or the importance of trading partners contemplated. ...
>
> The underlying assumption of these early policies was the belief that a temporary sacrifice of economic independence (i.e. by maintaining colonial ties) would, by attracting significant western capital, produce a quicker rate of economic development which would lead ultimately to independence.

(Rweyemamu, 1973, p.39)

Economic policy therefore sought to build on inherited comparative advantage from the colonial past. However, according to Rweyemamu, policy makers assumed that, given an open-door policy to foreign investment, 'foreign private capital would easily flow into Tanzania' (Rweyemamu, 1973, p.39). This would thereby provide the impetus for an economic development process that would transform the structure of the economy, and would lead eventually to more independence in the sense of economic and political autonomy from external pressure. Industrialization was thus left to the initiative of private (largely foreign) enterprises.

Take another look at Figure 11.1 and, expressly, at the growth performance of the early years 1961–66. A remarkable feature of these early developments is the volatile nature of the growth rates in this period – they ranged from very high to very low. This resulted from the vagaries of rain-fed agriculture. The growth performance was by no means bad – in fact, historically, this period witnessed some of the highest growth rates – but growth in real GDP did not always translate into increased incomes or foreign exchange earnings because of adverse movements in the international prices of cash crops – in particular, of sisal.

Moreover, the assumption that foreign direct investment would be easily forthcoming proved unwarranted, and the government quickly became disillusioned with a development strategy which relied on outside initiative to foster economic growth. The policy climate, therefore, changed dramatically with the adoption in 1967 of the Arusha Declaration. This set the stage for Tanzania's own brand of a more inward-looking socialist development strategy, characterized by a state-led investment drive for import substitution industrialization.

3.1 The attempted transformation of the economy through a state-led investment drive

The Arusha Declaration signalled a new era in Tanzania's economic development, characterized both by some remarkable successes and some notable failures (Doriye, 1992). Notwithstanding considerable reliance on foreign aid, this period witnessed the emergence of a Tanzanian developmental state. Economic policy was firmly directed from within the country under the leadership of Julius Nyerere, Tanzania's first president, who had led the mainland's struggle for independence. As Doriye (1992, p.98) explained, 'the three main aims established for governmental action after 1967 were:

- to increase industrial growth through direct state investment in industry
- to promote widespread and egalitarian access to state-provided social services
- to promote collective and cooperative agricultural development.'

Furthermore, this was, as Figure 11.3 shows, a period of high investment from the mid 1970s sustained by foreign aid and aimed at developing the country's transport infrastructure, creating industrial capacity to substitute manufactured imports, and improving provisioning of basic social services.

Question

Look back at Sections 2.2 and 2.3. In what ways could aid boost investment?

First, aid, along with savings, together finance investment (see Section 2.3). Without aid, domestic savings would set a limit on total investment; aid breaks that constraint. In addition, aid can finance imports over and above those bought by the foreign exchange earned by exports; these can include investment goods such as machinery and materials needed to build roads or railways, establish new production facilities, or construct hospitals and schools. Consequently, aid breaks a constraint on investment generated by exports and hence foreign exchange (Chenery and Strout, 1966).

The high investment rate from the mid 1970s shown in Figure 11.3 was fuelled in particular by Tanzania's Basic Industry Strategy (BIS), formulated in 1974 as part of the third Five-Year Plan. This strategy sought to step up the process of import substituting industrialization by investing in those industries with the most linkages to the rest of the economy – especially linkages with agriculture (for example, fertilizers), between industries (for example, supplying industrial inputs), and with final demand for mass consumption goods. The stated policy objective was that by concentrating on these 'basic' industries, industrialization could proceed without meeting a constraint created by import needs for raw materials and intermediary inputs that rise more rapidly than could be financed.

In this period, foreign aid (apart from food aid) was largely given in the format of project aid. Typically, the Tanzanian government would draw up development plans and on that basis articulate a 'shopping list' of investment projects. Donors would pick and choose which projects to finance. The recipient government could propose but donors disposed, exercising their own selectivity. Most projects were managed from the donor side; the aid financed imports of capital goods and the provision of technical and management expertise. One consequence of this, however, was that actual investment projects often turned out to be far more import- and capital-intensive than initially envisaged.

Nevertheless, this relationship with donors did leave macroeconomic policy firmly in local hands. Tanzanian macroeconomic policy in this period was basically investment planning, a focus that was to have severe longer term costs. To see why, we need to look at the effects on the local economy. The investment projects financed by aid also required local expenditure. The local partner in the project, usually the government or a public sector enterprise, had to raise the necessary domestic finance (called 'counterpart' finance) in the local currency, the Tanzanian shilling, to fund the costs of local labour, materials, rental of buildings and so on (Wangwe, 1983; Wuyts, 1994). As more project aid became available, more counterpart finance was required.

The result was inflation. As Chapter 8 explained, inflation is a *general* rise in prices in an economy. In Tanzania in the late 1970s, the method of raising the counterpart funds for investment was severely inflationary. To understand why that was so, first look back at Figure 11.3. Aid, represented by the trade gap, was significant as a source of finance for investment, but a similar, if not larger portion had to be supported by domestic savings.

How were those savings extracted from the local economy? If a large element of GDP is saved, that means those resources are not being consumed as food, clothing, and other consumer goods. But Tanzania was and is a very poor country; voluntary saving by individuals, in bank accounts, is low. The government can impose taxes and spend the revenues on investment (this is shown in national accounts as government saving), though that expenditure was also difficult because the government was spending its funds expanding health and education provision. The result was that the government, in order to keep up the rate of investment, resorted to borrowing from the Tanzanian central bank in order to provide the counterpart funds.

When governments borrow heavily in this way from their own central bank, in excess of available voluntary individual savings, it is called 'printing money'. This is a phrase you may have heard. It does not necessarily mean running the printing presses at the mint (though it may). It does mean injecting lots of extra purchasing power into the economy. The more donor aid in this period, the higher state money creation of this type (Doriye and Wuyts, 1992). If output of goods fails to rise in response to the extra purchasing power thus arising within the economy, the result is likely to be severe inflation.

And this is what happened. As prices rose, the government imposed price controls and rationed basic goods such as food and soap. Traders circumvented the controls, selling goods on parallel (illegal) markets at high prices. People's real incomes dropped sharply. In effect, by driving down real levels of consumption via higher prices, domestic savings were being forced out of the economy to support investment. The result was increasing economic hardship which turned severe in the crisis years of the early 1980s.

At first though, achievements of this industrialization policy were impressive. Economic growth averaged about 5 per cent during 1961–78, while social provision such as health care and education developed fast. But agricultural sector investment was neglected in the effort to industrialize. A process of forced 'villagization' of rural communities added to agrarian

351

problems, and the government had created a larger public administration than could be sustained without rapid growth which, after 1975, was no longer forthcoming (see Figure 11.1).

The final catalyst of crisis was faltering export earnings in the late 1970s and into the early 1980s (Wuyts, 1994). Export agriculture had a vital role to play within the industrialization strategy: while foreign aid paid for the foreign exchange costs of investment projects, export agriculture was supposed to pay for recurrent imports – in particular, raw materials and intermediate inputs. Yet export agriculture received relatively little investment and few incentives. Cash crop production for export fell from the mid 1970s onwards, but export earnings were briefly sustained by a favourable movement in the terms of trade due to a boom in coffee prices in 1976 and 1977 resulting from frost in Brazil. Once this boom fell away, oil price rises in the late 1970s and early 1980s turned the terms of trade against the country and the ratio of exports to GDP stayed stubbornly low. The rate of imports, including imports of inputs for manufacturing, was pulled down, worsening the scarcity of goods.

The effect was that the industrial capacity created by investment could not be used effectively (Wangwe, 1983). Production of manufactured consumer goods fell and consumer goods could not be imported because of a lack of foreign exchange. This 'goods famine' was experienced in both urban and rural areas: farmers had little incentive to sell crops if there was little to be bought with the money.

The industrial strategy thus ran out of steam only a few years after it was initiated because of its failure to address the importance of sustaining export earnings to pay for needed imports. The result was the crisis years of the early 1980s (Wuyts, 1994).

Those crisis years left a deep and lasting imprint on the economy and society, eroding the credibility of past policies. At first, the government merely tried to weather the storm, as Samuel Wangwe explains in Chapter 12. It tried to safeguard public sector employment but did so at the expense of a collapse in real wages. The goods famine created a situation where goods at officially controlled prices were mainly accessible to the political elite and civil servants who administered the distribution networks. The large majority of the population depended on parallel markets where inflation was rampant.

Life was difficult for most people, and households looked for multiple ways to survive: for example, doctors kept chickens and sold their previously free services for cash at the door; and car owners would double up as impromptu taxi drivers whenever the opportunity arose. The drop in GDP growth, and even the fall in GDP depicted in Figure 11.1, are but a poor reflection of what was happening to people's livelihoods. Consequently, the coherence of and support for the political platform that had carried the commitment to socialist ethics and policies in the 1960s was rapidly eroded as hardship spread. There was a widespread feeling of disenchantment with a government which was seen to be intransigent – unwilling to change in view of the new realities.

In the early 1980s, moreover, 'aid fatigue' set in as donors became disenchanted with the economic policies of the government. Declining aid drove down the investment rate and the savings rate, as Figure 11.3 shows. The harsher financial climate of the early 1980s only made matters worse as attempts by the government to borrow its way out of the crisis became increasingly unsustainable. Donors called for economic reform. The Berg Report articulated this need for change and its message found resonance, not only among the donors but also within the Tanzanian society at large. The policy initiative swung from inside to outside, and macroeconomic policy came to be steered by the IMF and the World Bank, supported by the other (bilateral) donors. Chapter 12 describes the political shifts this involved; the next sub-section examines its economic content and consequences.

3.2 Economic reforms in the era of structural adjustment

As Chapter 10 noted, the term 'structural adjustment' came to be used in the 1980s to describe a policy framework which aimed rapidly to recreate developing countries' economies as competitive, export-oriented and market-led. Exports were to be based on existing comparative advantage, the role of the state reduced, and private initiative was to become the prime force in economic development (Demery, 1994; Helleiner, 1994; Toye, 1994).

Structural adjustment was in some ways a misnomer. The term was first used in the sense currently understood to designate a particular form of lending by the World Bank: exceptional (crisis-led) balance of payments financing backed by strict and economy-wide policy conditions (Demery, 1994, p.29). However, John Toye, a development economist, explains that structural adjustment 'was an old phrase which had suddenly been given a new meaning' (1994, p.18).

> Until 1980, structural adjustment had been a task for developed countries. It had connoted the state-assisted run-down of their old industries (such as textiles, leather goods and light engineering) which could no longer compete with the industrial capacity in the developing countries. Since the birth of development economics in the 1940s this kind of structural adjustment had been seen as an essential policy component of the achievement of world economic development. ... The responsibility for industrial readjustment or adaptation was placed on the countries which were already the most economically advanced, as a way of avoiding the damaging protectionist practices which had characterized the Depression

era. The new meaning given to an old term in 1980 was significant ... as a sudden and dramatic reversal of the locus of responsibility for ensuring successful world development, from the shoulders of the economically strong to the economically weak.

(Toye, 1994, pp.18–19)

As Thandika Mkandawire explained, it was in Africa that the multilateral agencies most extensively experimented with this policy of 'adjustment' by the weakest economies. The key macroeconomic ingredients for adjustment of concern to our argument here are the following.

First, the adoption of *stabilization* policies aimed to maintain overall macroeconomic discipline within the economy and to reduce inflation. The key objective of stabilization policies is to reduce domestic absorption, forcing the economy 'to live within its means'. In technical jargon, these policies are often referred to as 'demand management' since their aim is to reduce domestic expenditure on (and, hence, the domestic demand for) final output to bring it in line with available means. A second key element was the promotion of trade liberalization and, expressly, of import liberalization to open up the domestic economy to foreign competition. A third key element was 'getting prices right', as described in Section 1. This meant aligning relative prices within the economy more closely to relative prices on world markets. The big shifts in relative prices that this entailed in Tanzania were a major cause of structural change in the whole economy in the adjustment years.

Bilateral aid donors lined up behind the IMF and World Bank to refocus their attention on macroeconomic policy. Instead of promoting investment support for import substituting industrialization, donors turned to using aid to open up domestic economies to competition from world markets. Donors recognized that stabilization alone, based on further reducing domestic expenditure, was bound to push fragile developing economies closer to despair. Therefore, they offered aid as balance of payments support – to fund a trade deficit to allow imports to exceed depressed levels of exports – as a way of underpinning and promoting a transition to market-based, open economy development.

This new form of aid, called 'programme aid', was conditional upon the acceptance by the recipient country of the new macroeconomic policy framework for structural adjustment. Consequently, the driving seat of economic policy design was handed over to the IMF and the World Bank, backed by other donors, while the recipient government was relegated to the back seat, entangled in a web of conditionality.

The initial phase of structural adjustment in Tanzania, in macroeconomic terms, was characterized by three policies. Imports were liberalized, initially mainly through the lifting of controls on imports and only later through tariff reductions. 'Demand management' was imposed in the form of reductions in government spending, and also by imposing limits on bank lending. In addition, the Tanzanian shilling was rapidly devalued. This last policy had a dramatic effect on the structure of the Tanzanian economy, as explained in Section 4.

Question

Look back at Figure 11.2. How did trade respond?

Both the import and export coefficients rose in the later 1980s, with the import coefficient growing more rapidly. Thus, the trade gap widened. Look back at Figure 11.3. During the late 1980s and early 1990s, the trade gap is more or less equal in height to the investment rate. Domestic savings had in effect more or less vanished. If you find this puzzling, have another look at the answer to Activity 11.3 before reading on.

Investment in the adjustment years was almost exclusively financed by aid. Subsequently, towards the turn of the century, domestic savings reappeared, but this time against the background of a falling trade gap. Therefore, one consequence of 'adjustment' was that aid ceased to drive investment in quite the same way as in the pre-reform period. The dynamics of aid, investment and trade changed in the era of the economic reforms.

There were a number of reasons for this change. The imposition of strict demand management and the reduction in state economic activity meant that the earlier practice of financing investment through money creation was brought to a halt. Programme aid was used to pay for imports of consumer goods, revitalizing private consumption. For example, private consumption formed only 62 per cent of GDP in 1979, the last year of the state-led investment boom; it rose to about 70 per cent in 1982, the depths of the economic crisis, against a background of falling GDP and particularly of falling investment. By 1987, however, the share of private consumption had risen to about 82 per cent. The greater availability of consumer goods pushed private consumption up in real terms and reduced the savings rate.

The structural adjustment period, then, saw falling inflation and a rising share of consumption in GDP, accompanied by a sharp move away from investment-led industrialization. Instead, donor-driven macroeconomic policy sought to open up the domestic economy and integrate it more deeply within world markets. The aim was to stimulate export production, especially in agriculture, and to attract private foreign investment to a newly competitive economy. A key policy instrument to open up the economy was 'getting the prices right' and, expressly, to establish a new exchange rate policy in the expectation that this would boost export performance and thus increase the standard of living of the Tanzanian population at large. To this we now turn.

4 Creating transition to an open economy: foreign exchange and exchange rate policies

In the pre-reform era in Tanzania, foreign exchange was largely allocated through non-market (planning) mechanisms, in accordance with government priorities. Structural adjustment policies engineered a transition to a market-led process of allocating foreign exchange. This was one of the major policies that opened the economy to the influence of world markets, and this section tells this story. I start by examining what happened to Tanzania's exchange rate and I then explain the working of demand and supply once there is a market for foreign exchange in a country like Tanzania. Finally, I explain what is meant by the real exchange rate: the key relative price addressed by structural adjustment policies.

4.1 Devaluing the shilling: the move from fixed to floating rates of exchange

The nominal exchange rate of a country (what we mean when we say 'the exchange rate') can be defined in two distinct ways: either as the *price of foreign currency* in terms of the home currency or, alternatively, as the *value of the home currency* in terms of the foreign currency. One is the reciprocal of the other. It is common practice in most countries (including Tanzania) to define the exchange rate as the price of foreign currency in terms of the home currency; a few countries (of which the UK is one) define the exchange rate as the value of the home currency in terms of foreign currency.

In this chapter, I shall follow the Tanzanian convention of defining the exchange rate as the price of foreign currency – say, the dollar – in terms of the home currency, in this case the Tanzanian shilling (Tshs). It is the price Tanzanian residents must pay to acquire foreign currency. Hence, when more Tanzanian shillings are paid for a dollar, the exchange rate (the price of the dollar in terms of shillings) increases or rises and, consequently, the value of the shilling in terms of the dollar declines – that is, we say that the shilling *devalues*. There is a whole set of exchange rates, one for each currency used in international trading or finance such as the dollar, the euro, the pound sterling, the yen or the rand. I shall use the dominant trading currency, the dollar, in this discussion.

Figure 11.4 shows how the shilling/dollar exchange rate has evolved in Tanzania from the mid 1970s to the turn of the century. I have used a logarithmic scale for this graph because a log scale makes it easier to see what is happening at the bottom and top ends of the graph. A logarithmic scale has another useful property: an equal vertical distance between any two pairs of points means that the rate of increase in the exchange rate is the same between both pairs.

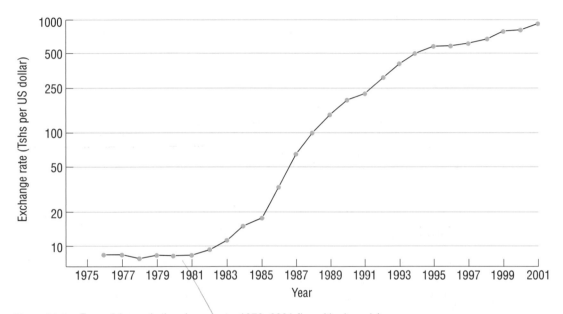

Figure 11.4   Tanzania's nominal exchange rate, 1976–2001 (logarithmic scale)

Source: World Bank, 2002e, Table 6.6; National Bureau of Statistics, Tanzania, 2002, Table 17

When you run your eyes over this graph from left to right, you will note that during the latter half of the 1970s and in the early 1980s the curve remains virtually flat, indicating no or only minor changes in the nominal exchange rate. Consequently, in the pre-reform period, the exchange rate was largely dormant. Tanzania had a policy regime of fixed exchange rates, while imports were largely rationed in accordance with government priorities. Under a regime of fixed exchange rates, the officially determined exchange rate is normally kept constant over a considerable period of time, but can occasionally be adjusted through either devaluation or revaluation.

In Figure 11.4, in the second half of the 1980s the vertical distances between successive points increase markedly. The distances narrow in the early 1990s, and after the mid 1990s the curve rises more gently. This means that the nominal exchange rate rose in the reform period, the rate of increase accelerating in the early reform era, then slowing down but remaining positive throughout.

Fixed exchange rates
A fixed exchange rate is an exchange rate chosen by government as an element of macroeconomic policy; all (legal) currency exchange must be at that rate.

This rise was policy-induced. During nearly a decade from the mid 1980s, the Tanzanian shilling was rapidly devalued.

Question

What does it mean to say that the shilling was 'devalued'. Why did that cause the exchange rate shown in Figure 11.4 to rise?

Devaluation means that the Tanzania shilling will buy less foreign currency than before. Consequently, the value of the shilling declines and, hence, the price of foreign currency in terms of the shilling – that is, the exchange rate – increases. The vertical axis in Figure 11.4 shows the number of shillings needed to buy a dollar. As the shilling's value falls, Tanzania's dollar exchange rate – the mirror image of the shilling's value – rises accordingly.

Floating exchange rates
Floating exchange rates vary as a result of changing supply and demand on foreign exchange markets.

Finally, during the 1990s and into the present century, Tanzania went over to a regime of floating exchange rates, indicating a shift to a more market-based allocation of foreign exchange. This was achieved through a process of dismantling the old structures of state control of imports and currency exchanges and through the emergence and consolidation of the institutional basis for foreign exchange markets. Foreign currency was no longer rationed through administrative allocation, but sold freely by banks and bureaux de change in accordance with demand and supply.

When the exchange rate is left entirely to market forces without government interference, economists will say that a regime of flexible exchange rates prevails. In practice, there is always an element of 'managing the exchange rate' on the part of monetary authorities. In Tanzania, this element was (and continues to be) quite important, not least because a sizeable share of the available foreign exchange derives directly from foreign aid and therefore its supply to domestic markets can be managed quite readily by the monetary authorities.

The move from a fixed to a floating exchange rate, therefore, reflected the difficulties of creating institutions and behavioural changes in a context of transition. Changing the exchange rate administratively could be done overnight. The series of large and rapid devaluations simply required decisions by the Tanzanian monetary authorities subject to World Bank and IMF policy conditionality. By contrast, dismantling the old system of exchange controls and building up the new institutions for market-based allocation of foreign exchange took time. The initial currency devaluations and import liberalization therefore aimed to subject the economy to new 'market signals' from the start. Producers, consumers and investors, it was intended, would start to respond to market price signals rather than government plans. Only toward the end of the 1990s did the organizational infrastructures for more market-based foreign exchange allocation emerge, allowing for greater flexibility in the exchange rate in response to market forces.

4.2   The demand for and supply of foreign exchange

Supply and demand for foreign exchange (backed by an appropriate macroeconomic policy environment) was put forward as the prime mechanism to regulate the economy's insertion in world markets. To understand the effect on the Tanzanian economy, we first need to take a more careful look at the operation of foreign exchange markets in an economy that is very small and poor relative to world markets.

Let us imaginatively situate ourselves at the end of the process of transition to an open market economy, when the foreign exchange market has become somewhat consolidated and foreign exchange allocation is largely market-based. Residents and foreigners can (more or less) freely exchange dollars into shillings (and vice versa) in the foreign exchange departments of banks, in the bureaux de change, or even in restaurants, hotels and some shops.

To simplify the argument, I shall start by considering only the demand for and supply of foreign exchange arising from cross-border private current account transactions, and specifically from exports and imports. The effects of foreign aid on foreign exchange markets are left out of the picture for the time being.

In what follows, keep in mind that for each traded commodity there are always two prices: its dollar price and its Tanzanian shilling price.

Question

Do you think it likely that a change in the exchange rate in Tanzania will affect the dollar prices of Tanzanian exports and imports?

Small, primary commodity exporting countries are generally *price takers* on world markets. That is, they can increase their export sales or import demand without affecting world prices, simply because their trade is very small relative to the world market. By contrast, large primary and industrial exporters are often *price makers*. A sharp increase in sales can drive down prices (see Chapter 3, Section 6), and very large firms have some discretion in pricing their products in relation to competing producers' pricing decisions, even on world markets.

For each of its main exports, Tanzania's export share in the corresponding international market is generally small. Consequently, the country is largely a price taker. The same is true for its imports: its import demand is insignificant within world markets. Thus, in dollar terms – or indeed in euros, yen and pounds – the prices of Tanzania's exports and imports are given, that is, they are independent of Tanzanian production and sales decisions. An important implication follows: changes in the exchange rate will change domestic prices (in shillings), but not foreign (dollar) prices for imports and exports. The purpose and effect of devaluation then is to change price relationships in the *domestic* economy.

What determines the demand for and supply of foreign exchange? And how do these influences affect the exchange rate?

Economists call the demand for foreign exchange a derived demand. What this means is that dollars are demanded, not for their own sake, but to be able to pay for imports. How then will this demand for dollars, which reflects the demand for imports, vary with the price of foreign exchange? To answer this question, economists make use of a demand schedule, as shown in Figure 11.5. The demand schedule D depicts the hypothetical relationship between the demand for foreign exchange (on the horizontal axis) and the price of foreign exchange (on the vertical axis), assuming that all other things (such as incomes and all other prices not directly affected by the change in the price of foreign exchange) are held constant.

Economists assume that this demand schedule D slopes downwards (not necessarily in a straight line). The reasoning is that since dollar prices of goods are unchanged, a rise in the exchange rate will make the prices in Tanzanian shillings of imported goods and services more expensive. Buyers of imported products are likely to shift their demand away from imports to similar goods and services produced domestically, or to reduce their demand for these types of goods if there is no domestic production. Thus, the total demand by Tanzanian residents for dollars will fall.

Question

Using Figure 11.5, explain what will happen if the exchange rate rises from E_1 to E_2.

Aggregate demand for dollars in the economy will be reduced from Q_1 to Q_2 as people decide to buy fewer imported goods. You can think of the economy as moving along the demand schedule D, from point A to point B.

In Tanzania (as distinct from, for example, Britain), the production structure of the economy is rather limited and rigid. Much of what is imported into the country is not locally produced, or it requires high levels of imported inputs. Buyers have limited options, therefore, for shifting from imports to similar locally produced goods and services. Tightening the belt is the more likely market mechanism curtailing the demand for dollars when the price rises.

The supply of dollars onto the foreign exchange market is also derived, from exports. Exporters sell their products abroad and obtain dollars which they want to change back into Tanzanian shillings. As Figure 11.6 shows,

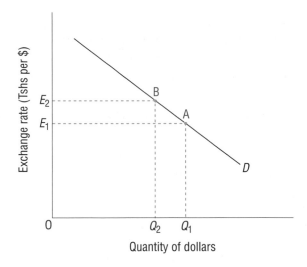

Figure 11.5   The demand for foreign exchange

economists assume that the supply curve for dollars *S* slopes upwards (not necessarily in a straight line). Dollar prices of exports, remember, do not change. A rise in the exchange rate (that is, a devaluation of the shilling), other things being equal, will lead to an increase in the prices in Tanzanian shillings of exported goods and services.

This shilling price rise should lead to an increase in exports because producers find exporting more profitable and produce and export more. Furthermore, the rise in the price of the goods in shillings discourages home consumption of the goods, leaving more production to be exported. More exports, at the same dollar price, mean more dollar earnings. In the economy as a whole, the aggregate supply of dollars increases. In Figure 11.6, if the exchange rate rises from E_1 to E_2, the supply of dollars in the economy rises from Q_1 to Q_2. You can think of the economy moving along the supply schedule *S* from point C to point F.

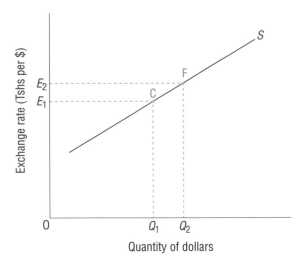

Figure 11.6   The supply of foreign exchange

Activity 11.4

Before reading on, check your understanding as follows. Suppose the Tanzanian shilling is revalued, that is, its value rises and so the price of a dollar falls from E_2 to E_1 on Figures 11.5 and 11.6. Explain what happens to the demand and supply of dollars respectively in the Tanzanian economy.

Tanzania's export structure is not very diverse: it consists mainly of coffee, tea, and other cash crops, some minerals, and tourist services. In such a poor country, there is little domestic demand for such products, and the main adjustment mechanism at work to increase the supply of dollars when the price rises has to be an increase in the volume of output of export products.

Demand and supply schedules give us the building blocks; now let us introduce a market mechanism. Suppose that the Tanzanian authorities cease to determine the price of dollars and let the foreign exchange market in Tanzania do the job. Bringing the demand and supply schedules from Figures 11.5 and 11.6 together in Figure 11.7 gives us an analysis of the market.

Question

Study Figure 11.7. What will happen if the exchange rate is at E_1?

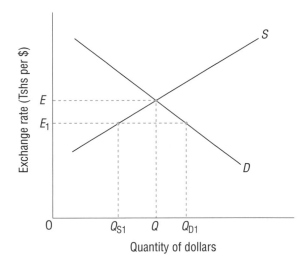

Figure 11.7 The demand for and supply of foreign exchange

At E_1, the demand for dollars is Q_{D1}. The supply of dollars however is lower at Q_{S1}. Supply and demand do not balance. Put differently, this is a situation where disequilibrium prevails.

Now think of the foreign exchange market as a bidding process – this is not unrealistic. If there is an excess demand for dollars, those who can make most profitable use of them bid up the price. Conversely, an excess supply of dollars, at any exchange rate above E will lead to a fall in the price. Consequently, only in one point, where demand and supply intersect at quantity Q and are equal to each other, will there be no market pressures at work on the exchange rate. The corresponding price E is the equilibrium exchange rate in our simplified market model.

One simplification I have made is particularly important. The equilibrium exchange rate is based on the assumption of 'all other things being equal'. That assumption helps to separate out how in theory a market price – in this case, the exchange rate – interacts with the quantities demanded and supplied under given conditions. We can also use the model to see how the market shifts when prevailing conditions change.

Question

What would happen to the equilibrium exchange rate if there was a bumper harvest of export crops, rather than a normal harvest, other things remaining the same?

You can think of a bumper harvest in this way: farmers have produced more than they planned at all dollar prices. So the bumper harvest of export crops shifts supply of exports – and therefore of dollars – to the right on Figure 11.8

Figure 11.8   Change in market equilibrium after a bumper harvest

at all exchange rates. The supply schedule shifts from S to S_1. The result is that the market equilibrium, where the demand and supply coincide, moves from point A to point B. There is a new lower equilibrium exchange rate E_1.

Activity 11.5

Now imagine that Tanzania's tourist trade suddenly declines. Another destination has become more fashionable, or perhaps tourists are less willing to travel abroad because the international security situation is thought to have worsened. Use Figure 11.7 to show what will happen to the equilibrium exchange rates, everything else remaining the same.

With the demand and supply framework to hand, we can now study the effect of a net inflow of foreign aid on the economy.

Question

Let us assume that previously all foreign exchange in the country was earned from exports. Now suddenly there is a net inflow of foreign aid. What happens to the foreign exchange market?

As aid dollars flow into the country, the supply of foreign exchange increases. You can think of this as a shift of the supply curve of dollars to the right, as in Figure 11.8. In this case, you can think of S as the supply schedule of dollars from exports with no aid, and S_1 as the supply schedule of dollars from both exports (unchanged at each exchange rate) and foreign aid. Consequently, the equilibrium exchange rate will be somewhat lower with aid than without – that is, dollars are cheaper once aid comes in, so the Tanzanian shilling has been revalued upwards. And, most important, the total dollar resources coming into the country rise, from Q to Q_1. The country can import more goods and services to ease the transition to market-based, open economy development.

4.3 The real exchange rate and structural change in the domestic economy

So, what were the effects of foreign exchange market liberalization within the Tanzanian domestic economy? Bear in mind the point emphasized above: exchange rate movements in Tanzania do not affect dollar prices, but instead change domestic prices. A devaluation forces up the prices of *traded* goods and services – imports and exports – relative to other prices in the domestic economy. Provided that domestic markets for goods and services are liberalized, a change in the exchange rate provokes domestic price changes, and these changing price signals from the world market reach down to every part of the domestic economy.

The message of the Berg Report was just that: domestic and foreign trade should be liberalized, and exchange rate policy – notably currency devaluation – should be directed at improving incentives for export production while ensuring that imports were used sparingly and in ways that took account of their proper dollar values. In Tanzania, this would mean that producers of coffee, tea, cotton, sisal, tobacco or cashew would gain better shilling prices from exports; food crop producers would face better prices too because imported food prices would rise, reducing competition in domestic food markets and allowing them to charge higher prices. However, the price of fertilizers, tractors and fuel would rise, favouring more labour-intensive production and careful husbandry of imported resources. Overall, price signals would favour exports and agriculture while enhancing efficiency in production.

Domestic industry would then have to compete with imported goods on world market terms and have to become more efficient or close down. In effect, industry would lose its favoured position under import substituting industrialization. In the early years of structural adjustment, this effect was less noticeable than might have been expected since the inflow of programme aid lifted the country out of its goods famine and provided domestic industry with much-needed imported inputs. Nevertheless, from the early 1990s onwards the competitive squeeze on industry from liberalized imports of goods became more noticeable.

For domestic prices to change in the way expected, there is one more condition to be met that has not yet been explained: when the nominal exchange rate rises (and hence the shilling devalues), shilling prices of internationally traded goods must rise relative to prices of goods produced and sold solely on the domestic market. If there is domestic inflation at the same time as the devaluation, then that price effect may be cancelled out, with all goods prices rising together. The intended structural changes in the economy then cannot occur.

Real exchange rate
The real exchange rate is the nominal exchange rate adjusted for the difference between domestic and world market inflation rates.

Another way of saying this is that for the intended effects of structural adjustment policies to occur, the real exchange rate must rise (and hence the shilling must devalue in real terms) – not just the nominal exchange rate.

The real exchange rate is calculated by correcting changes in the nominal exchange rate for changes in domestic and foreign price levels (Helmers, 1988, p.12). Specifically, let:

P_W be the dollar price index of world prices (in practice, creating this index involves a fairly complex calculation of a weighted index of the wholesale price indices of a country's major trading partners)

P_D be the shilling price index of domestic prices (usually the consumer price index)

E_N be the nominal exchange rate – the price of the dollar in terms of shillings (in practice, this usually involves calculating a weighted index of exchange rates with different currencies)

Then the real exchange rate (RER) is defined as:

$$ \text{RER} \equiv E_N \times \left(\frac{P_W}{P_D} \right) $$

This is approximately equivalent (you will have to trust me here) to defining the real exchange rate as the ratio of the prices of traded to non-traded goods.

Activity 11.6

If the nominal exchange rate remains fixed but domestic inflation runs ahead of world inflation, what happens to the real exchange rate?

Figure 11.9 shows the evolution of the real exchange rate in Tanzania over the period 1976 to 1998 (the period for which data were available).

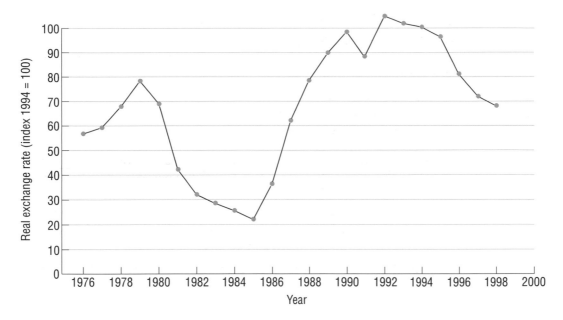

Figure 11.9   The real exchange rate, 1976–98

Source: World Bank, 2002e, Table 6.6; Rutasitara, 1994, Table 3.3

Question

Compare the evolution of the real exchange rate with the nominal exchange rate (Figure 11.4) during the pre-reform years. Can you think of an explanation for the differences?

The nominal exchange rate did not vary much during the late 1970s and early 1980s, the period of fixed nominal exchange rates. Nevertheless, the real exchange rate fell rapidly just before and during the crisis years. This was largely the result of rampant inflation (described in Section 3) in the midst of a 'goods famine'. The result was that the bias against export production intensified in the crisis years.

In the reform years, the nominal and real exchange rates both increased, meaning that the shilling value of the dollar rose in nominal and in real terms. That is, this period witnessed large shilling devaluations (the shilling becoming worth less in terms of the dollar). The increases in the nominal exchange rate were reinforced by falling domestic inflation. Restrictions on government spending and borrowing reduced domestic demand. Most importantly, the greater availability of goods for sale, financed by foreign aid, reduced prices sharply on the parallel markets – illegal markets operating outside government controls. Since the large majority of the population had been forced to survive by buying on these parallel markets in the crisis years, this might explain why no food riots or other forms of strong popular opposition to the imposition of structural adjustment policies occurred in Tanzania at the time. Life was by no means easy during these years of rapid change – the squeeze on real incomes and the effect of job losses in the formal sector clearly had their impact – but it certainly felt better than under the earlier years of severe goods shortages.

Thus, the major prescriptions of the Berg Report were implemented in Tanzania, engineering huge changes in internal prices. So far I have told quite a positive story about the immediate domestic macroeconomic effects: more goods available and falling inflation. But as structural adjustment unfolded, what happened to the structure of the economy? How did the trade sector and domestic production respond to the changing incentives? And, to come back to the theme at the beginning of this chapter, what about the premise that trade integration should lead economic development? The Berg Report strategy aimed to enhance the greater trade openness of the Tanzanian economy to world market prices and competition along the lines of existing comparative advantage. Did that work? Was the Berg Report right to assert, contrary to Rweyemamu's views, that there was no need to try to change comparative advantage?

5 Does structure matter under structural adjustment?

One of the most remarkable features about structural adjustment is that it appears to pay so little attention to economic structure. In fact, as pointed out in Section 1.1, the Berg Report explicitly argued that the fears about declining terms of trade were exaggerated and that economic development should be rooted in the pursuit of existing comparative advantage, even if based on an existing economic structure largely dependent on the production of an often narrow range of primary commodities. In this sense, the Berg Report was quite dismissive of African developmentalism during the earlier years with its explicit call for structural transformation through import-substituting industrialization.

Yet, in another sense, the key message of the Berg Report was by no means devoid of its own specific structural premises, especially where African economic development was concerned. Indeed, the report and its advocates explicitly called for an agriculture-led development strategy, rooted in existing comparative advantage. 'Getting the prices right' and trade liberalization were aimed at giving incentives, in terms of better shilling prices, to rural producers, particularly export crop producers, and thus at provoking growth in primary export production. Moreover, increasing rural incomes derived from export growth were expected, in turn, to generate internal demand for domestically manufactured consumer goods, local handicraft products and services, agricultural inputs and implements, and locally marketed food crops, fruits and vegetables. This would boost off-farm employment in rural areas as well as stimulate industrial output and service provisioning in urban areas to satisfy rural demand. Put differently, the basic premise was as follows.

> Only growth in comparative-advantage sectors affecting large numbers of people can provide the widespread and recurrent income source needed for a broad and economically sustained rural growth process affecting the demand-constrained sectors.

(Delgado *et al.*, 1994, p.1170)

Therefore, in the African context in general, and in Tanzania specifically, only traditional broad-based export agriculture could be seen to be large enough in terms of the numbers of people it employed to promote widespread linkages to other sectors, carrying the rest of the economy upwards as it grew.

Thus, this is an argument about the structure of the economy. It contains a certain image of the way links between sectors of the economy can promote economic development. What is distinctive about this argument, however, is that it does not call for an initial adjustment in the economic structure of Tanzania as a way of promoting economic development via trade integration. On the contrary, the argument asserts that existing comparative advantage should lead the way. The reasons given are the immediate financial viability of such a strategy in terms of generating export earnings, and the scale of its impact on the economy because of the sheer numbers of people whose livelihoods depends on agriculture.

This is a powerful argument, not least because of its explicit emphasis on promoting broad-based economic development. It is indeed hard to see how significant poverty reduction can be achieved if macroeconomic policies do not reach down to the large majority of people, especially those located in the poorer rural areas. This premise underlying structural adjustment policies is something that we should be careful not to dismiss too readily. It is an important insight into priorities which we should retain when thinking about development strategy.

However, is the strategy sufficient to achieve these ambitious objectives? Did it work? Furthermore, what about the fear of adverse terms of trade and its inherent potential to undo much of what is gained in increased production?

To answer these questions we need to see what happened to Tanzania's export performance in general and, in particular, to agricultural exports in the period of economic reforms. We also need to look at what happened to the terms of trade during the period of reforms, and assess their impact on incomes. Finally, we can try to infer how robust this strategy of adjustment really was in generating broad-based development.

5.1   A shift away from agricultural exports?

Figure 11.10 displays the percentage shares in total Tanzanian goods exports of the major cash crops, of minerals, of their sum (exports of primary produce), and of manufactures from 1980–2001. It shows that until the later 1990s, Tanzania relied on a narrow range of agricultural primary commodity exports: coffee, cotton, cashew, sisal, tea, tobacco and cloves. Nonetheless, the end of the period near the turn of the century witnessed the rapid growth in the share of primary exports of minerals (gold, diamonds and precious stones), mirrored by the dramatic fall in share of the major cash crops. The share of manufactured exports peaked at about 24 per cent by 1990, but subsequently declined to about 7 per cent in 2001.

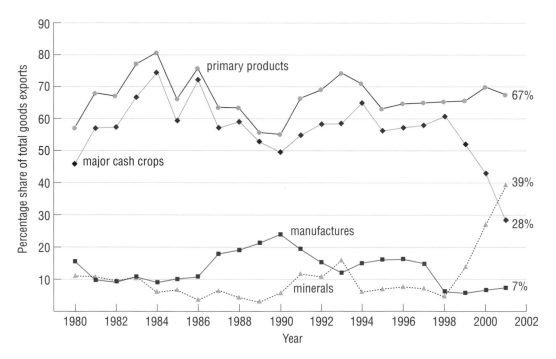

Figure 11.10   Composition of Tanzanian goods exports, 1980–2001

Source: World Bank, 2002e, Table 3.2; Bank of Tanzania, 2001, Table 4.3 (author's calculations)

In addition to commodity exports, Tanzania also exports services (primarily tourism, but also transport). The share of services in total exports of goods and services was rather low, around 20 per cent, until the mid 1990s. It then rose remarkably fast and, at the turn of the century, the share of services (notably tourism) was about 45 per cent of total export earnings.

In sum, it is not surprising that at the turn of the century a World Bank report referred to mining and tourism as 'the new pacemakers for growth' in Tanzania (World Bank, 2002e, p.8). Tourism has grown sharply and, like the mining industry, is largely driven by foreign investment. The economy has been diversifying in the wake of economic reform. But what happened to agricultural export development, which, as envisaged by the Berg Report, was to be the main pacemaker of economic development?

Tanzania certainly did not cease to be a predominantly agrarian economy. The larger part of its population still remains heavily dependent on agriculture to secure its livelihoods, including cash cropping for exports. And, as shown in Section 2.1, agricultural growth accounted for around half of total GDP growth since the era of economic reforms.

To see what happened, we need to look at the evolution of both the prices and volumes of major cash crops. Figure 11.11 shows the fluctuations in the

Figure 11.11   Export price index for major cash crops, 1980–2001

Source: World Bank, 2002e, Table 3.3; Bank of Tanzania, 2001, Table 4.3 (author's calculations)

export price index (based on dollar prices per ton of produce, using 1992 as the base year) of Tanzania's main cash crops – coffee, cotton, cashew, tea, tobacco and sisal – over a 20-year period.

Figure 11.11 illustrates the extent to which Tanzania, and its rural producers specifically, continued to be highly vulnerable to swings in incomes caused by the volatility of externally determined prices. Particularly noticeable is the sharp decline in the price index of agricultural commodity exports from the mid 1990s onwards – by 2001 the price index of cash crops stood at around 54 per cent of its level in 1994.

Figure 11.12 shows the evolution of the volume of exports of these cash crops (expressed as an index with base year 1992). The most remarkable feature is the rapid rise until about 1996–97, and the subsequent fall. The steep fall in export prices is likely to have been a major factor in driving this decline in output volume.

The combined effects of falling export prices and output volumes during the latter half of the 1990s and into the first decade of the new century suggest that the changing composition of Tanzania's exports noted in Figure 11.10,

Figure 11.12   Export crops: volume index, 1980–2001

Source: World Bank, 2002e, Table 3.3; Bank of Tanzania, 2001, Table 4.3 (author's calculations)

and the fall in the share of agricultural exports in particular, is in part due to genuine diversification in export production and in part due to the sharp reduction in export earnings from export crops.

5.2 The terms of trade and the purchasing power of exports

So what happened to Tanzania's overall terms of trade during this period, that is, the ratio of export to import prices? Figure 11.13 shows the story for the period 1987 to 2001. It shows the terms of trade:

■ between all exports and all imports (overall terms of trade)

■ between the exports and imports of goods only (goods terms of trade)

■ between agricultural exports and goods imports (agricultural terms of trade).

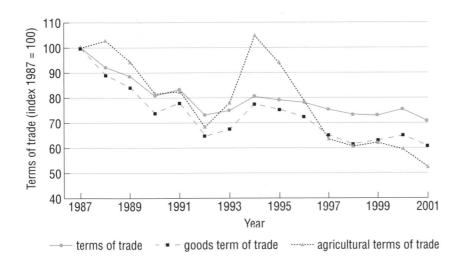

Figure 11.13   Tanzania's terms of trade indices, 1987–2001

Source: World Bank, 2002e; Bank of Tanzania, 2001; National Bureau of Statistics, Tanzania, 1999, 2002 (author's calculations)

Question

Take a careful look at Figure 11.13. What happened to the terms of trade for each of these three categories? Which fared the worst?

The general picture is of a rather dramatic decline over the period since the economic reforms under structural adjustment, indicating that Tanzania was receiving less and less for its exports relative to the prices of its imports. Between 1987 and 2001 the overall terms of trade dropped by nearly 30 per cent, while the terms of trade for goods dropped by nearly 40 per cent. The agricultural terms of trade show much greater volatility in their year-to-year fluctuations and dropped by about 50 per cent over the period as a whole.

A decline in the terms of trade implies that a country needs to export progressively more in volume terms just to be able to afford the same volume of imports (Chapter 3 discussed the poverty trap this process can create). The fundamental concern of macroeconomic policy makers seeking economic development is not export volume but the 'purchasing power of exports': what amount of imports (manufactured consumer goods, equipment and agricultural inputs) the exports will buy from abroad. 'Export volume' is a measure of production effort; the purchasing power of exports is a measure of the reward for this production effort, assessed in terms of the imports which the export earnings can buy.

The purchasing power of exports is measured by the volume exported, multiplied by the terms of trade:

$$Purchasing\ power\ of\ exports \equiv Terms\ of\ trade \times Export\ volume$$

Table 11.3 gives a summary of the growth rates in the purchasing power and volume of Tanzanian exports for each of the three groupings used above. It also shows the growth rates in GDP and percentage changes in import volume for the period 1987–2001.

Table 11.3   GDP and trade: average annual growth rates, 1987–2001

Summary table	Growth rates per annum (%)
GDP	3.6
Import volume	
goods and services	2.4
goods only	1.6
Export volume	
goods and services	9.9
goods only	7.8
main cash crops	3.6
Purchasing power of exports	
goods and services	7.2
goods only	4.0
main cash crops	−1.0

Source: author's calculations from sources for previous figures and tables

Table 11.3 tells an interesting but complex story:

- First, by and large, export volumes increased quite substantially over the period as a whole (despite some fluctuations). The economic reforms, therefore, appear to have had the desired effect of stimulating export production.

- Second, total exports of goods and services grew faster than exports of goods only, indicating the faster growth of services during the 1990s. Agricultural exports grew least of all, but still in line with GDP growth.

- Third, the rate of increase in export volume was not matched by the rate of increase in the purchasing power of exports.

- Fourth, import volume grew much less than either export volume or the purchasing power of exports.

- Finally, for agricultural exports the growth in purchasing power was actually negative!

Over the period as a whole, from 1987 to 2001, the aggregate export volume rose by 274 per cent (implying a growth rate of 9.9 per cent per annum, on average), while its purchasing power rose by 164 per cent (7.2 per cent per annum, on average). Similarly, but more modestly, aggregate goods export volume increased by 187 per cent (7.8 per cent per annum, on average), while the purchasing power only rose by 74 per cent (4.0 per cent per annum, on average). Additional efforts to boost exports, consequently, did not pay off proportionally in terms of additional ability to pay for imports and for debt servicing. This failure was also true for agricultural exports, which grew in volume terms by about 3.6 per cent per annum over the period concerned, while their purchasing power fell by 1 per cent per annum.

In contrast to export performance, the growth in import volume was modest, even when compared with the growth in the purchasing power of exports. Total imports rose by 39 per cent (2.4 per cent per annum, on average) over the period 1987 to 2001. Over the same period, imports of goods increased in volume terms by only 24 per cent (1.6 per cent per annum, on average). Both these growth rates were well below GDP growth. This lower growth of import volume is reflected in the narrowing of the trade gap observed in Figure 11.3, despite the falling terms of trade.

So did the terms of trade matter after all? Yes, they did. Moreover, what does this really mean in terms of people's livelihoods? The impact is akin to making people such as producers run faster to stay in the same place. The effect was particularly strong for the poorest agricultural export producers. Thus, the possibility, as predicted by the Berg Report and its advocates, of the beneficial effects of agricultural export-led growth generating further

secondary income growth to promote broad-based development is unlikely to be forthcoming. The reason is that real income growth from cash crop production has been severely eroded or has actually declined in the wake of the downward movement in the terms of trade and its negative impact on the growth in the purchasing power of agricultural exports.

Calling, as some do (World Bank, 2000d, p.xiv), for further devaluations of the shilling, both in nominal and in real terms, thus raising the dollar price in terms of shillings, does not solve the underlying problem. Indeed, inserting this policy into a context of falling terms of trade can constitute a potent force for extracting more work from people – including, in this case, some of the poorest people in the world – without a commensurate gain in their incomes and standards of living. The importance of structural weaknesses, such as concentration on a few primary exports, and the need for structural transformation to diversify the economy cannot be dismissed so easily. How to meet the challenge of combining trade integration with structural transformation still remains a valid and unresolved question for economic policy in a country like Tanzania.

6 Conclusion

This chapter took you on a journey through the macroeconomic analysis of the relation between trade integration and economic development in a low income country, using Tanzania as its source of evidence and debates. In the process, you have become acquainted with basic tools of national income accounting that allow you to locate aid and trade in relation to domestic production, investment and consumption. You have also studied the analytical apparatus economists use to understand the macroeconomic effects of the exchange rate policies that are key to the structural adjustment framework.

Our main concern was to use these tools to ask whether economic development should follow or lead trade integration. I argued that simple recipes can and do contain hidden traps. Perhaps you now expect me to pull the rabbit out of my hat by offering a feasible strategy to Tanzania's dilemmas? No such luck – I do not pretend to be a magician. Nevertheless, three important lessons can be learned from the analysis presented in this chapter.

First, the fact that the Nyerere regime in post-independence Tanzania gave an inappropriate or perhaps erroneous answer to an important question should not lead us to dismiss the question altogether. The brief attempt at import substituting industrialization scarcely got going before it ran aground in the turbulent days of the late 1970s and the early 1980s. Contrast this with India's much longer period of import substituting industrialization after independence. Yet this failure does not mean that the concerns of the early developmentalism were irrelevant. The structure of a country's integration within world markets – the goods it can produce, the diversity of resources and capabilities of its firms – matter a great deal in terms of the possibilities they offer and the constraints they create. A limited range of exports, mainly primary exports, and reliance on very diverse industrial imports exposes the country to the vagaries of adverse terms of trade coupled with volatile commodity prices.

To render the country less vulnerable, therefore, there is a need for greater export diversification through the structural transformation of the economy. As this chapter has shown, the expansion of mining and tourism since the economic reforms has undoubtedly allowed for faster growth in exports and has partly cushioned the economy from the effects of the sharply declining terms of trade of agricultural export commodities since the latter half of the 1990s. The same cannot be said, however, of industrial exports, which declined significantly as a share of total exports. Yet this book has shown that countries that have managed to pull themselves out of a low-level poverty equilibrium have generally done so by relying on industrial development as one essential ingredient of their policies. Nyerere's attempt to industrialize proved to be unsuccessful, but the need for industrial development cannot be put aside so easily.

However – and this is my second lesson – this in turn should not lead us too readily to dismiss the importance of agriculture for rural development. A large majority of Tanzania's population still relies and will continue to rely on agriculture in general, and on export agriculture in particular, to secure their livelihoods. Agriculture matters, not only in its own right but also – as the Berg Report asserted – because the income generated from broad-based growth in agricultural cash crop production is an important stimulus to rural diversification, including rural industrialization. It is indeed hard to conceive of a viable strategy of development with poverty reduction that would not address the importance of agriculture, its present predicament and its potential to generate broad-based rural development, through both on- and off-farm activities.

This leads me to my third and final lesson. Structural adjustment policies shifted the burden of adjustment wholly onto the shoulders of the poorest nations. The problem – the Berg Report argued – was the inappropriate policies pursued by these countries. The older notion, therefore, that structural adjustment should instead fall mainly on the shoulders of the rich countries, by making room for increasingly diversified exports from poorer countries, was conveniently set aside.

Part 1 of this book set out arguments that the present-day world trade regime is stacked rather heavily in favour of the economically powerful. Agriculture-led (or, more generally, primary commodity-led) growth, including its possible dynamic development by incorporating further stages of processing and marketing, is unlikely to generate sustained income growth if the richer countries are unwilling to accommodate the consequent growth in processed primary-based exports from the developing countries. If the so-called donor countries are serious in promoting policies aimed at poverty reduction, their policies will have to tackle the problems inherent in the relation between trade integration and economic development. Merely channelling aid resources towards social services and road building is unlikely to create a way out of poverty unless aid policies link up with trade policies and effectively provide greater room for manoeuvre for the poorest countries, including market space for both agriculture-based and industrial development.

As will be argued in Chapter 12 for the case of Tanzania, there is at present a growing space for a more productive development dialogue between donors and aid recipients in poor countries, but the boundaries of this dialogue still remain largely set by the industrialized countries. In particular, issues of structural transformation that could strengthen the returns to the poorest countries from the interplay between trade and economic development remain at the margins of, if not outside, these boundaries. Successful poverty reduction must come to terms with the question of how a country like Tanzania can realistically build upon its comparative advantage and, above all, how it can change its comparative advantage in ways that promote productivity and higher standards of living rather than exacting increased efforts for uncertain returns.

Further reading

For more about the relation between trade integration and economic structure, particularly with respect to its importance for poverty reduction in low-income countries, see UNCTAD (2002) *The Least Developed Countries Report 2002. Escaping the Poverty Trap*, New York and Geneva, United Nations. Chapter 3 'Patterns of trade integration and poverty' (pp.69–100) and Chapter 4 'Commodity export dependence, the international poverty trap and the new vulnerabilities' (pp.137–66) are especially relevant.

A useful reflective reading on structural adjustment in Africa is Toye, J. (1994) 'Structural adjustment: context, assumptions, origin and diversity' in Van der Hoeven, R. and Van der Kraaij, F. (eds) *Structural Adjustment and Beyond in Sub-Saharan Africa: Research and Policy Issues*, The Hague, Ministry of Foreign Affairs (DGIS) in association with London, James Curry / Portsmouth, N.H., Heinemann, pp.18–35.

Finally, to read more about the plight of agriculture under economic reforms in Tanzania, you may want to browse through Ponte, S. (2002) *Farmers and Markets in Tanzania. How Policy Reforms Affect Rural Livelihoods in Africa*, Oxford, James Curry / Dar Es Salaam, Mkuki na Nyota / Portsmouth, N.H., Heinemann.

Chapter 12 The politics of autonomy and sovereignty: Tanzania's aid relationship

Samuel Wangwe

1   Introduction

Chapter 10 examined, across a broad sweep of African post-colonial experience, the political debates concerning the role of the state under changing economic circumstances. It traced how the very possibility of state-led developmentalism in Africa was challenged in the years of structural adjustment. Chapter 11 explored the economics of structural adjustment and aid-dependence, and the nature of national economic vulnerability, using the example of Tanzania. I now examine, also from a Tanzanian viewpoint, a political issue at the centre of Chapter 10: the engagement of aid donors – both governments and multilateral institutions – in the process of redefining the role and purpose of the African state.

I argue that the sovereignty of the Tanzanian state has been redefined and reconstructed through the actions of aid donors and their relationships with internal political forces in Tanzania, between 1980 and 2000. The politics of this process can be understood as a struggle over the autonomy of the Tanzanian state to decide on policy options, and traces both the loss of this autonomy and the attempt by the Tanzanian state to regain its autonomy and voice in the international arena. The reshaping of the state and its approach to development in these years is profound, but it is not definitive: as I write this chapter in early 2003 the rethinking and renegotiating I describe later in this chapter is continuing.

Section 2 examines and develops the concepts of sovereignty and autonomy from earlier chapters. Section 3 recaps the nature of Tanzanian aid-dependence, discussed in Chapter 11, and examines in more detail the pressure for change in the form of the state. I then trace the politics of sovereignty and autonomy in this aid-dependent state through four historical phases that reflect the periodization in Chapter 10: the early years of aid with few 'strings' attached; the challenge to Tanzanian autonomy in the early 1980s; the structural adjustment programmes and the loss of 'voice' (1986–94); and the late 1990s when there seemed a real prospect of a regaining of voice and leverage despite continuing aid-dependency. The theme throughout is one of *interaction*: the struggle over autonomy involved both

379

internal and external forces – overseas actors and Tanzanian actors, and debates which were conducted within Tanzania and between Tanzanians and outside agencies.

The Tanzanian case

The Tanzanian case is indeed a remarkable one, illustrative of the complexity of the determinants of sovereignty and autonomy of states. Tanzania presents us with a state which, over the course of 20 years, was transformed from one with the ability to pursue distinctive policies in the international and domestic arenas to one which conformed in large measure to prescriptions of powerful, Western-dominated international institutions. Tanzania is one of the most aid-dependent countries in Africa, yet historically, Tanzania has been associated with a high degree of independence in policy making, including its foreign policy.

This is a country which proclaimed the policy of socialism and self-reliance in 1967, six years after attaining political independence from Britain in 1961, and one which was prepared and able to take a firm stand on matters of principle. Tanzania for a time broke diplomatic relations with Britain, the former colonial master, over its policy towards Rhodesia (later Zimbabwe) and forewent economic aid from West Germany over its policy towards (communist) East Germany. Tanzania has been a very active player in the politics of Africa, in particular in the liberation of Southern Africa, and actively engaged in supporting liberation movements in Mozambique, Angola, Rhodesia, Namibia and South Africa, in spite of its weak economic base. Its post-independence leader, Julius Nyerere, commanded widespread international respect and influence.

Domestically, the state initially played a central and highly interventionist role. From 1967 to the early 1980s Tanzania followed a socialist path to development, nationalizing the major means of production and making the bulk of subsequent investments in the public sector. The policy of self-reliance was declared with the intention to shift from aid-dependence to independence. Aid was to be accepted only on the understanding that it was necessary to help Tanzania move through the transition towards self-reliance. The role of aid therefore was essentially to enable Tanzania to build the capacity to stand on its own feet and be independent of other nations. As such Tanzania was expressing an aspiration shared by many other post-colonial states.

By the 1980s, however, the country was still aid-dependent, the socialist development model was coming under stress and pressure to change course was building up. The Tanzanian leadership initially resisted pressure to change its policies; however, the government found itself in a dilemma. Yielding to pressure from the international community would not only amount to losing all the achievements that had been made along the socialist path but would also mean an erosion of its autonomy over policy making and its ability to determine an independent development strategy. However, continuing to hold on to an economic system which was failing to deliver goods and services would progressively lose the political regime domestic credibility and legitimacy.

Tanzania resorted to extensive internal policy debates. It is a country which has a tradition of debates and discussions, not only during the times when it had a multiparty system before 1965 and after 1992, but also when it had a single party system from 1965 to 1992. Nevertheless, from the mid 1980s the influence of the international donors grew to the extent that it was they, not Tanzanians, who were setting the development agenda. Later, in the 1990s, there was an attempt to regain this lost 'voice'. Throughout, a complex interaction of domestic and international players has combined to redefine the purposes and role of the state in Tanzania.

Throughout the period since the early 1980s, Tanzania has remained an independent sovereign state. Yet the changes in development strategy effected over this period have had profound consequences for the nature and activities of the state – the relationship of the state to the domestic economy, the nature of Tanzania's insertion into the international economy, and even the constitution of the state itself. In short, the nature of Tanzania's sovereign statehood has been redefined.

So can a sovereign state maintain an independent voice while it is highly aid-dependent? How do we understand the relationship between internal and external forces in the construction of state sovereignty and the constraint they impose on its autonomy? And what are the implications for sovereignty of a loss of autonomy over development strategy? These are the questions with which this chapter is concerned.

These issues have been played out in the post-independence struggles between the international community and Tanzania over control and ownership of development policy under conditions of high levels of aid-dependence. This chapter narrates the story and interpretation of the developments in aid relations which reflect that struggle. That is, it shows us a struggle over the attempt to maintain a distinctive voice in a context where both internal and external factors contributed to the loss of that voice. In this chapter I demonstrate that the process of making policies or deciding to make major policy shifts is essentially a political process involving domestic and international players.

Tanzania's approach to receiving international development aid is that it is a means to complement its domestic efforts and realize faster development. Aid is therefore regarded as one way of delivering development to its people faster than would have been the case if relying on its domestic resources alone. For its part, the international community sees itself as having the obligation to assist poor countries to develop out of poverty. However, donors are accountable to their own constituencies – donor institutions such as the IMF and World Bank to their member states, and Western states to domestic political actors. They may therefore have their own expectations of what the results of aid should be. Where there is a divergence between recipient and donor of aid, as there has been for much of the time between 1980 and 2000 in Tanzania, aid becomes a crucial arena of contestation over the terms on which aid is given, with far-reaching implications for the receiving state and society. It is an arena in which the capacity of the state to make strategic decisions about the position the country wants to occupy in the global economy and international system, while remaining dependent on foreign aid to achieve its development ambitions, is forged. While for much of the time under consideration, Tanzania has been engaged in adjusting its economy under duress from the principal donors, nevertheless it has striven to regain control over development policy without losing these essential external sources of finance.

The extent to which Tanzania has determined its fate and owned the decision-making process, and indeed how far the economy has in fact been transformed, is debatable. However, its annual rate of growth has been better than that of some countries in sub-Saharan Africa. As Figure 11.1 in Chapter 11 shows, after the dreadful recession years of the mid 1980s, the growth rate rose to around 4 per cent on average from 1985 to the early 1990s. After another dip, it rose again from the late 1990s to above 5 per cent in 2001. In addition, the donors' attitude to aid has changed over time. The poor economic performance of African economies under adjustment led some (donors and recipients) to argue that receiving states in fact needed greater autonomy and 'ownership' of development strategies in the 1990s. This, combined with efforts of states such as Tanzania to regain control and ownership, holds out a prospect of the reclamation of voice. The extent to which this is the case will be reviewed at the end of this chapter.

A participant's assessment

This chapter is written from an African perspective in that I was an active participant in the process I describe and an analyst of the situation, involved in the debates throughout. So this may be taken as a kind of 'participatory research'. I draw extensively from the experience of Tanzania, where I taught at the University of Dar es Salaam from 1972 to 1991. Then, after three years studying several African countries (1991–94) as a researcher at the United Nations University, I returned this time as Executive Director of a policy think-tank in Tanzania, from 1994 to 2002.

During the period when the government was resisting pressure from the donor community to change course on development policy (1981–85), I had the opportunity to interact with policy makers and participate in debates and policy workshops in various efforts to search for alternative policy options. From 1984 scholars from the university, led by economists, organized annual workshops to debate in greater detail the status of economic policy, performance and policy options. At this time, as Dean of the Faculty of Arts and Social Sciences, I was an organizer of the workshops.

After reaching an agreement with the IMF in 1986, the country lost much of its autonomy over policy decisions between 1986 and 1995. Following a crisis in aid relationships in the early 1990s the Tanzanian government started making efforts to reverse this situation (1996–2002). During this period, I contributed to analysis of policy in the struggle to regain the lost ownership of development policy and to respond to the evolving aid relationships. The Economic and Social Research Foundation for which I was Executive Director (1994–2002) was one of the active players in shaping aid relationships. In 2002 the Foundation was formally appointed by the government of Tanzania and donors to co-ordinate initiatives for the independent monitoring of the evolution of aid relationships.

2   Autonomy, sovereignty and the loss of voice

In this section I revisit the meaning of 'sovereignty' and distinguish between a loss of sovereignty and a loss of autonomy, and I begin to apply these concepts to the aid relationship. My argument is that, even if state sovereignty per se is not lost through the aid relationship, the redefinition of sovereignty from outside nevertheless constitutes 'a loss of voice' for the state and the political community it claims to represent, and consequently an undermining of some of the purpose of 'being sovereign'.

Activity 12.1

Review Chapter 5, Section 5.3. What are the key points made about sovereignty?

It follows from the list in the answer to Activity 12.1 that sovereignty is 'socially constructed'. That is, it is the product of the interaction of social agents, such as states, populations, other powers and institutions, and corporate bodies. The varieties of sovereignty, or what we might call different 'forms of sovereignty', can therefore be understood as the product of the 'variety of ways in which states are constantly negotiating their sovereignty' (Biersteker and Weber, 1996, p.11).

It follows that what being sovereign means will vary from state to state and over different historical periods, depending on the particular bundle of claims which states make. Furthermore, for any state, sovereignty is something that faces two ways – inwards toward the domestic sphere and outwards to other states and the international system. The social construction of sovereignty is therefore always the product of an interaction between a state and both domestic *and* international actors about what it has the right to exercise its authority over. In this sense, sovereignty is not a single, absolute, elemental feature of states that they *independently* do or do not possess, but is a *relational* feature of states which always has to be specified in terms of the particular rights and obligations states claim in respect of other actors.

Question

Taking this explanation into account, why do you think the issue of sovereignty arises in the aid relationship between a recipient country and the donors?

The imposition by donors of conditions attached to aid has, as Chapters 10 and 11 suggested, contributed to a quite dramatic reshaping of the states at the receiving end: their constitution, the things that they claim a right to do and their ability to do those things, and their policy choices. For many post-colonial states, therefore, the aid relationship is a central nexus around which the sovereignty of those states is constructed and reconstructed and is a highly significant external constraint on policy options.

On the other hand, the issue of the sovereignty of such states is an acute political issue – the very term 'sovereignty' is part and parcel of the content of political debate around aid. For many states, aid conditionality represents a redefinition from outside of the nature of the state's sovereignty, and consequently a loss of 'voice' for the state domestically and in the international system. For states which emerged from a history of colonial subjugation, such issues are at the very core of the state's identity and purposes in the international system. For states such as Tanzania, which until the 1980s had a prominent and highly distinctive international position, this loss of voice is particularly acute.

Activity 12.2

Now look back at Chapter 10, Section 2.2. How does this issue of the sovereignty of states relate to their autonomy?

Autonomy
Autonomy refers, in an external sense, to the state's ability to rule: its ability to make independent decisions, such as policy choices about economic development strategy.

Chapter 10 explained that, while sovereignty is about rights to authoritative rule, autonomy refers to the ability of states to make independent choices. A denial of sovereignty – a denial of the right of a state to make such choices in the first place, as was the case in the colonial era – removes autonomy. So sovereignty is a necessary condition for autonomous action. But sovereignty is not a sufficient condition for autonomy. There are many constraints on independent choice of policies: lack of resources can make some choices impossible, as can the absence of the technical or bureaucratic capacity to formulate policy options. High costs of one course of action compared to another, and 'informal' influence over policy formation by particular political actors also constrain choices in practice, though they do not imply a loss of sovereignty per se. While all states in this respect operate in the context of some constraint – no state has ever had total freedom of action and all policy choices involve opportunity costs – it is states in the developing world that have been particularly subject to deliberate attempts to restrict their policy choice through aid conditionality.

Question

Which of the two concepts of 'autonomy' explained in Chapter 10 am I using here?

Aid conditionality is an example of the loss of state autonomy in the first sense: autonomy from external pressures. Indeed the debate over the African developmental state, traced in Chapter 10, and the discussion of Indian post-colonial politics in Chapter 6, sharply illustrate the interaction of sovereignty with autonomy in this sense.

The construction of sovereign states in much of the developing world after the Second World War was a product of the interaction between domestic political forces (the nationalist, anti-colonial movements such as India's Congress Party), the retreating colonial powers, and the rise of new anti-colonial norms at the international level. The sovereignty of the new states encompassed many of the basic features of modern sovereignty common to most states in the international system – the supremacy of the state to make laws internally, the sanctity of borders, the recognition of the new states by other states in the international system and so forth.

However, as both Sudipta Kaviraj (in Chapter 6) and Thandika Mkandawire (in Chapter 10) explain, states reclaiming sovereignty from colonial powers made development one of their central purposes. Externally, many developing countries claimed a *right* to determine national development, demanding resources from the industrialized countries, the Bretton Woods Institutions and the UN to realize their development strategies. Internally, this stance was often associated with state claims to a right to control economic resources – through direct production, price controls or controlling the terms of resource flows across national borders. The struggle for sovereign independence from colonial rule was thus seen as a necessary step to exercising autonomy in deciding the strategy for economic and social development.

However, claims to such autonomy *as a right*, were given only partial recognition and support from outside. In international law, states have a generally recognized right to decide on economic policy options. But for a state to exercise such a right with relative freedom, that is, for the state to have effective choice, requires resources, particularly funds for investment in productive capacity, infrastructure and social development. And while donor states generally do profess to share an obligation to support development through development aid, the aid has rarely been given unconditionally. As Oruka has argued, should one state decide to aid another then the donor state is given some kind of mandate to assume the right to decide the terms (Oruka, cited in Juma and Ojwang, 1989).

From the 1980s, as Chapter 10 outlined, aid in the form of grants and loans became highly conditional on agreement by the recipient state to implement far-reaching reforms of economic policy and the re-organization of the administrative apparatuses of the state itself. By deciding to attach strong conditions on aid, donor states and institutions were deliberately tightening the existing constraint on autonomy created by African states' limited domestic resources and their need for development aid. While formally recognizing the right of the recipient state to choose development strategies, donors made it clear that resources to fund development were available in support of some choices and not others.

While the sovereignty of the state was not questioned directly – indeed international donor institutions *require* sovereign states with which to do business – the state's autonomy in making policy choice was tightly constrained. I trace in the next section the pressure from donors to push the role of the Tanzanian state in a 'liberal' direction, relinquishing direct control of resources in favour of more market-based allocation. In such a circumstance, the external sovereignty of the state – its ability to maintain constitutional independence in relation to external sources of authority – remained. But the form of its internal sovereignty was pushed in a liberal direction away from attempts to exert direct, authoritative control over the economy. One might argue that while the state remained sovereign, autonomy was so tightly constrained from outside that some of the *purpose* of being sovereign was lost. The distinctive 'voice' of the state was submerged beneath the demands of powerful external actors and the economic constraints facing the state.

Naeem Inayatullah has argued that such loss is important as it relates to the 'moral and psychological power of independence' or more simply, 'who speaks for whom?' (Inayatullah, 1996, p.73). Conditionality appears to frustrate what those in power in the states concerned, and others, see as the legitimate expressions of national projects – development, self-reliance, independence or whatever. As Inayatullah put it:

> Sovereignty means more than just having access to resources on a territory and being juridically recognized as an equal among equals. In the context of colonialism, it means speaking for and representing oneself ... This sense of self-determination allows for a pride and dignity that were among the greatest losses under colonialism and the greatest virtues of independence.

(Inayatullah, 1996, p.73)

3 The pattern of aid to Tanzania and the pressure for a liberal state

Development co-operation in Africa goes back to the early 1960s, as the independence era was beginning. Tanzania has been a partner in development co-operation from the 1960s and its relationships with donors and the politics of aid have been evolving over time. The evolution of the politics of aid in Tanzania can be categorized into four distinct phases.

The first phase is that of the 1960s and 1970s, when a combination of factors led to Tanzania enjoying a relatively high degree of autonomy in policy making. The period 1981–85 is the second phase, a period of struggle between the government of Tanzania trying to preserve its approach to development and pressure from donors for Tanzania to change. The third phase (1986–95) was a period of defeat, when Tanzania effectively lost much of its control over macroeconomic and development policy. The fourth period (1996–2002) was a period of struggle to regain ownership of policy and reassert Tanzania's voice in negotiations with donors and internally through the consolidation of democracy and the improvement of governance.

In this section, as a background to the narrative of aid politics, I show that changing patterns of aid flows to Tanzania – from whom, how much and in what form aid was received – have been closely associated with the shifting politics of aid and development policy.

During the early post-independence era, Tanzania, like many developing countries, was able to exercise a significant degree of influence over the purposes for which aid was granted. Certainly, aid allocations were influenced by political considerations – Western states directed more aid at countries that were on their 'side' in the Cold War, and former colonial powers biased their aid towards former colonies. After independence in 1961, Tanzania became, and has remained, one of the largest recipients of aid in absolute terms in sub-Saharan Africa, and has received considerably more aid as a percentage of GDP than most other countries in the region.

Figure 12.1 shows the evolution of the net inflow of total official development assistance (ODA) from all donors, in millions of current US dollars, for the period from 1973 to 2001 (the period for which data are available).

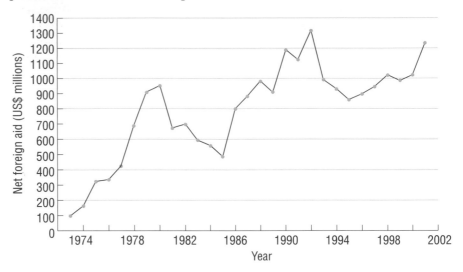

Figure 12.1   Net inflow of official development assistance (US$ millions)

Source: *OECD Report*, various years

Question

Take a careful look at Figure 12.1. Describe the evolution of foreign aid, noting periods of growth and decline. How do those periods relate to the different phases – outlined above – of the evolution of the politics of aid?

There is a noticeable correspondence between the different phases of the politics of aid and the pattern of net inflow of aid. The 1970s – the period in which Tanzania enjoyed a high degree of autonomy in policy making – was characterized by a veritable aid boom, particularly during the years of the industrialization strategy (thereby making the latter possible). This boom ended abruptly in 1980, after which the net aid inflow fell sharply up to 1985. Politically, these years were a period of government resistance to donor pressures for change in economic policy, coupled with donor fatigue (withdrawal of aid).

The subsequent period of structural adjustment – 1986 to 1995 – witnessed a second aid boom, which reached its peak in 1992, after which the inflow of aid declined again. This was the period of aid conditionality backed up by donor funding, but the later years witnessed a quite considerable retreat in donor support. However, in the subsequent phase after 1995, where the government sought to regain ownership of policy in the context of partnerships with donors, there was once more a revival in the inflow of aid. Historically, therefore, the politics of aid largely determined its availability. As we shall see, it also shaped the sources and nature of the aid.

During the 1970s most of the aid flows to Tanzania came from bilateral sources, that is, individual governments. Scandinavian countries were (and remain) important donors of bilateral aid, while donors of multilateral aid contributed an average of about 10 per cent annually of total aid. Much of this aid, as Marc Wuyts explained in Chapter 11, was in the form of project aid. For most of the 1960s and 1970s, assistance to investment projects comprised more than two-thirds of the total aid. Project aid put emphasis on aid to capital investment as a major source of growth. This chimed with early developmental strategies, and was preferred to programme aid by both donor and recipient states for several reasons. First, projects appeared to be easy to plan, design, control and supervise and hence ensured visible results, to which donors and recipients could point, allowing direct accountability. Second, unlike programmes, projects are easy to tie to the procurement of goods and services from the donor, creating benefits for firms in donor countries and raising support for aid (but at the cost of limiting the choice of supplier). Third, projects provided donors with opportunities to bypass national institutions in recipient countries and to pursue their own objectives.

While development strategies emphasized capital investment and donors were supportive of Tanzanian development strategy, donor/recipient interests could be reconciled. The sectoral distribution of aid in the 1960s and the early 1970s was directed to the agricultural and transport sectors, but during the second half of the 1970s the emphasis shifted from agriculture towards industry and energy, reflecting shifting Tanzanian development strategies and the interests of donors.

However, from the 1980s many aspects of the aid relationship changed. One aspect of the aid relation is that different donors have different interests. Part of the autonomy of the state in conditions of aid dependence therefore lies in its ability to increase its room for manoeuvre in policy making by drawing upon different donors to achieve different components of its overall strategy. The ability to play on the different interests of the diverse set of donors was indeed a major characteristic of the Nyerere years.

Historically, Tanzania relied on both multilateral and bilateral donors to obtain aid resources. Tanzania has received aid from over 50 bilateral sources. The Nordic countries (Sweden, Norway, Denmark and Finland) have been the major donors, accounting for over 30 per cent of the country's total ODA receipts between 1970 and 1996. Sweden has provided almost half of that amount for most of this period. The second group of major bilateral

Bilateral aid
Bilateral aid is aid given by one state to another state, and it is allocated according to the priorities of the donor state.

Multilateral aid
Multilateral aid is aid given by multilateral institutions such as the World Bank and IMF, regional development banks, such as the African development bank, and UN bodies such as the United Nations Development Programme. While the funding may originate from individual donor states, it is allocated by the institutions themselves, (in theory at least) according to the rules, procedures and constitutions of the organizations.

donors has been Germany and the Netherlands, each contributing around 8 per cent of total aid over the past 20 years. The third major group consists of Canada, the USA and the UK, each accounting for about 6 per cent of Tanzania's total aid receipts. Italy and Japan became important new donors in the late 1980s. Among socialist countries, the Soviet bloc and China in particular played an important role in the earlier period, but they drastically reduced their aid programmes for Tanzania starting from the 1980s. As I discuss below, the really big change in Tanzania's room for manoeuvre between donors came when the important bilateral donors fell into line with the multilateral agencies in terms of policy conditions on aid from the 1980s onwards.

At first, the stand-off between the government and the IMF and World Bank during the early 1980s provoked increased disenchantment with government policies on the part of bilateral donors. The crisis years of the early 1980s, therefore, came to be characterized by donor fatigue. From the mid 1980s onwards, with the introduction of structural adjustment, the proportion of multilateral aid in total aid also rose.

Such a shift in the sources of aid, from bilateral to multilateral institutions such as the World Bank or IMF, can have a significant effect on the nature of the aid relationship. If one source of aid predominates, the recipient state has less scope to bargain over the conditions on which aid is given; diverse sources of aid give the recipient more choice and leverage. The rising influence of multilateral donors such as the IMF and World Bank from the mid 1980s in Tanzania was partly built on their rising share of aid. After the mid 1980s, the form in which aid was given to Tanzania shifted markedly from project aid to programme aid, as explained in Chapter 11, Section 3.

Question

Look back at Chapter 11, Section 3. Why did this shift occur?

The change came in the midst of deep economic crisis. Donors moved from supporting investment for growth to using aid to support macroeconomic stabilization. Aid to finance balance of payments deficits, in order to allow imports to be sustained and increased, was made conditional on sweeping policy measures to promote a market-led, open economy development model. Donors developed increasingly close monitoring and control of the use of funds and the way the use was accounted for. The debates and negotiations between Tanzania and the donor community around these issues are explored in Section 5.

In political terms, this sharp change in the form and use of aid, and the conditions put upon it, were directed at pushing the role of the state in a liberal direction. Liberalization affects the very nature of the relationship between state and economy. By forcing the state to relinquish economic leadership and control, it creates a constraint on state autonomy that helps to reshape the domestic and international form of sovereignty in a liberal direction. The liberal state no longer claims a right to allocate resources directly, but instead seeks to regulate more at arms length and to provide the framework of law within which markets operate. For aid-dependent states such as Tanzania, aid conditionality gave donor institutions the ability to influence what states try to do in terms of the management of their domestic economies, the form and extent of their insertion into the international economy, and indeed the very political structures of the state itself. In Tanzania, the previous policies of self-reliance and a socialist model of development were an expression of what Tanzania (or rather those who were powerful in Tanzania) defined as 'the national project'. The redefinition of a new 'national project' in which others outside of Tanzania played a crucial role thus represented a challenge to the extent to which Tanzania could 'speak for itself'.

As Chapter 10 makes clear, the Tanzanian experience was quite typical of that of economically vulnerable developing countries facing an economic downturn. They were in a weaker position than before from which to negotiate the 'aid contract'. From the donor side, the dominant philosophies or ideologies about development held by the Reagan and Thatcher administrations in the USA and UK in the 1980s were crucial in shifting the stance of the international community, regarding the type of development that was deemed acceptable, in a liberal direction. Theirs was the ideology underpinning donors' much more robust stance in specifying restrictions on aid that constrained the policy space within which the recipient country could operate. Their influence was mediated through the international community of multilateral and bilateral donors. The 'aid bargain' was thus tilted in a way that limited developing country autonomy, yet was accepted because the need for external funding had increased.

Aid conditionality does not always work as intended, however. Even if conditions are specified on the receipt of aid, they may not be implemented – what has been agreed to formally is circumvented in practice. Furthermore, even if followed, they may have effects unintended by donors or recipients. For these reasons, through the period of structural adjustment, donors revised and extended economic policy conditions into institutional reform of the state itself, leading to a seemingly ever more intrusive influence in developing countries. As Chapter 10 noted, the perceived consequences, including sluggish economic growth and the limitations of imposed policy, have led to a rethink and to talk of 'partnership': the idea of policy reform as a shared project and not something imposed from outside.

Tanzania, once again, became a noted player internationally in this rethinking despite its small size and economic weakness: the scope for real change towards more autonomy of decision making is reflected on in the last section of this chapter.

These debates in the mid to late 1990s in Tanzania occurred during another downturn in the inflow of aid (Figure 12.1). The sectoral pattern of aid shifted as well, towards infrastructure (transport and communications and energy), agriculture (long neglected) and human resources development and health (closely relevant to the new focus on poverty noted in Chapter 10) (Mutalemwa *et al.*, 2000).

Aid, then, provides both potential benefits and dangers for recipient states. You might draw an analogy with international trade as discussed in Part 1, where states may gain from trading by becoming better off yet also become more vulnerable by coming to rely on others in a relationship of interdependence. So, similarly in aid, gains come at a cost of lost autonomy and such potential vulnerability may be exacerbated by the asymmetry of the relationship. States may choose the benefits of additional resources provided by the donor, but also have to negotiate over the conditions attached to such funds. The alternative exists – of doing without international aid – but that too carries the price of reduced funds with which to pursue development objectives.

The issue, therefore, is the terms of the aid contract. I have suggested that the aid contract is influenced by the sources, form and level of aid, and the uses to which it is put. Sections 4 to 7 examine how Tanzania has striven to maintain flows of aid while limiting the loss of autonomy that this threatens. I shall use the concepts of sovereignty and autonomy, and in particular the idea of aid conditionality representing a 'loss of voice' for the recipient state, to investigate Tanzania's political experience of bargaining over the aid contract in the 1980s and 1990s.

In this narrative, a strong theme is the way in which 'external' conditions on aid contribute to, and combine with, domestic policy discussions and political conflicts. While donors may influence the outcome of those processes, they are not the only players in the game. Tanzania's experience is therefore analysed here by examining the complex interaction between the nature of domestic politics and the impact of international politics. These interactions have been complicated by the lack of homogeneity of both the international players and the domestic players, and the shift over time in their relative roles and power relations.

4 The first phase (1967–79): aid with relatively few strings

Aid flows in the form they are known today started in the post-independence period in the 1960s and increased through the 1970s. During this early period aid was allocated to countries on the basis of broad endorsement of the development philosophy adopted, rather than on the basis of detailed policy frameworks and policy prescriptions. Project aid dominated and for Tanzania much of it came from bilateral donors.

The aid contract in this era thus gave significant room for manoeuvre for recipient countries including Tanzania. One reason was that developing countries that had recently thrown off the colonial yoke were forceful in asserting their new-found independence, and to an extent donors respected this. In addition, donors were often less concerned about the internal policies and politics of developing countries than the international balance of forces in the Cold War, creating a space in the international arena for states to voice their independence. This was also, as Chapter 10 argued, a period of optimism in development, when it was thought that an increase in investment in productive capacity, partly funded through project aid, would yield significant results in terms of development.

In the case of Tanzania, the volume of aid grew quickly in this period. In addition to the general international climate just described, there was a coincidence of interest between Tanzania and a number of important donors. Tanzania generally found it possible to attain supplies of external aid without having to seriously modify its development strategy. The trade-off between seeking aid and losing autonomy was less problematic than it later became.

In large part this success was due to Tanzanian development policies of the time. The country's emphasis on self-reliance and growth with equity, the targeting of government programmes on basic needs, and the emphasis on co-operatives and collective villages ('ujamaa' villages, from a Swahili word for family) motivated many donors to extend aid to Tanzania during this period. Tanzania's development policy struck a chord with social democratic governments in the North, notably the Nordic countries, West Germany (under Willy Brandt) and Canada. Tanzanian development policy was also consistent with the 'basic needs' approach to development, which gave priority to needs such as food, shelter, primary health and education and was put forward by the International Labour Office, and it was consistent with the policies that the World Bank was advocating at the time. Indeed, the World Bank doubled its lending programme to Tanzania between 1973 and 1977. The then President of the Bank – Robert McNamara, who was a personal friend of Tanzania's President Nyerere – had adopted a development policy framework of 'growth with equity' which was in line with Tanzania's development strategy.

In sum, Tanzania had a high level of aid-dependence even in this period. However, the combination of a coincidence of choice over the broad thrust of development strategy between Tanzania and donors, and the generally lower level of policy conditionality attached to aid at the time meant that this dependence did not confront Tanzania as a serious constraint on its policy formulation or development strategy. Multilateral and bilateral donors therefore supported Tanzania's development without imposing policy-based conditionalities and without eroding its ability to express the country's own choices about national development.

5   The second phase (1980–85): the challenge to Tanzania's autonomy

During the early 1980s this situation changed drastically. Donor countries such as the USA, UK and West Germany, under new right-wing conservative governments, shifted away from Keynesian interventionist and welfare state-oriented policies towards more pro-market, non-interventionist, neo-liberal policies. The donor institutions too adopted this stance and insisted that recipient countries liberalize their macroeconomic policy. For Tanzania, the shift of attitude started with the IMF which suspended its aid programme with Tanzania in 1980. In the negotiations it soon transpired, to the surprise of Tanzania, that the IMF sought to question the broad thrust of Tanzania's policies rather than negotiate over the use of existing policy instruments to deal with balance of payments problems and the budget deficit. The IMF became increasingly critical of the country's development policies and, following the breakdown of negotiations in September 1980, an increasing number of Western donors argued that aid to Tanzania could not be effective unless the country agreed to redress 'inappropriate' domestic macroeconomic policies (see Chapter 11).

Thinking that the problem was confined to the IMF, President Nyerere went public in criticizing the IMF and rejecting its policy prescriptions. The president made a speech in which he accused the IMF of trying to set itself up as an 'International Ministry of Finance' and rejected their demands. Tanzania then turned to the World Bank for assistance, but although the World Bank had been supportive throughout the 1970s it now refused to support the Tanzanian government. The World Bank indicated that it could provide quick-disbursing aid only if certain policy changes were undertaken and an agreement was reached with the IMF. The IMF demanded a devaluation of the currency by 50 to 60 per cent, a significant reduction of the budget deficit, removal or reduction of consumer and producer subsidies, positive real interest rates, and higher agricultural prices and import liberalization – measures which cut to the heart of Tanzania's development strategy and to which it was not prepared to accede.

Tanzania argued that the source of its economic problems was external rather than internal and lay in the changes in the international economy, such as a rise in the price of oil, a decline in the price it received for its commodity exports, and the wider international economic recession. Yet it remained heavily dependent on aid to deal with the immediate economic problems it faced and to continue to pursue its development aims. Over the next four years (1981–85) Tanzania sought to resist this challenge to its autonomy.

Question

In such a situation, what avenues might be open to a state in Tanzania's position?

Tanzania pursued four routes to try to avoid the choice it faced. First, it formulated its own home-grown recovery programme (1981–82). Second, it invited an independent group of experts to try to find some middle ground between itself and the donors (1982). Third, it sought aid from friendlier donors and to resist the pressure from the 'Bretton Woods' Institutions (BWI: the IMF and World Bank) and their supporters. Fourth, initiatives were taken to engage in internal debates on policy options and on whether to agree with the pressure to change policies or not. We shall now review each of the four initiatives.

5.1 Devising a home-grown programme to deal with economic crisis

In 1981–82 Tanzania designed a home-grown recovery programme known as the National Economic Survival Programme (NESP). The goals stated in the programme were to increase export revenue and to eliminate food shortages through encouraging production, and to reduce public expenditures by tighter state control of spending. However, despite its good intentions the plan did not put forward any credible policy options and instead amounted to little more than exhortations. The plan also needed external support but the IMF claimed that it did not address the areas of policy which it thought needed reform.

For its part, the Tanzanian government's position was that Tanzania was a structurally weak economy and that the remedies proposed by the IMF amounted to dismantling the state's socialist policies. The major cuts in social spending on education, health and water, and the removal of price controls which the IMF proposed, amounted to a far-reaching revision of Tanzania's development strategy and the role of the state in the economy. The government rejected these liberalizing reforms and the IMF, along with most other donors, refused to support the NESP. Implementation of the home-grown strategy therefore failed.

5.2   Finding a middle way

The country was now in a desperate situation with the exchange rate greatly overvalued and exports at very low levels (see Chapter 11). The World Bank and other donors, together with the Tanzanian government, agreed to appoint a Technical Advisory Group (TAG) of experts to try to find some middle ground between the government and donors. I was among those who worked with this group. TAG proposed a structural adjustment programme which entailed a more moderate set of reforms than those demanded by donors, including a more modest devaluation of the currency and some reform of the parastatals: that is, the state-owned enterprises and those enterprises in which the state held a majority stake.

However, internal politics in the Tanzanian state watered down the proposed plan. The leadership in the Ministry of Planning, who had the ear of the president, edited the plan, removing portions which proposed substantial change in domestic policy. In particular, the Minister of Planning, Kighoma Malima, resisted the idea that the parastatals should be restructured and instead argued that the private sector was the source of the problem (presumably by supplying the state sector with overpriced goods and services and engaging in other forms of corruption). As a consequence, the document which TAG presented to the government was diluted so much that its main thrust was distorted. Not surprisingly, the document, in the revised form, was not accepted by the multilateral agencies or by most donors. An agreement was not reached with the IMF and major donors withheld their financial support to the programme.

The lack of external support for this plan underlines a number of important points about the relationship with donors and internal politics in Tanzania. As noted above, the demands of donors amounted to a dismantling of the development strategy followed by the Tanzanian state, and the interventionist role this entailed for the state in the Tanzanian economy. Not surprisingly, many, including influential figures in the state, resisted these demands. However, clearly there was a debate growing inside Tanzania as to what, if any, changes should be made (a debate we return to in the fourth initiative, below) and some independent experts accepted the need for some policy changes.

Furthermore, Tanzania's continuing aid-dependence meant that some alternative policy avenues to those proposed by the multilateral agencies were cut off since they required external finance that was not forthcoming. As a result, aid declined further and so therefore did imports, worsening the level of utilization of productive capacity in industry and therefore leading to a shortage of goods for sale. Furthermore, the sparse foreign exchange that was available was spread too thinly across existing development projects rather than being re-allocated to improve efficiency. As a result, the implementation of the programme did not take off as it did not have the requisite external financial support.

However, the attempt to resist donor pressure in a situation of aid-dependency undermined domestic political support for the government. The worsening shortages prompted increasing criticism of the government. The state, in resisting pressure from outside to liberalize, resorted to ever tighter economic controls to attempt to deal with the crisis. Controls were intensified over the marketing and distribution of goods, over the acquisition of foreign exchange and import licences, and over prices in the domestic economy.

These controls became breeding grounds for new avenues of corruption. Business people, especially those engaged in illicit trade, appeared to have taken control of state organs. The government responded in 1983 with a campaign against those it branded as 'economic saboteurs' and hundreds of suspects were apprehended. A month after the launching of the campaign, Parliament passed the Economic Sabotage (Special Provisions) Act to give legal force to the exercise, later repealed and replaced by the Economic and Organized Crimes Control Act. This repressive clampdown failed in so far as most of those arrested were later released on grounds of insufficient evidence. Corruption continued largely because the fundamental causes of shortages of goods was not addressed, and public discontent with the shortages and repression increased.

In seeking to maintain the state's existing role and purpose in the face of donor demands for economic liberalization, the Tanzanian state had thus become both more interventionist and more repressive. However, maintaining this situation for long was untenable. In 1984 the first moves towards liberalization were taken. The government began to introduce partial trade liberalization measures, starting with freeing the importation of pickup trucks for those who had their own foreign exchange. This experimentation demonstrated that liberalization could reduce goods shortages, adding to domestic support for more liberalization measures. This situation reduced further the credibility of the government's continuing policy of economic control, and put its legitimacy into question, weakening the position of the forces which were opposing domestic policy change.

5.3   Turning to friendlier donors

The third initiative taken was to turn to other donor governments to try to fill the gap left by the cut-off of aid from the BWI. In principle, if a variety of donors follow a variety of different policies, there is more room for recipient states to gain external finance without being subject to the conditionality imposed by some and the restraint on autonomy that this would imply. It was shown in the previous section that Tanzania had traditionally received aid from a wide variety of donors. However, in the early 1980s, a remarkable cohesion began to emerge among Western donors. Through what was termed 'cross conditionality' (bilateral donors making their release of aid dependent on agreement to IMF conditions), the multitude of donor states became transformed into a 'donor community', sharing a relatively unified position in pressing recipient states to reform.

The power relations behind the aid negotiation were thus further tilted towards domination by donors, as individual developing countries found themselves facing a united external body of donors. Tanzania was shocked by this development. The government had turned to the Nordic countries – previously sympathetic to Tanzania's development strategy – but they too were becoming increasingly critical, and wanted Tanzania to reach agreement with the IMF. The government's hope that it could isolate the friendly donors from the multilateral agencies and from the less friendly donors was therefore dashed. What the Tanzanian government only came to realise later was the extent to which the donors had transformed themselves into a community who acted in unison, in pressing Tanzania to undertake a major shift in policy and to adopt the IMF package. At this stage efforts to play off one donor against another could no longer work.

5.4   The resort to internal policy debates

The fourth initiative taken was to engage in substantial internal debates about the possible ways forward. In a context in which the government was resisting change in its policies while donors, led by the multilateral agencies, were insisting on major shifts in domestic policy, struggles and debates about policy reforms raged. Scholars from the University of Dar es Salaam played an important role in these debates and, led by economists, organized annual policy workshops which addressed various policy options. The workshops attracted a broad range of participants, including policy makers, representatives of the ruling party, trade unions and the private sector.

Initially the debaters consisted of three identifiable groups. The first group advocated that the government should adopt the IMF package. The second group advocated continuation of existing domestic policies, a total rejection of the IMF package and blamed the economic problems on external factors. The third group advocated a major policy shift but not to the extent the IMF package was proposing. The debates became very polarized around the issue of whether the domestic policies needed to be changed according to the IMF package or not. As the debate raged, the first and third groups came together to form a more forceful alliance advocating a major policy shift. In the meantime a technical group was working with the government's technical staff and the IMF in trying to soften the hard-line stance of the IMF package, for example proposing a more modest devaluation of the Tanzanian shilling based on economic models deemed more appropriate to the Tanzanian economy at the time.

Finally, in 1986, Tanzania reached agreement with the IMF on an Economic Recovery Programme (ERP – also supported by the World Bank) to run from 1986 to 1989, marking the end of official resistance to a major change in development strategy.

Question

What were the factors pushing Tanzania to come to an agreement with the IMF?

As you have seen, a variety of factors contributed to Tanzania reaching an agreement with donors. The underlying aid constraint which is a basic feature of states such as Tanzania meant that it was very difficult for the government to achieve economic recovery on its own. In addition, the domestic initiatives (the NESP of 1981–82 and the subsequent policies described above) failed to attract external resources as they were perceived not to have gone far enough in shifting the domestic economic policy stance. The debates were taking place at a period of very low inflows of aid resources; once agreement was reached, these flows would rise sharply.

The failure of the earlier initiatives cultivated the ground for acceptance of the ERP of 1986–89. Tanzania was unable to gain support from the friendlier donors and faced a united front of donors – including the Nordic countries – insisting on a substantial change in direction. The worsening economic situation that resulted – shortages and corruption – eroded the domestic credibility of the very policies that the government was seeking to defend in the face of outside pressure. Finally, the thrust of the internal debates, reinforced by the role of the technical groups in reducing the gap between the hard-line stances of the government and the IMF, made agreement possible. The government of Tanzania therefore succumbed to pressure from outside and inside to change policy.

While much of the pressure came from donors, it is worth noting the role of the internal forces which helped to tip the balance. Internally, the fact that domestic voices, especially economists from the University of Dar es Salaam, engaged in policy debates advocating the need to shift the domestic policy stance helped to strengthen the position of those, within government and the ruling party, who wanted change, and weakened the position of those who were resisting any domestic policy change. The positive results of the partial liberalization measures of 1984 added to this. But these internal voices and the technical arguments they formulated, also helped to soften the hard-line stance of the IMF on specific measures such as the magnitude of devaluation.

The fact that there were internal forces which were advocating change was important.

In the end what was adopted was a compromise policy package which was closer to what the IMF had initially proposed than the programmes the government had proposed. In fact the hard-liners within the government felt the agreement was a sell-out while the hard-liners within the IMF felt the same. Some circles within the IMF had wanted Tanzania to be treated more harshly, partly to avenge the unprecedentedly strong public critique that President Nyerere had made of the IMF, and partly because the IMF believed in a 'shock-therapy' policy approach. With hindsight, some of us who were advocating a major policy shift on technical grounds did not recognize at that time that the adoption of the new policy package would entail the degree of loss of voice in decision making over domestic policy and the development agenda that then occurred, as we shall see in the next section.

6 The third phase (1986–94): the loss of voice

The agreements with the multilateral agencies in 1986 – a standby agreement with the IMF and a structural adjustment programme with the World Bank – helped to restore donor confidence. Under the ERP, a broad range of policies was adopted aimed at liberalizing internal and external trade, unifying the exchange rate, reviving exports, stimulating domestic saving and restoring fiscal sustainability. The ERP met with strong donor support. Bilateral aid was resumed leading to a second aid boom, which peaked in 1992. The agreement with the IMF was renewed in 1987, 1988 and 1990. In 1989, the reforms entered a second phase under ERP II (1989–92). This second wave of reforms continued earlier efforts at trade and exchange rate liberalization and macro-economic stabilization, but was widened significantly to include institutional reforms in the banking system, agricultural marketing, the parastatal sector and the civil service, together with a targeting of the social sectors.

The period 1986–94, when three-year economic recovery programmes were being implemented, was one where donors effectively muffled Tanzania's voice. The state seems to have conceded defeat in its struggle with donors and its capacity to determine the course of policy developments had been eroded. The government was locked into the three-year programmes in which the release of aid resources was conditional upon meeting tight, closely monitored, implementation schedules. In terms of policy formulation, the period 1986–94 was essentially one of rolling back the state and rolling forward the donor community led by the BWIs.

Question

Look back at the discussion of the concepts of autonomy and sovereignty in Section 2. What does the above account say about Tanzania's autonomy and sovereignty in the period in question?

During this period Tanzania's autonomy was at its lowest ebb. The government was preoccupied with meeting conditions on aid that were required to renew the agreement from time to time, so that resource inflows could be maintained. These developments were the consequence of a weak and aid-dependent economy and its implications for autonomy in policy making and development strategy. One consequence of the policy reforms that have been pursued in Africa under the leadership of the multilateral institutions has been the loss of autonomy in policy making and even in defining the development agendas of African countries. In the case of Tanzania, during the period of economic reforms, some essential macroeconomic stabilization was achieved and macroeconomic management tightened up (Chapter 11), but at the same time domestic ownership of the policy agenda was eroded considerably. With or without intending it, the policy-making machinery paid so much attention to meeting targets agreed between the government and the BWIs that the policy-making process itself – in principle a collaborative effort – became in practice dependent on external agencies.

In terms of sovereignty, the picture is more complex. Donor institutions and governments require sovereign states with which to do business: it is with governments of sovereign independent states that donor agencies such as the IMF and World Bank make deals, agree projects and provide loans. However, Tanzania's constitutional independence was not being explicitly challenged. What the Tanzanian state sought to do, even in the domestic arena (that is, to pursue a socialist development agenda based on direct state allocation of resources under the control of a single ruling party), was under fairly sustained assault, effected through the levers of influence afforded to donors by Tanzania's aid-dependence. In turn, because of the particular conditions on aid – conditions which specified that the Tanzanian economy should be liberalized – the very nature of the relationship between state and economy in Tanzania, and the role of the state in Tanzania's development, was being reshaped. The exercise of sovereign independence was therefore being pushed in a liberal direction (Section 3). However, we should also note that internal forces were at work as well as external. The (re)construction of the form of Tanzania's sovereignty in this period thus included both internal and external actors.

Policy relationships began to change from 1993 onwards. During 1993–94 relations between the government and major donors deteriorated seriously over disagreements concerning the domestic mobilization of resources and use of aid. The government had, in the donors' view, failed to increase tax collection efforts, and had failed to collect the local currency payments required from importers in return for foreign currency allocated to support imports (the so-called 'counterpart funds'). Donors argued that their aid resources were not being utilized effectively and there were increasing suspicions of corruption.

Donors started to question the effectiveness of their aid, for example, in evaluation studies carried out by the Nordic countries and The Netherlands in 1993 and 1994. The government's commitment to reform was questioned and failure to conclude a new agreement, called the Enhanced Structural Adjustment Facility (ESAF), with the IMF in 1994 worsened donor fears. The government, on its part, felt that the donors' demands were often unrealistic and too intrusive in matters that were essentially domestic. In other words, the government felt that the erosion of autonomy had gone too far and that the low level reached was no longer tolerable. The shift of accountability for policy from its own people to the donor community had gone beyond what was acceptable and was causing a real threat to their own position in the eyes of local constituencies. A stop to further erosion was to be applied.

The Tanzanian government and one of the Nordic donors now took an initiative that came to have a high international profile. Denmark commissioned an independent group of local and international advisers to investigate how the climate of confidence between the two sides could be restored. The group was headed by Professor Gerald Helleiner, a well-known Canadian economist with long experience of African policy debates. Helleiner commanded respect and was acceptable to both the government and donors. The report that the group produced in June 1995 – the Helleiner Report (Helleiner *et al.*, 1995) – became an important policy document for both the donors and the government, strongly influencing the evolution of aid relationships in Tanzania.

7   The fourth phase (1995–2002): regaining voice?

The concerted attempt from the mid 1990s to re-formulate the aid relationship between Tanzania and international donors, symbolized as well as partly shaped by the Helleiner Report, was driven by a number of factors. These encompassed linked developments in donor policies and aid delivery, and in the political system in Tanzania. I will outline these factors before reviewing how the changed context played out in Tanzania's aid relationship.

7.1 Changes in the international context

In the second half of the 1990s, the multilateral agencies took the lead in reconsidering their policy stance of the 1980s and the conditions they had applied to aid. Donors had already become more concerned with the effectiveness of aid, and had given increasing attention to institutional reforms of the state – what has been referred to as the 'governance agenda' – to sit alongside the reforms to macroeconomic policy. This signified an admission that structural adjustment in its original form was not delivering development and there was a need for a return to development issues.

Now, however, donors began to question how far the conditionality relationship – demanding recipient countries adopt certain policies before aid is released – actually achieved the results intended. Donors began to talk of the need for recipient states to actively 'own' the policies being implemented. This meant that the aid relationship, so donor rhetoric maintained, should be based on 'partnerships' between donor and receiving state. This rethinking of their previous policies, despite being something of a *volte face* in relation to previous practice, allowed donors to be more flexible and responsive to recipient states' initiatives. In Tanzania this contributed to an improvement in aid relationships.

Furthermore, donors shifted their emphasis on the purpose of aid from stabilization and adjustment (and ultimately economic growth) to 'poverty reduction'. This shift was expressed in particular by the OECD (1996) and by the World Bank in its proposals for a Comprehensive Development Framework, and it allowed development issues which had been sidelined by the earlier focus on macroeconomic reform – some such as health and education familiar from the 'basic needs' framework of earlier days – to come back on the agenda.

These two concerns, with 'ownership' and with poverty relief, affected the way aid was delivered. Section 3 noted that for Tanzania, as for many other countries, programme aid had grown in importance relative to project aid in the 1980s and 1990s as macroeconomic reforms were promoted. Towards the end of the 1990s developing countries were encouraged to formulate Poverty Reduction Strategies and submit Poverty Reduction Strategy Papers (PRSPs) to the multilateral institutions. PRSPs were intended to be the product of inclusive consultations between the government and a variety of 'stakeholders' in society – opposition parties, private sector actors and non-governmental organizations – to outline a comprehensive package of policies and development projects to which donors would then give support.

As discussed below, the reality somewhat qualified this rosy picture. Nevertheless, PRSPs reflected the new donor rhetoric of partnership and ownership and became one of the key arenas in which the aid relationship with the BWIs was played out. In addition, so long as donors felt they could trust the transparency of the state's administration of aid, and that it could demonstrate accountability as to the uses of aid, programme aid could be further increased through direct contributions from donors to the state's budgets. This new aid picture implied both a new kind of relationship with external donors and a new kind of relationship between the Tanzanian state and domestic society.

That this could be suggested owed much to the wave of political liberalization that occurred in developing country political systems in the early 1990s. The end of the Cold War and the collapse of one-party states in Eastern Europe and the Soviet Union had had a widespread impact. Some donors also began to argue more openly that developing countries should democratize and institute multiparty systems of governance, as well as giving more force to longer standing demands for respect of human rights and civil liberties. The experience of life under adjustment also weakened the hold on power of some of the one-party states in Africa. These external forces therefore combined with already existing internal campaigns for democratic reform in many states and led to some far-reaching changes in how many countries were ruled.

As these broad changes played out in Tanzania, they contributed to some significant changes in the nature of the state's relationship with international donors.

7.2   Changing aid relationship in Tanzania

The effectiveness of aid came to be an issue of debate in the discourse of development and discussions of the role of aid in development. The impact of aid – especially relatively large amounts of aid – is mediated through the organizations that manage it and the institutions that it affects. The capacity of these institutions and the human resources for running them often falls short of requirements.

There are two approaches to this problem in the context of Africa. The first approach posits a pessimistic view about the capacity of African states and of donors to change their ways of managing aid, and their capacity to improve governance and management of development. According to this approach, if institutions are problematic, as they frequently are in Africa, aid can undercut rather than hasten development. Since reforms to the management of large amounts of aid cannot be implemented effectively, the policy proposal for both donors and recipients of aid is to reduce dependence on aid.

The second approach posits an optimistic view about the capacity of African states and donors to learn from past failures, to change their ways of managing aid and to improve governance and management of development.

Only if aid is seen to be effective can more of it be justified in the initial phases, in order to build the capacity to manage the economy and manage a transition towards less aid in future periods. The implication is that aid management needs to change considerably from past practices on the part of recipients and donors alike. The interaction between aid and institutional learning by the recipient is important, and has to be cultivated in a way that will promote institutional capacity building rather than capacity erosion. The Helleiner Report (Helleiner *et al.*, 1995), adopted both by the government of Tanzania and donors, essentially opted for this second approach as the way forward.

Based on the Helleiner Report and following a change of government in November 1995, concerted efforts were made to redefine the aid relationship, through a dialogue between the government and donors initiated in 1996. This was followed by an agreement with the Nordic countries in September 1996 and a few months later (in January 1997) between the government and its development partners to set out jointly a programme to redefine the terms of their development co-operation. The set of 'agreed notes' stated, among other things, that there was a need to ensure enhanced Tanzanian government leadership in development programming, and increased transparency, accountability and efficiency in aid delivery. This initiative to change the relationship between donors and the government of Tanzania resulted in a Partnership Agreement in which a list of fundamentals was specified: the need for the government to produce a policy platform; adherence to democracy and human rights; the fight against corruption and for good governance; an emphasis on macroeconomic stability and domestic resource mobilization; and the focusing of government activities on specified 'core' functions such as infrastructure development, basic services for those on low incomes and creating a regulatory framework with complementary roles for civil society and the private sector.

In this new aid situation, government dialogue with donors and with 'stakeholders' outside government such as non-governmental organizations and private businesses, increased. This was manifested in a more participative approach to budget management in which accountability and transparency were improved. Donors, civil society organizations, the private sector and individual citizens were able to have their say concerning budgetary priorities.

The same was true of the consultative mechanisms that have grown up around the Poverty Reduction Strategy (PRS) and its aid-based budgetary support, for those participating in this process. There were efforts to increase the domestic 'ownership' of aid projects and programmes in different sectors such as health, and to improve the co-ordination of aid between different donors contributing to provision in particular sectors. The aim has been to channel external support through the government budget and through mechanisms of co-ordination that involve the government in prioritizing and creating policy coherence, in return for a transparent accounting process that allows donors to track the use of aid. This activity is a mix of changes in technical budget management associated with potentially a real shift in the balance of political leverage over the uses of aid towards the government.

As will be apparent from this review, the redefinition of how dialogue around aid was conducted changed not only the relationship with donors, but also that between the government and domestic political actors. That this was possible was due to the radically changed domestic political situation in the 1990s.

7.3   Political change, multi-party politics and aid

As noted above, a series of international changes helped to promote a wave of political liberalization across the developing world, particularly in Africa in the early 1990s. In Tanzania, these combined with already existing groups campaigning for multi-party politics. The Tanzanian response was to set up a commission to look into the possibility of moving to a multiparty system. In fact, of those surveyed 80 per cent wanted to maintain single-party politics. However, in the event it was decided to move to a multiparty political system on the grounds that if 80 per cent approved the ruling party then they would have the option of continuing to express their loyalty to it, while multi-party politics would also give the remaining 20 per cent the right to choose their preferred parties.

Multiparty politics was introduced in 1992 with further elections held in 1995 and 2000 during which the former ruling party – the CCM (*Chama Cha Mapinduzi*; Revolutionary State Party) – remained in power. At the same time there were other moves towards political liberalization, including more freedom for the mass media and organized groups in civil society.

However, the extent to which these changes led to a democratic system is debatable. Many of the new parties (fourteen in all) did not distinguish themselves clearly on grounds of policy, providing no alternative agenda to that of the government. Many also lacked genuine internal democracy. In addition, corruption affected the internal choice of party candidates. This was most pronounced in the ruling CCM (Mpangala, 2002) which, as the most dominant party, may have been perceived by many as the party offering the best prospects for entry into desired political positions. This led to some of the better qualified candidates stepping down in favour of better financed opponents (Kawa, 2002).

The move to multiparty politics has also changed the base of political support of the ruling party. Prior to economic liberalization, the ruling party relied on economic 'rents' generated by the economic wing of the party; this meant that import licences could be obtained to import goods at the official exchange rate and sell them at market prices. This activity created a parallel (unofficial) market exchange rate, at which the goods were sold, which was a multiple of the official exchange rate. It made huge profits for those involved.

Activity 12.3

Look back at the discussion of 'rent seeking' in Chapter 10. Is this an example of 'rent seeking' in the sense in which it is used there?

Trade liberalization and freeing of the exchange rate killed that source of financing. Furthermore, under more transparent government budgeting, the ruling party could not obtain as many funds as they had been used to acquiring under less scrutinized budgetary processes. New rules allocated government funds to parties according to the number of seats they had in Parliament. Under these new conditions alternative sources of financing for the ruling party had to be sought. The private sector, and especially those parts of it which gained from liberalization policies, became the one major target of fund raising. The Asian business community, which otherwise had a very limited role in Tanzanian politics, was one source, sponsoring candidates so that it had 'friends' in government and generating support for policies from which it benefited.

In addition, multiparty politics opened the way for external actors to become involved. Allegations were made that some parties received funding from allies in other countries, including Europe and the Middle East, and that that funding might undermine the extent of accountability of politicians to their local constituencies. This practice gave space to foreign actors to influence the decision-making processes within the government and the political parties. Opposition parties also resorted to appealing to donors to intervene against government actions they opposed, instead of mobilizing the support of local constituencies for this purpose. This suggests that political parties attach considerable weight to the influence of donors on the government and the ruling political party. Indeed, donors' contribution to financing elections was noted in the analysis of the 2000 elections (Chambua *et al.*, 2002).

Perhaps paradoxically, given that a liberalized political system is necessary for the new inclusive partnership approach to aid to work, the operation of multiparty politics also worked to limit some of these new developments. This particularly affected the extent to which programme aid replaced project aid. The government had expressed an official preference for programme aid and budget support over project aid. However, there were forces on both sides (Tanzania and donors) limiting this shift and indeed working against it.

Many donors have always tended to see project aid as more conspicuous and more amenable to accountability to their constituencies in their home countries. It is easier to attach a flag to specific projects.

However, on the Tanzanian side, not only did some of the 'sectoral' or 'spending' ministries prefer project aid, going against the wider government stance, but many politicians did too. Indeed, many politicians approached donors individually and requested them to fund specific projects in their own constituencies. The projects are more conspicuous, in terms of showing what the political representatives have done for their constituencies, than programme aid. To have conspicuous projects to show enhances their political positions and chances of re-election are greater. Politicians therefore need donor-financed projects in their constituencies in order to show results. The power an individual has in attracting donor projects becomes political capital in the eyes of their respective constituencies.

This situation complicated the balance between accountability to the electorate and that to the financing donors. It is in this context that scholars such as Mafeje (cited in Mpangala, 2002) have argued that liberal democracy can give rise to what is called 'compradorial' democracy. That is, it can create a political class that benefits from both its position of power within the country and also from its relationship with international capitalism or the international aid donors. The politics of aid therefore is likely to influence the speed at which the forms of aid will shift from project aid to programme aid and budget support – and hence towards more government policy control.

7.4   Increasing autonomy?

Question

Do you think these changes constitute a rebuilding of the autonomy of the Tanzanian state?

There are some reasons for optimism. The 'partnership' framework has endorsed the idea of recipients and donors jointly determining the development agenda, and this constitutes genuine progress towards increasing Tanzanian state influence from its lowest level in the late 1980s and early 1990s. Sharing responsibility is more effective than the previous case of complete donor domination, even if the donors still largely do exercise dominance.

Furthermore, the pattern of donor collaboration, which goes as far as pooling some aid resources between donors, and jointly putting aid through the budgetary mechanisms, does increase and perhaps lock in programme aid, and has been reinforced by visible improvements in budget management. So it seems there is some assertion of government autonomy, and activity as a sovereign partner in policy making and aid management.

Hence, in principle, the combination of a revised approach to aid delivery from donors emphasizing the need for ownership by recipient countries, coupled with internal political changes allowing greater participation in discussions around aid, should provide a basis on which countries such as Tanzania could regain their national 'voice'. On this basis an approach in which the recipient country would first develop its own development strategy, programmes and projects, primarily in consultation with its own population but also in dialogue with donors, could be achieved. It would then present its plans to the donors who would put unrestricted funding into a common pool (Kanbur *et al.*, 1999).

The common pool of development assistance together with the recipient's own resources would then finance the overall development strategy. Such national control of a state's own development programmes could ensure effective donor co-ordination whereby aid programmes would fit into national priorities. At that point true ownership and leadership would have been achieved. Is such an approach a possible way of reworking the aid bargain, so that the trade-off between loss of autonomy and access to aid is less unfavourable to Tanzania?

There are a number of factors that might militate against such an achievement. The new approach to aid which emerged in the later 1990s and the process of political liberalization not only changed the relationship between state and external donor but also redefined how the national 'voice' was itself constructed and expressed. Participation of the broader sections of stakeholders is an important dimension of the new definition of ownership of development strategy. To that effect, policy makers have been opening up the policy-making process. The degree of accountability has been enhanced by the establishment of a free press and the opposition parties, and broader participation in the policy-making process has been given greater attention.

In addition, in Tanzania, the preparation of key policy documents in the post-1995 period has been participatory, engaging the civil society, private sector and other actors outside government. However, the limiting factor is the capacity of the actors outside government. The civil society actors and the private sector have yet to build the capacity to articulate their positions from a point of strength. In addition, the approach to participation is rather weak in terms of its institutionalization in democratic institutions of elected representatives. If aid relationships are to be changed in a more sustainable way then the role of democratic institutions must be enhanced and participation processes will need to continue to be strengthened, especially among democratic institutions in the country.

Furthermore, many groups in civil society, particularly NGOs and consultants on policy matters, are themselves highly dependent on donors. In their work they are not likely to be critical of the donor practices provided they get the resources they need to run their business. Private sector associations also depend on donor support for running their operations. Some of these business associations have some financially strong members but as associations they are financially weak. They therefore seek donor funding to help run their offices.

For the government's part, too, a tension exists between the development of genuinely nationally-owned strategies and the need for these to be endorsed by the boards of the World Bank and the IMF. This has been particularly apparent in the poverty reduction strategy process whereby some governments were preparing PRSPs with a preconceived view of what was likely to be endorsed by the Washington institutions in order to gain access to aid. Here the danger is that endorsement from external donors will still take priority over that of domestic stakeholders. In this respect, for voice to be reclaimed donors will have to adjust aid policies, procedures and delivery mechanisms so as to allow national ownership to occur.

8 Conclusion

Let me return to my point of departure. The single most important limiting factor to genuine Tanzanian state ownership of the development agenda remains the high degree of aid-dependence with which I started this chapter. In Tanzania the government remains highly dependent on aid for a substantial part of its recurrent budget and for a very high share of its development budget. Government officials are very much aware of this situation and know that without foreign aid many programmes would not be implemented and their survival would be at stake. This awareness makes officials shy away from taking ownership as seriously as they might. In fact there is a limit to how much they can push the ownership agenda when the government is so dependent on donors for its budget. Unless the high degree of aid-dependence is addressed, it will be very difficult to change substantially the aid relationships to achieve genuine ownership.

The central theme of the last three chapters has been the international and national determinants of state capability – a concept first introduced in Chapter 5. The African viewpoint of Part 4 has illuminated the importance of international constraints on the content and exercise of national sovereignty, while emphasizing the ways in which international agencies interact with national economic management and domestic political processes. The relevance of macroeconomic management and economic policy-making capacity to the nature of the constraints on the autonomy of state action has been traced through the Tanzanian case, as has the direct involvement of international agencies and aid donors in reshaping an African state. For African states such constraints are crucial. This is partly because of the far-reaching effects that such restructuring has for those living within those states. But it is also because, as Inayatullah put it, much of the *purpose* of attaining sovereign independence is to act and speak for oneself. These lessons have much wider relevance than the African subcontinent; the social construction of state autonomy through international political and economic interactions affects all states. The African perspective helps us to see these processes more clearly.

Further reading

A useful collection of essays on the social construction of state sovereignty is Biersteker, T.J. and Weber, C. (eds) (1996) *State Sovereignty as Social Construct*, Cambridge, Cambridge University Press. See especially the Introduction and the essay by Naeem Inayatullah.

For a World Bank view on Africa's prospects and aid see World Bank (2000) *Can Africa Claim the 21st Century?*, Washington, DC, World Bank.

For a study of different experiences of adjustment in Africa, including a number of case studies, see Engberg-Pederson, P., Gibbon, P., Raikes, P. and Udsholt, L. (eds) (1996) *Limits of Adjustment in Africa: The Effects of Economic Liberalisation 1986–1994*, Copenhagen and Oxford, Centre for Development Research in Association/James Currey.

A study of Tanzania's changing aid relationship is Mutalemwa, D., Noni, P. and Wangwe, S. (2000) *Managing the Transition From Aid Dependency: The Case of Tanzania*, Nairobi, AERC/ODC Project on Managing the Transition from Aid in Sub Saharan Africa.

Part 5 International collective action

In Part 1, we drew a contrast between models of anarchy and of international governance. Both economics and politics use models of anarchy, and both are concerned in different ways with problems of governance of international relationships. Part 1 concentrated on the exposition of theories of anarchic order. In Part 5 we now pick up the contrasting theme in its own right, and examine economic and political theories of collective action.

The problem of collective action arises when individual decision making, of the sort examined in models of anarchic action, *cannot* achieve our objectives. We cannot, for example, individually ensure that we are protected from infectious diseases. That protection requires not only our own decision to be vaccinated but also the vaccination decisions of others and the development of the public health infrastructure to identify, diagnose and organize the response to outbreaks and sources of infection. Individual states, however militarily strong, cannot individually protect the stocks of fish in the sea for their citizens to consume; that involves co-operation between countries and abiding by agreed rules for fishing. Individual states cannot close the hole in the ozone layer or stop global warming: only international collective action could do that. The world is full of such collective action problems, and globalization increases the number of such dilemmas that cross national borders.

It is perhaps not surprising that it is in the analysis of collective action that economics and politics come closest together. In trying to understand how people and states can work together, how decisions can be taken that require co-operation, and how institutions can be created to implement those decisions, economics needs to take into account the political processes of co-operative action while politics needs to take on board the importance of material and strategic incentives. Both disciplines use the technique of game theory to explore the incentives that facilitate or block collective action. Both recognize that the resolution of collective action problems goes beyond getting the incentives right, into the fields of political organization and the strategic and cultural determinants of behaviour.

In Chapter 13 Judith Mehta and Rathin Roy examine the theory of collective action. They introduce game theory, and show how it can be used to understand how collective action problems arise. Game theory also helps us to distinguish different types of collective action dilemmas, and hence to understand how they might be resolved, and why some are much knottier than others. The authors show how game theory can be applied to a very wide range of international collective action problems, from coping with international epidemics to trying to avoid nuclear war. They go on to identify the limitations of the game theoretic analysis, and to outline a range of approaches to overcoming collective action dilemmas at the international level.

In Chapter 14 William Brown draws on this analysis to tackle one of the very largest and most contested of those dilemmas: global warming. It uses an explanation of this particular case to show how the tools of game theory can help to shed some light on collective action problems. The focus of the chapter is on the failure of states to agree a collective response to the challenge posed by global warming. Aspects of this failure, particularly the withdrawal of the United States from the Kyoto Protocol (the main international agreement dealing with global warming), are illuminated by deploying two of the games introduced in Chapter 13. The games are also used to contrast the failure of collective action on global warming with the much more successful response to the ozone problem. However, as well as illustrating some of the barriers to co-operation posed by global warming, the chapter also discusses some of the limitations of the game theory approach to analysing global warming.

Chapter 13 The collective action problem

Judith Mehta and Rathin Roy

1   Introduction

States, like people and firms, make choices among mutually exclusive alternatives. People choose between working, studying or holidaying; between saving and consuming. Firms go for what appear to be the most profitable export markets, or focus limited investment budgets on providing services for home consumers. States decide where to procure guns or supplies for government hospitals. These can all be thought of as 'private' choices. That is, these are decisions that can be made individually, and in a manner independent of the choices of others, even though over time one decision feeds back onto what others can do (by changing market supply, for example, or by creating a welfare system that other states wish to emulate or avoid). Economists, and realist theorists in politics, root their analysis in this world of private choice.

But there are some choices that an individual cannot make alone. If you or your government want an unpolluted environment, then you and they will have to co-operate with others. If another large pollution-emitting state has no intention of reducing emissions, then you cannot make your choice to breathe clean air. If you want your grandchildren to eat cod, then states with fishing fleets will have to act collectively to rescue the remaining stocks of codling. A cure for AIDS or a vaccine for a new infectious disease may require firms to pool research resources, or to work co-operatively with governments and charitable trusts. Choices like these, then, are *collective*, not private choices.

In other words, collective choices are those we cannot make alone. They pose questions about who should make the decisions, how, and in whose interests. When there are conflicts of collective choice, how should they be resolved? These problems of *collective action* are the topic of this chapter, and the answers to these questions are absolutely fundamental in shaping our lives and those of others in the communities in which we live.

1.1 Public goods

So what is it that distinguishes the objects of collective choice from private goods? An example may help to answer this question, so let us look at the ozone problem. Ozone is an unstable gas which forms a layer in the earth's stratosphere, operating as a 'shield' absorbing short wave UV(B) radiation. Without ozone, increased levels of radiation from the sun would cause mutations in cell structures of human, animal and plant cells. Removal or depletion of the ozone layer poses the risk of increased cancers and cataracts and disruption of the immune system in humans, extinction of many species, and serious disruption to the food chain through effects on the photosynthesis process in phytoplankton (the base of the food chain in the oceans).

In 1974, scientists claimed that a group of chemicals – chlorofluorocarbons or CFCs – could be causing the depletion of the ozone layer. CFCs were used in a wide range of applications from aerosols, refrigerators and air conditioning systems to cleaning products and foam insulation and, being extremely stable, remain in the atmosphere for up to 100 years. Later discoveries added other gases to the list of ozone-depleting substances. However, because of their usefulness, production of CFCs rose rapidly in the 1960s and 1970s (Benedick, 1991). While some states, led by the USA, took some measures to control CFC production, the calls for international co-operation to tackle the issue were initially frustrated. The issue became one of the most high-profile environmental collective action problems of the 1980s, and is analysed further in Section 6.

Question

What characteristics of the ozone layer distinguish it from private goods (the objects of private choice)?

No one owns it. The only way to have it is to share it. My benefits from an intact ozone layer do not reduce your benefits: on the contrary, once it is intact everyone can benefit at once. Nor can I prevent you from benefiting if I benefit.

Economists have slightly more technical terms for those characteristics. Goods like the ozone layer are:

■ *non-rival* in consumption: that is, my consumption does not affect your consumption

■ *non-excludable*: that is, no one can be prevented from consuming it once it is produced.

These characteristics imply two more. These goods are:

- *joint in supply*: that is, producing it provides for everyone

- *not congested*: that is, additional people consuming the benefits do not reduce your benefits.

Things which display all these characteristics – and the ozone shield is a very good example – are called public goods. The ozone layer can be called a global public good, affecting everyone on the planet.

Public goods
Public goods are non-rival and non-excludable.

> *Question*
>
> Think of some more examples of global public goods.

This is not very easy. Big environmental goods such as a stable climate come in this category. Others, such as vaccination for highly infectious diseases, are partly 'public' (my being vaccinated increases your chances of avoiding the disease, and I cannot stop you benefiting even if I wish to), and partly 'private' (vaccination benefits me directly, and is a service with limited capacity, so my being vaccinated might shut you out until too late). But eradication, for example of smallpox, is a global public good. Stocks of codling are owned by nobody, but more for me is certainly less for you: it is the restraint from consumption, to allow stocks to recover, that is the public good. The greater the extent to which a particular good or service exhibits the above characteristics, the greater its degree of 'publicness'.

Activity 13.1

Think of some global 'public bads': things that display the above characteristics on a global scale, but are bad for us all.

1.2   Disentangling collective action dilemmas

To decide how much of a public good is to be produced, we need a process of collective decision making – and that may mean we need an institution of some kind to organize and police the process. We explore this collective action problem in several stages.

First, we examine a classic statement of the collective action problem: the 'Tragedy of the Commons' (Section 2). We then use game theory to distinguish three key types of collective choice dilemma, as follows:

1   There is general agreement about the most desirable outcome, but the incentives facing states or other actors are such that independent action leads to an undesirable outcome.

2   There is general agreement about the most desirable outcome, but states or other actors have insufficient confidence in the likely behaviour of others to achieve that outcome.

3   There is disagreement about the most desirable outcome, and the problem is to find an outcome to the conflict that is not disastrous.

We introduce three different games that allow us to explore these different dilemmas, applying them to problems of international collective action (Sections 3–6).

We then go on in Section 7 to examine what can be done to overcome collective action dilemmas, and end by considering the extent to which the search for solutions to international collective action problems takes us beyond the game theory framework as it is presented here (Sections 7 and 8).

The objectives for the chapter are that you should:

■   understand the nature and significance of collective action problems

■   gain familiarity with tools of game theory that can be used to analyse behaviour in the context of a collective action problem

■   acquire a critical appreciation of the insights generated by a game-theoretic approach to the collective action problem, including the limitations of this conceptual framework

■   consider some implications of collective action problems for the construction of institutions of governance including the 'rules of the game'.

2   The Tragedy of the Commons

Tragedy of the Commons
The Tragedy of the Commons offers an explanation for the tendency for open-access resources to be over-exploited.

To illustrate the classic problem of collective action we begin with the Tragedy of the Commons. This oft-recounted tale has acquired the status of a political and economic parable – part of our shared understanding of the problems of environmental degradation and collective action. It shows what can happen when private self-interest dictates one course of action, while self-interest as part of a larger group or collectivity requires another.

2.1 Cod fishing as a Tragedy of the Commons

The 'commons' in the parable traditionally refers to common grazing land in agrarian communities. However, the consequences of fishing behaviour under common sea fishing rights can be recounted in precisely the same vein, illustrating an international version of the tragedy. In the early 1990s, cod fishing on the Grand Banks off Newfoundland in the North Atlantic was closed completely, but at the time of writing (2003) fish stocks have not recovered: the Banks were fished out. Now it is the turn of the North Sea.

Cod is caught in the North Sea by European fishing fleets. The key measure of a fishery's viability is the spawning stock biomass: the stock of fish of reproductive age. Figure 13.1 shows what has happened to cod spawning stock biomass in the North Sea since the early 1960s; the horizontal line, labelled Bpa, shows the level of biomass, on a precautionary approach, that scientists calculate is needed to ensure stable stocks. The figure illustrates the appropriateness of the language of tragedy. While pollution has played a role in the decline, the main culprit has been overfishing, including the taking of immature fish before they reproduce (Commission of the European Communities, 2000). In the early 1970s, around 350 000 tonnes of cod were landed; in 2001 it was 49 000 tonnes (Commission of the European Communities, 2003).

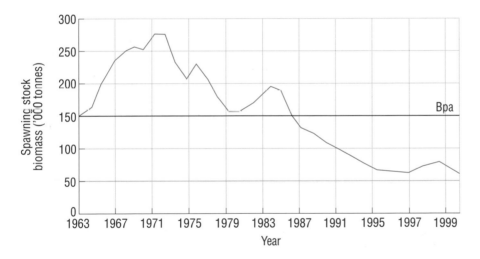

Figure 13.1   Spawning stock biomass of North Sea cod, 1963–2000

Source: Commission of the European Communities, 2000, p.5

Let us now tell the 'Tragedy of the Commons' parable about North Sea cod fishing. The parable takes the form of a story from which much of the fine detail of real fishing situations is stripped out. Picture a number of fishing fleets from a variety of European countries (all with populations liking to eat fish). The questions facing each boat or fleet are how large their maximum catch should be, and how small the minimum size of fish caught should be (which is affected by the mesh of the nets). On the one hand, it is in the best interests of each individual fishing captain and fleet owner to achieve as large a catch as possible, including small fish. But on the other hand, when everyone acts in this way, the result is overfishing, which in the end renders the fishing grounds useless to all.

How would we expect people to behave in this situation? It can be argued that, surely, rational individuals can work out the consequences of their actions, and this will be sufficient to discourage overfishing including the use of fine-mesh nets to trap small immature fish? However, there is a compelling rebuttal to that argument. Each individual can also work out that everyone else is likely to catch as many fish as possible, so he or she should do that, too. After all, the private gain from selling one more tonne of fish is greater than the private loss from fish stock depletion that extra tonne causes – since the loss is shared among all the fishing fleets. So the overfishing continues. The conclusion of the parable is that it is the tendency to act in individual self-interest that acts as a barrier to securing the benefits of co-operation.

Question

Are the sea fishing grounds – the 'commons' of the parable – a public good?

They do not quite fit the definition. As the parable is set up they are non-excludable: there are no impediments to putting to sea. But they are not entirely non-rival. While fishing is below a certain threshold the resource is non-rival – its ability to renew itself is not threatened – but once it passes that threshold, the fishing grounds become 'congested': more cod for you becomes, over time, less for me – and eventually less for you too.

The 'commons' are therefore not pure public goods: they are characterized by free access, being shared by everyone but owned by no one, but they are depletable in the face of intensive use. We can distinguish local commons – such as local woodlands and inland seas – from the global commons: the international benefits from such important resources as major fish stocks, the great tropical forests, and a great many wild animals.

Global commons
The global commons are resources of international importance, the benefits from which are shared by everyone but owned by no one, and which are depletable in the face of intensive use.

In the face of this 'tragedy', the issue for policy makers is how to entice individual members of a community or group (fleet owners and fishing captains) to take actions which are not in their best private interests in order to secure their interests as members of the collectivity (the fishing industry – not to mention the community of fish-eating humans).

2.2 Interdependence and strategic action

Note, first, that a *market* solution will not work. The source of the problem of overfishing, in our parable, is that fishing fleets consider only their own immediate incomes, and not the impact of their actions on others. So they respond only to the *private* returns from fishing, comparing them no doubt to the costs of fitting out and running the boats, and do not take into account the full *social* costs – that is, the impact on others. In those circumstances, one kind of solution sometimes proposed is to divide up the 'commons', so each user has to maintain just their share. But the sea cannot be privatized in this way, allocating a section for each boat, since fish swim across boundaries.

Within countries, state regulation may be a response to collective action problems and we return in Section 7.3 to this understanding of the state as a collective action institution. Here, we consider the international aspects of the problem. A single state – say, the UK – could restrict the size of the mesh and nets that its fishing industry is permitted to use, with the aim of reducing the quantity of fish, especially small fish, caught. But with open access to fishing waters and fish, such a policy would have little or no impact. Every other country with a fishing industry would have an incentive to exploit the benefits of the UK's action while bearing none of the costs. We describe such behaviour as 'free-riding' on the contributions of others. There is, then, no incentive for a single country to impose restrictions on its fishing industry in the first place and we are back to where we began. A solution that is in the common good calls, instead, for international collective action, in this case by the European Commission, which in 2002 proposed to cut cod-fishing quotas – the total each country could take – by 80 per cent.

Notice that for each country involved in this problem, the outcome is dependent, not only on their own actions, but on the actions of all the others. The quantity of fish available to a particular country depends, not only on the quantity of fish that this country's fleet chooses to harvest, but on the quantity of fish harvested by every other country with a fishing industry. Under these conditions, we say there is an *interdependence* in decision making, as Chapter 9 explained. When the number of participants is relatively small, as it is for the relevant group of nation states, it is reasonable to assume that each participant will be aware of their interdependence; that they will take the decisions of others into account in deciding how to act themselves; and that they will expect others to do the same. We describe such behaviour as *strategic*, and we say the participants are parties to a 'game' situation, or a situation of strategic interaction.

Game theory was developed to model situations of strategic interaction. The principles of game theory were originally laid down in 1944 by two mathematicians with an interest in the analysis of economic problems, John Von Neumann and Oskar Morgenstern. Many of the early game

Strategic interaction
Strategic interaction exists when the actions of one party perceptibly affect the welfare of another, and vice versa, and all parties act in the knowledge that this is the case.

Game theory
Game theory provides conceptual tools to analyse situations of strategic interaction.

theorists were employed to support North American military strategists in the 1950s and 1960s in their analyses of behaviour during the Cold War. Nuclear arms were proliferating at this time and there was the very real possibility of a 'preventative' war with devastating consequences. In Section 4.1 of the chapter, we examine a game-theoretic model of the nuclear arms race.

However, it was soon realized that strategic interaction arises in a much wider range of settings of interest to economists, political scientists, sociologists, and philosophers – even to biologists who devised their own branch of the theory (evolutionary game theory) to explain facets of animal behaviour. Contemporary game theory is, therefore, a product of the contributions of many different disciplines and it has wide-ranging applications. In this chapter, we focus our attention on the application of game theory to the collective action problem.

3   The Prisoners' Dilemma

In this and the next two sections, we look at three different games that are widely used to model collective action problems. The thought behind this approach is that key insights into classes of collective action problems are revealed when the situations are stripped down to their essential characteristics. Later in the chapter, we ask whether anything is lost by omitting so much detail.

Each of these three games has a key characteristic: it assumes that each 'player' acts independently. Players cannot make bargains because there is no way to hold another player to an agreement. Game theory of this kind is thus quite different from the kind of bargaining models that Rafael Sanchez discussed in Chapter 9. The models in Chapter 9 also addressed behaviour in situations of interdependence, but assumed that bargains could be made and kept. Here we look at the consequences of dropping that assumption, and modelling independent strategic interaction by states (or other players).

The classic game used by game theorists to analyse the problem of collective action at the heart of the Tragedy of the Commons is the *Prisoners' Dilemma*. The name comes from the story most famously used to explain the game: two prisoners, held in separate cells without communication, trying to decide whether to confess to a crime or deny it. We tell a different story here to explain the same situation: a story of nation states who find themselves 'prisoners' to the logic of the collective action problem in the context of an international public health dilemma.

3.1 The story: international infectious disease surveillance by nation states

International surveillance and reporting of infectious diseases is a long-established global public good (Zacher, 1999). It was established in the late nineteenth and early twentieth centuries, in a period when international epidemics of infection were widely feared killers: 'Spanish flu' killed about 22 million people in 1918–19. The early reporting obligations focused on yellow fever, cholera and typhus, diseases the Western Europeans who set up the system feared importing from Asia, Africa, Latin America and Eastern Europe. After 1945, the World Health Organization took over management of the system, but until the 1990s the process was quite low key: there was a general presumption that infectious disease had been beaten.

The 1990s changed all that. Old and new infectious disease outbreaks, associated with a huge rise in speed and extent of international travel, have put disease surveillance back in the news. As we write, the outbreak of SARS (severe acute respiratory syndrome) has illustrated both the dangers of infectious disease and the importance of having the capacity to identify outbreaks fast. Effective surveillance has the characteristics of a public good, and brings with it the capability to use international expertise to contain outbreaks.

Activity 13.2

Look back at the definition of a 'public good' and decide whether you agree with that last statement.

To create and benefit from the public good however, states have to co-operate. They have to identify and report outbreaks. And there are incentives not to do so. The most important are the economic costs. The SARS outbreak identified in February 2003 was predicted, just two months later, to knock US$165 billion off the GDP of the nine Asian countries most affected, and to reduce China's growth rate by one or two percentage points. Both Toronto (where the first serious non-Asian outbreak occurred) and China (where the outbreak began) saw a huge decrease in tourism and other international travel-dependent revenues including trade fairs. The temptation to keep quiet and hope to stop the outbreak before it is internationally reported is therefore enormous, particularly as other, uninfected countries have in the past strongly overreacted to public information about quite limited cases of diseases such as cholera.

So let us now set this up as a 'game' (which carries no suggestion of a lack of seriousness!). Imagine two states, we will call them China and Canada. Both have identified an outbreak of disease. They have two choices: comply with the regulations, or cheat (hide the outbreak). If both comply, both will face only limited economic problems since the outbreak will be contained quickly. If one country cheats while the other complies, the country complying expects to lose out heavily, facing large economic costs but still finding itself threatened by imported disease, while the cheater keeps their economic growth and hopes to clear up the problem secretly. If both cheat, the disease spreads out of control and both lose badly. Because of the incentives for secrecy, each country is taking its decision independently. Each has the same information, and considers only its own interests as it perceives them.

This two-country model of the situation is highly simplified. International collective action problems typically involve larger numbers of countries, but for simplicity, all the games you'll meet in this chapter involve just two players. The results of the two-player Prisoners' Dilemma can however be generalized to situations involving more than two players. What matters for the analysis is that the relationship between parties is one of interdependence, and that the parties know this to be the case and take their interdependence into account in deciding what to do.

3.2   The rules of the game

In order to analyse behaviour in a game, we first need to specify the rules of the play. That is, we need to identify:

- the participants, whom we refer to as the *players*

- the different possible actions that each player can take, which we refer to as the players' *strategies*

- the gains or losses to each player arising from each possible combination of strategies, which we describe as the *payoffs*. A payoff can be anything which is valued by a player (for example, wealth, security, or staying out of prison), and it may be expressed positively or negatively.

In this Prisoners' Dilemma game, the *players* are China and Canada. Each player has the same two *strategies* available: to comply or to cheat. Since it is the relationship between players which is at issue (and not between a player and, say, the World Health Organization), compliance can be understood as the 'co-operative' strategy, while the alternative is the cheating or 'defecting' strategy. The *payoffs* to the players are expressed in terms of total benefits to their economies of their decision; negative benefits are losses. Since the players are assumed to be interested only in their own citizens, each will try to maximize their payoff; that is, to secure the best economic outcome. One further rule of play applies to all the games featured in this chapter: each player must choose their strategy without knowing how the other has chosen.

Beyond these rules, we shall make a simplifying assumption. We shall assume that the game is played once only; this kind of game is described as a one-shot game. In a one-shot game, the players have no history and no future; it is as if they meet to play the game and then disappear never to interact again. In Section 7, we relax this assumption and see whether the analysis generates different results.

One-shot game
A game that is played only once.

The next step in game-theoretic analysis is to present information about the game in a tabular form which is described as a payoff matrix. A payoff matrix for the Prisoner's Dilemma is given in Figure 13.2.

The convention in constructing a payoff matrix is for the first player (in this case, China) to be the 'row' player on the left, and for the second player (Canada) to be the 'column' player at the top. Each cell in the matrix contains the payoffs to a particular combination of strategies, where China's payoff appears as the first entry in the cell, and Canada's payoff as the second entry. Since each of the two players has two strategies available to them, there are $2 \times 2 = 4$ possible outcomes, and so there are four cells.

The top left-hand cell of the matrix describes the payoffs to each state when both comply. The numbers represent billions of dollars. Each country faces an economic loss of US$1 billion, from lost tourism and medical costs, from a quickly contained outbreak. The top right-hand cell describes the payoffs when China complies and Canada cheats: Canada has a zero cost – its continuing economic growth cancels out the medical costs; China faces large losses of $3 billion from a prolonged outbreak and economic decline as cases

Canada

		Comply	Cheat
	Comply	−1,−1	−3,0
China	Cheat	0,−3	−2,−2

Figure 13.2   A Prisoners' Dilemma game between two countries

continue to be imported. The bottom left-hand cell, conversely, describes the payoffs when China remains silent and Canada complies: this time, China avoids a loss while Canada faces losses of $3 billion. Finally, the bottom right-hand cell describes the payoffs when both cheat: each face losses of $2 billion from a prolonged epidemic in which they keep exporting the disease to each other.

What matters about these payoffs, for the purpose of the game, is not their absolute values but the relationship between payoffs. In a Prisoners' Dilemma, the individual payoffs are ranked as follows. Unilateral cheating, while the other co-operates, has the best payoff. Mutual co-operation is the next best. Mutual cheating gives the third best individual payoff, and unilateral co-operation while the other cheats is the worst; this last is known as the 'sucker's payoff'. It is this relationship between the individual payoffs which produces the particular structure of the game which is described as a Prisoners' Dilemma.

3.3   Finding a solution

Now we are ready to consider how Canada and China will behave: will they comply or cheat? In seeking to answer this question, game theory is not concerned with any moral or ethical issues such as what the states should do. And, given the rules of the game, there are no shared norms of behaviour or enforcement agencies to take into account. Thus, all the information deemed to be relevant to the decision making of self-interested players appears in the payoff matrix.

Question

How do you think Canada and China will each choose? Remember that neither 'player' knows how the other will choose at the time of making a choice.

One approach to games like this is to ask: What are the properties which a solution to the game ought to have? The game theorist's response is to say that, once the players have chosen their strategies, neither of them should have any regrets about their choice, having seen how the other player has chosen. If you have ever been in a situation where you have had to make a difficult choice, you may find this property appealing! It is equivalent to saying that the solution to the game should have the property that no player can improve on their payoff by unilaterally adopting an alternative strategy.

Where this is the case, we say that each player is playing their *best reply*. Such a strategy combination is described as a Nash equilibrium after the famous game theorist John Nash who devised this approach. It follows that, once strategies have been chosen, any player whose position can be improved by a change of strategy cannot have chosen their Nash equilibrium

Nash equilibrium
A Nash equilibrium is a set of strategies, one for each player, such that, given the strategies being played by the others, no player can improve on their payoff by adopting an alternative strategy.

strategy in the first place. Nash equilibrium is used in this chapter because it is commonly regarded as the most powerful of the range of 'solution concepts' devised to identify the solution to a game.

Let us see if the Prisoners' Dilemma has a solution satisfying the requirements of a Nash equilibrium. There are two steps to the procedure. Step 1 is to consider each of the players in turn, to work out each player's best reply to each of the other player's strategies. To help you do this, you should put yourself in the shoes of one of the players (countries) and begin by asking: *If the other country decided to comply, which of my strategies would be best for me?* The answer to this question describes your 'best reply' to the other country's compliance. You should then ask what would be best for you if the other country decided to cheat. Then put yourself in the shoes of the other country and repeat the process. Step 2 is to look for a strategy combination where each strategy is a best reply to the other – that is, a Nash equilibrium solution.

Step 1: the strategies of each player

Consider the game from China's point of view

China can work out that if Canada were to comply (left-hand column), China would lose $1 billion if it also complied, but lose nothing if it cheated. So China's best reply to Canada's compliance is to cheat. (You may like to pencil a circle around China's payoff of 0 bottom left-hand cell to indicate that this is China's best reply to Canada's compliance.)

On the other hand, if Canada were to cheat (right-hand column), China would face losses of $2 billion if it also cheated, and of $3 billion if it complied. So China's best reply to Canada's cheating would be to cheat too. (Circle China's payoff of –2 in the bottom right-hand cell to indicate that this is China's best reply to Canada's cheating.)

Notice, then, that cheating is China's best reply to both of Canada's strategies, and so it makes sense for China to cheat.

Now consider the game from Canada's point of view

The payoff matrix is symmetric (that is, the payoffs are the same for each player) and so the same arguments apply. Canada can work out that if China complies (top row), Canada will lose nothing (zero payoff) if it cheats, but lose $1 billion if it complies. So Canada's best reply to China's compliance is to cheat. (Circle Canada's payoff of 0 in the top right-hand cell.)

But if China was to cheat (bottom row), Canada would lose $2 billion if it also cheated, and $3 billion if it complied. So Canada's best reply to China's cheating is to cheat too (Circle Canada's payoff of –2 in the bottom right-hand cell.)

Thus, cheating is Canada's best reply to whatever China chooses to do, and so we may conclude that Canada will also cheat.

Step 2: finding a solution

When China and Canada each play their best reply to whatever the other does, both of them cheat. The payoff to this particular strategy combination is given by the bottom right-hand cell: both players lose $2 billion. You will notice that this is the only cell in which both payoffs are circled indicating that each strategy is a best reply to the other and, hence, that this strategy combination is a Nash equilibrium.

Question

Nash equilibrium analysis leads us to conclude that China and Canada will both cheat. Do you think either state will regret its choice of action once it has seen how the other has chosen? In other words, could a player have done any better for itself?

Given that one player has chosen to cheat, the other player is always worse off from compliance than from cheating: it loses $3 billion instead of $2 billion. Thus, neither player could have done any better by unilaterally choosing the alternative strategy. This satisfies the condition for a Nash equilibrium.

The appeal of the Nash equilibrium solution is that it is individually optimal for both China and Canada. Yet it can be argued that this solution doesn't make sense. Look at the payoff matrix again. There is a strategy combination which is better for both players when their interests are considered jointly; this is where the players co-operate with one another by both complying. The result is losses of only $1 billion each instead of $2 billion each. We describe that latter strategy combination (both complying) as the social optimum of the collective action game because it is the solution which maximizes the total benefits to the players.

Social optimum
The social optimum in a collective action game occurs when the sum total of the players' payoffs is at a maximum.

Achieving the social optimum would therefore be analogous to joint restraint by fishing fleets to overcome the Tragedy of the Commons: that is, the outcome when the fishing fleets co-operate with one another by restricting the number of fish and minimum size of fish taken, so that overfishing does not take place. At issue, then, is whether players who are motivated solely by self-interest can achieve the social optimum.

The problem is that in the Prisoners' Dilemma it is in neither player's individual interests to play the co-operative strategy required to achieve the social optimum. The argument can be developed as follows.

Let us change the story a little by relaxing the assumption that the players cannot communicate. Suppose the two countries communicate with each other before either finds any infections. They agree that, were they to find cases, they will be better off if they both immediately comply with regulations by reporting the outbreak. Both states promise each other that this is what they will do.

So far, so good. But once the new disease has appeared in both countries, China can work out that if Canada keeps its promise to comply, China's best reply is to break its promise and cheat. China would then get the best individual payoff available, sometimes called the 'temptation' payoff, of zero cost of the outbreak; Canada would get the 'sucker's' payoff, the worst of all, losing $3 billion (the outcome in the bottom left-hand cell). If Canada cheats, China's best reply is also to cheat. Since the payoff matrix is symmetric, exactly the same argument applies to Canada: whatever China does, Canada's best reply is to cheat. The result is that both countries cheat and we are back to where we began! Allowing the players to communicate before playing the game does not change the equilibrium outcome.

It is not enough, then, that the players in a Prisoners' Dilemma recognize the collective benefits at stake in the game. Nor can the co-operative outcome be secured when the players are permitted to communicate with one another beforehand, since there is no mechanism by which a player can commit to a promised course of action and no external agency to enforce an agreement. Because each player can work this out, it is rational for both of them to ignore the content of communications; we therefore describe the content of any pre-play conversation as mere 'cheap talk'.

We must conclude, then, that the Nash equilibrium solution to the Prisoners' Dilemma, in which both players cheat, is the only outcome which is sustainable amongst self-interested players.

The Prisoners' Dilemma is one of several games used to demonstrate that the social optimum is not automatically realized by self-interested players; games like this are known as collective action games. The defining characteristics of a Prisoners' Dilemma are threefold. First, it is a game in which there is a co-operative strategy and a cheating strategy; in our example, complying is the co-operative strategy, and hiding the outbreak is the cheating strategy. Second, the game has a single Nash equilibrium solution in which both players cheat. And third, the Nash equilibrium outcome is worse for both players than the non-equilibrium outcome in which both players co-operate. Any situation with these three characteristics can be modelled as a Prisoners' Dilemma.

To illustrate the application of the Prisoners' Dilemma game to other collective action problems, let us apply it to the 'tragedy' of North Sea cod. To do that we reduce the story to two countries and use the game to identify the

Collective action game
A collective action game is one in which the socially optimal outcome is not automatically realized by self-interested players.
Prisoners' Dilemma
The Prisoners' Dilemma describes a game in which: (1) there is both a co-operative strategy and a cheating strategy; (2) there is a single Nash equilibrium outcome in which both players cheat; and (3) the Nash equilibrium outcome is worse for both players than the non-equilibrium outcome in which both players co-operate.

core of the tragic dilemma. So suppose there are two countries fishing for cod, Britain and the Netherlands. Figure 13.3 shows a blank matrix that can be used to analyse a cod-fishing Prisoners' Dilemma game. Each country has the choice of complying with an EU ruling to cut fleet sizes, to reduce catches drastically and widen the mesh of nets to avoid catching immature fish – or to cheat. Both countries know that catches above the EU maximum will cause the fish stocks to decline terminally. Both know that compliance is very hard to police. Each country's fishing fleets prefer more fish to less and each government faces political costs of scrapping fleet capacity.

Looking at it from the point of view of each government, the payoffs look as follows. The worst outcome for a government is that it takes all the political and economic pain of reducing catches, and the other country cheats. Fish stocks still decline, you have the sucker's payoff – and may lose an election. Suppose that payoff is –2. The best payoff (elected governments tend to have a rather short time horizon) results from cheating while the other country complies. Suppose that payoff is 2. The second worst payoff is when both cheat – no immediate political pain but long-term disaster. Suppose that payoff is –1. The social optimum – both agree – is for both countries to comply. Call that a payoff of 1. In Figure 13.3, the social optimum, where each country complies, curbing its fishing to the legal maximum of adult fish, is therefore the top left-hand cell.

Activity 13.3

Fill in the payoff matrix in Figure 13.3. Explain the solution to the game.

		Netherlands	
		Comply	Cheat
Britain	Comply		
	Cheat		

Figure 13.3 A Prisoners' Dilemma game showing a cod-fishing tragedy

Activity 13.4

Finally, before we move on to two different collective action games, pause and check that you have understood the key game theory concepts which have been introduced so far. There is no answer to this activity at the back. Instead, look back through Section 3 and check that you have understood the following:

- strategic interaction

- players

- strategies

- payoffs

- payoff matrix

- a one-shot game

- best reply

- Nash equilibrium.

4 Assurance

In a one-shot Prisoners' Dilemma game, a player who complies (co-operates) is ripe to be 'suckered'. The payoff from cheating is better than the payoff from co-operating, whatever the other player's strategy. That is the root of the dilemma. We now turn to a different game: one which still contains a collective action dilemma, but where the outcome depends on the confidence we have in the likely behaviour of the other player. This second game is known as the *Assurance game*.

4.1 The nuclear arms race as an Assurance game

The Assurance game, set out below, has been used to model the nuclear arms race which took place during the Cold War. Throughout the Cold War, there was little explicit communication between the USA and the Soviet Union. Each country suspected that the other wanted to live in peaceful coexistence, yet each country came to perceive the other as hostile to their own interests. Neither country was sure whether the other would risk a war; but in the event of a war, neither country wanted to be vulnerable to the superior nuclear capacity of the other. Thus, while sensitive to the huge financial costs of armament, each country felt it had an interest in building up its own nuclear capacity.

The rhetoric of the time suggests that game theory, and the concept of strategic behaviour, might have been in the minds of generals as they weighed up the parameters of the situation and tried to decide what to do. For example, George Stratemeyer, the US Commanding General of Air Defense Command, warned:

> Because of the fact that play may be resumed at any time, we must keep our winning team strong and intact – ready to take the field at a moment's notice. We are not blind as to whom the opposition may be, and shouldn't be blind as to the price we will have to pay if we should lose.

(Poundstone, 1992, p.80)

Notice that Stratemeyer was very much aware of the costs of being a 'sucker' if the Soviet Union were to act aggressively while the USA had failed to build up its armaments. We can imagine that his opposite number amongst the Soviet generals would have been thinking along the same lines in trying to decide what to do.

Once this situation has been stripped of its fine detail, it can be modelled as follows. There are two players in the Assurance game, the USA and the Soviet Union (USSR, Union of Soviet Socialist Republics), each of whom has the same two strategies available to them: to expend resources on building up their nuclear arsenals (the cheating strategy), or to refrain from doing so (the co-operative strategy). Once again, this is a one-shot game and each player must choose their actions without knowing how the other has chosen. The payoff matrix is given in Figure 13.4. In this game, payoffs represent the well-being of a country's population. Each player is concerned as before to maximize their payoff from the game.

Let us think about how we can interpret the different possible outcomes to the game. The best outcome for both – the social optimum – is where both players refrain from building up their arsenals and expend their resources on welfare-enhancing projects such as improving the health and education of their respective populations; this outcome is given by the top left-hand cell in which both refrain, yielding payoffs of 4 to each player.

The worst outcome for each player is where the other player builds up their arsenal while they refrain leaving them in a weak position if the other should attack; this outcome is given for the USA by the top right-hand cell (yielding payoffs of 1 to the USA and 3 to the USSR), and for the USSR by the bottom left-hand cell (yielding payoffs of 3 to the USA and 1 to the USSR).

		USSR	
		Refrain	Build
USA	Refrain	4,4	1,3
	Build	3,1	2,2

Figure 13.4 An Assurance game

The outcome in which both players build up their arsenals is given by the bottom right-hand cell, yielding payoffs of 2 to each player. This outcome has the merit of preserving the balance of power but, should a war actually occur, the build-up of nuclear capability means there is the potential for mutual destruction.

4.2 Solving the Assurance game

Question

Using Nash equilibrium analysis, see if you can work out the solution to the game. Do this before reading on. (Remember that it is helpful to circle best replies as you proceed through the analysis.)

Nash equilibrium analysis requires that we consider the game from the point of view of each player in turn, to work out each player's best reply to each of the other player's strategies. The USA can work out that if the USSR chooses to refrain (column 1), the best reply of the USA is also to refrain (4 is better than 3). But if the USSR chooses to build (column 2), the best reply of the USA is also to build (2 is better than 1). Since the payoff matrix is symmetric, the same arguments apply to the USSR. That is, the USSR can work out that if the USA chooses to refrain, the best reply of the USSR is also to refrain. But if the USA chooses to build, the best reply of the USSR is also to build.

If you have managed to get this far in your analysis, you will have realized that we have a new kind of problem: inspection of the players' best replies reveals there are *two* Nash equilibria! One is the social optimum in which both players refrain, yielding 4 to each player; the other is the outcome where both build up their weapons, yielding 2 to each player.

Activity 13.5

Stop here and check that you understand that last paragraph. Define a Nash equilibrium and explain why the top left and bottom right cells in Figure 13.4 are both Nash equilibria.

An Assurance game has two characteristics which distinguish it from others in the class of collective action games. First, it has two Nash equilibria. And second, both players prefer the same Nash equilibrium. In the example in Figure 13.4, the mutually preferred equilibrium is the social optimum, where both players refrain. Any situation with these two characteristics can be modelled as an Assurance game.

Assurance game
An Assurance game is one in which: (1) there are two Nash equilibrium outcomes, and (2) both players prefer the same equilibrium.

4.3   Choosing between equilibrium outcomes

The collective action dilemma in the Assurance game is thus different from the Prisoners' Dilemma. The difference lies in the structure of individual payoffs. In an Assurance game there is no 'temptation' payoff: to cheat ('build') does not yield a higher payoff than to co-operate ('refrain') when the other player co-operates. As a result, in the Assurance game, the social optimum is a Nash equilibrium; in the Prisoners' Dilemma it is not. However, in the Assurance game it is not the only equilibrium: the dilemma is how to reach the preferred equilibrium outcome.

It is true to say that, *after* the event, neither player would regret their course of action if they had done their part in arriving at one of the Nash equilibria. Thus, if both players in Figure 13.4 refrained, or if both players built up their arsenals, both players would have the satisfaction of knowing they could not have improved upon their chosen strategy by unilaterally choosing the alternative strategy. However, *before* the event, it is unclear which, if any, of the two equilibria will be played.

You might want to argue that, given that both players prefer the same equilibrium, the problem posed by an Assurance game must be easy to resolve. Intuition suggests that awareness of the collective benefits at stake in the game ought be sufficient to entice each player to do their part in the socially optimal outcome. But remember that, before the event, neither player knows how the other will choose a strategy. And if, for whatever reason, one of the players believed there was some chance that the other would build, then it would be individually rational for that player to choose to build too.

Question

Imagine that the USA and the USSR meet to discuss the situation and each promises the other that they will refrain from building up arms. How will these promises influence behaviour?

In its answer to that question, game theory yields an important insight into the collective action problem. Our analysis of the Prisoners' Dilemma revealed that any promises made prior to play constitute mere cheap talk and, hence, cannot be expected to influence behaviour. This result also applies to the Assurance game. Once again, there is no mechanism by which a player can commit to a particular action, nor is there an external enforcement agency to make sure that promises are kept. Thus, no amount of pre-play discussion alone can provide the players with the 'assurance' required for them to do their part in the socially desirable outcome. (You can see now why this is called 'the Assurance game'.) Each player will need more than cheap talk to assure them that the other will not build.

Looking beyond the model, we may speculate that the inability of each party to assure the other of their good intentions could have played an important role in the Cold War, leading to the build-up of nuclear armaments to the detriment of the welfare of both the USA and the USSR. Remember that, in the Cold War, both countries were superpowers and there was no superior authority capable of enforcing 'good' behaviour; this institutional arrangement within which decision making takes place is reflected in the structure of the game.

What the Assurance game tells us is that to entice co-operation in situations like this, promises are insufficient. In the absence of an external enforcement mechanism, each participant needs the *firm assurance* that all the others will co-operate and to *firmly* assure the others that they will co-operate themselves; only then can collective benefits of the preferred equilibrium be secured. In Section 7, we examine the means by which this assurance might be achieved.

5   Chicken

Our third and final game is known as the *Chicken game*. The situation it models may be familiar to you if you have seen the Hollywood movie *Rebel Without a Cause*.

In a test of bravado, two teenagers are driving towards each other down a long, straight highway. As they approach on a collision course, each must choose either to stay in the middle of the highway or to swerve to one side. If a player is the only one to swerve, he or she 'loses face' (the 'chicken'), while the player who stays the course in the face of the other swerving gains prestige amongst his or her peers. If both players swerve, both suffer from mild embarrassment. And if neither player swerves, they crash into one another losing their cars and possibly their lives. Neither player knows how the other will choose at the time of making their choice.

5.1 The Cuban missile crisis as a Chicken game

An analogous confrontation arose during the Cuban missile crisis in 1962. The crisis arose after the USA discovered that the Soviet Union was secretly placing nuclear missiles on Cuba within easy reach of the US mainland. The USA demanded their removal and instituted a naval blockade to prevent Soviet ships, carrying equipment for the missile bases, from reaching Cuba. As a deadline approached a tense stand-off developed with Soviet ships and US gunboats yards apart.

For the USA to give way (swerving), the loss would have been to concede a crucial political gain to the USSR and to lose credibility as the leader of the anti-communist world. For the USSR to give way would mean defeat in its attempt to establish the ability to strike the USA at short notice and loss of credibility as a powerful rival to the USA. For both to 'swerve', Soviet withdrawal would have taken place in exchange for a US concession elsewhere. But for neither to give way would have led to armed conflict, an invasion of Cuba by the USA and, almost certainly, nuclear war. It was very probably the most dangerous episode in the Cold War.

We can model this famous stand-off as follows. The payoff matrix is given in Figure 13.5. Each player has a tough strategy and a weak strategy. For the USA, the tough strategy is to maintain its blockade while the weak strategy is to remove the blockade. For the USSR, the tough strategy is to try to break through the blockade and the weak strategy is to turn its ships around. Payoffs represent the political and military gains which the USA and the USSR are each concerned to maximize. Once again, this is a one-shot game.

		USA	
		Maintain blockade (tough)	Remove blockade (weak)
USSR	Break blockade (tough)	–3,–3	2,0
	Turn ships away (weak)	0,2	1,1

Figure 13.5   The Chicken game

Question

Using Nash equilibrium analysis, see if you can work out what the USA and the USSR will each choose to do.

Consider the game from the point of view of the USA. If the USSR breaks the blockade (top row), the USA's best reply is to remove the blockade since 0 is better than –3. But if the USSR turns its ships away (bottom row), the USA's best reply is to maintain the blockade since 2 is better than 1. Now consider the game from the USSR's point of view. If the USA maintains the blockade, the USSR's best reply is to turn its ships away since 0 is better than –3. But if the USA removes the blockade, the Soviet's best reply is to break through since 2 is better than 1.

Inspection of the players' best replies reveals that, once again, there are two Nash equilibrium outcomes. One equilibrium is where the USA maintains the blockade and the Soviet ships turn away, yielding 2 and 0 respectively in the bottom left-hand cell; the other equilibrium is where the USA removes the blockade while the Soviets break through, yielding 2 to the USSR and 0 to the USA in the top right-hand cell. Each of these cells describes strategy combinations that are best replies to each other.

A Chicken game has four defining characteristics. First, the game has both a tough strategy and a weak strategy. And second, the structure of payoffs is such that the game has two Nash equilibrium outcomes. But third, and in contrast to the Assurance game, the players' preferences over equilibrium outcomes are opposed. Thus, notice that the Soviets would prefer the equilibrium outcome in which they act tough and the USA acts weak, while the USA would prefer the equilibrium outcome in which it acts tough while the Soviets act weak. Finally, each player prefers another (non-equilibrium) outcome to the equilibrium outcome in which they act weak while the other acts tough. In our example, the Soviets and the USA each prefer the non-equilibrium outcome in which both give way (bottom right-hand cell) to the one in which they yield while the other stays tough. Any situation with these four characteristics can be modelled as a Chicken game.

In the Chicken game, as in the Assurance game, after the event neither player would regret their course of action if they had done their part in reaching one of the Nash equilibria. Thus, if one of the players gave way while the other stayed the course, both would have the satisfaction of knowing they could not have improved upon their chosen strategy. But before the event, it is unclear which, if any, of the two equilibria will be played.

Chicken game
The Chicken game describes a game in which: (a) there is a tough strategy and a weak strategy; (b) there are two Nash equilibria; (c) the players' preferences over equilibria are opposed; and (d) each player prefers another (non-equilibrium) outcome to the equilibrium in which they act weak and the other acts tough.

In the Chicken game, the collective action problem posed by multiple Nash equilibria is compounded by the players' conflicting preferences over outcomes and by the potential for disaster. Thus, at issue for each player is how to achieve their most preferred outcome while avoiding the worst possible outcome.

Question

Can one player achieve their preferred equilibrium by threatening tough action?

In advance of the game, a player could threaten to act tough in an attempt to induce compliant behaviour from the other. If the other player knew for sure that their opponent really would act tough, then it would make sense to give way. But, as we know, talk is cheap and so, when it comes to the crunch, neither player can be sure of what the other will do.

This means that acting tough is a very risky action to pursue. What happens if both players try to act tough? In a Chicken game, each player is sharply aware that if both of them act to try to bring about their most preferred solution, there is the distinct possibility that the worst possible outcome will result. In the Cuban missile crisis game, this would mean a war in which the USSR tries to break the blockade and the USA tries to enforce it, yielding payoffs of −3 to each.

In the event, both sides in the Cuban missile crisis were highly uncertain of each other's intentions, and even had difficulty communicating with each other. But, ultimately, the Soviets 'swerved'; that is, they turned back their ships and the missiles were eventually removed from Cuba.

Interestingly, even some of the politicians involved viewed the crisis in terms of a game. Dean Rusk, Kennedy's Secretary of State, claimed:

> At that point I remarked that 'we were eyeball to eyeball and the other guy just blinked'. This was an expression borrowed from a children's game that we used to play in Georgia where two children would stand three feet apart and stare at each other's eyes and the first person to blink lost the game.

(BBC, 1992)

However, it emerged later that the USA had agreed not to renew its missile bases in Turkey. This 'deal' arguably meant that the real outcome was a 'both swerve' situation. Indeed, the deal was done partly so that the Soviet leadership could claim to rivals at home that it had got something out of the confrontation. The USA meanwhile kept the deal quiet and argued (with some justification) that it had 'won', claiming that the withdrawal of obsolete missiles in Turkey was only a token gesture.

6   Intermediate review: analysing collective action problems

Sections 3, 4 and 5 of this chapter have introduced you to three games which can be used to model problems of international collective action: the Prisoners' Dilemma, the Assurance game, and the Chicken game. Each game has distinct characteristics which turn on the particular relationship between payoffs. But all three games reveal that an outcome which is in the best interests of the community of players is elusive when behaviour is motivated by self-interest: that is the collective action problem.

So let us return to a collective action problem introduced earlier: the hole in the ozone layer caused by CFCs. Section 1 argued that the ozone layer is a global public good. In the late 1970s and 1980s, international negotiations tried – and eventually succeeded – in getting international co-operation to stop the loss of the ozone layer.

The activity in Section 6.1 asks you to apply game theory to this collective action problem. The activity will help to consolidate the ideas developed so far, and you should attempt it before reading on.

6.1   An ozone depletion collective action game

You are asked to analyse the collective action problem posed by the depletion of the ozone layer when it is modelled as a game, and then to interpret your findings. For the purposes of much of the negotiations on ozone depletion, the member countries of what was then the European Community acted as a single bloc, thus allowing us to treat them as a single player. And much of the disagreement about what to do about ozone has been between the USA and the Europe. We shall, therefore, represent the problem as involving two players only, Europe and the USA.

In this game, each player has the same two strategies: banning CFCs which is the co-operative strategy, and not banning them which is the cheating strategy. The payoff matrix is given by Figure 13.6.

Each payoff represents the net benefit (benefit less cost) to a player from a particular combination of strategies. Each player is concerned, as before, to maximize their payoff to the game. The logic of the relation between the payoffs is the following. The costs of unchecked emissions of CFCs were potentially very high – particularly increased health care costs in developed countries as a result of increased cancers and cataracts. Hence the negative effects of not banning the chemicals. However, banning CFCs was, initially, also costly, especially for the European countries who were significant producers of the chemicals. Hence the temptation to continue to produce

USA

		Ban CFCs	Don't ban CFCs
Europe	Ban CFCs	6, 6	−5, 10
	Don't ban CFCs	10, −5	−2, −2

Figure 13.6   An ozone depletion game

while the other player reduces the threat by a ban. The biggest net cost is to a country that bans CFCs while the other does not ban them.

Activity 13.6

1   Use Nash equilibrium analysis to identify the solution or solutions to the game.

2   Which of the three games you have been introduced to best describes this game? Explain your answer.

3   State carefully the collective action problem identified by the game.

6.2   Alternative formulations of the collective action problem

Game-theoretic analysis points to the underlying cause of the collective action problem: in each of the games we have looked at, it has not been in an individual player's private interest to do their part in an outcome which is in the common good. In the Prisoners' Dilemma, there is a single Nash equilibrium outcome, but this outcome diverges from the social optimum. In the Assurance game, there are two Nash equilibrium outcomes. There is no conflict over which of these equilibrium outcomes the players would prefer: both have a strict preference for the equilibrium which represents the social optimum. Yet there is no mechanism to ensure the social optimum will prevail. The Chicken game is similar to the Assurance game in so far as the analysis generates two Nash equilibrium outcomes. But in Chicken, the problem of avoiding the worst of all possible outcomes is exacerbated by the players' conflicting preferences over equilibria. Finally, all three games face us with the problem posed by cheap talk. That is, threats and promises which aim to influence behaviour are shown to be ineffective in the absence of an enforcement mechanism or some means of binding a player to a promised course of action.

We have already seen that a wide variety of international situations of concern to policy makers can be modelled as one of our three games. On these grounds, it can be argued that game theory provides a conceptual apparatus that can help us understand the causes of international collective action problems, and the consequences for society if the self-interest of states is not reined in.

However, we need to be circumspect when modelling real-world situations as games. We have seen that, for each game, the potential for co-operation – or, indeed, disaster – turns on the structure of the payoff matrix – that is, on the relationship between the payoffs to the different possible combinations of strategies. Yet it is not always clear, in analysing particular situations, what the relationship between payoffs should be; this is equivalent to saying that we may not know the nature of the game being played.

This uncertainty is acknowledged by game theorists and reflected in their debates. For example, Ward (1993) argues that the problem posed by ozone depletion is better represented as a game of Assurance rather than as a Prisoners' Dilemma. To develop the implications of Ward's argument, consider the payoff matrix for an ozone depletion game given by Figure 13.7. Once again, there are just two players, each of whom faces the same two strategies, with payoffs representing net benefits.

		USA	
		Ban CFCs	Don't ban CFCs
Europe	Ban CFCs	4, 4	−8, 0
	Don't ban CFCs	0, −8	0, 0

Figure 13.7 An alternative ozone depletion game

> ### Question
>
> Show that the game in Figure 13.7 is an Assurance game, and identify the equilibria.
>
> *Hint:* have a look at Activity 13.6 and repeat the steps you took there to identify the game structure illustrated.

We hope you have shown that the alternative ozone depletion game in Figure 13.7 is an Assurance game. There are two Nash equilibria (where both ban CFCs, and where both do not), and both players would clearly prefer the former (top left-hand cell). So, in contrast to Figure 13.6, in this game the social optimum *is* an equilibrium outcome. But there is no assurance that it will be reached. On the contrary, the desire to avoid the worst payoff (from banning CFCs while the other continues to use CFCs) may drive both countries towards the worse equilibrium outcome of continuing depletion.

As we saw in Section 4, the socially optimal outcome can be achieved in an Assurance game only if both players gain a *firm* assurance that the other will co-operate. Indeed, in negotiations over the ozone layer such assurance was gradually built up. The USA led the way, limiting its use of CFCs from the late 1970s, and in 1985 the leading producers of CFCs signed the Vienna Convention for the Protection of the Ozone Layer under the auspices of the United Nations Environment Programme (UNEP). The Vienna Convention was a 'framework' agreement and identified collective aims – to protect the ozone layer – but not the binding cuts in CFCs which were needed. However, within a short space of time the states involved did adopt binding targets in the Montreal Protocol on Substances that Deplete the Ozone Layer in 1987. These were later strengthened by amendments at meetings in London in 1990 and Copenhagen in 1992. The negotiating process generated what some have referred to as 'the most effective treaty in the history of international environmental diplomacy' (Victor, 2001, p.14).

Changing the relationship between payoffs leads to a change in the results of game-theoretic analysis. The problem for the analyst of international collective action is to identify which model is the most appropriate for a particular situation.

7 What can be done to elicit co-operation?

Game-theoretic analysis, using the one-shot game, may appear to leave little room for optimism with respect to collective action – yet there is a hopeful feature of recent events. This is the observation that some states do sometimes act co-operatively in order to secure collective benefits even when it is not in their best immediate private interests to do so. This was exemplified by the unilateral decision on the part of several countries (the

USA and the 'Montreal Group') to reduce CFC production in the early 1980s, even when it was not clear how others would act.

Another source of optimism is evidence of co-operative behaviour derived from 'laboratory' experiments, in which real people have been faced with a one-shot collective action game and their behaviour has been observed (Davis and Holt, 1993; Frey, 1997). To make the incentives players face in the laboratory setting as appropriate as possible, experiments are carefully controlled and real monetary incentives offered (for example, in the form of tokens that each individual can exchange for money at the conclusion of the experiment, contingent on the choices that have been made by all the participants). In one-shot prisoners' dilemma games in the laboratory, players often co-operate, though theory predicts they will not.

Such evidence of co-operative behaviour suggests we should be careful how we model international collective action situations. We should be sensitive to the assumptions upon which game theory is constructed and the institutional arrangements in which 'games' are played. It may be that the parties are not always as self-interested as game theory (and realist and liberal political theory) assumes, or it may be that so-called cheap talk can in some way influence behaviour. It may be that factors deemed to be extraneous to the game really do matter in a real-world situation.

We examine in this final section three ways in which the collective action dilemmas identified above can (sometimes) be resolved, and then go on to consider the limitations of the game-theoretic approach to the collective action problem.

7.1 Repeated play

Let us now drop the assumption that games are only played once. Most international policy-making activity, such as the negotiations between the USA and Europe over CFCs, takes place not once but in a series of rounds, with each round calling for decisions to be reached. What difference does it make to the outcome of game-theoretic analysis once the assumption of a one-shot game is relaxed?

In a repeated game, players play the same game more than once. For each 'round' of the game, the players, the strategies available to them, and the payoffs to the different combinations of strategies are all the same. We describe each round as a stage game in the overall game. This means we can represent the repeated game using the same payoff matrix as we would for a one-shot game. This payoff matrix now represents one stage of the larger game. We shall build on a game you are already familiar with: the Prisoners' Dilemma, as applied to cod fishing. The payoff matrix is given by Figure 13.8. It is the same as the payoff matrix you analysed in Activity 13.3.

Repeated game
A repeated game is one in which the same game is played more than once.
Stage game
A round of a repeated game is described as a stage game.

Netherlands

	Comply	Cheat
Comply	1,1	−2,2
Cheat	2,−2	−1,−1

Britain

Figure 13.8   A Prisoners' Dilemma: the stage game in North Sea cod fishing

If by any chance you skipped that activity, go back and work through it now, as we build on the answer here.

Let us consider how we can interpret the payoff matrix to the stage game and its relationship to the overall game. Once again, there are two countries. They meet annually to decide whether or not to co-operate by curbing fishing in the coming year.

Each country can cheat or comply ('co-operate') as before. For each stage game, each player (country) must choose their strategy without knowing how the other has chosen. The players are aware of the outcome of each stage game before they move on to the next one.

What will the countries do in this repeated game? We've seen that, in a one-shot game, there is no means by which the players can co-ordinate their expectations on the co-operative solution and, hence, that the only solution which is sustainable amongst self-interested players is mutual cheating (both countries contribute to overfishing and disaster). But in a repeated game, each play of the game adds to the sum of potential gains from co-operation. Does the presence of these larger potential rewards mean we can expect to observe more co-operation? Repeated play also opens up the possibility of observing the behaviour of the other player; and of rewarding good behaviour (offering a 'carrot') and punishing bad behaviour (wielding the 'stick') Could these features of the game improve the chances of co-operation?

First of all, we consider what happens when the stage game is repeated a specified number of times: we describe this as a finitely repeated game. Let us imagine that the stage game is to be repeated three times, at which point all interaction ceases. In these conditions, each player will want to consider

Finitely repeated game
A finitely repeated game is one in which the stage game is repeated a specified number of times which all the players are aware of.

the game as a whole; that is, to project forwards to work out what the other player will choose to do in each round of the game, and then work backwards to determine their own best reply in each round. This kind of reasoning is known as backwards induction.

Application of backwards induction requires that we start by considering what the players will do in the third and final round of the game. With the tools of analysis at your disposal, you should be able to work out what the players will do!

The final round is equivalent to a one-shot game since there is no future to consider. As a consequence, there is no incentive to play co-operatively in the hope of eliciting co-operation in further rounds of the game and there is no potential for the promise of reward or the threat of punishment to have any influence on behaviour. Knowing this, it makes sense for both players to cheat.

In the second round of the game, both players know that the other will cheat in the third round. Thus, once again, there is no incentive to play co-operatively and we must conclude that both players will cheat.

And what will the players do in the first round of the game? Exactly the same arguments apply: since the players know that both will cheat in the second round, it makes sense to cheat in the first round. We have therefore reached the conclusion that, in a finitely repeated game, the only outcome that is sustainable amongst self-interested players is mutual cheating in every round of the game. This result applies regardless of the number of repetitions of the stage game, say, three or 300.

However, now consider a game in which the stage game is repeated an unspecified number of times: we describe this as an infinitely repeated game This is equivalent to assuming the game does have a fixed end point but the players don't know when it will occur.

Under these conditions, the principle of backwards induction cannot be applied since there is no final round with which to start the analysis. It may now be possible for the players to use a 'carrot and stick' in the form of a trigger strategy to try to elicit co-operation. A player playing a trigger strategy will co-operate until the other player cheats, then cheat too as a punishment.

One well-known trigger strategy is known as the grim strategy. This entails a player co-operating in the first round of the game, and following this up with co-operation in all subsequent rounds of the game *as long as* the other player also co-operates. If co-operation meets with co-operation, all well and good and the players go on to reap the benefits of sustained mutual co-operation. But if the other player should cheat at any point, their bad

---

Backwards induction
Application of the principle of backwards induction implies that each player looks *ahead* to work out what the other will do in each round of the game and, in the light of this reasoning, looks *back* to work out their own best reply in each round.

Infinitely repeated game
An infinitely repeated game is one in which the stage game has an unspecified number of repetitions.

Trigger strategy
A trigger strategy entails playing co-operatively until such time as the other player cheats, at which point cheating 'triggers' a period of punishment.

Grim strategy
Under the grim strategy, a player responds to cheating by themselves cheating in every subsequent round of the game.

behaviour 'triggers' cheating thereafter in response; in other words, play reverts to the one-shot Nash equilibrium in every subsequent round.

What is a player's best reply to the other playing the grim strategy? Look at the payoff matrix in Figure 13.8. Cheating gives a one-period gain of 1 (the cheater gets 2, rather than the 1 they would get from mutual co-operation). But the gains to 'temptation' are won at the cost of losing 2 in all subsequent rounds.

Question

Explain why this is so.

Compare the payoffs to mutual cheating in the bottom right-hand cell (–1, –1) to the payoffs to mutual co-operation in the top left-hand cell (1, 1). Assuming payoffs in all rounds of the game are equally valued, it would appear that cheating doesn't pay.

However, we're not yet in a position to conclude that the grim strategy necessarily elicits sustained co-operation in response. In deciding on their best reply, a player will also want to know if the threat of punishment implicit in the grim strategy constitutes a credible threat – that is, if there is an incentive for the other country to punish cheating. In this case, the answer is yes, because cheating is the best reply to cheating (yielding a payoff of –1 rather than the –2 from co-operation). Given that the threat of punishment in the next round is real, then cheating in the face of co-operation doesn't pay and we may expect co-operation to meet with co-operation. Since the payoff matrix is symmetric and so the same arguments apply to both countries, we may conclude that the best reply to the grim strategy is also to play the grim strategy.

The results so far apply to a wide range of infinitely repeated games and lead to greater optimism than in finite games with respect to the chances of achieving the social optimum of a collective action game. However, it's still not possible to predict exactly what the players will do. This is because repetition opens up such a wide range of equilibrium outcomes.

Tit-for-tat
Under tit-for-tat, a player responds to cheating with just one round of cheating, and so the punishment phase only lasts as long as the other player continues to cheat.

For example, the grim strategy is just one of several trigger strategies; of the alternatives, the best known is tit-for-tat, where a player responds to cheating by cheating only for one round, reverting to co-operation if the other player co-operates. Tit-for-tat can also elicit co-operation. However the bad news is that mutual cheating throughout the game also constitutes an equilibrium and is therefore a candidate which we cannot dismiss. Indeed, any strategy yielding an average payoff no worse than could be achieved by mutual cheating is possible!

We should also bear in mind that the equilibrium outcome to a repeated game is highly sensitive to the values assigned by the players to the payoffs in each round. In the preceding analysis, it was assumed that payoffs in all rounds of the game are equally valued. But if players heavily discount the value of future benefits – that is, they value benefits now more highly than benefits in the future as governments with short time horizons to the next election may do – then trigger strategies are unable to sustain mutual co-operation.

Can we draw any further conclusions from these Prisoners' Dilemma games about the circumstances in which a framework of repeated play may support co-operation? One answer is provided by a Harvard economist called Mancur Olson (1971) in a book called *The Logic of Collective Action*. Olson argued that the larger a group is, the less likely it will further its common interests. To see why this might be so, look back at the North Sea 'tragedy'. First, with only two countries fishing it would be easier to monitor defaulters than with more countries (which is in fact the case). Second, the costs of cheating by one country are not spread over many other countries – as in the general story of the 'Tragedy of the Commons' as told in Section 2 – but fall on only two. Hence the benefits of default for an individual country may not so greatly outweigh the costs, or outweigh them for so long in a repeated game, as in the case where many countries are fishing. For both of these reasons, free-riding is much more difficult with just two players than with many. Third, communication is easier and cheaper with just two players than with many countries. While 'cheap talk' may not change the incentives, in repeated Prisoners' Dilemma games better communication may increase understanding of others' behaviour in ways that reinforce the effectiveness of trigger strategies.

7.2 Side payments and selective incentives

Does the Olsonian logic just outlined mean that all large groups will fail to provide public goods? Not quite, fortunately. There are two ways in which large groups can work. We will deal with the first in this section and look at the second in Section 7.3.

The first way in which large groups can achieve co-operation has to do with how different players value the outcomes. Not all contributors to the production of a particular public good value it equally. Consider the following extract which reports on a change in an international agreement about the ivory trade:

> Conservationists deplored a decision yesterday to allow Namibia, South Africa and Botswana to sell off up to 30 tonnes of their legally held ivory stockpiles. The decision taken by delegates to the UN convention on international trade in endangered species (CITES) in Santiago, Chile, falls short of the complete opening up of the controversial trade which southern

African states have wanted for many years, but was widely interpreted as the beginning of the end of the 13-year ban on all ivory trading. As the three countries celebrated a potential windfall of up to £13m, many conservationists said the decision would send a message to poachers that full ivory trading had resumed. This, they said, could mark a return to the level of slaughter that saw African elephant numbers halve from 1.2 million to 600 000 in just over a decade before all trade was stopped in 1989. ... However, non-governmental groups in several African countries welcomed the decision. ... 'Kenyans are currently barred from using their natural resource', said James Shikwati of the Sustainable Development Network in Nairobi. ... 'African people should be allowed to escape their poverty by making use of their resources – even elephants – without the interference of elitist eco-imperialism by NGOs who are only interested in protecting animals and not human beings'.

(*The Guardian*, 13 November 2002, p.15)

Questions

1   What is the nature of the international collective action problem associated with the ivory trade?

2   What difficulties stand in the way of reaching an agreement on what should be done about this problem?

3   How could these difficulties be addressed?

The argument being put forward by conservationists suggests that the African elephant is one of our global 'commons' and that, as long as there is a market for ivory, there will be an incentive to slaughter the animal leading to the depletion of numbers. This sets up the situation as a Prisoners' Dilemma: the social optimum arises when each country co-operates by not slaughtering elephants, while traders (in some countries) and poachers and game-managers (in others) have an incentive to slaughter and sell. Conservationists argue that to entice co-operative behaviour, international collective action is required to halt all trade in ivory, even in legally acquired stockpiles, so that killing elephants is no longer privately profitable.

But this conception of the problem is contested. Governments in countries with elephants do not want them all slaughtered – in that sense they agree with the conservationists – but they see elephants as a resource that they own, to be used for the benefit of local populations. Some local groups go further, seeing them as *only* a local resource for local use – and treating the overseas conservationists as 'eco-imperialists'.

Let us begin with the governments on both sides. Rich country governments have a vocal conservationist lobby. Poor countries with elephants have acute needs for foreign exchange (and some local conservationists). In other words, international relationships are characterized by inequalities among states, including inequalities of size, income per head, the level of dependency on particular industries, the extent of industrialization and the kind of technology a country has access to. Inequalities lead to differences in the costs and benefits of co-operation. For example, conservationists would argue that the benefits associated with protecting the African elephant are distributed across countries and even across generations. But, as James Shikwati points out in the extract above, the costs of a ban on the ivory trade fall disproportionately upon those countries that provide the elephant's natural habitat and for whom ivory trading has provided much needed extra income.

One way of addressing the collective action problem amongst a community of unequal players is to change the payoffs to the game; that is, to increase the incentives to co-operation through a system of bilateral side payments. Side payments may arise when one player values the public good more than another, and is able to pay to induce the other player to co-operate. Side payments need to be reinforced by binding contracts specifying the terms of the arrangement, including the penalties to be paid for 'cheating'. Thus, large, high-income countries can make payments to small, low-income countries which ameliorate disparities in the costs and benefits of co-operation.

Side payment
A side payment is a bilateral arrangement in which one party offers a financial inducement to a second party to change their behaviour in order to secure mutual gains.

This was one way in which co-operation against ozone depletion was reinforced. A side payment was used in the London Amendments to the Montreal Protocol, in the form of the Global Environment Facility (GEF). This was financed by the high-income countries to fund technology transfer, in order to give low-income countries an incentive to avoid developing production of CFCs and, in the longer term, to meet the obligations of the treaty.

In the case of ivory trading, Namibia, South Africa and Botswana might be given payments in the form of aid; the payments might replace the funds to be earned from ivory trading, and might in part be used to develop further a tourist industry which exploits worldwide interest in seeing the African elephant in its natural habitat, including ensuring that local populations benefit.

Side payments do not provide the perfect remedy for every collective action problem. In a situation of uncertainty, it may be difficult to determine the size of the side payment necessary to induce co-operation. Moreover, where information is imperfect, countries have an incentive to exaggerate the costs of compliance in order to increase the size of payment. Assuming an agreement can be negotiated, the problem then arises of monitoring and enforcing behaviour. This is because, as long as there is an incentive to cheat, and the strong possibility of getting away with it, we would expect to observe the persistence of cheating. One solution is to make further payments to entice the recipient to 'self-monitor', say, by providing the wages of game wardens where payment is conditional on a growth in the number of elephants.

We return below to other aspects of the ivory-trading problem. First, note a variation on the side payments approach: selective incentives and disincentives. A selective incentive exists where a desired private good is available only to those doing their part in creating a desired outcome of collective action such as a public good. A disincentive is therefore a sanction such as a fine, or exclusion from access to a desired private good.

Selective incentive
A selective incentive associates a private good with co-operation in resolving a collective action problem.

For example, consider the idea that respect for human rights is an international public good. A prerequisite for entry to the European Union is that applicants must demonstrate a respect for human rights. This condition can be understood as a private incentive (the envisaged economic benefits of access to the EU market) to comply with the creation of a public good. The net benefits from compliance rise sharply for the applicant for EU accession, increasing the likelihood of compliance. After accession, co-operative behaviour might be sustained through the use of sanctions (selective disincentives) such as withholding tax-based transfers for economic development projects.

7.3   Collective action institutions

Let us now look in more detail at Olson's proposition about the problem of collective action. His argument could be summarized as follows:

- The larger the group the less likely that all members will abide by the 'rules of the game', because the larger the incentives to free-ride.

- The larger the group the greater the 'organization costs' of providing the public good (i.e. the costs of communication, agreeing rules and monitoring payment for the public good).

- Collective action works with large groups only when selective incentives and/or disincentives are applied to individual members who abide by the rules/break the rules.

The implication of these reflections is that when collective action among large numbers is needed, it requires institutional change: the creation of a supra-national authority with the power to monitor behaviour and to enforce co-operation in the international public interest. Many of the examples used so far involve such a collective action institution to:

- define the framework and the rules of the game within which international collective action decisions are taken

- provide the mechanism which allows individual members (usually states) to express their acceptance or rejection of collective decisions.

You have seen an argument in this form before, applied *within* rather than between countries.

Question

Look back at Chapter 5. Which philosopher made an argument for the need for a state that reflects the inability of citizens to resolve a problem of collective action?

Hobbes justified a state in terms of its effectiveness in resolving the problem of collective action – Simon Bromley called it the problem of 'co-ordination' on a desired outcome. Hobbes argued in effect (he did not use this language!) that the most important public goods were peace and security over one's own life. Without these public goods, life would not be worth living and uncertainty would be so great that no one would invest in a better tomorrow, simply because no one could be sure that there would be a better tomorrow. But citizens faced a Prisoners' Dilemma situation: in the absence of a state, individuals acting on their own would use violence to pursue their interests, ultimately destroying their world. Hence, Hobbes argued, a state was necessary to provide peace and security.

A similar case can be made for giving some powers of enforcement to institutions of supranational governance such as the United Nations, to reduce the risk of mutual destruction, and to provide other collective goods.

Activity 13.7

Make a case for the WTO as an agency set up to create and sustain the continuation of a public good.

Some collective action institutions work by creating a context for negotiation and agreement rather than as formal organizations. CITES, for example, is a United Nations Convention (the Convention on International Trade in Endangered Species). The UN acts in this area not by coercion, but by providing a forum for the discussions that facilitate agreement in the first instance, and then by policing behaviour.

Other supranational collective institutions, such as the European Union, focus on providing public goods to their *members*, rather than creating or defending global public goods. They take collective decisions on behalf of their membership on the basis of agreed rules of the game, and they decide who can and cannot be members based on their acceptance of the agreed articles of association. This also means they have coercive power: they can throw out individual members by a collective decision thereby denying them the benefits they provide.

7.4 Limits to collective action

The creation of a collective action institution does not resolve a collective action problem – it only facilitates its resolution. The institution still has to make co-operation work, which requires the consent of the members or 'players'. What are the main reasons why effective co-operation may be blocked?

One important reason emerges from the extract about CITES in Section 7.2: there has to be agreement on the problem to be addressed and on the socially desirable outcome. In the debate around the conservation of African elephants, some positions identify a conflict of interest between those who want to protect animals and those who want to put human beings first, raising moral and ethical issues that game theory is not equipped to address – and that can paralyse collective action institutions. It may not be clear that all parties agree on the nature of the public good, or indeed are willing participants in the same 'game'.

More generally, Olson's arguments suggest that the closer the preferences of individuals comprising a particular community, the greater the probability of successful collective action without resort to selective incentives and disincentives. But this statement presumes in turn that we have resolved the question of who are the members of 'the community'.

Question

Is it acceptable that an infant in the Congo dies of hunger? If not, is it acceptable that Britain should spend some of its money on ensuring that a Congolese infant does not die of hunger?

The answer to this question plainly depends on the constitution of 'the community'. What distinguishes a hungry Congolese infant from a hungry European infant, apart from their geographical location? One answer is membership of different states, to which each child's parents pay (or do not pay) taxes. But if freedom from malnutrition in infancy is in the international public interest – is regarded, for example, as a human right – then the very concept of the community to which the public good should be provided is redefined as an international one. This problem of the constitution of the community is not dealt with at all in the game-theoretic analysis.

A second reason why collective action may be blocked is that all those engaged in collective action must have the *ability to pay* for their contribution to the public good. This is often not the case, as several examples have illustrated. Many of the world's 'global commons' are located in the low-income countries, while many of the most powerful conservation groups are located in the affluent countries of the northern hemisphere. The balance between benefits and costs is quite different in the two camps. Hence the parties may be divided on whether the benefits to co-operation outweigh the private costs, even if they agree on the nature of the problem. To resolve this, side payments are needed, or a more general agreement that contributions shall be in proportion to ability to pay – an agreement that is hard to capture in a game, and which in itself may require a sense of community and confidence among the parties to the agreement that may not be present.

Finally, acute uncertainty about the costs and benefits from co-operation makes response to a collective action problem very difficult. The next chapter contemplates just such a problem where the existence and nature of the problem is strongly debated, as are the implications of action: global warming.

8 Conclusion

We hope that we have persuaded you of the usefulness of game theory in modelling the collective action problem. We summarized our definition in Section 6.2: a collective action problem exists when it is not in an individual player's unambiguous private interest to do their part in an outcome which is in the common good.

This chapter has illustrated the enormous range of international policy problems that can be analysed as collective action problems. We have sought to demonstrate that game-theoretic modelling can help to distinguish different patterns of 'private' interests that shape behaviour in different collective action situations. It can also indicate the likelihood that different individual strategies – for example in situations of repeated interaction – can help to resolve collective action dilemmas. Hence game theory can help to formulate appropriate policy towards individual state strategies, and towards international institution-building.

Furthermore, the collective action problems examined are important enough to demand this kind of detailed examination: decisions taken by government representatives in negotiations over global commons affect not just the current generation but future generations' livelihoods too.

However, in harnessing game theory to develop an understanding of how to resolve problems, we need to be sensitive to the theory's limitations. It may not be clear how to model many situations. Context and history matter, and many of the keys to resolving collective problems lie beyond the reach of game theory modelling. We have raised several important issues in Section 7:

reaching agreement on shared objectives of public interest; the constitution of a sense of international community; the need to overcome the implications of vast international inequality; and the problem of building appropriate international collective action institutions.

We are left therefore with some hard questions that lie outside of the modelling framework. To what extent are the kinds of norms of behaviour which, between individuals, may assist co-operation, such as 'good manners', altruism, and shared concepts of 'fair play', relevant to interactions between states? Is there any international 'community' of states that can be appealed to? To what extent (if at all) do institutions of supranational governance such as the UN have the legitimacy and resources to enforce collective action in the international public interest? The case study in the next chapter, of the very difficult collective action problem posed by global warming, gives us more opportunities to examine these kinds of questions.

Further reading

If you want to read more about game theory, a good readable introduction with lots of examples of its uses is Hargreaves Heap, S.P. and Varoufakis, Y. (1995) *Game Theory: A Critical Introduction*, London, Routledge.

The history of the development of game theory can be found in Poundstone, W. (1992) *Prisoners' Dilemma: John Von Neumann, Game Theory, and the Puzzle of the Bomb*, Oxford, Oxford University Press.

A classic study using game theory to study international security issues and arms races is Schelling, T.C. (1997) *The Strategy of Conflict*, Cambridge, MA, and London, Harvard University Press.

A wide-ranging exploration of collective action problems including environmental ones is Sandler, T. (1997) *Global Challenges: An Approach to Environmental, Political and Economic Problems*, Cambridge, Cambridge University Press.

Chapter 14 Global warming, the USA and the failure of collective action

William Brown

1   Introduction

Among the most difficult contemporary challenges for international collective action are conflicts relating to the global environment. As Hurrell and Kingsbury put it: 'Can a fragmented and often highly conflictual political system made up of over 170 sovereign states and numerous other actors achieve the high (and historically unprecedented) levels of co-operation and policy co-ordination needed to manage environmental problems on a global scale?' (Hurrell and Kingsbury, 1992, p.1).

Perhaps nowhere is this challenge more sharply posed than in the case of global warming. The record of attempts to tackle global warming might suggest that the answer to Hurrell and Kingsbury's question is no. The announcement by the USA in 2001 that it was withdrawing from the Kyoto Protocol, the main international agreement created to address the problem, seemed to vindicate those who argue that there are major obstacles to the international system of states acting in concert. Tackling global warming does indeed require potentially very high levels of co-operation and the issue is replete with conflicting interests and priorities of different states.

In the last chapter, you studied international collective action problems faced by states in the international system. You examined some of the conceptual issues collective action problems raise and some of the tools of analysis used to understand them. In particular, you used some elementary game theory to model different kinds of problem and applied these tools in order to analyse what different solutions to collective action problems might be sought.

In this chapter I will take a close look at global warming. I investigate how the conceptual understanding of collective action problems and the tools of game theory developed in the last chapter can help to shed some light on this important problem. In particular, I will seek to show how modelling such problems as games can help to illuminate explanations of the failure to tackle collective action problems. We shall also note at various points along the way some of the limits of game theory and what it can and can't do. As part of this project, I will also ask why global warming has been such a difficult problem to tackle when other global environmental problems like depletion of the ozone layer have been the focus of more successful efforts.

1.1   The problem of global warming

In the rest of this section I want to provide a brief background on global warming. As you will no doubt be aware, attempting to sketch out the main features of such a complex problem cannot be entirely neutral and almost every aspect of the problem of global warming is contested. What follows in this section is mostly based on what can legitimately be termed 'the mainstream' of scientific and political opinion. I will note some of the main scientific disputes a little later on.

Global warming refers to the process whereby certain gases in the earth's atmosphere allow the sun's warming energy (in the form of light rays) to pass through on their way in but prevent the reflection, or 're-radiation', of this energy (as infrared radiation) from the earth's surface back out through the atmosphere, thus trapping some of the sun's energy. This 'natural' process (also referred to as 'the greenhouse effect' as it mimics the way a greenhouse works) is essential for life on earth. Without it, the earth would be about 30 degrees centigrade ($^{\circ}$C) cooler than it is.

The gases that cause this effect are referred to as 'greenhouse gases' (GHGs) and include water vapour, carbon dioxide, ozone, methane and nitrous oxide as well as several artificial chemicals. While most of the major GHGs occur naturally, the levels of all these gases (with the possible exception of water vapour) have been rising as a result of *human* activity: increases in carbon dioxide due to burning fossil fuels such as oil, coal and natural gas; an increase in ozone due to car exhausts; and increases in methane and nitrous oxide due to agriculture and changing land use. Together these increases create the 'enhanced greenhouse effect', trapping more energy within the earth's atmosphere and causing warming of the earth's surface and lower atmosphere. This enhanced effect is likely to have very severe knock-on impacts on the climate, including effects on rainfall and wind patterns, cloud cover and sea level, all of which could pose serious problems for different societies across the world.

Scientists calculate that since the late nineteenth century the global mean temperature has risen by between 0.3 and 0.6 $^{\circ}$C. While this may not seem a lot, it is estimated that the global mean temperature (the average temperature of the earth's atmosphere) has not varied by more than 1–2 $^{\circ}$C in the last 10 000 years, and only a few degrees of average temperature separates the climate today from the last ice ages (Elliott, 1998; Victor, 2001). Thus, small changes in mean temperature could have a huge impact on climate.

Furthermore, it is estimated that if no specific policies are adopted to change greenhouse gas emissions – and making some complex assumptions about technological change, economic growth and population levels – global mean temperatures may rise by between 1.4 and 5.8 °C between 1990 and 2100 (UNFCCC Climate Change Secretariat, 2001).

The most important GHG to our discussion is carbon dioxide (CO_2). Carbon dioxide is central to the global warming issue because:

- It is the most important contributor to global warming – it contributes an estimated 60 per cent of the 'enhanced greenhouse effect' (with methane contributing about 20 per cent and nitrous oxide, ozone and a number of industrial gases contributing the remaining 20 per cent) (UNFCCC Climate Change Secretariat, 2001).

- Controlling carbon dioxide emissions is at the centre of international discussions about how to combat global warming. It is thus the most important pollutant in debates over collective action on global warming.

- The centrality of carbon dioxide in the global warming process is one of the main reasons why global warming is such a contentious issue.

This last point is explained by the fact that the increase in carbon dioxide emissions is closely associated with industrialization. Industrialization has relied historically on massively increased energy usage, and this energy (whether in the form of coal, oil, gas or electricity) has come mainly from burning fossil fuels which release carbon dioxide into the atmosphere. It is thought that carbon dioxide levels varied by less than 10 per cent in the 10 000 years before industrialization, but, in the 200 years since England's Industrial Revolution, levels have risen by over 30 per cent (UNFCCC Climate Change Secretariat, 2001). Short of new non-polluting forms of energy, or radically cleaner technologies, controlling carbon dioxide emissions would entail curbing processes of industrialization in those countries which are not yet industrialized, or limiting industrial production in those which are. Alternatively, firms could adopt alternative energy technologies which are currently more expensive than fossil fuels. Tackling global warming is, therefore, potentially a very costly thing to do, and it could result in lower growth in industrialized and non-industrialized countries. The latter, in particular, might frustrate key policy aims of countries seeking to industrialize.

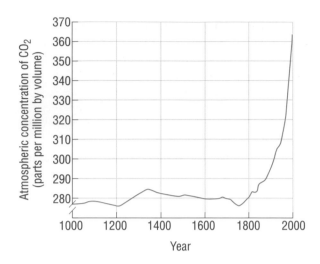

Figure 14.1   The impact of industrialization on the level of carbon dioxide (CO_2) in the atmosphere is particularly marked if one takes a long timeframe (here of 1000 years)

Source: Brown and Flavin, 1999, Figure 2.2, p.26

On the other hand, not doing anything about global warming could also be costly. The effects of rising global temperatures are hard to predict, but it is thought (UNFCCC Climate Change Secretariat, 2001) that these could include:

■ a rise in sea levels which imperils coastal communities and even the survival of some island states like the Maldives, as well as causing salination of fresh water supplies

■ changes in rainfall patterns causing droughts and loss of food production in some areas and flooding in others

■ an increase in severe weather events like hurricanes and droughts

■ the possibility of rapid and unexpected climate transitions like a collapse in the Antarctic ice sheet or reversal of the Atlantic Gulf Stream which warms Western Europe

■ increased rates of extinction of species as some fail to adapt to changing climate and habitat

■ an increase in migration as communities seek to cope with a changed environment

■ a wider incidence of diseases once limited to the tropics.

However, while the costs of global warming are likely to be high, they are also likely to be highly uneven. In part, they will depend on the geographical location of the country in question and the rate and magnitude of change. But the costs will also depend on a particular society's vulnerability and adaptability to change in climate. Rapid and large-scale negative effects on vulnerable agricultural systems, for example, are likely to create greater social and economic dislocation than slow and gradual change in developed economies with the infrastructural wherewithal to adapt to change. Some adaptation to change is inevitably going to be necessary given that warming of the atmosphere is already under way and, even if emissions were cut today, various built-in time lags mean that current GHGs will continue to create climate change into the future.

It is for these reasons that the political heat around global warming is so intense. The problem, and the proposed solutions, impact on every level – from individuals' livelihoods and everyday activities, to the interests of large multinational corporations, to the economic and developmental aims of nation states. I am going to focus on this last level as it is among states, in international negotiations, where most effort to address global warming has been expended and it is here that the problem of international collective action is most clearly illustrated.

2   Global warming as an international collective action problem: a first look

Having broadly outlined the global warming problem (I'll add more detail to this picture as I go on), in this section I want to start to analyse it as a collective action problem using some of the tools developed in the previous chapter.

Question

Why might you define global warming as a collective action problem? And why is global warming a public bad?

In the previous chapter you have seen that international collective action involves choices that one country cannot make for itself. In global warming, GHG emissions come from many different countries and it requires cuts in emissions by all or a large number of states to combat it. Furthermore, the object of global warming is public, not private; the atmosphere is shared, that is, owned by no one state and cannot be divided up. In Chapter 13 you saw that public bads are the other face of public goods. In the terms economists use, global warming is non-rival (one state suffering the consequences of global warming does not diminish the ill effects on another) and non-excludable (negative effects on one state do not exclude another from feeling them too). Furthermore, global warming is jointly supplied in that once it is set in train, all are vulnerable; and it is not congested in that negative effects on one will not reduce negative effects on another. (Review Section 1.1 of Chapter 13, and Activity 13.1 if you want to refresh your memory about this.)

You also saw in Chapter 13 that we can analyse international collective action problems using some of the tools of game theory. As was discussed there, different games can serve as models, or metaphors, for different collective action situations – Prisoners' Dilemma, Assurance and Chicken are the ones you have studied. These games allow us to strip out much of the complexity of collective action problems in order to reveal some of the basic features of the problem. In particular, using these games helps us to think through explanations for failure to achieve socially optimum outcomes and to consider how solutions to the problems of collective action might be found.

In my outline of global warming in Section 1, I argued that most people think that global warming will cause a series of negative impacts on the world as a whole. However, I also noted that the costs of cutting GHG emissions may be significant – cuts in GHG emissions (particularly CO_2) may have a negative impact on economic growth in particular. The majority opinion is that if states act together to cut GHG emissions, these costs are worth bearing because they will ultimately deliver enough benefits in the future from the avoidance of global warming. That is, there are net benefits (benefit minus cost) from cuts to GHG emissions. Note that here I am assuming (as has been the case in the games you have been using) that states act in a way that maximizes the net benefits to themselves, in this case economic benefits. Taken together, this economic rationality would lead states to cut GHG emissions and avoid global warming.

However, for any *individual* state, the most desirable scenario would be to avoid the costs of GHG emissions reductions, while getting the benefits of a curb on global warming through the efforts of other states. There is, therefore, a temptation to cheat. However, if each state knows this and acts accordingly, none will cut its emissions and global temperatures will continue to rise. This means that the incentives facing states may be such that independent action by states leads to a collectively sub-optimal outcome.

Question

What kind of game could be used to represent a situation where states agree on a desired outcome but, due to the incentives facing them, independent action leads to an undesired outcome?

As outlined in Chapter 13 (Section 1.2), such a situation can be modelled as a Prisoners' Dilemma. The Prisoners' Dilemma is used to represent a situation where states agree on the most desirable outcome but in which the temptation to cheat and free-ride (see Chapter 13, Section 2.2) on the efforts of others leads to an undesirable outcome. For these reasons it seems sensible to begin my analysis by using this model (in Section 5 I consider what difference it makes to our understanding if we represent global warming as a different kind of game).

Figure 14.2 depicts global warming as a Prisoners' Dilemma game. In this representation of the problem, I have portrayed it as involving just two players – the USA and the EU. As with the ozone problem that you encountered in the previous chapter, for much of the negotiations on global warming, the member countries of the EU have acted as a single bloc, thus allowing us to treat them as one actor. The EU and the USA are leading industrial economies and therefore responsible for a large amount of GHG emissions. Indeed, the USA alone accounts for nearly a quarter of all CO_2 emissions, making it the single most important state in global warming (more figures on CO_2 emissions are given in Table 14.1, Section 4.3 below). Not surprisingly, therefore, much of the disagreement about what to do about global warming has been between the USA and the EU bloc.

	USA	
	Cut emissions	Don't cut emissions
EU Cut emissions	6, 6	–5, 10
Don't cut emissions	10, –5	–2, –2

Figure 14.2   Global warming as a Prisoners' Dilemma

In this game, each player has the same two strategies: cutting emissions of GHGs (the co-operative strategy), and not cutting emissions (the cheating strategy). Each payoff represents the net benefit (benefit less cost) to a player from a particular combination of strategies. Accordingly, higher numbers are better for a player than lower ones.

Question

Explain why this is a Prisoners' Dilemma game.

The easiest way to start to think through this model of the problem is to consider the position of each player in the game. Put yourself in the place of the EU. If the USA cuts emissions (the co-operative strategy in the left-hand column), what would the EU do? The EU would not cut emissions because 10 is greater than 6; that is, the EU gets the benefits of a curb on global warming while the USA bears all the economic pain of cutting GHGs. If the USA did not cut emissions (the cheating strategy) the EU would not cut emissions either, (–2 is greater than –5); that is, it wants to avoid being 'the sucker' bearing the costs of GHG emissions while the USA free-rides. Thus, whether the USA cuts emissions or doesn't cut them, it is in the interests of the EU not to cut emissions. In Chapter 13 this was described as the EU's 'best reply' – whatever the USA does, it wouldn't change its strategy. Given that the payoffs are symmetric you can see that the same will go for the USA.

As you have seen, the situation in which both players' strategies are best replies, and neither player can improve their payoff by adopting an alternative strategy, is called a Nash Equilibrium. In this model of global warming, the Nash Equilibrium is in the bottom right-hand corner where neither player cuts emissions. Yet here, each player gets –2 rather than the 6 each would get if both cut emissions. In addition, you will notice that total net benefits (where payoffs of each are added together) are greatest where both co-operate, and least where both cheat. Independently rational calculations by each player therefore lead to a collectively sub-optimal outcome. (You might find it useful to refer back to Section 3 of the last chapter if you haven't followed the above explanation.)

Before I go on to discuss possible ways out of this problem, let us consider the representation of global warming offered in this example. As was noted in the last chapter, games are models of particular patterns of interaction that portray certain aspects of strategic interaction very clearly. In this case, our model displays a situation where independent decision making based on the pursuit of self-interest cannot realize the social optimum when the payoffs to the parties are of the kind represented in the Prisoners' Dilemma game. However, while this reveals something of the global warming problem, it, like all models, is based on a number of simplifications and we should always be aware of what those are.

Question

Have another look at the representation in Figure 14.2 and list some of the simplifications involved.

The key simplifications I noted were that: there are only two players in this game; the co-operative outcome is defined in terms of cutting emissions and it is a one-shot game. In addition, the payoffs assigned to the players are symmetric. Do these simplifications affect the value of the explanation of global warming that the Prisoners' Dilemma model gives us?

The first simplification is that there are only two players. As you will know, there are over 170 states in the world, the economies of which, to varying extents, all emit carbon dioxide. It is partly because tackling global warming both affects, and requires concerted action by, so many states that it is such a complex collective action problem. However, it would be possible to construct a model of global warming with more players. As Chapter 13 noted, the results of the two player Prisoners' Dilemma game can be generalized to situations involving many players. If we were to create a many-player model of the Prisoners' Dilemma game, it would help to group the states according to their different interests and hence payoffs. Matthew Paterson has argued that in the actual negotiations over global warming there have been broadly seven groups of states (Paterson, 1996, pp.101–8; also see Paterson and Grubb, 1992) as follows:

1   The USA – against large cuts in GHG emissions because of the domestic economic cost.

2   The EU and other industrialized countries – for stronger binding targets for GHG emissions because they are generally lower emitters of carbon dioxide.

3   Large developing countries (China, India, Brazil) – against binding cuts because these would be obstacles to further industrial development.

4   Newly Industrializing Countries (NICs) – against binding cuts which limit industrialization (as in (3) above).

5   Association of Small Island States (AOSIS) – for strong binding targets because of the threats faced due to sea level rises.

6   Less Developed Countries (LDCs) – against binding targets for developing countries and for action to be taken first by the developed countries.

7   Organization of Petroleum Exporting Countries (OPEC) – against large-scale cuts in GHG emissions because of the knock-on effects on demand for oil and hence their earnings.

To model global warming using these groups would mean assuming that each group acted as a single player (much as I have done with the EU). In itself, this is problematic as some of them are even more diverse and less able to act in unison than the EU is. However, putting this issue aside, we could in principle analyse the global warming problem as a many-player Prisoners' Dilemma situation, in which the non-cooperative outcome is the equilibrium outcome, even though all players (despite their differing interests) would have preferred the outcome where all co-operated to achieve a reduction in emissions. For that reason, the two-player simplification has been a useful way to analyse the global warming problem.

However, the grouping of countries just proposed raises some other problems for modelling global warming as a Prisoners' Dilemma game. Given the different interests noted among these seven groups, it may be that, for some, not cutting emissions would be preferable to cutting them, whatever any other player did. For example, there may be states which act on the belief that the non-cooperative outcome is better for them than any outcome that requires them to cut emissions. In this case, the game would cease to be a Prisoners' Dilemma. To see why, look back at the definition of the Prisoners' Dilemma in Chapter 13, Section 3.3: the game is defined by the preference of all players for the co-operative outcome over the equilibrium non-cooperative outcome.

Furthermore, a large number of players raises problems once we turn to ways of overcoming the Prisoners' Dilemma and achieving co-operation. The game shown in Figure 14.2 is a one-shot game. Given the ongoing nature of the problem, it may be that the sustained interaction represented by a repeated game would be more appropriate. You have seen in the previous chapter that, in some circumstances, repeating the game can change the outcome. However, a large number of players makes a co-operative outcome even harder to reach than co-operation in a two-player game, as the larger number of players makes it harder to achieve the monitoring and sanctioning necessary for co-operation to emerge. In Section 3.1, I shall discuss repeated games and the problem of the effect this has on the potential for co-operation to emerge over global warming.

The other simplification mentioned in the game represented in Figure 14.2 is the single co-operative option, to 'cut emissions'. In fact, as I go on to discuss in Section 4, much of the debate over global warming is over how to define what constitutes 'co-operation' as well as how cutting emissions should be effected, not simply about whether or not to co-operate.

Finally, in Figure 14.2 I have assigned payoffs that are symmetrical, which is the same as saying that the relative costs and benefits are the same for each party. As Paterson's list illustrates, and I have already noted above (Section 1.1), this is unlikely to be the case – climate change is likely to affect different areas of the world differently, as will action to cut GHGs. In particular, so far as the EU and the USA are concerned, the costs of cutting GHGs are greater for the USA than the EU (as the USA has an economy that is much more heavily dependent on the use of cheap oil supplies and may gain less from avoiding global warming than the EU). The list of groups of states given above illustrates more of these differences. If we were to change the payoffs in our model to reflect this asymmetry, it may or may not affect the conclusion which we draw. The problem could still be usefully modelled as a Prisoners' Dilemma, even if the payoffs are not symmetrical, so long as the key criteria of a Prisoners' Dilemma are still met. As you saw in Chapter 13, the key defining feature of the Prisoners' Dilemma game is the existence of a single non-cooperative equilibrium outcome in a situation where players would all prefer the co-operative outcome that is not an equilibrium. However, as noted above, this may not be the case for some players. We therefore need to remain open to the possibility that modelling global warming as a different kind of game, with different payoffs, might be a better representation of the problem.

2.1 Science and uncertainty

One of the central difficulties faced in global warming, and in our attempts to model it, is that costs and benefits for states are uncertain. This reflects some significant scientific uncertainty as to the process, its causes and consequences, and the relative costs and benefits of different courses of action. Much of the controversy around global warming in fact relates to arguments about these issues (for example, see Lomborg 2001).

The mainstream of scientific opinion is represented by by the International Panel on Climate Change (IPCC) – a large, international group of scientists established by the World Meteorological Organization (WMO) and the United Nations Environment Programme (UNEP) in 1988 and mandated to conduct research into different aspects of climate change. Its claim that global temperatures have been rising is generally accepted although there are differences of opinion about how extensive this is.

More controversial is the question of whether there is a human cause to global warming. The key issue here is that the temperature of the earth's atmosphere fluctuates independently of human activity due to changes in the earth's orbit and the sun's intensity. Some scientists claim that this natural fluctuation can account for any increase in temperatures over the last 100 to 200 years. So even if there has been an increase in carbon dioxide levels in the atmosphere, and some global warming, the two may not be causally linked. However, the IPCC's Second Assessment Report, published in 1995, concluded that the increase in temperature since the late nineteenth century was 'unlikely to be entirely natural in origin', and that 'the balance of evidence ... suggests a discernible human influence on global climate' (IPCC, 1995, paragraph 2.4). This conclusion that there was anthropogenic global warming (that is, originating from humans) played an important role in galvanizing efforts internationally to agree a common plan of action to limit the threat, ultimately leading to the Kyoto Protocol. The IPCC strengthened this conclusion in its third report in 2001, stating that 'there is new and stronger evidence that most of the observed global warming over the last 50 years is attributable to human activities' (IPCC, 2001).

It is even less clear what effects global warming might have in the future. The predictions all rely on complex computer models of global climate and assumptions about future human activity, economic growth and technological change. Furthermore, some of the impact of rising temperature may well be 'non-linear': namely, it is possible that increases in GHGs beyond a certain threshold will result in disproportionately large-scale and rapid changes. For example, the North Atlantic drift, which circulates warm water from the Caribbean past Europe's west coast, may slow or reverse, causing a severe drop in temperature in Western Europe, or the polar ice caps might melt leading to a sudden rise in sea levels. The implication of such environmental thresholds, if they exist, is that the ability of societies to adapt to a changing climate is seriously impaired if change is large-scale and sudden rather than slow and gradual. However, identifying such thresholds before they are crossed is extremely difficult. Different scientific predictions and public debate about risks can have significant consequences for the perception of the need for collective action.

Perhaps not surprisingly, the scientific debate is also highly politicized. Different actors in the global warming debate – whether states who face large costs in cutting emissions, or firms in particularly heavy carbon dioxide-emitting sectors of the economy, or environmentalists with a particular view on protecting the natural environment – have all played a role in promoting particular scientific theories, research and political responses. For example, at least some of the research that is critical of the global warming thesis has been funded by the oil and car industries, particularly in the USA – they wish to avoid policies that cut back on oil and car use. Others claim that scientists on the IPCC have vested interests in playing up the global warming problem in order to generate additional research funding.

I cannot judge the science of this debate here. However, I can make three points about the implications of scientific uncertainty for our understanding of the politics of global warming. First, the majority opinion among scientists – that global warming is a potential problem, that humans play at least a contributory role, and that controlling carbon emissions is a good idea – is widely accepted and has helped to prompt states and politicians to talk about how to co-operate on global warming. Thus most accept that there is a collective action problem to be faced.

Second, scientific uncertainty means that trying to model the collective action problem is difficult as it is not obvious what relative payoffs we should use. In reality (as opposed to in our models) states may not have a very clear idea of the costs and benefits of different courses of action. Yet, game theory assumes that the players know the payoffs to different combinations of strategies. As was noted in the last chapter, this assumption can have important consequences for how we understand particular collective action problems and what solutions might be available. It means that we are in a position of thinking, '*If* we model the problem as a Prisoners' Dilemma, then what kind of solutions might be sought?' This is what I will do in the next two sections. However, as relative payoffs may be different, we should also think about asking what the problem would look like if we used a different game to interpret it (something I come to in Section 5).

Finally, we also need to keep in mind that the bits of game theory you have been using assume that states will act in a self-interested way to maximize economic gain and will make independent calculations about their own and other states' behaviour. Yet, arguably, the environmental issue has done more than most international issues to raise awareness of a 'common destiny for mankind'. Indeed, such language is often used in international environmental negotiations and agreements. It may be that such an awareness could shift states' focus from their own self-interest to the collective interest. I will return to these issues and their implications at the end of this chapter.

3 Achieving co-operation? The obstacles to overcoming a global warming Prisoners' Dilemma

However, let me set these thoughts aside for now and see how, if we stick with the Prisoners' Dilemma as our model, we would explain the obstacles to achieving co-operation on global warming.

The record of attempts to forge international co-operation over global warming is a chequered one. Scientific enquiry into global warming dates back to Fourier's research into the greenhouse effect in the early nineteenth century (Paterson, 1996, pp.16–29). But it was in the 1970s that research increasingly focused on the role of human activity in climate change, particularly fossil fuel burning. In the mid 1980s a growing scientific consensus developed. Indeed, one of the first international responses was to try to consolidate the state of scientific knowledge. As noted above, the UNEP and the WMO set up the IPCC in 1988 with the task of assessing the scientific information, assessing the likely impact of climate change and formulating realistic response strategies to climate change (Paterson, 1996, pp.41–3). The IPCC's role was intended to establish a firmer basis on which international negotiations about a collective response could proceed (there had been calls for an international convention on climate change from as early as 1985). Indeed, IPCC assessment reports (of which there had been three by 2001) are viewed as the 'official word' on climate change. Furthermore, the IPCC explicitly set out to be internationally representative, with participation from developing as well as developed country scientists and policy makers (Paterson, 1996, pp.41–4). In a field in which there is considerable disagreement about what action to take, and significant scientific uncertainty, the setting up of the IPCC represented a strategy to try to narrow down some of the disagreements.

These early efforts bore fruit with the signing of the UN Framework Convention on Climate Change (UNFCCC) at the Rio summit in June 1992.

The Convention was the product of a series of often acrimonious and highly charged negotiations held between 1990 and 1992 by the UN's International Negotiating Committee. The main focus of the negotiations were conflicts over whether the Convention should specify 'targets and timetables' for countries to reduce their GHG emissions and what place within the Convention developing countries should have. The Convention settled on a broad aim to 'achieve ... the stabilization of greenhouse gas concentrations in the atmosphere at a level that would prevent dangerous anthropogenic interference with the climate system' (United Nations, 1992, Article 2), without specifying what constitutes 'dangerous'. Significantly, the largest emitter of GHGs – the USA – was resolute in opposing the setting of any targets or timetables for reductions. The then US president, George Bush (senior), famously proclaimed to the Rio summit that the US way of life was not up for negotiation. The Convention commits parties to various 'policies and measures' aimed at cutting GHG emissions, to further scientific research, and to national reporting of GHG emissions and efforts to reduce them. The onus on developing countries was even weaker and the developed countries committed themselves to provide 'new and additional' funding and technological transfers to help them meet their obligations under the treaty.

The UNFCCC was heavily criticized by environmentalists, and the USA in particular was held to blame for the absence of more stringent commitments. However, by the time the Convention had entered into force (1994), there was both a change of administration in the USA, with an environmentalist (Al Gore) as vice president, and stronger scientific opinion from the IPCC as to the causes of global warming. Follow-up meetings of the UNFCCC are known as a 'Conference of the Parties', or COP. At the first, COP-1, in Berlin, a mandate was agreed to create binding targets for GHG emissions reductions. These were eventually agreed at COP-3 in Kyoto in Japan in 1997.

The Kyoto Protocol forms an addendum to the UN Framework Convention on Climate Change (United Nations, 1998). It specifies the targets and timetables for GHG emissions that were missing from the UNFCCC and began to identify the mechanisms by which these could be brought about, monitored and enforced. There is a more detailed discussion of the Protocol in Section 4.2, so for now I shall just note the four main elements agreed at Kyoto (see Greenpeace, 1998):

1 *A cap on GHG emissions*. This set targets for cuts in GHG emissions applying to 39 industrialized countries listed in Annexe B, itemized as percentage cuts from a 1990 base year. In effect this established permits to emit a certain amount of GHGs for each of these countries and a commitment from them not to exceed their permitted emissions.

2 *Emissions trading*. This mechanism allows trade in permits to emit GHGs and is explained below (Section 4.2). For now, note that it is an approach

which is designed to allow cuts in GHG emissions to be made where it is least costly to do so.

3   *Joint Implementation (JI).* This allows Annexe B (industrialized) countries to gain credits for investment projects in other Annexe B countries that reduce emissions.

4   *Clean Development Mechanism (CDM).* This allows emissions-reducing projects in developing countries to count as emissions credits.

By committing states to some concrete action, Kyoto was a major step forward in efforts to achieve collective action on global warming. However, the targets were condemned as 'purely political' in that they were the minimum that could be agreed between the parties, rather than being driven by any scientific or 'objective' criteria as to what should be done (some scientists and environmentalists argued that cuts of 60 per cent would be required to stabilize global temperatures). Furthermore, developing countries, including those with an important role in carbon dioxide emissions such as China and India, were excluded from all binding targets. Additionally, all of the key mechanisms to realize these aims were left to later COPs to decide. As Victor noted, 'Speedy agreement in Kyoto was possible only because a great veil of uncertainty put all the critical details in the shadow' (Victor, 2001, p.26). At the following COPs 4–7, the mechanisms needed to make the Protocol work were thrashed out. By COP-6, in the Hague in 2000, two weeks of 24-hour-a-day negotiations failed to break the deadlock between the EU and the USA, and negotiations were dramatically suspended. It was while preparations were under way for a resumption of COP-6 at Bonn, in the summer of 2001, that the USA, under the new Bush administration, announced its withdrawal from the Protocol. The remaining parties to the agreement persisted with negotiations into the autumn of 2001 (COP-7 at Marrakech), at which most of the remaining issues were settled, even though environmentalists argued that these agreements weakened the targets still further. And although negotiations proceeded among the remaining parties, the absence of the USA, the exclusion of the larger developing countries from the targets for GHG reductions, and a tortuous road to ratification of the Protocol meant that it had a mountain to climb if it was to have any real impact on global warming.

3.1   Analysing the obstacles

Why should co-operation on global warming be so elusive? I want to begin to analyse this by sticking for now with the idea that global warming presents the international community with a Prisoners' Dilemma-type of problem. In the previous chapter (Section 7.1), you saw that, even in a Prisoners' Dilemma, co-operation may still emerge if the game is indefinitely repeated. Here, I will assess whether adding repetition to my model increases our expectations that co-operation could emerge over global warming.

In their discussion, Judith Mehta and Rathin Roy identified a number of criteria which would allow co-operation to emerge in a repeated Prisoners' Dilemma. They included:

1   players (states) believe that the interaction will continue indefinitely or do not know when it will end

2   future gains from co-operation will be valued highly enough in the present for it to influence players' current behaviour

3   the number of players is reasonably small.

Question

In the case of global warming, to what extent are these criteria satisfied?

First, clearly, states believe that interaction over global warming will continue indefinitely. While cleaner energy supplies may be developed in time, most energy needs will continue to be met through GHG-emitting activities. Consequently, the effects of these emissions will remain a contentious issue for an indefinite number of years.

Second, you saw in the previous chapter (Section 7.1) that in a repeated Prisoners' Dilemma, 'each play of the game adds to the sum of potential gains from co-operation'. In repeated games states can also observe the actions of others over a number of stages and adopt strategies to try to elicit co-operative behaviour in order to realize these larger gains. However, such incentives to co-operate will only be effective if these gains from future co-operation are valued highly enough by states. This is particularly relevant for global warming where the gains from co-operation are mostly in the future while the costs are in the present. Many would argue that the impacts of global warming will be so great that all states have an interest in co-operation – that the costs of inaction will *eventually* outweigh the costs of action. Indeed, the further into the future one looks, the more likely this is as the negative impacts of global warming are likely to grow the further ahead one looks, and the likelihood of crossing some of the key environmental catastrophe thresholds increases.

However, two problems arise here. First, the scientific uncertainty about global warming makes these future benefits uncertain. Second, for such future gains to elicit co-operation also requires that states take into their present-day calculations these future benefits. For many policy makers and politicians, short-term considerations such as the next election may have a greater impact. The problem with global warming is that it requires costs to be borne today that may yield returns only in the relatively distant future. Arguably, it is this kind of calculation which led the Bush administration to withdraw from the Kyoto commitments which the Clinton Presidency had entered into.

Third, achieving co-operation in an infinitely repeated Prisoners' Dilemma game is easier if the numbers of players is relatively small. As the previous chapter discussed, this is mainly to do with the ability of players to observe the behaviour of others and to use trigger strategies to elicit co-operation by punishing players who cheat and rewarding those who co-operate ('grim' and 'tit-for-tat' were the ones discussed). However, the use of trigger strategies requires accurate information about what a player has done in a previous round and what they are doing in the current round. In particular, monitoring is important as there remains a temptation for states to cheat. Trigger strategies will only work if other states believe the threat of the 'stick' is credible. If they think they can get away with cheating they will do so. Here the two-player simplification in my Prisoners' Dilemma model of global warming becomes more problematic, as such monitoring of others' behaviour is far more difficult in a world of 170 states than in a world of two states. Issues to do with monitoring and sanctioning bedevilled the Kyoto negotiations.

The upshot of this analysis is that, if the payoffs involved in global warming resemble those of a Prisoners' Dilemma, there is every reason to suppose that co-operation will be difficult to achieve. These problems are brought into sharp relief if you contrast global warming with the negotiations over damage to the ozone layer.

3.2   The contrast with the ozone problem

Many of those involved in negotiations around global warming sought to emulate the success of the ozone layer agreements. However, you saw in Chapter 13 that ozone negotiations resulted in much more successful efforts at co-operation than have global warming ones. Modelling the problem as a game helps to identify some of the reasons why this is so. In Chapter 13 (Section 6), the authors showed how the problem of the depletion of the ozone layer could be represented both as a Prisoners' Dilemma and as an Assurance game. Here I want to note that, even if the ozone layer problem is represented as a Prisoners' Dilemma, there are good reasons for thinking that co-operation was more likely to emerge than in the case of global warming.

Question

Referring to the three criteria listed above (Section 3.1) that support the emergence of co-operation in a repeated Prisoners' Dilemma game, identify the factors which helped states to achieve the co-operative outcome over banning CFCs. (Refer back to Chapter 13, Section 6 if you need to refresh your memory about this.)

As with global warming, it is reasonable to assume that states would think that interaction over emissions of ozone depletion would continue indefinitely, and it is therefore more realistic to model the situation as an indefinitely repeated game.

In principle, this means that if the payoffs were those of a Prisoners' Dilemma game, then the gains from co-operation in the future could be substantial. Furthermore, unlike global warming, these potential gains became clearer as the scientific evidence about the problem clarified. Most notably, the scientific uncertainty around ozone depletion was rapidly overcome by the discovery in 1985 by the British Antarctic Survey of a hole in the ozone layer and subsequent research on the actual processes that depleted ozone in the upper atmosphere. The potential costs to human health also became more widely known. Thus, the risks associated with doing nothing became more certain, and the impact more immediate, than for global warming. Indeed, the nature of these risks – as a real perceived threat to personal health – had a significant impact, particularly on public opinion in the industrialized world. Compare this to the uncertain, varied and diffuse threat posed by global warming. Such clarity helped to focus governments' attention on taking action in the present. The net benefits from co-operation were also increased as the costs of banning CFCs came down as alternatives were developed by the chemical industry.

Finally, there was a relatively small number of states involved, making monitoring and sanctioning simpler, and thereby allowing states to respond appropriately to any defections. Production and consumption of CFCs was heavily concentrated – just 12 states accounted for over 78 per cent of emissions (Sandler, 1997, p.112), there were relatively few companies involved, and the range of activities that would be affected by a ban was much smaller than for carbon dioxide emissions. As Benedick (1991) has outlined, the bulk of the negotiations over the ozone layer was actually conducted between just two parties – the USA and the EU (although internal conflicts in the EU complicated this somewhat) – and agreement between just these two could deliver real effective progress on the problem.

4   Co-operative options on global warming

So, what are the possibilities for progress on global warming? If the above analysis of global warming as a Prisoners' Dilemma is appropriate, this should give us reason to be pessimistic about global warming. In this section, I will take a closer look at why the halting efforts at co-operation that produced the Kyoto Protocol have not followed the path of the ozone layer negotiations in evolving into a more far-reaching co-operative outcome. Indeed, by 2001 Kyoto had failed to keep on board the single most important state – the USA

– and excluded other key players like China and India from any binding commitments.

Up to now, we have assumed that the co-operative option is simply to 'cut emissions'. However, the 'mode' of co-operation on global warming has an effect on:

■ the net benefits accruing to any state (that is, some approaches may increase the costs of taking action relative to others)

■ the certainty that states have about those payoffs (that is, some ways of framing international agreements on the issue lessen uncertainty while others may increase it).

Now, we know already that global warming is surrounded by uncertainty in any case. But different models of co-operation have been at the heart of much discussion about what to do about global warming and have affected the level of this uncertainty. I want to look at these different approaches to co-operation before seeing how two of them are reflected in the actual international conflicts over global warming.

4.1 What kind of action is possible in response to global warming?

In principle, there are three basic options open to states. The first option would be to do nothing. This option is sometimes referred to as 'business as usual' and would be the outcome if states didn't agree to take any action at all. As a deliberate strategy it could be justified either on the basis that it is the rational path to take in the light of expectations about what other states will do (see above), or on the basis that the threat from climate change is not significant enough to warrant action and that the normal processes of adaptation and change in society will cope with any threats that do occur.

The second option would be to mitigate GHG emissions. This approach recognizes that it would be prudent to try to control or reduce the emissions of GHGs below a business-as-usual level. However, measures would be taken to reduce GHGs emissions to 'lower than they would otherwise have been' rather than to specify an actual physical target for GHG emissions. That is, states may be able to agree on a 'degree of effort'. However, as economic output and technological change will vary, what effect this has on actual physical amounts of GHGs in the atmosphere will be unpredictable. With a stagnant economy, a certain degree of effort may produce falls in GHG emissions, but with a fast-growing economy, they may increase, just not as fast as otherwise. For instance, changes in technology may reduce energy use per unit of GDP. While such efforts might include a variety of actual policies (for example, taxes on fossil fuels and subsidies for energy efficiency projects), in principle, the degree of effort could be expressed as a monetary value (for example, the amount of resources states are prepared to commit to tackling GHG emissions).

The third option would be to adopt policies aimed at avoiding an environmental threshold. Some of the scientific evidence points to the possibility that accumulations of GHGs in the atmosphere might lead to environmental thresholds being crossed, in turn leading to rapid, unpredictable and extensive changes in climate. This implies that it might be possible to identify ceilings defined in terms of actual amounts of GHGs in the atmosphere. If such ceilings could be identified, then another course of action might be to adopt measures that prevent GHG emissions exceeding a particular level defined in physical terms and thus avoid such an environmental threshold being crossed. In contrast to mitigation, international agreements to avoid a threshold would be based on governments committing to meeting absolute targets defined as physical levels of GHG emissions.

Environmental threshold
Environmental threshold here means a point at which accumulations of GHG in the atmosphere will trigger more rapid and far-reaching climate change.

Question

What effect do these different options for action have on the two issues identified above – *costs* to states of taking action on global warming; and the *uncertainty* states face with respect to those costs?

Of these three options, one dividing line is between option 1 and options 2 and 3. Option 1 – business as usual – clearly imposes no costs in the short term although it runs a risk that large-scale negative effects from global warming will not materialize. In principle, option 2 doesn't necessarily imply lower costs to states than option 3 – states could agree a high degree of effort, or could set physical targets at a low level. However, in practice, in terms of the actual negotiations over global warming, mitigation has generally been interpreted as implying a weaker commitment (lower costs in the short term) than specifying actual physical targets for GHG reductions.

More importantly, perhaps, these two modes of co-operation (options 2 and 3) do imply potentially significant differences with regard to the uncertainty states face (Victor, 2001). If states were to agree a 'degree of effort', then they would have a reasonably sound idea of how much pain they would have to bear in the short term. The uncertainty of the benefits from this – avoidance of negative impacts of global warming – would remain, but one side of the calculation would be more concrete. If states were to follow option 3 and set actual physical targets, however, the certainty of costs would not be achieved. Setting a target typically involves specifying a percentage reduction in GHG emissions relative to some common baseline. While this makes the level of GHG reduction more certain (assuming targets are met), the unpredictability of economic growth and technological change means that the cost to the state in terms of economic growth foregone is much less

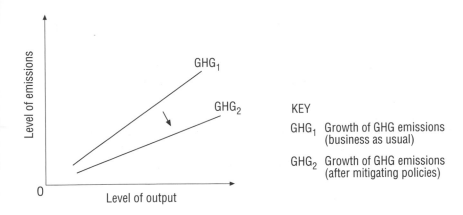

Figure 14.3   Mitigation of GHG emissions

predictable given that emissions rise as economic output rises. A high level of economic growth will potentially make meeting physical targets very costly for some states.

As Figure 14.3 indicates, in order to mitigate GHG emissions, states can try to reduce the rate at which the emissions increase relative to output. Both lines (GHG_1 and GHG_2) show that emissions of GHGs will rise as output rises. However, before mitigation policies (GHG_1) this rise is steeper than after mitigation policies (GHG_2). This shift to lower emissions per unit of output is typically achieved through increasing the price of emissions by imposing carbon taxes or subsidizing the cost of non-carbon-emitting alternatives. However, note that the absolute physical level of emissions will ultimately depend on the general level of economic activity, which is determined by a host of other factors. In this approach, the costs to governments of any agreed policies will be relatively predictable but their ultimate impact on GHG emissions will be less so.

Contrast this with option 3, avoiding a threshold. Here, in order to avoid crossing a threshold, an attempt can be made to specify an actual physical ceiling of GHG emissions which must not be exceeded. For most industrialized countries these ceilings are below current emissions, so agreements will be about targets for emissions reductions to be met at some specified date in the future in order that, globally, GHG emissions do not lead to environmental thresholds being crossed. This delivers certainty about the physical amount of GHG emissions (assuming targets are met). However, the cost of achieving these targets will vary depending on, among other things, what happens in the economy. For example, if a physical target is set and the economy then grows very quickly, resulting in higher emissions, the costs of meeting this target will consequently be much higher (bigger reductions will be necessary by the target date) than if the economy had grown more slowly.

Out of options 2 and 3, which approach to global warming would you advocate taking?

The distinction between options 2 and 3 reflects some of the very real alternative approaches to addressing climate change (most industrialized country governments accept that some action is needed on the issue, so option 1, business as usual, is put aside). In fact, if one contrasts the Kyoto approach with that advocated by the US administration at the time when it rejected the Protocol, one can see the outlines of this choice between options 2 and 3.

For environmentalists campaigning for an international agreement on global warming, the demand has consistently been for governments to set clear targets for specified physical levels of GHG emissions reductions. The UNFCCC was widely criticized for not having these and Kyoto was hailed for achieving binding targets, albeit with calls for targets to be more far-reaching. Environmentalists and some states argued that, without these, increasing economic output would leave the levels of emissions rising (even if more slowly) and the underlying problem in place. They argued that this was risking the future on a gamble that global warming thresholds would not be crossed. However, if you put yourself in the position of one of the players in the global warming game discussed above – a government negotiator, say – your incentive to co-operate rests on the balance between costs and benefits being right. The problem with avoiding a threshold, *in a situation of uncertainty*, is that both costs and benefits are unknown – the *costs* of meeting the target rest on the unknown future performance of the economy and the *benefits* of meeting the target are not clear either. On the other hand, the mitigation strategy has the advantage of governments having more certainty about the short-term costs (levels of carbon taxes, for example, would be agreed in advance), even if this would leave the absolute level of emissions unspecified, and therefore the risk of catastrophic climate change would remain a real possibility.

4.2 Kyoto targets versus US mitigation?

In fact, the choice between these two options is a reasonable reflection of the real-life debate between those advocating the Kyoto Protocol method of cutting GHG emissions and the advocates of the alternative suggested by the Bush administration in 2001. The following illustrates the contrasting approaches.

The Kyoto Protocol comes closest to the 'avoiding a threshold' approach to tackling global warming (option 3 above). Indeed, even the much more general UN Framework Convention on Climate Change mentioned earlier (Section 3) implies such an approach. Article 2 of the UNFCCC commits the parties to avoid 'dangerous anthropogenic interference with the climate system', although, significantly, it does not specify what such 'dangerous interference' amounts to. However, the Kyoto Protocol, which constituted an addendum to the UNFCCC (United Nations, 1998), was based on the notion that a specific level of GHG emissions should not be exceeded.

Box 14.1 The jargon of Kyoto

Caps: physical limits on GHG emissions expressed as CO_2 equivalents.

Emissions trading: buying and selling of permits to emit CO_2.

Sinks: activities which store carbon (negative emissions or emission credits).

Banking: emissions credits can be earned if states reduce net emissions by more than their target. Any surpluses are counted as emissions credits and can be carried over into a subsequent period of new targets.

Bubbles: groups of countries pooling their obligations under the Protocol (mainly the EU).

Hot air: under-specifying targets effectively allowing 'business as usual' to count as a reduction in emissions.

As noted above (Section 3), the core of the Kyoto Protocol is a 'cap and trade' approach to cutting GHG emissions. The two principle elements are:

1   *A cap, or physical limit, on the emissions of GHGs for all of the Annexe B countries.* The Protocol sets targets for cuts in GHGs and dates by which these are to be achieved. These are expressed as a percentage of a country's GHG emissions in the base year of 1990. The cuts average 5.3 per cent and are to be achieved between 2008 and 2012. However, the targets are set only for the 39 more developed countries listed in Annexe B of the Protocol. All developing countries are exempt from such binding targets. The protocol covers carbon dioxide and five other GHGs, which, due to their differing impact on global warming, are expressed as 'carbon dioxide equivalents'. While the cap specifies targets for reductions in *emissions* of GHGs, it includes provision for what might be termed 'negative emissions' or 'sink activities'; that is, those actions which take carbon out of the atmosphere (such as changes in land use or extension of forest and woodland).

2   *Emissions trading.* The Protocol establishes that trading in 'emissions permits' (the targets for each state effectively create a right or permit to emit a certain amount of GHG) can take place in order that the reductions can be achieved at the lowest global cost. Emissions trading is a method of ensuring that cuts in pollutants occur where it is most

efficient (least net cost) to do so. It has been used in reducing sulphur emissions from electricity-generating power stations in the USA. Kyoto sets these amounts by specifying the upper limit (or cap) on what each Annexe B country can emit. While some countries may relatively easily meet these targets and have some 'spare emissions' – that is, they may emit less than their target – others would only meet their target through very costly domestic measures. Trading allows the latter countries to buy the spare emissions from the former at a cost below that of the expensive domestic measures. For global warming it is the total global amount of emissions that matters, so, as long as the global target is met, it doesn't matter which country actually emits the GHGs. With emissions trading, the total amount of emissions meets the global target, but at a lower cost than if each country had to meet its target entirely by domestic measures.

To see how this might work, consider two countries. One country, let us say Russia, has a target of reducing GHGs by 5 per cent on its 1990 level. Its 1990 emissions were 100 000 tonnes, so this translates into a physical cap of 95 000 tonnes of GHGs (the numbers are hypothetical). Due to other circumstances – the collapse of its economy after the fall of communism – significant parts of its heavy industry have shut down since 1990 and, therefore, it will easily meet its target, emitting only 80 000 tonnes of GHGs. It thus has a spare 'permit' to emit 15 000 tonnes. This has been achieved without Russia taking any action to reduce its emissions of GHGs – a business-as-usual strategy, except that many businesses went bust!

Another country, let us say the USA, also has a target of reducing GHGs of 5 per cent on its 1990 level. Its 1990 emissions were 500 000 tonnes (it is a much bigger economy), so it has to find a way to cut emissions by 25 000 tonnes. Some of this, say 5 000 tonnes, can be achieved relatively easily by domestic measures (getting businesses to adopt some important new kinds of energy efficient technology, say). However, further cuts necessitate much more costly actions which impose serious constraints on economic activity and standards of living (limits on car and energy use, for example). However, if it can buy the spare permits from Russia at a price lower than the cost of these measures, it can move towards its target. Of course, even then, assuming that it buys all of Russia's spare permits (15 000 tonnes), it would only have achieved cuts in emissions of 20 000 tonnes. So, the USA will either have to buy other permits from other countries, or adopt at least some further domestic measures in order to meet its obligations.

There is an international market in which emissions permits are traded and prices of permits (US$/tonne) are set. The theory is that, as the spare permits are bought up, the price will rise, making domestic measures more cost effective. The initial allocation of targets, determined ultimately by the negotiations at Kyoto, is therefore crucial in determining who will have spare permits and who will seek to buy them. In effect, this initial allocation creates potentially valuable property rights to pollute. In Kyoto, the targets set for the former communist countries (particularly Russia and the Ukraine) were generous and did not take adequate account of the collapse of their economies, while the USA experienced a period of high economic growth, making targets easy to meet for the former and hard for the latter.

In addition to the two main mechanisms outlined above, the parties to the Kyoto Protocol adopted two further mechanisms to accompany the cap and trade system:

3   *Joint Implementation (JI)*. Under Article 6 of the Protocol, it is possible for Annexe B (developed) countries to gain credits for emissions reductions by implementing, jointly with another Annexe B country, investment projects that reduce GHG emissions. These may be either projects that reduce emissions (energy efficiency projects, moves from fossil fuels to renewable energy and so on) or projects that enhance carbon sinks (reforestation, for example). However, these projects have to be shown to be 'additional' to what would have happened in any case (a routine upgrading of a power plant should not count, therefore, as it would simply be 'business as usual').

4   *Clean Development Mechanism (CDM)*. The CDM allows Annexe B countries to gain credits for emissions reductions by funding projects in non-Annexe B countries (developing countries), thereby aiming to promote sustainable development in the developing world. Such projects must deliver real, measurable and additional reductions to business as usual.

It has been argued that a cap and trade system is an efficient way to organize international co-operation in order to stop emissions of GHGs going above a certain threshold (Victor, 2001) – it sets a physical level of GHG emissions and then establishes mechanisms to meet these in the most cost-effective way on a global level (via trading and the other mechanisms). Of course, some of the actual policies that would come under mitigation may also be taken by individual states in order to meet their emissions targets, but the *basis of international co-operation* is to cap a physical level of GHG emissions. One problem with this is that, because there is disagreement about the future impact of climate change, meeting this target delivers uncertain benefits. Meanwhile, because targets are set in advance, the cost of achieving them is dependent on the performance of the economy (as higher economic growth generally means higher emissions).

The paradox is that an approach which was advocated by environmentalists (and some states, including some in the EU) as ensuring a 'cast iron' deal on GHG reductions because it specified actual physical reductions in GHG emissions, ended up delivering commitments to cut emissions which were far less than most environmentalists thought necessary. States, well aware of the uncertain benefits to be gained from emissions cuts, 'played safe' and bargained for the lowest targets they could get (Victor, 2001). The negotiations resulted in states which wanted slightly higher targets (mainly the EU) trying to persuade those who wanted lower or no targets (the USA, Eastern European countries and Australia) to agree to some emissions cuts, producing a deal based on a minimum agreeable (Paterson, 1996). Even then, for some countries the deal was too shaky and the payoffs too uncertain. The problems are well illustrated by the position of the USA.

4.3   The US position

Question

Read the quotation below from a speech made by US President George W. Bush in 2001 about his administration's rejection of the Kyoto Protocol. Identify the reasons President Bush gives for this decision:

> The approach taken under the Kyoto protocol would have required the United States to make deep and immediate cuts in our economy to meet an arbitrary target. It would have cost our economy up to US$400 billion and we would have lost 4.9 million jobs. As President of the United States charged with safeguarding the welfare of the American people and American workers, I will not commit our nation to an unsound international treaty that will throw millions of our citizens out of work.

(*The Guardian*, 14 February 2002)

The main message is that the costs to the USA of the Kyoto targets were too high and the administration believed that they would restrict economic growth too much. Note also the use of the word 'arbitrary' – a clue that the USA believed the science and the economic calculation supporting a cut in emissions of the magnitude suggested by Kyoto were not proven. President Bush also believed – following in the footsteps of his father's policy in the early 1990s – that the *method* of tackling global warming which Kyoto represented was 'unsound'.

The reasons why the Bush administration took this line are not hard to find. In contrast to the ozone depletion problem, the USA had been one of the most reluctant parties in the global warming negotiations. The USA (under Bush senior) successfully opposed binding targets in the negotiations for the UNFCCC in 1992 and, even though it agreed to the principle of binding targets in the Kyoto negotiations (under the Clinton Presidency), it persistently argued for lower reductions than other countries. Even then, the Clinton administration's acceptance of Kyoto faced increasing hostility at home from a range of domestic actors – big business, particularly oil and car companies, motorists and trade unionists fearing job losses. But it was the rate of growth in the US economy, and consequently of GHG emissions, which really stoked opposition in the USA to Kyoto. The result of the high economic growth between 1990 and 2000 was that, according to the White House, the 7 per cent cut on 1990 emissions (that it had agreed to in 1997) would translate into a 30 per cent cut on actual emissions by 2012, with the consequent knock-on effect in terms of growth and jobs that President Bush highlighted in the quotation above (United States Department of State, 2001). The USA bargained hard for an interpretation of the Kyoto mechanisms – sinks, trading and so on – which would reduce this burden, and it was on these issues that COP-6 at the Hague eventually became deadlocked. Environmentalists and the European negotiators were therefore accurate in arguing that the USA was trying to 'water-down' the treaty. But it is highly unlikely that the US Congress would have ratified the Protocol in any case and, in 2001, the new President, George W. Bush, announced US withdrawal.

The Bush administration's initial proposed alternative to Kyoto was a set of unilateral policy aims set out in a *Global Climate Change Initiative* (United States Department of State, 2002). The cornerstone of this policy was the aim of reducing GHG *intensity* by 18 per cent over 10 years (between 2002 and 2012). 'Greenhouse gas intensity' is the ratio of GHG emissions to economic output defined as metric tonnes of GHG per million dollars of GDP. As such, it is a measure used to reduce the pace at which emissions rise alongside economic growth. In fact, the USA has a particularly high ratio of GHG emissions to GDP, largely because of the low taxation (and hence prices) of carbon fuels as compared with other developed countries. The White House claimed that this approach of reducing GHG intensity 'puts America on a path to slow the growth of greenhouse gas emissions, and – as the science justifies – to stop, and then reverse that growth'. It would aim at, 'stabilizing GHG concentration in the atmosphere in the long run, while sustaining the economic growth needed to finance our investments in a new, cleaner energy structure' (United States Department of State, 2002). The measures to achieve this focused on developing new technologies and investing in further research into climate change, as well as providing some funding for cleaner energy development in developing countries.

Question

What kind of strategy is this in terms of the options identified in Section 4.1?

In the terms discussed above (Section 4.1), the proposed US alternative is a 'mitigation strategy' – in so far as it seeks to make GHG emissions lower than they would otherwise be – compared with the Kyoto Protocol's setting of physical targets. The aim of policy is to reduce the ratio of GHG emissions to economic output, not to set a specific physical limit on GHG emissions. More economic growth will mean higher emissions, just not as high as otherwise. It rejects an approach that would severely curtail economic growth and indeed argues the need for economic growth in order to generate the kind of investment in new technologies that would be required to further reduce GHG emissions. The White House also clearly came down on the more sceptical side of the scientific debates.

For the more sceptical, all this might seem like an excuse for getting out of any commitments to address climate change. Many commentators criticized the US action. Some accused Bush of being in hock to oil companies who bankrolled his election campaign and who were strident opponents of Kyoto. Others argued that the USA was acting selfishly, was wilfully turning its back on international co-operation and was refusing to shoulder its share of the burden. Gerhard Schroeder, the German Chancellor, castigated the USA, stating, 'It is important that US accepts its responsibility for the world climate. They are the biggest economy in the world and the heaviest energy consumers' (*The Guardian*, 29 March 2002). However, if we are to follow the assumptions underlying our analysis of collective action and of game-theoretic attempts to represent such problems, then we can see that it is precisely *because* the USA is the largest economy and energy consumer, and because states will act in their own selfish interests, that it rejected the Kyoto deal. To argue that this approach might seem 'unfair' or a neglect of America's responsibilities may be appropriate. However, note that arguing such a line would be to directly challenge one of the core assumptions of the elements of game theory you have been using (and an assumption that is shared by both realist and liberal theories of international politics) – namely, that states act in their own self-interest and not for some other reason (ethical motives, upholding international responsibilities or in the common interests of humankind).

Indeed, the US perspective extended beyond objecting to the costs to itself. It also wanted to avoid being 'the sucker' – having to cut emissions while others did nothing. This argument was particularly directed at the omission of the larger developing countries like China, India and Brazil from Kyoto. It has long been an argument of developing countries that, from the point of view of equity, the onus for tackling global warming should reside with the industrialized world. As I noted in Section 1.1, one implication of tight curbs on carbon dioxide emissions, in the view of countries like China and India, is to threaten their industrialization strategies, and these countries have been successful in being accorded special treatment under international agreements – including both Montreal and Kyoto – that bind them to fewer obligations than the industrialized countries. Indeed, these exemptions (a total exemption from targets under the Kyoto Protocol) constitute the kind of large 'side payment' that has been necessary in order to ensure these countries' participation in the CFC reduction regime (side payments were discussed in Chapter 13, Section 7.2).

Against this background, the problem for the USA was twofold. First, the non-participation of the larger developing countries in GHG reduction may actually undermine any moves being made by the industrialized countries. That is, even if the industrialized countries cut their emissions, the effect on global warming will be limited by rising emissions from the developing world. But second, the exemption of larger developing countries from targets was deemed 'unfair' if others were having to meet targets. Bush claimed that 'developing countries like China and India already account for a majority of the world's greenhouse gas emissions, and it would be irresponsible to absolve them from shouldering some of the shared obligations' (*The Guardian*, 14 February 2002). This view was supported by businesses and labour unions in the USA who argued that they would have to meet costs of GHG reductions while competitors abroad would not. The problem is well illustrated if you look at Table 14.1.

Table 14.1 Share of top 10 emitting countries in global CO_2 emissions

World ranking	Percentage share of world population	Percentage share of world CO_2 emissions	Percentage cumulative share of CO_2 emissions
1 USA	4.76	24.45	24.45
2 China	21.47	13.91	38.36
3 Russia	2.55	6.44	44.81
4 Japan	2.18	5.07	49.88
5 India	16.97	4.75	54.63
6 Germany	1.42	3.70	58.33
7 United Kingdom	1.03	2.43	60.76
8 Canada	0.52	2.09	62.85
9 Italy	1.00	1.86	64.71
10 Mexico	1.65	1.68	66.39

Source: data compiled from World Bank, World Development Indicators 2003, *online*

As you can see from the table, while the USA is the biggest emitter of CO_2, responsible for nearly a quarter of emissions while accounting for under 5 per cent of the world population, other large developing countries are also crucial to curbing carbon emissions: China, Russia and India are all in the top five emitters, and Mexico is in the top 10, yet of these four, only Russia is among the Annexe B countries. Even here, Russia's target was set very low (following the collapse of heavy industry after the fall of communism), and it stood to benefit greatly from the emissions trading system.

The USA also objected that the initial allocation of targets was arbitrary. Because of the collapse of their economies consequent upon the demise of communism, both Russia and the Ukraine would have had valuable emission permits to trade, even though they had taken no direct action to reduce GHGs. If the USA purchased some of these to meet its obligations, this might have involved large transfers of income from US citizens to those of Russia and the Ukraine. Many critics in the USA asked why the USA should pay for the failure of communist economies.

However, the Bush administration was not proposing an alternative *international* regime to replace Kyoto. Partly, this reflected the opposition of other industrialized countries to the US action – they simply rejected any abandonment of the Kyoto deal. But it also reflected the US concern that a new and wider deal, which included the developing countries, would be unsound because there would be too much likelihood of cheating. Even the Kyoto deal is based on the premise that it is possible to monitor and enforce the targets that were agreed. Indeed, emissions trading is impossible without some robust method of ensuring that countries are meeting their obligations, otherwise a country could claim it was emitting less GHGs than it in fact was and then sell bogus spare permits on the international market. This would undermine the credibility of the entire system. For an international system of permit trading like Kyoto, there is no international authority analogous to the national state to enforce the rules of the market.

The US *Global Climate Change Initiative* therefore also included funding to develop better methods of accurately measuring GHG emissions and funding for developing countries so that they could develop improved systems for monitoring their GHG emissions. It was also part of the US perspective that, while the industrialized countries had well-developed and often similar legal systems which could be used to enforce emissions trading contracts, these were less robust in the non-industrialized world (see Victor, 2001). The US rejection of Kyoto thus extended beyond a rejection of the particular method of co-operation adopted by the Protocol, to a scepticism about the potential for *any* robust system for international co-operation over this most complex collective action problem. It is therefore a unilateral strategy, which represents the *most* that the USA was prepared to do, assuming that others would act in a similarly self-interested manner.

5 Reconsidering the analysis of collective action

I want to conclude our analysis of global warming by reconsidering some elements of the problem as we have looked at it so far. I want to do this in two ways: first, by asking what impact it has on our analysis if we model the problem differently; and, second, by considering some more far reaching questioning of the assumptions on which such models are based.

5.1 Playing different games?

I have analysed the global warming problem as a Prisoners' Dilemma-type of problem and indicated some reasons why we might expect co-operation to tackle global warming to be hard to achieve. However, as was pointed out in the previous chapter, we do not always have a clear idea of what the payoffs to the players are, we do not always know the nature of the game being played. And for global warming, where there is a high degree of uncertainty about both the costs and benefits of different courses of action, this problem is particularly acute. What I want to consider now is, if we model the problem as a different game, how does this affect our understanding of the potential for co-operation?

> Question

Consider the matrix of payoffs for global warming given in Figure 14.4. As before, I am concentrating on two actors faced with the option of cutting or not cutting emissions of GHGs. What kind of game is being played here?

As you have done before, you can begin to identify the game by thinking about each players' best response and thus identifying the Nash Equilibria. If the USA plays 'don't cut' emissions, the EU's best response is to 'cut' as –2 is better than –5; if the USA plays 'cut', Europe's best response is 'don't cut' as 6

	USA	
	Don't cut emissions	Cut emissions
Don't cut emissions	–5,–5	6,–2
Cut emissions	–2,6	4,4

EU (label on left side between the two rows)

Figure 14.4 Payoff matrix for global warming

is better than 4. Since the payoffs are symmetric, the same applies the other way around. If you have circled the best responses on Figure 14.4 you will see that there are two Nash Equilibria. One is in the bottom left-hand cell, where the USA doesn't cut emissions and the EU does; the other is in the top right-hand cell, where the EU doesn't cut emissions and the USA does. The first equilibrium is clearly preferable to the USA (it gets 6 instead of –2) and the second equilibrium is preferable to the EU. There is thus conflict over which equilibrium is preferred. However, note that both players would prefer either equilibrium (even the one where they get –2) to the situation where neither player cuts emissions (the top left-hand cell) where both get –5. The choice for each player is therefore how to get their preferred equilibrium. That is, the choice of strategy for each player is between whether to play 'tough' (not cut emissions) or 'weak' (cut emissions). If the EU were convinced that the USA will play tough, then it is in the EU's interests to play weak. Additionally, both players would prefer the other non-equilibrium outcome, where both cut emissions and get 4 each, to a situation where they both play tough, and to the situation where they play weak and the other plays tough.

These characteristics share those of a Chicken game: there are two equilibria, the players are opposed over which equilibrium they prefer and they have two strategies – to play 'tough' or 'weak' (see Chapter 13, Section 5).

Question

What are the main differences if global warming is modelled as a Chicken game, compared to my previous model of global warming as a Prisoners' Dilemma?

One of the crucial differences of a Chicken game is that the least preferred option for both players is the situation where neither cuts GHG emissions. This catastrophic outcome is analogous to the head-on crash in the original Chicken metaphor. In the Prisoners' Dilemma the situation where neither player cuts emissions is the single Nash Equilibrium. However, as in the Prisoners' Dilemma game, in the Chicken game the social optimum, where both players cut emissions and total benefits are maximized (4 + 4 = 8 in Figure 14.4) is also unlikely to be realized. Each player prefers an outcome where they do not cut emissions while the other does. Hence they prefer different equilibria. The danger in that situation is that independent decision making may fail to reach either equilibrium, generating the 'catastrophe' outcome of passing a threshold and generating severe climate change.

In fact, Ward (1993) has argued that global warming may be better represented as a game of Chicken than as a Prisoners' Dilemma, and there are some good reasons to think that this may be so. Ward claims that for the USA, as well as Russia and China, their strategy has been a successful one of 'refusing to swerve' in which case the EU's best play would be to cut emissions – thus delivering the benefits of cuts in GHG emissions to Russia,

China and the USA while the EU bears the costs. If we look at the situation at the time of the signing of the UN Framework Convention on Climate Change (when many European countries made unilateral commitments to reduce GHGs and the USA refused) and after the US announcement of its withdrawal from Kyoto (after which the other parties to the agreement continued in their efforts to complete and implement the Kyoto agreement), then the outcome would seem to accord with the Chicken game. If it had been a Prisoners' Dilemma, we would have expected to observe a different combination of strategies; that is, mutual cheating (withdrawal from the agreement by the EU as well as the USA). Ward argues that the USA has used 'commitment tactics' (such as publicizing the costs of cutting GHG emissions) to try to persuade the other parties that its stated intention to withdraw from the Kyoto Protocol was not just cheap talk but deeply serious (Ward, 1993, pp.203–5). Publishing an alternative policy – the *Global Climate Change Initiative* – also helped to reinforce the idea that it was going to continue to 'act tough'.

If global warming does in fact have similar characteristics to the Chicken model, then the prospects for an agreement to cut GHGs are not good; indeed, a solution to the problem may be even harder to find. The more entrenched the US position becomes, the more the EU will think that the USA will continue to refuse to cut emissions, and the more the EU will continue to play weak. While this avoids the 'head-on crash' of neither party cutting GHG emissions, the absence of the USA from the co-operative strategy means that the social optimum – of both cutting emissions – is not realized. Furthermore, it is difficult to see what the EU can do to persuade the USA to change strategy.

Of course, things can change. One possibility is that, if the costs of global warming become clearer and US calculations of its preferences change, then the Chicken game may not be an appropriate analytical tool. Changes in this kind of information may have far-reaching effects on the states' perceptions of the kind of problem that confronts them. One of the factors that led to the solution to the ozone layer problem was precisely the reduction of uncertainty, as you saw in the last chapter. And the alternative representation of the ozone problem as an Assurance game gave an even stronger explanation of how co-operation eventually emerged.

However, we might note one further contrast here. In the ozone layer problem, the costs of banning CFCs were particularly acute for key developing countries such as China and India: they had plans for the development of refrigeration capacity and didn't have access to the new technologies which European and US multinationals had developed as alternatives to CFCs. In this situation, the developed countries offered a side payment to the developing countries in the form of a longer timescale in which to outlaw CFCs, and aid and technology transfer to lower the costs of such a ban (side payments were discussed in Chapter 13, Section 7.2). However, for global warming, such a side payment is much more difficult to realize – the magnitude of the costs and the numbers of activities which would be affected by tight curbs on emissions mean that this solution may well not be available. Indeed, as we have seen, the 'side payment' offered to developing countries to sign the Kyoto agreement was simply that they would not face any binding targets at all. In the event, this was simply too great a price to pay for the USA.

5.2   Extending the analysis and reconsidering the models

In the previous chapter, Judith Mehta and Rathin Roy argued (Section 7) that, while game theory is a valuable tool of analysis,

> we should be careful how we model international collective action situations. We should be sensitive to the assumptions upon which game theory is constructed and the institutional arrangements in which 'games' are played. It may be that the parties are not always as self-interested as game theory (and realist and liberal political theory) assumes, or it may be that so-called cheap talk can in some way influence behaviour. It may be that factors deemed to be extraneous to the game really do matter in a real-world situation.

In the above game-theoretic analysis, I have proceeded based on the assumption that, 'If the payoff structure is of this pattern, then we can interpret the collective action problem in this way'. I have focused the analysis mainly on the Prisoners' Dilemma but briefly noted the features of a Chicken game. This modelling allowed certain issues to be clarified – in particular, those relating to the barriers to co-operation. I then took those insights and showed how they might lead to an interpretation of the problems of the Kyoto Protocol and why the most important player in this game refused to co-operate.

However, you have just seen that much then rests on the 'if' in the assumption in the previous paragraph. In fact, assigning payoffs in such a complex problem is very tricky indeed, will change over time, and will pose different issues for different states. One way in which you might extend the analysis presented here is to investigate more deeply how different states come to formulate their positions on global warming. As you know from Chapter 13, the game-theoretic analysis presented above assumes that the players are rational and self-interested actors. I have interpreted this to mean that the players (states) concerned will seek to maximize their net benefits (the benefits of stopping global warming minus the costs of reducing emissions) in terms of national income. The rational calculation states make in the above models is whether cutting emissions is 'worth it'.

One obvious, limited way to extend and complement the analysis of the problem given by this game-theoretic approach is therefore to 'go behind the payoffs' and concentrate on explaining what it is that states value and why. As I have noted along the way, some states – like the USA – may put a low value on cutting GHGs because of the economic consequences of doing so; others may value highly even very severe restrictions on GHGs because they are particularly at risk from global warming. Indeed, Paterson has argued that different states' differing stances on global warming come down to three factors: the energy dependency of the state concerned (whether they are heavy fossil fuel users, for instance); the level of development and position in the international political economy (for example, whether they are intent on promoting industrialization); and the level of risk faced from climate change (Paterson, 1996, Chapter 4).

As you also know from Part 2, state preferences – the outcomes they seek in respect of the international system – are formed by a range of political and economic factors and social forces and processes of social change both within and outside of states. Any explanation of an individual state's policies in respect of global warming would need to include these factors. For example, in discussing the policy of the USA, I have already made reference to multinational companies and labour unions opposing Kyoto and environmentalists in the USA supporting the treaty, and to development strategies in the developing world and processes of industrialization which might be frustrated by a curb on GHG emissions in other countries.

Question

Does this mean that a game-theoretic approach to collective action problems is inherently limited?

Well, yes and no. Yes in the sense that in any modelling of a collective action problem, certain things are taken for granted; that is, assigning payoffs involves 'bundling up' all these factors into a single value, and an explanation of that 'bundling up' will add to the analysis. However, in a sense, that is why modelling is useful – precisely because it strips out some of the 'fine detail' and allows the structure of a collective action problem to be identified. In short, a defence of the game-theoretic models might be that while this extended analysis is all relevant, the end point of this process is still that those acting as representatives of the state come to a calculation, in which there may be many influences, but which is nevertheless something analogous to the single rational player weighing up different courses of action. At the end of the day, the Bush administration had to decide whether or not to withdraw from the Kyoto Protocol.

However, game theory also assumes that such calculation is independent and strategic – that is, informed by an awareness of the fact that one player's actions affect the payoffs of another, and vice versa. Perhaps a more far-reaching argument, therefore, is that the ways in which states formulate their preferences is itself a product of their experience of interaction with each other. There are two ways in which one might take this point. The first is to see states as involved in a process that is an attempt to create, rather than play, a game. The game theory image is that states have preferences over outcomes and then come to the 'playing field', knowing the strategies open to each other, in order to play. With a relatively new issue like global warming, however, states may not know how to define the available strategies. As Paterson has argued, what constituted 'co-operation' and 'defection' in the early years of the negotiations was uncertain. In this sense, the rules of the game – who the participants are, the strategies available, and the payoffs – only emerge over time. We have seen that the 'game' that actually emerged came to be defined as one about who would or wouldn't adopt binding targets on GHG reductions – and, as Ward argued, it was a game better modelled as a game of Chicken with the EU as the weak player.

The second way in which states' experience of interaction with each other has been important is the way that previous histories of interaction impinge on states' expectations of each other and the influence this exerts on the co-operative solutions they might seek to a given dilemma. One example of this is the way that the global warming problem emerged in the first place. You know already that the problem of global warming emerged from scientific enquiries that were largely conducted under the auspices of two already-existing international organizations – the WMO and the UNEP, and their joint body the IPCC. These organizations have, partly due to the way the UN operates, significant participation from states and individuals from the developing world. From very early on, the climate issue was defined as involving a significant North–South dimension. This dimension of the problem was even highlighted in the way that supposedly 'neutral' scientific data were presented. For example, per capita carbon emissions were used as a measure and this helped to emphasize the disparities in emissions between North and South. The problem was, therefore, framed in a way that made it very difficult for northern countries to define co-operation as involving equal obligations for all states. This became enshrined in the Kyoto Protocol in the form of the absence of targets for developing countries, something that the USA in particular continued to object to. Had the problem been framed differently, then the debate over different states' co-operation or defection would look very different (Paterson, 1996, pp.124–5).

Another example of the impact of states' interaction with one another is that, in the case of global warming, the prior history of co-operation over the ozone layer problem exerted a major influence on the kind of co-operative solutions that states sought to agree on. Global warming negotiations followed on from, and overlapped with, the ozone depletion negotiations. Importantly, many of the scientists and diplomats involved in the global warming issue had also been involved in the ozone layer negotiations.

Perhaps not surprisingly, especially given that politicians and governments had also just emerged from negotiating this successful global environmental agreement (The Montreal Protocol), the discussions on a climate change convention came to focus on creating a similar kind of agreement. As you have seen in detail above, the fact that efforts to tackle global warming focused on a similar kind of agreement to the Montreal Protocol, with its emphasis on targets and timetables for emissions cuts, stored up a host of problems. Thus, while game-theoretic analysis can help to shed some light on how the two problems differed in terms of the structures of the payoffs, we should always bear in mind the context in which collective action problems, and states' actions in relation to them, are defined.

6 Conclusion

The analysis of collective action presented in Part 5 has sought to identify the extent to which individual states in the international system are able to co-operate in pursuit of socially optimal collective decisions. You have seen that in many instances states seem unable to achieve what would be in each state's self-interest by acting independently. You have also looked in detail at one way of explaining why this might be the case, using tools of game theory to analyse the global warming collective action problem. However, as I have noted, this approach rests on some far-reaching assumptions about how states behave, including that they will make independent decisions based on a rational calculation of self-interest. However, at the end of Section 2 I noted that one of the particularities of the environmental issue (which only came to feature prominently on international political agendas in the late twentieth century) is that it has helped to engender the idea that humanity shares a common destiny. Even if one maintains the realist view raised in Part 1 – that the primary goal of states is survival – the genuinely global problem of climate change confronts all states, albeit unequally. The question this prompts is whether, in the face of a common threat, states' behaviour will move away from the assumptions of non-cooperative game theory toward the pursuit of collective decision making.

Such a prospect seems a long way from the behaviour of George Bush (his rejection of Kyoto was, after all, not based on concern for China or India, but for the US economy, firms and citizens). It would imply a transformation in the states system and would challenge some of the basic assumptions that have been made about it in economic and political theory.

Further reading

A readable general account of various global environmental issues and the international politics around them is Elliott, L. (1998) *The Global Politics of the Environment*, Basingstoke, Macmillan.

A detailed study of the politics of global warming and some of the international relations issues it raises (written before the Kyoto Protocol was signed) is Paterson, M. (1996) *Global Warming and Global Politics*, London, Routledge.

A critical review of the Kyoto Protocol from one of the leading environmental campaign groups is Greenpeace (1998) *Guide to the Kyoto Protocol*, Amsterdam, Greenpeace International.

A review of a number of global problems and the prospects for solutions, using some game-theoretic analysis to identify different issues in international co-operation, is Sandler, T. (1997) *Global Challenges: An Approach to Environmental, Political, and Economic Problems*, Cambridge, Cambridge University Press.

A sophisticated analysis of the problems that the Kyoto Protocol created is provided in Victor, D.G. (2001) *The Collapse of the Kyoto Protocol and the Struggle to Slow Global Warming*, Princeton, NJ, and Oxford, Princeton University Press.

Chapter 15 International political economy and making the international

Simon Bromley, Maureen Mackintosh, William Brown and Marc Wuyts

1   Introduction

Economic analysis and political theory develop independently as separate disciplines, yet they draw on each other and they study the same world. Indeed, the experience of economic interdependence drives many of the debates about international politics and governance. And political arguments, as well as the capabilities and interests of states, profoundly influence – in ways often unacknowledged – the policy proposals of economists as well as the operations of markets. As an intellectual endeavour, therefore, international political economy lies in the interweaving of these ideas; as an object of study, it consists of the complex interaction of the economic activities of states and firms with political institutions, actors and initiatives.

So, in this text, we have tried to institute a conversation between economists and political scientists. We have brought together an international group of authors prepared to engage with closely related topics from distinct intellectual traditions, and have structured the contributions, in part, around regional perspectives on major international issues. In this concluding chapter, we seek to explore briefly, but in more depth than the book's structure has allowed so far, some of the cross-cutting themes that connect the various parts of *Making the International*. In the process, we hope to establish the outlines of a broader argument that relates to the interplay of the book's two main characteristics: bringing economics and politics together in the study of the international, and the juxtaposition of an internationally shared terrain of theoretical debate with the diversity of voices across that terrain (see Chapter 1). In so doing, we also hope to draw attention to some of the key concepts and models that you will have already met.

2   Economics and politics

One simple way to think about the difference between economics and politics is to consider the counterposition of markets and governance. We trust that this book has made it clear that the difference between the disciplines is more complicated than that, although it remains a useful starting point. The economics you have studied has emphasized a number of lessons for our thinking about the making of the international, but we want to draw your attention to two key points. First, market incentives – the opportunities and constraints that markets offer to profit from production and trade – are enormously powerful influences on the actions of firms and people. They also serve to shape the context in which public policy operates, whether nationally or internationally and in organizations such as the WTO, NAFTA and the IMF. And second, people, firms and even states come to markets on highly unequal terms. This has been a running theme throughout the economics you have studied in *Making the International*. Small economies, countries with low purchasing power, have little influence on the development of international markets: they are 'price takers', driven by the production and trading decisions of others (Chapters 2, 3 and 11). As international markets change, the positions of different countries shift: for example, Mexico found that lower income countries were influencing its competitive position in the 1990s. Markets are both a sphere of anarchic interaction – a terrain for independent trading among buyers and sellers – and a vehicle for the concentration of resources and income in a relatively small number of hands (countries, firms and individuals).

At the same time, however, the politics you have studied demonstrates that states are actors that make special – that is, sovereign – claims for their authority in relation to the activities of individuals and firms, as well as in relation to other social institutions and groups. States engage with the international economy but they are primarily institutions of territorial control and political order. These sovereign claims serve to structure the international system as a *states-system* and as an international economy. The production of political order within states and the processes of co-operation, competition and conflict among states in the states-system relate to markets and market processes in complex ways. Once again, there are, perhaps, two key lessons to draw in this respect. There is, first, an important argument, developed in Chapter 5, that the extended forms of interdependence – that is, mutual dependence – created by markets are sustainable only on the basis of a prior and continuing guarantee of basic physical and material security established by the state. The realist version of this argument suggests that voluntary specialization and trade between countries will be limited in those areas that bear directly on the security of the state, as the international realm is essentially anarchic. In this context, strong states may be able to *impose* interdependence on others; and for some this is precisely what is represented by the macroeconomic policy changes associated with aid-conditionality and the moves towards freer trade and investment. Others – liberal theorists of interdependence, for example – argue that arrangements such as the WTO and NAFTA represent a more positive-sum form of interaction, allowing some co-operative governance of this growing economic interdependence (see especially Chapter 9). Still, both perspectives insist on the importance of governance for market processes.

The second key point from the politics you have studied is that the construction of agents as market actors, able and willing to engage in market processes, is also a profoundly political accomplishment. States not only regulate markets, they also make markets. Chapter 6 emphasizes that 'treating people as "economic individuals" with atomistic self-interested inclinations is not to respond to a natural human trait, but to build a policy on a cultural construct'. Something similar can be said of countries, as the political struggles over the nature of African states discussed in Chapter 10 demonstrate. People and countries are not simply economic actors, and different societies embed economic relations in different ways in their social, cultural and political settings, so many of the contests at the international level turn on how the 'economic' is to be politically constituted. The political objectives at stake in these contests may vary widely – for example, India's attempt to pursue a policy of non-alignment or, perhaps, the USA's attempt to maintain its relative position vis-à-vis other states. What is sometimes seen as a co-operative process is often a process in which the powerful are able to impose their wishes upon others.

3   Specificity and difference

We have emphasized that markets create interdependence, but that the gains of specialization and trade are distributed unequally. We have also noted that governance, whether nationally or internationally, involves collective choices, but that these can be marked as much by the exercise of power as by co-operation. Another way of putting all this is to say that difference matters acutely in the shaping of the international political economy: the differences between the resources various agents bring to production and trade, and the differences in power in the political sphere. This implies that countries enter the international arena from different and thus specific vantage points. There are at least three distinct dimensions to the variation in specific contexts that together constitute the international as a heterogeneous ensemble: size, conjuncture and location.

The GDP of the European Union is roughly equivalent to that of the USA but militarily speaking the latter is the sole superpower capable of deploying conventional military forces extensively and intensively across the world. Russia has only a fraction of the GDP of the USA but its possession of nuclear weapons makes it an important international power. Switzerland has a higher GDP per capita than the USA but this is unlikely to cause sleepless nights in Washington given the relative sizes of the economies. The weight of the US economy within world markets by far overshadows that of Switzerland, despite the higher standard of living in the latter. Conversely, as is shown in Chapter 14, China has relatively low level of carbon dioxide emissions per capita, but its total contribution to world levels is substantial. And so on. Economic size and political and military power matter in structuring the international, although they matter in complex ways.

Compare, for example, India with Tanzania. The sheer size of the home market in India has created possible avenues for processes of industrial investment and development through import substituting industrialization (see Chapter 7), which Tanzania, given its size, could only dream about (see Chapter 11). Similarly, it is not surprising that Chapter 6, on the politics of liberalization in India, stresses the role that internal domestic processes have played in reshaping the definition of the national interest to open the door to liberalization. In contrast, Chapter 12 focuses on the extent to which liberalization under structural adjustment in Tanzania was largely dictated from abroad. Similarly, the bargaining relations between the USA and Mexico, on the one hand, and the European Union, on the other, are likely to differ considerably, given the considerably smaller size and lower per capita GDP of Mexico's economy.

The remaining ingredients that make for specificity within an international context are associated with historical conjuncture and geographical (or, better still, geopolitical) location. Countries do not develop in parallel along similar trajectories or phases, even when they evolve in broadly similar directions such as, for example, the road to industrialization. A major theme of this book has been that the making of the international is shaped by the dynamic evolution of economic interdependencies and by the prevailing nature of the international political order. A country's trajectory, therefore, depends not only on its own history but also on the histories of other countries that have gone before and others that are lagging behind. It is also shaped by the contemporaneous trajectory of the international as a whole, as fashioned by its most powerful political and economic members. That is to say, historical evolution takes place in the context of conjunctures marked by distinct patterns of geopolitical power and geo-economic influence. The location of countries in relation to a given conjuncture is an important aspect of the international environment.

Take, for example, the process of industrialization in East Asia, which is analysed in Chapter 3 using the 'flying geese' paradigm: a set of countries, in a hierarchy of followers and leaders, moves in formation in a process of industrialization whereby the leaders move successively towards higher skilled, higher technology manufacturing and exports, leaving the followers to occupy the space left behind for lower skilled, lower technology manufacturing and exports. The industrialization efforts of different countries in the region became mutually reinforcing in this process.

Furthermore, countries such as South Korea or Taiwan (but also India and others), which embarked on this process of industrialization in the aftermath of the Second World War, benefited from the prolonged boom that followed the War from the 1950s to the early 1970s and from an international political climate that was far more conducive to active industrial policies (such as infant industry protection and, more generally, import-substituting industrialization) than has been the case in recent years.

Thus, politics and geopolitical alignments played a key role. In the case of India, for example, Chapter 6 argues that the impetus of decolonization and the Cold War rivalry between the Soviet Union and the USA created a space in which, as Chapter 7 shows, the state was able to lay the foundations on which new comparative advantages could be forged. By contrast, latecomers, such as Tanzania and other African countries, began industrializing at a time when the tide was about to turn, both economically and politically, and soon found their attempts aborted through economic crises and donor-induced political conditionality (Chapters 10, 11 and 12). Looked at from a political angle, these contrasting fortunes may be described in terms of the degree of autonomy of the Indian state compared with most African states, and its consequent ability to give voice to its distinctive conception of national sovereignty in the international order. Similarly, the autonomy of African states and their abilities to give voice to their own sovereign claims to development have varied over time, especially before and after the dramatic changes of the 1980s (as Chapter 10 argues).

The interplay between Mexico and the USA provides another example of the importance of historical conjuncture and geopolitical reality in shaping the options open to a country within the international arena. As Chapter 9 explains, the end of the Cold War (1989–1991) and the rapid changes this provoked within Eastern Europe opened up new opportunities for foreign investors, creating a new context within which Mexico, under President Salinas, came to abandon its traditional conception of sovereignty as something exercised unilaterally (and, especially, independently of ties to the USA) in favour of becoming part of an economic trading block, NAFTA, with the USA and Canada. More generally, as argued in Chapters 2 and 4, in recent years the political arrangements crystallized within the WTO have severely limited the scope of low income countries to follow in the trade policy footsteps of the current industrialized and newly industrialized countries, thereby 'kicking away the ladder' – as Ha-Joon Chang (2002) put it – which had allowed the latter to rise to prosperity.

4   Interdependence, asymmetry and power

From what we have said so far, it is apparent that international economic interdependence and the anarchic structure of the international political system coexist with highly asymmetric relations of population size, per capita GNP and political and military power. In the making of the international, asymmetry is the rule not the exception. This is in fact a corollary of the points we have already made about the relevance of difference, specificity and context. When asymmetry prevails, averaging conditions or outcomes across countries (or groupings of countries) can give results that are neither typical nor particularly meaningful. Consequently, making generalizations from evidence becomes a tricky exercise in the presence of asymmetries.

Chapters 2 and 4, for example, look at the WTO from the perspective of the 'developing countries' – a generic term which suggests the prevalence of sufficiently homogeneous conditions to warrant grouping them together (if only in comparison with 'developed countries'). This is a useful device that often allows us to bring out the differences between groups more sharply, in terms of both the economic resources they command and the political power they wield. But, as Parts 2, 3 and 4 demonstrate, there are considerable differences among developing countries: in terms of the benefits they can derive from membership of the international economy, and in terms of the influence they can exert in shaping the rules of international political institutions such as the WTO. India can afford to fight costly legal battles in Western countries to prevent the patenting of products whose medical properties have been known since ancient times. Similarly, Brazil and South Africa can induce pharmaceutical companies to supply drugs at lower prices within developing countries. Many of the least developed countries, however, lack the resources or the expertise to engage in battles of this sort and are consequently left with the choice of whether to participate in an arrangement that they have little ability to influence (see Chapter 4).

The developing countries share certain common interests (particularly in contrast with the OECD countries), but there is also considerable heterogeneity among them. Moreover, in the second half of the last century this heterogeneity – and hence its associated asymmetries – became more pronounced. Thus Section 8 in Chapter 3 asks whether the recent era of increased globalization and greater market openness has reduced poverty. The answer is mixed: globalization appears to have led both to falling total numbers in poverty in the world and to a severe worsening of poverty in a large number of countries. The reason is that successful development in a few large countries such as India and China can disguise, in calculations and political commentary, the plight of smaller, less fortunate countries, such as many in sub-Saharan Africa. In a context in which asymmetries are increasing, drawing conclusions based on the average performance of increasingly heterogeneous nations can be seriously misleading.

Asymmetric interdependence is not important only when considering economic comparisons, it can also be a source of political power between and among states as discussed in detail in Chapter 9. The relations between Mexico and the USA can be analysed in terms of the interplay between asymmetric interdependence, bargaining and coercive power. Interdependence may create scope for positive-sum interactions and mutually beneficial bargaining. But asymmetric interdependence between two (or more) parties may give rise to coercive power, the ability of one party to impose costs on another, in which the dominant party can 'go it alone'. This form of power is in addition to the kind of power realists have in mind when they speak of the unequal distribution of (military) capabilities among states (Chapter 5). Both are sources of power, but the former may operate even in the absence of direct physical coercion.

One possibility that arises in this context is that asymmetries become a source of power and, in turn, that power is then used to reinforce asymmetry. Chapter 10 argues at length that this was the experience of Africa, faced with powerful aid donors in the 1980s and 1990s. Chapter 11, picking up this point, contains a quotation from John Toye arguing that 'structural adjustment' as a concept acquired a whole new meaning once it became adopted and transformed by the World Bank in the late 1970s and early 1980s. Previously, Toye argued, structural adjustment referred to the process in which developed countries made room to accommodate industrial exports from industrializing developing countries. In essence, this earlier concept of structural adjustment is akin to the 'flying geese' paradigm. It takes asymmetry as its point of departure, but seeks to *diminish* it over time by slanting the burden of adjustment towards the more advanced countries, pulling up the less developed countries in the process. The later (and now dominant) concept of structural adjustment, however, involved shifting the burden of adjustment back to the economically weak, calling on them to adjust their economic policies towards greater market openness – a process that has much greater potential to increase asymmetries, not just between the developed and developing countries but also among the latter.

Another possibility is that increasing asymmetries of power in the system of states may be the *object* of international policy, as when states are concerned, not with their absolute position, but with their economic and political performance vis-à-vis other states, that is, when states focus on relative gains. Consider, for example, the reasons for the withdrawal of the USA from the Kyoto Protocol discussed in Chapter 14. There it was suggested that, given the structure of the incentives in a setting of strategic interdependence, it was not in the USA's 'private' interest to cut emissions of carbon dioxide. An alternative explanation, however, might be that the USA was concerned to avoid doing anything that might constrain its economic (and hence, in the long run, its military) lead over future potential rivals such as China, India and even the European Union. As Chapter 9 argues, when countries evaluate their positions relative to the performance of others, that is, when they focus on their share of the total gains available, even positive-sum interactions can take the form of zero-sum conflicts.

Asymmetry and power are not only apparent between countries, they also operate within them. Consider, for example, the asymmetries of power between capital and labour. Chapter 8 argues that, in the formation of NAFTA, the power of capital became greatly enhanced (including legal enforcement), while that of labour was rendered considerably weaker. In a similar vein, Chapter 2 points out the remarkable asymmetry between capital and labour with respect to the institutional arrangements of the WTO, governing the free movements of goods and capital but not of labour. More generally, the changing resources and powers available to social groups within states may affect how states define their national interests and seek to fashion international alignments – as Chapters 6, 9, 10 and 12 all illustrate.

5   Anarchy and governance

We began *Making the International* with some models of anarchic order, both in economics and politics. The theory of comparative advantage assumes an anarchic system: it examines the gains from trade between independent national economies (countries). And the underlying model of specialization and trade on markets is also anarchic, in the sense that the outcomes of market processes arise spontaneously from the interaction of many independent decisions taken by firms, consumers and so forth. And the realist theory of Waltz is explicitly a theory of international politics as an anarchic order. At the same time, we noted that international trade is governed, to some extent, by states acting both nationally and internationally, and that critics of realism argue that there are forms of governance beyond the state in the international political system, of which institutions such as the WTO, NAFTA and the European Union are examples (Chapters 3, 5 and 9).

In Parts 2 and 4 we see that states are not the passive bearers of these anarchic forces, but that they make (often strenuous) efforts to shape the terms on which they trade and to give voice to their own distinctive national priorities. That is to say, the social purposes that states seek to realize internationally are derived, in part, from the agency of groups within distinct national cultures and histories, and that these purposes change as the cultures and histories evolve and develop (Chapters 6 and 12). Similarly, many states have pursued economic policies to transform and expand their production possibility frontiers, whether in the form of import-substituting industrialization or, more generally, under the guise of developmental states (see Chapters 7, 8 and 10). State policy towards the international is derived not only from the position of the state and its economy in the system as a whole but also from the agency of national forces and groups. As part of that process, states often seek to govern aspects of their 'external' environment, individually and collectively.

In short, at both the national and international level, individually and collectively, states attempt to govern aspects of the international political economy and to change the terms on which they engage with it. This raises the possibility that the institutions of co-ordination and governance that develop in an anarchic states-system may act upon and transform the international to produce a modified anarchy, in which rules operate to constrain and enable the actions of member states. Sometimes this governance is based on co-operative relations founded in the ability to negotiate bargained outcomes in positive-sum games. At other times, independent decision making leads to outcomes that fail to realize the social optimum (as is explored using game theory in Part 5). This may or may not lead to attempts to resolve these collective action problems (see Chapters 13 and 14). On occasions, some may be in a position to 'go it alone' and impose forms of governance that suit their interests without worrying about the interests of poorer and weaker countries (Chapter 9). To be sure, richer economies and states that are more powerful have a greater capacity to do this than others do. The making of the international involves all of these interactions, in different combinations in different contexts. The degree to which the international can be governed in the interests of many, rather than subject to the power of a few, is one of the most contested and difficult questions of international political economy.

6   Models as metaphors

The complexity just described is one reason we have given so much attention to developing models in *Making the International*. Throughout this book, you will have come across the use of models – both in economics and in politics. You will have noted that models in economics often make use of diagrams and graphs, numbers and equations. In politics, models tend to be confined to words (but not always – see, for example, Chapter 9). Despite these apparent differences, there are certain common threads that are characteristic of the use of models in analysis.

A good model is akin to a sketch (or even a caricature) but it is not a mirror. Models are about the inspired simplification of the reality around us. Such simplifications are based partly on judgements about what is important and partly on the modelling techniques available. Consequently, do not judge models by whether they explain every nook and cranny of the phenomenon under study but by the insights they yield and the relevance of those insights to the problem at hand. Models demand that you see the point they make. In other words, to get the point, you have to work through the analytics of a model. To understand a model, you have to be able to use it. That is one reason why we have provided a range of activities and questions for you to work through. This is true whether you are dealing with the arithmetic of comparative advantage, the pessimistic logic of the Prisoners' Dilemma, the implications of viewing the international arena through the eyes of a realist, or the use of bargaining games to think about power.

Models focus your attention on a particular aspect, isolate it, and investigate its logic. They are an attempt to make our metaphors more rigorous, to bring out the essential logic connecting assumptions to conclusions, and (sometimes) to make arguments testable in the light of empirical evidence. The insights they yield can often be quite surprising. For example, it is not immediately obvious that two countries can benefit from trade even if one of them has higher productivity all round. Similarly, it can come as a bit of a surprise when first confronted with a Prisoners' Dilemma game to find that the stable outcome is not an outcome that any player prefers. Thus, these kinds of intellectual exercises throw light on complex realities.

Models vary in their design and purpose, and you have seen several different types of models. The different 'games' in Chapter 13 are all examples of a broad class of game theoretic models, widely used now in economics and politics to investigate strategic behaviour. They all assume independent, self-interested and 'anarchic' strategic behaviour by the 'players'. The assumption of independent decision making is also shared by a number of the economic models of markets that you have also studied. The theory of comparative advantage, related models such as the 'immiserizing growth' model (Chapter 3), and the competitive market models of the labour market (Chapter 8) and the foreign exchange market (Chapter 11) all assume that countries, people and firms act independently in their own interests. Like the realist model of the political behaviour of states in the international arena (Chapter 5), they are anarchic models. Nevertheless, if you compare the theory of comparative advantage with the realist model, you will see that each highlights a different aspect of international interdependence: the theory of comparative advantage highlights the gains to countries arising from economic interdependence, while realist theory draws one's attention to the ways in which security may be compromised by the resulting forms of dependence on others.

In contrast, the bargaining models developed in Chapter 9 make a different assumption: that 'players' (countries in Chapter 9, but it might be people or firms) can make agreements and then stick to them. In other words, they assume that governance processes can be created and will 'stick' once players have decided on their best decision in the circumstances that face them. Other models too assume that governance processes exist and structure economic and political interaction. The model of market segmentation in Chapter 8, for example, assumes that labour market institutions and the laws and regulatory agreements that govern labour markets in a corporatist country influence wages and employment conditions. The trick, in using models, is to pick the set of assumptions and the modelling approach that best highlights key aspects of the problem or situation you are analysing.

Models yield insights but – particularly when part of dominant discourses – they can also structure what is considered to be politically feasible or possible. In other words, models restrict our view because they focus on particular aspects and ignore others. The contrasting notions of structural adjustment referred to earlier, for example, redefine what are considered feasible policy options. Looking at a problem as a Prisoners' Dilemma game leads to different conclusions from looking at the problem as an Assurance game (Chapter 13). The realist theory of international anarchy suggests that the scope for co-operative international governance – as opposed to domination by the powerful – is inherently limited, yet liberal theories of interdependence argue that the games states can play include positive-sum as well as zero-sum games.

7 Theory and voice

In a world marked by specificities of scale and conjuncture, and by vast asymmetries of income and power, different locations and different intellectual traditions employ the concepts and models of economic and political analysis in a wide variety of ways, to varying ends. You have seen, for example, that the economic analysis of trade can support both the claim of the WTO that comparative advantage can benefit all and the assertion that countries may trade themselves into increasing poverty. Politically speaking, the scope for international governance looks very different if one assumes that states' national interests are given by their position in the system of states or if one assumes that they are derived from the social purposes of powerful groups in society (compare Chapters 5, 6 and 9). Viewing liberalization and growing economic openness to international markets from Indian, Mexican and Tanzanian perspectives yields a rich range of contrasting insights. The ways in which countries are able to give a distinctive voice to their sovereignty, either nationally or internationally, varies considerably from case to case, depending upon the state's freedom from domestic and international pressures. Judgements about the most important international collective action problems are likely to differ in Washington, Brussels and Dar es Salaam.

Accordingly, our aim has not been to present a set of packaged views of the international. Rather, we wanted to give you a flavour of this diversity and to show you that an analysis of how the international is made can be conducted in many relevant ways. So you have studied a variety of models and concepts in particular contexts, presented from different vantage points for diverse purposes. As we said at the outset, however, these tools of political and economic analysis are of general, international applicability. And as we have emphasized throughout, they can be deployed in other contexts for other purposes. If *Making the International* enables you to think about some of the questions of international political economy for yourself in new ways, our main objective will have been realized.

Answers to activities

Activity 2.1

You will have used your own example. As an illustration, think of the emotive issue of child labour. If this were to be effectively banned in developing countries, the costs of export industries (such as garment making) would rise in those countries, as employers either closed down or hired adult workers at higher wages. Firms and workers in developed countries who produce garments that compete with imports would gain; consumers in those countries would lose by having to pay more. In developing countries, the child workers would lose (if no better alternative were provided), as would those making a living from the occupations in which the displaced children would end up (typically, begging, street vending and domestic services), where competition would increase. The adults who replaced the children would gain, but they would have to be paid higher wages and the industry's sales would be reduced, so they would be fewer in number than the children they had displaced.

Rather than an outright ban, a better way to tackle the problem might be to provide funding to improve the education, health and nutrition of the children who are withdrawn from work, so as to prepare them for more productive jobs through which they could contribute to their families when they grow up. To improve these employment opportunities, it is important to dismantle the barriers that developed countries have imposed on simple manufactures exported by developing countries. Temporary financial compensation could also be provided to the families; this would not amount to large sums, as the children's cash contribution to their families is typically small.

Activity 3.1

The answer is that nearly 30 per cent of low and middle income countries' exports go to other low and middle income countries. To calculate this, you need to express the share of world trade that is between low and middle income countries as a percentage of the share of world trade that originates in such countries. That is:

$$\frac{7.1}{24.2} \times 100 = 29.34 \text{ (to two decimal places)}$$

In other words, low and middle income countries *are* important trading partners for each other, despite the low share of *world* trade their trading relations represent.

Activity 3.2

The tariff on tomato concentrate is removed. The price of imported concentrate in Senegal drops to the world price, now that the overseas exporters do not have to pay a tax at the border. The local producers are forced to reduce prices to match, or lose their customers. The local producers lose part of their share of the market, and cut back output. If they cannot produce profitably at the world market price they will close down. Consumers gain from lower prices;

overseas producers gain larger sales; Senegalese producers lose output and revenue; Senegalese workers lose jobs; and the Senegalese government loses the tariff revenue. As many European exporters are still benefiting from EU subsidies, the world market price may be too low for unsubsidized Senegalese producers, despite the lower wages in Senegal compared with Europe. If neighbouring countries were liberalizing too, prices would be falling in those markets as well, preventing Senegalese producers from continuing to export profitably.

Activity 3.3

The height of the first bar from the left, for example, shows that the average tariff paid by imports coming into South Asia between 1980 and 1985 was about 65 per cent of the sales value of the imports.

Activity 3.4

If the low income country produces no medicine, it can produce 30 000 bags of food (point A); if no food, 1500 boxes of pills (point B). Or it can produce any mix of food and medicine along the solid line AB joining those two points, such as point C. The line AB is the country's production possibility frontier. If the country fails to use some of its available labour, then production might be inside the frontier, at a point such as D.

Activity 3.5

If both countries specialize according to their comparative advantage, world output is 30 000 bags of food produced by the low income country and 4000 boxes of pills produced by the high income country per month. If both countries had produced at point C instead, output would be 25 000 bags of food and 2750 boxes of pills.

Activity 3.6

The country's production possibility curve shifts outward only along the horizontal axis, from AB to AE. Its maximum production of food is unchanged. The shift changes the country's opportunity cost of production of each good – lowering the opportunity cost of producing medicine in terms of food – and increases the amount of goods available to the population under autarky by raising the medicine available at each level of food produced.

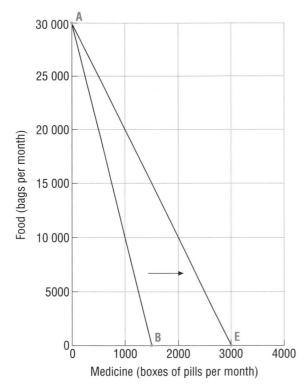

Figure 3.10   An outward shift of the production possibility frontier of the low income country

Activity 4.1

The requirement for consensus effectively gave the rich countries a veto, and the principal supplier principle excluded developing countries from the negotiations.

Activity 5.1

If you were to follow Aristotle and see politics as involving a co-operative endeavour to collectively formulate rules and pursue a shared notion of the good life, then you would tend to the view that the member states conform to the WTO's rules because they are their rules and that they are free to leave with their rights intact. On the face of it, this seems to be what the supporters of the WTO are saying. As you know there are good reasons to doubt this rather comforting view of the WTO and of politics in general. In the WTO there would appear to be considerable disagreement about the good life and how to achieve it, and some doubt as to how easily and at what cost developing countries could stay outside of the WTO.

Activity 5.2

1 The basic source of violent conflict among individuals is that people's judgements or decisions about what is necessary for their self-preservation are partial and, therefore, different from one another. The result is that everyone lives in fear of others.

2 If everyone agreed to transfer his or her right to decide what is necessary for self-preservation to a sovereign power, which was empowered to making binding judgements for all, then there would be only one such judgement and hence no conflicts over what conduces to self-preservation among the people so constituted.

3 Since peace is obviously preferable to war, people should take the second step noted above.

Activity 5.3

One of the key things Waltz adds is that states will only trade to the extent that they don't become vulnerable by becoming dependent on others for their physical and material security. The extent to which a state will specialize – concentrate on producing medicines rather than arms, say – will thus be limited. The overall gains from trade, according to the theory of comparative advantage, will also thus be limited but this is the price to be paid by states for their security, according to Waltz. You might question this by asking how realistic it is. Many states are dependent on imports for key goods such as arms and food. Do Waltz's conclusions apply only to the most powerful states?

Activity 5.4

Hierarchical systems are characterized by the existence of legitimate authority; a degree of specialization among political actors; and a relative indifference to comparisons of power, since the security of all is guaranteed. Anarchical systems are characterized by the absence of legitimate authority among political actors; functional equivalence between actors; and a concern with relative power, as security is maintained on a self-help basis.

Activity 5.5

1 My answer to this question would include noting that trade will only be engaged in if (a) it does not increase vulnerability, particularly in areas central to a state's security (for example food or armaments) and (b) it does not weaken a state's relative power vis-à-vis others. The rules governing trade should be understood as reflecting the interests of the most powerful states.

2 For Waltz, clearly, international interactions are anarchic rather than governed. Within states, Waltz, following Hobbes, sees the anarchy of the state of nature replaced by a hierarchy. Between states, Waltz claims this doesn't happen and interactions between states are determined by considerations of power. Section 5 begins to question why this is so and whether Waltz's argument holds up under scrutiny.

Activity 5.6

This will vary a great deal but some examples might be the debates in the European Union about whether economic integration threatens member states' sovereignty; whether WTO rules on intellectual property rights infringe developing countries' sovereignty; or whether the actions of the United Nations with respect to Iraq infringe that state's sovereignty. All of these are examples in which international processes are involved in shaping the nature of domestic sovereignty.

Activity 5.7

The standard realist reply is that while states can indeed co-ordinate their interests, and may even come to share common values, the scope and depth of co-operation that these can induce is always limited by the inherently competitive striving for relative power in a system in which the means of coercion remain decentralized. Hobbes argued that only the creation of a sovereign power, which monopolized the means of coercion and embodied a unity of judgement as to what conduces to self-preservation, could lift individuals out of the state of nature. Realists contend that the absence of these features among states at the international level renders co-operation based on co-ordinated interests or consensus as to values highly precarious. The idea that WTO rules are based in any fundamental sense on genuine co-operation would therefore be rejected.

Activity 6.1

To some extent both are important, but the emphasis here is on changing forms of discourse – in a context of the 'activation of the common people' as strong party control of national government is replaced by more unstable coalitions drawing on regional forces – and on new forms of collective identification based on notions of community defined in caste, religious and tribal terms.

Activity 6.2

Answers will depend on judgement about the nature of political activity. One counter to the view advanced in the text is that identity politics based on attachments to particular communities (say, the Black community in the UK or the gay community) are part of politics in Western states. By the same token, it might be suggested that significant elements of individualistic, interest-based politics are present among the common people in India. The difference may be more one of degree, than of kind.

Activity 6.3

I have been appealing to the (changing) interests of different social groups in order to identify how they might relate to different policy options.

Activity 6.4

One way of describing the politics of the BJP, in this respect, is to see it as an attempt to redefine and re-imagine some identities in new terms – to define India as a Hindu nation rather than a secular state, for example. At the same time, the BJP has had to recognize that the interests of some groups – businesses with a big stake in liberalization and economic openness to foreign capital and firms – place constraints on this process. In other words, the field in which actors seek collectively to define and symbolize interests is a contested one.

Activity 7.1

This activity requires you to use the formula for calculating the rate of growth and the completed table should read as follows.

Year	Production (in units)	Year on year rate of growth (%)
1995	120	–
1996	90	–25.00
1997	110	22.22
1998	160	45.45
1999	100	–37.50

The growth of production in 1996 over 1995 is $90 - 120 = -30$. Production has fallen by 30 units. Computed as a percentage of income in 1995, this is a fall (hence the minus sign) of 25 per cent:

$$\left(\frac{-30}{120} \right) . 100$$

The growth for income in 1997 over 1996 is an addition of 20 units. Computed as a percentage of income in 1996, this is a growth of 22.22 per cent:

$$\left(\frac{20}{90} \right) . 100$$

The growth for income in 1998 over 1997 is an addition of 50 units. Computed as a percentage of income in 1997, this is a growth of 45.45 per cent:

$$\left(\frac{50}{110} \right) . 100$$

The growth for income in 1999 over 1998 is a reduction of 60 units. Computed as a percentage of income in 1998, this is a growth of –37.5 per cent:

$$\left(\frac{-60}{160} \right) . 100$$

Activity 7.2

The figure should look like Figure 7.6.

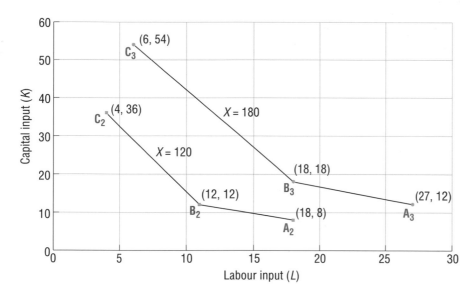

Figure 7.6   Isoquants for $X = 120$ and $X = 180$

On the horizontal axis we measure the labour input and on the vertical axis we measure units of capital. Note the co-ordinates of (L, K) shown for each point and relate them back to Table 7.2b. You will see that the lower isoquant shows the (L, K) combinations required for producing $X = 120$ units of output. Similarly the isoquant that lies above shows the (L, K) combination required for producing 180 bales of textiles.

Activity 7.3

If producers use technique A, then nine more people are needed to produce 60 more bales; with technique B, six more workers are required; and with technique C, two more.

Activity 7.4

1   The main elements of Indian industrial policy in the 1960s were as follows:

(a)   A large role for the public sector in industrial investment, especially in the capital goods and infrastructure sectors.

(b)   Tariffs on consumption goods to protect the domestic market for domestic producers.

(c)   The use of licensing to regulate the quantity and direction of private sector industrial investment.

(d)   The use of import licences and quotas to regulate private sector imports into the economy.

2   In the mid 1970s and 1980s the following changes were introduced.

(a)   The Monopolies and Restrictive Trade Practices Act was introduced to monitor the behaviour of big business houses and foreign firms.

(b)   Some industries were reserved for production in the small-scale sector and by small firms.

(c)   Import quotas and licences were liberalized.

(d)   Industrial licences were granted more easily.

Activity 7.5

1   This is similar to Activity 7.2, except that the numbers are different for the (*L*, *K*) combinations. You should get a figure like Figure 7.7. I have labelled the new points with their (*L*, *K*) combinations.

2   Comparing these isoquants with the ones you drew in Activity 7.2, you will find that in each case (*X* = 120, 180), the isoquant in 2000 lies lower than the isoquant in 1980 and closer to the origin. The inward shift is due to the increased productivity caused by technological change.

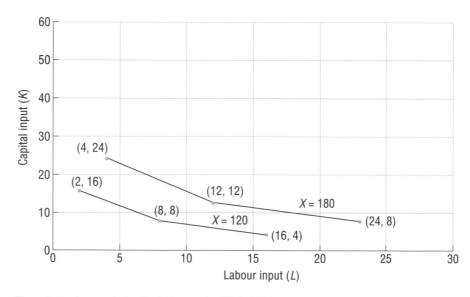

Figure 7.7   Isoquants for *X* = 120 and *X* = 180 in 2000

Activity 8.1

We cannot answer for the author of Chapter 2, but it seems to us that the answer to the first question is no: the Kukdong case is different. In this case, international activists were supporting local labour organizing in pursuit of basic labour rights and working conditions the local workforce thought decent. This seems to be much closer to Aditya Bhattacharjea's recommendation to support local activism and local action in support of better standards. However, some of the anti-sweatshop campaigning may have the protectionist effect of closing markets to goods made by very low wage workers. There are no easy answers here.

Activity 8.2

To construct the cumulative share of the poorest 60 per cent of the households (third row of column 4) add the share of the middle 20 per cent (11.8 per cent) to the share of the poorest 40 per cent (10.4 per cent): total, 22.2 per cent. The share of the poorest 80 per cent is then 22.2 per cent plus the share of the next richest fifth (19.1 per cent): total 41.3 per cent. All 100 per cent of households finally have 100 per cent of the income. (The calculation does not quite add to 100 because of the effect of rounding the data on the table to one decimal place.)

Activity 8.3

The best way to check your understanding is to draw this for yourself. Take a piece of graph paper and plot the data in column 3 against the data in column 4 of Table 8.8.

Activity 8.4

Your calculations for 1984 should look like this (Table 8.11).

Table 8.11   Cumulative monetary income distribution, 1984

(1) Percentiles of households	(2) Share of total of monetary income	(3) Cumulative share of households	(4) Cumulative share of total monetary income
Lowest 20%	3.9	20	3.9
Second 20%	8.2	40	12.1
Middle 20%	13.1	60	25.2
Fourth 20%	21.2	80	46.4
Top 20%	53.4	100	99.8

Graphing the two years together should then give you a figure like Figure 8.5

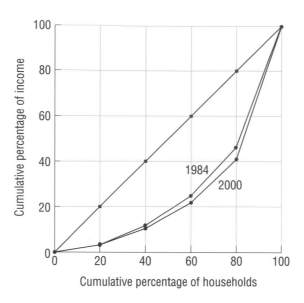

Figure 8.5 Lorenz curves: monetary income distribution in Mexico, 1984 and 2000

The curve for 1984 is closer to the diagonal (representing equal incomes) than the curve for 2000. Monetary incomes were therefore more equally distributed in 1984 than in 2000.

Activity 9.1

1   It is a negative-sum game. To see this, start at O and move to R, where Mexico has lost $20 billion and the USA has gained nothing. Then move from R to Q, at which point Mexico has lost $40 billion and the USA has gained $20 billion (a net loss of $20 billion).

2   At any point along the line PR the gains of the USA are less than Mexico's losses, so the USA cannot afford to compensate Mexico. Mexico will not 'play'; it will stay at the origin.

Activity 9.2

The frontier OT lies in the bottom left-hand quadrant. At any point on the line both countries lose. As I have drawn it, it represents a game in which Mexico's losses are greater than those of the USA. At T, for example, Mexico loses $60 billion and the USA loses $40 billion.

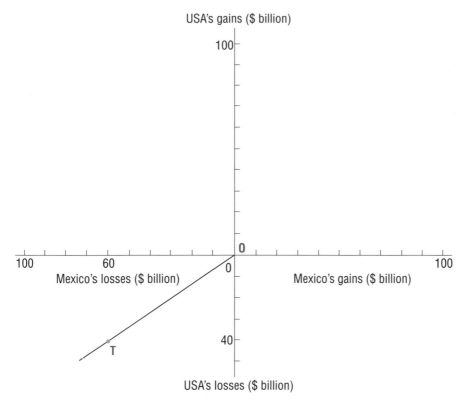

USA's gains ($ billion)

100

0

100 — Mexico's losses ($ billion)

0

Mexico's gains ($ billion) — 100

40

T

USA's losses ($ billion)

Figure 9.3   A trade war game

Activity 9.3

Salinas's ranking of the alternatives was as follows (1 = least favoured; 4 = most favoured):

1   maintain tariffs to support import-substitution

2   develop a strategy of negotiated liberalization in the GATT

3   open the economy unilaterally

4   negotiate bilaterally with the USA.

As the president preferred unilateral liberalization to liberalization under the auspices of the GATT, he was unable to use the GATT negotiations as a fall-back position in his negotiations with the USA.

Activity 9.4

Before the gains are shared, the USA has $9 trillion (90 per cent of $10 trillion) and Mexico has $1 trillion (10 per cent of $10 trillion); the absolute gap is $8 trillion. The USA then gets 90 per cent of $1 trillion, that is, $900 billion; Mexico gets $100 billion. So the USA has $9900 billion and Mexico $1100 billion; the absolute gap is $8.8 trillion. The absolute gap has increased.

Activity 10.1

In the development years, there was a higher proportion of high growth countries than in any subsequent period. (Note, however, that the number of countries in the data varies by period.)

In the crisis years, the number of high growth countries fell only slightly – since the oil-producing countries did well – but the proportion of low growth countries rose.

In the adjustment years, the vast majority of countries fell into the low growth category.

The recovery years were characterized by some countries moving back to medium or high growth rates. The lowest growth rates, however, remained sharply negative in each period after the development years.

Activity 11.1

In Table 11.1, on the left-hand side:

GDP + Imports = 100 + 24.5 = 124.5% of GDP

Domestic absorption + Exports = 108.5 + 16 = 124.5% of GDP

The two sides balance: all the resources available from production and imports (left-hand side) are used as either domestic absorption or exports (right-hand side).

Activity 11.2

Private plus public consumption equalled 84.5 + 6.3 = 90.8% of GDP. Domestic savings were therefore 9.2 per cent of GDP in 2001.

Activity 11.3

Investment was at its highest in relation to GDP in the late 1970s. It fell steeply in the early 1980s, and after that fluctuated. There were smaller peaks in the early 1990s, and then a steep decline to a level of 15–18 per cent in the late 1990s. The trade gap fluctuations mirrored those of investment, but the trade gap rose as a proportion of GDP to its highest levels in the later 1980s and early 1990s. It then fell steeply after 1994 to its lowest levels since the mid 1970s at the turn of the century. From 1976 to the mid 1980s, the trade gap was smaller relative to investment (both measured as percentages of GDP), so domestic savings played an important role in sustaining investment but fell along with it in the crisis years of the early 1980s. After the mid 1980s, investment and the trade gap were almost equal: all the investment in the economy was being financed by the aid inflow that supported the trade gap. Domestic savings virtually disappeared and turned negative in some years. Only in the late 1990s did some savings again emerge to finance investment.

Activity 11.4

As the price of a dollar in Tanzanian shillings falls from E_2 to E_1, the demand for dollars in the economy rises from Q_2 to Q_1 on Figure 11.5. Dollar prices of goods do not change. The rise in demand for dollars is explained by the lower prices of imported goods (since each dollar translates into fewer Tanzanian shillings). People will buy more imported goods, and may switch to them from local goods.

As the price of a dollar in Tanzanian shillings falls from E_2 to E_1, the supply of dollars in the economy falls, from Q_2 to Q_1 on Figure 11.6. Dollar prices of goods do not change. Exported goods earn fewer Tanzanian shillings for each dollar and so exporters are likely to have less incentive to produce for export and may curtail production, or switch sales to the home market; the former mechanism is likely to have the larger effect.

Activity 11.5

A fall in travel reduces demand for Tanzania's holidays at all levels of the exchange rate. This is equivalent to a decline in exports. The country has a lower supply of dollars at all exchange rates. So the supply schedule shifts to the left at all exchange rates, from S to S_1 as shown in Figure 11.14. The result is that the market equilibrium, where the demand and supply coincide, moves from point A to point B. There is a new higher equilibrium exchange rate E_1; that is, the effect is to reduce the value of the Tanzanian shilling by raising the price of the dollar in shillings.

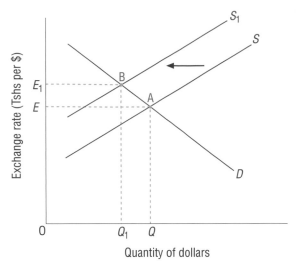

Figure 11.14   The effect of a decline in tourism in Tanzania on the equilibrium exchange rate

Activity 11.6

The real exchange rate falls. The real exchange rate falls, implying a revaluation of the shilling in real terms – its value increases in terms of the dollar. In the equation that defines the real exchange rate, E_N the nominal rate stays the same, but the ratio of world prices to domestic prices falls since domestic inflation is faster than world inflation. Thus, the whole expression

$$RER \equiv E_N \times \left(\frac{P_W}{P_D}\right)$$

becomes smaller.

Activity 12.1

Simon Bromley makes a number of points in Chapter 5, Section 5.3. I noted the following.

■   Sovereignty is a particular kind of authority: it is a claim to a *right* to rule that, to be successful, requires *recognition* from those to whom such claims are directed.

■   Sovereign claims by states are directed both internally and externally, that is towards the population and other agents within the territory of the state, and to other states outside.

- The sovereignty of any particular state is in fact made up of a 'bundle' of different claims receiving varying levels of recognition, rather than a single fixed entity which either is or is not present.

- Finally, since sovereignty is a relationship constructed around a state making a claim and seeking recognition of this from others, it is never an accomplished fact but an ongoing history motivated by political aspirations. That is, people seek to achieve sovereignty for some purpose, purposes which others may resist.

Activity 12.2

As Chapter 10 explains, sovereignty is to do with a state's claim to a right to rule, autonomy with the de facto constraints on a state's ability to achieve its aims.

Activity 12.3

Yes it is. The controls on exchange rates create opportunities for enrichment. Politicians spend funds seeking to gain control of these rents, rather than spending funds productively, on investment or the outputs of local productive activity.

Activity 13.1

'Global public bads' are the other face of public goods: environmental disaster; pandemics of infectious disease; depletion of essential resources. These are also non-rival (my getting ill does not reduce your chances, quite the contrary); non-excludable (once they occur we are all vulnerable); joint in supply (produced once for everyone); and not crowded (a lack of cod affects everyone).

Activity 13.2

Surveillance provides information and allows an international response. Once the information is publicly supplied, it is a public good: supplied to all, non-rival (anyone can use it without depleting it) and non-excludable (because published).

Activity 13.3

Figure 13.9 (overleaf) shows the completed matrix. We could have chosen many different numbers for the payoffs so long as the relationships between them produced a Prisoners' Dilemma. The essential property of the Prisoners' Dilemma game is that the 'temptation' payoff (to cheat when the other co-operates, here 2) is the highest payoff, and the 'sucker's' payoff (to co-operate when the other cheats, here –2) is the lowest; the social optimum, the highest joint payoff (here 1, 1) must be unattainable though it is preferred by both parties to the solution (here –1, –1).

Netherlands

		Comply	Cheat
Britain	Comply	1, 1	−2, 2
	Cheat	2, −2	−1, −1

Figure 13.9   A Prisoners' Dilemma game showing a cod-fishing tragedy

The Nash equilibrium is the lower right-hand corner: both cheat. Start from the point of view of Britain. If the Netherlands complies, Britain will cheat (it prefers a payoff of 2 to 1). If the Netherlands cheats, Britain will prefer to cheat (it prefers a payoff of −1 to −2). So Britain will cheat. The same argument applied from the point of view of the Netherlands. So the bottom right-hand cell (−1, −1) is the Nash equilibrium. But in this story, both countries would have preferred both to comply, with a payoff of (1, 1) saving the fish stocks. But individual decision making by governments on the basis of their own interests prevents it.

Activity 13.5

The definition of a Nash equilibrium is 'a set of strategies, one for each player, such that, given the strategies being played by the others, no player can improve on their payoff by adopting an alternative strategy' (marginal definition, Section 3.3). In the top left-hand cell, if the USSR refrains, the best reply of the USA is to refrain (4 is better than 3). The same is true for the USSR. So this is a Nash equilibrium. In the lower right-hand cell, if one country builds, the best reply of the other is to build (2 is better than 1). So this is also a Nash equilibrium.

Activity 13.6

1   The Nash equilibrium outcome to the game is the situation when both players choose not to ban CFCs. Starting with Europe's point of view: if the USA chooses not to ban CFCs, Europe's best reply is not to ban them (−2 is better than −5); if the USA bans them, Europe's best reply is not to ban them (10 is better than 6). The game is symmetric, so the US viewpoint is the same. The Nash equilibrium is therefore the bottom right-hand cell.

2   The ozone depletion game has the structure of a Prisoners' Dilemma. A Prisoners' Dilemma has three defining characteristics: it is a game in which: (1) there is both a co-operative strategy and a cheating strategy; (2) there is a single Nash equilibrium outcome in which both players cheat; and (3) the Nash equilibrium outcome is worse for both players than the non-equilibrium outcome in which both players co-operate. The ozone depletion game has all three characteristics. Both players would prefer the top left-hand cell — the social optimum — where both ban the CFCs.

3   Given the assumptions: that states act to maximize their own (rather than collective) benefits; that there is uncertainty about how the other will choose to act; and that there is no higher authority to ensure any promises to co-operate are kept, there will always be the temptation to free-ride. That is, each state will try to get away with not banning CFCs while benefiting from the efforts of the other. Given the symmetry of the situation, each state will also expect the other to try to free-ride, and will want to avoid the worst-case scenario of banning CFCs and being caught out by the other defecting on the deal (the 'sucker's' payoff). Thus, no state will ban CFCs. The result is the sub-optimal outcome of unchecked depletion of the ozone layer.

Activity 13.7

The public good in this case is the benefits of free trade in the form of higher joint incomes than could be sustained by autarky. The WTO exists to provide the framework for enforcement of the 'rules of the game' in international trading that sustain those joint (though unequal) gains. As Part 1 of Book 1 discussed, for this collective action institution to be legitimate, there have to be genuine gains for all members.

References

Ai Camp, R. (1999) *Politics in Mexico: The Decline of Authoritarianism*, New York, Oxford University Press.

Ahluwalia, I.J. (1985) *Industrial Growth in India: Stagnation Since the Mid-Sixties*, New Delhi, Oxford University Press.

Ake, C. (1996) *Democracy and Development in Africa*, Washington, DC, The Brookings Institution.

Akyüz, Y. (1996) 'The investment–profit nexus in East Asian industrialization', *World Development*, vol.24, no.3, pp.461–70.

Amin, S. (1972) *Neocolonialism in West Africa*, Harmondsworth, Penguin Books.

Amsden, A. (1989) *Asia's Next Giant: South Korea and Late Industrialization*, Oxford, Oxford University Press.

Aristotle (1996 edition) *The Politics and The Constitution of Athens* (edited by Stephen Everson), Cambridge, Cambridge University Press.

Arora, A. (2000) 'Software development in non-member countries: the Indian case' in *OECD Information Technology Outlook*, Paris, Organisation for Economic Co-operation and Development.

Aryeetey, E., Harrigan, J. and Nissanke, M. (eds) (2000) *Economic Reforms in Ghana: The Miracle and the Mirage*, London, James Currey.

Athreye, S. and Kapur, S. (2001) 'Private foreign investment in India: pain or panacea?', *World Economy*, vol.24, no.3, pp.399–424.

Bajpai, N. and Sachs, J.D. (1997) 'India's economic reforms: some lessons from East Asia', *Journal of International Trade and Economic Development*, vol.6, no.2, pp.135–64.

Baldwin, D. (1989) *Paradoxes of Power*, Oxford, Basil Blackwell.

Baldwin, R.E and Martin, P. (1999) *Two Waves of Globalisation: Superficial Similarities, Fundamental Differences*, NBER Working Paper No.6904, Cambridge, Mass., National Bureau of Economic Research.

Bank of Tanzania (2001) *Economic Bulletin For the Quarter Ended 31 December 2001*, vol.32, no.4, Dar es Salaam, Bank of Tanzania.

Bardhan, P. (1984) *The Political Economy of Development in India*, Oxford, Oxford University Press.

Barzel, Y. (2002) *A Theory of the State: Economic Rights, Legal Rights, and the Scope of the State*, Cambridge, Cambridge University Press.

Bates, R. (1981) *Markets and States in Tropical Africa*, Berkeley and Los Angeles, Calif., University of California.

Bates, R. and Krueger, A. (eds) (1993) *Political and Economic Interactions in Economic Policy Reform*, Oxford, Basil Blackwell.

Bayart, J. (1993) *The State in Africa: The Politics of the Belly*, London, Longman.

BBC (1992) *Timewatch Special: The Cuban Missile Crisis. Part 2: Eyeball to Eyeball*, BBC2, 14 October 1992.

Benedick, R.E. (1991) *Ozone Diplomacy: New Directions in Safeguarding the Planet*, Cambridge, Mass., and London, Harvard University Press.

Bhagwati, J.N. (1993) *India in Transition: Freeing the Economy*, Oxford, Clarendon Press.

Bhagwati, J.N. and Desai, P. (1970) *India: Planning for Industrialization – Industrialization and Trade Policies Since 1951*, Oxford, Oxford University Press.

Bhattacharya, A., Montiel, P.J. and Sharma, S. (1997) 'How can sub-Saharan Africa attract more private capital inflows?', *Finance and Development*, vol.34, no.2, June, pp.3–6.

Biersteker, T.J. and Weber, C. (1996) 'The social construction of state sovereignty' in Biersteker, T.J. and Weber, C. (eds) *State Sovereignty as Social Construct*, Cambridge, Cambridge University Press, pp.1–21.

Blackhurst, R. (1999) 'The capacity of the WTO to fulfil its mandate' in Krueger, A.O. (ed.) *The WTO as an International Organization*. New Delhi, Oxford University Press.

Blasi, J. (2003) *Kukdong: A Case of Effective Labor Standards Enforcement*, Berkeley, Calif., John F. Henning Center for International Labor Relations/ University of California [online]. Available from http:// henningcenter.berkeley.edu/gateway/kukdong.html [Accessed 10 July 2003].

Boyce, J.K. and Ndikumana, L. (2000) *Is Africa a Net Creditor? New Estimates of Capital Flight From Severely Indebted Sub-Saharan African Countries, 1970–1996*, Amherst, Mass., University of Massachusetts Political Economy Research Institute.

Brown, L.R. and Flavin, C. (1999) *State of the World 1999: A Worldwatch Institute Report on Progress Toward a Sustainable Society*, London, Earthscan Publications.

Bull, H. (1995) *The Anarchical Society* (second edition), London, Macmillan.

Business India (1992) 'A survey of the computer industry', 31 August–13 September 1992.

Buzan, B., Jones, C. and Little, R. (1993) *The Logic of Anarchy: Neorealism to Structural Realism*, New York, Columbia University Press.

Cain, G.C. (1976) 'The challenge of segmented labour market theories to orthodox theory: a survey', *Journal of Economic Literature*, vol.14, no.4, pp.1215–57.

Cairncross, F. (1997) *The Death of Distance: How the Communications Revolution Will Change Our Lives*, Boston, Mass., Harvard Business School Press.

Cairnes, J.E. (1974; first published 1874) *Some Leading Principles of Political Economy*, London, Macmillan.

Callaghy, T. (1987) 'The state as lame leviathan: the patrimonial administrative state in Africa' in Zaki, E. (ed.) *The African State in Transition*, London, Macmillan, pp.423–42.

Cameron, M.A. and Tomlin, B.W. (2000) *The Making of NAFTA: How the Deal was Done*, Ithaca, NY, and London, Cornell University Press.

Cardoso, F.H. and Faletto, E. (1979) *Dependency and Development in Latin America*, Berkeley, Calif., University of California Press.

Carr, B. (1999) 'Globalisation from below: labour internationalisation under NAFTA', *International Social Science Journal*, no.159, March, pp.49–60.

Carrillo, J. and González, S. (1999) *Empresas Automotores Alemanas en México. Relaciones Cliente–Proveedor*, Cuadernos del Trabajo No.17, Mexico, Secretaría del Trabajo y Previsión Social.

Castañeda, J.G. (1988) 'Mexican foreign policy' in Pastor, R.A. and Castañeda, J.G. (eds) *Limits to Friendship: The United States and Mexico*, New York, Alfred A. Knopf, pp.167–92.

Chambua, S.E., Kihiyo, V. and Mpangala, G.P. (eds) (2002) *Multiparty Elections and Corruption in Tanzania with Special Reference to the 2000 Elections*, Dar es Salaam, Dar es Salaam University Press.

Chang, H.-J. (2002) *Kicking Away the Ladder: Development Strategy in Historical Perspective*, London, Anthem Press.

Charnovitz, S. (2002) 'The legal status of the Doha declarations', *Journal of International Economic Law*, vol.5, no.1, pp.207–11.

Chatterjee, P. (1994) *The Nation and its Fragments: Colonial and Postcolonial Histories*, Princeton, NJ, Princeton University Press.

Chenery, H.B. and Strout, A.M. (1966) 'Foreign assistance and economic development', *American Economic Review*, vol.56, no.4, pp.679–733.

Cheng, T., Haggard, S. and Kang, D. (1996) *Institutions, Economic Policy and Growth in the Republic of Korea and Taiwan Province of China*, Geneva, United Nations Conference on Trade and Development.

Clemens, M. and Williamson, J. (2001) *A Tariff-Growth Paradox?: Protection's Impact on the World Around 1875–1997*, NBER Working Paper No.8459, Cambridge, Mass., National Bureau of Economic Research.

Collier, P. and Gunning, J.W. (1997) *Explaining African Economic Performance*, Oxford, Centre for the Study of African Economies.

Collier, P., Hoeffler, A. and Patillo, C. (1999) *Flight Capital as Portfolio Choice*, Washington, DC, International Monetary Fund.

Commission of the European Communities (2000) *Recovery Plans: Background Information* [online]. Available from http://europa.eu.int/comm/fisheries/news_corner/press/inf01_72_annex1_plan_en.pdf [Accessed 4 August 2003]

Commission of the European Communities (2003) *Report of the Scientific, Technical and Economic Committee for Fisheries: Review of Scientific Advice for 2003*, Commission Staff Working Paper SEC (2003)102, Brussels, Commission of the European Communities.

CONAPO (Consejo Nacional de Población) (2000) *La Situación Demográfica de México 2000*, Mexico, Consejo Nacional de Población.

Cortés, F. (2001) *Evolución de la Desigualdad en la Distribución del Ingreso en México, en el Último Cuarto de Siglo*, México, Consejo Estatal de Población.

Cully, M., Woodland, S., O'Reilly, A. and Dix, G. (1999) *Britain at Work*, London, Routledge.

Dahl, R. (1970) *Modern Political Analysis* (second edition), New Jersey, Prentice Hall.

Davis, D.D. and Holt, C.A. (1993) *Experimental Economics*, Princeton, NJ, Princeton University Press.

Delgado, C., Hazell, P., Hopkins, J. and Kelly, V. (1994) 'Promoting intersectoral growth linkages in rural Africa through agricultural technology and policy reform', *American Journal of Agricultural Economics*, vol.76, pp.1166–71.

DeLong, B.J. (2001) *India Since Independence: An Analytic Growth Narrative* [online]. Available from http://ksghome.harvard.edu/ ~.drodrik.academic.ksg/ Growth%20volume/DeLong-India.pdf [Accessed 3 June 2003].

Demery, L. (1994) 'Structural adjustment: its origins, rationale and achievements' in Cornia, G.A. and Helleiner, G.K. (eds) *From Adjustment to Development in Africa*, London, Macmillan, pp.25–48.

Desai, A.V. (1981) 'Factors underlying the slow growth of Indian industry', *Economic and Political Weekly*, Annual Number, March 1981.

Devarajan, S., Easterly, W. and Pack, H. (1999) *Is Investment in Africa Too Low or Too High? Macro and Micro Evidence*, Washington, DC, World Bank.

Doeringer, P.B. and Piore, M.J. (1971) *Internal Labour Markets and Manpower Analysis*, Lexington, Mass., D.C. Heath.

Doriye, J. (1992) 'Public office and private gain: an interpretation of the Tanzanian experience' in Wuyts, M., Mackintosh, M. and Hewitt, T. (eds) *Development Policy and Public Action*, Oxford, Oxford University Press, pp.61–116.

Doriye, J. and Wuyts, M. (1992) *Aid, Adjustment and Sustainable Recovery: The Case of Tanzania*, Working Paper No.6, London, Department of Economics, The School of Oriental and African Studies (SOAS).

Dresser, D. (1996) 'Mexico: the decline of dominant-party rule' in Dominguez, J.I. and Lowenthal, A.F. (eds) *Constructing Democratic Governance: Mexico, Central America, and the Caribbean in the 1990s*, Baltimore, Md., and London, The Johns Hopkins University Press, pp.159–84.

Dreze, J. and Sen, A. (1995) *India: Economic Development and Social Opportunity*, Oxford, Clarendon Press.

Dunlop, J.T. (1957) *The Theory of Wage Determination*, London, Macmillan.

Dunn, J. (1996a) 'The history of political theory' in Dunn, J. (ed.) *History of Political Theory and Other Essays*, Cambridge, Cambridge University Press.

Dunn, J. (1996b) 'Political obligation' in Dunn, J. (ed.) *History of Political Theory and Other Essays*, Cambridge, Cambridge University Press.

Dunn, J. (2000) *The Cunning of Unreason*, London, HarperCollins.

Elliott, L. (1998) *The Global Politics of the Environment*, London, Macmillan.

Ergas, Z. (1986) 'In search of development: some direction for further investigation', *Journal of Modern African Studies*, vol.24, no.2, pp.303–33.

European Commission (2000) *Background Information on Fish Stock Recovery*, Information Sheet, February, Brussels, European Commission.

Evans, P. (1992) 'The state as problem and solution: embedded autonomy and structural change' in Haggard, S. and Kaufman, R. (eds) *The Politics of Structural Adjustment: International Constraints, Distributive Conflicts and the State*, Princeton, NJ, Princeton University Press, pp.139–81.

Findlay, R. and O'Rourke, K. (2001) *Commodity Market Integration 1500–2000*, NBER Working Paper No.8579, Cambridge, Mass., National Bureau of Economic Research.

Finger, J.M. and Schuler, P. (2000) 'Implementation of the Uruguay Round commitments: the development challenge', *The World Economy*, vol.23, no.4, pp.511–25.

Finger, J.M. and Schuler, P. (2002) 'Implementation of WTO commitments: the development challenge' in Hoekman, B.M., English, P. and Mattoo, A. (eds) *Development, Trade and the WTO: A Handbook*, Washington, DC, World Bank.

Fischer, S., Hernández-Catá, E. and Khan, M.S. (1998) *Africa: Is This The Turning Point?*, Washington, DC, World Bank.

Foweraker, J. (1996) 'From NAFTA to WHFTA?: prospects for hemispheric free trade' in Nishijima, S. and Smith, P.H. (eds) *Co-operation or Rivalry: Regional Integration in the Americas and the Pacific Rim*, Boulder, Col., Westview Press, pp.150–69.

Fowler, M.R. and Bunck, J.M. (1995) *Law, Power, and the Sovereign State: The Evolution and Application of the Concept of Sovereignty*, Pennsylvania, Pennsylvania State University Press.

Frey, B.S. (1997) *Not Just for the Money: An Economic Theory of Personal Motivation*, Cheltenham, Edward Elgar.

Gereffi, G. (1996) 'Mexico's "old" and "new" maquiladora industries: contrasting approaches to North American integration' in Otero, G. (ed.) *Neoliberalism Revisited: Economic Restructuring and Mexico's Future*, Boulder, Col.,Westview.

Gerschenkron, A. (1962) *Economic Backwardness in Historical Perspective*, Cambridge, Mass., Harvard University Press.

Goldsmith, A.A. (2001) 'Institutions and economic growth in Africa' in McPherson, M.F. (ed.) *Restarting and Sustaining Growth and Development in Africa*, Cambridge, Mass., Harvard Institute for International Development.

Goozeit, M.J. (1973) 'The Corn Laws and wage adjustment in a short-run Ricardian model', reprinted in Cunningham Wood, J. (ed.) (1985) *David Ricardo: Critical Assessments Vol. III*, London, Croom Helm.

Gordon, D.M., Edwards, R. and Reich, M. (1982) *Segmented Work, Divided Workers: The Historical Transformation of Labour in the USA*, Cambridge, Cambridge University Press.

Greenpeace (1998) *Guide to the Kyoto Protocol*, Amsterdam, Greenpeace International.

Grieco, J. (1993) 'Anarchy and the limits of cooperation: a realist critique of the newest liberal institutionalism' in Baldwin, D.A. (ed.) *Neorealism and Neoliberalism*, New York, Columbia University Press, pp.116–40.

Grindle, M. (1996) *Challenging the State: Crisis and Innovation in Latin America and Africa*, Cambridge, Cambridge University Press.

Gruber, L. (2000) *Ruling the World: Power Politics and the Rise of Supranational Institutions*, Princeton, NJ, Princeton University Press.

Grugel, J. (1996) 'Latin America and the remaking of the Americas' in Gamble, A. and Payne, A. (eds) *Regionalism and World Order*, London, Macmillan, pp.131–67.

Hardin, R. (1999) *Liberalism, Constitutionalism, and Democracy*, Oxford, Oxford University Press.

Harris, N. (1986) *The End of the Third World: Newly Industrialising Countries and the Decline of an Ideology*, Harmondsworth, Penguin Books.

Helleiner, G.K. (1994) 'From adjustment to development in sub-Saharan Africa: consensus and continuing conflict' in Cornia, G.A. and Helleiner, G.K. (eds) *From Adjustment to Development in Africa*, London, Macmillan, pp.3–24.

Helleiner, G.K., Killick, T., Lipumba, N., Ndulu, B. and Svendsen, K. (1995) *Report of the Groups of Independent Advisers on Development Cooperation Issues Between Tanzania and its Aid Donors* (the Helleiner Report), Copenhagen, DANIDA.

Helmers, F.C.H. (1988) 'The real exchange rate' in Dornbusch, R., Leslie, F. and Helmers, F.C.H. (eds) *The Open Economy: Tools for Policy Makers in Developing Countries*, EDI Series in Economic Development, Oxford, Oxford University Press for World Bank, pp.10–36.

Henderson, J.P. (1997) *The Life and Economics of David Ricardo*, Boston, Mass., Kluwer Academic Publishers.

Hernández-Catá, E. (2000) *Raising Growth and Investment in Sub-Saharan Africa: What Can Be Done?*, Washington, DC, International Monetary Fund.

Hertel, T.W. and Martin, W. (2001) 'Liberalising agriculture and manufactures in a Millennium Round: implications for developing countries' in Hoekman, B. and Martin, W. (eds) *Developing Countries and the WTO: A Proactive Agenda*, Oxford, Blackwell.

Hirschman, A.O. (1945) *National Power and the Structure of Foreign Trade*, Berkeley, Calif., University of California Press.

Hirst, P. (1997) *From Statism to Pluralism*, London, University College Press.

Hoekman, B. and Kostecki, M.M. (2001) *The Political Economy of the World Trading System: The WTO and Beyond* (second edition), Oxford, Oxford University Press.

Hume, D. (1994, first published 1741) 'Of the first principles of government' in Haakonssen, K. (ed.) *David Hume Political Essays*, Cambridge, Cambridge University Press.

Hume, D. (1994, first published 1752) 'Of the balance of power' in Haakonssen, K. (ed.) *David Hume Political Essays*, Cambridge, Cambridge University Press.

Hurrell, A. and Kingsbury, B. (1992) *The International Politics of the Environment: Actors, Interests and Institutions*, Oxford, Clarendon Press.

Hutchful, E. (2002) *Ghana's Adjustment Experience: The Paradox of Reform*, Geneva and London, UNRISD/James Currey.

Inayatullah, N. (1996) 'Beyond the sovereignty dilemma: quasi-states as social constructs' in Biersteker, T.J. and Weber, C. (eds) *State Sovereignty as Social Construct*, Cambridge, Cambridge University Press, pp.50–80.

INEGI (various years) *Encuesta Nacional de Empleo*, Aguascalientes, México, Instituto Nacional de Estadística, Geografía e Informática.

Institute for Development Policy and Management (2003) *Indian Software Labour: Cost Breakdown and Comparison* [online]. Available from http://idpm.man.ac.uk/rsc/is/isi/isicost.shtml [Accessed 8 July 2003].

Internet Economy Indicators (2002) [online]. Available from www.internetindicators.com [Accessed 30 October 2002].

IPCC (1995) *Second Assessment Report: Climate Change 1995*, Geneva, International Panel on Climate Change.

IPCC (2001) *Third Assessment Report: Climate Change 2001, Synthesis Report*, Geneva, International Panel on Climate Change.

Jackson, J.H. (1997) *The World Trading System: Law and Policy of International Economic Relations* (second edition), Cambridge, Mass., The MIT Press.

Johnson, C. (1981) 'Introduction: the Taiwanese model' in Hsiung, J.H. (ed.) *Contemporary Republic of China: The Taiwanese Experience*, New York, Praeger.

Juma, C. and Ojwang, J. (eds) (1989) *Innovation and Sovereignty: The Patent Debate in African Development*, Nairobi, African Centre for Technology Studies.

Kanbur, R., Sandler, T. and Morrison, K. (1999) *The Future of Development Assistance: Common Pools and International Public Goods*, Essay No.25, Washington, DC, Overseas Development Council.

Kaplinsky, R., Morris, M. and Readman, J. (2002) 'The globalization of product markets and immiserizing growth: lessons from the South African furniture industry', *World Development*, vol.30, no.7, pp.1159–77.

Kawa, I.H. (2002) 'Corruption in the 2000 local and parliamentary elections in Morogoro Urban District Constituency: the local people's perspective' in Chambua, S.E., Kihiyo, V. and Mpangala, G.P. (eds) *Multiparty Elections and Corruption in Tanzania with Special Reference to the 2000 Elections*, Dar es Salaam, Dar es Salaam University Press.

Kerr, C. (1954) 'The Balkanisation of labour markets' in Bakke, E.W. *et al.* (eds) *Labour Mobility and Economic Opportunity*, New York, Wiley.

Krasner, S.D. (1985) *Structural Conflict: The Third World Against Global Liberalism*, Berkeley, Calif., University of California Press.

Krishna, R. (1984) *Growth of Aggregate Unemployment in India: Trends, Sources, and Macroeconomic Policy Options*, New York, World Bank.

Krugman, P.R. (2000) 'Technology, trade and factor prices', *Journal of International Economics*, vol.50, pp.51–71.

Kuznets, S. (1966) *Modern Economic Growth*, New Haven, Conn., Yale University Press.

Lewis, J.P. (1962) *Quiet Crisis in India: Economic Development and American Policy*, Washington, DC, The Brookings Institution.

Lewis, P. (1996) 'Economic reform and political transition in Africa: the quest for a politics of development', *World Politics*, vol.49, October, pp.92–129.

Lindert, P.H. and Williamson, J.G. (2001) *Does Globalisation Make the World More Unequal?*, NBER Working Paper No.8228, Cambridge, Mass., National Bureau of Economic Research.

Lomborg, B. (2001) *The Skeptical Environmentalist: Measuring the Real State of the World*, Cambridge, Cambridge University Press.

Lubeck, P. (1987) 'The African bourgeoisie: debates, methods and units of analysis' in Lubeck, P. (ed.) *The African Bourgeoisie: Capitalist Development in Nigeria, Kenya and the Ivory Coast*, Boulder, Col., Lynne Rienner Publishers, pp.3–26.

Luxembourg Income Study [online]. Available from http://www.lisproject.org/ [Accessed 14 April 2003].

Madavo, C. and Sarbib, J.-L. (1997) 'Africa on the move: attracting private capital to a changing continent', *The SAIS Review*, vol.7, no.2, pp.111–26.

Maddison, A. (2001) *The World Economy: A Millennial Perspective*, Paris, Organisation for Economic Co-operation and Development.

Malhotra, K. (2002) 'Doha: is it really a development round?', *Trade, Development and Environment*, vol.1, Washington, DC, Carnegie Endowment for International Peace.

Marx, K. (1981; first published 1894) *Capital: Vol.III*, Harmondsworth, Penguin Books.

Marx, K. and Engels, F. (2002; first published 1848) *The Communist Manifesto*, Harmondsworth, Penguin Books.

Mill, J.S. (1976; first published 1848) *The Principles of Political Economy*, New York, Senator Press.

Milner, H. (1993) 'The assumption of anarchy in international relations theory: a critique' in Baldwin, D.A. (ed.) *Neorealism and Neoliberalism: The Contemporary Debate*, New York, Columbia University Press, pp.143–69.

Moody, K. (1995) 'NAFTA and the corporate redesign of North America, *Latin American Perspectives*, vol.22, no.1, pp.95–116.

Morales, I. (1999) 'NAFTA: the institutionalization of economic openness and the configuration of Mexican geo-economic spaces', *Third World Quarterly*, vol.20, no.5, pp.971–93.

Moravcsik, A. (1997) 'Taking preferences seriously: a liberal theory of international politics', *International Organization*, vol.51, no.4, pp.513–53.

Moravcsik, A. (1998) *The Choice for Europe: Social Purpose and State Power from Messina to Maastricht*, London, UCL Press.

Morgenthau, H.J. (1985) *Politics Among Nations* (sixth edition, with Thompson, K.W.), New York, Alfred A. Knopf.

Mpangala, G.P. (2002) 'Growth of corruption in Zanzibar elections of 1995 and 2000' in Chambua, S.E., Kihiyo, V. and Mpangala, G.P. (eds) *Multiparty Elections and Corruption in Tanzania with Special Reference to the 2000 Elections*, Dar es Salaam, Dar es Salaam University Press.

Mutalemwa, D., Noni, P. and Wangwe, S. (2000) *Managing the Transition From Aid Dependency: The Case of Tanzania*, Nairobi, AERC/ODC Project on Managing Transition from Aid in Sub-Saharan Africa.

Nabudere, D. (1985) 'The role of the state in the economic transformation of the African states', paper presented at AAPS symposium on 'The Problems of Transition to Socialism in Africa', Harare, Zimbabwe.

Narlikar, A. (2001a) *WTO Decision-Making and Developing Countries*, Trade Working Paper No.11, Geneva, South Centre [online]. Available from www.southcentre.org [Accessed 6 May 2003].

Narlikar, A. (2001b) *Back to the Excluded: A Focus on Developing Countries in the WTO (Post Seattle)*, Manchester Papers in Politics No.4/01, Manchester, Department of Government, University of Manchester.

Narlikar, A. (forthcoming in 2003) *International Trade and Developing Countries: Coalitions in the GATT and WTO*, London, Routledge.

National Bureau of Statistics, Tanzania (1995a) *Selected Statistical Series 1951–1992*, March, Dar es Salaam, National Bureau of Statistics (Table 7.1).

National Bureau of Statistics, Tanzania (1995b) *Revised National Accounts of Tanzania 1976–1990* (the results of the National Accounts Project in Tanzania implemented on behalf of Eurostat and Sida through Statistics Sweden), April, Dar es Salaam, National Bureau of Statistics.

National Bureau of Statistics, Tanzania (1999) *National Accounts of Tanzania 1987–1998* (third edition in the revised series of GDP), December, Dar es Salaam, National Bureau of Statistics.

National Bureau of Statistics, Tanzania (2002) *Hali ya Uchumi wa Taifa Katika Mwaka 2001* (*The Economic Survey 2001*, Swahili edition), June, Dar es Salaam, National Bureau of Statistics.

Nauman, A.K. and Hutchinson, M. (1997) 'The integration of women into the Mexican labor forces since NAFTA', *American Behavioural Scientist*, vol.40, no.7, pp.950–7.

Nester, W. (1995) *International Relations: Geopolitical and Geoeconomic Conflict and Co-operation*, New York, HarperCollins.

Ng, F. and Yeats, A. (2000) *On the Recent Trade Performance of Sub-Saharan African Countries: Cause for Hope or More of the Same?*, Washington, DC, World Bank.

O'Day, P. (1997) 'ATC phase out – a few big winners, long list of losers', *International Fiber Journal*, vol.12, February.

OECD (1996) *Shaping the 21st Century: The Contribution of Development Cooperation*, Paris, Organisation for Economic Co-operation and Development.

OECD (2002) *Main Economic Indicators* [online]. Available from http://www.oecd.org/home/0,2605,en_2649_201185_1_1_1_1_1,00.htm [Accessed 6 May 2003].

OECD Report (various years) [online]. Available from http://www.oecd.org [Accessed 6 May 2003].

Office for National Statistics (2002) *Labour Market Trends*, vol.110, no.2, London, The Stationery Office.

Olson, M. (1971) *The Logic of Collective Action*, Cambridge, Mass., Harvard University Press.

Olson, M. (2000) *Power and Prosperity*, New York, Basic Books.

Organisation for African Unity (1980) *Lagos Plan of Action*, Addis Ababa, Organisation for African Unity.

Ortiz Muñiz, G. (1992) 'Reflexiones respecto al avance conocido en las negociaciones del TLC', *Revista Latinoamericana de Economía*, vol.XXIII, pp.30–6.

Ostry, S. (2000) 'The Uruguay Round North–South Grand Bargain: implications for future negotiation', paper presented at conference 'The Political Economy of International Trade Law', University of Minnesota, September [online]. Available from http://www.utoronto.ca/cis/ostry.html[Accessed 6 May 2003].

O'Toole, G. (2002) 'Integration and nationalism in Mexico during the Salinas Sexenio', paper presented at the Society of Latin American Studies Conference, University of East Anglia, 22–24 March 2002, 16P.

Pastor, R.A. (1993) *Integration with Mexico: Options for US Policy*, New York, The Twentieth Century Fund Press.

Paterson, M. (1996) *Global Warming and Global Politics*, London, Routledge.

Paterson, M. and Grubb, M. (1992) 'The international politics of climate change', *International Affairs*, vol.62, no.2, pp.293–310.

Pigato, M. (2000) *Foreign Direct Investment in Africa: Old Tales and New Evidence*, Washington, DC, World Bank.

Poundstone, W. (1992) *Prisoners' Dilemma: John Von Neumann, Game Theory, and the Puzzle of the Bomb*, Oxford, Oxford University Press.

Prebisch, P. (1959) 'The role of commercial policies in underdeveloped countries', *The American Economic Review*, vol.49, no.2, May, pp.251–73.

Pritchett, L. (1997) 'Divergence, big time', *Journal of Economic Perspectives*, vol.11, pp.3–17.

Raghavan, C. (2000) 'After Seattle, the world trade system faces an uncertain future', *Review of International Political Economy*, vol.7, no.3, pp.495–504.

Raghavan, C. (2002) 'Developing countries call for principles and procedures for WTO ministerial conferences' [online]. Available from http://www.twnside.org.sg/title/twr141c.htm [Accessed 6 May 2003].

Rege, V. (2000) *WTO Procedures for Decision Making: Experience of Their Operation and Suggestions for Improvement*, Background Paper, 21 January, London, Commonwealth Secretariat.

Reich, R. (1990) *Wall Street Journal*, 18 June, p.A10.

Rodrik, D. (1997) *Has Globalization Gone Too Far?*, Washington, DC, Institute for International Economics.

Rodrik, D. (2001) *The Global Governance of Trade as If Development Really Mattered*, New York, United Nations Development Programme.

Rostow, W.W. (1960) *The Stages of Economic Growth: A Non-Communist Manifesto*, Cambridge, Mass., Harvard University Press.

Rowthorn, R. (1996) *East Asian Development: The Flying Geese Paradigm Reconsidered*, East Asian Development Lessons for a New Global Environment: Study No.8, Geneva, United Nations Conference on Trade and Development (UNCTAD).

Rubery, J. and Wilkinson, F. (1994) *Employer Strategy and the Labour Market*, Oxford, Oxford University Press.

Rubio, L. (1996) 'Mexico, NAFTA, and the Pacific Basin' in Nishijima, S. and Smith, P. (eds) *Co-operation or Rivalry: Regional Integration in the Americas and the Pacific Rim*, Boulder, Col., Westview Press, pp.76–96.

Rutasitara, L. (1994) *Real Exchange Rate Behaviour and Merchandise Exports in Tanzania*, Ph.D. thesis, Dar es Salaam, University of Dar es Salaam.

Rweyemamu, J. (1973) *Underdevelopment and Industrialisation in Tanzania: A Study of Perverse Capitalist Industrial Development*, Oxford, Oxford University Press.

Sachs, J. and Warner, A. (1995) *Economic Reform and the Process of Global Integration*, Washington, DC, The Brookings Institution.

Sandler, T. (1997) *Global Challenges: An Approach to Environmental, Political and Economic Problems*, Cambridge, Cambridge University Press.

Schelling, T. (1960) *The Strategy of Conflict*, Cambridge, Mass., Harvard University Press.

Schiavo-Campo, S. (1996) 'Reforming the civil service', *Finance and Development*, vol.43, no.3, pp.10–13.

Schmitter, P.C. (1979) 'Still the century of corporatism?' in Lehmbruch, G. and Schmitter, P.C. (eds) *Trends Towards Corporatist Intermediation*, London, Sage Publications, pp.7–52.

Schott, J. (2002) 'Comment on the Doha Ministerial', *Journal of International Economic Law*, vol.5, no.1, pp.191–5.

Scruton, R. (1982) *A Dictionary of Political Thought*, London, Macmillan.

Sen, A.K. (1986) 'How is India doing?' in Basu, D.K. and Sisson, R. (eds) *Social and Economic Development in India: A Reassessment*, New Delhi, Sage Publications.

Shadlen, K.C. (2000) 'Neo-liberalism, corporatism, and small business political activism in contemporary Mexico', *Latin American Research Review*, vol.35, no.2, pp.73–106.

Skinner, Q. (2002) 'From the state of princes to the person of the state' in Skinner, Q. (ed.) *Visions of Politics. Volume I: Renaissance Virtues*, Cambridge, Cambridge University Press.

Smith, A. (1982; first published 1776) *An Inquiry into the Nature and Causes of the Wealth of Nations*, Harmondsworth, Penguin Books.

Smith, P.H. (1996) 'The United States, regional integration, and the reshaping of the international order' in Nishijima, S. and Smith, P.H. (eds) *Co-operation or Rivalry?: Regional Integration in the Americas and the Pacific Rim*, Boulder, Col., Westview Press, pp.27–51.

Sridharan, E. (1995) 'Liberalisation and technology policy: redefining self-reliance' in Sathyamurthy, T.V. (ed.) *Industry and Agriculture in India Since Independence*, New Delhi, Oxford University Press.

Stiglitz, J. (2001) 'Two principles for the next round, or how to bring developing countries in from the cold' in Hoekman, B. and Martin, W. (eds) *Developing Countries and the WTO: A Proactive Agenda*, Oxford, Basil Blackwell.

Stokke, O.S. (1997) 'Regimes as governance systems' in Young, O.R. (ed.) *Global Governance: Drawing Insights From the Environmental Experience*, Cambridge, Mass., MIT Press.

Strange, R. and Newton, J. (2002) 'From rags to riches: China, the WTO and world trade in textiles and clothing', paper presented at conference 'The WTO and Developing Countries', London, Kings College, September.

Sundaram, J.K. (1996) *Lessons from Growth and Structural Change in the Second-Tier South East Asian Newly Industrialising Countries*, Geneva, United Nations Conference on Trade and Development (UNCTAD).

Tandon, P. (1980) *Return to Punjab*, Delhi, Vikas Publishing House.

The Guardian (2002) 'George Bush's global warming speech: The US president unveils his clear skies and climate change initiatives at the National Oceanic and Atmosphere Administration, Silver Spring, Maryland', 14 February [online]. Available from http://www.guardian.co.uk/bush/story/0,7369,650820,00.html [Accessed 20 February 2002].

Toye, J. (1994) 'Structural adjustment: context, assumptions, origin and diversity' in van der Hoeven, R. and van der Kraaij, F. (eds) *Structural Adjustment and Beyond in Sub-Saharan Africa: Research and Policy Issues*, The Hague, Ministry of Foreign Affairs (DGIS) in association with London, James Curry / Portsmouth, NH, Heinemann, pp.18–35.

Tuck, R. (1989) *Hobbes*, Oxford, Oxford University Press.

Tuck, R. (1996) 'Introduction' in Tuck, R. (ed.) *Thomas Hobbes: Leviathan* (revised student edition), Cambridge, Cambridge University Press.

Tuirán, R. (ed.) (2000) *Migración México–Estados Unidos: Continuidad y Cambio*, Mexico, Consejo Nacional de Población.

Tussie, D. and Lengyel, M.F. (2002) 'Developing countries: turning participation into influence' in Hoekman, B.M., English, P. and Mattoo, A. (eds) *Development, Trade and the WTO: A Handbook*, Washington, DC, World Bank.

UNCTAD (1995) *Foreign Direct Investment in Africa 1995*, Geneva, United Nations Conference on Trade and Development.

UNCTAD (1996) *Trade and Development Report 1996*, Geneva, United Nations Conference on Trade and Development.

UNCTAD (1998) *Trade and Development Report 1998*, Geneva, United Nations Conference on Trade and Development.

UNCTAD (2000) *World Investment Report 2000: Cross-Border Mergers and Acquisitions and Development*, Geneva, United Nations Conference on Trade and Development.

UNCTAD (2001) *UNCTAD Handbook of Statistics 2001*, Geneva, United Nations Conference on Trade and Development.

UNCTAD (2002a) *The Least Developed Countries Report 2002: Escaping the Poverty Trap*, Geneva, United Nations Conference on Trade and Development.

UNCTAD (2002b) *Trade and Development Report 2002*, Geneva, United Nations Conference on Trade and Development.

UNFCCC Climate Change Secretariat (2001) *Climate Change Information Kit* [online]. Available from http://unfccc.int/text/resource/iuckit/fact02.html [Accessed 1 July 2003].

UNFCCC Climate Change Secretariat (2002) *A Guide to the Climate Change Convention Process* [online]. Available from: http://unfccc.int/resource/process/guideprocess-p.pdf [Accessed 1 July 2003].

United Nations (1992) *United Nations Framework Convention on Climate Change* [online]. Available from http://unfccc.int/resource/conv/conv.html [Accessed 1 July 2002].

United Nations (1998) *Kyoto Protocol to the United Nations Framework Convention on Climate Change* [online]. Available from http://unfccc.int/resource/docs/convkp/kpeng.pdf [Accessed 21 July 2003].

United States Department of State (2001) *White House Report: Climate Change Review – Initial Report*, 11 June [online]. Available from www.whitehouse.gov/news/releases/2001/06/climatechange.pdf [Accessed 21 July 2003].

United States Department of State (2002) *Fact Sheet: White House Unveils Two Environmental Initiatives* [online]. Available from http://usinfo.state.gov/topical/global/climate/02021402.htm [Accessed 21 July 2003].

Victor, D.G. (2001) *The Collapse of the Kyoto Protocol and the Struggle to Slow Global Warming*, Princeton, NJ, Princeton University Press.

Villegas, A. (1986) *Reformismo y Revolución en el Pensamiento Latinoamericano*, México, Siglo XIX.

Von Neumann, J. and Morgenstern, O. (1944) *Theory of Games and Economic Behavior*, Princeton, NJ, Princeton University Press.

Wade, R. (1992) *Governing the Market: Economic Theory and the Role of Government in East Asian Industrialisation*, Princeton, NJ, Princeton University Press.

Waltz, K. (1959) *Man, the State and War*, New York, Columbia University Press.

Waltz, K. (1979) *Theory of International Politics*, New York, Random House.

Wangwe, S.M. (1983) 'Industrialisation and resource allocation in a developing country: the case of recent experiences in Tanzania', *World Development*, vol.11, no.6, pp.483–92.

Ward, H. (1993) 'Game theory and the politics of the global commons', *Journal of Conflict Resolution*, vol.37, no.2, pp.203–35.

Weber, M. (1978) *Economy and Society: Volume One* (edited by Roth, G. and Wittich, C.), Berkeley and Los Angeles, Calif., University of California Press.

Wight, M. (1986) *Power Politics* (second edition), Harmondsworth, Penguin Books.

Wilkinson, R. (2000) *Multilateralism and the World Trade Organization: The Architecture and Extension of International Trade Regulation*, London, Routledge.

Wolfensohn, J.D. (1997a) 'The challenge of inclusion', address to the Board of Governors of the World Bank, Hong Kong.

Wolfensohn, J.D. (1997b) 'Preface' in World Bank (ed.) *The State in a Changing World: World Development Report 1997*, Oxford, Oxford University Press.

Woods, N. and Narlikar, A. (2001) 'Governance and the limits of accountability: the WTO, the IMF and the World Bank', *International Social Science Journal*, vol.53, no.170, pp.569–83.

World Bank (1981) *Accelerated Development in Sub-Saharan Africa: An Agenda for Action* (the Berg Report), Washington, DC, World Bank.

World Bank (1993) *The East Asian Miracle: Economic Growth and Public Policy*, Washington, DC, World Bank.

World Bank (1998) *Assessing Aid: What Works, What Doesn't and Why*, Oxford, Oxford University Press.

World Bank (2000a) *World Development Indicators 2000*, Washington, DC, World Bank [online]. Available from http://www.worldbank.org/data/wdi2000/index.htm [Accessed 30 October 2002].

World Bank (2000b) *World Development Report 2000: Building Institutions for Markets*, Washington, DC, World Bank.

World Bank (2000c) *Can Africa Claim the 21st Century?*, Washington, DC, World Bank.

World Bank (2000d) *Agriculture in Tanzania Since 1986: Follower or Leader of Growth?*, Washington, DC, World Bank, The Government of the United Republic of Tanzania, and IFPRI (International Food and Policy Institute).

World Bank (2001a) *World Development Indicators 2001*, Washington, DC, World Bank [online]. Available from http://www.worldbank.org/data/wdi2001/index.htm [Accessed 30 October 2002].

World Bank (2001b) *Global Economic Prospects*, Washington, DC, World Bank.

World Bank (2002a) *World Development Report 2002: Building Institutions for Markets*, Washington, DC, World Bank.

World Bank (2002b) *World Development Indicators 2002*, Washington, DC, World Bank [online]. Available from http://www.worldbank.org/data/wdi2002/index.htm [Accessed 30 October 2002].

World Bank (2002c) *Globalization, Growth and Poverty: Building an Inclusive World Economy*, Washington, DC, World Bank.

World Bank (2002d) *World Development Indicators 2002 CD-ROM*, Washington, DC, World Bank.

World Bank (2002e) *Tanzania at the Turn of the Century: Background Papers and Statistics*, Washington, DC, World Bank and Government of Tanzania.

World Bank (2003) *World Development Indicators 2003*, Washington, DC, World Bank [online]. Available from http://www.worldbank.org/data/wdi2003/index.htm [Accessed 7 August 2003].

World Trade Organization (2000) *WTO Directory*, Geneva, World Trade Organization.

World Trade Organization (2002a) *Trading into the Future* [online]. Available from www.wto.org [Accessed 30 October 2002].

World Trade Organization (2002b) *What is the WTO?* [online]. Available from www.wto.org [Accessed 30 October 2002].

Wuyts, M. (1994) 'Accumulation, industrialisation and the peasantry: a reinterpretation of the Tanzanian experience', *The Journal of Peasant Studies*, vol.21, no.2, pp.159–93.

Yanagihara, T. and Sambommatsu, S. (eds) (1997) *East Asian Development Experience: Economic System Approach and Its Applicability*, Tokyo, Institute of Developing Economies.

Zacher, M.W. (1999) 'Global epidemiological surveillance: international co-operation to monitor infectious diseases' in Kaul, I., Grunberg I. and Stern M. (1999) *Global Public Goods: International Co-operation in the 21st Century*, Oxford, Oxford University Press.

Zapata, F. (1997) 'The paradox of flexibility and rigidity: the Mexican labour market in the 1990s' in Amadeo, E. and Horton, S. (eds) *Labour Productivity and Flexibility*, London, Macmillan.

Index

Note: an index reference in **bold** type indicates a marginal note.

Acknowledgements

Grateful acknowledgement is made to the following sources for permission to reproduce material in this book.

Every effort has been made to contact copyright holders. If any have been inadvertently overlooked the publishers will be pleased to make the necessary arrangements at the first opportunity.

Text

pp.447–8: Vidal, J. (2002) 'Ivory vote sparks new fears for elephants', *The Guardian*, 13 November 2002. Copyright © *The Guardian*.

Tables

Table 3.3: Hertel, T.W. and Martin, W. (2001) Table 1 in 'Liberalising agriculture and manufactures in a Millennium Round: implications for developing countries', in Hoekman, B. and Martin, W. (eds) *Developing Countries and the WTO: A Proactive Agenda*. Blackwell Publishers Limited; Table 3.5: *The Least Developed Countries Report 2002: Escaping the Poverty Trap*. Reprinted with permission of United Nations Conference on Trade and Development. Tables 8.2–8.5, 8.7–8.8: © INEGI (Instituto Nacional de Estadística, Geografía e Informática).

Figures

Figure 3.2: From *Globalization, Growth and Poverty* by Paul Collier and David Dollar. Copyright © 2002 The International Bank for Reconstruction and Development/The World Bank. Used by permission of Oxford University Press. Figure 3.6 and 3.9: *The Least Developed Countries Report 2002: Escaping the Poverty Trap*. Reprinted with permission of United Nations Conference on Trade and Development. Figure 13.1: European Commission (2003) Information Sheet, *Background Information on Fish Stock Recovery*. Copyright © European Communities , 1995–2003.

Photos

(p.12, left): © Eric Draper / Associated Press. (p.12, right): © Khue Bui / Associated Press. (p.55): © Jeremy Horner / Panos Pictures. (p.219): © EPA / PA Photos.